DRAMATIC SOUNDINGS

DRAMATIC SOUNDINGS

Evaluations and Retractions
culled from 30 years
of dramatic criticism

by

JOHN GASSNER

Introduction and Posthumous Editing
by
GLENN LONEY

CROWN PUBLISHERS, INC., NEW YORK

ACKNOWLEDGMENTS

Permission has been received from the indicated original sources for reprinting the following articles and reviews:

"Oresteia: Dramatic Form and Vision." *Varieties of Literary Experience*, ed. Stanley Burnshaw, New York University Press, 1962.

"The Modernity of Shakespeare's Theatre." *Prairie Schooner* (Fall, 1964). Reprinted from PRAIRIE SCHOONER. Copyright © 1964, by the University of Nebraska Press.

"Strindberg: Pearl and Oyster." Introduction to *Strindberg: The Origin of Psychology in Modern Drama*, by Franklin Klaf, The Citadel Press, 1963.

"Shaw on Shakespeare." *The Independent Shavian* (Fall, 1963; Winter, 1963/64).

"Shaw on Ibsen and the Drama of Ideas." *Ideas in the Drama*, ed. John Gassner, Columbia University Press, 1964.

"The Dramatic Vision." Reprinted from *Impromptu* by permission of Occidental College.

"The Source, the Path, the Vision: A Relativistic View." *Educational Theatre Journal* (December, 1959). Reprinted by permission of the American Educational Theatre Association, Inc.

"Aristotelian Literary Criticism." Preface to *Aristotle's Theory of Poetry and Fine Art*, ed. and trans. by S. H. Butcher, Dover Publications, Inc., 1951.

"William Archer." Introduction to *Play-making*, by William Archer, Dover Publications, Inc., 1960.

"Playwrights and Playwriting." Introduction to *Playwrights on Playwriting*, ed. Toby Cole, Hill & Wang, Incorporated, 1961.

"Theory and Practice for the Playwright." *First Stage* (Spring, 1962). Used by permission of the Purdue Research Foundation.

"Theatre Arts in a Free Society." *Educational Theatre Journal* (October, 1954). Reprinted by permission of the American Educational Theatre Association, Inc.

"Eugene O'Neill." A modified version of the pamphlet *Eugene O'Neill*, University of Minnesota Pamphlet on American Writers Series, No. 45, © 1965, University of Minnesota.

"The Influence of Strindberg in the United States." *World Theatre* (Spring, 1962).

"Anouilh's *Valse Triste*: A Minority Opinion." *The New Republic* (February 11, 1957). Reprinted by permission of THE NEW REPUBLIC, © 1957, Harrison-Blaine of New Jersey, Inc.

"The Two Worlds of Thornton Wilder." Modified version of Introduction to *The Long Christmas Dinner*, by Thornton Wilder. Copyright © 1963, by Harper & Row Publishers, Inc. By permission of the publishers.

" 'There Is No American Drama'—A Premonition of Discontent." *Theatre Arts* (September, 1952). Used by permission of the representatives of Theatre Publications, Inc.

"Our Lost Playwrights." *Theatre Arts* (August, 1954). Used by permission of the representatives of Theatre Publications, Inc.

"The Winter of Our Discontent." *Theatre Arts* (August, 1955). Used by permission of the representatives of Theatre Publications, Inc.

"The Stage and the City." *Theatre Arts* (April, 1956). Used by permission of the representatives of Theatre Publications, Inc.

"Futile Editorial: A Theatre for the People." CURRENT HISTORY, INC. (October, 1941).

"The Public Is to Blame." *Drama Critique* (November, 1961).

"Too Many Judges?" *The New York Times* (July 21, 1963). © 1963, by The New York Times Company. Reprinted by permission.

"Playwrights of the Thirties." *Theatre Arts* (September, 1960). Used by permission of the representatives of Theatre Publications, Inc.

"Paul Green: Playwright on Native Ground." Introduction to *Paul Green: Five Plays of the South*, Hill & Wang, Incorporated, 1963.

"The One-Act Play in the Revolutionary Theatre." *The One-Act Play Today*, ed. William Kozlenko, Harcourt, Brace, and World, Inc., 1938.

"Politics and Theatre." Introduction to *Drama Was a Weapon*, by Morgan Himelstein, Rutgers University Press, 1963.

"Social Realism and Imaginative Theatre." *Theatre Survey*, 1962.

"The Group Theatre." *Theatre Arts* (October, 1940). Used by permission of the representatives of Theatre Publications, Inc.

BROADWAY IN REVIEW. Excerpts from Professor Gassner's quarterly "Broadway in Review" articles in the *Educational Theatre Journal*, 1960 through 1966. Except for a few exceptions, as noted by footnote, all the reviews in Part Five of this volume are from this source. Used by permission of the American Educational Theatre Association, Inc.

"*Who's Afraid of Virginia Woolf?* on LP." *Saturday Review* (June 29, 1963).

"The Playwright and the Contemporary World." *Theatre Arts* (January, 1964). Used by permission of the representatives of Theatre Publications, Inc.

"Bernard Shaw and the Making of the Modern Mind." *College English* (April, 1962). Used by permission of the National Council of Teachers of English.

"Forms of Modern Drama." *Comparative Literature* (Spring, 1955).

"The Modern, the Modernist, and the Absurdist." *Drama Critique* (Spring, 1963).

"*Avant-Garde*: Real or Fancied?" *Kenyon Alumni Bulletin* (January–March, 1965).

To MOLLIE

whose companionship

and help

made all this possible

Other Books by JOHN GASSNER

BEST PLAYS SERIES

Edited by John Gassner

(Containing the complete texts of the plays, introductory matter, etc.)

25 BEST PLAYS OF THE MODERN AMERICAN THEATRE:
Early Series, 1916–1929

20 BEST PLAYS OF THE MODERN AMERICAN THEATRE, *1930–1939*

BEST PLAYS OF THE MODERN AMERICAN THEATRE: *Second Series, 1939–1946*

BEST AMERICAN PLAYS—THIRD SERIES, *1945–1951*

20 BEST EUROPEAN PLAYS ON THE AMERICAN STAGE

BEST AMERICAN PLAYS—FOURTH SERIES, *1951–1957*

BEST AMERICAN PLAYS—FIFTH SERIES, *1958–1963*

BEST AMERICAN PLAYS—SUPPLEMENTARY VOLUME, *1918–1958*

BEST PLAYS OF THE EARLY AMERICAN THEATRE

THE THEATRE IN OUR TIMES

MASTERS OF THE DRAMA

PRODUCING THE PLAY

OUR HERITAGE OF WORLD LITERATURE

A TREASURY OF THE THEATRE (3 VOLS.)

ENGLISH COMEDIES

COMEDIES OF MOLIÈRE

HUMAN RELATIONS IN THE THEATRE

FORM AND IDEA IN THE MODERN THEATRE

TWENTY BEST FILM PLAYS

BEST FILM PLAYS OF 1943–44

BEST FILM PLAYS OF 1945

THEATRE AT THE CROSSROADS

THE NATURE OF ART (with Sidney Thomas)

FOUR NEW YALE PLAYWRIGHTS

CONTENTS

PREFATORY NOTE

The word "soundings" in the title of this book calls for a brief explanation. With a little temerity I could have substituted the word "criticism," since the volume contains critical essays from 1935 to 1966, either written or spoken. In the loose terminology long current in these days of literary journalism, almost every review, often mostly summary, of a play or book passes for criticism. I may have myself labored under such a delusion from time to time, and was encouraged in that belief by friends who were in the business of reviewing.

That this notion could have arisen is not difficult for me to understand since in a varied career in letters and theatre that started in the mid-twenties I did write at different times, and often with considerable regularity for such periodicals as *The Forum, New Theatre, One-Act Play Magazine* and *Theatre Review, Poetry World, Theatre Time, Theatre Arts, Directions, Current History,* the *Quarterly Journal of Speech, Theatre Survey,* the *Tulane Drama Review,* and the *Educational Theatre Journal,* and I have written a large number of prefaces and introductory essays at the request of authors and publishers. Some of these pieces have been included in two earlier volumes, *The Theatre in Our Times* (Crown Publishers, Inc.) and *Theatre at the Crossroads* (Holt, Rinehart, and Winston), and still others are presented here. But I believe "soundings" is a better term than "criticism" for most, if not indeed all, of the essays and addresses in this volume.

I offer this opinion not because I wish to trick myself out in the roles of false modesty or genuine penitence, but in order to define the nature of the present endeavor. I don't in fact believe much in "pure criticism." I don't believe it is "pure" at all, but partisan (I, too, was once a partisan, in my salad days in the thirties), and this is the case whether the partisanship is explicit or is concealed under a cotton-packing of alleged universal or of academic categorizing, to which I, too, find myself addicted from time to time. At its "purest," such criticism ascends to *esthetics,* a realm in which one will encounter men of fine intelligence, such as William K. Wimsatt, Jr., of Yale, whom I wish I were equipped to emulate, and others of high reputation whom I wish I could comprehend.

Above all considerations that occur to me at this writing, however, I must mention a special circumstance. I refrain from making large claims here for several related reasons. One is that I simply could neither afford nor achieve criticism because I could not stand apart from a play or a production, a playwright or a producing organization, to do more than approximate an objective view. Fate cast me in the role of a participant in theatre production (chiefly through the Theatre Guild after 1929 and Erwin Piscator's Dramatic Workshop of the 1940's), and empathy, at least, with the Group Theatre and the New Theatre League, on the one hand, and on the other hand as an instructor in several educational institutions (New Theatre School, the Dramatic Workshop, Columbia's School of Dramatic Arts, and Yale's School of Drama), and these two roles may have made me at times more or less "useful" to the theatre but too engaged with the particular individual's or institution's endeavors and problems. In this respect I was thrust at an early age, in my mid-twenties, into the untimely and, I may add, unenviable role of midwife and mentor.

Since understandably in an age of flux and uncertainly not one of the playwrights I sponsored and may have aided, and not one of the institutions with which I became associated, had an uncheckered career, but bogged down in some kind of stalemate or failed to survive the thirties, forties, or fifties, the present volume must be largely retrospective. This makes it history more than criticism, and if this is a defect in the opinion of young friends and associates, I shall simply have to bear their disapproval. I shall perhaps console myself, too, with a suspicion that if they are lucky enough to survive in an age hurtling to disaster, and if their endeavors become or remain strenuous enough, they too will become embalmed in "history." That is, they will find that their critical writings have become considerably historical, and the mood with which they assemble and assess them will be reflective. Embarrassing, perhaps? Possibly! But then only those who never put pen to paper or froze an opinion in printer's ink will be secure from embarrassment.

Still, there is this, too, to be said by way of preface: I believe that some chapters here can have the interest, and perhaps the value, of generalization based on a period's time-conditioned endeavor; that we may learn something from both its exertions and defeats; that it is possible to achieve perspectives and draw conclusions; and that past evaluations invite useful corrections and re-evaluations, as my subtitle suggests and supplementary comments in the text indicate here and there. Moreover, it is my hope that scattered in the essays that follow and in some hortatory or admonitory pieces are some guidelines for the present situation in dramatic art; and this may be the case even when some part, or a large part, of an essay here and there, such as the one on Aristotle or William Archer, deals with a general subject usually referred to as "academic."

In conclusion, I am pleased to have the opportunity to acknowledge with continued gratitude my wife Mollie's continued collaboration in putting another volume into press. And in the publishers' precincts I am especially grateful to Herbert Michelman's encouragement to collect these "disjected membra," to Nick Lyons for valuable help in both selecting and putting them together in some semblance of intelligible order, and to Mrs. Naomi Rosenbach for supervising publication.

—JOHN GASSNER

New Haven, Conn.
August, 1966

INTRODUCTION

Those who love the theatre—both those who work in it and those who still go to it—can be grateful for John Gassner. Whether he wrote for the *New York Times* or a periodical, his reports and critiques were always well considered, thoroughly documented, and wisely phrased. Even occasional pieces, written nearly four decades ago, still make interesting reading, though the plays and players they celebrate have long since been forgotten. More than that, though, those critical analyses constitute invaluable records of the period.

On April 2, 1967, John Gassner died at New Haven in the sixty-fifth year of his life.

His passing was the sad signal for the customary survey of credits and contributions, for eulogies and encomia. In his case, the list of achievements and honors is truly notable. It parallels the unfoldment of the American theatre of his time, a development that his unfailing aid to theatre people and his thoughtful criticisms of their work did much to influence. The tributes that have been paid him by family, friends, colleagues, and students have been distinguished by the depth of personal feeling revealed. Unlike so many eulogies, they have also been memorable in that every word of praise was thoroughly deserved, justly earned.

Although he periodically urged the necessity for, and the purgative value of, destructive criticism, as a critic, teacher, and friend he always tempered his judgments with humor, hope, and encouraging alternatives. This was nowhere better testified to than at his funeral service in New York City.

Among the speakers, playwright Robert Anderson and Yale School of Drama Dean Robert Brustein, their voices revealing the shock of loss, spoke not so much of his achievements—which were too well known to need repeating—but rather of the things he had done for them: how his help, advice, and friendship had influenced their lives and careers. Later, at a memorial service at Yale, held in front of the then unfinished set for the Robert Lowell adaptation of *Prometheus Bound,* the same thread was picked up by a number of sorrowing friends and students. The sense of loss was not purely that of a great teacher gone, a distinguished critic departed, but also that of a dear, beloved friend vanished from sight. A rabbi, Robert Goldberg, spoke of Professor Gassner's wide-ranging Humanism. His editor, Herbert Michelman, stressed his extensive knowledge and boundless interests. The noted French scholar, Henri Peyre, evoked his wisdom and wit so warmly, so richly that those present were moved to smiles, even to laughter. That, one feels, is what John Gassner would have wanted. Tears and mourning are wasted, for he is still with us in spirit.

Dramatic Soundings is an effort to prevent the erosions of time—to preserve important and insightful essays on theatre by one of its most devoted critics and teachers. The present volume is actually the third in a series of Professor Gassner's collected reviews and comments. The genesis of the project is typical of life with John Gassner, and it is worth telling the story in Mollie Gassner's own words:

> For years I had been annoyed that John's magazine and lecture contributions were gathering dust in the basement of the old homestead on Dahill Road in Brooklyn. Since we were always a "talking-it-out" family, I mentioned this to John many times, but his answer to getting the material between the covers of a book only got a vague, "We'll see, darling."
>
> I was still bothered by the thought of the dust collectors, facing me on my return home after four months abroad, and, on our last day in Paris, I decided to talk the matter over with Caroline [the Gassners' daughter]. My opportunity came when Caroline and I took a walk along the Champs-Elysées that very night. We finally came up with the idea of Caroline doing a book about growing up in our particular home, with a father who was a genius, but who never neglected his role as a man at the head of a household; always with a twinkle in his eye and time for friends and students; always aware of their problems. She was to weave John's articles into her book. It *seemed* like a good idea.
>
> Two or three days out at sea, Caroline was about to mention this project to John when she and I began to laugh out loud, for the idea suddenly struck us that she could not do this particular kind of book while her father was alive. Poor John! Now he was really in for it; he was not only confronted by a nagging wife, but by a daughter— fresh out of Smith College and whom he adored and respected—who agreed that Mother was right. *He* agreed to put the essays into a book. Accordingly, Caroline got all the articles together, dated them, sorted them, and piled them on a table. They collected dust again, while she went off to Columbia for her M.A. She and I nagged again and again, and finally the manuscript [*The Theatre in Our Times*] went off to Crown and was duly published. *Theatre at the Crossroads* followed later, and now *Dramatic Soundings*.

A representative selection of essays and reviews was made; structural divisions were established; the copy was edited and set. Unfortunately, at this time Professor Gassner was recovering from an illness that had greatly weakened him, though it did not decrease his appetite for work. His obligations to his students at the Yale School of Drama, his commitments as a regular Broadway reviewer, as well as several pressing publication projects prevented him from making final corrections, additions, and deletions to the galley proofs. It was his intention to do this work on a summer trip to Europe in 1967.

He could not have known that this would be a posthumous book. He was, in so many ways, still a young man in spirit and outlook. More books were planned, to add to the already lengthy shelf of Gassner titles.

In the summer before his passing, I visited him in New Haven to discuss the Broadway and Off-Broadway reviews on which I collaborated with him for the *Educational Theatre Journal*. Noting my avid interest in opera and operetta at home and in Europe, he urged me to write a book about the problems and practices of musical production. And then, slowly and thoughtfully, he said, "If I live, I'd like to do a book with you in a year or two."

Now that can never be. My small part in helping finish the editing of *Dramatic Soundings* must suffice. Credit for the work goes, of course, to its author and to his loving wife, Mollie. She accompanied him to the theatre constantly. He was fond of pointing out how often, in discussing a production with her, she was able to help him make a more balanced evaluation. Since his method of composition was generally to scribble his always well-organized thoughts in a kind of hieroglyphic on various pieces of paper he found at hand, Mrs. Gassner was more his translator than his amanuensis. This was a working partnership in every sense. *Dramatic Soundings* is, therefore, not only a memorial to its creator, John Gassner, but also a tribute to Mollie Gassner. He intended to dedicate the book to her as a small token of the years of productive collaboration and happy marriage.

Students and friends of the Gassners can testify that it is impossible to think of John without Mollie. One of his favorite prescriptions to angry young bachelor playwrights and critics, smarting from rejection and frustration, was to urge prompt marriage with a young woman with the qualities of Mollie Gassner. This is excellent advice, but the prescription is unfortunately not easy to fill.

Much of the arrangement of this book and most of the editing is the work of Nick Lyons, of Crown Publishers, Inc. My contribution has been to study the marginal indications Professor Gassner made on the galley proofs, as reminders to himself of the alterations he would effect on that summer trip he was never to make. I have deleted where he wished deletion, shifted some material where he wished it shifted, and added the explanations he indicated. In general, instead of trying to outguess him, I have merely cited his notations, offering an additional comment where I believe it represents his point of view. A span of decades separates some of these essays, and, while Professor Gassner's appreciation of innovation always kept pace with theatre development, it is remarkable how the central tenets of his criticism do not waver. Rather, they are adapted to new subject matter and new periods with wisdom and wit, instead of the dogmatism and peevishness of some younger critics. This means, however, that repetition of concepts or judgments occasionally may occur.

Professor Gassner was intent on removing as much reiteration as possible. Some essay proofs were heavily marked with marginal deletion signs. Others were not touched, although favorite anecdotes recur, as they so often do in professorial lectures. If a good story makes a point in 1942, it may still serve in 1962. Besides, the lecturer-writer will probably have a different audience—or, if the same eyes and ears are present, at least he will have few with total recall. As much as possible, repetitions of quotes, illustrations, and judgments have been removed, but there are several instances where the same story or fact make quite good, even essential, points in different essays. Also, in discussing certain periods and specific playwrights, Professor Gassner often qualifies his remarks by noting typical plays or outstanding features of content and style of the period. This creates a potentially irksome sense of the *déjà vu* the umpteenth time one encounters references to, say, Paul Green's *Hymn to the Rising Sun,* in the series of essays on the thirties; but trial excision of such repetitions damaged the wholeness of individual essays, which were usually not conceived in relation to each other and which were, in some cases, written years apart.

Since *Dramatic Soundings* is just that, the depth varies, as do the inland waters and the high seas on which Professor Gassner is navigating. The first section, "Soundings in World Theatre," surveys and judges the work of a number of masters from the distant and the recent past. The second, "Dramatic Theory and Practice," shifts its focus from playwrights to the crafts of writing plays and evaluating them. The third division, "Perspectives on American Theatre," is a rough chronology of American drama, seen through essays and reviews, from the beginnings to the present. "The Thirties," the fourth section, is separated from the previous sequence because its bulk and particularity are not balanced by that of any other period in American theatre represented; it is a young book, by itself, and it has special interest in that it mingles Gassnerian appreciations written during the heat and fever of the Depression with the sober reevaluations of later years. For readers who were too young to know the years of the Federal Theatre, Professor Gassner's contemporary evocation of this time of ferment and experiment may prove more immediately informative than recent works written very much after the fact. The fifth section, "Broadway in Review," covers productions of the sixties, and represents typical reviews written for the *Educational Theatre Journal,* for which the author was drama critic from 1951–1967, generously donating his services to this professional quarterly. It is divided into two parts, the first being those selected by Professor Gassner himself, prior to 1965, and the second being those I have chosen from later reviews. The latter are arranged according to subject matter, and, where possible, chronology, to provide a more effective display of the author's critical practice. The sixth section, "The Modern Vision in Drama," treats new movements and modes in thinking about and writing for the theatre. If some of the essays, especially those dealing with poetry in the theatre—a subject *aficionados* periodically urge on a generally disinterested public—seem slightly dated, it may well be that the search for novelty has become as feverish on stage as it has on canvas. This year's fad is next year's ancient theatrical history.

A curious discovery may be made by the careful reader. Professor Gassner, in person, was the epitome of courtesy, interest, and kindness. These qualities are also present in his writing. He has, in fact, been criticized by younger critics for being too kind, too forgiving, too soft. The general impression of gentleness, of thoughtfulness, is not an incorrect one, but it does not tell the whole story. Reading the reviews in Section Five ought to dispel the notions that he was a purely avuncular figure or a critical Santa Claus, despite his enthusiastic championing of experimental plays and new playwrights. When he was displeased, he could voice his displeasure in very definite, stinging terms. When he was dissatisfied, he was able to make that quite apparent, demonstrating the whys and hows. He shows, for example, a real admiration for the talent of Edward Albee, but he also takes him vigorously to task for his carelessness in construction, his casualness in thought. Professor Gassner, it can be seen from his reviews, was in the lead in appreciating new ideas and methods. He did not mourn the loss of a theatrical tradition: he begged for the establishment of a new one.

If he needed any defense from charges of conservatism—which he does not—one would only have to cite the Pulitzer Prize affair. In 1963, he and John Mason Brown, acting as the Pulitzer Drama Jury, recommended *Who's Afraid of Virginia Woolf?* for the annual drama award. Their 1960 choice, Lillian Hellman's *Toys in the Attic,* had already been passed over, so it was no great surprise when the Pulitzer Advisory Board did not honor the selection. As a result, the Columbia University trustees made no award in drama, not wishing to risk the moral dangers attendant on loading with laurels a work that contained real "four-letter" words. Not only did the Jury resign; they also made their disgust known. Professor Gassner's "Too Many Judges?"—reprinted in Section Three, from the *New York Times*—vigorously discusses the issues.

Several months after this introduction had been composed, and shortly before final changes and additions were sent to the printer, Professor Gassner's Preface was discovered among notes for work in progress. It excellently sums up his character and career. If anything, he has been too modest. His distinctions between reviewing and criticism are significant, worth remembering. Regardless of the general truth of his remark that "almost every review, often mostly a summary, of a play or book passes for criticism," the careful reader can see that Gassner critiques are seldom plot summaries. Indeed, when a synopsis of dramatic action is offered, it is usually necessary for a subsequent analysis of the virtues and/or defects of the structure, an analysis for which Professor Gassner's work as a play editor for the Theatre Guild and later for Columbia Pictures especially qualified him. At Mrs. Gassner's wish, the Preface has been printed exactly as written, without corrections or additions.

To me, Professor Gassner's friendship, interest, and aid was especially welcome, if unexpected. I was never a student of his, and my first contact with him was the result of a testy letter I had written, suggesting that Yale School of Drama graduates seemed to have a corner on all the grants, awards, and recommendations to be had. I was amazed to find how embracing his concern could be and how many people, also not Yale alumni, had profited from his interest and intervention. He was, I was astonished to discover, genuinely anxious to know what I thought of his criticism, his choice of plays in *A Treasury of the Theatre,* and the prospects of various young American playwrights. Now, in reading over and over the proofs for *Dramatic Soundings,* I understand at last that I *was* his student.

Everyone who has read any of his books—*Masters of the Drama, Producing the Play, Form and Idea in Modern Theatre,* or *Theatre at the Crossroads*—has been his student. And it is through them that John

Gassner continues to be among us. He will live as long as his books are read, as long as his students create, write, and teach with the curious mixture of humility and audacity, scholarship and humor, incisiveness and generosity that marked his life and work.

—GLENN LONEY

New York
November, 1967

Part One

SOUNDINGS IN WORLD THEATRE

ORESTEIA: DRAMATIC FORM
AND VISION*

Comparative studies may serve different purposes. It is my present intention to illustrate the close relationship that exists in a play between "dramatic form" and the "vision" or point of view it embodies. We might describe this relationship as the connection that can be found, without especial straining for subtlety or thoroughness, between the inner form of a dramatic work and its manifest content of ideas and attitudes. Even the term "inner form" is intended here in a limited sense—that of the choice, treatment, and arrangement of the events and other dramatic elements—in contrast to the external form determined by the conventions of a period that distinguish a classic Greek tragedy, for example, from a Japanese Noh play, an Elizabethan drama, or a modern realistic play.

I have selected three well-known treatments of a famous dramatic theme—the Oresteian, which culminates first in the murder of the Homeric king Agamemnon by his unfaithful wife Clytemnestra and, many years later, in the vengeance of his children—the high point of which is the murder of the queen by her son Orestes. Many writers from Aeschylus and Sophocles to Giraudoux and Sartre have treated the theme with significant differences. In order to limit the inquiry as narrowly as possible, I have selected three extant works from the same period. Three distinctly different treatments were made, by Aeschylus, Sophocles, Euripides, expressing markedly divergent points of view and producing more or less different species of dramatic literature—the epic, the tragic, and the nontragic realistic—within the compass of the same dramatic and theatrical conventions. The plays are the *Oresteia* trilogy by Aeschylus and the *Electra* plays by Sophocles and Euripides.

A few introductory remarks are in order. The plays of Sophocles and Euripides appeared almost a half century after the production of Aeschylus' trilogy in 458 B.C. They were produced during the declining years of the Athenian democracy, whereas the Oresteian trilogy was writ-

* From *Varieties of Literary Experience,* ed. Stanley Burnshaw (New York: New York University Press, 1962). [Apparently Professor Gassner felt this essay, in the context of this collection, begins rather abruptly. He queried in the margin of the proofs: "Introduction needed?" Because it is not known what he might have used as a prelude to the discussion, and because the directness and clarity with which the essay opens is typical of his criticism, no additions have been made. *Ed.*]

3

ten when Athens was the supreme Greek state, enjoyed unrivaled prestige, and was without question the one important outpost of Western civilization. Since the Greek tragedians were expected to deal exclusively with legendary and mythical matter, there was no question of imitation when Sophocles and Euripides took up the same theme. Moreover, they drew upon the same storehouse of literary material, which even for the Greeks of the fifth century was not always strictly distinguishable from history. The events are set in dimly dated Homeric times and concern a famous dynasty.

A vaguely defined curse rests upon the family in question; a strong feeling of fate (*moira*) hovers over its history of multiplying error, infatuation, and crime (*ate*) which leads, in one way or another, to retribution (*nemesis*). Tantalus, the mythical ancestor, had offended the gods by offering them the flesh of his own child: he was cast into the infernal regions of Tartarus, there to be tortured with thirst and hunger. His son Pelops, after successfully wooing the daughter of a king by winning a chariot race, ungratefully threw the charioteer who had helped him gain the victory into the sea. The dying Myrtilus cursed Pelops and his race for this treachery, and his curse was said to be responsible for the subsequent misfortunes of the family. The evil disposition, or hereditary guilt, was compounded in the next generation when the two brothers Atreus and Thyestes became mortal enemies: Thyestes had seduced Atreus' wife. Pretending to forgive Thyestes and inviting him to a feast of reconciliation, Atreus slew two of his brother's children and fed him their flesh. Escaping with another child, Aegisthus, Thyestes nursed a vengeance that attained fruition in the next generation when Aegisthus seduced Clytemnestra, the wife of his cousin Agamemnon. Agamemnon had sacrificed his daughter Iphigenia to enable the Greek expedition under his command to set sail for Troy; in revenge for this action, as well as in furtherance of her adulterous lust, Clytemnestra, with the help of Aegisthus, murders Agamemnon upon his return from the war. The family vendetta is carried yet one step further when Agamemnon's son Orestes, upon arriving at manhood, murders Aegisthus.

I

Aeschylus gives the legendary story a full-scale treatment, whereas his successors deal solely with the vengeance of Orestes and his sister Electra. He devotes separate plays to the murder of Agamemnon, the death of Clytemnestra at the hands of her son Orestes, and the sufferings and final release of Orestes. This treatment constitutes the trilogy, and only a trilogy could have projected his ruling idea, which concerns the development of private and public morality in the Greek world. As in most of his other extant work, Aeschylus is here concerned with the evolution of beliefs, principles, and institutions.

The first part of the trilogy, the *Agamemnon,* is on the simplest level a domestic tragedy, but it introduces the main theme and carries it forward. Vengeance is a prime *motif* since Aegisthus, who has won Clytemnestra and helps her in her project of murdering Agamemnon, is simply carrying on his father's (Thyestes') feud with Agamemnon's father (Atreus). There is a further parallel between the past conflict and the present: just as Thyestes seduced his brother Atreus' wife, so his son Aegisthus has possessed himself of the wife of Atreus' son, Agamemnon. Moreover, Clytemnestra claims to have turned against her husband only after his sacrifice of their daughter Iphigenia to his military ambitions. To justify her calculated murder of her husband, she maintains that she is simply avenging that death. Other possible motivations are subordinated, if not indeed suppressed, in the *Agamemnon.* Although love or sexual attraction for Aegisthus and aversion to Agamemnon must have played a part in her adulterous conduct, the romantic interest a modern reader might expect is simply nonexistent in Aeschylus' play. Although she resents Agamemnon's bringing home a concubine and kills her after slaying Agamemnon, jealousy is not presented as a motive in the betrayal and murder of the king. Clytemnestra's adultery, hinted at by the Watchman who appears in the Prologue and by the Chorus early in the play, had occurred long before Agamemnon's return home. Her private complexities and inner struggles do not concern the playwright either; it is enough for his purpose to portray her as strong-willed and resourceful—and unscrupulous. If Clytemnestra is to be considered an instrument of justice and of Zeus, then (as so often happens) a criminal character has been chosen to serve their ends and she is in no moral sense vindicated. Aeschylus does not ignore the compounding of evil by human beings and the punishment of crime by agents of justice (*dikê*) who incriminate themselves by their very actions in the service of divine purpose.

Criminal psychology does not concern Aeschylus beyond the service that the particular character renders to the governing ideas of his work. The returning Agamemnon, too, is given only as much character dimension as is needed for the drama's argument, and no more. He evinces a certain arrogance in bringing his concubine home and casually telling Clytemnestra to take good care of her, although we should note that

concubinage and the bringing home of a captive woman from a successfully waged war do not seem the least unusual to the Chorus. Later he
exhibits a conventional fear of committing the sin of pride (*hybris*) lest
he offend the jealous gods, but he allows Clytemnestra to play on his
vanity and inveigle him into walking into the palace on a purple carpet.
He questions her about Aegisthus, for he has heard the news that his
cousin has been received by her as a guest. But he does not press the
question, because Clytemnestra distracts him; and here it is especially
apparent that Aeschylus is disinclined to turn his play into a tragedy of
jealousy. We go on, instead, to the main action—to the murder of Agamemnon—and to the prophetic allusions of the captive priestess-princess
Cassandra, who recalls the long chain of guilt antecedent to the impending murder and foretells the continuance of retribution in the sorry history
of the "house of Atreus." Cassandra, in accordance with a curse laid on
her by the god Apollo, is unable to prevent the murder and, therefore,
steeling herself to the inevitability of her own death, she goes into the
palace, which she had previously refused to enter at Clytemnestra's urging. In killing her, Clytemnestra adds another sin to her criminal record,
just as Agamemnon had enlarged his own by taking the virgin Trojan
priestess for his mistress.

In one respect or another we are always made aware of an old disposition to evil that renews itself in the present action of the characters;
we are never allowed to forget that even the historic, heroic actions that
form the background of the immediate action have been steeped in guilt.
Through the choral odes that bring the past into the present in a manner
no less dramatic than poetic, we observe the sinfulness of both the abduc-
tion of Helen and the ensuing war led by Agamemnon. The latter is
actually, according to the Chorus, punished *in advance* for the crimes he
will commit in the conquest of Troy, since he is "compelled" before sailing
to Troy to sacrifice his daughter. The war itself is strongly disapproved
by the Chorus; it was apparently regarded as a mistake from the beginning. Not only does evil beget evil; it gives rise to complex questions as
to the heriditary nature of sinfulness and the circuitous course of punishment, which itself engages evil agents (such as Agamemnon and Clytemnestra) as its executants.

The vendetta theme of private or tribal justice is clearly presented
as the hurdle to be overcome by humanity in its progress toward civilization. At the end of the play, Clytemnestra, standing over the corpses of
Agamemnon and Cassandra, claims the deed for her own and urges the
justice of her action in accordance with the principles of private vengeance. Aegisthus, who arrives on the scene after the murder and is roundly

denounced by the Elders as a lecher and coward, justifies himself by crisply reciting the details of the feud between his father and Agamemnon's father. Ignoring his love for Clytemnestra (and we must assume that he loves her), he, too, stresses only the claims of justice—that is, the privilege of the blood feud. The Elders do not actually know how to refute this claim, for as yet there is no alternative to the primitive right of retribution, which will now, of course, pass on to the murdered Agamemnon's next of kin.

How then can this endless round of vengeance come to a halt? In the second play of the trilogy, *The Libation Bearers* (*Choephoroi*), the blood feud is carried to its ultimate horror. If the obligation of taking revenge devolves upon the next of kin, Agamemnon's son, Orestes, now grown to manhood, must kill his own mother. Apollo himself, at his Delphic shrine, orders Orestes to carry primitive law to this dreadful but inevitable conclusion. Moreover, there is no honorable or even safe alternative as yet for the unfortunate son. The case becomes clear when presented in terms of primitive belief: if he had refused to avenge his father, he would have been subject to punishment by the Furies arising automatically from his father's blood. Orestes is, as it were, trapped between his father's and his mother's Furies.

We first encounter Orestes as a character in literature when Homer refers to him a number of times in the *Odyssey* as a heroic young man who performed a meritorious deed. There are no dire consequences for Orestes in this early report; on the contrary, Pallas Athena holds him up as an example to Telemachus, Odysseus' son: "Haven't you heard what a great name Orestes made for himself in the world, the fine young fellow, when he killed the traitor Aegisthus who had murdered his famous father?" (Book I). And in Book III, the wise Nestor includes Clytemnestra's fate in his report saying, "When Orestes killed him [Aegisthus], he gave a funeral feast to the people over his hateful mother and Aegisthus the coward."[1] Moreover, Sophocles, long after the Homeric period, also elected to present the matricide without following it with retribution. Can we doubt that Aeschylus was bent upon undermining the primitive institution of the vendetta by devoting the second play of his trilogy to a major crisis in moral history?

Despite the static quality of its opening, *The Libation Bearers* makes an extremely moving experience out of the crisis. Seven years have elapsed since the murder of Agamemnon when Orestes returns. Retribution comes even though Clytemnestra took the primitive precaution of mutilating the

---

[1] Rouse translation, except for a slight change in the spelling of "Aegisthus" in order to keep it uniform in the present essay.

king's corpse before burying it, apparently in order to render her victim's spirit powerless. And vengeance falls even though, warned by a frightening dream that she has given birth to a viper that draws blood from her breast, she sends her servants with libations for the tomb of Agamemnon in the hope of placating his angry ghost. Aeschylus spares no effort to make the rule of Clytemnestra and Aegisthus abominable. Clytemnestra's daughter Electra, who had entrusted young Orestes to relatives in the distant city of Phocis some time before Agamemnon's death, has now been degraded by Aegisthus and Clytemnestra. The common people have apparently been oppressed, and the foreign serving-women or slaves who make up the Chorus of *The Libation Bearers* are so resentful that they have become the natural allies of Agamemnon's children.

Electra and the slave women pray for vengeance against their oppressors; and another round of prayers in the form of a great choral lyric follows once Orestes has revealed himself to his sister. He also reveals that he has been commanded by Apollo's oracle to perform the deed, and he prays for guidance to Zeus, the supreme god. At what we could consider the cost of much delay, the groundwork is laid for the vengeance that falls swiftly when it finally falls: Aegisthus and Clytemnestra are slain. Most of the delay is caused by the preliminaries to this action, which apparently must give every possible sanction for Orestes' deed—a god has ordered it; supplications have been made at the murdered king's tomb, where his spirit is supposed to reside; the avengers themselves have been greatly wronged; there is collective approval from the Chorus; and as the Chorus reminds us, "It is but Law that when the red drops have been spilled upon the ground they cry aloud for fresh blood" (Lattimore's translation). Also, the young avengers—the new agents of the old law—are a breed different from Clytemnestra and Aegisthus: they are pure of heart. And Orestes is by no means an unfeeling killer when he confronts his mother—as he cries out "What shall I do?" he has to be strengthened in his resolve by his hitherto silent companion Pylades, who warns him to heed the oracle and not to make an enemy of the gods.

Nevertheless the consequences are dreadful, and it is plain that Aeschylus would have it so. He prepares for the impact of his indictment of the old order of justice by raising the scene of the murder to an acute pitch of human drama. The excitement produced by the rhapsodic manner in which the avengers work themselves up to their task is followed by a scene which, although hardly sympathetic to Clytemnestra, stresses the appeal she makes to her long-absent son. Her appeal is so strong that it weakens his resolution until he is reminded to obey the god. As if this were not enough, the outrageousness of the deed is climaxed by the conclusion. Orestes justifies himself effectively before the populace in another highly dramatic scene, when he displays the robe in which Clytemnestra had cunningly entangled Agamemnon preparatory to slaying him. But his reasoning is of no avail; Orestes' mind begins to wander, terror overcomes him, and he runs away pursued by the Furies, the vengeful spirits whom he alone notices. The result of his unnatural act is madness, human nature having been brought to the breaking point by the inflexible operation of the law of the vendetta. Significantly enough, Electra has no role in this last scene despite her importance in the earlier action, nor does she appear in the last play. For all her sufferings, she is not directly involved in the evolutionary drama of *dikê*. It is Orestes in his public role of avenger, not Electra in her private role of sufferer, who is important to the central question of Aeschylus' trilogy.

Its resolution is the theme of *The Eumenides,* the concluding play, which now introduces some interesting changes. For one thing, the Furies are entirely objectified. They are first seen in all their repulsiveness in the sanctuary of the Delphic Oracle as they surround Orestes, who has taken shelter at the altar. They have been put to sleep by Apollo, who sends Orestes away to Athens under the guidance of his brother-god Hermes. We next see them awakened by the enraged ghost of Clytemnestra, who expects to be avenged by them even against her own son. On finding themselves robbed of their prey, the Furies protest bitterly that the upstart Olympian god has deprived them, the elder powers, of their rights. Apollo drives them out of his temple scornfully; but, undeterred by his contempt and claiming their ancient prerogatives, they run off in pursuit of Orestes, intent upon tracing him by his mother's blood. Apollo, in turn, declares that he will continue to assist *his suppliant*—whence the shift in emphasis in the trilogy. What was up to this point a conflict between human beings has now been transformed into a conflict between supernatural forces; or, in the familiar terms of Hegelian dialectics, into "a conflict of two rights." The moral position of the old goddesses of retribution, the Furies, is clear enough: they are avenging a horrible, unnatural crime. As for Apollo's position, although it is morally admissible in a patriarchal society and especially in a world in which revenge by the nearest of kin is lawful, it has its weaknesses—not only because its consequence has been the horrendous crime of matricide but also because the Furies have every right to make themselves the mother's avenger if vengeance for the father is justified.

In the next part of the play, Apollo will argue quite explicitly for a patriarchal point of view, but it is doubtful that he could convince any audience, ancient or modern, with his contention that the mother does not create the child but merely carries it. Aeschylus obviously sees little merit in Apollo's argument: it is not successfully pleaded and it fails to win an acquittal for Orestes. Moreover, Apollo's last speech to the Furies in the first part of *The Eumenides* implies a shift in his own position. He does not exculpate Orestes; he declares, instead, that he intends to assist and try to save a *suppliant*. Apollo's words are important not simply because it is noble for a god to help those who appeal to him for protection but also because it is only such an act of grace—in Christian terms, the mercy of God, and in the *Oresteia,* as we shall see, Pallas Athena's vote— that can redeem a guilty man.

In the *Oresteia,* however, redemption is not a religious mystery and Pallas Athena's mercy is tendered only after she has instituted the legal machinery of a trial, presumably the very first, in Athens. The trial that takes place is political, in being an act of the *"polis,"* or Greek city-state. Due process of law, as administered by the specially created court of the Areopagus, takes the place of private retribution. The great event in the final play of the trilogy is the institutionalization of *dikê* as a function of the *polis.* And this comes to pass in the City of Reason, the city of Athens presided over by the goddess of wisdom and the paragon of reasonable-ness, a virtue she displays abundantly throughout the second half of *The Eumenides.* Mercy, reason, and reasonableness form, as it were, a triad which ensures social evolution. It is both reasonable and merciful to keep retribution within bounds. Where reason prevails, retribution ceases to be blind, automatic, and without term.

Time is an important factor in the resolution of the *Oresteia,* and the last play of the trilogy, *The Eumenides,* is that rare thing, a Greek tragedy that violates the so-called unity of place. The scene shifts from Delphi to Athens; considerable time is supposed to elapse before Orestes succeeds in reaching Athens. The development of a new type of justice— the new *dikê* of the *polis*—is a historical process, and it is the product of "knowledge won by suffering," as the Elders of Argos in the *Agamemnon* put it. The passage of time, moreover, is associated with simultaneous processes of punishment by the matricide's conscience, which cannot in all decency be brief, and of the healing or the recovery of reason, which can-not be effected in a moment. When Apollo put the Furies to sleep and told Orestes to make his escape, he did not tell him that the way to "Pallas' citadel," or, if you will, the City of Reason, was going to be easy or short. The "repulsive goddesses," says Apollo, "will track you down . . . and your driven feet forever pound the earth, on across the main water and the circle-washed cities" (Lattimore translation). Declaring, "I have been beaten and been taught," Orestes later tells Pallas Athena that he has come to request her favor "blunted at last, and worn and battered on the outland habitations and the beaten ways of men" (Lattimore). Moreover, after the performance of lustral rites at Apollo's hearth, he is no longer an unpurged suppliant whose very presence brought pollution, and he is confident that the stain of blood on his hand is fading. Facing the Furies who have caught up with him in Athens, he proves himself once again sound of mind by his freedom of spirit and by the rationality of his behavior.

Nevertheless, the playwright's prime concern here is not with the individual but with the generations of men. Athena's course consists of *two* significant actions: she establishes a court for trying cases of homicide, apparently for the first time in history, and she casts a vote for acquittal, which proves decisive when the votes of the jury, made up of the worthiest citizens of Athens, are counted. In the first instance, she takes the administration of justice out of the hands of individuals, families, and tribes when she establishes the court on the Hill of Ares (the Areopagus) that shall henceforth try all cases of homicide in Athens. This is tantamount to creating the true City of Man, a viable political union of rival interests. Significantly enough, one of the "moral teachings" of the play is its explicit denunciation of *civil war,* which is followed by the assurance that Athens shall forever escape this calamity.

Athena's second decision is, as previously noted, truly an act of grace. The reason she gives for favoring Orestes at the trial is of course casuistical—having been born of no mother but of the brain of Zeus, she confesses herself a partisan of the male against the female. Such reasoning may have had considerably more force in fifth-century Athens than in twentieth-century New York, since the Athenians associated their success as a political unit with the substitution of a hard-won patriarchal society for a primitive matriarchal one. Nevertheless Athena's vote transcends any narrow sexual bias in the context of the humanistic character of the trilogy; what is important is that with her vote for an acquittal the patron goddess of Athens puts an end to blind vindictiveness and primitive retribution.

One thing remains: what to do with the Furies. A determination must be made after Orestes departs for Argos to assume the throne of Agamemnon. The reasonable Athena resorts to her great gift of persuasion, the civilized alternative to violence which is an indispensable instrument of the democratic *polis.* She succeeds in pacifying the Furies by offering them a hillside sanctuary in the city and converts them into spirits of benevolence—henceforth they will be known no longer as the "Erinyes" (Furies) but as the "Eumenides": the Kindly Ones. Their new benevolence, however, emanates from their old function as punitive goddesses; they are the representatives of conscience, without which civic order and civilization can be neither attained nor preserved. *The Eumenides* concludes with a torchlight procession of citizens conducting the mollified goddesses to their sacred habitation in the *polis*. Aeschylus' dialectical thinking ends in a "synthesis" of the conflicting forces represented by the bright, essentially amoral, young Olympian gods (especially by Apollo) and the primitively exacting earth-goddesses of retribution.

So ends the *Oresteian* trilogy of Aeschylus, one of the profoundest and most majestic works of literature. The more we ponder it the profounder it grows, and the grander it also grows; the visual components of stage action and spectacle—the varied and striking use of ceremonial acts, processions, choral recitation, and song—may well stagger the imagination of anyone but an expert in Wagnerian opera. We have said almost nothing about the theatrical qualities of the trilogy, though they are in fact commensurate with the impressive governing idea of the work.

There is no loss of dramatic power in the work as a result of Aeschylus' moral and philosophical intention. When the trilogy ceases to be a drama of persons and becomes a conflict of forces the action rises to new peaks of suspense and intensity. This is evident in the passages of moral fervor throughout the trilogy. It is also apparent in *The Eumenides,* first in the argument between the Furies and Apollo at Delphi, then in the suspense-laden trial, and finally in the scenes in which Athena placates the enraged Furies after Orestes' acquittal.

Each of the three plays, we must observe further, is a complete dramatic work and has a unique character, revealed in part by its structure. The *Agamemnon* is a great lyrical tragedy in which a crucial action in the present is enveloped in dramatic recitatives that fuse the past, present, and future. *The Libation Bearers* verges on character drama in the last two scenes, when Orestes kills his mother and is overcome with terror. *The Eumenides* veers toward the earliest form of Greek drama, in which the Chorus was the main actor.

In the *Agamemnon,* the Chorus of the Argive Elders, although it speaks with superb excitement, is primarily reflective; it fails to act while Agamemnon is being slain and makes a vain show of action only toward the end, when Aegisthus arrives to gloat over the death of the king. In *The Libation Bearers,* the Chorus of foreign slave women, sympathetic to Electra, is privy to the design against Clytemnestra and even prevails upon the old Nurse to mislead Aegisthus so that he will come to the palace unattended; the action, however, belongs not to the Chorus, but to an individual—to Orestes. In *The Eumenides* the action, except for a few minutes when Orestes speaks, is carried by the Chorus of Furies, with which Apollo and Athena have to contend; Athena's moral importance is great indeed, but even her role is dramatically secondary, because the Chorus is the aggressor. There is also a second choral group in *The Eumenides,* consisting of the Athenian citizens who act as judges at the trial and later make up the torchlight procession that accompanies the Furies to their shrine.

The Eumenides culminates as a fundamentally collective drama relating the private fate of the house of Atreus to the larger realities of moral law. The "people" have been on the stage in the first two parts of the trilogy; and the "people" and the gods take over entirely in the third play. A work that Richmond Lattimore has aptly called "a grand parable of progress" could have no other effect than that of a collective issue and action, and this was bound to be especially evident in a work permeated by an imagination that is not only moral and political, but, be it noted, *religious.*

The Oresteia is the work of a poet and thinker steeped in the mystery cults of classical antiquity. The trilogy is anagogical, so to speak, although in a fundamentally Greek sense, in which human reason and divine mystery—the "City of Man" and the "City of God"—are neither polarized nor even distinguished sharply. It is hard to avoid the thought that whereas the *Agamemnon* and *The Libation Bearers* are human tragedies, the trilogy as a whole is a sort of Divine Comedy. The outcome is a happy one and it bespeaks the operations of some dimly discernible divine plan associated with the Father-God Zeus. Apollo and the other gods, including of course the Athenian goddess of wisdom, are partial realizations of this All-God Zeus, who is the underlying creative and moral force of the world. Moreover, since it is an *evolving* force, Apollo may be described as a manifestation of Zeus at *one* evolutionary stage and Pallas Athena at *another, more advanced,* stage. The Furies distinguish themselves from the Olympian gods, but their conflict is not with Zeus himself. Everything that happens seems to occur through his will or with his permission as part of a divine plan identifiable perhaps with a spiritualized concept of the Destiny which, according to the Greeks, ruled gods and men alike. Zeus is fundamentally undefinable by men. "Zeus, whatever he be, if this name suits him" (Lattimore translation) is how he is invoked by the Chorus of Elders in the *Agamemnon.* But he reveals himself partially again and again, in specific events and in the overall course of *dikê;* present at the decisive trial of Orestes, says Athena, is "the luminous evidence of Zeus."

II

The distinctly narrower vision in the Oresteian dramas of Aeschylus' immediate successors, Sophocles and Euripides, produces narrower plays (just as the later treatments, including O'Neill's *Mourning Becomes Electra* and Sartre's *The Flies,* are narrower). Sophocles attains dramatic perfection in his *Electra* at the cost of a marked limitation of scope, imagination, and perhaps even sensibility. He seems to have gone out of his way to avoid moral complexities and theological commitments. He seems impervious to the outrageous character of Orestes' deed, so that the work invites the charge of moral callousness on the author's part. (An attempt has been made to explain this seeming detachment in regard to the murder on the grounds that Sophocles had set out to write an archaic heroic drama. Another explanation maintains that he presented his *Electra* as a corrective to Euripides' version, presumably written before Sophocles' play. These explanations, whether right or wrong, can have no particular bearing on our analysis, which is concerned solely with the effect of the play.) Euripides, on the other hand, unmistakably wants us to be outraged by the murder of Clytemnestra, but except for one speech that informs us that a common man can possess noble traits, he virtually exhausts his moral and intellectual (though not his dramatic) content with his explicit denunciation of the murder. There is no particular profundity in the work, although it can be praised for possessing other qualities. Sophocles gives us a heroic, Euripides an antiheroic drama. Sophocles creates character drama, whereas Euripides, carrying realism to naturalistic extremes, offers pathology and melodrama.

When Orestes in *The Libation Bearers* addresses the people of Argos in self-justification, he declares brokenly, "I have won; but my victory is soiled, and has no pride" (Lattimore translation). Then he perceives the Furies and, crying out to the Chorus, "You cannot see them, but I see them," he runs, presumably mad, out of the city he should be ruling. Sophocles' Orestes, on the contrary, is not at all overwhelmed with a sense of defilement and guilt. There are simply no postmortems, recriminations, or complications in Sophocles' *Electra.* Evil has been put down and the city freed from its tyrants; the play is, in effect, a heroic drama of liberation. (It is perhaps noteworthy that in a later treatment of Orestes' deed as an act of liberation, in Sartre's existentialist drama *The Flies,* Orestes is also in full control of his faculties and devoid of feelings of guilt; the liberation from the sense of guilt is, in fact, a principal theme and the resolution of Sartre's play.) The subject of *dikê* presents no particular problem to this younger representative of the post-Aeschylean "Enlightenment," the Periclean Age: Sophocles takes the rise of the well-ordered *polis* as a matter of course rather than as a hard-won victory for civilization. His sole concern appears to be with the individuals who became involved in an historic situation that taxed their human resources and tested their spirit or virtue (their *aretê*). *"Electra"* is the best possible name for this play since it is concerned chiefly with her character. Her suffering is of long standing, her situation is the desperate one, her endurance is tested in the extreme, and she is contrasted with more easy-going, opportunistic, humanity in the person of a sister, Chrysothemis, who does not appear in the plays of Aeschylus and Euripides. Sophocles invented this unheroic character apparently to help create a tragically isolated *heroic* Electra. His tragic vision focuses on the question of how integrity can be maintained and at what price.

Electra's sense of wrong disintegrates her essential womanliness, turning her into the virago of the later part of the play who stands guard outside the palace while her brother, Orestes, kills her mother inside; who calls out to him to strike her again, and then urges him to dispatch Aegisthus, too, and throw his body to the dogs. The most tragic element in the play lies *within* the character of Electra, where nobility (*aretê*) and femininity are in conflict. That the womanliness is there is carefully established in the recognition scene between Electra and Orestes, to which Sophocles assigns more weight than either Aeschylus or Euripides. Electra's happiness at recovering a long-absent brother, her clinging to him at the risk of endangering their plot, and the total humanization of this scene contrast vividly with what the embittered woman has been throughout the long years of waiting and what she will be soon again in the moment of vengeance. The dramatic design of the work is masterly in its simplicity as a result of Sophocles' dramatic tact and simplification of issues. The only complexity is complexity of character. Sophocles' play is not epic but individual tragedy; moral and religious, let alone metaphysical, problems have no place in it.

His *Electra* ends with a sense that a serious wrong has been righted, and with only a natural recoil by his son and daughter to save the action from melodrama. Serenity of a considerable degree is secured for the young Orestes, who arrives at dawn (a dawn full of singing birds) in the company of a wise tutor, the Paidagogos. Orestes is in all respects the composed and confident young aristocrat, and this is particularly evident in his superior bearing toward Aegisthus before he kills him. Electra is a more troubled character indeed, but she remains well within the bounds of sanity even when desperate. She manifests nobility rather than madness or some obsessional neurosis when she resolves to enact vengeance with her own hands on being told that Orestes is dead.

Sophocles, who limits the action to strictly human dimensions (he never brings the gods on stage, for instance, and avoids all supernatural manifestations), also limits the extent of his protagonists' disturbance before, during, and after the deed. If his Electra suffers from "tragic excess," it is an excess of spirit. Her tragic flaw is that she cannot live at peace with her father's murderers, cannot accept her mother's sensuality, and cannot endure seeing Aegisthus sitting on her father's throne and wearing her father's royal robes. She readily admits to the sympathetic Chorus of Mycenean women that she has let life slip by her and that she has invited the harsh treatment she has received. Unable to accept their advice to live moderately, "neither forgetting nor hating too much," she can only affirm her sense of obligation not to rest until she has avenged her father's death. She is plainly modeled after Sophocles' earlier heroine Antigone, to whom he also assigned an unheroic foil in the person of a compromising sister (Ismene).

III

Electra, we may conclude, is (like Antigone and Oedipus) one more character Sophocles has forced to the limit of endurance in order to dignify humanity rather than to degrade or reprove it. He has transmuted tragic excess into tragic victory in this tragedy with a nontragic conclusion. His *Electra* reflects all that was both splendid and contracted about the culture associated with the short-lived Periclean period.

Sophocles' younger contemporary, Euripides, was one of the most persistent of the challengers of Athenian society when it started to deteriorate, and his readiness to question conventional values and expose heroic characters to realistic scrutiny is abundantly evident in his *Electra*. The contrast with Sophocles' tragedy is all the more apparent because Euripides too makes Electra the central character, though he gives Orestes a greater share in her anguish. Like Aeschylus, he totally deplores the murder of Clytemnestra. But his dramatic focus is no less, and perhaps even more, contracted than Sophocles'. Euripides' treatment of the Oresteian theme does not take any evolutionary view of humanity's moral history and institutions. He dwells upon the religious problem in attributing to Apollo's orders the murder of Clytemnestra by her children, and is concerned only with showing what crimes are committed in the name of religion. There is no prophetic inspiration in his treatment of the moral impasse that arises when a son is required to execute his mother as his father's slayer. In the *deus ex machina* Epilogue of Euripides' *Electra* one may find, it is true, a wisp of Aeschylean evolutionary thought. Since the young gods Castor and Pollux, who come down to earth to assist Electra and Orestes in their blackest hour, deplore not only the murder but also Apollo's part in the crime, we may conclude that a more humane dispensation is somehow taking hold in heaven. But Euripides is not engaged by this subject; he does not develop it.

Euripides concerns himself, as does Sophocles, with the *agents* of the action; and toward the action itself he brings neither religious nor political vision, but a distinctly disdainful and antiheroic (as it were, "debunking") attitude. His approach is comparable to that of a liberal newspaper reporter covering an especially repulsive murder case, writing a realistic and somewhat lurid account—except that Euripides happens to be a dramatist of genius writing poetic drama for a theatre that has formal and ritualistic features. And this of course makes quite a difference; it is the difference between poetic drama (even when deliberately stripped of poetry so far as the murderers are concerned) and yellow journalism. Realism—within the framework of formal and poetic drama—dominates Euripides' *Electra;* it is visible in every significant aspect of the work up to the epilogue. The speeches are unelevated, though at the same time so shaped to fit the characters and their feelings as not to remain on a dead level of insensibility or mediocrity. Euripides also draws a sharp contrast between a commoner, the small farmer Electra was forced to marry, and the royal children of Agamemnon. Electra's husband respects her person and is the superior of any aristocrat in the play. As to the details of the murder, they are made especially repulsive: they reflect no glory whatever on the avengers. In this respect, Euripides works on us largely as a naturalistic writer, establishing an inglorious Orestes and a self-pitying, neurotic Electra, who does not exhibit a single attractive feature.

Euripides' Orestes, unlike his Sophoclean counterpart, is a nervous youth whose heroism is extremely doubtful. As if bent upon degrading him altogether, Euripides assigns him a rather dastardly and repulsive action. Aegisthus, playing the gracious host, has invited Orestes to partake of a sacrifice of a bull to the Nymphs. He offers him a knife or cleaver with which to perform the ceremony. As Aegisthus bends over the sacrificial animal in order to examine the entrails, Orestes assaults him with his butcher's instrument, breaking his spine and leaving him to die in agony. Aegisthus is hacked down like an animal in the midst of religious observances, and this rather sacrilegious action stands in sharp contrast to Orestes' dignified conduct in Sophocles' *Electra*. As for Euripides' Electra, her role is no less contemptible. Euripides actually evinces sympathy not for her, as Sophocles does, but for her victim, Clytemnestra. Electra traps her mother, who is portrayed as a remorseful middle-aged woman, by sending word that she has given birth to a child and calling upon Clytemnestra to perform the necessary rites. At the end, Electra is further implicated in the murder by Euripides. Not only has she bullied the hesitant Orestes into killing his mother but, as we now learn, she actually pushed Orestes' sword toward her mother's breast when he drew back from the deed. That both Electra and Orestes should later be appalled at what they have done is completely believable.

Moses Hadas does not speak too strongly for our modern sensibility when he calls Electra "a self-pitying slattern obsessed with sex" and Orestes "a timorous young ruffian." Euripides' Electra and Orestes are caught in a web of destiny—or, if you prefer, of circumstances and "conditioning"—worse than any that Clytemnestra wove for their father, but one cannot be stirred by these characters. Their situation, which is melancholy at the start of the play, remains depressing throughout. The action no doubt becomes dramatically intensified but it is hardly elevated as Electra reveals her pathology and Orestes his inadequacy for heroic action. A great deal of powerful *drama* but very little *tragedy* results from Euripides' naturalistic undercutting of the old Oresteian saga. There is much that is pathetic or subtragic in this essentially modern play. Indeed, we may well wonder whether such a work agrees with the formalistic nature of classic tragedy; whether, as it were, the "inner form" of the play harmonizes with its external choral, and more or less lyrical, structure. I am not disturbed by this disharmony, which actually contributes to the tension of the work, because here the "inner form"—the weave of the style, the characterizations, and the incidents—powerfully realizes Euripides' evident intention of showing what conventional heroism amounts to when observed closely.

One structural feature may be cited as additional evidence of Euripides' procedure in the service of his objective: In the sequence of events in *The Libation Bearers,* Aegisthus is killed *before* Clytemnestra: Aeschylus forces the appalling act of matricide into the foreground. Sophocles reverses the sequence, so that the action of his play comes to a climax with the slaying of the tyrannical usurper of the throne, Aegisthus, by the legitimate heir, an act that the Athenian audience could approve unreservedly. Euripides adopts the sequence followed by Aeschylus and concludes with the death of Clytemnestra. After the climactic matricide, the epilogue, with its condemnation of Apollo and its compassion for misguided humanity, is entirely appropriate.

In spite of critical animadversions against Euripides—the most famous and fatuous appear in August Wilhelm Schlegel's *Lectures on Dramatic Art and Literature*—we may wonder indeed who works with greater skill toward a particular end by means of tone, characterization, and structure, Sophocles or Euripides. Concerning Sophocles' *Electra,* the British scholar A. J. A. Waldock exclaims with admiration, "How a horror can be sapped of its strength, how a crime can be so drained of its power to shock that we are left in full sympathy with the criminals, how an offence against nature can be smothered and we can be led to accept an atrocity—this is the technical lesson of the *Electra."* True enough! But how horror can be magnified, how a crime can be made repugnant even when committed in the name of justice, so that we are left utterly dismayed by the experience—this is the technical lesson of Euripides' *Electra.*

Euripides also reflects an attitude expressive of his times, which happened to be Sophocles' times as well. His play is not a mere *tour de force* of realistic denigration, but a radical writer's protest against vengefulness and hysteria in the midst of the deteriorating morale of Athens. Both Sophocles and Euripides produced their Electra plays toward the end of the twenty-seven-year-long Peloponnesian War, a war that Athens was to lose once and for all in 404 B.C., at about the time when both playwrights died, the older in the fullness of years and honors in Athens, the younger in self-imposed and apparently expedient exile in distant Macedonia. Sophocles, who had reached manhood in the high noon of Athenian culture under the leadership of Pericles, could draw upon reserves of humanistic faith, confidence, and balance. Euripides had no such reserves to draw upon, and the heroic tradition of the Greeks lost much of its glamour for him when the war between Athens and Sparta was senselessly protracted. (We know that Euripides became a member of the Athenian peace party that endeavored to put an end to the conflict.) The older man celebrated traditional heroism, the younger looked askance at it; the former achieved exultation, the latter pathos. Aristotle, we may recall, considered Euripides "the most tragic of poets on the stage"; he was certainly the master of pathos. Euripides achieved it in his *Electra,* as in several other plays, despite his realistic characterizations; it was for humanity as a whole that he had compassion—for the guilt-laden Clytemnestra as well as her appalling children. Like his skepticism, his critical spirit, and his fondness for disputation, Euripides' "humanitarian" and "liberal" sentiments belong to the twilight of the Athenian state, not to its high noon. But his less "classic" and more "modern" disposition attained authority and integrity in the plays, such as his *Electra,* in which he successfully translated pity into passion and argument into human experience.

An effective agreement between means and ends, moreover, is apparent in the *Electra* even if one adopts a radically different interpretation, which holds that "there is no focus of sympathy" left in the play, "only a pervasive bad taste which leads to disgust with all forms of violence," and that Euripides simply demonstrates here that "justice can be as ugly as crime," or that his sole, if brilliantly accomplished, objective has been to alienate us from the conventionally regarded "right side."[2] It is hard to believe, besides, that the playwright who invites this alternate interpretation has not actually introduced humanitarian and liberal principles into his work and demonstrated compassion, no matter how bleakly, for bedevilled humanity. Even the *deus ex machina* Epilogue strengthens agreement between form and content, for it is only proper that the young gods be brought onstage to deplore the conduct that an older god sanctioned and to mitigate its consequences for the misguided avengers. Having first resorted to naturalism in depicting gross human action, Euripides has gone on to challenge its religious basis with a suitable epiphany; both the naturalistic and poetic elements serve the same end—the work is "structured," as it were, by its ruling idea. Dramatic form and dramatic vision, then, are interdependent in Euripides' drama just as they are in the parallel by Aeschylus and Sophocles.

   2 Emily Townsend Vermeule, "Introduction to *Electra*," *The Complete Greek Tragedies,* ed. David Grene and Richmond Lattimore (Chicago: University of Chicago Press, 1959), IV, pp. 390–94.

■

LOPE DE VEGA*

At a peasant wedding in Ocaña, in the kingdom of Toledo in the year 1406, a young peasant, Pedro, says to his bride Casilda in public:

> You are more beautiful to me than an olive grove laden with fruit or a meadow full of flowers at dawn on a May morning. No riper red apple can compare with you, nor can golden olive oil gleaming in jars give me more delight. The scent of your lips is sweeter to me than the breath of the best white vintage wine. A courtier would compare you to a rose, but to a peasant wine smells better. . . . With you in my house I shall not mind what time of year it is or what the weather is like.

To which the pretty bride Casilda, who I suspect is about the same age as Juliet, if not actually younger, replies:

> No music that ever set my feet tapping can thrill me as much as you do, however hard the drummer beat his stick or blew on his pipe. Myrtle and vervain were never so sweet, nor are the horses whinnying on Midsummer morning as exciting to me as the sound of your voice. What gay, tinkling tambourine or psalm in church can equal you? A processional power with all its bobbles and shiny silk cord is not as fine as you in new red hat. Your love is better than clean feet in new shoes.

And since her enthusiasm is not easily exhausted, she continues:

> Out of a million boys you are the Easter cake—covered all over with little chicks and sugar eggs. You are like a young red bull in a green

* An address given at Princeton University on March 28, 1963, in commemoration of the quadricentennial of Lope de Vega's birth. [Unusual and effective as the opening of this essay is, Professor Gassner intended to lead up to it—and the achievement of Lope de Vega—with an historical prelude that would help to put these sentiments in better perspective. His notations read: "Introduction. Explain significance of proletarian theatre in Spain!! Cf. anti-feudalism in Sh[akespeare] and Lope, etc. Workers' plays!! Medieval!"

Despite frequent assumptions that the Golden Age of Spain's drama grew from religious *autos,* the evidence is that the secular tradition was also very strong—even, at times, invading the ritual plays to the annoyance of the Church. Interesting details are provided in Hugo Rennert's *The Spanish Stage in the Time of Lope de Vega* (New York: Dover Publications, 1963). The comic *pasos* of Lope de Rueda—first heard of as an actor-manager in 1554—exploit simple daily situations with wit and insight characteristic of the people, rather than the court. As Lope de Vega's antecedant and as a founder of Spanish theatre, De Rueda's influence should not be overlooked. *Ed.*]

field or a new white shirt in a golden basket with jasmine all around
it. You are like Easter candles and almond paste at a christening.

The officiating priest suggests a halt, since the guests are eager to
dance, and Pedro asks their forgiveness, saying, "We were carried away!"
A peasant courteously says, "Don't let us stop you!" But the country dance
starts up and a singer accompanies it with a song promising the couple an
idyllic life to which nature itself will provide suitable courtesies—"Green
alders will salute them, and the heavy almond shall bow down before
them."

These rhapsodies in the opening scene of Lope de Vega's famous play
Peribañez and the Commander of Ocaña signify a great deal. The play
was once translated and adapted by a protégé of mine at the Theatre
Guild under the title of *Peter among the Horns.* Lope de Vega was himself among the horns, so to speak. By temperament as well as chronology
and the historical situation, he stood between the Middle Ages and the
Renaissance in many respects; and, like the Golden Age of Spain itself,
he tended to live, feel, and think himself into a synthesis of both worlds.

In the scene from which I have quoted, as elsewhere in *Peribañez*
and other plays, we find feeling and form, impulse and formality, naturalness and elegance, closeness to nature and closeness to rhetoric. And in
some of Lope's most important plays from the modern point of view—in
Fuente Ovejuna as well as in *Peribañez and the Commander of Ocaña*—
Lope stood between medieval collective conscience and Renaissance individual will, between an ideal of submission and an ideal of self-assertion.
And the historical situation is such that Lope can be both for the common
man and the king, who stands above both the peasantry and the feudal
nobility but shares with the former a desire for justice and opposition to
the self-will of the feudal nobility claiming absolute power over the peasantry and independence from the central authority of the king.

An especially significant detail in *Peribañez,* in which the peasant
Pedro kills his feudal overlord the Commander of Ocaña for trying to
seduce his young wife, is that instead of stressing the conflict between
peasant and nobleman as class conflict Lope minimizes it. The Commander tries to get Pedro out of the way by appointing him leader of the
company of peasant soldiers he is sending to the King of Castile. But
before departing for the King's campaign, Pedro gets his social status
elevated in being knighted by the Commander. Therefore, when he kills
the Commander later on in the play for laying siege to Casilda, Pedro
attacks the Commander as his social equal. And Pedro, indirectly warn-

ing the Commander, of whom he already has reason to be jealous, is fully
aware of his new status. He says to the Commander:

> This sword I wear, which *you* put on, now represents my new estate.
> I take my leave *your equal*. See that you protect my honor, or I shall
> hold you responsible and acquit myself according to the rules and
> code of your behavior.

It is as a knight privileged to avenge his injured honor, and not as a
peasant, that he is acquitted by the King. And the King, who releases
him, refers to a conventional class distinction between a nobleman and a
peasant in saying:

> It is strange that one so humble should hold his honor so high.

And after announcing that Pedro is to be retained as captain of the
company of peasants from Ocaña, the King confirms his rise in rank,
saying:

> And last, Peribañez, I give you leave to carry arms as a gentleman.

It is in *sentiment* that the play is so exhilaratingly democratic—in
Pedro's and the other peasants' self-respect and the pride their women take
in them as they march off to war beside a company of nobles. One peasant
girl declares, "I think our men look better"; and another adds, "Their
clothes may be finer, but the men inside them are not."

It is this abundance of sympathies, this fusion of the new and the old,
of originality and conventions, in Lope's plays, that accounts for a good
deal of their variety and vivacity, and that enabled their author to mediate,
it would seem effortlessly, between the popular theatre of the Middle Ages
and the rising courtly theatre in Spain, and to combine the freshness of
folk speech with the refinements of literary drama, often (as in *Peribañez*)
in the same work. This variegated talent made him a playwright for his
own age as well as a playwright for ours, and secured his twentieth-
century reputation as the greatest Spanish dramatist.

I recall my extreme excitement in the 1930's when I first came across
a play by him that, for all its formalism, and despite the fact that its
action was set in the year 1476, seemed to belong essentially to the contemporary world. The play was *Fuente Ovejuna,* or *The Sheep Well,*
and I came to it, after having previously formed the impression from an
early translation that the play was much too stiff and remote to justify
my recommending it for production by the Theatre Guild, then the country's leading theatrical organization. I was impelled to give the play a

second reading only several years later when, on leafing through the foreign periodicals and newspapers that came to my Theatre Guild office regularly, I found favorable notices on *Fuente Ovejuna* in two publications rarely in agreement on anything. There must be something to a play, I said to myself, if it can be praised within a week by both *The London Observer* and *The Moscow Daily News!* Although somewhat unwieldy for production on Broadway, the play came close to getting a production from us, and *Peribañez* came even closer when Ramon Naya made the adaptation we optioned and knew under the piquant title of *Peter among the Horns*. Although *Fuente Ovejuna* has not yet reached Broadway, and it is unlikely that it will, it has already reached a number of American communities through university productions. I narrowly missed seeing one of the most recent of these at the University of Texas, in Austin. Thus the wheel turns full circle round, and Lope, who had enjoyed great esteem and success in his own day but came to be overshadowed in later times by his successor, Calderón de la Barca (1600–1681), resumed his place as the principal Spanish dramatist.

Peribañez is perhaps the simplest of the three best-known more or less historical plays that comprise a small percentage of Lope's enormous output. With an energy that could have put his contemporaries the *conquistadores* who gave Spain its overseas empire to shame, Lope wrote in addition to voluminous nondramatic works close to a thousand long and short dramatic pieces, and he himself claimed to have written more than fifteen hundred. Among these are many trivial and devotional pieces, cloak and dagger adventure plays, comedies of manners and tragicomedies, dramas of intrigue, pastoral and mythological plays, religious dramas, and short allegories called *autos sacramentales*. The works that have attracted the greatest interest beyond Spain are the plays largely based on Spanish history, and balladry, the historical material supplying the occasion for freely invented romantic events and metrically varied poetic dialogue, as well as vivid characters. In these plays, moreover, the dramatic action is strongly marked and rapid, as might be expected from the vitality of his times, the period of Spanish world empire—and from the man himself, concerning whom it has been said that "had he devoted every single minute of his life to his writings—which include lyrics, epic poems, prose fiction, treatises, and so on—it still would be difficult to believe that a single human being could have written these millions of lines, most of them in verse. But what is especially amazing is that Lope did not devote even half of his time to his literary endeavors, for he was extremely fond of the ladies and devoted many hours to them." To which one would have to add that there was a great deal he was devoted to, including theatre management and religion—a rather unlikely combination. It is no wonder that Lope's greatest contemporary, Cervantes, called him "The Prodigal [or Monster] of Nature"—the *Monstruo de la naturaleza*.

In an age of striking personalities, he was one of the most colorful. Born on November 25, 1562, about two years before his greatest contemporary, Shakespeare, Lope outlived him by nearly twenty years, dying in 1635. He could apparently read Latin and Spanish and compose poetry at five; he entered the Imperial College in Madrid at fourteen, having also become adept at music, dancing, and fencing. But he soon ran away from the college, traveled across northwestern Spain with a classmate, enrolled as a soldier, and participated in an expedition against Portugal. Taken under clerical patronage, he then went to the University of Alcalá, took his bachelor's degree there at the age of seventeen, and would have entered the Church had not his nature, which was highly impressionable and inflammable, decreed otherwise. He was on the verge of becoming a priest, he wrote in a letter, "but I fell blindly in love, God forgive it; I am married now, and he who is so poorly off has nothing else to fear."

After participating in a successful naval expedition, he came to Madrid to lead the arduous life of letters and soon acquired a genteel reputation for wit and began to write plays professionally. At the same time, he fell in love with his producer's married daughter and began to celebrate her in ballads under the name of "Filis." If we are not misinformed, the lady in question, who was married to an actor, reciprocated by giving Lope both her love and her jewels. This happy arrangement apparently lasted five years, when it was terminated in 1587 by a violent quarrel with the lady's father, the producer, whom he proceeded to lampoon. A libel suit ensued and Lope was sent to prison and then exiled from the kingdom of Castile. But at the risk of being arrested and sent to the galleys, he reentered Castile, and promptly eloped with the daughter of a prominent courtier in Madrid. He married the girl, but having heard the call to arms and adventure, he left her in Madrid and promptly joined the Spanish Armada as a soldier.

Fortunately, the ship on which he embarked, the *San Juan,* was one of the few galleons to return from this ill-fated effort to conquer England. The débâcle was singularly favorable to the theatre, of course: it left England free to evolve the Elizabethan theatre and brought Lope back to resume his career and develop the Spanish national theatre, a bustling popular, yet also literary, enterprise like the Elizabethan theatre. It must be noted that Lope had not been so greatly disturbed by the historic episode that he could not settle down to some sturdy writing during the long voyage that lasted some six months and included the circumnavigation of the British Isles. It was on this precarious trip that he wrote one of his longest and most ambitious pieces—a romance in verse called *The Beauty of Angelica*. Recovering from both the voyage and the romance, within about a month he went to Valencia to resume his theatrical career. His plans, however, failed to include resumption of his married life with the young wife he had left in Madrid. Instead, he assumed a new attachment closer to the stage when he fell in love with the married actress Micaela de Luján, who had five children by him and to whom he evidently remained constant for a long time—despite his marriage in 1598 to the well-dowered daughter of an affluent pork merchant. He was rewarded in 1605 by the birth of a son by his wife and a daughter by Micaela, and two years later by the birth of a talented son by her who attained considerable reputation as a poet under the name of Lope Felix del Carpio y Luján. After the death of his wife in 1613, Lope de Vega, who was an affectionate father, brought his legitimate and illegitimate children together under the same roof in Madrid. A year later he also took minor orders with the Church and became an official or "familiar" of the Inquisition, though without any noticeable interruption of his amatory and literary careers. His lady loves included a spirited actress whom he nicknamed *la loca*, "the mad one," and a young married woman whom he celebrated under the pastoral pseudonym of "Amarilis," who also enlarged his paternity when he was well past fifty. He continued to be a prolific worldly playwright, too, although he continued to write religious drama as well. Anyone not a psychoanalyst would be hard put to reconcile this career, too, with the religious fervor that apparently impelled him to scourge himself regularly for the good of his soul—until the walls of his room were spotted with blood. Lope himself does not appear to have made any noteworthy effort to reconcile the contradictions in his life and careers. Although often remorseful, he merely let the contradictory elements run parallel courses; perhaps the same thing can be said about Spain itself in the "Golden Age."

To arrive at a just estimate of Lope's labors, it is necessary to realize that it was virtually his genius alone that presided over the transition from medieval to Renaissance drama in Spain. Imitations of Roman comedy and Greek tragedy had a brief vogue, but only among the learned, who were mainly interested in the study of the humanities as an academic discipline. Comic interludes and related entertainments flourished in the fifteenth century, but they lacked literary artistry and were too crude for the intellectual and artistic flowering of the next century graced by Lope and Cervantes, his senior by fifteen years. Romantic drama began to take shape before Lope's success on the stage but still needed the ingenuity and vivacity that he cultivated in this type of comedy, which came to be called *capa y espada,* cape and sword (or cape and dagger) drama. Yet the theatre itself was ready for plays of some substance and professional competence. The public theatres in Spain, which resembled the open-air theatres in London, were crowded with both common playgoers and gentry. The platform, still the most important feature of the stage, jutted out into the audience and allowed a flow of continuous dramatic action uninterrupted by the raising and dropping of act and scene curtains and by changes of stage settings for separate scenes or acts. Now the important thing, as in Shakespeare's ample Globe Theatre, was to unroll upon this stage a series of vivid and varied actions that would make a good story and provide an amusing or exciting experience.

More than crude entertainments and simple pious scenes were needed once plays came to be produced in permanent theatres, known as *corrales,* rather than by traveling companies on hastily assembled stages, which Cervantes described as being "composed of four benches, arranged in a square, with five or six boards laid across them, that were thus raised four palms above the ground."

In the permanent theatres that grew in number and comfort in Valencia and Madrid during the latter half of the sixteenth century, rudimentary stage productions also would no longer do, and underwent Baroque elaboration of the *mise en scène* on multiple acting areas and with the gradual pictorial enrichment of painted scenery. Moving well ahead of his predecessors in the theatre since the middle of the century, including Cervantes, Lope proceeded to satisfy the needs of the day with bustling action and bold invention. Without exactly overestimating the value of his dramatic work (he took considerably more pride in his other writings) he defended it as entertainment and genially defied the pseudo-classical rules laid down for the drama by scholars of the fifteenth and sixteenth centuries. The scholarly code called for the strict separation of tragedy and comedy, forbidding the intrusion of humor into a tragic play. They ordered playwrights to avoid scenes of violence on the stage and to relegate unpleasant events to narration—that is, to messengers' reports. They called for the strict observance of the rule of the three unities of action, place, and time, according to which playwrights were required to present only a single story in a play, confine the action to a single place and limit it to events transpiring in a single day. Defending his use of multiple and shifting action, Lope composed an apologia in rhymed verse, *The New Art of Writing Plays,* in 1609, that speaks for the Elizabethan playwrights as well as for Lope and his Spanish contemporaries of the nonacademic stage. It contains apt passages. The most famous of these is, although indirectly and ironically formulated, a veritable declaration of independence for playwrights. Addressing the Spanish Academy in Madrid, and referring to the precepts of neoclassic theory, he says:

> True it is that I have sometimes written in accordance with the art which few knew [that is, with the neoclassic precepts]. But no sooner do I see coming from some other source the monstrosities full of painted scenes where the crowd congregates and the women who canonize this sad business, than I return to that same barbarous habit, and when I have to write a comedy I lock in the precepts with six keys. I banish Terence and Plautus from my study that they may not cry out at me; for truth, even in dumb books, is wont to call aloud; and I write in accordance with that art which they devised who aspired to the applause of the crowd; for since the crowd pays for the comedies, it is fitting to talk foolishly to it to satisfy its taste.

Following which, Lope goes on to deal with technical matters with the practicality of an expert contriver of entertainments.

These consumed no less of his time than the exciting melodramas he fashioned so well. Literary fame is not easily achieved by these means, of course, even if there is much sense in Lope's insistence, as Brander Matthews puts it, that "the stage is intended primarily for story telling, for presenting in action a serial tale which shall excite the constant interest of curiosity." Without doubt, Lope de Vega made himself vulnerable to strict criticism in fabricating unexpected plot complications and keeping up the suspense until the last moment possible. It is also true that his "cape and sword" plays are only whirling affairs of love-making, intrigue, and confusions; that in being limited to plot interest, his dramas of passion and crime bear a resemblance to minor Elizabethan tragedies and do not rise to the high order of tragedy; that his flair for romance leaves little room for depth of thought or characterization. But this is not all that can be said about the bulk of his dramatic work; and it is too much to say with Brander Matthews that Lope "lays all his stress upon adroitness and ingenuity of plot building." This is certainly not true of *Peribañez* and the other social dramas involving the peasantry, the feudal nobility, and royalty. Nor is it true of even the lighter works with which I am familiar. Not only must one reckon with the style, metrical virtuosity, and flair of the writing, but with much verve in the plot that derives from (and defines) the spirited characters. This should be apparent, for example, in a summary of *A Certainty for Doubt,* one of the swaggering romances.

The play describes the rivalry of King Pedro the Cruel and his brother Don Enrique for the love of Doña Juana. Although Pedro has the advantage of royal power, which allows him to banish his brother, and Enrique the disadvantage of being troubled by two other women, Doña Juana favors the dashing cavalier Enrique and rejects the King's advances. Thereupon, Pedro impulsively tries to have his brother assassinated, and then tries to marry Doña Juana forcibly. But Enrique unexpectedly appears at the wedding ceremony and somehow gets himself married to her, whereupon Pedro discloses a royal nature and pardons the lovers.

Another, and lighter, example in which plot improvisation is the primary factor, in the story of Belisa in *Madrid Steel*.

The spirited Belisa falls in love with the young spark Lisardo, and being watched by an argus-eyed duenna Teodora pretends to be ill. A doctor is called in, who is none other than the young lover in disguise, while Teodora is engaged in the park by the young hero's friend, Riselo, who pays court to the astonished but nonetheless grateful elderly lady. As this intrigue is a prolonged one, the lovers are in danger of losing each other. Also, young Riselo's lady-love frets at his neglect of her while he is distracting the duenna from her watch, and Belisa's father is already laying plans for marrying the girl to someone else. But Belisa flees from her father's house to her lover's quarters, and a double wedding ends all difficulties.

And it was not impossible for Lope to find an effective combination of character development and action in the same work. This is the case in *The Dog in the Manger,* in which a high-born lady is shown struggling against falling in love outside her class. The proud Countess Diana is loved by her secretary Teodoro and is attracted to him in turn. But his humble rank proves an impediment to her affections, and she fluctuates between love and scorn for him until Teodoro's roguish servant makes up a sufficiently distinguished family tree for Teodoro—which the lady knows to be false. A nobleman is tricked into believing that the young man of humble birth is his long-lost son.

The Dog in the Manger is, of course, limited in depth of feeling by its very excellence as a comedy of manners based on the barriers of caste that the noblewoman in love with her secretary has to overcome. Only a certain degree of psychological impasse adds weight to the comedy, the title of which refers to the fact that the Countess cannot allow herself to love Teodoro and yet cannot tolerate his being loved by anyone else. The reference is to the dog in the manger that begrudges anyone's consuming the food it does not eat itself. But, in fact, *The Dog in the Manger* can do very well without "psychology" in any but the most superficial sense, since the multiple complications arising from the heroine's concern with family honor are lively, and the play is raised well above ordinary romantic comedy by its irony. The heroine's real honor was never threatened or affected since this is a matter of personal worth and scruple; only the false honor of belonging to a favored social class and keeping up appearances was affected. The play, then, constitutes a satirical comment on the worthlessness of appearances and insuperable class distinctions. This is the most modern feature of the play and its most serious substance.

High seriousness appears in Lope's work when the theme of honor is utilized with tragic overtones and tragic resolution. Strict principle drives his heroes to extravagant actions, and when this leads to extremes of conduct that belong to neither comedy nor romance, there are only two alternatives—namely, melodrama and tragedy. Often the result may be entirely melodramatic from our modern point of view, but melodrama is not the exclusive effect when the extreme actions required by the protagonist's sense of honor sound the depths of his character and he is caught in the vise of contradictory emotions. In that case, Lope *achieves* tragedy for his times and *approaches* tragedy for our own. The best example known to me is his *Justice without Revenge* (*El Castigo sin Venganza*), one of Lope's latest and most powerful plays. The play dramatizes the conflict between the promiscuous Duke of Ferrara and his natural son Federico as a result of the son's falling in love with the Duke's new young wife Cassandra. The Duke continues his amorous ventures after his marriage and neglects Cassandra, and his son had met Cassandra before he could know that she would become his stepmother. The Duke goes off to war, leaving the young lovers opportunities they are not reluctant to exploit. When the Duke returns as an apparently reformed character and discovers their love affair, he regards it as an ironic punishment for his own immoral conduct in the past. But horror overtakes him at the thought of the dishonor—that is, the jeopardy to his reputation.

"Oh God of Justice," he cries out, "my house shall this day see more than you decree. . . . I do not avenge my injury. I will not invite your divine displeasure by taking vengeance, for to do so against my own son would be a double cruelty. I must act as a father, not as a husband, and administer punishment without revenge to a sin that was beyond shame. The laws of honor demand that much . . ." And he concludes that "Love must not stand against me, when honor, presiding in the court of reason, pronounces its implacable sentence."

Thereupon he bullies his son into stabbing the bound and covered body of his wife, then accuses the young man of having murdered his stepmother, and has him murdered. Though the Duke does not die in the play, his responsibility for the death of his son causes his life to lose all meaning.

Even a play such as this Phédre tragedy, which approaches tragic reality even closer in not painting the stepson and his stepmother in colors of absolute innocence, does not introduce us to the Lope de Vega who attained his greatest magnitude for our times. The values upon which the tragic action is based are not immediate to us; they do not redeem the Duke convincingly. His Borgia-like strategy in encompassing the murder of the stepmother by the son, and the deliberate murder of the son as a murderer, reduce the Duke's tragic stature in addition to diminishing the credibility of the plot. And another play veering toward tragedy, *The Knight from Olmedo,* in depicting only the private action of the assassination of the hero by his rivals in love, misses tragic magnitude. It is one of Lope's most appealing plays, starting with romantic comedy, then deepening in tone with the employment of a sinister bawd who practices witchcraft, climaxing in murder, and ending with the ironical revelation that there need have been no tragedy at all if the heroine had told her father of her love. The lovers actually had no reason for the fatal concealment of their love since the heroine's father would have approved their marriage.

It is, in fact, not in pathos or tragedy that Lope excells most for our generation but in the works that may actually puzzle us with their curious modernity. They are the works in which class relations, at times intensifying into class conflict, constitute an important dramatic element. Political implications are present in these dramas and the theme of honor introduces the theme of social justice, which is still very much with us. They are plays, too, in which poetry and the folk spirit appear in combination with strong characters and significant issues, and in which formal structural and stylistic features co-exist with both realistic detail and realistic viewpoint. *Peribañez and the Commander of Ocaña* is such a play; it is perhaps the earliest, and may have been written as early as 1605 and was published in 1614. *Peribañez* illustrates Lope's historical genre most simply, although in my opinion less successfully than one could wish because the happy resolution is too uncomplicated and too easily encompassed when the King instantly pardons the peasant who, sensible of his honor, killed his feudal overlord.

A more complex work is *The King the Greatest Alcalde,* which Lope based on the history of Alfonso VII of Castile, a ruler renowned for his sense of justice. This play also has a peasant hero, Sancho. In compliance with feudal regulations, young Sancho goes to his master, Don Tello, to obtain permission to marry a pretty girl, Elvira, whom he brings with

him to his overlord. But Don Tello abducts the girl, and when Sancho
endeavors to plead with him to return Elvira, Don Tello has his servants
drive away the peasant suitor. After vain efforts to get justice, Sancho
and his prospective father-in-law appeal directly to the King, who not
only orders the knight to release the girl but, on being ignored by Don
Tello, goes to the scene of the crime himself, retrieves the girl for the
peasant bridegroom, and has the refractory nobleman executed. A noteworthy point is that the nobleman behaves as an irresponsible, willful
individualist. He violates not only his obligation to treat the peasant as
a responsible master should, but also his duty to obey the King as the
King's vassal. This makes the play a drama of class relationships in a
framework of personal relations, but it also establishes a larger historical
context. On one side stands the wronged peasant; on the other side stands
the willful feudal master, while mediating between them stands the King,
the embodiment of impartial justice.

   Fuente Ovejuna, or *The Sheep Well,* is the most developed of these
social and historical dramas. Like the others, it is technically a tragicomedy; that is, it moves toward a catastrophe but escapes it and ends
happily for the protagonists, and the author, furthermore, makes his public approve this conclusion. In this play (and also in the pieces mentioned
earlier) our sympathies are engaged in favor of the conclusion in which
morality and justice score victories, the peasantry is vindicated, the villainous feudal overlord receives condign punishment, and the King exercises
his royal prerogatives royally. Thus the divinity that "doth hedge a king"
manifests itself on earth, and divine order is maintained by God's duly
appointed representative. After a temporary disturbance of that order by
the willfulness of the feudal nobleman who has yielded to lawless passion
and anarchic desire, the balance of human relationships—and of the relationship of the social classes—is restored. To put this in terms especially
meaningful for Lope de Vega's and Shakespeare's times, we may say that
the "Great Chain of Being" that stretches from divine providence to the
ordered world of human society has been kept intact. Shakespeare speaks
to the point memorably, almost as if he has intended to speak the last
word on the moral essence and the politico-social principle of Lope's plays,
especially *Fuente Ovejuna.* Protesting against the dissention among the
Greeks, in *Troilus and Cressida,* Ulysses says:

> when the planets,
> In evil mixture, to disorder wander,
> What plagues and what portents! What mutiny!
> What raging of the sea! shaking of earth!

> Commotion in the winds! Frights, changes, horrors
> Divert and crack, rend and deracinate
> The unity and married calm of states
> Quite from their nature.

Social stratification is not eliminated or overlooked by Lope but actually intensified. He emphasizes *obligation* or relationships of duty and at the same time of self-respect, which enable even the peasant to respect himself as a man and insist upon his honor no less than a nobleman— and to earn the right to his sense of honor by living up to it. The peasants of the village of Fuente Ovejuna violate their duty to their feudal master, but only after he has violated his duty to them and has failed to respect their rights as self-respecting men. A third force, the King's, must therefore assert itself, close the rift in social relationships, and restore the order which if disturbed in the village can start discord in the kingdom and then in the world as a whole. In this sense, *Fuente Ovejuna* (in which a revolution is actually started) is not a revolutionary play, but a profoundly conservative one. The stability of social relationships, of the state, and of the world itself is at stake when this chain of obligations and rights based upon regard for social "degree" is violated.

> O, when degree is shak'd [Ulysses continues]
> Which is the ladder to all high designs,
> Then enterprise is sick. . . .
> Take but degree away, untune that string,
> And hark, what discord follows! Each thing meets
> In mere oppugnancy. . . .
> Then everything includes itself in power,
> Power into will, will into appetite;
>   [as in the case of Lope's lustful overlords]
> And appetite, an universal wolf,
> So doubly seconded with will and power,
> Must make perforce an universal prey,
> And last eat up himself.

All this business about "degree" is, of course, more than a philosophical conceit. It is a practical matter for Lope's and Shakespeare's times (a period of transition from political feudalism to the establishment of a centralized monarchy), and perhaps a more practical condition for the preservation and pacification of the world today than we are apt—or want!—to realize. Moreover, such is the interpenetration of poetry and prose, of informal and the formal qualities in dramatic art, that *Fuente Ovejuna* is realistic enough to fit comfortably into the modern theatre while retaining its character as a play for the Golden Age of Spain. *Fuente Ovejuna* can indeed be set down by historians of the theatre as a modern social drama with a collective character—that is, with the village as the protagonist—while at the same time it is this collectivity that provides the emotional force of the play, its dramatic vibration, and its pulsing theatricality.

Fuente Ovejuna may therefore be regarded as especially representative of the dual grasp of reality and theatre, and also of the amplitude and vigor, that distinguish its author and qualify Lope de Vega as one of the major figures of the theatre. It helps to explain his great influence in his own day and his continuing influence, whether direct or indirect, in twentieth-century drama (which I find in some of the plays of Lorca) or the fascination with which he is still regarded. By a coincidence I shall not endeavor to explain, I was just about to close my notes on this subject when my eye lighted on a passage in a collection of Brooks Atkinson's essays called *Tuesdays and Fridays,* an advance copy of which had just reached me. The passage dealing with Thornton Wilder reads as follows: ". . . Mr. Wilder now proposes to seek asylum for about two years in an obscure community in Arizona, near the Mexican border. He would like to squander his time and energy on a project that has stirred his imagination since the end of World War II—the plays, the time, and the character of Lope de Vega."

THE MODERNITY OF
SHAKESPEARE'S THEATRE*

The opportunity has always existed to write about Shakespeare without having to leave the contemporary theatre, because Shakespeare has always been contemporary. But the opportunity has been enlarged ever since departures from Victorian pseudorealism have made it possible to be contemporary with Shakespeare without depriving his work of its original theatrical reality. To put it briefly, today, more than ever before, it is possible to accept Shakespearean drama in terms of Shakespearean, rather than eighteenth- or nineteenth-century, theatre. The dream of Shaw, William Poel, Gordon Craig, and others to divest Shakespearean drama in production from elephantine standards of decorative realism can now be realized. It is possible at last to bridge the gulf that always lay between Shakespearean drama and the prevailing production style of any post-Shakespearean stage. It is possible now to produce one of Shakespeare's plays with the same theatrical freedom and fluidity that his own platform stage allowed and required. Moreover, such a production, given today, need no longer be odd or antiquarian but truly contemporary.

The reason for the modernity of Shakespeare is simply that wherever the theatre is alive, or even half-alive, the open stage, whether or not it is an arena stage, has its place. More than that, the open-stage theatre is considered the most advanced theatre of the age, especially by contrast with its vestiges of realistic writing and stage production. Another way of putting it is that wherever we have epic theatre of one sort or another, and wherever we have some form of arena-stage production, we have advanced theatre, which is tantamount to comprising Shakespearean theatre; the kinship with Shakespeare is manifest. Brechtian drama by Brecht, as in the case of *Mother Courage,* or by the Duerrenmatt who wrote *The Visit,* or by Max Frisch in *Andorra,* or by Robert Bolt in *A Man for All Seasons,* is very much closer to Shakespearean drama than to anything Ibsen wrote after *Emperor and Galilean* in the 1870's. This is also true of many another progressively structured play produced within the past quarter of the century, such as Giraudoux' *The Trojan War Will Not Take Place,* presented in English under the title of *Tiger at the Gates,* and Anouilh's *The Lark,* not to mention the numerous historical

* From *Prairie Schooner* (Autumn, 1964).

or biographical plays of our time that have a fluid chronicle structure, such as Robert Sherwood's *Abe Lincoln in Illinois* and Christopher Fry's Moses-drama *The Firstborn*.

Especially marked is the Shakespearean mode of play structure called *theatricalistic*—because the author frankly acknowledges that his play is a theatrical structure rather than a consistent realistic illusion of life observed through the peephole of the proscenium arch, which by naturalistic convention constitutes an invisible fourth wall. I have in mind the imaginary wall between the actors and the audience in front of the stage predicated by Diderot in the eighteenth century and observed in directorial practice in the late nineteenth by Antoine and his naturalist successors, such as Otto Brahm, director of the *Deutsches Theater,* who vainly attempted to put Shakespearean drama behind the wall; they might as well have tried to confine Puck and Ariel and all the angels and ministers of grace in Shakespeare's cosmology.

Maintained by the production, this realistic illusion calls for a certain kind of acting known as Stanislavskian or Method acting, which has proved so inadequate for Shakespeare except as an element in performances histrionically augmented and poetically transfigured. But this kind of acting requires an intelligent balance rarely understood or undertaken until recently, as when one of our foremost teachers of acting, Robert Lewis, who grew up in the Group Theatre of the thirties but escaped its naturalistic bias, declared at the conclusion of his book *Method—or Madness:* "I feel that all art must have form, that theatricality must grow out of, and be built on, real substance, and that truth need not be drab or limiting if it is clothed with a sense of form and nurtured by our imagination."[1] And this is what Michael Redgrave, a good man with a Shakespearean role, must have had in mind in saying that he found Stanislavskian training helpful in playing Shakespeare. Nevertheless, Redgrave concluded after a long career in the theatre that "for acting Shakespeare an approach must be found which makes use not only of the Stanislavskian method—which would seem to be psychological plausibility but whose main objective, I will nevertheless remind you, is to find the creative mood, but also of something similar to Meyerhold's 'bio-dynamics,' "[2] which stresses the external possibilities of acting, involving, whenever necessary, formalism and stylization of posture and movement.

External acting is acting for form, which concerns the meaning and

[1] Robert Lewis, *Method—or Madness* (New York: Samuel French, 1958), p. 165.

[2] Michael Redgrave, *The Actor's Ways and Means* (New York: Theatre Art Books, 1953), p. 76.

character of the play as a whole, rather than acting for realizing a particular character; it is acting for effect and involves an awareness on the part of the actor, as Michael Redgrave put it, that "if I do this and this, so and so will be the effect." And there have been many other artists, of course, who have placed the stress elsewhere—on form in the performance rather than on mere motive-hunting combined with (and confined by) verisimilitude and ordinary plausibility. Sir Henry Irving's admonition to his actors to "Speak clearly and be human" covers much ground. There is much to be said, too, for the demand of the great Italian Othello, Ernesto Rossi, for "Voice, voice, and then more voice" from players in Shakespearean tragedy, provided it is not mere elocution that the call for voice implies. Shaw, as an erstwhile music critic, said substantially the same thing when he referred with admiration to Shakespeare's long speeches as "arias" and when he required of his actors more than anything else that they should stand up and say the words clearly enough for everyone in the audience to hear them; the popularity of Maurice Evans as a Shakespearean actor has depended largely, as an admiring elderly lady was overheard saying at one of his *Hamlet* performances, on one's being able to hear every word he uttered. Margaret Webster, who directed some of the most successful Shakespeare productions, several of which had Evans in the principal role, belonged to the same school of thought in maintaining that "the actor needs better enunciation, more breath, and a greater sense of the rhythm and musical value of the English language," and that the director should aim for the "exact and proper blend of melody and meaning in the lyric and epic passages" and "orchestrate the voices."[3]

Today, certainly, both actors and audiences are increasingly grateful (if only out of desperate need in a theatrical morass of commonplace realism) for some transcendence of mere illusionism in the performance as well as in the décor of the production as a whole. Watching and *hearing* a good contemporary Shakespearean production, a playgoer can well exclaim, as did the famous nineteenth-century American star Joseph Jefferson, "I am grateful for this life of illuminated emotion." The playgoer may also be grateful for a Brechtian interruption of illusion and an intensification of unique or even abrupt moments of theatre that provide the "moments of truth," the dramatic realizations or recognitions, that give significance to a play beyond the suspense of story and the interest of plot. In the case of Shakespeare, most English-speaking playgoers will agree, these recognitions are not only the most beautifully expressed in

[3] Margaret Webster, "On Directing Shakespeare," in John Gassner's *Producing the Play* (New York: Holt, Rinehart and Winston, 1953), pp. 440–442.

the language but are numerous enough to constitute the main pattern of
each of the better plays, whether we judge them by the imagistic standards of literary analysis or by essentially histrionic standards.

But we must realize that the effect of Shakespearean drama is greatly
dependent upon the basic Shakespearean structure, which is theatricalist
rather than realistic in any narrow sense. It can properly be conveyed only
by productions that are theatricalist rather than illusionistic. This accounts
for many occasions of gratification with semi-amateur productions which,
whatever their defects or crudities, at least do not stand in the way of
Shakespeare's theatricality and the vitality which accompanies it, because
the producers cannot afford to overproduce the play. Thus, some of the
best-liked recent Shakespearean productions have been those given out-
doors during the summer in New York's Central Park (Joseph Papp's
"Shakespeare in the Park") and London's Regent's Park; and some of
the most approvable productions available for perhaps a dozen years in
New York City were given almost entirely on a platform stage in the
basement of a Czech house of worship, the Jan Hus House, by a group
that called itself "The Shakespearwrights." These productions were, so
to speak, the cleanest or trimmest Shakespeare I have had occasion to see
in New York; they had the streamlined look of ultramodernity. It is by
no chance either that the best *Twelfth Night* I ever attended in New York
was produced with only the most fragmentary scenic set-pieces, in the
manner of a Brechtian production in which the scenery consists of small
half-open sets placed on platforms that can be brought on or whisked off
quickly, as, for example, in the Washington Arena Stage opening production of Brecht's *The Caucasian Chalk Circle,* staged by Alan Schneider.

Significantly, this *Twelfth Night* (given in the small auditorium of
the New School for Social Research designed by the late Austrian designer
Josef Urban, who also designed the sumptuous Ziegfeld Theatre in the
twenties), was staged by a young lady, Chouteau Dyer, formerly of Bryn
Mawr College. Moreover, the production was under the supervision of
the famous co-creator (with Brecht) of "epic theatre" and one of the most
progressive of European stage directors, Erwin Piscator, then a political
exile from Germany. In this instance, there was a clear and effective meeting of modern and Elizabethan dramatic art.

In the fields of comedy and romance, I should add, a decorative element is not necessarily antithetical to either Shakespearean or modernistic
theatre, provided the essence of the production is theatrical. I do not mean
pretty but *dynamic,* and not *decorative* but *vivid, playful,* and *blithe* in
make-believe. Provided, too, that the point of the particular play or of
any particular scene is not smothered in a flood of adolescent high spirits,

which is the special fault of amateur or, if you will, undergraduate dramatics and approximates idiocy rather than poetry. A certain degree of ceremonialism appears in many Shakespearean plays. Shakespearean comedy, as has been noted recently by C. L. Barber, Leslie Hotson, and William Green[4] (and probably others), has a strong festive element that belongs to the domain of unconcealed masquerade and make-believe. Contemporary theatricalism in comedy and romance thrives on the same masquerades and festive processions (if not of formal ceremonialism) that distinguished celebrations of May Day and Twelfth Night in Tudor times. A vivid example is a production of the famous French farce, *The Italian Straw Hat,* as staged by Gaston Baty for the Comédie Française, which consisted of an almost continuous procession of guests in search of the bridegroom. It was a romp from beginning to end, Gallic and gay to such a degree that one could feel, as I did in 1950, that a special glory had descended upon him. Even memories of the German occupation of Paris could not darken it. That, I imagined, is what Shakespeare's comedies must have felt like when untrammeled by Bardolatry or the kind of reverence for his genius that fears a caper. This is the kind of production in which I remember the Lunts when my theatrical organization* presented *The Taming of the Shrew* in the middle thirties. Well-known recent examples have been productions of Anouilh's *Thieves' Carnival,* mostly somewhat less than professional, and the same author's *L'Invitation au Château,* originally staged by Peter Brook in England and the United States in a Christopher Fry adaptation titled *Ring 'Round the Moon;* this lark of confused identities involving a pair of twins is probably familiar on every campus in the country.

There is no longer any justification for the nineteenth-century convention of staging the comedies and romances as excuses for mindless and heavily sentimental spectacles or—in the case of, say, *Cymbeline*— for overstuffed melodrama topped by a lavish happy ending. I suspect,

[4] C. L. Barber, *Shakespeare's Festive Comedy*—"A Study of Dramatic Form and its Relation to Social Custom" in *A Midsummer Night's Dream, The Merchant of Venice, Love's Labour's Lost, As You Like It, Twelfth Night,* and *Henry IV*— (Princeton: Princeton University Press, 1959).

Leslie Hotson, *The First Night of Twelfth Night* (London: Rupert Hart-Davis, 1954). Professor Hotson's contention is that the play was commissioned for performance on Twelfth Night, January 6, 1600/1601, as an entertainment at Queen Elizabeth's court. The general festive occasion was Twelfth Night, or Feast of the Epiphany or the Three Kings—the climax of the Christmas holiday.

William Green, *Shakespeare's Merry Wives of Windsor* (Princeton: Princeton University Press, 1962). This study develops Leslie Hotson's hypothesis, made in 1931, that the play was performed in 1597 at a celebration of the Knights of the Garter.

* [The Theatre Guild. *Ed.*]

even if I cannot prove, that the *Cymbeline* I saw two summers ago at Stratford-on-Avon is the first completely gratifying and consistently tolerable *Cymbeline* to be seen by several generations of Englishmen. Had Shaw seen such a production he might not have denounced, as he did in reviewing Sir Henry Irving's 1896 production of *Cymbeline,* its author's "monstrous rhetorical fustian, his unbearable platitudes, his reduction of the subtlest problems of life to commonplaces." He would not have cried out with pretended desperation that "with the single exeception of Homer, there is no eminent writer, not even Sir Walter Scott, whom I despise so entirely as I despise Shakespeare when I measure my mind with his." And he wouldn't have gone to the trouble of publishing a revised and presumably corrected *Cymbeline* himself. Shaw, who was never insensible to fun and fancy and was never a stickler for realism in his own plays after he got *Mrs. Warren's Profession* out of his system— Shaw would have taken much less umbrage at *Cymbeline* (he might have even grudgingly liked it, for he admired its heroine) had he seen a contemporary Stratford rather than a late Victorian production at Irving's Lyceum Theatre in London. He would have enjoyed the make-believe stage reality of the play if it had been presented as spirited make-believe. It is especially worth noting here that the recent *Cymbeline* to which I refer so enthusiastically was commended in England as a Brechtian production—this at a time when a successful *Caucasian Chalk Circle* was on view at the Aldwych Theatre in the West End and the Bristol Old Vic had brought to London a surprisingly effective epic-theatre production of *War and Peace* that Piscator had carved out of Tolstoy's novel and had originally staged toward the end of his exile in New York during the forties.

Finally, if any doubt exists as to my meaning when I refer to Shakespeare's highly modern theatricality—and if I have raced along at so fast a clip that the concept of theatricalism is being confused with theatricality in general, which is not a modern discovery but the oldest thing in the history of theatre—I can only emphasize that "theatricalism" exposes and even proclaims the artifice of the dramatic projection rather than attempts to conceal it, which has been the customary thing ever since the advent of realism. Brecht, to cite an example, used a theatricalist approach in a variety of ways. He even used half masks in *The Caucasian Chalk Circle,* in which all action save a dispute over the possession of a valley in Russia after World War II constitutes a visualized folk tale recited by a folksinger. It is a dramatized *exemplum* to drive home the folksinger's lesson

That what there is shall belong to those who are good for it, thus
The children to the maternal, that they thrive;
The carriage to good drivers, that they are driven well;
And the valley to the waterers, that it shall bear fruit.[5]

Anouilh, in a radically different manner, gives a theatricalist version of *Antigone* when he introduces it with a Narrator's speech in Act One and interrupts the action later to lecture the audience on the nature of tragedy. Cocteau does the same thing in his Parisian Oedipus version, *The Infernal Machine,* by means of a Voice coming over a loudspeaker to announce the theme and later to comment on the action. And Giraudoux interrupts the action of his *Electra* play with an address to the audience by a character who says that he feels free to speak to the public since he is no longer in the play.

Clear examples of this type of theatricalism, aside from the standard Elizabethan devices of the soliloquy and aside, violations and interruptions of stage illusion, appear in *Romeo and Juliet* and *Henry V.* I refer of course to the sonnet prologue of the first act of *Romeo and Juliet,*

> Two households, both alike in dignity,
> In fair Verona, where we lay our scene . . .

which introduces Shakespeare's "two hours' traffic" of the stage; and to the Act III prologue, also in sonnet form, which rhapsodizes over the "young affection" of the lovers. Another example is the Prologue to the first act of *Henry V* that calls for

> a Muse of fire, that would ascend
> The brightest heaven of invention;
> A kingdom for a stage, princes to act
> And monarchs to behold the swelling scene.

The Prologue, spoken by a single actor, then calls attention to the limits of the stage; he requests the gentles of the audience to pardon

> The flat unraised spirits that have dar'd
> On this unworthy scaffold to bring forth
> So great an object,

knowing, as he openly admits, that the "cockpit" of an Elizabethan theatre cannot hold "the vasty fields of France" and that the actors cannot cram the battle of Agincourt into the "wooden O" of his Globe

---

[5] Tranlation by James and Tania Stern, with W. H. Auden, in *Bertolt Brecht: Plays,* Vol. I (London: Methuen & Co., Ltd., 1960).

Theatre. And the Prologues to acts Two, Four, and Five eke out the scene for the audience with other histrionic recitations.

Certainly there is no lack in Shakespeare and his theatre of parallels to modern dramaturgy and stage practice, and we would even be better advised to substitute the term *"modernistic"* for "modern" in order to account for the theatricalist devices, style, and structure that are both Shakespearean and ultramodern by contrast with humdrum realistic drama and naturalistic staging. Even the soliloquy and the aside have been restored to grace in our century. O'Neill, for example, employed the former in the next-to-the-last scene of *Ah, Wilderness!* (first produced in 1935) in order to project the inner thoughts of his harassed adolescent hero alone on the beach. And O'Neill also exalted the aside, using it as a pattern of inner expression to accompany the dialogue of *Strange Interlude*—by convention, a character's asides in O'Neill's play are not supposed to be heard by the other characters. Giraudoux, Anouilh, Samuel Beckett, and other French modernists also have resorted to these means of externalizing interior tension and adding dimensions to the surface action.

The interpolation of songs into the dramatic action has been a resource of Brechtian drama; Brecht actually makes more varied and dramatic use of these interpolations than Shakespeare did. And Brecht has not been alone among the modernists to follow this practice. Lorca employed it with noteworthy lyric and dramatic effect in his plays, using songs for soliloquy in *Blood Wedding* and enlarging song into chorus especially well in *Yerma* to contrast the barrenness of his heroine with the fecundity of nature and her neighbors. Even allegory and symbolistic "showing," including the "dumb show" of which the "Murder of Gonzaga" scene in *Hamlet* is the famous example, are now modernist rather than antiquated devices. A case in point is Adamov's *Spring 71,* a play about the French Commune presented in London and Paris within the past few years, in which the allegorical figure of Liberté is both commentator and actor. The actress playing Miss Liberty unifies the episodic action of the play and also telescopes the action by taking part in it as a collective character. When the Commune falls at the end, for example, the allegorical figure of Liberté, wearing the liberty cap and carrying a red flag, falls to the ground presumably dead.

Other procedures once considered unmodern, but standard Shakespearean practice, are now regarded as ultramodern features. One of these is the play-within-the-play device present in *A Midsummer Night's Dream* and *Hamlet.* It has been a staple of the modernist theatre for a long time now in such varied work as Molnar's comedy *The Play's the Thing;*

Schnitzler's brilliantly structured one-act play about the French revolution, *The Green Cockatoo;* Edna St. Vincent Millay's *Aria da Capo;* Pirandello's paradoxical dramas, such as *Six Characters in Search of an Author* and *Tonight We Improvise;* Anouilh's *The Rehearsal* and his Joan of Arc drama *The Lark,* in which the story of Joan is presented as a show that is being put on with ironical overtones, an idealistic counterpart of which appeared in Maxwell Anderson's rehearsal play, *Joan of Lorraine,* concerning the endeavor of an actress starring in the role of Joan of Arc to understand the character she is playing.

We have also drawn considerably upon the intermingling of dream and reality, upon the suspension of characters between reality and illusion so magically present in *A Midsummer Night's Dream* and *The Tempest.* The erosion of boundaries between reality and appearance, or life and theatre, has been a modern subject and has been used as modern dramatic technique since Strindberg's *A Dream Play* (1902) at the beginning of the century.[6] A large number of expressionist plays in Central Europe, such as Kaiser's *From Morn to Midnight* and Capek's *The Insect Comedy,* and even in the pragmatic United States, as in the case of O'Neill's *The Emperor Jones, The Hairy Ape,* and *The Great God Brown,* manifest this more or less metaphysical interest. So does, of course, the major work of Pirandello and his followers in an imaginative genre of so-called Pirandellism represented by such plays by Pirandello himself as *Six Characters in Search of an Author, Right You Are, If You Think So,* and *Henry IV.* The mingling of reality and fantasy absorbed Giraudoux from the beginning of his career in the theatre, in *Siegfried, Intermezzo, The Madwoman of Chaillot,* and *Lucréce (The Duel of Angels).* It has occupied Anouilh in a number of popular plays, and it has attained, within the past decade, a remarkable climax in the work of that perverse genius of French Bohemianism, Jean Genet. In the latter's provocative trio of plays, *The Maids, The Balcony,* and *The Blacks,* nearly all distinction between reality and make-believe is obliterated by the author's theatrical virtuosity. In *The Blacks,* in fact, it has been necessary for the director to stage two worlds, that of the white colonialists and that of the African natives, in such a way that white and black are interchangeable.

These examples are sufficient to establish the fact that far from being alienated from Shakespearean dramaturgy and its underlying imaginativeness, we have drawn closer to it. "What fools these mortals be," "All the world's a stage," and the magical world of Prospero are no longer poetic reflections but the very substance of much modernist drama,

[6] Preceded by Strindberg's earlier trilogy, *To Damascus,* written some five years earlier.

which in a relativistic world-picture and in an unstable, Kafkaesque socio-political world, constitutes a veritable metaphysics or *Weltanschauung,* regardless of whether the author presents it comically or tragically—or tragicomically.

I would conclude, then, that since the old realistic outlook of the theatre has been displaced or supplemented in numerous respects, Shake-spearean theatre is now more than ever since the early seventeenth century *modern* theatre. Due to the realization that there are no longer impedi-ments other than economic ones to the creation of multiscened plays expressive of the variety and ambiguity of life, the Shakespearean theatre is very much back with us, even if the results have fallen considerably below any attained by Shakespeare himself. It is true, of course, that the loose Elizabethan play structure returned to the European theatre earlier. It was brought back in late-eighteenth-century "Storm and Stress" *(Sturm und Drang)* dramaturgy of which such ultraromantic plays as Goethe's *Goetz von Berlichingen* and Schiller's *Die Räuber* are representative. But an *unromantic* open type of dramaturgy is with very few exceptions (such as Hauptmann's late-nineteenth-century work *The Weavers* and his peas-ant-war chronicle *Florian Geyer*) a twentieth-century achievement. A vital rather than academic or antiquarian use of multiscened dramaturgy has manifested itself in such dramas as O'Casey's *The Plough and the Stars,* Brecht's *Mother Courage* and other plays, Claudel's *The Satin Slipper (Le Soulier de Satin)* and Sartre's *The Flies* and *The Devil and the Good Lord.* And it is important to note this fact, for Shakespeare's dramaturgy itself was neither academic nor antiquarian. If it had been academic in his time it would have observed the new-classic unities advo-cated by Sir Philip Sidney in his *Defense of Poesie.*

"Bardolatry" is the term Bernard Shaw invented in the 1890's to describe the indiscriminate Shakespeare-worship that prevailed in nine-teenth-century England. In claiming Shakespearean theatre for ourselves we do not have to succumb to Bardolatry. We do not have to overlook imperfections in the poet's workmanship or in his time-conditioned think-ing and even taste, as in the case of the bed-trick with which *Measure for Measure* is resolved. In claiming contemporaneity for Shakespeare we are under no obligation to acclaim him as a paragon of private and public wisdom and as the purveyor of timeless truths. In fact, it is in respect to content, very much dependent upon the fictive and historico-biograph-ical sources of the plays as well as upon Renaissance political and psycho-logical theory, that we are least likely to claim Shakespeare for the modern age.

This was Shaw's own view. As an Ibsen partisan, he could approve of almost everything in Shakespeare except his thought. Yet even Shaw could appreciate the ideas imparted in Shakespeare's work without precisely calling it "thought." He found, for example, a vein of modernity in Shakespeare's treatment of young women endowed with un-Victorian initiative and candor in matters of loving and wooing. When he acclaimed the species of young womanhood represented by Benedick's Beatrice, Rosalind, and Viola as "Shakespeare's mighty huntresses," Shaw found in these characterizations the élan of modern feminism that made him a champion of Ibsenism, and the libidinal energy, or Life Force, he associated with Lamarck, Bergson, and Nietzsche.

But it is actually first in the war-torn contemporary world that the modernity of Shakespeare assumes its proper impact. Old liberal doctrine and social-democratic optimism stood between Shakespeare and Shaw as they no longer stand between Shakespeare and our more or less disillusioned contemporaries. Shakespeare's concern with social order, naturally expressed in medieval and Renaissance terms of a "chain of being" and of interrelated social status, or "degree," is a major concern of our divided modern world. The intellectual of today takes a more sober view of political democracy than was the case fifty or seventy-five years ago, when men were put off by Shakespeare's alleged aristocratic bias. The aftermath of two world wars parallels the aftermath of the Wars of the Roses and the religious contentions of the reigns of Edward VI and Mary Tudor. We no longer sense a great ideological gulf between Shakespeare and ourselves; we can no longer boast superiority in social conscience and vision. Our idioms are different but our variously expressed longing for order and unity brings us together with Shakespeare. The contemporary world's experience with war and genocide, civil and racial strife, and with the undulant fever of demagoguery is too recent and too acute for us to miss the urgency of Shakespeare's histories and tragedies of social disorder.

And, finally, it is no less a matter of content that the psychological orientation of drama has such marked kinship to Shakespearean drama despite the outdated crudities of the Elizabethan psychology of humours collected in Burton's *Anatomy of Melancholy*. The fascination of *Hamlet* increased rather than diminished after the advent of Freudian psychoanalysis, culminating in Ernest Jones's famous essay on *Hamlet and Oedipus* in 1949. It is worth noting that the outstanding performance of Hamlet for the past forty years or more has been John Gielgud's, which was considerably influenced by Dr. Jones's premise of an Oedipally disturbed personality—the neurotic Hamlet in this case superseding the romantic Hamlet fostered by Goethe, Coleridge, and others early in the previous century.

A number of characters in the Shakespeare canon continue to absorb our attention even at the considerable risk that we fail to see them, as E. E. Stoll warned us we should do, in the context of the entire play containing them and the literary-theatrical tradition of motives and artifices to which the plays or plots belong. In this connection one readily thinks of Macbeth and his lady, Othello and Iago, Angelo in *Measure for Measure,* Leontes in *The Winter's Tale,* and Richard II, in addition to Hamlet. It is not without significance that British Public Library statistics on the greatest demand for books on personalities ranked the figures in the following order of popularity—1) Jesus Christ, 2) Hamlet, 3) Napoleon Bonaparte.

To summarize what is meant by the "modernity of the Shakespeare theatre," a brief historical review will be in order. *Modernity* has been claimed with respect to the staging of Shakespearean drama in various and even conflicting ways. First there was the antiquarian approach which started in England with the efforts of the actor-managers John Philip and Charles Kemble during the first three decades of the nineteenth century to achieve accuracy in settings and costumes. It is worth recalling that the great actor-manager David Garrick, who presented twenty-four of Shakespeare's plays, at the Drury Lane Theatre under his management between 1747 and 1776, and who played in seventeen of them himself, wore the costume of an eighteenth-century brigadier general in *Macbeth.* The production was, so to speak, a modern dress *Macbeth.* This fairly general practice was superseded only half a century later in England by the collaboration of J. R. Planché and Charles Kemble in 1823 on the production of *King John,* which was advertised as using "the precise habiliments of the period"—that is, of the historical period of King John's reign in the Middle Ages.

After the spread of the antiquarian, more or less historically accurate, presentation of the plays had culminated with Sir Henry Irving and others in a blend of romantic and naturalistic staging, a reaction took place in favor of a selective rather than detailed, suggestive rather than literalistic, investiture of Shakespearean drama. By the end of the nineteenth century it was no longer considered "modern" to present the plays realistically, much having occurred to discredit this procedure. Shakespeare had written for an open stage and had designed the bulk of his dramatic action and narration for the Elizabethan platform rather than for the peepshow box-set established in English theatrical practice by 1870. The butchery of Shakespeare's multiscened plays that occurred when managements tried to fit the text into realistic settings, which were supposed to be changed for each scene set in a new locale, outraged Shaw when he wrote dramatic criticism for Frank Harris's weekly, *The Saturday Review,* in the 1890's. The amputation as well as the long waits between scene changes became a scandal. The modern Shakespeare of surface realism or naturalism was only "a half-Shakespeare" despite the exertions of a succession of superb English star actors from the Kembles to Irving.

The next move to modernize the productions was to simplify them, and this process virtually brought stage production back to the Elizabethan stage itself. The effort was greeted with enthusiasm. In observing the experiments of simplification and in noting the transfer of emphasis from visual illusionism to Shakespearean speech by William Poel, which gave rise to the Elizabethan Stage Society in 1895, Shaw declared that the Poel productions (Poel produced twenty Elizabethan plays) were the only Shakespearean productions that had ever really moved him. Although Poel's attempts to return the plays to the Elizabethan platform stage tended to become academic, the revived emphasis on speech at the expense of pictorialism proved substantially rewarding. This practice has continued to be the general one throughout our century. The results, provided the acting and direction are up to snuff, have continued to be satisfactory.

We have had, however, special types of modernism briefly in fashion; we have had symbolist, expressionist, constructivist, and strenuously theatricalist productions in rapid succession in our century. They have proved arresting now and then and have occasionally been memorable. Symbolism prevailed in the 1921 Arthur Hopkins production of *Macbeth* with symbolist partial scenery against a black cyclorama by Robert Edmond Jones. A majestic monumentality of tall screens appeared in the early Moscow Art Theatre production of *Hamlet* designed by Gordon Craig, the chief proponent of theatrical symbolism in Europe. In the early 1920's, expressionist directors, such as Leopold Jessner in Germany, played Shakespeare on steep platforms known as Jessner-steps, and at breakneck speed, as in the case of a notorious *Richard III.*

But the main contrast remains that between a generally theatrical style and a realism that confines Shakespeare even when it prettifies his comedies and localizes his histories and tragedies. The contrast of two kinds of modernity may be illustrated in principle by two programs about seven decades apart, the first announced by the actor-manager Charles Kean for his production of *The Winter's Tale* in 1856 and the second by the American producer Arthur Hopkins for his famous Macbeth production in 1921.

MR. CHARLES KEAN	MR. ARTHUR HOPKINS
PRESENTS—1856	PRESENTS—1921

[Shakespeare] has left the incidents of *The Winter's Tale* alternating between Sicily and Bohemia, without assigning any specific date to the time of action. Chronological contradictions abound throughout the five acts; inasmuch as reference is made to the Delphic oracle, Christian burial, an Emperor of Russia, and an Italian painter of the sixteenth century. It is evident that when an attempt is made to combine truth with history, conflicting epochs cannot all be illustrated; and I have therefore thought it permissible to select a period which, while it accords with the spirit of the play, may be considered the most interesting, as well as the most instructive. . . . An opportunity is thus afforded of reproducing a classical era, and placing before the eyes of the spectator *tableaux vivants* of the private and public life of the ancient Greeks, at a time when the arts flourished. . . .

To connect the country known as "Bohemia" with an age so remote would be impossible; I have therefore followed the suggestion of Sir Thomas Hammer by the substitution of Bithynia. The difference of name in no way affects the incidents or metre of the play, while it enables me to represent the costume of the inhabitants of Asia Minor at a corresponding period. . . .

The architectural portions of the play have, as on many former occasions, been kindly superintended by

In our interpretation of *Macbeth* we are seeking to release the radium of Shakespeare from the vessel of tradition. To us it is not a play of Scotland or warring kings or of any time or place or people. It is a play of all times and all people. We care nothing about how Inverness may have looked, neither do we care about all the conscious motives that have been ascribed to Macbeth and Lady Macbeth. We believe them all to be of no importance, because we believe the real causes were deeper seated than conscious motive, and, furthermore, that the same causes exist today in all people.

We believe the witches are the evil forces of life, forces that have hovered about for all time.

We find Macbeth a man of whom there has been no previous ill-account, walking along a road. A hand reaches out and touches him. From that moment he becomes as one in a dream. He is possessed. He is picked up and whirled through a torrent of blood and agony. Never once does he seem accountable for the things he is doing. . . .

So, to us the tragedy of *Macbeth* is not the series of incidental murders and deaths, but it is that strong people can be picked up by forces they do not understand, are helpless to combat, and by which they are dashed to utter destruction.

George Goodwin, Esq., F.R.S., . . . and my thanks are peculiarly due to George Scharf, Esq., Jun., F.S.A. (author of the Handbook to the Greek and Pompeian Courts at the Crystal Palace), . . . whose pictorial mind has suggested many important details. The vegetation peculiar to Bithynia is adopted from his private drawings, taken on the spot. . . .

This we believe to be the immortal phase of *Macbeth,* since it is a tragic condition of all time.

As to settings, we have left behind all compromise with realism. They are just the barest beginnings of things. We believe there will be great beauty. . . .

So there is our dream. It may prove wonderful or terrible, but it at least expresses our feeling for the play. No other consideration has interefered.

It requires no great astuteness to determine in which direction will be found the modernity of Shakespearean theatre, even if we can understand the historical necessity of the Charles Kean program as an experiment in bringing Shakespeare's plays closer to the modern public. We can view realistic stage productions as the culmination of efforts since Garrick's time and even earlier to perform Shakespeare naturally. And for this the cue was memorably given by the poet himself when he made Hamlet warn the players not to "saw the air too much with their hands," not to "tear a passion into tatters," and not to split the ears of the groundlings but "suit the action to the word, the word to the action" and to observe that the purpose of playing was "to hold . . . the mirror up to nature" (III, i). Fortunately Hamlet's admonitions, so agreeable even to enemies of realism, can be heeded today without an obligation to employ the cumbersome impedimenta of naturalistic scenery and staging. That many a contemporary production has not yet divested itself of them is an error of taste; it was Hollywood taste in the case of the Olivia de Haviland production of *Romeo and Juliet* about a decade ago. But the principle of realistic staging as the modern way of staging Shakespeare's plays has been almost interred with the bones of the great Victorian actor-managers.

The opposite mistake of believing that the way to keep Shakespearean theatre modern is to give it a mystical symbolist production, an hysterical expressionist, or a constructivist mechanical one has proved, on the whole, even more deplorable. The temptation to do so vanished after the brief vogue of the symbolist, expressionist, and constructivist styles. It is regrettable only that many productions still employ more mist, quasi-Craig mist, than plain meaning—that, as Eric Bentley puts it, we still respect "something vague, sweeping, impressionistic" on the presumable assumption that "what is ill-defined must be deep and what is other-worldly must be sublime."[7] The only basic style of Shakespearean production is both the newest and the oldest, the most sensible and the closest to the original style. It is a semi-formal theatricalist style which is apparently gaining ground in the modern arena-stage type of productions on view at Central Park, the Guthrie Theatre in Minneapolis, and the theatre in Stratford, Ontario. This is so even if Stratford in England still compromises now and then with Victorian pictorialism, and even if the directors of Stratford in Connecticut seemed to assume until recently that the art of Shakespeare cannot be conveyed to the American public without transferring the scene of *Much Ado About Nothing* to Texas and transposing the Trojan War in *Troilus and Cressida* to the Civil War in the United States. We have come to realize more and more clearly that the only reliably modern Shakespeare is the Elizabethan Shakespeare, and that the only modern theatre for his plays is in one way or another an equivalent or analogue of the open stage which they suited so well, and for which they were mainly written. A modern theatre for Shakespeare is a theatre loyal to Shakespeare that allows him to have his say directly and clearly.

[7] Eric Bentley, *In Search of Theatre* (New York: Alfred A. Knopf, Inc., 1953), p. 117.

THE WORLD OF MOLIÈRE*

Molière has been excelled only by Aristophanes and Shakespeare in the possession of the fused talents of writer and showman. As a writer, he is distinguished by wisdom, wit and grace; as a showman, by improvisation, ingenuity and vitality. His work exhibits a unique combination of intellect and spirit, of sober judgment and gaiety, of orderliness and vigor.

Molière's eminence was comic. He was most at home on those foothills from which one can observe the valleys where the mass of mankind proliferates. At that distance, one is not too far removed from the average sensual man who is the ideal subject of comedy. At that remove, it is possible to escape the passion for the infinite that often blurs vision, and yet to stand sufficiently above the procession of fallible humanity to possess perspective. From that moderate height, one can also reduce man to proper scale, as a creature neither as insignificant as he would look when viewed from the heights nor as towering as he fancies himself. At the same time, differences in stature become less pronounced; the great and the small become subject to the leveling process of comedy, to the infallible democracy of humor.

Men of Molière's stamp always leave the valley by gradual stages, they even appear to be *of* the valley, though by temperament they must have always stood on some private elevation invisible to others. Some men may be born to judgment, but it takes a great deal of experience before a temperament takes discernible shape, and it takes much labor before that temperament is translated into art. It is no wonder that Molière came to the peak of his powers slowly. Nature, one may add parenthetically, abhors any exemption from its sway almost as much as it abhors a vacuum, and life took sardonic vengeance on one who tried to follow reason as his exclusive deity. It filled the comedian, for example, with a desire to write, and act in, tragedy. It led him to commit the mistake of marrying a flirtatious wife many years younger than himself, and placed him on the same rack of jealousy on which he had stretched many of his comic characters. But this, we may fancy, was after all only nature's left-handed compliment to his perspicacity, and merely substantiated his own premise that mankind is ruled by Unreason. If it were otherwise, there would be no matter for high comedy and a Molière could not have written.

* Introduction to *Comedies of Molière,* trans. by H. Baker and J. Miller (New York: The Book League of America, 1946).

51

Jean Baptiste Poquelin, born on January 15, 1622, to one of Louis XIV's *tapissiers,* or upholsterers, traversed the life and intellection of his times. He displayed an unappreciated talent for mimicry in childhood, was left on his own at an early age by the successive deaths of his mother and stepmother, and came close to following his father's trade. But prosperity smiled upon the upholstery business, and the boy was entered in the Collège of Clermont, the best school in Paris, conducted by those accomplished instructors the Jesuits, whose policy of sharpening the intellect probably produced more skeptics than did all the explicit teachers of heresy. As the curriculum included instruction in Latin comedy and acting, Jean Baptiste was also introduced at an impressionable age to the theatre and the continuing tradition of European comedy. Here, moreover, he struck up a friendship with a Parisian banker's illegitimate son that enabled him to share his friend's private lessons with an early philosopher of modern science, Gassendi, the friend of Kepler and Galileo. It is not without significance that the future playwright's first literary effort should have been a translation of Lucretius' paean to the scientific attitude, *De Rerum Natura.* When, after a brief encounter with legal studies, he embarked upon an acting career he had considerably more equipment than the ordinary player's bag of tricks.

It was, however, as a strolling actor, who had changed his name to Molière in order to spare his father some embarrassment, that the young intellectual served his apprenticeship to the theatre. It was as a comedian —physically suited to that role by a swarthy complexion, wide-set eyes, long legs and a short torso—that he first made his mark; and his first essays at authorship were short, contrived farces, written for his company during its fourteen-year-long tour through the provinces. Still, these years were far from wasted. Hard necessity taught him the requisites of success in comedy, liveliness and inventiveness. By the time he brought his company back to Paris in 1658, giving a first performance before the King in the great hall of the old Louvre, he had mastered the medium which he was to enrich with his critical faculties.

Paris was not only a location, and a very profitable one for the showman, but also a challenge. Here, in the cultural capital of the world, he had the most critical audience. Here, moreover, to replenish his quiver he needed only to cast his eyes on the most resplendent court in Europe, on the fashionable set at its periphery, and on the *nouveau riche* bourgeoisie that played the sedulous ape, and had, besides, foibles of its own, peculiar to its Philistinism.

Its common aspect is one of unsolicitous observation, as if surveying a full field and having leisure to dart on its chosen morsels, without any fluttering eagerness. Men's future upon earth does not attract it; their honesty and shapeliness in the present does; and whenever they wax out of proportion, overblown, affected, pretentious, bombastical, hypocritical, pedantic, fantastically delicate; whenever it sees them self-deceived or hoodwinked, given to run riot in idolatries, drifting into vanities, congregating in absurdities, planning short-sightedly, plotting dementedly; whenever they are at variance with their professions, and violate the unwritten but perceptible laws binding them in consideration one to another; whenever they offend sound reason, fair justice; are false in humility or mined with conceit, individually, or in the bulk; the Spirit overhead will look humanely malign, and cast an oblique light on them, followed by peals of silvery laughter.

George Meredith's description of high comedy fits Molière's comic art in all respects. It is important only to qualify that his plays reveal no trace of the moral indifference that limits the English comedies of the Restoration period. It is idle to pretend that there is no strong element of chastisement in his laughter, and that it possesses no special friendliness for those whom the perverse world threatens or frustrates. Molière was, essentially, a critic of his age, although he had enough of its courtly spirit to refrain from impassioned protest. His contemporaries smarted under his lash, even though he wrapped it in velvet and wielded it with urbane grace.

Unnatural refinement, actually a false conception of manners, is the butt of his first mature satire, *Les précieuses ridicules,* or *The Romantic Ladies.* It was aimed at the reigning courtly cult, or, as he maintained in self-defense, at its inept imitators. A pedantic conception of education and cultivation is the object of his masterpiece *The Learned Women.* The accepted and legalized view of marriage as a relationship of convenience, to be determined by parents or guardians, draws many of the brightest shafts of his derision. *The School for Husbands* and *The School for Wives* are wholly given over to the subject, but it is present to varying degrees in most of his plays. He is forever waging war against those who would dam up or deflect the channels of nature; he is forever on the side of wholesome young lovers in their conflict with parental pig-headedness or self-interest.

The classes and the professions are constantly under sardonic scrutiny. Molière looks askance at the flourishing middle classes and shows them being hoist with their own petard: by their greed, in *The Miser,* and by their social ambitions in *The Would-Be Gentleman* and *George Dandin.* The corruptions and the arrogance of the nobility, as well as its pretensions to culture, come under his purview in *The Misanthrope, Don Juan,* and the aforementioned *George Dandin*. The pedantry and bombast of a medical profession still remote from scientific knowledge evoke his laughter in his *Doctor in Spite of Himself* and *The Imaginary Invalid*. His major masterpieces cut deeply into the social integument. *Tartuffe* has for its subject religious hypocrisy, as well as the universal theme of human credulity; *The Misanthrope* exposes a world in which titled fools parade as wits, conversation is a continual flow of perfumed bile, truth-telling a social disgrace, and justice a commodity to be bought and sold. It took many years before the opposition of the Jesuits could be surmounted and *Tartuffe* could be shown outside the court; *The Misanthrope* was a failure when first produced.

Because Molière was a consummate showman, because his urbanity rarely deserted him, and because he had enough human inconsistency or practicality to vary his diet for the public, his career was, on the whole, enormously successful. But his genuine greatness was something that only time and perspective could establish. His king, Louis XIV, took a friendly interest in him but only as a superior clown. His plebeian public loved him ingenuously as a showman. The Church preferred to regard him as a disreputable player, and was disinclined to grant him religious burial.

On the European continent, Molière's sway has been undisputed since the eighteenth century. In the Anglo-Saxon world his influence has also been enormous; his ghost has lurked in the wings of our comic theatre whenever it has been at its best. We have heard echoes of his laughter frequently within recent memory; almost continually in the plays of Shaw, and not infrequently in the comedies of younger playwrights. We heard it, for example, when the young radical in *The Philadelphia Story* who protested needlessly that he was not a communist was set down as "just a pinfeather on the left wing" by his mistress; and when the mercenary physician in Behrman's *End of Summer* explained that he took up psychoanalysis only after realizing that whereas the poor have tonsils the rich have neuroses. Molière's comedies have not, however, been often enough, and successfully enough, revived on Broadway. They are, at their best, perhaps too cool and remote for popular taste. Moreover, they have not been available in sufficiently good modern translations;* loose prose and antimacassar phraseology are painful to one who knows his Molière in French.

* [A manuscript notation by Professor Gassner indicates he intended to qualify the remarks in this paragraph with comment on Richard Wilbur's translation of *Le Misanthrope*. Ed.]

ENGLISH COMEDY IN THE
CLASSIC AGE*

The simplest matters can cause the greatest whirl of complication when we elect to ponder them. Take the cast of comedy. It would seem that so simple a statement as Max Eastman's that the first law of humor is that "things can be funny only when we are in fun" would cover the case sufficiently. But even Eastman, who has written three hundred and fifty pages on the sense of humor, has succeeded only in raising the ghosts of more questions than he has laid. The esthetics of comedy has filled many books, some so formidable that it is certain the authors were temperamentally unqualified to write on the subject. Even if we limit inquiry to English comedy, the morasses lie all around us. It is simply impossible to generalize on anything as varied as life itself. English comedy has run the entire gamut from horseplay to laughter of the mind, and the two have, as often as not, overlapped.

The classic period covered by the plays in this volume is fortunately more distinctive than any other. The purest English distillations of the comic spirit make their appearance in the years between the restoration of the monarchy in 1660 and the production of Sheridan's *School for Scandal* in 1777. That is, we can allow the claim, provided we concede that there were decades of drought even within this century, and that some of the worst comedies and most deleterious influences upon the art appeared then.

If the world were well ordered, excellence would never have to be explained. The world is not well ordered. Moreover, past and present are not co-existent for most of us, and especially in the case of humor the gap between two eras can be very wide. When John Palmer wrote that "laughter is the real frontier between races and kinds of people," he was not guilty of much exaggeration. The best comedies of the Restoration period and the eighteenth century differ from those to which we are habituated in one cardinal respect: their humor is *disengaged*. We are accustomed to admixtures of comedy and sentiment: to social satires, rooted in moral indignation or disapprobation; and to plays in which the laughter is gross rather than subtle. In the masterpieces of English classicism, we encounter

---

* Introduction to *English Comedies* (Eau Claire, Wisconsin: E. M. Hale and Company, 1945).

a view of comedy largely or wholly free from contamination by either sentimentality or the moral faculty. Its world is small, for it consists of the social set. The characters who whirl about in it are always dressed in the height of fashion, as if for a continuous Easter parade, and they exhibit virtually no life beyond the puppetry of their social comportment. The one exception afforded by *The Beggar's Opera* and its sequel *Polly* proves to be no exception at all; John Gay's underworld characters do not differ in essence from Wycherley's and Congreve's dandies.

If, however, you take exception to this mode of characterization, if you protest that these peruked figures are egregiously unreal, they will smile at you with a disconcerting air of superiority. If you could follow the imputations of their periodic sentences, paraphrase them in the less impeccable speech of our times, you would know why they smile. "At most," you would hear them say, "we wear our cap and bells at a more rakish angle, the cap is made of better cloth, the bells are of silver not earned in the sweat of our brow. But no matter how low you descend in the social scale, or how far you forage in time and space, you will find humanity wearing the same unmistakable adornments. You will find the same unwarranted pretensions, the same egolatry and selfishness, and the same illogic and lack of balance. The difference at best is that our foibles and follies are more openly exhibited because we are less inhibited, and because our creators, the pestilential authors, were men of our kidney. Expecting no more from us than we could deliver, they enjoyed the spectacle we provided with untroubled eyes. Is it art you want to discuss? *Their* artistry was more complete because more single-minded, and more single-minded because less adulterated with anger or pity. We did not take the world more seriously than it should be taken, and neither did our authors. In any case, let us alone and don't try to touch our hearts with the tears of things; we cannot even cope with our follies! And if you press your social or private anguish closer, we will have to tell you that we have no heart at all. It won't be entirely true, but you will believe us, for we, who had the benefit of breeding, are past masters in the art of concealment."

One could have quite a conversation with this breed. And no wonder, since their creators were masterly conversationalists in an age of salons and coffee houses where the English tongue was filed to a fine cutting edge. It is some such conversation that George Meredith, whose ear was singularly attuned to it, tried to reduce to a number of critical distinctions in his famous essay on comedy. "If you detect the ridicule," he wrote, "and your kindliness is chilled by it, you are slipping into the grasp of satire. . . . if you laugh all around him [the ridiculous person], tumble him, roll him about, deal him a smack, and drop a tear on him . . . it is the spirit of Humor that is moving you." Comedy is more objective or disengaged than either moral fervor or humanitarian sympathy will allow. It does not hover on the altitudes where the thunder is grown, nor does it snuggle in the valleys where humanity teems with activities and experiences that obliterate aloofness; it clings close to the temperate foothills of reason. The comic spirit, writes Meredith, is "the perceptive, the governing spirit, awakening and giving aim to those powers of laughter—" that is, to satire and humor. But it differs from satire "in not sharply driving into the quivering sensibilities," and from humor "in not comforting them and tucking them up." Its laughter is "impersonal and of unrivaled politeness, nearer a smile, often no more than a smile."

Comedy, so defined, is the peculiar possession of an epoch, more particularly of a class, and most particularly of specially slanted personalities. The class is what Veblen aptly termed "the leisure class"—the conglomeration of gallants or society folk augmented by a small intelligentsia that wrote for a living, when it had to, but greatly preferred patronage. The rare individuals who possessed this gift of comedy were the so-called wits, not all of whom committed their talent to paper. Those who wrote have a secure place in the history of English letters; Dryden, Pope, Swift, Addison, Steele, Fielding, Samuel Johnson, and others contributed verses, essays, and novels that we would not willingly relinquish from our literary heritage. A few of them wrote comedies for the stage—Wycherley, Congreve, Gay, and Sheridan, who are represented in this collection; and there were a number of others, including Goldsmith, John Dryden, George Etherege, Mrs. Aphra Behn (the first woman to write for the English stage), Sir John Vanbrugh (the architect of Blenheim castle) Fielding, the novelist, and George Farquhar.

Their type of comedy—aptly termed, for the most part, "comedy of manners"—was the product, and the luxury, of an age that supported a settled upper-class devoted to the amenities. The world seemed very stable to its members. No new frontiers seemed necessary, no great adventures lay before them, no great changes seemed imperative. The Elizabethan world of promises and fluctuations of fortune, of wonder and of challenge, was past. That world had produced a comedy of romance, as in *As You Like It, A Midsummer Night's Dream,* and *Twelfth Night;* and when social strife and insecurity darkened the horizon, it brought forth Shakespeare's "dark comedies" (*All's Well That Ends Well, Measure for Measure*) and Ben Jonson's angry satires. There was a portent in these works. There came revolution—the Puritan revolution, the beheading of Charles I, and the flight of the nobility to France. When Charles II returned, he took care to walk a political tightrope by interfering with government as little as possible, by confining his prerogatives to the bed-chamber and the world of fashion. There was method in the merriment of the "Merry Monarch." The aristocracy followed suit and led its own life as something apart, adhering to the maxim of *carpe diem* with fine living and frivolity, partly as a safe way of thumbing noses at an entrenched bourgeoisie, partly because their vigor had been sapped. They became gallants and courtiers, and, by a process of sublimation, wits instead of explorers and buccaneers and military conquerors. The larger world of politics and economics also settled down. England favored gradualism rather than violent upheavals, evolution rather than revolution, and inched along the road of constitutional monarchy. And the England of the middle class settled down to a business-as-usual policy whose rewards filled horns of plenty. "Whatever is, is right," Alexander Pope's maxim, expressed the prevailing attitude, the smugness of which probably helped to drive Jonathan Swift mad, since he could not share his "savage indignation" with anyone. To this we may add another maxim, tacitly held by the leisure class, that "Whatever is, is funny." Indolence, of a kind, no doubt contributed to this state of mind.

The period's masters of comedy were supremely intelligent, but their moral laziness—call it indifference, if you will—kept them from seeing much that wasn't in the least funny, such as the hangings for petty crimes, the baiting of the hapless insane that passed for entertainment, and the delight in unmitigated malice that made Pope's enemies twit him because he was of dwarfish stature. "Humor," Ludovici writes in *The Secret of Laughter,* "is the lazier principle to adopt in approaching all questions." The questions, moreover, barely existed for them, and a certain degree of petty malice, a little sadism, was actually a component of their laughter. In a catastrophic age like our own, we are likely to feel very critical of these carefree writers. They took for granted that they were possessors of civilization, and could be easily refuted. They were strong believers in cultivation, in the manner of Lord Chesterfield's letters to his son; they neglected to realize that the value of culture lies in its effect on character. They made tolerable with laughter that which the moralist or the social critic would find intolerable. We can reflect that the social graces could blossom only by fortuitous benefit of freedom from want. We can note that the actual field of observation was often as narrow as the Mall or Mayfair, that their microcosm could be engraved on a guinea.

Nevertheless, their merits are considerable. Their concentrated light promotes crystal clarity. There is something undeniably civilized in their urbane detachment; their cerebral approach is bracing, and provides a tonic to frayed nerves. Their wit, a creation of unintimidated intellect, enables us to triumph momentarily over the confusions and intimidations of reality. It is always pleasurable, if not always useful, to make an excursion with someone who doesn't try to inform us. Above all, these writers were a merry lot. They knew what many of their colleagues, past and present, have overlooked—that the primary function of comedy is to entertain.

To varying degrees, the writers in this collection answer to this description. William Wycherley (1641–1715) had an unhappy marriage, fell upon evil days, had a long sojourn in debtors' prisons, and wrote one bitter play, *The Plain Dealer,* based on Molière's *The Misanthrope.* But he was a dashing blade when he returned to England with the other royalists in 1660, enjoyed the exalted friendship of Charles II's mistress, the Duchess of Cleveland, was presented to the King, and had success with his first play, *Love in a Wood,* in 1671. His third play, *The Country Wife,* produced four years later, reveals him at the peak of his talent for sophisticated comedy. It is perhaps the most amusing treatment of jealousy in the English language, and Mistress Margery Pinchwife is an ingenue who has not been frequently surpassed.

William Congreve, the genial "Phoebus Apollo of the Mall," was wholly a son of the Restoration period. He was born in 1670 and surrendered himself completely to the spirit of the age. Excellently educated, the protégé of the reigning arbiter of letters, John Dryden, he had his first play, *The Old Bachelor,* polished by Dryden and performed by the leading stage couple of his time, Betterton and Mrs. Bracegirdle. His two masterpieces *Love for Love* (1695) and *The Way of the World* (1700) are generally considered the supreme achievements of the comic spirit in England. At any rate, they are the best examples of comedy of manners in the language. They may be caviar to the general, but they are the very best caviar.

Comedy began to decline from its zenith after these two productions. A withering blast from a polemical clergyman, Jeremy Collier, silenced its purveyors, and public taste, now largely dictated by the sedate burghers, favored sentimental plays. This change in the moral climate is a chapter in social history, as well as in the English theatre. But, fortunately, the comic spirit rallied for a few more pirouettes on the boards in the eighteenth century. It found an able and willing master of ceremonies in John Gay (1685–1732), an indolent fellow but an irrepressible wit, whose ballad-operas *The Beggar's Opera* (1728) and its sequel *Polly* are imperish-

able. Congreve, who died in 1729 after a life of pleasant patronage, sine-
cures, and friendships without writing another play after *The Way of the
World,* lived to witness the return of the unruly muse he had briefly
served. Gay's comedies were political satires aimed at England's first prime
minister, Robert Walpole, but their blithe insouciance and amorality are
undated. Their prime subject is the comedy of villainy. *The Beggar's
Opera* fits any period. It was adapted for the German stage shortly before
the advent of Hitler and his gang.

Henry Fielding, who is better known for the notable novels with
which he stemmed the tide of sentimentalism, also took a stand against
false art in the drama. *Tom Thumb the Great* (1730), one of several
comedies by Fielding, is a burlesque on fulsome heroic drama to which
the public had been partial. It is one of three literary satires (Bucking-
ham's *The Rehearsal* and Sheridan's *The Critic* were the other two) the
like of which was not to be seen in the English theatre until Gilbert and
Sullivan created Bunthorne. Then came the last capers with Oliver Goldsmith's *She Stoops to Conquer* (1773) and Richard Brinsley Sheridan's
two masterpieces *The Rivals* (1775) and *The School for Scandal* (1777),
none of them free from traces of concession to sentiment, but sufficiently
lively and perceptive to deserve their hold upon the English-speaking
world.

After these productions comes the deluge of lachrymose comedies,
romantic claptrap, and knockdown farce that lasts until the closing decades of the nineteenth century. Wit is banished for a century or more as
either indecent or unfeeling. Sophistication becomes improper in the Victorian period, and the public would no doubt have answered any imperti-
nent admirer of the older comedies with the dear Queen's own words on
Gilbert and Sullivan: "We are not amused." The renascence of English
comedy comes late, with Oscar Wilde, Gilbert and Sullivan, and Bernard
Shaw. On the nonmusical stage, moreover, comedy becomes subject to a
major transformation, in keeping with the climate of an age of rapidly intensified social awareness. Wilde's one successful effort to return strictly
to the Restoration, *The Importance of Being Earnest,* is not in the mainstream of further development. And yet we can go too far in denying the
continuance of the Restoration and eighteenth-century spirit since 1890.
The wit and the comedy of manners are abundant in the work of Shaw,
Maugham, Coward, and the less celebrated practitioners of our day. The
comic spirit, in the twentieth century, no longer finds, and no longer
creates, so artificial a world. But it still makes use of dispassionate observation, and a certain degree of artificiality in background and behavior. It

also still derives entertainment from man's divergences from common sense. Only the implications of such divergence are different today—larger and charged with the travail of a world in transition. At least this has been apparent in Shaw and Behrman, though still too infrequently in the work of other contemporaries.

STRINDBERG: PEARL AND OYSTER*

What I like most about Dr. Franklin Klaf's book is its interest in *health,* not disease. Although he is chiefly concerned with the nature and etiology of Strindberg's mental disturbance, Dr. Klaf makes it clear that Strindberg's immense literary labors kept him from permanently crossing the tenuous border between sanity and insanity, facilitated rapid, if incomplete, recovery when he did overstep, and preserved him as a literary master when simple recovery might have produced merely a subdued and delicately balanced discharged patient. "Genius plus application to creative work" might prove a good formula for psychotherapy if only one knew how to provide genius and make sure that it is creatively employed.

Dr. Klaf's formidable collection of data concerning the imbalance of Strindberg's psyche will be interesting as a case history to those who are professionally interested in case histories. I cannot imagine it to be otherwise, although I must own up to a personal distaste for words like "insanity" and "schizophrenia" when applied to men of productive talent. But the struggle for health in Strindberg's case possesses a fascination for the lay reader that ranges far beyond the psychiatric clinic and the psychoanalyst's couch. The mother fixation that flared up periodically in Strindberg's life, the accompanying exaggerated expectations and disappointments of his matrimonial ventures, the paranoid delusions of grandeur that made an alchemist of him, and the delusions of persecution that bereft him of peace and perspective in personal relations—these and other morbid manifestations can become decidedly tiresome as clinical phenomena. Only in so far as he made distinguished fiction, drama, and literary autobiography with them can they be considered more than tolerable to any but clinically interested readers.

In appreciating Strindberg the *artist,* even his admirers have sometimes evinced irritation with Strindberg the neurotic, as when the British critic Desmond MacCarthy referred to the playwright's well-aired domes-

---

* Introduction to *Strindberg: The Origin of Psychology in Modern Drama,* by Franklin Klaf (New York: The Citadel Press, 1963). [Here again, Professor Gassner indicated on the proof copy the possibility of an added introduction for this essay, though no comments were noted regarding its content. The "Pearl and Oyster" of the title refer to an image of a pearl being produced by a diseased oyster, used by the author in "Strindberg and the Twentieth Century" (in *The Theatre of Our Times,* Crown Publishers, Inc., 1954). He pointed out that ". . . we prefer to dissociate the oyster from the pearl," but that "We cannot easily dissociate the two in Strindberg's work. . . ." (p. 173). *Ed.*]

tic conflicts as "the sorrows of a henpecked bluebeard." Even when the two Strindbergs, the genius and the psychopath, appear to be the same individual, we prefer to divorce the infirm creator from his properly crystallized creation; we like to separate the pearl from the sick oyster. In the case of Strindberg, it is gratifying to observe his artistic victories over disease and exhilarating to find him transforming common enough morbidity into uncommonly absorbing drama. His symptoms, as Dr. Klaf relates them, are the classical ones in psychopathology, but we are ultimately interested in those powers of resilience, projection, and transformation observable in his writing that distinguished Strindberg from other patients and made him the father of modern psychological drama. He had *illness* in common with them, but they did not have *genius* in common with him; and in his possession and exercise of genius lay, in fact, his essential *health*.

Dr. Klaf perceives all this and presents it with professional authority. He therefore follows Strindberg into the world of his art and leads us into it appreciatively instead of allowing himself to be mired in the minutiae of neurosis and psychosis. Although his excursions into literary and dramatic criticism are necessarily limited, he makes it abundantly evident that it is there, in Strindberg's works, that we shall find what is unique about his subject. In this sense it is possible to say that Dr. Klaf studies the patient's health while recording his disease. What this consists of, aside from the end-result of social acceptance as a distinguished writer, is an endowment also possessed by "normal" men who became distinguished authors, although it was probably less hard-won in their case. It could be said of Strindberg that in possessing powers of acute sensibility, vivid externalization, vigorous projection, and keen perception he was like other good writers, only *more so*. If this had not been the case, indeed, his dramatic work could not have been superior, as it indisputably is, to the work of all but possibly two or three modern dramatists.

Insight, into himself and into others, is an especially significant attribute of his art, and therefore of his health, too. (Disease may have, of course, sharpened insight even while subverting it in some of his writings and producing the abnormal suspicions and delusions of persecution from which he suffered to various degrees virtually throughout his life.) He manifests this insight early in his work, and it even increases and deepens with experience. This is, of course, what the mentally disturbed lack and what it is hoped therapy will enable them to attain at least so far as their illness is concerned. If Strindberg lost insight or perspective from time to time, his recovery was usually swift and was followed by renewed creativity. He had a major psychotic episode in 1897, but it is remarkable how after leaving his sanatorium (and leaving it by no means completely liberated from tensions and delusions) he was able to produce an entire series of objective historical dramas such as *Gustav Vasa* and *Gustav Adolf,* along with fantasies of the order of *To Damascus,* in which deep-seated guilt feelings are objectified and the troubled spirit is temporarily pacified.

Many who appear to possess insights are unable to articulate them. In this respect Strindberg could not be faulted even at the first great stage of his career in the late 1880's, when he created naturalistic psychological drama, and his growing confidence in his craftsmanship enabled him within a decade to undertake deeper probings than any previously attempted that affected dramatic form itself. The deeper he mined the human psyche the more he resorted to complex and original techniques with which to present the apparitions of subjective experience. Only a writer confident of mastery of the dramatic medium would have dared to depart, not once by accident but many times by design, from the norms of imitation and stage representation as Strindberg did in moving from realistic to expressionist drama—from the dramatic style of *The Father* or *Miss Julie,* for example, to that of *A Dream Play* and *The Ghost Sonata.*

Strindberg penetrated with his expressionist plays into the very recesses of the Unconscious or the dream so usefully explored in twentieth-century metapsychology and psychopathology. And although he had but recently recovered from his psychotic crisis he was completely aware of what he was doing when he wrote his series of nonnaturalistic dramas beginning with the first two parts of *To Damascus* in 1898. His understanding of means and ends is especially evident in his celebrated Preface to *A Dream Play,* in which he describes his use of dream technique in that play and in *To Damascus.* He tells his readers that he has resorted to "the detached and disunited—although apparently logical—form of dreams." In *A Dream Play,* time and space have no reality and anything is possible and will seem probable: "On a flimsy foundation of actual happenings, imagination spins, and weaves in new patterns: an intermingling of remembrances, experiences, whims, fancies, ideas, fantastic absurdities and improvisations, and original inventions of the mind." And in the play dominated by the dreamer, "the personalities split, take on duality, multiply, vanish, intensity, diffuse and disperse, and are brought into focus" (Arvid Paulson's translation).

Intention and execution matching, Strindberg not only introduced a new subject matter in giving primacy to psychological conflicts but created a new dramatic form. He fathered not only modern psychological drama but modern expressionist style, which has had a constant direct and indirect effect on the theatre since the end of the nineteenth century second only to that of dramatic realism.

When in an earlier period, during the late 1880's, Strindberg favored strict realism in his plays as a dedicated naturalist he was no less aware of intent and procedure than when he became an expressionist, as may be particularly observed in his Preface to *Miss Julie*. In fine, he had a way of crystalizing experience and emotion as "form," which was nothing less than an uncommon aptitude for knowing what he was doing in art even if he had a considerably less reliable aptitude for knowing what he was doing in life. He had "a will to form," one might say, and a concomitant "will to objectivity" which is particularly apparent in his confessional autobiographies from *The Son of a Servant* in 1886 to *Inferno* in 1897. And here again we may observe health or, as Bernard Shaw put it, "the sanity of art" supervening therapeutically upon disease, for nothing is so outer-directed and related to what is called "the reality principle" than conscious creativity. Dramatic writing is an especially exacting discipline. However unreasonable Strindberg's attraction-repulsion relationship with the women in his life and the reflection of the duel of the sexes in his literary work, he mastered a large portion of his inner disorder with his mastery of dramatic form. If this had not been the case, we might have known Strindberg as a magisterial psychopath but hardly as a master playwright.

Ego-centered to a greater degree than most men, but less blinded by concern with his ego than minor artists whose narcissism dooms them to be forever "minor," Strindberg could look over the fence of his egotism and see "other people," especially the women who were the antagonists in his plays and books. He could create characters instead of limiting himself to inquisitions and disquisitions, or to a dialectic of the mind, in dealing with the duel of the sexes. Consequently, too, his insights carried conviction, penetrating as they did into life—that is, into people as they are apt to be in their complexity and contradictoriness. Few playwrights have been as concerned with the tangle of causation, as if Strindberg had been heedful of the Viennese psychoanalyst Robert Wälder's later formulation of a "law of multiple motivation." Strindberg made much the same formulation in his remarkable Preface to *Miss Julie,* in which he wrote that "A happening in life—and this is a fairly recent discovery!—is generally brought by a whole series of more or less deep-lying motives," and added, "I commend myself for the introduction of this multiplicity of motives" (Paulson translation). Strindberg was one of those nineteenth-century observers, mostly poets, playwrights and novelists, who contributed subtleties of well-nigh diabolic perception to European romanticism and realism alike. He belonged to the company of Kleist, Novalis, Stendhal, Dostoevsky, and Nietzsche, among others.

Had Dr. Klaf been so minded or so lavish with space as to provide a close analysis of some of Strindberg's best-known dramas, he could easily have provided evidence of impressive artistic balance in Strindberg's works even when he presented literary surrogates of himself as victims of feminine parasitism and guile. In the first of his dramatic masterpieces, *The Father,* for example, Strindberg shows his hero the Captain inviting defeat by his wife with his own flaws of character, and he makes Laura, the husband-destroying Clytemnestra of the play, considerate to nearly everybody but the Captain, her would-be master. In the sex duel central to *The Father,* the Captain is no match for his wife, despite his superior intelligence, because he is insecure in his masculinity and parenthood, while Laura pushes her conflict with him to an extreme of destructiveness beyond her original intention and will. Villainess she may be, as well as representative of Strindberg's paranoid conception of women created in the image of his first wife, Siri von Essen, but it is essentially her husband's masculine self-assertiveness that arouses her compulsive, irrational enmity.

Strindberg, although greatly perturbed by the course of his first marriage while writing *The Father* in 1887, keeps antagonists in balance. There is no villainy or melodrama in the play in spite of the extreme violence of the interior and exterior action; there is only the action of characters driven to destruction and self-destruction by psychic forces Strindberg associated with a universal conflict between male and female. In other plays, too, such as *The Creditor, The Link* (or *The Bond*), and *The Dance of Death,* Strindberg's husbands are not innocent martyrs, and individuals of both sexes are driven by impulses beyond reason and control. With that kind of treatment of character-motivated action Strindberg served reality, produced art, and created psychological drama all at the same time instead of simply projecting a psychosis or a series of psychotic reactions. I do not say that Strindberg was ever a happy man for long, but I believe it would be hard to find better examples of the transcendence as well as utilization of mental suffering in literary history.

Strindberg, we know, also went beyond individual psychology in his work and adopted the still wider perspectives of "social drama." He related domestic conflict to the social factors reflected and represented by the turn-of-the-century feminism and the rise of the so-called "new woman." He observed the growth of feminine domination of society in modern times. Like D. H. Lawrence decades later, he viewed sexual conflict as a special struggle for power. Conflicts between the upper and lower classes also came under his observation, and were both actually and symbolically represented in his writings. In *Miss Julie,* for example, the antagonists of the sex duel are a valet and a countess who exemplify characteristic differences of class as well as of sex. Strindberg, indeed, found a parallel to the "war of the sexes" in the "class war," to which European literature became increasingly attentive after the revolutions of 1830 and 1848. Strindberg projected this conflict not only in his naturalistic plays but even in his expressionist fancies, as in the contrast he draws between the worlds of the rich and the poor in *A Dream Play,* and in the vampire character of a household cook in *The Ghost Sonata* who drains the strength out of her master's food. There is an *outside* world in Strindberg's consciousness, no matter how distorted it happens to be in certain periods of his life, and this is especially evident in his fiction and in his noteworthy series of historical plays.

So we come, I repeat, to the ineluctable conclusion that it is the *sanity* of art, not its insanity, that is exemplified in the career of Strindberg; its order, not disorder; its relatedness to reality, not evasion of reality; and the artist's mastery of chaotic tension, not a psychotic submission to it. The final result is integration, not disintegration. The fragments of a frequently exploded life are reassembled in Strindberg's art, conflict is momentarily stilled in the very process of being revealed, and a temporary reconciliation with existence is achieved even in the act of showing life to be as intolerable and illusory as it is in *A Dream Play.* These are the paradoxes of creativity and among major modern writers will be found few who exemplified them so conspicuously and persistently as Strindberg did. More than anything else, this is what constitutes the modernity of the most "modern" of the theatre's writers, this dramatist of modern man's division and alienation.

Dr. Klaf's chronicle of Strindberg's struggle for mental health, lapses, and recoveries, pertains to the base upon which Strindberg erected works of recognition, projection, and transcendence besides which clinical facts alone must appear routine no matter how accurate and relevant. Dr. Klaf himself, and this is greatly to his credit, wants us to turn from the disease to the frequently won and precariously held sanity of the modern master. (I wish only that he had been more disposed than he is in the last chapter to do justice to the dramatic labors of the latter-day O'Neill.) Dr. Klaf does not gloss over the presence of neurosis and psychosis in his subject, but he knows that the creative power of the artist, the basis of his social value and distinction, lies in the deepest recesses of his personality. He could have said with Lionel Trilling that the one part of the artist that is healthy is "that which gives him the power to conceive, to plan, to work, and to bring his work to a conclusion." And he realizes that, like other major artists, Strindberg (as John Keats would have put it) was more than a dreaming thing and a fever of himself.

THE MODERNISM OF CHEKHOV*

It is possible, and advisable, to consider the modernism of Chekhov in both general and specific, more or less philosophical, and more or less technical, terms. As the technical aspects of Chekhov's artistry are probably familiar to so cultivated an audience as the present, I shall refer to it first and shall do so with the utmost brevity.

Nor is the subject particularly complicated by the fact that Chekhov made himself the master of *two* crafts, whereas even the mastery of a single craft is beyond the compass of ordinary writers. Chekhov is a master of both the modern short story and the modern drama. But the same man appears in the mature artistry of both his stories and plays, and the style is the man in both cases. Chekhov places wonderfully alive characters in the center of his work. He relates them to their environment, but without allowing the environment to obscure or diminish the individual, and without allowing the dissonances of social reality to drown out the human voice. Chekhov supplants the external action of commonplace fiction and drama with *inner* action, thus producing the plotless story and plotless play we associate importantly with modern literature and theatre. In reducing the role of plot, however, Chekhov does not diminish—he actually enlarges or intensifies—character revelation and the action of society upon the individual. It may be said that Chekhov performed the extremely difficult feat of maintaining the reality of character and the reality of environment in delicate equilibrium.

Both in fiction and drama, Chekhov is a master realist who did not content himself with surfaces but observed and created in depth. And he is a master naturalist who escaped the aridity of most naturalistic writing. That is, he observed human reality with detachment but did not congeal it with indifference. He could be detached and compassionate at the same time. Like other naturalists, he provided many a slice of life, but each slice was alive whereas the usual slice of life possesses everything but life.

In both fiction and drama, Chekhov wrote with extreme simplicity—with the simplicity of one who is constitutionally incapable of imposing on anyone. He wrote neither verse nor purple prose. Yet the result of his mature writing, full of delicate shadings of characterization and emotion, has the effect of poetry. The effect is evidently so sure that it even survives

* A lecture delivered on March 11, 1960, at Brooklyn College, commemorating the hundredth anniversary of Chekhov's birth.

translation. Especially in his chief plays, the poetry is one of complex design, which is what is meant when we advert to the *contrapuntal* character of the work. And, finally, Chekhov is that rare naturalist who actually writes naturally. It is not only that his writing flowed easily, but that he managed to write masterly stories and four major plays in which the characters behave and speak as if they were completely unaware of having been caught in the net of literature. They seem immersed in their own life rather than in the complications or situations assigned to them by an author. They feel for themselves, think their own thoughts, and dream their own dreams. Which is what we mean when we say that Chekhov's dramatic characters tend to fly away from the center of the action—that the dramatic roles are *centrifugal.*

And one more technical point of some significance. It has often been noted that Chekhov is a great humorist yet also a profoundly moving writer. What this amounts to in terms of artistry is that his writing has a rich texture, that it exists on several levels of experience at the same time, and that his simplicity masks considerable complexity. But it means more than this: Chekhov is especially modern in this one respect that his mature work belongs, in the main, to a *mixed genre.* Whereas in past ages comedy and tragedy tended to exist separately, they tend to blend in modern writing.

In his work, comedy may infiltrate tragedy, and tragedy may infiltrate comedy, producing controversy on the part of those who like to busy themselves with the fine points of literary classification. Chekhov is the master of the mixed literary form, of the double mode, of what for want of a better term we may call *tragicomedy* or *"drame."* He was so effective in this blended genre partly because his attitudes and moods blended so naturally. He was so effective also because he had such high spirits that grief could not subdue him; and because he had a rich vein of humor, even a tendency toward prankishness—a vein he cultivated buoyantly and profitably in many a humorous story and in a number of delightful vaudeville pieces, such as *The Bear.* Whatever the reason, however, Chekhov brought to its culmination the modern art of blended styles and literary structures; and in doing so, advanced the truthfulness and subtlety, the complexity and penetrativeness, of modern writing.

We can perhaps best approach the romantic fiction that Chekhov is the laureate of modern spiritual bankruptcy by noting that there have indeed been two major modes of modernism. It seems as if the modern world has been divided between a modernism of *Thanatos,* or *Death,* and a modernism of *Eros,* or *Life.* It is becoming increasingly evident even in England and the United States that Chekhov belongs to the positive mode of modernism in spite of the tendency to associate him with moribund and negativistic modernity. We have begun to associate him with strength rather than weakness, and we have thus begun to do justice to one of the most buoyantly vital of modern writers—a man equally free from twilight Slavophile mysticism and the mystiques of Western decadence.

Chekhov, in brief, possessed "the even-tempered soul" Matthew Arnold attributed to Sophocles. He was compassionate, but he had a sharply critical mind and temperament, too. He was critical of the old regime in Russia, of the general lack of progress in that country, of its dispirited intelligentsia, its ignorant peasantry, and the inhumanity of the law, including the barbaric penal system in Siberia. Certain it is that Chekhov did not allow himself to be overpowered by the enervation and gloom he attributed in his stories and plays to the Russian gentry of the provinces. Nor did he believe that others were doomed to triviality and uselessness if they did not doom themselves. He was essentially an optimist. For Chekhov, as Gorky noted, there were "no completely hopeless cases." As Gorky further noted, Chekhov "was always himself inwardly free."

Stanislavsky, often blamed for filling Chekhov's plays with tragedy, also felt the optimism and healthy outlook of his author. Chekhov merely disdained being obvious and platitudinous about his point of view—or, indeed, about *any* point of view. Referring to his story "The Horse Thieves," he wrote to a correspondent, "You scold me for my objectivity, calling it indifference to good and evil, lack of ideas, and so on. When I describe horse thieves you would have me say: 'Stealing horses is evil.' But that was known long ago without me."

But he could be roused to indignation and protest. He was outraged by symptoms of corruption and injustice, he was especially pained by the stalemate of educated people. He believed, as he said, that each man must work for mankind despite his misfortunes. He himself had known suffering and privation, but had refused to be suffocated by his circumstances. "In my childhood," he once wrote, "I had no childhood."

He was compelled, moreover, to assume at an early age the extreme burden of supporting his parents and brothers. As Lillian Hellman writes, Chekhov "became the father of his family and remained the father the rest of his life." He wrote continually—fluently, but under great pressure—while studying medicine. It is no wonder that envying Tolstoy and Turgenev their financial freedom he once wrote, "they receive as a gift what we lower classes buy with our youth."

Nevertheless, Chekhov succumbed neither to self-pity nor self-deception. "You hold that I am intelligent," he once wrote. "Yes, I am in-

telligent in that I . . . don't lie to myself and don't cover my own emptiness with other peoples' intellectual rays." And above all, he believed in
that sense of responsibility or outward direction that produces major
writers who belong to all humanity rather than to their own little egos
and their small fellowship of writers dedicated to the pursuit of purely
private sensibility. "Writers," he wrote to his editor, Suvorin, "who are
immortal or just plain good . . . have one very important trait in common: they are going somewhere and they call us with them." Passiveness,
despite his frequent concern with characters who suffer stalemate, was the
one thing he could not endure in a writer, declaring that "he who wants
nothing, hopes for nothing, and fears nothing cannot be an artist." It is
for that reason as well as because of his social sympathies and medical
training that he rejected the indifference to science common among turn-
of-the-century art-for-art's-sake coteries. "Science and letters," he declared,
"should go hand in hand. Anatomy and fine literature have the same
enemy—the devil."

It is evident, then, that Chekhov could not be content with mere depression in his writing even when he represented some extremely depressing characters and slices of life; it can be said truly that much of his
work is a marvelous combination of compassion and buoyant intelligence,
of much darkness but also many flecks of light in the darkness. Stanislavsky, for instance, noted how intensely Chekhov's submerged characters
reject total defeat or even mere submission to failure: "they dream, they
rebel and they reach out for what they want." Two significant lines originally in *The Sea Gull* reveal Chekhov's impatience with the passiveness
and mildness of weakling intellectuals. When the comic schoolmaster
Medvenko declares "The earth is round," Dr. Dorn asks him, "Then why
do you say it with so little conviction?" Characters with whom Chekhov
is in obvious sympathy are apt to advert to Chekhov's favorite *work
theme*—that is, to the belief that salvation for the individual or at least
balm for suffering lies in useful creativity. "If only one could live the
remnant of one's life in some new way," cries Uncle Vanya, and adds, "we
must make haste and work, make haste and do something." Irina, of
The Three Sisters, cries out at the end, "I will give all my life to those to
whom it may be of use," and her fiancé the Baron rejoices at the prospect
of exchanging his aristocratic profession of arms for simple, useful work:
"Something formidable is threatening us, the strong cleansing storm is
gathering us . . . it will soon sweep our world clean of laziness, indifference, prejudice against work and wretched boredom." It is not surprising
that unlike Western admirers of Chekhov who had singled out the list-
lessness and morbidity of his dramatic characters for sentimentalization,

the first great director of the plays, Stanislavsky, in *My Life in Art,* "they, like Chekhov, seek life, joy, laughter, courage . . . [they try] to overcome the hard and unbearable impasses into which life has plunged them."

Chekhov himself never ceased to exert himself as long as his health permitted, working among the peasants, and on one famous occasion taking an arudous trip to the Siberian peninsula of Sakhalin for the purpose of making a study of Russia's prison camps. And outstanding in his mind were the two necessities of social reform and the application of scientific knowledge to human suffering. "God's earth is good," he once wrote after many travels. "It is only we on it who are bad. Instead of knowledge, there is insolence and boundless conceit; instead of labor, idleness and caddishness; there is no justice, the understanding of honor does not go beyond 'the honor of the uniform' . . . the important thing is that we must be just and all the rest will be added to us." He could be eloquent on the subject; and he could be equally eloquent on the subject of science: "Surgery alone," he declared, "has accomplished so much that the very very thought of it is frightening. The period of twenty years ago appears just pitiful to anyone studying medicine nowadays. . . . If I were presented the choice of one of the two, the 'ideals' of the sixties or the worst community hospital of the present time, I wouldn't hesitate a moment in choosing the latter."

And in the end, these twin interests in social reform and science profoundly affected his work as a writer. In all his mature work he has the penetration and candor that distinguish great naturalistic writing. And these qualities are only enriched, rather than diminished, by the fine poetry of nuance and mood and atmosphere for which he is rightly renowned. He was for plain speaking on all occasions and held moral censorship in great contempt. "There are people," he wrote, "who can be corrupted even by children's literature." To the contrary, he considered the facing up to the realities of life an act of purgation, observing that there are people like good jurists and physicians "who the more they acquaint themselves with the sordidness of life, the cleaner they become." Such views could only serve to intensify the depth and scope of his naturalistic artistry and to support his ideal of the man of letters as a responsible person "under contract to his conscience" who is "in duty bound to battle with his fastidiousness and soil his imagination with the grime of life." Here, too, we find Chekhov reconciling the aims of literature with the principles of science, as when he declared: "To chemists there is nothing unclean in this world. A man of letters should be as objective as a chemist; he has to renounce ordinary subjects a little and realize that manure piles play a very respectable role in a landscape. . . .

I am not in the same camp with literary men who take a skeptical attitude of science; and I would not want to belong to those who handle every subject solely on the basis of their wits."

In conclusion, we can take the measure of Chekhov's stature and locate his position in modern literature by taking into account just these points of view, to which he reverted again and again in his most personal writings, his notes and his letters. Too often in our times, modernism has been equated with morbidity, negativism, and nihilism—or with a fashionable medievalism and a T. S. Eliot kind of stratification of persons into high and low, sheep and goats. Modernism after World War I, and indeed somewhat earlier, became equated with an infatuation with chaos on the one hand, as in European expressionism and surrealism, and with a mystique on the other hand, ranging from the cult of pure spirit to the cult of the flesh absolute. I am thinking of such writers as Maeterlinck and Claudel, on the one hand, and Arzybashev and the fascist Céline on the other. All this is not the modernism of Chekhov.

Chekhov the man and Chekhov the writer belong to the clear and broad, if by no means untroubled, stream of progressive rather than retrogressive modernism—of hope, rather than of despair, and of activism, rather than pessimistic passiveness. His was the modernism of health rather than the modernism of disease, which has mostly been a cult of death or an indirect surrender to death—a form of romanticism in modern trappings, whether sporting a yellow flower in Oscar Wilde's London or a mildewed beard in a West Coast beatnik's paradise.

Chekhov's modernism, I should conclude, was actually a true classicism. This is true insofar as the mature and long experienced Goethe was correct in declaring that "the classic is health, the romantic, disease." It is also true, to the degree that, as the young Nietzsche of *The Birth of Tragedy* put it, classicism opposes order to the primal chaos of the passions—to the degree that Apollonian serenity supersedes Dionysian frenzy. Few writers saw evil as clearly as Chekhov did, or exposed it more thoroughly—as we observe in his full-length plays and in such realistic masterpieces of the short story as "The Peasants," "The Village Elder," "In the Steppe," and "Ward No. 6." But few modern writers were as little confused by error and few so little mesmerized and seduced by evil. And few writers, as we observe especially in his plays, looked at even attractive weakness and self-deception with so much ironic detachment. There was simply no divorce between intelligence and compassion in his plays and stories. For Chekhov's health—the health of a man who suffered from tuberculosis during half his lifetime and died at the age of forty-four—was not an easy possession. It was born of experience rather than ignorance; it was hard won, and it was heroically maintained. Chekhov, who stood on the brink of morbidity and despair, managed to keep his balance; and his wonderful sense of humor helped him to keep that balance, as did his scrupulously objective view of reality. Securing Chekhov for *positive* modernism was his soundness as a man—and his modesty. He was truthful, but without vanity and rudeness. He pared down his expectations to the possibilities of life instead of crying like a hurt adolescent for its impossibilities. Disappointment did not drive him to despair of life because he did not require of life more than it could give; he did not become a misanthrope because he did not expect of men what they were incapable of being or becoming. What they *were* capable of was sufficient; the problem was merely how to secure a favorable social climate for their potentialities.

In sum, the Chekhov we celebrate was a realist who transfigured the commonplace, and a naturalist who transcended the determinism and artlessness of the naturalist theory of art. He avoided the superficiality that often adheres to optimistic transcriptions of reality, and at the same time he escaped the morbidity that accompanies subjective pessimistic renditions of the so-called human condition. He stands virtually alone among the modern masters of literature after 1890—complex without obfuscation and mystique, and classically simple and clear in the midst of the fumes of a world in transition. He is both Sophoclean and modern —not, indeed, a Titan of letters nor an Olympian, but a wholly companionable and civilized human being. As man and artist he belongs at once to common humanity and to those irrepressible intellectual leaders, from Thomas Huxley to John Dewey, those dreamers of the modern dream who believed that mankind may yet save itself through the power of reason and good will.

SHAW ON SHAKESPEARE*

I

My title could just as well have been "Shaw *versus* Shakespeare," or, for that matter, "Shakespeare *versus* Shaw." This being the case, it may be to our advantage to start with a few stabilizing observations. The first of these could be some reassurance to anyone moved to inquire what profit can be expected from such a discourse. Can it be expected to throw any light on Shakespeare? I think it can, and this from an unusual angle— the mind of Shaw that was resolutely and, during the 1890's, almost pugnaciously modern. If anyone was naturally qualified to reject Shakespeare for the sociological modern spirit and for the realistic modern theatre, it was Shaw. And if any modern writer's acceptance or assimilation of Shakespeare could have significance, it would be Shaw's.

This much is certain: Shaw's reaction touches upon questions concerning both Shakespeare and Shaw. Among these, the important questions are Shaw's competence as a Shakespearean critic, which was considerable, and Shaw's incompetence as a Shakespearean critic, which was also considerable. As far as Shakespeare is concerned, the paramount question is how useful Shaw's criticism was in encouraging adequate stage productions and discouraging inadequate ones. The fact is that in these respects Shaw rendered Shakespeare a great service with the reviews he wrote in the 1890's, and his critical support was important to pioneers in the field of modern Shakespearean production such as William Poel and Granville-Barker. In America we have been greatly indebted to these experiments in stripped expressive stage production. And we would reap still greater benefit if more of our actors could speak Shakespeare's lines—or perhaps just *speak*.

Shaw related Shakespeare to the modern theatre in many ways, but chiefly with the close attention and withering candor he brought to every stage production he witnessed in London as a critic. Three volumes of collected criticism attest this fact. He was ardent in his denunciations of indiscriminate Shakespeare-worship—of what he called "Bardolatry." But it is one of the paradoxes of the odd relationship between Shaw and Shakespeare—the relationship, it would seem, of two bears in one den—that

* An address delivered on April 12, 1961, at the first Festival of the Arts, Queens College of the City University of New York. Reprinted from *The Independent Shavian* (Fall/Winter, 1963).

Shaw's scorn for bardolatry made him the best friend Shakespeare had in the British theatre. No one fought so vigorously to preserve "the bard" from his worshippers. Shaw was the sworn enemy of the Victorian actor-managers who in stressing plot and spectacle treated Shakespeare as if he were a contriver of nineteenth-century melodramas. And Shaw was equally scornful of admirers who tried to make a Victorian schoolmaster out of Shakespeare by reducing his plays to a string of platitudes on public and private conduct.

Shaw was particularly involved with the plight of a deified but abused Shakespeare while writing dramatic criticism in the pages of a London weekly, *The Saturday Review,* from 1895 to 1898. Recalling his vendetta against Shakespearean production in England in a valedictory essay, Shaw declared with characteristic extravagance, "When I began to write, William was a divinity and a bore. Now he is a fellow-creature." Shaw's most noteworthy generalization appeared in the article-review of the year 1895 captioned "Poor Shakespeare!" In it he deplored the long-standing tendency of the London actor-managers to abbreviate Shakespeare's plays in order to overproduce them—a tendency that grew more acute with the multiplication of cumbersome scenery. In order to make a Shakespearean play compatible with the realistic staging in vogue during the second half of the nineteenth century, the London actor-managers either omitted or telescoped or arbitrarily patched together scenes Shakespeare had innocently expected to follow each other on the Elizabethan platform stage in proper sequence. Shakespeare did not have to worry about changing to a new setting after each scene as did his nineteenth-century producers. According to new realistic requirements each of these scenes needed to have its own scenery; and in trying to abide by this principle of scenic illusionism, the managers reached an impasse. They simply had to chop up the scenes and rearrange and amalgamate them in order to reduce the number of scenes in the play.

The more the Victorian manager ignored the Elizabethan platform stage the more he was apt to perpetrate assault and battery on Shakespeare's text. Shaw was one of the first critics to take note of this fact and to protest against it; and it is significant, if not indeed also paradoxical, that so ardent a champion of modern realism as Shaw, England's foremost spokesman for Ibsen, should have deplored a realistic style of staging Shakespearean drama. Shaw had no difficulty in skirting the realistic bias of his age, for Shaw had no use for mere pictorialism or for a mere realism of surfaces. He scorned the substitution of spectacle for dramatic content.

Even the power of Shakespeare's tragedies, which the actor-managers

could not extinguish, did not reconcile Shaw to the customary tampering
with Shakespearean texts. We find Shaw as late as 1925 reproving John
Barrymore for drastically cutting *Hamlet*. He admonishes Barrymore to
"concentrate on acting rather than on authorship." Concerning a *Macbeth*
production of the year 1895, he declared with malice unconcealed: "I am
fond—unaffectedly fond—of Shakespeare's plays. I do not mean the plays
of actor-manager's editions and revivals. I mean the plays as Shakespeare
wrote them, played straight through, line by line and scene by scene, as
nearly as possible under the conditions of representation for which they
were designed." Badgering the offenders—especially the chief Victorian
actor-manager, Sir Henry Irving—became one of Shaw's ruling passions
as a critic. "In a true republic of art," he once wrote, "Sir Henry Irving
would ere this have expiated his acting versions on the scaffold. He does
not merely cut plays: he disembowels them."

It must be conceded that, in criticizing the plays, without benefit of
recent Shakespearean scholarship, Shaw overlooked some aspects of Shakespeare's dramatic poetry. Shaw wrote virtually all his Shakespearean criticism before the vogue of the great American image-hunt initiated by Miss
Caroline Spurgeon. Shakespeare's imagery presented no particular patterns or "clusters" for him and invited no special interpretations. Nor did
he, any more than most nineteenth-century writers, take any note of the
poet's recourse to symbolism and allegory. Although he himself paid close
attention to text, Shaw was not interested in Shakespeare for the library
but in Shakespeare for the theatre, where his work could come gloriously
alive or suffer indignity from those who butchered his text and mispoke
his lines. But in one important respect Shaw was in agreement with contemporary scholarship. Shaw was eminently concerned with Shakespeare's
language. At least two reasons can be adduced for Shaw's interest. As a
believer in discussion drama or the "play of ideas," he was bound to give
primacy to language. One cannot sustain much of an argument—much of
a Shavian argument certainly—with mere gestures. Moreover, in coming
to dramatic criticism after a brilliant, if brief, career as a music critic, he
could hardly fail to identify good language with the *sound* of words and
the *rhythm* and cadence of sentences.

Consistently, then, Shaw turned his attention to the speaking of
Shakespeare's lines on the stage, a large subject to which I can allude only
briefly. Shakespeare, in his opinion, was poorly spoken, and the fault lay
with the professional elocutionist who devotes his life, as Shaw put it, to
"the art of breaking up verse in such a way as to make it sound like in-
sanely pompous prose." Shaw even went further than many of us would
care to follow him.We can appreciate the gallantry but also question the

validity of some of his compliments to both Shakespeare and some rare actress—to "some happy fair whose eyes are lodestars and whose tongue's sweet airs more tunable than lark to shepherd's ear." No sooner does the actress, he says recklessly, strike up "the true Shakespearean music," no sooner does she feel her way to her role "altogether by her sense of that music," than "the play and all the music is there." This delightful creature "may make nonsense of the verses by wrong conjunctions and misplaced commas, which show that she has never worked out the logical construction of a single sentence in her part; but if her heart is in the song, the protesting commentator-critic may save his breath to cool his porridge: the soul of the play is there, no matter where the sense of it may be."

Nevertheless, it would be a mistake on our part to assume that Shaw entertained no other standards than those of opera for Shakespeare. Shaw did not reserve his appreciations exclusively for the passages to which he once so aptly alluded as Shakespeare's "verbal arias." It is true that he defended the dramatic poet in Shakespeare against elocutionism, but he also defended the playwright against every other manifestation of bad acting and wrong staging. Shaw spared none of the prominent performers of his day. Of the famous actor-manager Beerbohm-Tree in the role of Falstaff, he once wrote that Beerbohm-Tree needed only one thing to make him an excellent Falstaff—"and that is to get born over again as unlike himself as possible."

Shaw was apt to take note of virtually everything that went into the production, including even the play. His closeness to the text is attested indeed in many a detailed criticism. Details of staging concerned him no less than the details of speech and performance. In reviewing an 1895 production of *All's Well,* for instance, Shaw wrote that "The play, of course, was pulled to pieces in order that some bad scenery . . . might destroy all the illusion which the simple directions in the book create, and which they would equally have created had they been printed on a placard and hung up on a curtain." We know, in fact, that Shaw ardently supported the efforts of his contemporary William Poel, the founder of the Elizabethan Stage Society in 1895, to provide simplified staging as well as good speaking. Costuming also concerned Shaw; a characteristic protest is that which he worded so caustically in the *All's Well* review: "The dresses were the usual fancy ball odds and ends, Helena especially distinguishing herself by playing the first scene partly in the costume of Hamlet and partly in that of a waitress in an Aerated Bread Shop, set off by a monstrous auburn wig which could by no stretch of the imagination be taken for her own hair." And finally, I must repeat, there was the play itself to be protected from the usual Victorian production—that is, the "whole play," which, as

Shaw complained, was "vivisected, and the fragments mutilated, for the sake of accessories."

Even as late as the 1890's, there was also some need to protect the plays from bowdlerization on the grounds of public morality; and Shaw, of course, rose nobly to such occasions. In the case of an amateur production of *All's Well,* Shaw scorned the stock Victorian objection, as he put it, "that the heroine is a lady doctor, and that no lady doctor of any delicacy could possibly adopt a profession which involves the possibility of her having to attend cases such as that of the king in this play, who suffers from a fistula." This example of Nice-Nellyism drew a characteristic volley of rhetoric from Shaw, the confirmed feminist and practiced stump-speaker. He declares: "How any sensible and humane person can have ever read this sort of thing without a deep sense of its insult to every charitable woman's humanity and every sick man's suffering is, fortunately, getting harder to understand nowadays than it once was."

In Shaw's eagerness to claim Shakespeare for the modern theatre, he even looked for possibilities of saluting him as a predecessor. He especially liked Shakespeare's un-Victorian young heroines—those "mighty huntresses," as he called them, who, obeying the Life Force, pursue their prey in the form of a potential mate, as his own Ann Whitefield was soon to do in chasing John Tanner in *Man and Superman.* In reviewing *All's Well,* Shaw went so far as to write that Shakespeare's play "stands out artistically by the sovereign charm of the young Helena and the old Countess of Rousillon and intellectually by the experiment, repeated nearly three hundred years later in *A Doll's House,* of making the hero a perfectly ordinary young man, whose unimaginative prejudices and selfish conventionality make him out a very fine mean figure in the atmosphere created by the nobler nature of his wife." Praise from Ibsen's leading British champion could hardly rise higher!

Yet the account of Shaw's relationship with Shakespeare cannot end on this happy note. And by this I do not mean that Shaw exercised a critic's prerogative of separating the wheat from the chaff in the case of a particular play, or that he manifested that power of discrimination or "resistant flexibility" which made him call *Much Ado About Nothing* "on the whole, a very bad play, but a very enjoyable entertainment."

II

Shaw came to be known as Shakespeare's most formidable enemy rather than as his admirer and ally. There can be no doubt that he actually went out of his way to attain this dubious reputation. For one thing, Shaw made the elementary error of attributing a character's opinion to its author. If Macbeth, at the low ebb of his fortune, called life "a brief candle," Shaw was apt to attribute the statement to Shakespeare himself and to impugn what he considered to be Shakespeare's philosophy or lack of philosophy. Whereupon Shaw, the socialist, optimist, and the champion of the Life Force, cried out, "Life is no 'brief candle' for me. It is a sort of splendid torch which I have got hold of for the moment."

He could also perversely set Bunyan above Shakespeare because the hero of *Pilgrim's Progress,* Christian, calls out, "My sword I give to him that shall succeed me in my pilgrimage and my courage and skill to him that can get it," whereas the dying Hamlet only says, "The rest is silence." Shaw often indulged himself in formulating arbitrary judgments, for which the only explanation is probably that great men make great mistakes while little men make little ones. And Shaw did not care much about being fair when he buckled on his critic's belt, saying on one occasion that he hoped his dramatic criticism had no other fault than, as he put it, "the inevitable one of extreme unfairness." "I do my best," he declared, "to be partial." Had he been familiar with our current psychoanalytical jargon he might have also said, "I cannot help it if I am ambivalent." Shaw, the son of separated parents ("the upstart son of a downstart father," as he once called himself), was ambivalent toward nearly everything, from democracy to Marxism; and toward nearly everyone, from characters in his plays like that mother-image Candida (part Magna Mater and part minx) to the actress-objects of his epistolary passions, Ellen Terry and Mrs. Patrick Campbell. Nevertheless, there was also a more objective reason for his anti-Shakespearcanism.

Measuring the plays against the needs of the theatre to deal with modern ideas, Shaw found Shakespeare unsatisfactory. It is possible even that Shaw would have pressed artistic claims for Shakespeare less zealously if he could have wholeheartedly claimed him as an ally in the battle for modern ideas. He might have applauded Shakespeare's music less if he could have applauded his ideas more. In the puritanical Shaw there was plainly a division between love and suspicion of art; a conflict between artist and social reformer; an impulse to sacrifice the artist to the reformer, the literary genius to the sociologist.

Conscience, I believe, was at the root of this desire—conscience combined with a sense of immediacy. For he believed that society would have to reform itself or go down to destruction. Reason would have to create a brave new world of social justice if Unreason was not to plunge the world into murderous chaos. Like many giants of the nineteenth century, whether or not they survived into the twentieth, Shaw had a foreboding of disaster long before nuclear fission made it probable. To avert it was, in his opinion, the most urgent necessity of the modern age. And even his enormous evolutionary optimism, which he renounced only late in his long career, was not sufficient to insulate him against despair. Man would have to work out his salvation collectively with extreme exertions of intelligence and will. An art devoid of usable social content, according to Shaw, no less than to Tolstoy, was a luxury humanity could ill afford. Above all, art should not be allowed to lull modern humanity to catastrophic contentment. In this opinion, too, Shaw was, of course, by no means alone. In varying degrees, his regard for socially responsible and challenging art was shared by such modern writers as Tolstoy, Dostoyevsky, Zola, Ibsen, Chekhov, and Thomas Mann. I say *modern,* not *modernist,* writers because unlike these (unlike the Becketts and the Genets of our time) Shaw, the severe social critic, did not want to live by negations, and had too much vitality for Thanatos—or death—worship.

There was to come a time indeed in Shaw's lengthening career when hope was too like despair—when he could say of the aroused masses in his 1931 play, *On the Rocks,* that "they always break the wrong windows, poor fellows"; or when he would let the clergyman-hero of *Too True to Be Good* declare in one breath that Western civilization was, as he put it, "damned beyond salvation," and then add, "Is No enough? For a boy, yes; for a man, never. . . . I must preach and preach and preach no matter how late the hour and how short the day." Shakespeare, of course, did not preach and preach and preach. And in the days before hope and despair kept such close company Shaw was particularly eager not to allow Shakespeare-worship to impede the cause of Ibsen and the press of modern drama.

Priding himself on being a "true Puritan" in putting "moral passion" ahead of sexual attraction, Shaw could even wax stuffy at times. Aside from occasionally succumbing to a narrow moralism, moreover, Shaw did not realize how much Shakespeare had anticipated him in taking a critical view of the passion of the Roman soldier and the Egyptian queen. Indeed, Shaw generally failed to take a sufficiently ample view of Shakespeare's typical Tudor concern with the collective interest—with the interest of sound government and stable order. It remained for later students such as Tillyard to take cognizance of the political substance in Shakespearean drama, especially in the history plays and the tragedies. Shaw was not greatly mollified by this matter in the plays, apparently because of the medieval and Tudor cast of Shakespeare's political thought and the preponderantly poetic, rather than discursive or Ibsenist, mode of presentation. There is many a passage in the plays that invites a political interpretation, although it does not necessarily provide grist for Shaw's Fabian-Socialist mill. There is, for example, Ulysses' famous speech on "degree" or *order*, in *Troilus and Cressida;* there is Menenius' celebrated reproof to the discontented plebeians of Rome in his speech on "the body's members" in *Coriolanus*. There is also the entire tragedy of political failure in *Julius Caesar*, which, as some of us will remember, Orson Welles found it possible to present in 1937, in modern dress, as an antifascist drama. And there is in the history plays not only abundant illustrative action concerning right and wrong modes of government combined with ample characterization of good and bad rulers, but many an exhortation as well as some lesson-giving symbolism.

Shaw, however, was not greatly affected by such evidence in favor of Shakespeare as a responsible thinker. Bent on fostering a thoroughly modern type of drama, Shaw looked toward a different dispensation that Ibsen, not Shakespeare, could provide. He explained his views in an important chapter of his *Quintessence of Ibsenism* called "The Technical Novelty in Ibsen's Plays"—the "technical novelty" being "discussion." The passage I have in mind is not particularly profound, but it is worth quoting precisely because it is free from the customary Shavian pyrotechnics and comic exaggeration. Shaw explains:

> When Ibsen began to make plays, the art of the dramatist had shrunk into the art of contriving a situation. And it was held that the stranger the situation, the more interesting the play. Ibsen saw that, on the contrary, the more familiar the situation the more interesting the play. Shakespeare had put ourselves on the stage but not our situation. Our uncles seldom murder our fathers; we do not meet witches; our kings are not as a rule stabbed and succeeded by their stabbers; and when we raise money by bills we do not promise to pay pounds of our flesh. Ibsen supplied the want left by Shakespeare. He gives not only ourselves, but ourselves in our situation. The things that happen to his stage figures are things that happen to us. One consequence is that his plays are much more important to us than Shakespeare's.

This is a distinctly moderate statement for Shaw, although it was made in defiance of Ibsen's enemies and flung in the teeth of Shakespeare's idolaters.

Shaw delivered extreme *obiter dicta* and one truly Olympian bit of thunder when he compared Shakespeare's mind with his own. The occasion was a production of Shakespeare's quite inferior drama *Cymbeline*. Shaw's exuberant diatribe starts with a description of the play—as "for the most part stagey trash of the lowest melodramatic order, in part abominably written, throughout intellectually vulgar, foolish, offensive, indecent, and exasperating beyond all tolerance." Then Shaw really let himself go. "There are moments," he declared, "when one asks despairingly why our stage should ever have been cursed with this 'immortal' pilferer of other men's stories and ideas, with his monstrous rhetorical fustian, his unbearable platitudes, his pretentious reduction of the subtlest problems of life to commonplaces against which a Polytechnic debating club would revolt"—and so on in one extravagant sentence. He topped it, however—a feat surely only Shaw himself could have managed—by concluding that "With the single exception of Homer, there is no eminent writer, not even Sir Walter Scott, whom I can despise so entirely as I despise Shakespeare when I measure my mind against his." As for the poor little play under review, Shaw's summation is surely a classic of either self-ignorance or tongue-in-the-cheek asseveration. "To read *Cymbeline* and to think of Goethe, of Wagner, of Ibsen, is, for me, to imperil the habit of studied moderation of statement which years of public responsibility as a journalist have made almost second nature in me."

Nevertheless, please hold your fire if you think these are Shaw's last words on either Shakespeare or *Cymbeline*. The very next paragraph, with its stunning dramatic reversal, starts as follows: "But I am bound to add that I pity the man who cannot enjoy Shakespeare. He has outlasted thousands of abler thinkers, and will outlast a thousand more." And Shaw goes on to expatiate on Shakespeare's "gift of telling a story [provided someone else told it first]; his enormous power over language, as conspicuous in his senseless and silly abuse of it as in his miracles of expression; his humor; his sense of idiosyncratic character; and his prodigious fund of that vital energy which is, it seems, the true differentiating property behind the faculties, good, bad, or indifferent, of the man of genius." And even the violently flouted *Cymbeline* is said to possess values by no means expendable: above all, the play's heroine, Imogen, when she is not an unspeakably virtuous person but the "Imogen of Shakespeare's genius" is declared to be "an enchanting person." After this, perhaps only one more point needs to be made. It is that in every comprehensive tribute Shaw grudgingly or generously pays will be found an underlying regard for Shakespeare's immense love of life and capacity for fellow-feeling.

It might be appropriate, indeed, to conclude with a reference to positive expressions of the humanism by both Shakespeare and his affectionate foe—who became his foe indeed, for humanistic reasons, in response to late-nineteenth- and early-twentieth-century idealism. We may take as suitable summations a well-known passage from *King Lear,* and one less well known from Shaw's *John Bull's Other Island.* They illustrate in both instances a characteristic humanism identifiable with humanitarianism and issuing in that unmistakable power of eloquence which Shakespeare and Shaw held in common—characteristically, the eloquence of memorable poetry in Shakespeare's case and of memorable prose in Shaw's. The outcast Lear, storm-battered on the heath, comes to realize what fellow-suffering can teach even an arbitrary king: "Poor naked wretches, wheresoe'er you are," etc. (III, 4). These words come naturally, indeed, from the poet who later made Lear exclaim with hard-won knowledge that "Through tatter'd clothes small vices do appear," etc. (IV, 6), the poet who exclaimed in his own person in Sonnet 66 against "captive good attending captain ill" and "art made tongue-tied by authority."

Shaw's unfrocked mystic, asked by the English Babbitt, Broadbent, what heaven is like in his dreams, answers: "In my dreams it is a country where the State is the Church and the Church the people; three in one and one in three. It is a commonwealth in which work is play and play is life: three in one and one in three. It is the temple in which the priest is the worshipper and the worshipper the worshipped: three in one and one in three. It is a godhead in which all life is human and all humanity divines: three in one and one in three." As a metaphorical expression of Shavian and turn-of-the-century optimism the "three-in-one" sentences, written in 1904, come naturally enough from an avowed apostle of the Life Force and an ardent believer in the perfectibility of man—a faith that, actually, originated in Shakespeare's own time rather than in Shaw's.

Shaw and Shakespeare then met more easily on the ground of common aspirations for humanity than Shaw was apt to realize. For one thing, Shaw, while adhering to Fabian sociology and Marxist ideology, was too easily put off by Shakespeare's alleged antidemocratic bias. There is considerable irony in the fact that Shaw, given to superman-worship throughout his life and growing impatient with social inertia after 1930, leaned toward authoritarianism as much as any apologist for Tudor absolutism in Shakespeare's time. Still, in claiming Shakespeare for art, in acclaiming Shakespeare primarily as a supreme poet, dramatist, and theatrician, Shaw did claim him for the modern world in terms far more potent than any he could have selected if he had discovered in him another Ibsen, another Sidney Webb—or even another Bernard Shaw.

In being so powerfully drawn to Shakespeare quite against his sociological zeal, Shaw, indeed, evinced the sensibility that made him, too, an artist. We shall probably remember Shaw the playwright long after we have forgotten Shaw the sociologist. Deep calls unto deep, and the artist in Shakespeare found a powerful response from Shaw the artist. This much must be granted in the case of the hardy iconoclast who wrote of

King Lear that "no greater tragedy will ever be written," of *Hamlet* that it marked "the beginning of modern drama," of *Othello* that it "remains magnificent by the volume of its passion," and of *Romeo and Juliet* that it has "lines that tighten the heart." Whether or not he was altogether aware of it, Shaw, in responding so wholeheartedly to Shakespeare as a dramatic poet while deriding him for lacking modern "ideas," willy-nilly embraced the total creative man. In our appreciation of the work of a supreme artist, there can hardly be a meaningful distinction between art and thought; and in yielding to the one, we submit to the other.

■

SHAW ON IBSEN AND THE
DRAMA OF IDEAS*

The rise of distinctly modern drama is usually associated with the development of "drama of ideas" during the last third of the nineteenth century. This is virtually an article of faith among theatre historians, and it has been left intact by a succession of revolutions in dramatic theory and criticism. Ibsen, it is maintained, created the genre of drama of ideas; Shaw promulgated and developed it. Ibsen was the creator, and Shaw was his prophet. In the English-speaking world there could be no doubt about the accuracy of either statement by the end of the nineteenth or the beginning of the twentieth century. Shaw's role was evident wherever Shaw's dramatic criticism penetrated and his early plays were seen or read. As for Ibsen's role, it could not be questioned by anyone startled by the content of Ibsen's plays, since drama of ideas meant, of course, drama of ideas that called attention to themselves.

These are, obviously, transparent simplifications. Shaw's advocacy of Ibsen was by no means the sole or even the first factor in the gradual acceptance of Ibsen as a major playwright in England. His interpretation of Ibsen's plays could be questioned, not to say improved upon, and it was not difficult to conclude that Shaw as critic and champion had created an ideal in his own image. It used to be said that his *Quintessence of Ibsenism* was actually a "Quintessence of Shavianism." If Shaw was useful to Ibsen as an advocate, Ibsen was useful to Shaw as a postfabricated forerunner. It was certainly unnecessary to accept Shaw in order to accept Ibsen, and a close student of the latter, such as William Archer, could not fail to realize that Ibsen and Shaw were two different breeds of men who differed radically in their dramatic artistry. But this much is certain: the concept of drama of ideas was to a considerable degree Shaw's contribution to dramatic theory; it was, in part, a Shavian discovery and, in part, a Shavian invention useful in the struggle for liberal principles and modern social drama.

To observe this phenomenon adequately we must do several things that cannot possibly be accomplished in a single paper. We must compare Ibsen's plays with Shaw's exegesis, which is no mean assignment, chiefly because of what Shaw left out of consideration more or less deliberately.

* From *Ideas in the Drama* (New York: Columbia University Press, 1964).

We cannot confidently match Ibsen's intentions with the intentions blithely attributed to him by Shaw, who spoke as one unacquainted with the obscure night of the soul of one of the theatre's most ambivalence-ridden authors. Shaw is not necessarily wrong or obtuse, but much that seems crystal-clear in a short Shavian analysis or synopsis of one of Ibsen's plays proves to be decidedly complicated and somewhat murky in the play itself.

In the history of Shaw's concern with Ibsen as "the onlie begetter" of modern drama of ideas it is, moreover, helpful to discriminate three main stages. The first appears when Shaw speaks on Ibsen to the Fabian Society in 1890 and publishes his lectures in 1891 under the title of *The Quintessence of Ibsenism;* the second, when Shaw, covering the London theatre between 1895 and 1898 for Frank Harris's periodical *The Saturday Review,* serves Ibsen in commenting on Ibsen productions, as well as on the plays of pre-Ibsenist playwrights such as Sardou and pseudo-Ibsenite dramatists such as Pinero; the third, when after long practice as a playwright himself and considerable observation of the theatre since his retirement from *The Saturday Review* in favor of Max Beerbohm, Shaw brings out a new edition of *The Quintessence of Ibsenism* in 1913. He brings this publication up to date by adding a section on Ibsen's last four plays (*The Master Builder, Little Eyolf, John Gabriel Borkman,* and *When We Dead Awaken*), published after Shaw's Fabian lecture, and develops his conception of drama of ideas by providing two new concluding chapters. In the first stage, Shaw writes as a Fabian reformer; in the second, as a journalist reviewer; in the third, as a critic and historian of the drama. In the first two stages he was effective (with others) in securing a victory for Ibsen in England. In the third stage he reflected on the victory, defined its nature, and described it as the decisive event in the making of modern drama.

Half a century has elapsed since then—a rather large interval of time in the life of literary theory and practice. It is hardly too soon, therefore, to reexamine Shaw's conception of drama of ideas and to test its application to the work of Ibsen and his successors. By piecing together Shaw's viewpoint from the aforementioned three stages of his engagement with Ibsen, we may hope to achieve a perspective that Shaw himself would not find objectionable, although nothing is more certain than Shaw's great disinterest in dramatic theory *per se* unless it is his readiness to resort to theory as an instrument of his socialist and argumentative inclinations.

As Shaw tells us himself, *The Quintessence of Ibsenism* was originally a *pièce d'occasion.* The Fabian Society decided to occupy its membership during the summer of 1890 with a series of lectures under the general title of "Socialism in Contemporary Literature," and Shaw volunteered to speak on Ibsen. His lecture was "duly read at the St. James's Restaurant on the 18th of July," and as duly laid aside by its author, who was probably correct in concluding that the series had added "nothing to the general stock of information on Socialism in Contemporary Literature." He decided to publish the lecture in 1891 only after concluding, as a result of disputes over Ibsen's plays, that an exposition of Ibsenism was greatly needed. *Rosmersholm,* produced at the Vaudeville Theatre by Florence Farr, *Ghosts,* presented as the inaugural production of the Independent Theatre, and *Hedda Gabler,* he recalled, had "started a frantic newspaper controversy, in which I could see no sign of any of the disputants having ever been forced by circumstances, as I had, to make up his mind definitely as to what Ibsen's plays meant."[1] Shaw proceeded to give his views to the public after candidly warning his readers in the Preface that he had not written "a critical essay on the poetic beauties of Ibsen, but simply an exposition of Ibsenism." He also admitted that his conclusions were drawn from the plays rather than from explicit comments by Ibsen himself—that, as Shaw put it, "the existence of a discoverable and perfectly definite thesis in a poet's work by no means depends on the completeness of his own intellectual consciousness of it."[2]

The essence of Ibsenism, according to Shaw, is that Ibsen offends his opponents and pleases his supporters because his plays invalidate old beliefs and propose new ones. His struggles and questionings propound a transvaluation of values in the interests of progress. For Shaw, echoing Marx, Butler, Nietzsche, and other leaders of nineteenth-century iconoclasm, "progress must involve the repudiation of an established duty at every step," and there is nothing new in "the defiance of duty by the reformer: Every step of progress means a duty repudiated and a scripture torn up."[3] This view is maintained against a representative of conservative dramatic criticism, Clement Scott, who led the opposition to Ibsen in London and demanded the suppression of *Ghosts* in the British theatre on the grounds that he, as spectator, has been exhorted by Ibsen "to laugh

---

[1] G. B. Shaw, *The Quintessence of Ibsenism* (New York, 1914), Preface, p. vi. Also, Shaw's *Major Critical Essays* (London, 1932), pp. 11–12. As a partisan for the luminous known and the readily manifest, Shaw could not, of course, evince much patience for anyone ill at ease in the presence of the dark unknown in Ibsen's work that made Henry James, for example, complain of Ibsen's "bewildering incongruities" in *Hedda Gabler* and refer to his "strangely inscrutable art" in *The Master Builder.*

[2] *Ibid.* This was a sound precaution, since Ibsen himself was inclined to disclaim political partisanship or any strong opinion.

[3] *Major Critical Essays,* p. 17.

at honor, to disbelieve in love, to mock at virtue, to distrust friendship, and to deride fidelity."[4] It is plain, then, that Shaw acclaimed Ibsen as a revolutionist and that drama of ideas could mean but one thing to Shaw, namely, subversive drama; for surely Clement Scott and his numerous followers also had "ideas," but conservative ones. Had these latter been expressed or demonstrated in a play, we may well ask, would they have qualified the play as a drama of ideas? Apparently not! For the operative word "ideas" we would have to substitute the word "challenges" to approximate Shaw's meaning.

This was tantamount to saying that a conservative position could not produce drama of ideas or had no ideas worthy of a modern intellect, a point of view to which G. K. Chesterton, T. E. Hulme, T. S. Eliot, and later neoconservatives could justifiably take exception. It could be argued that Shaw had got himself caught in a trap of his own devising in substituting an illiberalism of the left for the illiberalism of the right. This argument would not have disturbed Shaw, however, because he thought of criticism as a partisan tactic rather than as an end in itself. He was by training and inclination a debater rather than an arbitrator; and he was far more interested in disparaging Victorian moralism than in maintaining the dubious virtue of consistency.

It is also conceivable that conservatives reacting at a later time to a *status quo* of liberalism might take the offensive in the manner of T. S. Eliot's attacks on democratic disunity or, as he calls it in *The Idea of a Christian Society,* "a liberalized or negative condition of society."[5] But this eventuality would not have disconcerted the later Shaw, who became perfectly aware of flaws in democracy and hankered for government by superior individuals. His thinking was, as a rule, relativistic rather than absolutist, and he would have had no difficulty in admitting to the category of drama of ideas, at some later time than the 1890's, a play that *reversed* belief in the inevitability of progress and the worth of democratic government. In his old age he wrote such plays himself (*The Apple Cart, Too True to Be Good, On the Rocks,* and *The Millionairess*) without in the least depriving them of provocative ideas—which did not, however, make him revise his premise of the 1890's that the only sound ideas were modern ones. (It is this assumption that led him to assert superiority to Shakespeare in the realm of thought and to consider Ibsen "more useful" for his times than Shakespeare, and more "useful," too, than many a contemporary naturalist determined to record sordid details,

[4] *Ibid.,* p. 15.
[5] *The Idea of a Christian Society* (New York, 1940), p. 23.

as, for example, Zola, about whom Ibsen is said to have once declared "[He] descends into the cesspool to take a bath, I to cleanse it."[6]

First, then, Shaw announced the principle of relativism in the matter of morality and applied it to his defense of Ibsen against the conservative opposition. Ibsen was praised for having reduced Victorian morality to a tragic absurdity in *Ghosts*. The heroine in that play, Mrs. Alving, came to realize that she had been grievously wrong in adhering to the puritanical code of her times instead of leaving her profligate husband. The rewards of conventional virtue in her case had been years of humiliation in the past and a diseased son on the brink of feeble-mindedness in the present. If the worthy Victorian drama critic Clement Scott had allowed himself to be upset by a production of *Ghosts* in London to the point of wanting the authorities to withdraw the offending theatre's license, it was because the Victorian establishment had yet to surrender the notion that morals are unchanging and absolute in application. Ibsen's Mrs. Alving would have been more moral if she had been less submissive to moralistic absolutism in Norwegian society. Repudiation of "duty" by woman, Ibsen's implicit theme in *A Doll's House* and *Ghosts,* was justified by Shaw as an instance of the general validity of rejecting outworn mores and morals. The repudiation of established opinion and specious morality, we may note parenthetically, is recurrent in the work of such latter-day practitioners of drama of ideas as Brecht and Sartre. Brecht's work often culminates in revolutionary irony; Sartre's in existentialist tragedy.

Shaw started his apology for Ibsen rather laboriously in a chapter entitled "The Two Pioneers," by distinguishing two different types of pioneer: the reformer who declares something to be right that had hitherto been regarded as infamous, and the revolutionist who declares something to be wrong that had hitherto been considered eminently right. He calls the former an "indulgence preacher" and the latter an "abstinence preacher," although a particular individual (the poet Shelley, for example) can be both an "indulgence preacher" and an "abstinence preacher" in differing respects. Still, nothing particularly original came from this distinction in *The Quintessence of Ibsenism*. Shaw was considerably more successful in the second chapter, entitled "Ideals and Idealists," in which he divided men into three categories. There are the "Philistines," who are satisfied with things as they are and display neither intellectual curiosity nor artistic sensibility. They neither create nor challenge principles or ideals. Naturally, they constitute the great majority; in a thousand people, says Shaw, you are likely to find 700 Philistines. There are also

[6] A. E. Zucker, *Ibsen the Master Builder* (New York, 1929), p. 181.

the "Idealists" in considerable number (299 out of a thousand!) who mask realities with fancies and, says Shaw, "graft pleasure on necessity" with desperately defended illusions, making belief in them "a point of public decency." These are, in Shaw's terms, the idealists who are up in arms against Ibsen, who made his outspoken character Dr. Relling in *The Wild Duck* declare that "ideals" are pretenses and that a good old-fashioned Norwegian word for them is "lies"! And, finally, there is the third category, to which a man like Ibsen and no doubt Shaw himself belong, namely, the one man in a thousand whom Shaw calls a "realist," who dares to pull the masks off things that idealists have placed on them. For Ibsen and Shaw, then, the evil they fight is "idealism," and the enemy they encounter is not the Philistine but the idealist.

A pervasive anti-Victorian revolt, with or without Fabian socialist overtones for which Ibsen's middle-class drama provided hardly an occasion, would alone have provided a sufficient springboard for Shaw's advocacy of drama of ideas. So would have Shaw's general craving for an intellectually stimulating theatre, into which he was ready to pour the varied substance of his reading and enthusiasms. It is no accident that his first play, *Widower's Houses,* on which he had been working since 1885, should have been completed and staged in London within a year of the publication of *The Quintessence of Ibsenism.* But Shaw gave the argument in that tract a special Shavian twist that we can only ascribe to his gyroscopic intellect. He arrived at a piquant formulation of Ibsenism by means of the semantic device of calling conservative thinking like Clement Scott's idealism, and iconoclastic thinking like his own and Ibsen's realism. Some forensic advantages were patently inherent in a formulation that revised the usual nomenclature for conservatism and radicalism; here was indeed an early instance of Shaw's trick of turning things topsy-turvy that so upset his critics and delighted his admirers, and that was surely as much a habit of mind as a calculation on his part. In any case, the novelty of Shaw's revisionist definition was bound to be arresting and its patent irony entertaining.

Shaw's introductory comments and the summaries of the plays that follow the chapter on "Ideals and Idealists" present Ibsen as an imaginative writer, albeit a rather thin playwright, rather than as a humdrum reformer. Many a scrupulously written later study, as well as many a stage production after 1890, was to do less than that. Ibsen would have had to wink a little when Shaw attributed a comprehensive philosophy to him not many years before he himself declared in a public address that he had been "more of a poet and less of a philosopher than is commonly supposed." But he could well have been pleased with the dramatic élan and acute intelligence attributed to him by Shavian exegesis.

It has been all too possible to treat Ibsen as a prosaic middle-class writer. Shaw's timely intervention in behalf of Ibsen's reputation saved it from possible imputation of dullness. If there had been a grain of Shavian wit among the outraged conservatives who flouted Ibsen as the devil incarnate, they could have exchanged their hysterical denunciations for Shavian complaints that the devil was too unexciting and dull for them. They could have disposed of modern drama of ideas altogether by charging intellectual playwrights with static playwriting, argumentativeness rather than dramatic action, desiccation of feeling, and the substitution of mouthpieces for characters. This is the kind of criticism to which Shaw and many later dramatists of ideas such as Granville-Barker, Pirandello, Brecht, and Sartre were, indeed, to be exposed at one time or another. We may observe parenthetically that the best butt of truly Shavian criticism, curiously enough, turned out to be Shaw himself when he became the subject of a brilliant little book by G. K. Chesterton in 1909. Chesterton accused Shaw of an insufficient sense of paradox and of not quite understanding life because Shaw "will not accept its contradictions." Chesterton took plains to explain early in his book that by paradox he meant "truth inherent in a paradox" rather than simply "something that makes one jump," and he concluded that Shaw's "madness is all consistency, not inconsistency."[7]

An illustration of Shavian exegesis is Shaw's previously mentioned treatment of *Ghosts,* which was watered down into a second-rate tract on the dangers of heredity in more than one instance of both favorable and hostile criticism. Ibsen's admirers and followers were, in fact, especially inclined to interpret *Ghosts* as a naturalistic sermon and to imitate it as such. Hauptmann reflected this view when he started his dramatic career in 1889 with *Before Sunrise,* a crude naturalistic *pièce à thèse,* in which the hero refuses to marry the heroine because there is alcoholism in her family; and Echegaray won a specious reputation for modernism in the Spanish theatre with another variation on the heredity theme, *The Son of Don Juan,* in which Don Juan, now middle-aged and respectable, receives condign punishment for the profligacy of his youth when his about-to-be-married son turns out to be diseased.

It is refreshing to come across Shaw's comments on *Ghosts* after considerable unevenness in the early chapters of his discourse on Ibsen's play. This begins with a little chapter on Ibsen's *Brand* that presents an almost

[7] G. K. Chesterton, ed., *George Bernard Shaw* (London, 1948), pp. 173, 175, 177.

complete distortion of the play, although there is some evidence that he appreciated Brand as an heroic figure.[8] His next chapter on *Peer Gynt* appreciates the irony in that work and its reductive treatment of Peer the would-be self-realizer as a prototype, Shaw says, of "the pushing, competitive, success-craving man who is the hero of the modern world." In Peer, the characterless loafer and shabby opportunist, the idealizing tendency turns out to be nothing but "the romantic fancies of the born liar," and Peer's conception of himself as "a self-realized man" is exposed in the play as sheer self-delusion. In Shaw's acute little chapter, moreover, we get inklings of the possibility of having drama of ideas in poetic and fantastic form, that is, of not having to identify or associate this genre with problem plays and prosaic playwriting. Shaw does not make this point himself, but, as we may observe in his appreciation of the intellectual vitality of *Peer Gynt* as well as in his own later practice as a playwright whenever he resorted to fancy or extravagance, drama of ideas is anything but a restrictive genre. Those who would limit it to prosaic argument have not read Shaw well either as a critic or a playwright.

Shaw's next chapter, on Ibsen's *Emperor and Galilean,* is unsatisfactory. There is no flagrant distortion here, but considerable confusion, partly produced by Ibsen's historical double-drama itself and partly by Shaw's zealous recourse to Victorian freethinking and protest against the quasi-Darwinist doctrine of "natural selection" in sociology with its fatalistic *laissez-faire* doctrine of the "survival of the fittest" in society. Shaw's remarks are relevant to elucidation of *Emperor and Galilean* only when he refers directly to the character of Julian the Apostate, whom he aptly, if not altogether justly, defines as an early Peer Gynt.[9] The Emperor Julian, Shaw says, is with respect to the "antithesis between idealism and realism . . . a reincarnation of Peer Gynt."

Shaw insists on forcing *Brand, Peer Gynt,* and *Emperor and Galilean* into the mold of his thesis by referring to them as "three immense dramas, all dealing with the effect of idealism on individual egotists of exceptional imaginative excitability." And Shaw justifies the liberties he was taking in interpreting these plays by declaring that at the time of their creation Ibsen was still a subjective writer; his "intellectual consciousness of his theme was yet incomplete"; he was still "simply portraying sides of himself." Not so in the prose plays that followed *Emperor and Galilean,*

---

[8] *Major Critical Essays,* p. 48 ("Brand, made terrible by the consequences of his idealism to others, is heroic"), and p. 51 ("It is against this conception of God as a sentimental dupe that Brand rages"). See also the beginning of the second paragraph on p. 42.

[9] *Ibid.,* pp. 55, 59.

according to Shaw, because Ibsen, "having at last completed his intellectual analysis of idealism . . . could now construct methodical illustrations of its social working." In the plays of the postromantic middle period, says Shaw, "Ibsen could see plainly the effect of idealism [the effect, that is, of masking reality] as a social force on . . . everyday people in everyday life," and not merely on "saints, romantic adventurers, and emperors."[10]

This procedure started with Ibsen's satiric comedy *The League of Youth* in 1869 and more distinctly with the "first of the series of realistic prose plays," *Pillars of Society* in 1877, and, two years later, *A Doll's House*. And so impressive were the plays that followed in the Ibsen canon that neglect or scorn of the work of Dumas *fils,* Émile Augier, and other early problem-play writers could seduce one into believing that drama of ideas began its association with the realistic theatre in Ibsen's work. This is not the case, of course. Friedrich Hebbel, in reflecting Hegelian philosophy, for which he entertained a high regard, presented a conflict between old ideas and new as early as 1844, in his middle-class tragedy *Maria Magdalena;* and Hebbel made an important early observation concerning drama of ideas in his *Journals* when he wrote that "drama should not present new stories but new relationships," and that "ideas are to the drama what counterpoint is to music. In themselves nothing but the *sine qua non* for everything."[11]

There seems to be no evidence that Shaw was familiar with Hebbel's *Maria Magdalena*. The work of Dumas *fils,* however, was well known to Shaw. The younger Dumas began to write social drama almost as a journalist by about the middle of the nineteenth century and dealt with contemporary problems in *The Demi-Monde, The Question of Money,* and other once popular plays. A more skillful playwright, Émile Augier, followed him with topical plays such as *La Jeunesse,* an attack on materialism in society, and *Les Effrontés,* an exposé of yellow journalism. Dumas *fils,* in fact, came out strongly for drama of ideas, which he equated with moral and *useful* drama, in an open letter to the Parisian critic Sarcey.[12] If he could treat causes rather than merely effects, and if he could find the means to force people to discuss a problem and lawmakers to revise a particular law, he would be doing his part as a man as well as a poet. There was, of course, no poetry in such plays, only the surface realism of commonplace verisimilitude; and it is chiefly this kind

[10] *Ibid.,* p. 60.

[11] *Playwrights on Playwriting,* ed. Toby Cole (New York, 1959), pp. 287–88.

[12] Published in *Entr'actes* (Paris, 1877), and quoted in Barrett H. Clark's *European Theories of the Drama, with a Supplement in the American Drama* (New York, 1947), p. 382.

of social drama that prevails even today, varying only in degree of characterization and intensity of conflict. But Shaw could not be impressed with Dumas *fils,* because he devised intricate plots instead of providing provocative discussions and was humdrum rather than revolutionary in his thinking. The latter still employed the so-called "well-made play" technique, which emphasized a contrived and involved plot, popularized since the 1840's by Eugène Scribe. Moreover, the reforms advocated by the younger Dumas barely scratched the surface of society. It seemed, on the contrary, that the consuming interest of Dumas, Augier, and other pre-Ibsenite playwrights, as well as post-Ibsenite ones led in England by Pinero, was to defend middle-class interests and morals. If "ideas" functioned in their plays at all, they were conventional ones; like the late Calvin Coolidge's New England clergyman, they were simply against sin. (And since the sin was usually adultery, the scholar-critic Gilbert Norwood was once justified in claiming that they had reduced the Decalogue to a monologue.)[13] For Shaw, socially effective drama of ideas started not simply when Ibsen gave up writing verse drama and turned to everyday life and conversation, but when the drama became acutely critical rather than routinely reformatory, when it replaced interest in plot with interest in inquiry, conflict of values or ideas, and discursive action—that is, action of the intelligence.

This change was first apparent in *A Doll's House,* the full significance of which Shaw did not formulate as clear theory until some twenty-two years after his Fabian lecture, when he came to amplify *The Quintessence of Ibsenism* for a revised edition published in 1913. In the 1891 edition Shaw made some excellent small points. He pointed out, for example, that, whereas the fraudulent hero of *Pillars of Society* was a pillar only in the ironical sense of the word, the Philistine husband in *A Doll's House,* "the pillar of society who owns the doll," was by conventional standards "a model husband, father, and citizen."[14] But it is first in a chapter added to the 1913 edition, called "The Technical Novelty in Ibsen's Plays"[15] that Shaw made the important observation that a "new technical factor," the element of discussion, entered the theatre with *A Doll's House* and won a dominant position in the drama. Shaw's summation is too important not to be given *in toto:*

[13] Gilbert Norwood in *Euripides and Shaw* (Boston, 1911), p. 65. Norwood wrote: "Your pseudo-advanced writer invariably reveals his calibre by this assumption that 'the problem-play' must treat of marital infidelity: there is only one sin—the Decalogue has become a monologue."

[14] *Major Critical Essays,* p. 64.

[15] *Ibid.,* p. 135.

This technical factor in the play is the discussion. Formerly you had in what was called a well-made play an exposition in the first act, a situation in the second, and unravelling in the third. Now you have exposition, situation, and discussion; and the discussion is the test of the playwright. The critics protest in vain. They declare that discussions are not dramatic, and that art should not be didactic. Neither the playwrights nor the public take the smallest notice of them. The discussion conquered Europe in Ibsen's *A Doll's House;* and now the serious playwright recognizes in the discussion not only the main test of his highest powers, but also the real centre of his play's interest. . . . This was inevitable if the drama was ever again to be raised above the childish demand for-fables without morals.[16]

Shaw went on to explain that the ordinary plot-play, the dramatized fable that does not rise above "the commonplaces of the Newgate Calendar," would simply have to go, because intrigues and story contrivances were soon exhausted: "In twenty visits [to the theatre] one can see every possible change rung on all the available plots and incidents out of which plays of this kind can be manufactured."[17] And at this point we once more encounter evidence to the effect that it is not realistic technique or style that Shaw considers paramount in modern drama, whether by Ibsen or himself, but realism of viewpoint.

Early critics of Shaw could indeed go further and affect to regard the bulk of his dramatic writing as fantastic, a view pleasantly sustained by Chesterton while complimenting Shaw for excelling in "the difficult art of being at once modern and intelligent." This, indeed, was the burden of A. B. Walkley's clever review of a revival of *Candida* at the Court Theatre in the spring of 1904. The first paragraph of Walkley's review reads:

Fantasy has its place in the theatre, as well as realism, and that is one reason why the theatre has room for Mr. Bernard Shaw. His method of travestying life is to eliminate from it everything but pure intelligence. Just as Mr. H. G. Wells amuses us by supposing a world where the laws of gravity are suspended, or where there is no such thing as time or where space is of X dimensions, so Mr. Shaw amuses us by representing a world where conduct is regulated by thought, and men love women, as the civil servant in Pickwick ate crumpets, on principle.[18]

[16] *Ibid.*
[17] *Ibid.*, p. 136.
[18] A. B. Walkley, *Drama and Life* (New York, 1908), p. 214.

Walkley, reflecting that "our little exploits of coherent thought are mere bobbing corks on the great stream of life," concluded not unexpectedly that "the chief delight" of Shaw's plays was their "brilliant dialectics," and that on the whole *Candida* on the stage is "capital sport." He observed, it is true, that "Mr. Shaw takes care to give his fantasy a certain admixture of reality," as in the case of the recognizable parson Morell and of Candida herself as "the managing, mothering, thoroughly competent woman, who carries about innumerable bags and parcels, with an aggressive air of brisk usefulness, and cannot talk to a man without patting him on the back, or retying his cravat, or picking bits of cotton off his coat." And Walkley knew well enough that for Shaw's plays to be regarded as "capital sport" was not in the least satisfactory to Shaw. "Mr. Shaw," he wrote, "maintains that he is quite serious, an out-and-out realist; in short, that in saluting him as a merry sportsman one is like the young lady who when [the Reverend] Sydney Smith said grace, shook him by the hand with a 'Thank you so much, Mr. Smith; you are always so amusing.' "[19]

Walkley scores well here, and Shaw's view of himself as a realist extends to Ibsen in all editions of *The Quintessence of Ibsenism*. This may be observed in his summary of the dramatic action of *The Lady from the Sea,*[20] in which Ibsen's play is shorn of all its fancifulness and mystery, and of all its poetry too, in the interest of elementary clarity and humdrum credibility.

Shaw must have been himself aware that in explicating this play he was explaining away both its defect of mistiness and its merit of poetry or apt symbolism, just as he had underrated the poetry and imaginativeness of *Peer Gynt* in an earlier chapter. Referring to Ellida, the respectably married heroine of *The Lady from the Sea,* who is mysteriously drawn to the sea and is claimed by a sailor with "fish eyes," Shaw wrote that "she seems more fantastic to English readers than to Norwegian ones" and that "the same thing is true of many other characters drawn by Ibsen, notably Peer Gynt, who, if born in England, would certainly not have been a poet and metaphysician as well as a blackguard and a speculator." Shaw took exception to the tendency of British audiences to consider *Rosmersholm* and *The Lady from the Sea* as "more fantastic and less literal than *A Doll's House* and the plays in which the leading figures are men and women of action."[21] And in making this evaluation he did not differ greatly with Ibsen himself, even though the latter pre-

---

[19] *Ibid.*, pp. 214–18.
[20] *Major Critical Essays,* p. 82.
[21] *Ibid.*, pp. 84–85.

ferred to be considered a poet and not a realistic reformer. Ibsen does not appear to have drawn a sharp distinction between the plays of his middle period and the more or less symbolist works of his last period: *The Master Builder, Little Eyolf, John Gabriel Borkman,* and *When We Dead Awaken,* published between 1892 and 1900. The latter-day Ibsen did not enroll himself under the banner of the symbolists, even though they laid claim to him.

Maeterlinck's manifesto of the year 1896, "The Tragical in Daily Life," concludes with complimentary paragraphs on *The Wild Duck.* Maeterlinck referred to Ibsen as "the old master" who "freed certain powers of the soul that have never yet been free", and whose protagonists Hilda and Solness in *The Master Builder* were "the first characters in drama who feel . . . that they are living in the atmosphere of the soul."[22] There is, however, no evidence that Ibsen thought of himself as a symbolist when he invented the "white horses" of *Rosmersholm,* the wounded bird of *The Wild Duck,* or even the weird Rat Wife of *Little Eyolf.* Ibsen simply worked with whatever means were available to his imagination in elaborating and reinforcing a dramatic idea in a particular play. And he composed all his last plays, except *When We Dead Awaken,* with a realist's firm grasp on characterization.

But it is idle, if not in fact misleading, to raise the issue of realism here at all in the sense of verisimilitude and literalism, and this may be said no less of Shaw's own plays. For Shaw simply did not insist, as a Galsworthy would have, that the realism that really mattered, namely, realism of idea or viewpoint, was necessarily dependent on verisimilitude. Like Brecht, who opposed Stanislavskian acting and realistic dramaturgy several decades later, Shaw showed no inclination to accept the illusion-fostering machinery of theatre already well exploited in unintellectual Victorian melodramas and pantomimes as a substitute for strenuous analysis and disputation. The need for maintaining illusion was not to be allowed to serve as a deterrent to "discussion drama," if Shaw could help it. So, returning in 1913 to the campaign he had waged as a partisan drama critic of the 1890's against contrived surface realism more than fifteen years before, and sounding rather like Dr. Samuel Johnson defending Shakespeare against the proponents of neoclassicism, Shaw proclaimed in the chapter on "The Technical Novelty in Ibsen's Plays" that "the illusion of reality is soon lost; in fact it may be doubted whether any adult ever entertains it; it is only to very young children that the fairy queen is anything but an actress." Only drama of ideas or discussion

[22] Maurice Maeterlinck, "The Tragical in Daily Life (*Le Tragique quotidien,* 1896), in *The Treasure of the Humble* (New York, 1907).

drama can effectively displace the old-fashioned plays with involved plots full of what he called "the tomfooleries of action." Until fairly late in *A Doll's House,* Shaw declares in the new chapter, Ibsen's feminist play "might be turned into a very ordinary French drama by the excision of a few lines and the substitution of a sentimental happy ending for the famous last scene; indeed the very first thing the theatrical wiseacres did with it was to effect exactly this transformation."

A case in point, with which Shaw may have been unfamiliar, was the production of *A Doll's House* toured in the United States by the Polish actress Helena Modjeska in 1883 under the odd title of *Thora.* A reviewer for the Louisville *Courier-Journal,* who complained that the maimed play ended turgidly, provided a description of this ending, which resembled thousands of other play endings before and after Ibsen: Nora, here called Thora, "dons a street dress, and announces her intention of leaving her husband for ever. He expostulates, argues, and pleads in vain, but finally, through the medium of the children, some indefinite talk about 'religion,' there is a reunion and a falling curtain on a happy family tableau."[23]

"But," declares Shaw, "at just that point in the last act, the heroine very unexpectedly (by the wiseacres) stops her emotional acting, and says: 'We must sit down and discuss all this that has been happening between us.'" (Here the approving Shaw sounds as if he were anticipating Bertolt Brecht's theory of alienation, or *Verfremdung.* The emotional bond is abruptly broken while the plot action is interrupted in order that the spectator, repossessing his judgment from pure emotional involvement and mere absorption in the story, may start thinking and arrive at some judgment.) With Nora's sitting down and reexamining her marriage, there begins a new phase in European drama, which was modernized far more by Shaw himself, along with Granville-Barker, Galsworthy, Cocteau, Giraudoux, Sartre, Brecht, and others than by the merely technical innovators of naturalist, symbolist, and expressionist persuasion. As Shaw put it in 1912: "And it was by this new technical feature: this addition of a new movement, as musicians would say, to the dramatic form, that *A Doll's House* conquered Europe and founded a new school of dramatic art."[24]

Shaw, however, noticed a further development. "Since that time [since the writing of *A Doll's House*]," he continued, "the discussion has expanded far beyond the limits of an otherwise 'well-made' play." A dis-

[23] This review appears in *The American Theatre as Seen by Its Critics,* ed. by Montrose J. Moses and John Mason Brown (New York, 1934).
[24] *Major Critical Essays,* p. 138.

advantage of placing the discussion at the end was that it would be necessary to see the play for a second time if one was to follow the earlier acts in the light of the final discussion. The theatre, he observed, now (by 1913) has plays, including some of his own, "which begin with discussion and end with action, and others in which the discussion interpenetrates the action from the beginning to the end."[25]

In the new art beginning with *Ghosts,* the drama arises "through a conflict of unsettled ideals rather than through vulgar attachments, rapacities, generosities, resentments, ambitions, misunderstandings, oddities and so forth as to which no moral question is raised." Remembering Hegel perhaps as much as Ibsen, paralleling indeed Hegel's view that contradiction is the power that moves things and the Hegelian theory that tragedy is a conflict between two rights as exemplified in the *Antigone,*[26] Shaw elaborated upon his notion of a conflict of unsettled ideals: the conflict is "not between clear right and wrong; the villain is as conscientious as the hero, if not more so"—which is actually the case in Shaw's *Major Barbara,* in which Shaw makes out a better case for the munitions manufacturer Andrew Undershaft than for the Salvation Army. "Or," adds Shaw, "there are no villains and no heroes" in the new kind of discussion play, which he believes is exactly as it should be, as may be observed in the case of Hamlet, who would not have continued to hold our interest if he "never had any Ibsenist hesitations."[27]

According to Shaw, the one fault indeed to be found with Ibsen after *Ghosts* is that Ibsen still uses drastic *dénouements* such as may be found in the old-fashioned well-made plays. Shaw did not approve of Hedda's suicide at the conclusion of *Hedda Gabler* on the grounds that the really tragic fact about the Heddas of the world is not that they kill themselves but that they live on in all their aridity and uselessness. According to Shaw, "perhaps the most plausible reproach leveled at Ibsen by modern critics of his own school is just that survival of the old school in him which makes the death rate so high in his last acts," although he concedes that in Ibsen's latter-day work the play never exists for the sake of the catastrophe as it does in plays contrived solely for excitement. He cited the superior example of Chekhov's *The Cherry Orchard*—he was to emulate Chekhov a few years later in writing *Heartbreak House*—in which "the sentimental ideals of our amiable, cultured, Schumann-playing

[25] *Ibid.* "Plays that begin with discussion and end with action" may not be easily cited, but this is approximately true of Shaw's *The Apple Cart, Man and Superman,* and *Major Barbara,* and Sartre's *The Flies.*

[26] See Hegel's *Philosophy of Art* and John Howard Lawson's *Theory and Technique of Playwriting* (New York, 1936).

[27] *Major Critical Essays,* pp. 139, 142.

propertied class are reduced to dust and ashes by a hand not less deadly than Ibsen's because it is so much more caressing," a play in which "nothing more violent happens than that the family cannot afford to keep up its own house." Shaw maintains that it is "no true *dénouement* to cut the Gordian knot" and that "if people's souls are tied up by law or public opinion it is much more tragic to leave them wither in these bonds than to end their misery."[28] And Shaw indeed could have seen this viewpoint borne out before his death in Brecht's *Mother Courage,* in which the title character resumes following camp after losing all her children in the Thirty Years' War, and in Sartre's *No Exit,* in which the characters are doomed to have to endure each other's company forever.

In the same 1913 chapter on Ibsen's drama of ideas as contrasted with drama of plot action, Shaw justifies himself as well as Ibsen in writing: "I myself have been reproached because the characters in my plays 'talk but do nothing,' meaning that they commit no felonies." And we may again observe that in championing Ibsen and post-Ibsen playwrights like himself, Shaw anticipated in 1913 the anti-Aristotelian protests and practices of later playwrights and directors such as Brecht, Piscator, Cocteau, Giraudoux, Jouvet, Anouilh, Adamov, and Wilder. "Hence a cry has arisen," Shaw declares, "that the post-Ibsen play is not a play, and that its technique, not being the technique described by Aristotle, is not a technique at all."[29]

Just as Brecht and Piscator both claimed that their "epic" theatrical form was not actually new but was rooted in older, indeed in classical, dramatic form, so Shaw reminds his critical sparring-partner Walkley that "the new technique is new only on the modern stage," It is as a means of demonstrating an idea or arguing about it, "the technique of playing upon the human conscience, and it has been practised by the playwright whenever the playwright has been capable of it." He then goes on to describe it, and it seems to me that actually the description fits no particular play by Ibsen after *Peer Gynt* and *Emperor and Galilean.* It does apply, however, to plays by Shaw, Strindberg (beginning with the expressionist trilogy *To Damascus*), Pirandello, Auden, Eliot, Duerrenmatt, Frisch, Genet, Beckett, Ionesco, and other modernists. He concludes:

> Rhetoric, irony, argument, paradox, epigram, parable, the rearrangement of haphazard facts into orderly and intelligent situations, these are both the oldest and the newest arts of the drama, and your plot construction and art of preparation are only the tricks of theatrical

28 *Ibid.,* pp. 142–43.
29 *Ibid.,* pp. 143, 145–46.

talent, the shifts of moral sterility, not the weapons of dramatic genius.[30]

And what better description can we have of Shaw's *Back to Methuselah* and *Heartbreak House* or Brecht's *The Caucasian Chalk Circle* and *The Good Woman of Setzuan,* which incidentally are both called "parable plays." How much less this summary applies to the dramatic form of Ibsen's postromantic plays is apparent. The variety of modernist types of dramatic structure, the deliberate theatricalization of reality in plays, the abrupt shifts from representational to presentational drama (that is, from illusionistic realism to direct address to the audience by some formal narrator, explicator, or choral character, as in Giraudoux's *Electra* and Anouilh's *Antigone*), the injection of illusion-breaking lyrics and choral recitations into the dramatic action (as in T. S. Eliot's *Murder in the Cathedral* and in Brecht's plays), and the pattern of moving into and out of illusion in the same play—one will look in vain in Ibsen's tightly built plays for these violations of realistic play structure, and for the naturalistic fourth-wall convention that completely separates the actor from his audience by hypostatizing a real wall between the two at the curtain line. From a technical standpoint we can only describe the postromantic Ibsen as moving stolidly from point to point to tell his story, create his characters, and establish his argument or analysis. We may watch his artistry with admiration as he conceals his tendentious art behind everyday details of life, credible characterization, and compressed prose dialogue, punctuated now and then with telling yet natural metaphors like Hedda's asking Lövborg to return to her from a stag party as a Dionysian figure wearing "vine-leaves" in his hair. And in passing, we may note how natural Ibsen's visual symbols are after *Peer Gynt,* so that they are indistinguishable from the dramatic action, as in the case of Nora's dancing the tarantella in *A Doll's House* in order to distract her husband, or from mere stage furnishings and stage properties, as in the case of the deceased General Gabler's portrait and his daughter's brace of pistols in *Hedda Gabler,* even if the pistols may be said to also "symbolize" Hedda's frigidity and destructiveness.

Nevertheless, Shaw was not wholly mistaken in attributing to Ibsen some of the elements he ascribed to the "new drama." They are not, it is true, formally, or stagily, striking, as when an actor in Giraudoux's *Electra* steps out of his role as Electra's gardener-fiancé when the engagement is called off and tells the audience in a Pirandellian manner that now that he is out of the play he can say what he thinks: "I'm not in

---

[30] *Ibid.,* p. 146.

the play any more. That's why I'm free to come and tell you what the play can't tell you."[31] But Ibsen's dramatic strategies behind a screen of unfanciful middle-class and rather provincial drama were decidedly unsettling. Ibsen's conservative opposition was not entirely obtuse in accusing him of subversiveness, violation of natural action and feeling, and arbitrariness. Shaw was especially right in attributing to Ibsen the use of "irony" and "paradox," which so irritated Ibsen's conservative critics, and of "parable," which apparently confused them. It is ironical and paradoxical, for example, that Mrs. Alving's wrongdoing in *Ghosts* consists of *not* having left her husband and that the rewards of Victorian conformity in the play should prove to be, in her son Oswald's case, softening of the brain. In *Ghosts,* so to speak, the wages of virtue are paresis.

Moreover, Ibsen's "rearrangement of haphazard facts in orderly and intelligent situations," as Shaw puts it, is mordantly ironic when the memorial building erected in memory of the deceased philanderer Mr. Alving burns to the ground. The orphan asylum, besides, is uninsured. The same clerical oaf who had sent the young Mrs. Alving back to her husband in submission to convention many years before had dissuaded her from insuring the building on the grounds that to insure a charitable institution is to evince a sinful lack of trust in the Lord. If ever a playwright before Shaw contrived events for effects of rather diabolical irony while retaining an outward show of verisimilitude, it was Ibsen. In *Ghosts* a "realistic" indictment of society was accomplished with means that actually violated realistic technique. There was almost as much contrivance in *Ghosts* as in the well-made plays of intrigue and emotional forcing that Shaw the critic scorned so heartily that he dismissed their technique in one of his reviews (with reference to the work of the most efficient of the contrivers, Sardou) as sheer "Sardoodledom." The sole difference was that, as Shaw could not fail to observe, Ibsen contrived dramatic events in order to invalidate, rather than support, convention, and in order to achieve irony rather than heroics or sentiment.

It is because this was not at all the case when the most popular Victorian playwright Arthur Wing Pinero wrote a seemingly modern play such as *The Second Mrs. Tanqueray* that Shaw blasted him in a famous review. Pinero contrived to undo the marriage of a Victorian gentleman to a woman with a lurid past by having the man who once had kept her suddenly turn up as her stepdaughter's suitor. Coincidence could not have had a longer arm or a more serviceable one in reassuring a righteous Victorian family that society would not be contaminated in the long run.

---

[31] *Electra* in *The Modern Theatre,* ed. Eric Bentley, I (Garden City, N. Y., 1955), 243.

Poor Paula Tanqueray had to die in the play to prove that, although Pinero was a daring modern playwright in presenting a fallen woman on the stage, he could nevertheless be trusted to conclude that the marriage of a gentleman and a former courtesan could not possibly work out well.

Shaw's most conclusive summation may be given in Shaw's own words in *The Quintessence of Ibsenism,* and these take us, as previously noted, well beyond Ibsen to Shaw himself and to many a latter-day modernist playwright. The technical novelty of the Ibsen and post-Ibsen plays, Shaw concludes, is "first, the introduction of the discussion and its development until it so overspreads and interpenetrates the action that it assimilates it, making play and discussion practically identical"—which is surely the best general definition of drama of ideas. Following this, the summation lists the detailed strategies of the "substitution of a forensic technique of recrimination, disillusion, and penetration through ideals [*sic*] to the truth, with a free use of all the rhetorical and lyrical arts of the orator, the preacher, the pleader, and the rhapsodist."[32]

With Shaw's summary it is possible to define the rationale for this paper as an integral part of a program on "Ideas in the Drama." With his provocative definition of Ibsenism, Shaw introduced us to that considerable portion of the modern drama that exemplifies modern social and moral thought, and even philosophy—as in the case of existentialist drama represented by Sartre's *No Exit* and *The Flies.* The so-called ideas could be brought to the surface, as in Shaw's *Don Juan in Hell,* or imbedded in the characters and story, as in his *Saint Joan.* They could come to the surface as an assertion, as in Brecht's *Mann ist Mann,* or as a question and challenge, as in the same author's *The Good Woman of Setzuan.* They could be given a contemporary content, as in Shaw's *Major Barbara,* or a retrospective, quasihistorical one, as in his *Caesar and Cleopatra.* They could be propounded, as in *Back to Methuselah,* or dallied with, as in that delightful "farce of ideas," *Misalliance.* At times the result has been comedy, at times serious drama—only very rarely tragedy—and quite often a blend of the comic and the serious that constitutes, with the help of irony, as in the case of Friedrich Duerrenmatt's *The Visit,* a genre of modern "dark comedy" concerning which Shaw's declaration is perhaps the most apt: "The jests do not become poorer as they mature into earnest."[33]

[32] *Major Critical Essays,* p. 146.
[33] *Ibid,* p. 134.

Part Two

DRAMATIC THEORY AND PRACTICE

THE DRAMATIC VISION*

The dedication of a building devoted to play production is the proper occasion for viewing the theatre in the largest possible context. Soon, I trust, your new building will be humming with theatrical activity, and the probability is that you will be so busy with the many details that go into play production that you will have neither time nor inclination for theory.

Yet it is one of the constant perils of the theatre that its significance and potentialities may be assumed rather than realized. Counting the trees we miss the forest. We assume for the stage a justification we do not take the trouble to understand, and so we are apt to turn a high art into a trivial habit. We assume that the theatre can feed on itself alone and lapse into an outlook no wider than that afforded by the proscenium arch.

Recently a prominent stage director reminded me that he had studied under me and that he had never forgotten my once asking the class rhetorically, "What do they of the theatre know who only theatre know!" Many years have elapsed, but everything confirms me in my opinion that my question is still a valid one. I do not, in fact, believe there was ever a time when it was not valid. The great theatrical periods of the past always nourished themselves on the ideas, aspirations, and struggles of their age, and, at the same time, evolved or adhered to a central dramatic vision that is nothing less than a fundamental view of life itself.

The dramatic approach to reality is, to begin with, a view of life as a condition of disequilibrium, a state of crisis, conflict and change; and dramatic vision encompasses movement toward some new equilibrium, however temporary or tentative, or movement toward a reconciliation of opposites that makes survival or sanity possible. Without this essential quality, the art of the drama and the stage cannot be regarded as much more than a moment's play-acting and beguilement. But it is not for this that educational institutions, however greatly they may favor recreation, build playhouses and foster dramatic art. On the present noteworthy occasion I propose, therefore, to speak a little about the nature of the dramatic vision that gives the theatre much of its scope and justification.

* This article was first delivered on November 10, 1960, as an address to mark the dedication of the Willis H. Booth Music-Speech Center, Occidental College. It is reprinted from *Impromptu* (1961).

Dramatic vision, I submit, is actually a *tripartite* vision, although a fundamentally unified one, too, of man viewed mainly under the aspects of comedy, tragedy, and an admixture of the two for which the most comprehensive name is probably the French term *drame,* or in simple English, *Drama.* I would call attention to the rightness and the richness of this triple way of describing the human condition or reflecting our earthly pilgrimage—the human condition with its absurdities and contradictions or our mundane pilgrimage with its follies, miseries, and splendors.

I have in mind, to put it briefly, comedy's view of man as the creature of his limitations and pretensions, tragedy's view of him as the hero and victim of his aspirations, and nontragic drama's, or *drame's,* view of him as neither fool nor hero in many of life's situations and circumstances. I have also in mind the variety of attitudes we bring to human beings and the judgments we pass on them. I refer particularly to comedy's corrective laughter; to tragedy's apprehensive admiration; and to nontragic drama's, or *drame's,* sympathy, pathos, and blending of comic and tragic realizations.

These well-established categories of comedy, tragedy, and drama enable us to observe how dramatic art observes and evaluates humanity in general, and humanity in our own time and place.

I regard the high art of theatre, then, as primarily an instrument of the understanding, which assuredly justifies its study in a liberal arts program; and with this premise in mind we may also legitimately inquire into the present condition of an art that is so universal and yet so time-conditioned. Even the ideal theatre is not an absolute, it is not a Platonic idea suspended above our planet as an *a priori* ideal. Dramatic art is constantly made and remade by contemporary pressures; it is subject to the tensions experienced and the opinions entertained by contemporaries.

Thus as the times change, a certain type of comedy is apt to lose its edge or its glitter; and one period's tragedy may become another period's melodrama, its poetry turned to pomposity and its once acceptable heroics into pinchbeck heroics or hokum. Our notions of the absurd, the heroic and the pathetic change with the times or the epoch. Thus the absurd comes to be regarded as pathetic, as was the case when the detached or, if you will, "unsentimental" comedy of the Restoration period in England under Charles II became transformed into the so-called sentimental comedy of the eighteenth century under Queen Anne. And it may happen, too, that characters who could only be regarded as comic in one era became pathetic, and even tragic, in another. Just as the tragically jealous Othello of one age could become the comically betrayed husband of another period—(let us say in the Restoration Period or the age of Molière) so Arthur Miller's near-tragic Willy Loman, the twentieth-century common man, would have been the seventeenth-century ridiculed bourgeois or peasant. It is therefore relevant and even useful to ask ourselves here: Where does dramatic art stand today with respect to these fundamental variables of viewpoint and value? And with this question we could inquire into the very meaning and worth of our contemporary theatre.

Limiting myself to the American scene but without excluding theatre elsewhere in the Western world, I would say that comedy of manners or so-called high comedy has suffered a great decline; that tragedy, in the long accepted exalted and austere sense of the term, has virtually disappeared or appears only in distinctly diluted form; and that nontragic drama or *drame* has become the predominant form of serious theatre. Nor is the cultural significance of these features of the contemporary American drama difficult to spell out.

Thus, we no longer have an upper class that can foster comedy of manners with its extravagances or invite satire with its vices—but, let me add, without the bitterness of class conflict or the negativism of desperation. Upper-class manners and follies have become indistinguishable from the manners and follies of the rest of the population. We have comedy and musical comedy, of course, in great abundance in a land distinguished by comparative affluence and considerable optimism. But most of our recent comedies have lacked brilliance and wit because in our ultrademocratic world there is no longer any glittering society and congenial social climate for high comedy. Usually we produce only farce, low comedy, or, as we say, farce-comedy.

More is involved here than the erosion of an upper social crust in our age. The corrective or social value of high comedy has itself lost meaning. The contented middle-class public which has multiplied among us sees little need for correctives for its manners or values, while the dissatisfied part of the public has no trust in correction by comedy, or, for that matter, in the reformation of society through the reformation of manners. At the same time, there is scant liking nowadays for pure comic detachment from the scene of human emotion and endeavor. Such detachment seems an insult to the complacent because it implies superiority; and it betokens neutralism to the dissidents who are committed to programs of social reform or revolution and regard neutrality as treason. Trust in comedy has long been a low ebb since the economic depression of the 1930's even in English theatre. The brilliant writer of high comedy S. N. Behrman noted the difficulty of maintaining detachment as long ago as the 1930's and apologized for the persistence of the Comic Spirit in his play *No Time for Comedy.*

In the Victorian period, in which some decline was already noticeable until Wilde and Shaw gave comedy a new lease on life, George Meredith could still write trustfully of the Comic Spirit instead of apologizing for it. It may be instructive indeed to return to one of the famous paragraphs on comic detachment and exposure in his 1871 lecture on *The Idea of Comedy and the Uses of the Comic Spirit.*

Comedy's common aspect, Meredith wrote, "is one of unsolicitous observation, as if surveying a full field and having leisure [and who, I ask, has such leisure nowadays?] to dart on its chosen morsels, without any fluttering eagerness. Men's future upon earth does not attract it; their honesty and shapeliness in the present does; and whenever they wax out of proportion, overblown, affected, pretentious, bombastical, hypocritical, pedantic, fantastically delicate; whenever it sees them self-deceived or hoodwinked, given to run riot in idolatries, . . . planning short-sightedly, plotting dementedly; whenever they are at variance with their professions . . . whenever they offend sound reason, fair justice; are false in humility or mined with conceit, individually, or in the bulk; the Spirit [that is, the Comic Spirit] will look humanely malign, and cast an oblique light on them, followed by volleys of silvery laughter."*

How many today, we may ask, think there is enough time for the leisurely operations of Meredith's Comic Spirit? Are peals of silvery laughter enough to correct evil or save us from disaster? It has been quite some time since Europeans or Englishmen really thought so. Can we share Meredith's exuberant trust in reason as a purgative? The answer is bound to be in the negative. Even Bernard Shaw's better directed bolts of laughter no longer inspire confidence in their efficaciousness, and his so-called "comedy of ideas" is no longer particularly provocative in many instances. Shaw himself expressed serious doubts of his efficacy by the time he came to write *On the Rocks* and *Too True to Be Good* in the busy world of the 1930's. On the eve of World War II, Shaw survives as a dramatist on other grounds than those suggested by Meredith's paragraphs, and certainly not as a master of what Meredith called "unsolicitous observation." The politically engaged Shaw was, to the contrary, extremely solicitous.

But if my analysis of the fate of comedy of manners is substantially correct, does it follow that the theatre is now obliged to surrender that part of its dramatic vision which we call the comic? By no means! The

* *From An Essay on Comedy* (1897).

human race remains, even if the chic old upper classes have slipped from their eminence; and if cultivated sophistication has largely vanished, the critical spirit has not departed from us. New forms of comedy have been taking shape ever since the turn of the century, and have reestablished the theatre's comic vision. Thus, the old domestic type of comedy of manners has been bathed in atmosphere and brought close to pathos, though without any sacrifice of irony, ever since Chekhov wrote his *Uncle Vanya* in 1899.

Sean O'Casey explored the same possibilities with his masterwork *Juno and the Paycock* a quarter of a century later, and a rueful type of comedy continues to be written, whether in *Heartbreak House,* in which the old country-house locale of traditional English comedy was treated by Shaw during World War I symbolically as the ship of state, or in the fantastic and more or less philosophical vein of Pirandello and other writers of the Italian "school of the grotesque," the masterpiece of which remains Pirandello's piquant *Six Characters in Search of an Author*. In their work, comedy became mordant rather than playful, and modern morbidity has not been excluded in their work or that of the other writers. Modern experience injects a quality of anguish into Puck's exclamation, which is comedy's exclamation, too, "What fools these mortals be." During and after World War I the theatre also moved to extremes of extravagance in plays and productions of a dadaist, surrealistic, or expressionist character. Combined with social satire, these extravaganzas attained the inspired mockery of Erwin Piscator's *The Good Soldier Schweik* and Kurt Weill and Bertolt Brecht's *The Threepenny Opera,* first produced in Berlin in 1928 and which has been running in a Greenwich Village theatre for the past three years. Since the 1920's, in fact, several strands of fanciful comedy concerned with the social scene have had considerable vogue in a variety of works ranging from Giraudoux's urban comedy *The Madwoman of Chaillot,* in which a mad Countess liquidates French speculators by luring them into the sewers of Paris with the promise of oil underground, or O'Casey's general fanciful satire on Irish provincialism, *Cock-a-Doodle-Dandy,* to Jean Genet's fierce satire, *The Balcony,* running in New York in the spring of 1960, which reduces all political reality to illusions spawned in a brothel.

When we add to works of this order the ingenuities of an Ionesco, who spins out uncanny fables and converts his cult of the absurd and the eery into a species of theatre poetry, we observe a further enlargement or intensification of comic vision in the theatre. We also observe it, on the one hand, in a metaphysical direction with Samuel Beckett's Joycean masterpiece *Waiting for Godot* and, on the other hand, in a social-allegorical direction with Brecht's didactic masterpieces of the 1940's, *The Caucasian Chalk Circle* and *The Good Woman of Setzuan.*

My report on tragedy is less sanguine and can be briefer. Important as it has been to preserve and, if possible, expand the comic vision in the modern theatre, it has been, in some respects, even more important to cultivate tragic art. Playwrights have done so throughout the century but with meager results, unless we modify the established definitions of tragedy. There has been no dearth of imitators of old-style tragedy, from Stephen Phillips, whose first successful tragedy appeared in England in 1901, to Maxwell Anderson, who introduced elevated expression and romantic passion in the Elizabethan manner in *Elizabeth the Queen, Mary of Scotland,* and *Anne of a Thousand Days* and then tried to follow a tragic blueprint of purpose, passion, and recognition on the part of his chief character, followed by reconciliation to fate, in writing his drama on a contemporary subject, *Winterset,* in 1935.

Various claims to tragic eminence have been advanced for a number of contemporary playwrights, and with what has been called my characteristic generosity I have been disposed to endorse the claims until I realized that in many cases I had accepted *tragicality* rather than tragedy. I had succumbed to seductive tragic moods and pathos as substitutes for tragic vision, which takes an honest measure of man in his natural condition of strength and weakness, potency and failure. I do not subscribe to the school of thought that categorically denies that tragedy can be written in our times. But I find myself, in the end, more or less endorsing for tragic eminence only a few little known plays and a small number of well known ones, such as Shaw's *Saint Joan,* Lorca's *Blood Wedding,* and O'Neill's *Desire Under the Elms* and *Mourning Becomes Electra.*

Neither the time nor the occasion is propitious for describing my wavering struggles with the possibilities and perils of writing modern tragedy. The curious will find me wrestling with the topic at some length in two of my recent books *The Theatre in Our Times* and *Theatre at the Crossroads,* which reflect, in part, my own experiences in adapting Jeffers' *The Tower Beyond Tragedy* and Stefan Zweig's *Jeremiah* for the Broadway stage and, in part, my efforts to advance the early career of such earnest playwrights as Williams, Miller, and Inge.

What I discovered for myself—as others must have done for themselves—was that the question was not altogether whether the work was poetically conceived and written in verse or elevated language, but whether intensity of experience was attained in the work with some amplitude of thought and feeling. And another question was whether it was possible to emerge from the experience provided by the author with some enrichment or elevation of spirit—that is, with enhanced self-respect and respect for humanity as represented by the chief character or characters. When that was the case I did not feel trapped by the misery displayed before me, and I did not feel frustrated by the failure of the characters of the play. I did not feel futile in the face of the many impediments of circumstances and accident to self-realization, happiness, and survival that appear in mournful plays, but that do not really constitute *tragic* fate.

In truly tragic dramas, composed in any time or place, in experiencing evil and suffering, I emerged on the other side of despair; I arrived at inward victory in spite of outward defeat. These are big words and they have been made bigger by critics and poetasters; there is indeed a natural tendency to glorify tragic art, perhaps compensating for our human-all-too-human littleness and our insecurity in a hostile or at least indifferent universe. But I am not greatly worried by the bigness of the words because the representatives of humanity in genuine high tragedy reap as they sow and get away with absolutely nothing. True tragedy is never morally flabby because it is never basically unrealistic. In any case, the big words are the *best* words I can find, and that others have found, for the essentially inspiriting quality of tragedy; for the *paradox* of suffering and exultation that is tragedy; and for the imaginative art that transmutes into a healing and sustaining experience the bitterness of self-created evil and the humiliations of world-created suffering.

These are, however, precisely the experiences that many masterpieces of the past have provided and that most contemporary plays have not afforded us despite the seriousness of their subject and the somberness of the writing. I could not arrive at any other conclusion than that humanity's representatives in the plays were not enabled by the author to effect through their very nature and action and responses a greatly needed liberation from stalemate, and I was left to flounder in swamps of immobilizing and demoralizing misery. Why should this have been the case? Chiefly because they had not been made big enough to suffer arrestingly and meaningfully enough, which they could not really do without possessing a fine sensibility, a capacity for passion, a will for action, an inclination toward extremes having its source in a strong spirit, and an intelligence capable of arriving at perception or judgment—at recognitions or knowledge born of suffering, as Aeschylus, the father of tragedy, put it twenty-four centuries ago.

It is not that the little man of modern democracy is too little—and of course he isn't any larger in the totalitarian state—but that his littleness is so common. There is no quality of wonder in his endeavors and his reversals of fortune. He falls from no eminence and he strives toward none, his horizons for the future being no less common than his acquiescence of contentment in the present. It isn't simply that playwrights aiming at realism have been content to feature this at best pathetic creature in their plays as representative of humanity. They even identify themselves with him, down to his last monosyllable and grunt, whereas the great tragedians' heroes have generally spoken as if they were poets and tragedians themselves. The playwrights of past ages built their heroes up; with few exceptions the playwrights of the present have built themselves *down,* so that their talent may squat side by side with their subject.

Occasionally, as in Arthur Miller's *Death of a Salesman,* the author does pass judgment on the unheroic hero of his play; he brings to his study of the "low man," Willy Loman, not merely compassion but social and moral perspectives. But even Miller, observing realistic conventions in characterization while violating realistic play-structure with flashback scenes, wrote dialogue for Willy Loman and the other characters as if he were under some interdict against enriching their speech. And it is not, as older critics such as Joseph Wood Krutch used to complain, that the hero of modern drama is determined in his being and behavior, but that he is determined *downward* in the direction of petty desires and mean actions rather than upward, like Oedipus, toward excesses of will and action. The low-grade realism that prevails on our stage whittles down the dramatic stature of the individual until he becomes too trifling or banal to exhibit humanity on some appreciable elevation of mind and spirit. Ordinarily realistic drama presents him as altogether too passive or inept to engage in conflicts that engage our imagination and excite our passions. Moreover, this second-rate realism has found a new reducing agent for characters in the Western theatre to replace the old reducing agent of so-called "social causation."

I refer to *psychopathology* as a means for calling attention to a character by drawing him out of the limbo of averageness and yet still keeping in convenient proximity to averageness because neurosis has become the commodity of common conversation. Amateur psychiatry has become a substitute in the literary market for original observation and representation of human character—it has become an accessible formula and we are apt to lazily reach for it. As a result we have tended to present fragments of personality rather than personality itself, and complexes rather than complex individuals. If there is one thing tragedy needs it is complete characters, because only total characters can stand for total humanity and can provide sufficient richness of experience.

The old masters set us a different example. Thus, Oedipus in Sophocles' tragedy is not destroyed by an "Oedipus complex." When he expresses his dread of incest, Jocasta dismisses it with the statement that men have often dreamed of marrying their mothers, following which Sophocles blithely goes on with the course of discovery that is relevant to the action of the play. Sophocles concerns himself with a spirited man entangled in the mighty coils of Moira or Fate and not with an emotionally retarded mother-fixated character metaphorically entangled in his mother's arms. Sophocles is involved with imperious Fate itself, rather than with the messy clinical phenomenon of sexual regression. And entire worlds tumble with the fate of Shakespeare's tragic characters. Can we imagine high tragedy based, as it would very likely have to be in a contemporary play, on a jealous Othello's retentive anal-eroticism, on Lear's incestuous passion for Cordelia, or on a Cleopatra's insatiate nymphomania!

We must conclude that the prospects for high tragic art are no brighter now than they were fifty or a hundred years ago. We may also conclude that the reasons I have adduced suggest vulgarization and dilution of dramatic writing, and reflect upon society itself. But this does not mean that scattered tragedies may not be written or that tragic poets can no longer appear in the theatre. Genius transcends many a limitation and performs miracles, to which the only dampening reply can be that genius is rarely, if ever, abundant. It is even possible to add that a tragic afflatus, or an inclination toward the tragic, has appeared in the case of a number of twentieth-century playwrights.

I believe this may be said of Claudel, Montherlant, Sartre, and Camus in France, O'Casey, Eliot, and Fry in England, and O'Neill, Williams, and Miller in America. And the nature of tragedy itself is not so fixed for all time that we are compelled to make a burnt offering to Aristotle's ghost before applying the term to a variety of contemporary plays, realistic, poetic, or even partly clinical. It does not even follow that sociology and psychopathology are forever banished from the sanctum sanctorum of the high art of tragedy. How sociology and psychopathology are employed is the only real test.

After all, some great older tragedies from the Oresteian trilogy to *Antony and Cleopatra* have had a social or political dimension, and many a tragic character from Sophocles' Ajax to Shakespeare's Lear has been mentally afflicted. Finally, it is difficult to foresee a time when the old high tragedies will not be available to theatre, and whenever the most durable of these plays is placed on the stage with some measure of competence there will be audiences for it. A vital theatre is neither parochial nor time-bound; it is not exclusively subjugated to the present any more than it is to the past; it does not depend entirely upon the quality of the new plays.

Finally, we come to the intermediate theatre of *drame*. This mixed style of drama can border on the tragic but can remain fixed in pathos and blend with humor, fancy, and sociology—that is, documentary drama or discussion drama. In dealing with unusually affecting or remarkably stimulating characters and situations, however, it can make inroads into true tragic art. In that case, I for one would err on the side of generosity and accept the interloper: I can only disagree with the author of a recent book on tragedy, William C. McCollum (*Tragedy,* New York, 1957) when he writes that "Tragedy presents a poetic cosmology and is committed to a metaphysical attitude," and agree with him when he states on the same page (p. 8) that "The world of experience is in and around us, awaiting representation." But even nontragic drama can, and does, attain significant power.

Drame can raise the same questions as tragedy, though perhaps not to the same degree—questions Mr. McCollom has formulated as "What kind of world do we live in? How are we to judge man's life? Are man's values those of his world"—though I find the last question rather ambiguous. It is not perhaps even an answerable question.

The great value of the concept of *drame* lies in this, I think, that it does not constrict dramatic creation. It does not inflate it either. It is so comprehensive a concept of drama that it leaves room for present-day topical, social, and psychological interest without necessarily depriving them of the emotional and imaginative qualities of art. *Drame* is a mixed form of dramatic composition and provides occasion for a mixed kind of stage presentation, neither formal nor informal, and neither ritualistic nor frivolous. A good deal of life can be contained and revealed within the bounds of *drame,* and such a play can prove absorbing by reflecting our times. *Drame* provides the playgoer with abundant possibilities of recognition. It is the familiar transmuted into art and transferred to the theatre. Not surprisingly it is singularly the art of the twentieth century, so that it has abounded in our theatre. It is singularly suited to the experience of frustration, loneliness, and confusion, from *The Three Sisters* of Chekhov to *A Taste of Honey* by the young English playwright Shelagh Delaney.

Drame is also the peculiar tragicomedy of the twentieth century in such works of mingled humor and pathos, representative of a divided world and a divided sensibility, as *The Cherry Orchard* and *The Glass Menagerie. Drame* also hovers close enough to the tragic to appear as a sort of low form of tragedy, as in Paul Vincent Carroll's *Shadow and*

Substance, O'Neill's *The Iceman Cometh* and *Long Day's Journey into Night*, Odets' *Golden Boy*, Williams' *A Streetcar Named Desire*, and Miller's *Death of a Salesman*. *Drame* is also the vehicle for our psychological interest and for much of the social drama of the century, the drama of social situations and conflicts, such as Galsworthy's *Justice*, O'Casey's *The Plough and the Stars*, Odets' *Awake and Sing*, Lillian Hellman's *The Little Foxes*, Giraudoux's *Tiger at the Gates*, and Brecht's *Mother Courage*. *Drame*, indeed, is even the carrier of much of the speculative, metaphysical, and religious interest of the century, as in *Berkeley Square*, Barry's *Here Come the Clowns*, and T. S. Eliot's *The Cocktail Party*. To take stock of these and many other plays of subtragic but powerful and significant theatre is to realize that we have been living in the greatest age of *drame*. And without exhausting the subject we can let it rest for the present after conceding that like every other means of expression it can be abused as well as used; and indeed it has been abused, and it has been a convenient means for evading tragic realizations and driving through to uncongenial conclusions; as in certain "upbeat" Broadway, not to mention Hollywood, endings.

Thus Tennessee Williams' artistic conscience led him to publish two versions of the third act of *Cat on a Hot Tin Roof*, the "upbeat" Broadway version and his more convincing original "downbeat" version. I am myself about to publish in a forthcoming volume the original tragic ending of Paul Green's social drama *The House of Connelly*, which the 1930 Group Theatre production of that play scuttled in favor of an optimistic resolution. There is, in brief, a fertile field for uncertainty and confusion in the latitudes allowable by departures from strictly tragic art. Nevertheless, there can be no doubt from the evidence I have cited that *drame* can constitute authentic dramatic art. It is an authentic way of perceiving and revealing the multiple and contradictory aspects of life. It is, in fine, authentic dramatic vision.

With two modes of dramatic vision, those of reconstituted comedy and vital *drame*, amply available to us, and with *tragic vision* not entirely unavailable, we can confidently look forward to the continuing importance of dramatic art. It has weathered severe economical and political storms for half a century, and there is, undoubtedly, a great deal of stormy weather ahead. But the art itself has maintained notable vitality. It has also gained momentum in some directions while losing it in others. It is worth cherishing, and giving it one more home at the source of creative work and appreciation by new generations as here at Occidental College, is a noble and inspiring enterprise.

A NOTE ON THE FUNCTION
OF CRITICISM[1]

The artist, without respect to medium, is interested in criticism because it is a form of public opinion. Also, because it *creates* public opinion.

The artist is, of course, rarely satisfied with criticism. When it is not strictly adulatory it is frequently an affront to his ego, and what would any artist be without an ego? But even if he can, in the vernacular, "take" criticism, he can never be wholly satisfied with it. Even after he has written it off as one of the resistances he must encounter in the world, he cannot be entirely content with the critic's understanding of his work. No criticism ever quite translates the creator's unconscious processes and nuances into conscious ideas, just as no lyric is ever completely translated into another language.

Nevertheless, there are obvious functions that criticism can perform for the artist, and these can be performed well or ill.

Not to be despised is its function of publicizing his work. In order to wield an influence criticism must, however, be as authoritative as possible. It is well known that praise from certain of our critics bears a *cachet* of distinction not forthcoming from other sources. Equally important, though the artist may be inclined to object, is the value of criticism as a measure of his accomplishment and an aid to its improvement. Here, too, authoritativeness becomes an all-important factor in criticism.

Authoritativeness, however, means discrimination. Unpleasant as it may be to some artists and some managements (perhaps to all of them at one time or another), a critic must not withhold condemnation when he feels it is merited. Otherwise commendation from him becomes meaningless. To prevent criticism from winnowing the chaff from the wheat is to destroy its utility to both artists and their managements. This would be a truism were it not that, from time to time, discontent with certain kinds of criticism takes the form of castration wishes with regard to all criticism; and were it not also that the so-called "fascist-unconscious," which has always been operative but is particularly rampant in our era,[2]

[1] Published in *Theatre Workshop* (Fall, 1937) as a revised and extended report of an address given at the First Congress of the American Dance Association, May 15, 1937.

[2] The 1930's.

exhibits a tendency to eliminate the critical spirit in all departments of human activity.

Still, discrimination is not the simple process it is assumed to be. Two cardinal errors are uppermost in our time—the tendency to make discrimination a form of political judgment devoid of artistic significance, and the reverse tendency to disclaim all objective judgments. I do not wish to imply that these trends have never been operative in other times. They are merely pursued more deliberately and extensively in our own day and they have more ponderable effects in an age in which criticism reaches a relatively wide circle of readers.

Political judgment has been particularly rampant in the embattled sectors of the world and among sharply contending groups. It is reduced to an absurdity in fascist nations; nor has the other side been free from the taint, although it is my understanding that Marxist theory gives no support whatever to a crassly political approach to criticism. However, it is the reverse tendency that makes itself most felt, or most articulate, in our own cosmopolitan criticism. I am therefore confining my remarks to that type of helter-skelter criticism which admits no standards except those of personal impression.

Such criticism does pass judgment—of this there can be no question. Yet it claims no authority for judgments. Ostensibly such criticism merely registers an individual impression, a single person's simon-pure reaction to a work of art.

Granting that individual impressions cannot and should not be eradicated from criticism, it is nevertheless incredible that the theory underlying our cosmopolitan criticism should be taken at its face value. First of all, whether or not the critic claims authoritativeness for its opinion, the fact remains that it is invested with authority. Published opinions are the only ones that are articulate to any degree and most readers are in no position to question their validity. The critic cannot, therefore, seek immunity from responsibility. He *must* be responsible, he *must* strive for authoritativeness, and he must be judged by this criterion.

Impressionism is simply untenable in critical practice. As its ablest proponent, Anatole France, declared, "the good critic relates the adventures of his soul among works of art." When the critic is a literary artist, with rich resources of personality and experience, such impressionism justifies itself by the creation of beautiful literature—although it can never replace authoritative criticism, which makes the criticized object its main consideration. But genius does not grow on trees, and most impressionism can only result in a series of willful reactions of no interest as literature.

Criticism thus practiced becomes a stew of lazily sensed and arbitrarily expressed impressions.

Actually, moreover, this impressionistic approach, even when pursued conscientiously, is not the simple matter it is supposed to be. It is not a smooth, automatic process in an air-tight test tube. It must be obvious that the critic's impressions are conditioned by limitations of knowledge and temperament, and by resistances arising from its outlook upon life in general and society in particular.

Omitting the question of knowledge and temperament as too detailed a subject to be discussed here—even if it could be discussed, without uncertain personal evaluations—it is clear that the critic's social bias often plays havoc with the purity of his sensations. Too frequently it is apparent that if a work of art is merely pretty or entertaining it easily passes muster with the critic who has a comfortable relation to his environment. (Assuming that he is a free agent on the publication for which he writes!) Allowances for flaws and inadequacies come easily when a congenial view toward society permeates the work of art, whereas there is slight mercy for imperfections when the critic's roseate horizon is being threatened by storm clouds of disapproval and indignation. In the latter instance, every flaw becomes a major fiasco. The critic may be without conscious bias, but the nature of his reactions is not above suspicion. (It might be argued that the bias works the other way round when the reviewer is a radical. It *has* operated that way to some extent, but the proportion of such criticism in our country has been slight, it has often served a cathartic purpose, and it has been far less injurious than orthodox criticism's coddling of trivial mediocrity. For this reason I do not consider it in this address.)

A prominent critic once said to me, "I see no reason for being kind to a play just because it possesses social content." All plays were to be judged without regard for superiority or inferiority of content! That content makes no difference in a work of art is a curious view that might well deserve scrutiny. It is at least equally curious that the *single standard* advocated by my interlocutor has been honored only in the breach. In practice, the high-minded impartiality of criticism has been invoked only against drama of social significance. And indeed there has rarely been any kindness for significant material. But there has been plenty of kindness for fluff that tickled the funny bone and left the mind and conscience mercifully asleep. Also, many allowances have been made for work that merely skirted an issue at a comfortable distance.

To be perfectly fair, let us again admit that this partiality has not always been practiced with deliberate malice but more or less instinctively, in conformity with the critic's conditioning. Let us even go further and concede that when we are amused and sensuously gratified we are apt to find ourselves in an exceptionally tolerant mood. Nevertheless, we cannot avoid the conclusion that *actually there is a double standard of criticism and that it works the wrong way.*

In effect, impressionistic criticism, far from keeping itself aloof from the political arena, enters it—by the back door.

Needless to say, it is easier to criticize criticism than to prescribe a panacea for it. The form it takes is too greatly dependent upon the milieu in which the critic thinks and writes, upon his social allegiances, and upon the publication and the public for which he writes. The question of critical sensibility cannot be reduced to a formula. Differences of temperament cannot be eliminated, even if one were so mistaken as to wish to eradicate them. And we who see the mote in our neighbor's eye often do not see the beam in our own. Even the best of critics will make errors in judgment, just as even the best poet will write poor poems and the best dancer will stray from his highest standards. Even the great Sainte-Beuve was grievously mistaken in his opinion of Baudelaire.

Nevertheless, much may be gained by pricking the pretensions of our so-called impartial criticism, by discouraging irresponsible impressionism, and by clarifying critical standards.

In reaction to the obtuse moralistic standards against which criticism has had to struggle, here and in England, there prevails an unholy fear of all standards. Any effort toward coping with the question is bound to meet with resistance, and the unwary man who rushes in where angels fear to tread will be dubbed a fool or a prig. Moreover, it is true that any systematization of criticism is a task that calls for close and elaborate argument. But is it too much to ask that the objectives of a work of art should be studied with understanding care, and that judgments should have some stability? Such stability cannot but depend upon an appreciation of values. The value of a work of art depends upon some standards of execution; in the field of drama, for example, the criteria of execution comprise, in the main, depth of characterization, development of situation, and climactic inevitability and force. This is generally recognized in theory and practice.

The value of a work of art, however, must also depend upon some reference to external reality. In other words, its objectives must be evaluated in accordance with some hierarchy of general values. If the objective is mere entertainment along the line of least audience resistance, the work is to be commended when the task has been well accomplished. But should not the limits of that task be unequivocally recognized? Conversely, an artist is entitled to credit for the quality of his aims. If he has striven for significant expression, which is a matter of content as well as execution, he should not be treated as a flat failure simply because he has striven for more than he can accomplish with perfection. He is not to be relegated to the last row in preference to facile purveyors of trivialities and commonplaces as is so frequently the case at present. Not only should his intentions receive critical attention, but his achievement must be gauged with reference to the difficulties intrinsic in his aims and his material. Otherwise criticism will give aid and comfort to nothing but gilded mediocrity.

As a matter of fact, these expectations would not strike the critic as either novel or unwarranted. He may even believe that he is striving to fulfill them, and in the field with which I am most familiar such efforts have actually been made. In the main, the Drama Critics Circle Award operates precisely along these lines. Nevertheless, the daily review, which wields the widest influence, tends to operate in the opposite direction.

To make standards prevail in the field of criticism remains a major task for critics. But not only for critics. Creative workers in all fields must apply themselves to the effort—by criticism of criticism (at which no self-respecting critic can take offense), and clarification of their aims or program. This might entail entry into the field of criticism, a proposal which will find some artists exceedingly reluctant. But there is sound precedent for them, if we may cite such diverse examples as Leonardo da Vinci, Dante, Ben Jonson, Goethe, Wordsworth, Coleridge, Walt Whitman, Tolstoy, the French impressionists, Proust, Valéry, and Thomas Mann. The problem of criticism cannot be disregarded if creative work is to flourish.[3]

---

[3] [Professor Gassner noted in the proof margins of this essay: "Add?" No supplementary comments have been found among his papers, so it is impossible to indicate how the discussion would have been expanded. *Ed.*]

■

THE SOURCE, THE PATH, THE VISION:
A RELATIVISTIC VIEW*

It is characteristic of the theatre that it should begin to operate with all the apparatus of sound organization, that it should nevertheless succumb to all degrees of disorganization at some time or other, and that it should then frantically reorganize itself, fearing the worst, and hoping for the best. Everyone concerned with stage production is familiar with this process, which entitles the theatre to be politely described as a miracle of organized chaos. In the commercial world, no other business is so incalculable whether it succeeds or fails, and no other business gets the support of otherwise "solid" citizens who find horse-racing too tame for their blood. And in the academic world, no other part of the curriculum is so disconcerting to the orderly aspirations of a sane faculty yet so attractive to the long-inhibited that even presidents of universities have been known to put on greasepaint with their students.

Mr. John Wray Young, who arranged this year's program, gave months of scrupulous attention to its preparation and logical organization. This is apparent, of course, in the beautiful division of our discourse into "the Source," "the Path," and "the Vision." Mr. Young *organized* the show. Then he promptly made sure that it would become *disorganized* by selecting a "keynote speaker." The anarchist standing before you grew up in the early Theatre Guild, a mighty organization in its day, that could thrive only on disorder. The moment it became orderly it became commonplace; the moment it became temperate it ceased to be interesting; the more it became responsible to creditors, the less it became responsible to art. Oh, how we longed to find stability in the quicksands of theatrical enterprise, but how we dreaded stabilization! We were an institution that was mortally afraid of becoming institutionalized. An institutional theatre might have developed *character,* but we behaved as if we had been warned by the misfortune of the girl in a Jules Laforgue poem who, according to the translator, "was wed/To a certain gallant/With character/Instead of talent."

Another institution I had occasion to observe from not too great a distance, the Group Theatre of the 1930's, wanted to have character above

---

* This paper was the keynote address at the AETA convention, Chicago, 1958. It is reprinted from the *Educational Theatre Journal* (December, 1959).

all else, but so far as I could observe, its members could rarely agree on anything except general principles. Its membership dreamed of collectivism in art even more than of collectivism in economics, but "something there is that doesn't love a fence" in organic theatre and the artists of the Group were as remarkable a breed of individualists as any I have encountered, and I include the directors among them. Lee Strasberg, Harold Clurman, Robert Lewis, and Elia Kazan—each has been a distinctive personality in whatever work he has done in the theatre. Nor would these gentlemen be alarmed by this allegation, which I intend as a compliment, for the so-called Method they have variously endorsed calls, in their opinion, for individualized creation rather than the robotization of the artist-actor. And, finally, it was my curious fate to also spend nearly a decade under the shadow of one of continental Europe's most resolute theorizers and organizers, Erwin Piscator, an exile from Germany in the 1940's.

Herr Piscator believed in the dictatorship of the director long after he had lost his taste for the dictatorship of the proletariat. He also seemed single-mindedly bent upon converting the American theatre to his brand of "epic theatre" compounded of lectern-drama, revolving stages, ramps, and magic lanterns. Nevertheless, virtually every vital production engendered in his Dramatic Workshop was the consequence of somebody's pulling away from Piscator's epic-theatre principles. And I must say that Herr Piscator, an individualist and adventurer himself, seemed to be drawn continually to persons who could not and would not accept his ideological discipline. This was as true of his faculty, which at different times included Brooks Atkinson, Theresa Helburn, Harold Burris-Meyer, James Light, Valerie Bettis, Carl Zuckmayer, Stella Adler, and Herbert Berghof as well as his favorite students, among whom were Elaine Stritch and Marlon Brando, not to mention the motley crew of young playwrights Miss Helburn and I collected around him—Tennessee Williams, Arthur Miller, Norman Rosten, Sylvia Regan, Horton Foote, Barrie Stavis, and others. And may I say, in passing, that what we know of the history of far more important enterprises, such as the Abbey Theatre of Dublin and the Moscow Art Theatre, also fails to reveal unanimity of opinion or a planned economy in dramatic art.

I must declare, then, that I feel a strong impulse to upset the well-laid plans of our gracious Program Chairman if only in order to emphasize that in creative theatre hazard and individual talent are all, and that everything else is chaff in the creative process and chatter in the academic world —and that includes esthetics, with all its talk about empathy, esthetic distance, and *Verfremdung*.

I would have to be contradictory of principle at least to the extent of saying that what works in one production or play doesn't necessarily work in another, that orthodoxy in the theatre is always only one's own doxy, and that even so she cannot be trusted very long or very far. One man's "esthetic distance" is another man's intimacy; one man's realism is another man's romanticism, and one man's sympathy is another's antipathy. I would recommend caution in entertaining visions of only one path and one direction in the practice of theatre.

In considering the "Source," the present keynoter would have to brazen out a skepticism that may confuse the very young, affront the old, and contradict impressions no doubt created by his own writings and teachings, too. There is the question, for example, of "What Is Theatre?" I believe a session is to be devoted to this hardly irrelevant question. But how do I really know what is or what is not theatre until I have experienced, if not indeed created or helped to create, it. Theatre could be anything that constitutes a public dramatic experience; we have had readings of O'Casey autobiographies and of *Don Juan in Hell* that made for richer theatrical experience than many fully staged plays. I am, indeed, in mortal dread of being called upon to decide what is theatre and what is a play. I am even wary of the question of what isn't a play. I am reminded of the report that when *The Glass Menagerie* won the New York Drama Critics Award, Frank Fay in the rival company of *Harvey* declared in dismay, "But that isn't a play; it's a mood." It is laudable to inquire into the nature of things, but if the thing is characterized by protoplasmic variety and complexity this fact must be included in the definition. It seems to me inadvisable to try to determine what theatre is in advance, or to accustom students to *start* with the question. It would be wiser, I believe, to enable them to make theatre first and then try to discover what it is they have made.

As for "History," it is possible, of course, to learn much from the history of the theatre, and it is a pleasant and stimulating exercise. We can also learn from it how to put on a period piece as a period piece, or how to write a play in imitation of a Greek tragedy or of an Elizabethan history. The only thing we cannot learn from history is what matters most—how to make a play or a stage production come alive. I offer this reflection, of course, as a physic to pedantry and not as an insult to scholarship.

If we turn to the "Literature" of the theatre, meaning apparently the plays that have come down to us from past ages, we reach a quintessential subject. If we could make more use of our dramatic heritage, our theatre would not suffer from such a dearth of plays to produce after twenty-four centuries. Drama, unfortunately, continues to be taught almost exclusively as literature, and, even where it is not so taught, the resuscitation of even a fifty-year-old play remains a major task for the reader's imagination. And here again I am forced to look to individual talent rather than to standardization of instruction. The very plain fact is that it is difficult to read plays; there are too few signposts along the road of the action for the reader to form any but the most elementary impressions until he begins to create alongside the playwright. One reason why the vast treasury of dramatic literature remains hidden from the playgoer is because it remains hidden from the reader first. I doubt whether much of Ibsen's work, not to mention that of Corneille and Racine in English translation, yields more than an uninspiring elementary content, barren of irony and qualification, to most readers, including, I would say, most actors, directors, and producers. To unseal the treasure house of dramatic literature is undoubtedly an important task, and I believe it is already being performed by anthologists and translators. But there is another task without which much anthologizing and translating plays will have insufficient effect. We must first learn to *read*—and in the case of the drama, this means that we must first learn to create theatre with the text, which is no small order and a very large question. And then we must proceed to stage what we have read.

Taste and judgment are, of course, relative, and there are limits to the catholicity we may expect even under economic and social conditions that would make the production of every kind of play possible. But it is essential to refrain from setting narrow bounds to our taste, and from accepting defeat before we have been defeated. There is a mistrust of creativity in ruling out the master plays of the past, even if it is folly to assume that every play once alive somewhere can be brought to life again everywhere. If it is true that the success of yesterday may be the failure of today, it is also true that the failure of today may be the success of tomorrow.

We may fail indeed more from want of audacity than from want of caution. To be men and women of little faith is to cease being men and women of the theatre.

With respect to dramatic literature, then, I would conclude by recommending less certainty rather than more, less closing of the doors of judgment than opening of doors for hazard and discovery. I suspect, moreover, that the academic young among us need this admonition even more than the old, for if the latter have often been too infirm of judgment and too lax, the young today have tended to be too firm in judgment. I would recall, I hope not unfairly, that they had already drummed O'Neill out of the theatre a dozen years ago.

This brings me to "Dramatic Criticism," another subject with which we are expected to be concerned at this Convention. First and above all, a distinction is needed. For the most part, the theatre of today is not directly concerned with dramatic criticism but with *reviewerism,* which is a practical, box-office consideration. It is noteworthy that the greatest sufferer from the newspaper strike in New York has been the New York theatre. The problem of reviewerism, dutifully inspected and dutifully laid aside after brief flurries of concern by producing managements, directors, and playwrights, are familiar enough. For myself, I must register skepticism. If reviewers have hurt the theatre, they have also helped it; *The Glass Menagerie* and *A Member of the Wedding,* for example, could never have succeeded without journalistic support. And if reviewers have hurt the theatre with unfavorable reviews, they have also hurt it with favorable ones. If the reviewers have possessed too much power, as is alleged, they also have possessed too little power—otherwise we would surely see fewer inept productions on Broadway.

All suggested correctives for newspaper reviewing have been tried at one time or another, but without success. So long as tongues will wag and typewriters click, there will be no way of finding a solution for newspaper criticism. We shall have to rely upon the individual ability and taste of the reviewer, the intelligence of his readers, and the willingness of the latter to pit their judgment against his. I would suggest that producers attend to their own business and let the reviewer attend to his. They should not expect perfect justice, and, above all, they should never try to outguess the reviewers—or, for that matter, the public. That way madness lies!

There is of course such a thing too, as genuine dramatic criticism. It appears in books, periodicals, and, more rarely, also in newspapers. It has a long history that fascinates many of us, and some of us are indeed very much occupied with it as historians, teachers, and writers. Nevertheless, I doubt that the pure critic's responses are necessarily more reliable than the pure journalist's. A qualified endorsement is all that we may extend to dramatic criticism, which has been a maze of contradictions, half-truths, and, truths of limited application from Aristotle's *hamartia* to Hegel's dialectics of "two-rights-in-conflict," to the latest blueprints for drama or for tragedy. And the reason is obvious: the play as a work of art is an individual creation requiring individual assessment even when the playwright has made a commitment to specific principles. Granting the unfortunate confusions of our times and of our theatre, I am nevertheless unwilling to entrust dramatic criticism with the task of making the crooked paths straight. The results could just as well be the reverse of the expected—the few remaining straight paths could be made crooked.

Having gone thus far along the primrose path of relativism, I shall conclude with no greater trust in absolutes in the case of the "Path," which designates the practice of the theatre on the Convention program, and the "Vision," which designates our ideals and our expectations for the theatre of the future. There is obviously no single way of writing, acting, directing, and designing that will ensure any order of success—except success in mediocrity. Our most sensible approach is to abide by our experience and belief that there is no single infallible way of producing any new or old play, although this does not exempt us from exercising judgment instead of lapsing into a passive impressionism. What should concern us most, I think, is the tendency to expect theatrical salvation by stylization or style alone. You may arrive at the style that seems utterly right to you, and the results may be unfortunate. It is not the style, but the effectiveness of communication through that particular style, that matters, and this result does not follow with mathematical certainty. And this brings us to the question of teaching dramatic art, for we often present principles with such an air of confidence in the classroom and in the textbook that we offer certainty for uncertainty. We seem to be guaranteeing results it is impossible to guarantee because of the many intrapersonal and interpersonal complexities, the individual and collective character of the cast, and the special circumstances that intervene between a plan and its execution. We speak and write as if we were promising complete solutions when we should give heed instead to Paul Valéry's warning that "Every art can be learned, but not the whole of art." After every last calculation has been made, in brief, the practice of the stage remains an adventure, a discovery, and an exploration. Even a stage setting, we surely know, is a variable thing. The stage set is dependent not only upon the light that strikes it and the action transpiring on the stage, but upon the very personality, not to mention the costumes, of those who walk upon its boards. An ordinary drawing room could not have been ordinary when Eleanora Duse stood in it, whereas the loveliest setting may lose its loveliness when dolts instead of actors perform on it.

As for so-called Vision, who can be against it? We all desire a theatre that will gratify the heart and satisfy the spirit, that will increase our understanding and uplift our humanity. But how are we to agree upon Vision except in these general terms, which would still have to be translated into the specific terms of individual plays and stage productions in order to possess any force and meaning? This much is certain, we cannot depend upon agreement on objectives in a free society that would give us a uniform kind of theatre even if uniformity were a quality to be desired rather than deplored. The dictatorship of any "idea of theatre," even the worthiest, could indeed strangle creativeness far more easily than foster it. We cannot expect one kind of theatre for all kinds and conditions of men. We shall not, I trust, lapse into the error of postulating an eternal and inviolable theatre in a world of men who are neither eternal nor inviolable.

It is sufficient to recognize the theatre as a humanistic enterprise, to know that it is made by men for men, and to call upon our human resources in the making and teaching of theatre rather than upon a narrow craft-interest. I am convinced of this—as who among us here is not! Goethe once declared, *"Man muss etwas sein, um etwas zu machen."* It is surely true that in order to accomplish something, one must *be* something. We must also strive to make the stage in America a greater cultural force —though the creation of subsidized repertory, for example—and to teach the nation, the states, and the cities to support the theatre as a cultural institution. But we must not inebriate ourselves with extravagant notions. Theatre should not be regarded as religion even in the lukewarm Arnoldian sense of "morality tinged with emotion," lest we infect the stage with pretensions.

Even the word *philosophy* seems to me to promise too much when applied to the stage, which has room for all competently expressed philosophies but has no exclusive philosophy of its own. An "imitation of life" is not philosophy. I would conclude, rather, that when we ask so much of the theatre we are only a few steps away from asking too little of it. When the stage fails to live up to an impossible demand, the inevitable disappointment leads us to downgrade the theatre and prescribe only lowly entertainment for it. Dissatisfied with O'Neill, for example, we are apt to postulate musical comedy or French farce for a horizon. Starting with too much expectation, we may end up with too little.

But now both my reservations and my time run out, and I observe that something quite familiar in the theatre has transpired—and perhaps you saw it happening, too. *I seem to have organized my chaos.* My doubts and anxieties have *justified* rather than invalidated the program of inquiry initiated by our Program Chairman. The lack of certitude makes inquiry necessary, and the empirical character of dramatic art introduces precisely the subjects with which the convention will concern itself—that is, with history, literature, criticism, acting, directing, playwriting, teaching, children's and secondary school theatre, religious theatre, community theatre, musical theatre, and, may the ghost of Sophocles forgive us, television. If we are incapable—and I trust we are incapable—of organizing ourself into immobility, it does not follow that we must resign ourselves to indeterminate flux and to directionless movement. And if we are disinclined to marry our minds to theoretical absolutes, it does not follow that we should not examine the premises upon which we act or might act. And whatever aims we set before us, our policy is surely going to be suggestive rather than prescriptive, and our maxim, should we need one, would remain *"non vi, sed arte"—"not by force, but by art."*

ARISTOTELIAN LITERARY CRITICISM[1]

Half a century earlier, an introduction to a combined edition of Aristotle's *Poetics* and S. H. Butcher's notable commentary would have been unnecessary. Today, however, Aristotle's thoughts on art are apt to seem remote to the general reader and disputable to critics. The values of a moral and philosophical nature that interpenetrate Aristotle's esthetics have been challenged in our time, and it is yet to be determined by events beyond the control of both artists and philosophers whether such values will have much hold upon the century's turbulent generations. The arts, moreover, have been subject to such upheavals, both separately and collectively, that a classical theory may at first glance seem about as useful in sustaining art as a sieve is in retaining water.

What is it, then, that nevertheless still keeps mind and spirit fastened on a twenty-four-century-old document? For the *Poetics* still concerns us to a greater degree than a cursory glance at Western culture would suggest—this even in America, where the classical tradition is virtually extinct. We are attracted, I would suggest, by a way of looking equally at art and humanity as objects of rational inquiry and ideal expectations.

Call the *Poetics,* if you will, a mere manual on poetry in general and on epic and dramatic literature in particular. And a fragmentary manual at that! Yet implicated in it is virtually everything that makes esthetics truly and deeply practical rather than an airy exercise for life's and society's ineffectuals. No typical Greek thinker, and Aristotle least of all, was apt to exercise himself in a partial vacuum filled only with private sensibilities. A cool lucidity in the *Poetics* involves the total experience that is life.

I

In Aristotle's fragment we find an urbane, open-minded man of the fourth century B.C. observing the specific literary products of Greek civilization and drawing generalizations from them concerning the craft of writing. We find him inquiring into the nature of each literary medium

[1] Introduction to *Aristotle's Theory of Poetry and Fine Art,* trans. and ed. by S. H. Butcher (New York: Dover Publications, Inc., 1951).

and into its potentialities. Even more remarkably, we see him continually mingling with his judgments on art a sense of how man, the public
at whom every artist aims his effects, is apt to respond by nature, moral
bent, and emotional involvement. ("Audience psychology" is the popular
American term for this last-mentioned inquiry.) Here, then, is an eminently empirical approach that observes and appraises works of art in
terms of their forms, possibilities, and effects.

The *Poetics* is the first extant essay on art that is honestly exploratory.
Such criticism was unusual in Aristotle's time, and it continued to be
rare long after his death when he was considered the supreme arbiter in
esthetic judgment. It is, indeed, one of the ironies of history that Aristotle's
admirers from the sixteenth to the eighteenth centuries should have tried
to convert the explorer into an absolute lawmaker. It was their chief
ambition, next to that of establishing themselves as legislators, too, by
standing under the ample shadow of the great man's reputation. (Did
Aristotle say undogmatically that the action of a tragedy—that is, of
Greek tragedies—*tended* to be restricted, "as far as possible," to "a single
revolution of the sun"? That was not enough for the new arbiters; they
made it imperative for tragic action to transpire within twenty-four or
even within twelve hours. Did Aristotle take note of a tendency toward
concentration in tragedy? Instantly, although he never so much as mentioned "unity of place," they ordered playwrights to keep all their action
in a single place.) Nor has dogmatic criticism been so rare in a century
full of manifestoes from almost every conceivable school of art and politics
that the *Poetics* can no longer set us a good example of empirical criticism
today.

Still, it is one of the marks of the comprehensive Greek mind that
the practical involves the ideal. By viewing art in terms of its effect,
Aristotle places humanity squarely in the center of his esthetics. He makes
humanistic values paramount from the beginning by asking the right—
or, at least, the current, modern—question of how the artist can please
men. Since, moreover, man is a creature endowed with reason, art is
viewed by Aristotle under the category of rational procedure, and this
involves a sense of appropriateness, measure, and organization in artistry.
And in this respect, art is seen only as another aspect of an ideal of man
first developed in Greece and left as a legacy to civilization.

It is true that in stressing the pleasure-giving feature of art, this
dispassionate thinker broke with the moralistic attitudes of Plato and
asserted the freedom of the arts from moral censorship. Yet he also medi-
ated between the artists and the philosophers of Greece; and in doing so,
he found a perfect solution equally satisfactory to free men in fourth-

century Greek and twentieth-century Western civilization. The mediating concept is *ideality* or *universality*. The ideal, to Aristotle, is that which is free from idiosyncrasy or specialness, and art is an abstract—although not an unliving symbol—of what all men are in their humanity. For realism of detail such a view substitutes the ideality of significant outline. It is not, as Butcher rightly notes, the opposite of the real, but rather its fulfillment and perfection—in the sense that reality stands in clear relief and becomes meaningful.

Without actually crossing boundaries and employing the methods of discursive reason, true art is akin to philosophy in arriving at general truth and coordinating the data of existence. It is actually, says Aristotle, more philosophy than history. Art creates an idea of order where, to the inartistic or unphilosophical observer, life is only a whirl of action and a chaos of emotion. In literature, and especially in its highest form, which for Aristotle is tragedy, the writer creates a logical sequence and causal connection of events. The crude matter of life assumes significance from the shaping hand of the artist.

We also see the same connection between practicality and ideality in Aristotle's discussion of characterization and style. It is only plain sense for Aristotle to maintain that comedy revolves around men whose defects can provoke ridicule and that tragedy concentrates on characters that we can take seriously, for which reason they must possess some degree of importance in our eyes and be neither unregenerately villainous nor flawless. Other conclusions are inevitable from this premise, and it is little wonder, for example, that the Aristotelian principle of *hamartia,* or the "tragic flaw," should recur so frequently in our thinking about tragedy. Underlying Aristotle's thought, here as elsewhere, is his acute awareness of "final ends" or ultimate objectives. The tragedian's objective is to move us with the meaningful experience of human beings with whom we can identify ourselves to the extent of suffering with them—from which, in turn, other conclusions follow. All the reasoning is pragmatic, and Aristotle is disconcertingly bland by comparison with seventeenth- or twentieth-century authors who speak glowingly of the grandeur of tragedy. Aristotle, indeed, sounds flat and business-like. But we may never forget that the business in hand is that of stirring us with a presentation of human destiny, and there is no higher subject available to our experience. The *ends* of tragedy are implicit in Aristotle's discussion of the *means*.

The stress on the efficiency or, as Aristotle would have said, "the efficient causes," in art cannot, then, be our sole and final impression of the *Poetics*. The essay assumes standards by its very concern with the problem of affecting an audience. Success in this respect is measured by high humanistic standards, and Aristotle's frame of reference when he discusses tragedy is an "ideal" spectator—which does not, of course, mean a superhuman one. The writer of tragedies, unlike a Hollywood showman, is not expected to titillate everybody by resorting to sensational effects and to cater to the sentimentalism of the immature. The tragic effect must reside in the matter and mode of the written drama rather than in the "spectacle" on the stage; the tragedian works on the heart and the mind. Nor are we to be melted with "pity," as sentimentalists suggested, but stirred by the more exacting experience of "pity *and* fear." And so tragedy involves our capacity to feel for others and fear for ourselves, too, by knowing that we share in their humanity and that they share in ours, which rules out the possibility of our ever dismissing humane considerations concerning other members of the species.

Tragic art is for those who are not merely mature but humanely mature. It does not address itself to the storm trooper any more than to the sentimentalist. We can imagine men who would be pleased to see villainous and degraded individuals succeed and innocent and noble people destroyed. What can we *not* imagine concerning the taste and appetites, the delusions and frenzies, of the species? Nor do we have to conjure up these possibilities out of thin air when history—including, unfortunately, recent history—provides so many examples. Aristotle measures the effects of art with reference to reasonable men rather than lunatics, grownup men rather than infants, and men capable of sympathy rather than inveterate sadists. He also makes assumptions inherent in the Greek worldly, though not necessarily antispiritual, view. We can imagine, for instance, a convocation of saints exulting in the trials of the flesh as a preparation for the heavenly life or an assembly of yogis completely unmoved by tragic events because suffering is only "Maya" or illusion. It is more than possible, too, that a completely collectivistic society, as envisioned by Aldous Huxley or George Orwell, would consider individual misfortune inconsequential. But none of the antihumanist approaches to the human situation are entertained by Aristotle, and his standards have been potent for so long a time precisely because they have been those of Western humanistic society until now.

II

In reading the *Poetics,* nevertheless, we dare not be easily satisfied that we know what we are reading. There is the Aristotle of the bald text, now at last painstakingly established, and also the Aristotle of all the extant treatises correctly ascribed to him. The one without the other is obscure and incomplete. To know what the *Poetics* means at every point we must know what certain concepts meant to Aristotle in his other works. For example, what do the terms "imitation" and "action" mean to him? Only by determining this can we understand why he calls art an "imitation" and why he places "action" at the head of all the elements that constitute a play. Also, what particular process did he have in mind when he wrote that tragedy effects a *katharsis,* or purgation, of "pity and fear" by exciting "pity and fear" in the spectator? There is trouble, besides, with the very language he employs, since many Greek nouns lack distinct single equivalents in modern languages, and since Aristotle, the great synthesizer, is apt to subsume several ideas under a single term.

There is, moreover, a third Aristotle—the Aristotle of his many interpreters, who encrusted the *Poetics* with their own artistic and social attitudes. It is always a problem to determine how far we are to accept critics' adumbrations as consonant with Aristotelian thought. One might word the question simply as "whom are we following, Aristotle or his interpreters?" We can try to determine this, and we can succeed up to a point. But there is the Aristotle who is significant precisely because so many attitudes and ideas have accreted around his words. This Aristotle cannot be ignored either, without depriving ourselves of important stimulations and gratifications. Besides, it is almost impossible for most of us to read the *Poetics* now with pristine innocence.

It was in order to correct misconceptions and prevent further perversions of Aristotle's book that late-nineteenth-century English scholars undertook the exacting labor of preparing definitive editions and commentaries. The present book, a product of many decades of modern scholarship and revised continually between 1895 and 1911, is, along with Ingram Bywater's *Aristotle on the Art of Poetry,* the most reliable introduction to the *Poetics* available in English. Although it is still possible to disagree on particular readings of the text and on details of translation, the reader can turn to Butcher's memorable book with confidence. As the notes show us, Butcher substantiated disputable points with a painstaking scholarship that belongs to the grand tradition of English learning. Moreover, Butcher's commentary, "Aristotle's Theory of Poetry and the Fine Arts," appended to the Greek text and the translation, leaves nothing to be desired; nothing that Butcher could have supplied without venturing into unresolved discussions of modern drama. At all points the scholar appears to be as thoroughly in accord with Aristotle's mode of thinking as anyone can be over the wide chasm of the centuries. A mere smattering of Greek enables us to realize this, and no Greek is necessary for the reader to sense that this must be so.

We can avoid disappointment, however, only by resigning ourselves to the limitations of the text that has come down to us. It was written around 330 B.C., but the oldest surviving Greek text is dated about the year A.D. 1000, and a section on comedy was apparently lost by then. We have, besides a general introduction to the nature and types of literature, only that part of the treatise which deals with epic poetry and tragedy. And even this part is incomplete and apparently unrevised, as if it had been intended solely for the author's use in delivering lectures on the subject. It is frustrating not to be able to follow some of the illustrations cited by Aristotle from the literature known to him and lost to us, and it is disconcerting to be forced to resort to speculations on how he expected tragedy to purge us by means of pity and fear. Are we to assume that, according to Aristotle, many men are troubled by too much inclination toward pity and fear, and that in experiencing these emotions in the theatre we discharge them successfully by means of empathy? Are we to include other emotions too under the terms? Are we to content ourselves with the probability that, in accordance with the views of Greek medicine, Aristotle thought of the process of *katharsis* as a sort of homeopathic practice, whereby we are cured by taking a hair of the dog that bit us? Or are we to assume that the complex of pity and fear in us is transformed into an ennobling experience by being directed outwardly toward characters distanced by the stage and, at the same time, exalted by the tragic poet to such a degree that they sum up the human situation and universalize it? Are we, as Butcher maintains, "lifted above the special case and brought face to face with universal law and the divine plan of the world?" And, finally, is there no *katharsis* in comedy as well—no purgation, different in quality, by means of which our dislikes, our rebelliousness at social restraints, and our own tendencies to self-depreciation or self-criticism are discharged on the deserving object of a comically drawn character? On these and other matters Aristotle is by no means as explicit as we should have liked him to be. His students in Greece were probably better served than his readers have been since his spare essay was recovered for us.

Only when we know, indeed, what not to expect, can we make the most of the extant portions of the *Poetics* and pursue the lines of inquiry they open up to us. And we may be sure it will not be a fruitless inquiry when we reflect that it was undertaken with variable results by Ben Jonson, Milton, Corneille, Dryden, Lessing, and Goethe among other luminaries of the literary world. To this very day, in far from classically minded America, statements in the *Poetics* have engaged the interest of influential critics such as Joseph Wood Krutch and John Mason Brown and successful playwrights such as Maxwell Anderson and Arthur Miller. It is surely significant that a playwright so closely bound to the contemporary social scene as Miller should have attempted to reconcile his practice in *Death of a Salesman* with the Aristotelian criterion that a tragic hero should possess stature. Although Aristotle's knowledge of epic and dramatic literature was confined to writings in the Greek language before the end of the fourth century B.C., his essay has been found relevant to the literary production of later ages. Ever since the *Poetics* was translated into Latin by the Italian humanist Valla in 1498, we have tended to employ Aristotle's terms and standards even in our judgment of literary productions uninfluenced by the book: to oriental epics and plays, to medieval epics and romances, and to the work of Shakespeare, Lope de Vega, and other writers for the popular stage who were either ignorant of Aristotle's essay or indifferent to it. Nor have we hesitated to apply his ideas to the experiments of modern dramatists such as Ibsen, Strindberg, Chekhov, and Shaw, who struck out in their several new directions with scant respect, if any, for tradition. Whether or not we think we apply or should apply Aristotelian criteria, the fact is that we do apply them.

The problem is merely one of accommodation to the civilization and art of the latest transitional period the generations of Western man have experienced since the nineteenth century. Aristotelian esthetic theory is bound to be viewed in our time with the perspectives laid down by modern romanticism and realism, terms under which we may include the creative and critical approaches of symbolism, expressionism, surrealism, and modern psychological and social literature. Although at least one of Aristotle's ideas—the spiritual significance of tragedy—actually looms larger than ever in critical thought, many of his observations now require reconsideration. Whether we can mediate between them and our own observations is an important question to writers, critics, and teachers. I believe that, on the whole, we can. I am convinced, in fact, that Aristotle's thinking is still a useful corrective to whatever views we maintain on the subject of narrative and dramatic art, since he is free from our habits of excessive romanticization of ideas and ideals, including those we promulgate in his name.

III

Aristotle looks into the craft of writing with a lively interest, concerning himself with language, diction, style, the forms of literature, the characteristic qualities of the medium, the nature of effects, and how they are achieved. He sets later criticism a lesson in intelligent, systematic, and inductive procedure. But it is true that we shall not find in his work certain refinements of the modern critical approach, such as "levels of meaning," symbolization, and chains of association. He treats broad and generally direct or objective effects. He is no more concerned with the poet's unique personality or special creative processes than he is with the state of his own soul, for which he claims no notable uniqueness. Art is not a divine madness or a manifestation of subjective intimations. Nor is criticism a purely personal adventure among masterpieces.

The reason becomes apparent in the second paragraph of the treatise. Romanticists have stressed the element of self-expression in art, whereas Aristotle defines art as an "imitation," a term that Butcher's scholarship will clarify and broaden for us. An entire field of critical inquiry is opened up by the difference between the Aristotelian and the romantic view. For example, are the two views entirely irreconcilable? Does "imitation" necessarily exclude self-expression or, for that matter, even symbolization? Is there no possibility of self-expression *through* imitation, since we view reality through a temperament and we comment on it through the very acts of perceiving and representing objects and experience. Also, is not all communication and, indeed, the very apprehension of reality an act of symbolization on our part? Suzanne Langer's *Philosophy in a New Key* points out that even the eye and the ear make abstractions, so that these organs present our mental faculties with already symbolized data. At what point, too, does "self-expression" lead to private or coterie art as incommunicable to the average intelligent man as, let us say, *Finnegans Wake?* To what degree this is artistically and socially defensible became, in fact, the main issue in the arts of the twentieth century, a controversy as keen as was the "battle between the ancients and the moderns" in the eighteenth century. If Aristotle was aware of any such problem, and it is extremely doubtful that he could have been in his time, he gives no attention to it, and many centuries were to pass before even the literal sense of his theory of "imitation" would be challenged. Aristotle fastens our attention on everything that is directly communicable and socially digestible in artistic endeavor.

Next we may note that Aristotle stirs up a veritable beehive by maintaining that tragedy is "an imitation, not of men, but of action and of life, and life consists in action, and its end is a mode of action, not a quality," for which reason he gives preeminence to plot. Modern writers tend to bristle at this statement, overlooking the fact that he has earlier declared that the "action implies distinctive qualities both of character and thought; for it is by these that we qualify actions themselves, and these—thought and character—are the two natural causes from which actions spring." And Butcher, indeed, helps us to understand that by the term "action" he must have meant more than simply external events. Nevertheless, the phrase "not of men, but of an action" gives rise to the question of the relative importance of character and action; and, in extreme cases of modern theory and practice, even to the question whether external action or plot is needed at all. What could O'Neill, for example, have considered more important, action or inner stress, in *Strange Interlude*? He continually stopped stage activity in order that his characters might express their hidden feelings, and yet large audiences found the story of Nina and her lovers absorbing and dramatic. Did not Zola and other champions of modern drama, besides, make the subordination of "plot" to representations of human nature and environment the prime requisite for dramaturgy? Did not Shaw in the 1890's also proclaim the superiority of the "discussion play," as written by Ibsen and himself? And did not Galsworthy, actually a moderate iconoclast, declare that "character is the best plot there is?" The fact is that modern drama, as well as fiction, for we also have the "plotless" short story and novel, has conformed to prescriptions of priority for characterization, "psychology" and psychological analysis, environment, discussion, and mood—the latter, often by "symbolist" suggestion and subconscious association. Some playwrights—most conspicuously, Maeterlinck and Andreyev—even went so far as to condemn action as barbaric and to call for the representation of a "stasis" on the stage. In modern times, as Andreyev wrote in 1914, "life has gone within."

We can try to mediate, of course, between Aristotle and the latter-day writers by maintaining that the difference between the Aristotelian and the modern emphasis is only a matter of degree. It would seem, too, that the argument over the priority of characterization reduces itself to the absurd question of which comes first, the chicken or the egg. We may ask, besides, how character or psychological reality can manifest itself effectively, especially in the theatre, without a sequence of revelatory responses, decisions taken or evaded, and externalized feelings and thoughts. Does not this sequence, too, constitute "action" and "plot"? To what extent is the mental action of discussion, especially when Shaw presents it, *not* action? Or is the self-revelation of characters not action when Shakespeare writes a soliloquy in *Hamlet* or Strindberg a dramatic monologue in *The Stronger*? Is not even a succession of moods, as in Maeterlinck's *The Intruder,* "action," and is not the organization of the mood—with a "beginning, middle, and end," with a rising intensity and a final discharge of tension—"plot"?

It may have to be conceded, nevertheless, that a complete reconciliation cannot be effected between the introspective moderns and Aristotle. It is precisely matters of degree that are decisive in art, and a strong inclination in one direction or another determines the singular quality of an author's writing. We are forced back, as is Butcher, to the position that for Aristotle, too, action could not be consonant solely with external activity. Aristotle, moreover, does not think of action without characters —characters so fully realized, indeed, that he pays special attention to their ethical disposition, or *ethos,* and their intellectual content, or *dianoia.* It is because Aristotle kept his mind on the nature of the drama as the medium in which things are represented rather than narrated, and surely not because he was less interested in man than we are, that he gave priority to action. If he refrained from painting a nimbus around characterization as an element in drama, we may be certain that he took it for granted that tragedy's sole consideration was man and his destiny. Nor was there, indeed, any want of characterization or even "psychological interest" in the classical works he knew and admired. They are actually less plotty than many later tragedies. If character development is less marked in the Greek tragedies than in Shakespearian and some modern dramas, the main reason is structural: a Greek tragedy is shorter and starts closer to the crisis of the story.

Can we be so certain, finally, that the trend in modern literature has been in all respects contrary to the Aristotelian emphasis on action or that we may not actually come full circle round to it? Two nineteenth century ideas in criticism have proved seminal in our time. One is Hegel's dialectical view that a conflict of opposites is the driving force in tragedy, and the other is Brunetière's stress on the volitional factor in drama—specifically, that "drama is the representation of the will of man in conflict." Both concepts are more honored in the teaching and practice of playwriting today than is the romanticist Schlegel's preference for subjective experience and sensation; this in spite of later symbolist theory in literature and in spite of Gordon Craig's emphasis on nuance and suggestion in the art of theatrical production. Both ideas, "tragic conflict" and "the will of man in conflict," have found a specially active realization in social, especially "class-struggle," drama in our century; and this, in spite of theories of social determinism in human behavior. Today, in fact, the tide may often be seen running counter to introspective writing, which has been subjected to denunciation from both the political right and the political left. Activism in art has been propounded by Malraux during both his communist and De Gaullist phases. "Epic drama," as preached and practiced by the German poet-playwright Brecht, regards action as the very end of dramatic demonstration. So much so, indeed, that Brecht deprecates a *katharsis* or purgation of the emotions, lest the emotional involvement of the spectator blind him to courses of action and drain him of the will and ability to be effective in life! In Sartre's existentialism, too, action is considered the exclusive test of character. Propagandist "class-struggle" literature never fails, of course, to represent action and to clamor for it, and "socialist realism," entrenched in a large segment of the world, rules out subjectivity in the arts as a symptom of middle-class decadence. It is, indeed, a question whether, were Aristotle alive today, he would not be more disconcerted by those who could agree than by those who would disagree with him on the primacy of action.

IV

The largest area of discussion is opened up by Aristotle's special enthusiasm for tragedy as a literary form, although the subject might not have loomed as large as it does in his book if the *Poetics* contained the treatment of comedy promised by him. With the examples of the *Odyssey* and *Iliad* before him, Aristotle, it is true, esteems epic poetry highly. Yet after noting the attributes epic poetry has in common with tragedy, he gives his accolade to the latter as the more unified and concentrated art. It is possible to contend, as it has indeed been contended, that the novel, which is the present equivalent of the epic, is the superior form of modern literature. Weighty evidence can be collected in favor of this view if we confine ourselves only to *The Red and the Black, War and Peace, The Brothers Karamazov,* Proust's cycle of novels, *The Magic Mountain,* and, perhaps, *Ulysses,* in which Joyce paralleled the epic events and structure of the *Odyssey.* Those who, like T. S. Eliot, set a higher valuation on *The Divine Comedy* than on Shakespeare's work, can also throw Dante's epic into the scales. And it might also be contended that had Aristotle known *Hamlet, King Lear,* and *Antony and Cleopatra,* he might not have been able to draw the line between epic and dramatic form quite so sharply. Today, indeed, we find the school of "epic drama," led by Piscator and Brecht, maintaining that drama needs epic scope if it is to express modern life. But Aristotle's ideal tragic form does have a valid claim to esthetic superiority in so far as, other qualities being equal, a work that exerts a single concentrated effect is superior to a work that does not. As a logician, too, Aristotle could hardly resist favoring the tightly closed system of Greek tragedy, and we may also remember that he was the spiritual heir of the fifth-century Athenian civilization in which the classic drama attained its perfection after epic writing had lost vitality.

We are primarily concerned, then, with tragedy when we read the *Poetics,* and it is a subject full of pitfalls and miasmas largely of our own making since the sixteenth century. Involved in this subject are such matters as the character of the tragic hero, the manner in which tragic purification is effected, the matter with which tragedy can treat, and the varieties of tragic effect. The accepted view is that tragedy must concern itself with a character well above the common level, that we must be emotionally shattered and yet somehow purified by his experience, and that there is only one kind of drama—a character's downfall—that can effect all this. These ideas dominate most thinking about tragedy, judgments on plays, and prescriptions for the stage. We may wonder, however, whether these have not been employed too narrowly and without reference to correctives supplied by Aristotle himself. We shall not perhaps feel entirely reconciled to modern drama until we realize how broadly operative his thinking is by comparison with the tendency to seize upon one of his ideas and erect it into a taboo or a prescription.

When we talk of the uncommon nature of the hero, for example, as well as when we tend to think of tragedy occurring only in a rarefied atmosphere of conflict uncontaminated by ordinary life, it is useful to recall that for Aristotle the gratification of art comes first of all from "recognition." In harmony with his theory of art as an "imitation," he declares that our pleasure comes from "seeing a likeness," although he is not so dogmatic as to assert that gratification may not also have other sources, such as artistic execution. And surely, if this is so, is there not a place in tragedy for an ordinary man? Not merely for a man of low station, which is now granted by modern critics, but for a man whose *mentality* is common and whose spiritual endowment is not notably above the ordinary. Many effectively realized characters of serious modern drama fall into this category. Are modern plays that revolve around them, such as *Ghosts, Drayman Henschel,* and *The Lower Depths,* automatically ruled out as tragedies, as many a critic has maintained, or is there a type of "naturalistic tragedy" to which we owe respect as a high form of dramatic art even if it does not satisfy the standardized requirements for so-called high tragedy?

May we not wonder in the case of such a powerful example of intermediate drama as Arthur Miller's *Death of a Salesman* whether the audiences have not been more strongly moved and, indeed, uplifted by the superannuated salesman's close likeness to themselves and people they know than by anything extraordinary in the character? Here the critic for whom tragic experience is the prime requisite, if he does not rule the play out of the argument as pathetic rather than tragic, has only one recourse. He can maintain that Miller's drama scales the tragic heights because the character Willy Loman is extraordinary in the persistent efforts he makes to hold on to high evaluations of himself and his son Biff, in the passionateness of his nature, and in his exceptional capacity for suffering. Yet even if this contention is correct in every particular (and not everyone will grant this in America, while few have granted it in England), it is undeniable that the element of "recognition" is dominant and decisive in *Death of a Salesman.* Audiences would have dismissed Willy as simply an untragic, merely pathetic, dolt if he had not been so much like themselves and their relatives and acquaintances whose defects are neither heroic like Macbeth's nor ludicrous like Malvolio's. If his struggles and sufferings provided them with tragic exultation, it was less because Willy was eminent than because he epitomized their own lack of eminence. If they did not consider him ignoble, it was because they do not consider themselves ignoble. If he made large claims upon their sympathy, it was because, along with Arthur Miller, they attributed his failure, as well as their own, to entrapment in social delusions and circumstances. If they considered him heroic at all, they did so essentially in terms of their awareness of how much fortitude the soul must bring to common everyday situations, his and theirs. If our aristocratic sensibilities shudder at the thought of this democratization of tragedy, and if Aristotle himself, living in a society founded on slave labor, was actually unlikely to conceive of tragedies devoted to the Willy Lomans of the world, the trend in this direction has been nonetheless strong. And Aristotle's own plain words are less of a prohibition of tragic gratification on Willy Loman's democratic level than his interpreters assume when they rhapsodize, as he definitely did not, over the spiritual elevation of tragic heroes.

As for Aristotle's principle of *katharsis* through "pity and fear," continually stressed after him, should we not also limit the degree of emotional involvement required for purgation by tragedy? "Objects," Aristotle writes, "which in themselves we view with pain, we delight to contemplate when reproduced with minute fidelity." Implicit here is the doctrine of "esthetic distance" to wit, that we derive gratification in art from being able to stand at some remove from the object. The death of a character simulated on the stage or described in the pages of a book can be artistically gratifying whereas, in normal cases, the actual death of a person in our presence is only painful. If Aristotle does cite the arousing of "pity and fear" as the specific characteristic of tragedy, he does not insist that it is the *only* element that makes the pain of tragedy "pleasurable." *Katharsis* in tragedy is more dependent than has been generally realized upon this esthetic distance and upon the perspectives it affords. Otherwise it would be impossible to explain how we are to be liberated from the pity and fear we are supposed to experience in witnessing a tragedy. And to what end would Aristotle have made *dianoia* or the thought (or intellect) of characters an important dramatic element and described it as containing the subdivisions of "proof and refutation" and the "suggestion of importance and its opposite" if he had considered nothing but emotion important in tragedy?[2]

Merely being enabled by the artist to stand at some distance from a painful experience, to observe and understand it, can in itself afford some release from our tensions. And if it is our own tension or plight that we are able to discover and evaluate in others, our release from it is all the greater. In a sense, we master what we manage to observe objectively. In harping continually on the idea of "pity and fear," critics and writers, ever since the great critic Lessing hammered away at it in his *Hamburg Dramaturgy,* in order to discredit feeble neoclassic French tragedy, have virtually given the impression that tragedy is an emotional orgy. Unquestionably an orgy can exhaust us to such a degree that we are no longer capable of feeling our own and our fellow-creature's pain. But is this the most desirable way to be "released," and is it consonant with the dignity of tragic art, which is expected to sharpen our sensibilities instead of dulling or numbing them? Emotional involvement *and* detachment, "pity and fear" *and* objectivity, are present in tragedy, and to varying degrees in different plays, as well as in different effective productions of the same play.

Aristotle's thinking, indeed, allows for far greater latitude than is usually assumed in the major qualifying statement of the *Poetics* which reads: "Whether Tragedy has yet perfected its proper types or not, and whether it is to be judged in itself or in relation also to the audience— this raises another question." This single sentence, which gives us freedom to reconsider tragic art since his time, should certainly give pause to critics who maintain that playwrights since Ibsen have not written true

---

[2] In "Catharsis and the Modern Theatre," *European Theories of Drama,* ed. by Barrett H. Clark, rev. by Henry Popkin (New York: Crown Publishers, Inc., 1965), I have maintained that there can be no complete purgation for the spectator or reader without "enlightenment" ensuing upon the "pity and fear" he has experienced; and there can surely be no enlightenment concerning an experience that we cannot view from some emotional distance. Maxwell Anderson, in *The Essence of Tragedy,* postulated that the tragic hero must make some decisive discovery about himself and about the world that will alter his course of action. This, of course, affords realizations to the audience as well, and neither the tragic hero nor his audience can of course arrive at such realizations while engaged in purely emotional reactions.

tragedies because the plays fail to conform to the postulated absolutes for tragic art.

Cannot a problem play, for example, be a tragedy? Aristotle never had to consider this question in our particular terms because the problems he found in such Greek tragedies as *Antigone* and *The Trojan Women*— the rival claims of private conscience and obedience to the state or the inhumanity of war—were surely inherent in the traditional material upon which they were based. Is there not, besides, a genuine tragedy of *attrition,* best exemplified by *The Three Sisters* and *The Cherry Orchard,* as more or less distinct from the classic tragedy of a resounding fall from a great height? And have we not overstressed the "fall" as a tragic element even in the older drama? Is not attrition, or the "breaking down" process, actually an element in such plays as *Oedipus the King, King Lear,* and *Macbeth.* I may not be alone in reporting that I have been more deeply stirred by the manner in which Oedipus is deprived of his certainties and Lear is worn out as a human being than by a precipitate fall from greatness.[3] It is not that they are hurled down like Lucifer from heaven but that they crumble in some fundamental respect, as many men do, that moves me most. And I should have been so moved, I suspect, even if Oedipus had not gouged out his eyes at the end and Lear had not died. To be ground down is the most universal—the only truly universal— destiny. It can also be made just as pitiful and fear-inspiring as physical destruction. Even Macbeth, who falls like a tower, is most profoundly tragic in the gradual deterioration of his character, and the most plangent notes in the play come after his way of life is "fall'n into the sear, the yellow leaf" in the great "Tomorrow, and tomorrow, and tomorrow" soliloquy of universal disenchantment. The only difference between his end and that of such modern characters as "the three sisters" and the "cherry orchard" family is that he rallies his spirits to wage a final battle in which he is slain whereas they rally their spirits to endure the continuance of their misfortunes; and we may wonder which is the more trying experience requiring the greater fortitude.

It is pertinent, indeed, to observe that Aristotle, like the Greek play-

---

[3] J. Dover Wilson's description is to the point: "Lear is a king 'more sinned against than sinning.' Hell, in the person of his two daughters and in the symbol of the storm, seems to rise up in full panoply, first to crush the old man's pride, then to overthrow his intellect, and last of all to break his heart." This suffering does not, of course, deprive Lear of sublimity but actually enables his greatness to shine forth, just as fate brings out the greatness in that other, even more ensnared, king Oedipus. "The Lear that dies," writes Wilson, "is not a Lear defiant, but a Lear redeemed" in his late-won humility, presenting to God "the oblation of a broken heart" (*The Essential Shakespeare,* pp. 124–27).

wrights and the play-contest judges of the Theatre of Dionysus, does not insist that all the plays the Greeks called tragedies must end in disaster; he prefers a catastrophic ending as the best or "perfect" for tragedy, but refers to two possible sequences of events—"a change from bad fortune to good, or from good fortune to bad." We may be certain, for example, that Aristotle would have accepted *Anna Christie* as a tragedy in spite of the resolution in which Anna and her suitor are reconciled. The Greeks had no separate category for "tragicomedy." And does it really matter whether we insist upon a sharp distinction, as we have tended to do? There is more high seriousness in Sophocles' *Philoctetes,* which has a "happy ending," than in gory *Gorboduc* or *Titus Andronicus.* If we put a low estimation on, let us say, some of Fletcher's tragicomedies and *Cymbeline,* not to mention Hollywood drama, our criticism is surely founded on other considerations than "the change from bad fortune to good"; we object to the unconvincing manner in which the happy ending is effected and to the organization and quality of the work as a whole. Normally, as Aristotle noted, the disastrous conclusion is more tragic, but surely the tendency of modern drama to omit the last rites and come to rest on what Aristotle indefinitely calls "the scene of the suffering" is not inconsonant with tragic effect. Shaw actually regarded the fatal endings in Ibsen's plays as a defect. In taking exception to the suicide of Hedda Gabler, he held that the real tragedy of the futile Heddas of the world is not that they die but that they have to live on. To have to live on is also, in a sense, the ultimate tragedy of Oedipus at the end of *Oedipus the King.*

V

For all the qualifications we may or must, indeed, make concerning any narrow interpretation of tragedy that places most modern drama beyond the pale, it is, nevertheless, true that there is an irreducible minimum below which no play can fall without losing tragic distinction. The "letter" of prescription for tragedy is immaterial; the spirit is all important. Even those who put altogether too narrow constructions upon the concept of tragedy may be forgiven, because their eyes are fixed on the profoundly spiritual essence of the tragic experience.*

This essence is sometimes referred to as tragedy's "universality" but with questionable applications. The term has been used, for example, as

* [Apparently Professor Gassner had considered revising this paragraph to include some specific examples. A marginal note: *"Vide* Mary McCarthy." *Ed.*]

a weapon in the hands of critics of modern "problem plays." It is true enough that writers of such plays should be aware of the commonplace-ness and impermanence they risk when they present sociological matter. But it is not at all certain that the genius of a writer cannot under any circumstances transmute a present subject into a universal one. It was the problem Maxwell Anderson set himself in *Winterset,* even if he ulti-mately flew away from it on pseudo-Shakespearian wings. And, in any case, the fear of impermanence and "untragic" drama has not deterred, and need not deter, an able playwright from taking advantage of the com-munion that is theatre and from having his say in it. Greatness, like light-ning, strikes infrequently. While we wait for it, it is well at least to have a vital theatre that has interest and meaning for its own time. Nor is it certain that the worship of universality is not hedged about with its own dangers. The cult can encourage writing in a vacuum. It can divert the writer from his own times, about which he knows something by observa-tion, into a world he knows only through literature. He may also become a mere echo of the great writers of the past and intoxicate himself (as, for example, George Chapman, Schiller, and occasionally Maxwell Ander-son did) with his own high-sounding generalizations to the detriment of significant action and characterization. Concerning "universality," as con-cerning other matters, Aristotle's own words are, in fact, deflatingly mod-est. "By the universal," he writes, "I mean how a person of a certain type will on occasion speak or act, according to the law of probability or necessity." He does not impregnate the term with philosophical or spir-itual content. We must not lay at his door the sententious magniloquence of some genuine and many pinchbeck tragedians.

Universality, if not romantically misconstrued, is a quality of tragedy. But the most distinctive value of tragic art consists of the high valuation it places upon man as a species and upon the individual as its representa-tive. Tragic art predicates the *special* universality of man's capacity for greatness of soul and mind in spite of his *hamartia* or the flaw in his nature. Man is endowed with an acceptable or a deplorably perverse yet somehow admirable nobility (rather than eminence) in so far as his tragic representatives belong, in Edith Hamilton's apt words, "to the only true aristocracy, that of all passionate souls."[4] The French critic Saint-Évre-mond declared that tragedy induced "admiration," and it does, if not necessarily in the old-fashioned heroic sense of the term. Tragedy is a

---

[4] Aristotle's own spare words are that tragedy is "an imitation of persons who are above the common level" and should "preserve the type and yet ennoble it," which may mean simply that the character's traits should be carried to some pitch of intensity or be given more than inconsequential dimensions.

poetry of man. The individual is exemplified by the highest reaches of his humanity in erring and bearing the consequences, willing and suffering, groping and arriving at decisions, collaborating in his destiny (becoming its dupe when necessary but never its puppet), and affirming his personality even in defeat and dissolution.

Twentieth-century critics and playwrights have fixed their expectations for the drama almost exclusively upon this view of tragedy and have subordinated virtually every Aristotelian principle to it. Romantic Aristotelianism has been the keynote of our criticism.[5] The latter-day Aristotelians, have turned compulsively to tragedy as a way—as the only way —of asserting the stature or dignity of the human being in the face of the indignities of a world of real and fancied slurs on man. Whether or not they have been entirely correct in attributing the whittling down of the individual to the literature and plays, the psychopathology and psychoanalysis, and the science and philosophy, as well as the social pressures, of our time is a large question. The fact is that the critics express an unease and uncertainty characteristic of Western society in our century, and their romantic vocabulary betrays a sense of dismay, if not actually of defeat. They speak of the "reconciliations" and "conclusions" of tragedy in the accents of Schopenhauer, and even their strenuousness in affirming the strong spirit of man sounds compensatory in a familiar, Nietzschean vein. Be that as it may, their disenchantments combine with their protest against a petty world and against petty views of man to crystallize an attitude that later and perhaps happier times may set down as unduly romantic. Only theological thinking, on the one hand, and collectivist thinking, on the other, actually challenge this emphasis at present—the

---

[5] Even practitioners of the "New Criticism," who pay more attention to the "texture" of literature than to its explicit ideas, do not provide an exception. Their talented leader John Crowe Ransom arrives at the concept of ennoblement *via* his own close consideration of writing. In the stimulating essay "The Literary Criticism of Aristotle," *Lectures in Criticism* (New York: Pantheon Books, 1949), called to my attention by Dr. Dorothy Richardson of Queens College, Ransom holds that the poetry in tragedy diverts us from obsessive horror. We recover presence of mind when the mind resumes its "gallant and extravagant activities." And identification makes it possible for us to experience the tragic *katharsis* because the heroes of Greek tragedy "themselves were not terrified out of their wits but continued in the easy exercise of the most liberal powers of mind." With the tragic characters, we experience a suspension of mere animal suffering. Tragedy, then, enables our sensibility to triumph over "vile occasions."

For Ransom, "the heroic style is the thing." This is a poet's view of tragedy, and I am not certain that it is strictly applicable to plays where the characters are incapable of deathless poetry. But Ransom's view, too, gives primacy to the concept of tragedy as an exaltation of man's status in the animal world, and Ransom concludes that the tragic hero ends "in full character . . . perfect in his fidelity to the human career."

former by warning us that neither man nor art should be exalted without reservations, the latter by deprecating the stress on "individualism."

If Aristotle's book had not provided the fabric of this view of tragedy, it would have been spun out of the tragic literature of the past, as well as out of the needs of present-day critics and writers themselves. But it so happens that the fabric can be assembled from various elements in the *Poetics*—from Aristotle's references to the uncommon character of the tragic hero, the high style of tragic writing, and the distinctive function of tragedy in effecting a purgation of the soul. Aristotle's view that the spectator is to be cleansed specifically of "pity and fear" has been made to signify a general cleansing—a view that a classicist such as Aristotle would perhaps have disclaimed as fuzzy thinking. According to contemporary critics and dramatists—among whom Joseph Wood Krutch, Edith Hamilton, Philo Buck, John Mason Brown, and Maxwell Anderson have been representative—the tragic hero wins a final victory for mankind over pettiness and pain. His personality exalts the human race, his struggle exhilarates men, and even his death is an affirmation.

For Joseph Wood Krutch, in his chapter on "The Tragic Fallacy,"[6] tragedy was predicated upon the ability of men to believe "in the greatness and importance of men." The writer may "not believe in God, but he must believe in man." Tragedy is, then, a "profession of faith," although Mr. Krutch reflected that it could suffer the "fate of all faiths" and be "ultimately lost as a reality," as, indeed, he thought it had already been "in those distressing modern works sometimes called by its name." (And in this connection we may reflect that there have already been periods of world history in which the humanistic basis for tragedy was absent and no tragic literature was created.) Almost at the same time, in *The Greek Way to Western Civilization* (1929), Edith Hamilton maintained a similar view. For her, tragedy is "pain transmuted into exaltation by the alchemy of poetry," and the "dignity and significance of human life" is attested by the tragic hero's rich capacity for "the high estate of pain." For Maxwell Anderson, in *The Essence of Tragedy* (1938), a tragedy had to proceed toward a "spiritual awakening, or rejuvenation" of the hero. The tragedian must "so arrange his story that it will prove to the audience that men pass through suffering purified, that, animal though we are in many ways, there is in us all some divine, incalculable fire that urges us to be better than we are." Somewhat more ecstatically, John Mason Brown voiced the same faith in his *Broadway in Review* (1940), declaring that tragedy leaves us "spiritually cross-ventilated"; and even the less eloquent

[6] *The Modern Temper* (1929).

author of the present Introduction referred to the final tragic experience, in "Catharsis and the Modern Theatre" (1937, 1946), as "a state of grace . . . an Apollonian attitude . . . a clarity of mind and spirit, a resilience and cheerfulness even."

If such statements as these seem curiously rhapsodic by comparison with Aristotle's matter-of-fact notations, if they appear to be time-dictated intensifications of his bland analysis, they are, nevertheless, allied to the man-centered point of view in the *Poetics*. Provided we do not really turn tragic art or any form of art into an *ersatz* religion and believe that the substitute can actually take the place of the genuine article; provided, too, that we refrain from slighting the plain but serviceable humanism of good untragic drama, we serve Aristotelian humanism well with this stress on tragic ennoblement. And so it appears that the reverberations of Aristotle's book continue to be as strong as ever, and more clearly perhaps than ever before they ring out words that penetrate the heart of man. This has been a curious destiny for an incomplete first manual on literature, but it is surely the best evidence of its power of survival. Its survival can, indeed, be truly jeopardized only by the triumph of a philosophy that would abolish concepts of right and wrong and of individual responsibility, deny the possibility of free will, and reduce life to pure mechanism or to nihilistic meaninglessness. In such an event, the *Poetics* would be a mere relic from a vanished age. Because this possibility, indeed, seems no longer speculatively remote, there is all the more reason for interest in Aristotle's essay as a document in the history of civilization and as an affirmation.

The *Poetics* is, nonetheless, I repeat, a book through which a reader should move warily. We must avoid coming out of our reading with impressions either too strict or too loose. A "little knowledge" in the case of this book has proved "a dangerous thing" for many centuries and to many men, including even scholars. Butcher's *Aristotle's Theory of Poetry and Fine Art,* therefore, still makes large claims upon our attention.

■

WILLIAM ARCHER[1]

> The drama may be called the art of crises,
> as fiction is the art of gradual developments.
>
> WILLIAM ARCHER

Of the making of books on playwriting there is no end, for success in the theatre remains as much a mystery as ever; and plays, it is commonly asserted, are not simply "written" but "constructed." Everybody "knows," of course, that it is possible to succeed on the stage without a play—just playing the piano on stage is enough if you happen to be a Victor Borge—and the sad experience of centuries whispers that poor plays can succeed as well as good ones. Nevertheless, the search for a "good play" continues to be a major occupation in the theatre and the showman is rare who doesn't think he has found one; almost as rare as the individual who isn't convinced he has written one. As for the so-called construction of plays, an industry that turns a writer into a "playwright," it commands all the attention of a specialty reserved for experts but also mysteriously open to inspired, or perhaps only persistent, amateurs.

Playwriting continues to be looked upon as a craft that can be imparted and mastered. Capsuled instructions on writing for the stage are sought even by novelists and poets who in their own profession rely solely on individual artistry. In a world as insecure as that of the theatre, both the vendors and buyers of talismans are many, and they make a busy market. The impossible is believed to be possible in the theatre and sometimes becomes just that because incompetence in the department of playwriting may be decisively compensated for by talent in the departments of acting and stagecraft. So it happens that persons who would consider themselves grievously wronged if set down as pretenders expect to become "playwrights" without ever really becoming writers. They may even aspire to the rank of serious dramatists without deeming it necessary to function on a higher mental or emotional level than a producer of toilet articles.

One would be hard put to it to discover any other field of writing, unless it be the commercial short story, that attracts so many deluded aspirants. Those who confuse play-carpentry with creative writing and theatrical imagination want to be told how to fabricate a play as a commodity.

---

[1] Introduction to *Play-making: A Manual of Craftsmanship,* by William Archer (New York: Dover Publications, Inc., 1960).

There will always be some persons who seemingly will tell them, although the perspicuous advisers will try to make it plain to their readers that they have *not* told them. But if the naïve craving for a formula is certain to be frustrated, it does not follow that every book on playwriting is without interest and use. The subject itself continues to be an absorbing one, and the information that will not supply us with successful plays may allow insight into the problems of playwriting and provide a basis for sound criticism.

It is my pleasure to assist in the reprinting of a classic in the study of playwriting by a man to whom many persons in the theatre have been bound by a strong sense of obligation. William Archer, born in 1856, in the same year as Bernard Shaw, was Ibsen's most influential translator and, next to Shaw, his most effective champion in the English-speaking world. *Play-making* was the result of Archer's thirty years of experience as critic and translator between the 1880's and 1912, the year of publication. Ibsen became an international figure during those years, Shaw performed prodigious feats both as a critic and dramatist, Pinero and Henry Arthur Jones attained their maturity while Galsworthy and Barrie passed their novitiate, and the stage was revolutionized from Paris to Moscow. *Play-making* had its roots in this important period and represents it in dramatic practice, aspiration, and theory. No other work of its kind exerted an equal effect on the formative talent that was to turn the 1920's into the golden age of the American theatre within a decade. The only other influential work available to the same generation, George Pierce Baker's *Dramatic Technique,* appeared seven years later, in 1919.

Arbiter rather than partisan or revolutionist, Archer made himself the spokesman of a reasonable attitude toward playwriting that would serve "theatre" and "truth" in equal measure. He wanted to make theatricality plausibly realistic and realism effectively theatrical. With admirable clarity and accommodating catholicity he provided a craftsman's approach to dramaturgy that would fit the practice of the dominant realistic style of his day and ours. In this area of dramatic art his thinking operated with such clarity and precision that his observations in *Play-making* became as definitive as it is ever possible for dramatic theory to become. While making generous allowance for divergences of practice and granting independence to individual genius, Archer rarely allowed his thought to deviate into mistiness and never into *mystique.* He was eminently a man of nineteenth-century flexible practicality, and he was neither disingenuous nor clever enough to allow himself literary flourishes. When he gave *Play-making* the subtitle *A Manual of Craftsmanship* he meant exactly what he said;

the very preference for the word "play-making" in the main title signifies his concern with *craft*. If the book is, nevertheless, extremely well written for a "manual," the reason is that "play-making" was for him a subject to be treated with cultivated fluency as a matter of course. Archer did not confuse criticism with science, and he addressed mature minds he plainly had no intention of insulting with summaries, classifications, graphs, and charts.

Although filled with closely reasoned concepts, *Play-making* is discourse composed in a literary tradition as alien to the vulgarities of "show business" as it is to the desiccated profundities of academicism. And if I must confess to having felt considerable diffidence at first when I was invited to introduce the present edition, I was relieved on rereading the book to discover how well it holds up. If modifications of the text or additions to it are in order, they are suggested mainly by developments in dramatic art since the date of composition. Even my fear of contributing to our egregious cult of vocationalism was allayed by the author's unequivocal declaration that "there are no absolute rules . . . except such as are dictated by the plainest common sense," followed by the terse warning that "if any part of the dramatist's art can be taught, it is only a comparatively mechanical and formal part—the art of structure." "No teaching or study," he observes further, "can enable a man to choose or invent a good story, and much less to do that which alone lends dignity to dramatic storytelling—to observe and portray human character."

II

Although the author of *Play-making* was a public figure and had many eminent friends, one has to hear from Bernard Shaw of all witnesses before forming an estimate of the man. To become a leader of the *avant-garde* Archer had to possess qualities of mind and spirit of which there is nary a hint in the notices on him one normally encounters. We learn little when told that he was born in Perth, Scotland, in 1856, was educated at Edinburgh University, and died in 1924; that he held the post of drama critic on a succession of periodicals; that his translation of *The Pillars of Society* was the first Ibsen to be produced in England; that he published books on the actors Henry Irving and William Macready and a five-volume translation of *Ibsen's Prose Dramas* in 1890–91 (the complete "Archer-Ibsen" ultimately extended to eleven volumes in 1908, with a twelfth volume of early drafts, *From Ibsen's Workshop,* published in 1912); that he was himself the author of several plays, among which the melodrama *The Green Goddess* succeeded on both sides of the Atlantic in 1921. My discovery, not an exclusive one to be sure, that he wrote an inevitably dull play on Martha Washington is only a glorious irrelevancy.

The otherwise undistinguished volume *Three Plays by William Archer* contains a delightful introductory essay by Shaw written in July, 1926, some two years after the death of his friend. "How William Archer Impressed Bernard Shaw" supplies the winning portrait of "probably the most deceptive man of his time" who took in all his contemporaries with the air of a dour Scot, "hard, logical, with an ability that was always in cold storage" whereas he was actually a remarkably amiable person. The allegedly humorless man, says Shaw, was "like myself the victim of an unsleeping and incorrigible sense of humor." The young Shaw delighted him as "an incarnate joke," and Archer's sense of humor was proof even against personal misfortune. He was tickled, Shaw relates, when an oculist informed him he had amblyopia and explained that "there is no lesion or defect of any sort, a first-class eye, only it doesn't see anything." Archer, reports Shaw, "found this so funny that he thought half his sight well lost for the fun of repeating it." He needed hardly any comforts himself but conscientiously set to work to accumulate savings once he got married. Acting on the best advice, he invested all his money in Australian banks, which presently went bankrupt. The bad news from Australia arrived in the same mail that brought him an economic treatise from a friend entitled *The Fallacy of Saving*. Archer promptly acknowledged receipt of the treatise. "My dear Robertson," he wrote, "I am already completely convinced of the fallacy of saving, thank you."

The impression of puritanic rigidity he made on people was caused simply by the fact that in spite of his lifelong involvement with the stage he was "not a dramatic self-expressive person," and nobody could tell from his expression what he was thinking or feeling. Perhaps the amblyopic eye that saw nothing contributed to this impression of reserve which made him seem "a monster of insensibility" to those who did not know him intimately. But, also, "the reserve was real," a fact attributable, Shaw thought, to Archer's ultraseparatist Protestant ancestry: "Now of Separation there is no end until every human being is a Separate Church, for which there is much to be said." Archer was, in several respects, "separate," and he was, naturally, attracted to the "separativeness" of both Ibsen and Shaw, if not indeed to the spirit of independent inquiry that characterized the realistic movement in Europe.

Shaw proceeds at some length to describe the gangling Archer's marriage to a spirited little woman, who became a "new woman" and founded a "nerve training institution" in London, and his wonderfully playful friendship with his son Tom, later transferred, after Tom's death in the First World War, to the son's young widow—"and so, between daughter and son, the adventure of parentage never ended for Archer." Shaw sees the same gift of sympathy operative in Archer's nowadays much criticized translations on the grounds that "Archer understood and cared for Ibsen's imagination." Unimpressed by the latter's sociology, "undistracted by Ibsen's discussions," Archer "went straight for his poetry, and reproduced every stroke of imagination in a phraseology that invented itself *ad hoc* in his hands." And, finally, Shaw takes notice of the critic's far-flung journalistic activities that took him to the south of the United States, Mexico, and India as an observer of social and political conditions. For Archer the world did not begin and end with the theatre or even with imaginative literature. He may not have been particularly taken with Ibsen's sociological thinking, but his response to the new dramatic art of the 1880's was surely not unaffected by its concern with social realities. Archer's report on India, which hard-headedly resisted the romantic appeal of Hindu ritualism, was in keeping with his firm hold on reality, while his greatly esteemed "on the spot" investigation, in 1906, of the case of the Spanish radical educator, Francisco Ferrer, tortured and then shot by the Spanish military, attested to the liberal conscience that aligned Archer with the turn-of-the-century modernism. Shaw's tribute was as unfeigned as it was unstinted when he referred to him as "a friend of whom, after more than forty years, I have not a single unpleasant recollection," and added, "I still feel that when he went he took a piece of me with him."

That Archer's feelings for Shaw were equally warm is evident in the letter he wrote "My dear G.B.S." on December 17, 1924, just before submitting to an operation that proved fatal. He believed that his chances of recovery were pretty good. "Still, accidents will happen," and he considered it important the day before entering the hospital to say what he hoped Shaw didn't doubt, "that though I may sometimes have played the part of all-too-candid mentor, I have never wavered in my admiration and affection for you, or ceased to feel that Fate had treated me kindly in making me your contemporary and friend. I thank you from my heart for forty years of good comradeship."

The word "mentor" in the letter is doubly significant, in that Archer both helped Shaw with his early career and continually badgered him to write soundly constructed and character-based plays such as *Candida*. Their friendship began under interesting circumstances recalled by Archer long after. "In the winter of 1881–82 [for which read 1882–83], I used to go almost every day to the British Museum Reading Room in

London. I frequently sat next to a man of about my own age [26] who attracted my attention, partly by his peculiar coloring—his pallid skin and bright red hair and beard—partly by the odd combination of authors whom he used to study—for I saw him, day after day, poring over Karl Marx's *Das Kapital* and an orchestral score of Wagner's *Tristan und Isolde.*"[2] Early in 1884, Archer joined Edmund Yates's *World* as that London newspaper's drama critic and made his officially unemployed friend his colleague, starting Shaw on a brilliant journalistic career:

> The post of art-critic of the *World* fell vacant, and Edmund Yates asked me to undertake it. I told him I knew nothing about painting; he said that did not matter. I did the work laboriously and infamously for some weeks, until my conscience could endure it no longer. I then got Shaw to do a specimen article, which I sent to Yates, and thus easily secured him the post. He didn't know much more about painting than I, but he thought he did, and that was the main point. I had, as a matter of fact, already forced upon him a good deal of work as a reviewer of books. Then (some four years later) the post of musical critic fell vacant, and I secured it for Shaw by the simple process of telling Yates the truth: namely, that he was at once the most competent and the most brilliant writer on music then living in England.[3]

Nevertheless, as noted before, Archer remained the gadfly as well as the friend, disapproving so strongly of Shaw's dramatic skulduggery as to withdraw from collaboration in 1885 on a work which Shaw wrote alone some six years later under the title of *Widower's Houses*. It was the first of his plays and the first to be staged when the pioneering Independent Theatre of London presented it in 1892. Shaw thus embarked on his second and more important career as a playwright. Subsequently, the spirited friends exchanged views with heat and high spirit, Shaw in the position of playwright and Archer in that of critic and "all-too-candid mentor." One exchange has Shaw writing, "You are really the very blamedest dunderhead—explaining all the most exciting social phenomena of your times as mere aberrations of Shaw" (April 26, 1898). And Archer replies four days later:

> If you really want to "mow down" the critics, write a few more *Candidas*—that's the way to do it. Anyone can achieve the triumph of being misunderstood; it is only the bungler (sometimes, no doubt, a

---

[2] Charles Archer, *William Archer: Life, Work, and Friendships* (New Haven: Yale University Press, 1931), p. 119.
[3] *Ibid.*, p. 133.

bungler of genius) who makes a virtue of his limitations and pretends to aim at and rejoice in "mowing down" people. I ask for nothing better than to have it proved that my analysis of your limitations is wrong, imperfect, founded on insufficient or misread evidence. . . . But the evidenced want is good plays, not expositions of the excellence of your sociology. . . .

Nor would Shaw let the argument rest, writing:

Your *analysis* of my limitations! Why, you stupendous ass, you draw a line through my plays which represents your own limitations in your most fatuously lazy mood; and you then proceed to explain that everything outside that line is mere Shawism. . . , and everything inside is heaven-born genius. You are getting a great deal worse than Clement Scott; everything that is not a stagily sentimental *coup de théâtre* makes you simply petulant. . . .[4]

"It was my deliberate and unconsumable disregard of the rules of the art of play construction that revolted him," Shaw explained. "Archer did not agree with me that the form of drama perfected in the middle of the nineteenth century in the French theatre was essentially mechanistic and therefore incapable of producing vital drama." An intelligent observer, Shaw went on to say, was bound to realize that this dramatic style was "exhausted and, for the moment, sterile," but Archer "saw nothing fundamentally wrong with it. To the end of his life he considered it indispensable for sound playwriting, needing only an infusion of new ideas—needing only to be brought into a contact with life. . . ." Shaw held, on the contrary, that the plot-play or heavily "plotted" piece was of little worth. For him a play was "a vital growth and not a mechanical construction." A play should never indeed have a plot, because "if it has any natural life in it, it will construct itself; it will construct itself, like a flowering plant, far more wonderfully than its author can consciously construct it."[5]

Shaw, in brief, held an organic view of dramaturgy, if not indeed an improvisatory one to judge from many a wayward piece from the beginning of his career to his very last work, *Buoyant Millions,* written when he was in his nineties. Archer, who believed he could not remain a responsible critic or a reliable guide without rejecting this view, took the only sensible course of declaring that everything was allowable to genius, but that the proof of genius rested with the playwrights. In writing *Play-*

---

[4] *Ibid.,* pp. 243–44

[5] William Archer, *Three Plays: Martha Washington, Beatriz-Juana, Lidia* (New York: Henry Holt & Co., Inc., 1927), pp. xxix–xxx.

making he was willing to allow Shaw the genius liberties he was disinclined to extend to other playwrights. There can be no doubt that *Playmaking* does not satisfactorily treat "organic playwriting," the very nature of which would seem to defy formal discussion, for in so far as it is really organic it falls outside the province of craftsmanship. To write manuals about how to "feel" and how to be "inspired" would be ridiculous, and it would be no less absurd to offer instruction on how to bring about those "free" associations of thought, cadence, and imagery that have nothing to do with craftsmanship and apparently little to do with consciousness. The presumption would be instantly punished by exposure as sheer charlatanry.

In *Play-making,* Archer sensibly confined himself to matters susceptible of practical analysis and useful discussion. In giving so little attention to free-flowing playwriting, nevertheless, he did submit to an important limitation. His study gives no direct consideration to two significant types of organic playwriting, the Shavian type of discussion-drama or "play of ideas" and the Chekhovian "contrapuntal" play, also identified as "centrifugal" because its characters seem to fly away from each other and from involvement with a central problem. No more progressive approaches to modern dramaturgy have arisen within the bounds of realistic playwriting. No more rewarding ones either. To which Archer's reply might have been that works of this character are so uniquely associated with their authors that there is little point in discussing them in a manual. And until now, indeed, only Chekhov has succeeded in being Chekhov, only Shaw has succeeded in being Shaw.

"I classed constructed plays with artificial flowers, clockwork mice, and the like," wrote Shaw,[6] who did not perhaps look very closely at his own particular artifices. Archer, on the contrary, dealt with "constructed plays" exclusively, although he was resolute in his rejection of *contrived,* of implausible and unnatural, works. Archer might have also pointed out that many Shaw plays were actually "constructed," but *musically* rather than mechanically. In later years, Alfred Einstein likened Shaw's plays to Mozart's music, and Edmund Wilson, in the stimulating book *The Triple Thinkers,* noted the "theme with variations" structure of some of Shaw's discussion-pieces. A musical development indeed is conspicuous in the relentlessly discursive *Getting Married,* which proves to be engrossing without anything we may legitimately call "action," in *Back to Methuselah* and *Heartbreak House,* and in the superb *Don Juan in Hell* interlude of *Man and Superman.* Did not Shaw himself maintain that he learned his art

[6] *Ibid.,* p. xiv.

from "the masters of a universal language—Bach, Handel, Mozart, Beethoven, and Wagner." And musical structure is surely apparent, motif blending into motif, and mood following mood, in Chekhov's dramatic masterpieces, especially in *The Three Sisters*. On Chekhov's "delicate art of emotional orchestration" (William Gerhardi's apt description) there is also no comment in *Play-making*.

One should not perhaps blame Archer for failing to explain the inexplicable when even so close and admiring a student of Chekhov as Gerhardi can only write: "All the time he works on real life. But in his hands it becomes more than real life; and after Chekhov has done with it, it is still real life. What he has done with it we do not know, but it has become beautifully, strangely disturbing. . . ." Yet one cannot help regretting the absence of a larger perspective and finer sensibility in *Play-making*. If only Archer, the contemporary of both Shaw and Chekhov, had accredited an order of playwriting in which the music of ideas or the music of feelings creates its own order, it would be much less necessary to remind ourselves that there are more facets to dramatic art than those encompassed in the "manual."

III

Archer was also the contemporary of many a poetic playwright who employed imagery and verbal music dramatically. The names of Maeterlinck, Verhaeren, Hofmannsthal, D'Annunzio, Andreyev and, nearer to home, Yeats and Synge, come to mind. They need not have impressed Archer as much as Ibsen did, but among them there were surely several who deserved no less attention than he was willing to give to Pinero and Henry Arthur Jones. If only he had given some consideration to the use of "magic" and "suggestion" in the theatre, if only he had appreciated "symbolism." Surely even his beloved Ibsen could have drawn Archer's attention to poetic prose in playwriting with the symbolist plays of his last period. And if regrets are in order—and I think they are, if only out of regard for imaginativeness in dramatic art—we may also wonder at Archer's inattentiveness in *Play-making* to expressionist dramaturgy, fluid as dreams and as arbitrary with time and place. This dramatic style was already well marked in the late plays of Strindberg, *To Damascus, The Dream Play,* and *The Ghost Sonata,* all written between 1898 and 1907.

Expressionism, it is true, first came into prominence in Europe and America after the publication of *Play-making*. But the book having gone through many editions after 1912, its author could have taken sufficient notice of the new style, if he had cared to. Most of the noteworthy expressionist plays by Kaiser, Toller, and O'Neill (*The Emperor Jones* and *The Hairy Ape*) were already well known before Archer's death in 1924; and a scholar-critic such as Archer could be expected to take notice of Strindberg's experiments in dramatic form at the turn of the century instead of waiting for expressionism to become a newsworthy "movement." We know that Shaw had suggested to Archer that he translate Strindberg's plays by 1908. A postcard from Shaw to Archer, dated July 17, reports: "I achieved the impossible—a meeting with Strindberg—today. He said 'Archer is not in sympathy with me.' I said, 'Archer wasn't in sympathy with Ibsen either; but he couldn't help translating him all the same. . . .'" Nothing much came of this conversation, conducted half in French and half in German, and it was promptly terminated when Strindberg took out his watch and informed his guests, "At two o'clock I am going to be sick." The visitors, we are told, "accepted this delicate intimation, and withdrew." It is doubtful, in any case, that Archer could have brought himself to the point of translating a work like *The Dream Play*. Published in 1902, it was prefaced by "A Reminder" from the author which declares among other things that "Anything may happen" in this work imitative of dream-formation; that in it "imagination designs and embroiders novel patterns: a medley of memories, experiences, free fancy, absurdities, and improvisations"; that "the characters split, double, multiply, vanish, solidify, blur, clarify."

It is to be regretted, finally, that Archer, who was averse to traditional literary drama, on the one hand, did not, on the other, take into account the new theatricalist view of theatre, "the theatre theatrical," growing up under Gordon Craig's apostolate in England and, under the leadership of Copeau, Reinhardt, Meyerhold and other stage directors, in France, Germany, and Russia. We may say in his defense that he was hardly the man to wax enthusiastic about retheatricalizing the theatre after having given earnest support to efforts to detheatricalize it for the sake of "true-to-life," plausible and convincing, dramatic art. It would seem then that *Playmaking* is not an ideal handbook to put into the hands of contemporary enthusiasts of Cocteau, Giraudoux, and Anouilh (or, for that matter, Brecht), unless it be considered very much the ideal book because Archer's limitations were also his strength. We can count on help from him precisely because he remains fixed in the firm, if narrow, ground of essential dramaturgy which puts out no frills of "style." This is not to say that there is no need for a new *Ars Poetica* in the theatre, for there is. But although Archer was not the man to have written it at any time (and up to this writing, curiously, no one else has proved to be that man), we can be certain that it will need *Play-making* for its basis.

The problem of sustaining interest to which Archer gave great weight will never be less than primary in all writing for the theatre. The plausibility and conviction he set up as goals for modern playwriting cannot be neglected without peril even by writers of a fanciful and theatrical bent. Much of the failure of postrealistic experimentation in playwriting, much of the effect of confusion or triviality, may be traced to neglect of the essential elements of dramatic communication. Archer was preoccupied with these. His emphasis on the drama as the art of crises, which he elaborated with exemplary vigor (although at the precarious sacrifice of Brunetière's famous stress on drama as a clash of human wills), may not be safely minimized except in the case of short mood-pieces. If playwriting is often tepid in any style, whether realistic or nonrealistic, the chief reason is failure to present characters in states of crisis our intelligence can recognize as significant. Dramatic writing in our time has frequently amounted to the proverbial tempest in the teapot, and this without the justification of farce, in which the disproportion between cause and effect, or between ends and means, produces hilarity. And Archer's only slightly vulnerable concept of the "obligatory scene," the big scene the audience has been led to expect or desire, should prove equally useful to playwrights regardless of age and experience. It can only serve as a corrective to a vast quantity of slipshod writing by playwrights whose main occupation appears to be that of escaping from the consequence of their observation or from the logical conclusions of their argument.

Archer's bias in favor of characterization—he cannot write two consecutive sentences without making it evident—is apt to put both "theatricalists" and political propagandists out of countenance. They are disposed to subordinate multidimensional humanity to either theatrical or ideological uses; Archer feels a sturdy, old-fashioned preference for characters as against puppets, and he is often justified. If genius or great talent can occasionally dispense with characters in favor of "types" or of symbolic figures, we may be sure that usually the void we sense in unsatisfactory plays is the place that should have been occupied by a representative specimen of humanity.

We can only be grateful, finally, that Archer was old-fashioned enough to stress construction in the drama. If Shaw believed he got along without it, it is certain that most playwrights cannot. Should their plays occasionally succeed on the stage, we may be sure that somebody else—the stage director undoubtedly—organized their chaos for them. Usually, however, anyone who looks closely at seemingly "unconstructed" plays of merit—whether a Chekhov drama or a seemingly casual *My Heart's in the Highlands, Glass Menagerie,* or *Member of the Wedding*—will discover "structure" in them. We are apt to find in them a coherence of parts, from a beginning, to a middle, to an end or "resolution," as in any good conventionally written drama. Each part is merely likely to be less marked and separate, the scaffolding less conspicuous, the skeleton less obtrusive.

Sometimes a connection or transition may be lacking. Sometimes it is deliberately omitted, as in the case of a scene between the young heroine of *The Member of the Wedding* and a young soldier which was dropped from the play during the pre-Broadway tryout. In such instances an imaginative leap is required of the audience, and a properly prepared audience will make that leap willingly and well. Otherwise a movement of minor crises toward a cumulative central crisis of maximum intensity we call the climax characterizes both unconventionally and conventionally composed plays. It is merely a question of our acquiring sufficient insight into the play and possessing sufficient sense of theatre to be able to see the construction, although this does not at all mean that we can count on success for a play simply because it has discernible "structure." One distinction does always have to be made: it is the difference between "construction" and "contrivance"—that is, an implausible manipulation of events and people—in plays. And Archer makes that distinction altogether plain.

It needs only to be qualified in one respect. We must observe, specifically, that "contrivance" is relative to the style of the dramatic work and to the basic assumptions of the form. The development or incident we consider flagrantly artificial when it appears in a realistic play will be accepted as perfectly natural in a Greek play composed of alternating choral recitations and dramatic episodes, in an Elizabethan drama studded with soliloquies and asides, in a modern lyrical tragedy such as Lorca's *Blood Wedding* or *Yerma*. Which does not, however, mean that we are obliged to find plausibility in the heroine Yerma's extreme action in killing the husband who refuses to give her a child. We will accept the formal characteristics of the play without difficulty, but our acceptance or rejection of a human action will be determined by our knowledge of human conduct and our understanding of people. We judge formal details by the formal character of a work, but we judge characters by life. ("And let there be no mistake about this," I am tempted to say to art-intoxicated novices of the craft.) To return to "contrivance," what remains to be stressed is our readiness in the theatre to suspend or even scrap realistic requirements. The most derogatory comment I was wont to hear in councils of the early Theatre Guild was that a play was "contrived." To charge a realistically designed play with contrivance was tantamount to dismissing it from serious consideration. This did not, however, deter the same organization from staging such arbitrarily constructed expressionistic pieces as Kaiser's

From Morn to Midnight and Toller's *Masse-Mensch,* or *Man and the Masses.*

Archer's *Play-making,* we may conclude, is especially valuable in a period of unstable dramatic art, amidst inchoate strivings for new dramatic forms and for poetic drama in general. His chapters are useful precisely because he gave prominence to essential requirements we may designate as the classic ones. He will not allow us to be fobbed off with empty decorative graces and rhetorical pomp, whether in prose or verse. He demanded *drama* of the dramatic medium—not fiction, not poetry, not disquisition, not histrionic display, but simply drama. He expected playwrights to be capable of holding audiences instead of readers or students in the lecture hall. He wanted dramatic *order* from playwriting rather than mere displays of sensibility. He acknowledged the special nature of the art of drama and considered the specific means of attaining the concentration and impact proper to its nature. No one is likely to describe *Play-making* as an agreeable *causerie,* and Archer did not go out of his way to make himself ingratiating when he so plainly set out to be instructive.

That he is not, at the same time, outdatedly pedantic in touching upon such matters as probability, chance, coincidence, foreshadowing, climax, and anti-climax is evident from the fact that later-written books have rarely been less sparing of this kind of detail. Even so informal a writer as John Van Druten in his *Playwright at Work,* published some forty years later, is replete with practical tips on drawing up a scenario, dividing the play into acts of varying length (the first act to amount to no less than 30 and no more than 48 pages of dialogue!), avoiding extensive meals and large parties onstage, allowing time for changes of costume, using stage-time as against real time, writing time-cover lines or scenes, treating weather, and the like. Archer, in spite of his old-fashioned defense of *The Second Mrs. Tanqueray* and concern with many a deservedly forgotten play, occupied a position in 1912 not outdated by Van Druten in 1953 when the latter wrote that "I also want, nowadays, to be sure that the well-made play is something more than just well-made" (Archer wanted that, too) while asserting that "an acquaintance with the older rules of the well-made play is still a good basis for learning how to break them."[7]

Organic playwriting is still only the exception. It is so exceptional that a man with Van Druten's extensive theatrical experience could still consider such free-flowing pieces as *The Member of the Wedding* and

[7] John Van Druten, *Playwright at Work* (New York: Harper & Brothers, 1953), pp. 66–67.

The Glass Menagerie "forerunners" of a new art of playwriting.[8] Van
Druten might have added his own dramatization of Isherwood's Berlin
stories, *I Am a Camera,* as an example and a critic could observe in *I Am
a Camera* the same fragmentariness that Van Druten noted in *The Member of the Wedding* in calling attention to the lack of two obligatory
scenes. He objected to the relegation of two potentially vital scenes to a
shadowy off-stage existence—little Frankie's unsuccessful proposal to her
brother and his bride that she be allowed to join them on their honeymoon and her meeting with a soldier in a hotel lobby after her disappointment caused her to run away from home. Van Druten, while appreciating
Carson McCullers' preference for mood rather than plot, declares, "The
purpose of her play to some extent absolves her from blame though not, I
think, altogether." He correctly observes, however, that although he has
said something here and there that Archer would not have said because
"the plays were not there to say it from," he has gone only a little way
further than Archer: "I am still in the modern realistic theatre, and we are
still guided by its rules, even if we have stretched them a little."

Van Druten is still bound, as most contemporary playwrights are, by
the conventions of the imaginary fourth wall between the actor on stage
and the spectator in the auditorium, still bound by the necessity of maintaining the pretense "that the play is really happening somewhere." The
promise of expressionism as an alternative to realism faded rapidly,
the theatrical stylization with which Thornton Wilder broke through the
fourth wall brought a new way only for Wilder, and Van Druten doubts
that modern verse drama will be the door to a vital new dramaturgy. He
has seen that door tried too often before. He even begins to worry when
he hears critics clamoring for "a poetic approach" or for so-called heightened speech; "deliberately aspired to," it is likely to sound forced and
pretentious. "Beauty will not be caught that way," he believes, and he
wonders whether she will be caught in playwriting by anything but the
freshness of a playwright's sense of wonder. Nor was Van Druten, who
had much experience in staging as well as writing plays, content to let the
scene designer and the lighting specialist do the work of the playwright.
The nonverbal addition of "poetry of the theatre," *poésie de théâtre,* however welcome when appropriate, only begged the question of poetic playwriting. He placed greater reliance on language, calling attention to the
unpretentious beauty of the servant Berenice's speech in *The Member of
the Wedding* as she recalls the sad month in which her nephew Honey
was killed and the little boy John Henry died suddenly of meningitis:

[8] *Ibid.,* pp. 181–83.

"The most beautiful September I have seen. Countless white and yellow butterflies flying around the autumn flowers—Honey dead and John Henry suffering like he did—and daisies, golden weather, butterflies—such strange death weather."

John Van Druten may have been too pessimistic about the possibilities of nonrealistic experimentation in our own time just as Archer appears to have been too apathetic toward it in his, as if the strenuous struggle for realism in his nineteenth-century youth had been cause enough for him. But Van Druten was by no means alone in believing that realism has not been supplanted or transcended as the dominant style. It will be noted, for example, that the master of experimentation with masks, soliloquies, and expressionistic distortion, O'Neill, returned to realistic style in his last plays; and that the return to realism actually increased his stature *half a century* after the birth of the symbolist and expressionist styles of theatre in Europe. The most inspired poetic playwright of the second quarter of our century, Federico García Lorca, abandoned lyric tragedy after having written *Blood Wedding* and *Yerma*. He turned chiefly to domestic realism in his last work *The House of Bernarda Alba*. Sean O'Casey's experiments in dramatic stylization for the past three decades have not enabled him to excel the achievement of his naturalistic dramas *Juno and the Paycock* and *The Plough and the Stars*. And the strength of many younger writers here and abroad—one thinks of John Osborne, Jean Genet, William Inge, Arthur Miller, and Tennessee Williams—has lain in the realism, if not indeed naturalism, of their writing. We have been provided with noteworthy exemptions from realistic style by Wilder, Cocteau, Giraudoux, Anouilh, Brecht, Beckett, and Ionesco, yet their imaginative writing has not propelled the theatre as a whole into new directions. For better or worse, Archer still addresses majority practice in playwriting, and *Play-making,* except for its author's reliance on late-Victorian examples, remains a viable work.

IV

Close examination of the book will reveal the reasons for its continued vitality as well as moderate the stuffed-shirt impression affectionately disseminated by Shaw. A new reading could even mollify the Young Turks of criticism. The lucidity with which Archer wrote *Play-making* makes an attempt at detailed summary superfluous. But we may observe that intrinsically it is the author's humanistic outlook combined with flexibility and common sense that keeps the book alive today. Thus, he makes short shrift of closet drama with the assertion that only in relation to an audience does the drama have any meaning. He respects "theme" in plays and he agrees that it is possible, at a pinch, to assign one to every acceptable play. Yet he does not fanatically insist on one in every instance, observing that no theme expressible in abstract terms appears to have been present to the author's mind in the case of a number of successfully realized plays. He urges the importance of plot as much as Aristotle did, but doubts that it is the noblest element, "or that by which the value of a piece should be measured." And the puritan in Archer speaks out along with the humanist in maintaining that the action in a play should exist "for the sake of characters"; that "when the relation is reversed" the play may be "an ingenious toy, but scarcely a vital work of art"—at which advocates of many an *avant-garde* play from Jarry's *Ubu Roi* to Beckett's *Endgame* might well wince.

Unintimidated by the literary repute of verse drama from Elizabethan times to his own, Archer can declare flatly that whatever principles of conceiving and constructing a play apply to prose drama "apply with equal cogency to the poetic drama." He concedes only that soliloquies are "more acceptable" in verse drama than in prose, although it does not follow that the prospect of encountering a soliloquy anywhere entrances him. He favors active drama, but is dubious about the highly touted value of "suspense" ("our pleasure," he declares, "consists of a delicate blending of surprise with realized anticipation"), and is unwilling to require "conflict" at all costs from plays; some, he finds, get along well enough without a standup battle of wills as predicated in Brunetière's famous "Law of the Drama" (he might have cited *The Cherry Orchard* with better justification than the *Agamemnon*), provided the pivot of the play is a crisis. He may go all out for plot movement in the drama, taking special pains to stress "the joining of the issue" or "firing of the fuse" and the "obligatory scene," but is willing to grant success to plays that paint an environment primarily. Archer is even content to let the story stand still for a while if some phase of life is sufficiently absorbing. He also assents to the growing acceptance of quiet, indecisive endings. He favors naturalness in modern drama, although he admits that realism has imposed on its writers all sorts of hampering reticences.

It is well known that Archer goes into the problems of plot-making and allows himself no fanfares about the "eternal soul of the theatre" approachable only by "inspiration." Yet he can state unequivocally that the best plot is the plot that chooses the writer instead of being chosen by him. "Tension," that important element in playwriting, is by no means a mechanical effect for Archer, but "a stretching out, a stretching forward, of the mind." And there are in good plays "minor rhythms of tension and resolution like the harmonic vibration of a violin string" just as a play is "a great crisis worked out through a series of minor crises." It is a continuous vibration of increasingly intensified life rather than one grand histrionic stretching of the nerves and violent explosion. He is for order in the drama, but not for that arbitrarily forced arrangement of effects that is the mark of the "well-made play" school with which he has been identified. He finds merit, moreover, not only in tension, but in a suspension of tension; and not only in dramatic movement, but in the retardation of movement that produces a *rallentando* effect. But for this, he remarks sensibly, "our drama would have to be all bone and muscle, like the figures in an anatomical text-book."

There is patently a place in Archer's esthetics for the current of life with its accidents and divagations. And if he is, nevertheless, concerned with "the art of construction," a deceptive term I should like to see replaced by "the art of movement," what he means by it amounts to an eminently reasonable requirement whether the author has written in verse or prose, and whether or not he has used choruses, soliloquies, and flashback scenes. At bottom, Archer is not the mechanist he has been taken for. In his opinion, the art of dramatic construction consists "first, in giving the mind of an audience something to which to stretch forward, and secondly, in not letting it feel that it has stretched forward in vain." It is well to remember this definition, which is tantamount to a statement of principle, when we begin to weary of Archer's dutifully set forth technical considerations in the second half of his book.

Even there, however, we may have our patience rewarded with elucidations interesting in themselves, despite the occasional fussiness of the author, as well as potentially useful. In truth, he became fussy much earlier, though at the same time rewarding. I find this to be the case at the start of Book II when he discusses "the point of attack" and describes the two main ways of beginning a play—either at the start of the crisis, as in *Othello,* and *King Lear,* or at the beginning of the catastrophe, as in *Oedipus the King* and *Ghosts.* As he goes deeper into the labyrinth of dramatic technique he becomes vexatiously nice. In the beginning part of a play we should have "foreshadowing, without forestalling"; in the middle part, "expectation mingled with uncertainty," climaxed by one of several kinds of *scènes à faire,* or "obligatory scenes": "thematic," "dramatic," "structural," "psychological," "historic." And in discussing the end of a play Archer harasses us somewhat with observations on "climax and anti-climax" and modern endings that may look "affectedly unaffected, artificially inartificial."

Nevertheless, there is usually matter in Archer's mannerism. His explanation of the meaning of "character development," for example, may well be indispensable to bedevilled playwrights: By "development" of character, says Archer, we actually mean a "bringing out" of character comparable to "developing" a roll of film. Development means "not change but, rather, unveiling, disclosure." Nor are his observations on the modern obsession with "psychology," rather than "simple character drawing," less essential. I know he has my gratitude for the reminder that "character drawing," which gave us Falstaff among the cherished characters of world literature, is not necessarily inferior to "psychology," which has given us Strindberg's Miss Julie and Tennessee Williams' Blanche Du Bois. "The character-drawer's appeal to common knowledge and instant recognition" may be more than sufficient. At the same time, Archer does not deprecate "psychology" and goes so far as to declare that, in many plays, "Ibsen is a psychologist, or he is nothing,"—which takes Archer far indeed from Shaw's position in *The Quintessence of Ibsenism* that in Ibsen's plays it is the "ideas" that matter most. Who was the better judge in this case may be left to the judgment of the present-day reader.

And, curiously, the fussier he becomes the more liberties he extends to the post-Victorian playwright, the more he recognizes possibilities excluded by "well-made play" practice and conventional realism. Thus, he criticizes problem-play writers such as Hervieu and Brieux for their conception of dramatic art "in which the free rhythms of life are ruthlessly sacrificed to the needs of a demonstration." Thus, too, he is not only willing to accept nonrealistic methods of mirroring action through narration as in the Cassandra-Chorus scenes of the *Agamemnon,* but he adds that he is "much inclined to think that the dramatic effect of highly emotional narrative is underrated in the modern theatre." He also acknowledges "the difficulty of deciding that any form of scene is predestined by the laws of dramatic effect." Although making much of the value of "reversals of fortune" in plays and noting that "peripeties" are apt to be "great scenes," he does not hesitate to assert that there are admirable plays in which it is impossible to discover a distinct reversal. And although he fusses a good deal about the importance of probability and plausibility, he observes that there are plays (by Shakespeare, Maeterlinck, Barrie) in which the charm lies in "pleasant departures from probability."

Even in the formidable sections of *Play-making,* then, there is no want of evidence that, for all his partiality for Pinero and reserve concerning Shaw, Archer is anything but fixed in his realistic bias. The sense of humor Shaw applauded in his friend appears in the midst of a bumper crop of soberly monitory practical advice. On the question of concluding a play with a death, he admonishes the student-playwright, "Be sure you are an Ibsen before you kill your Hedwig," and he reminds novices that "A broken heart is no longer held to be necessarily fatal." He knows, too, when to stop giving advice. He observes that "the power to observe, to penetrate, and to reproduce character can neither be acquired nor regulated by theoretical recommendations." He concludes that "specific directions for character-drawing would be like rules for becoming six-feet-high."

For all the intricacies of his exposition, then, Archer understood what sooner or later we all come to realize in dealing with dramatic art: You can teach only those who already know.

V

Another way of testing Archer's views on "play-making"—we suspect the mechanical term in view of the above-given quotations and his colloquially put dictum "Either you have it in you, or you have it not"—is to inquire what others coming after him have been able to add. The inquiry, since the literature on playwriting has mounted exceedingly since 1912, would probably burst the already overstrained seams of this essay without attaining an impressive result. There have been *some* additions, the most successful being Kenneth Rowe's, as well as Macgowan's and Marian Gallaway's, stress on the need for *complications* in a play to ensure dramatic progress. The least successful addendum is probably his American friend Clayton Hamilton's attempt to displace both Brunetière's *will* and Archer's *crisis* with "contrast" as the common dynamic element in drama. George Pierce Baker's *Dramatic Technique,* of 1919 vintage, is the next classic treatise in English after Archer's, and Professor Baker's illustration of the condensed power of dialogue is especially valuable. One recalls specifically Baker's comparison of the early and the final drafts of Nora's "recognition scene" to show how a simple change in her egotistical husband's speech from "We are saved" to "I am saved" was decisive to dramatic development in *A Doll's House.* John Galsworthy's essay "Some Platitudes Concerning Drama," published in the same year as Archer's book, remains a provocative brief statement delivered from the lectern of the British naturalistic school. One sentence may well be the classical statement of that school on the subject of sustaining an "illusion of reality" on the stage: "The aim of a dramatist . . . is evidently to create such an illusion of actual life passing on the stage as to compel the spectator to pass through an experience of his own, to think and talk and move with the people he sees thinking, talking, and moving."

Reacting against marketable melodrama, Galsworthy, moreover, contradicted Aristotelian critics by awarding primacy to character rather than plot. Although guilty of loose thinking when he wrote that "character is the best plot there is," he achieved clarity in defining a good plot as "that sure edifice which rises out of the interplay of circumstance on temperament, or of temperament on circumstance." I have been partial, too, to various other points made by friends and colleagues such as John Van Druten, Samson Raphaelson, Kenneth Macgowan, Samuel Selden, Marian Gallaway, Arthur Hopkins, Maxwell Anderson, Alan Reynolds Thompson, Lajos Egri, and John Howard Lawson. I believe that the latter's refutation of Archer's rejection of "conflict" as the pivot of a play is an especially invigorating piece of criticism. And there is much to be said for Granville-Barker's terse reminder, in his 1930 Cambridge lectures *On Dramatic Method,* that playwriting is importantly linked to theatrical convention. Yet, with the exception of specifically Hegelian and Marxist theory from Hebbel to Lawson and Brecht, I cannot recall anything of importance that is not either explicit or implicit in Archer's book.

What needs to be added to *Play-making* to encompass developments since Archer's time is of course a legitimate question. We could, no doubt, use penetrating criticism of the "well-made play," a nineteenth-century product still current in the mid-twentieth, although Archer was well on the way to dismissing it in declaring that "the trouble with the well-made play is that it is nearly always, and of necessity, ill-made." Experience led him to observe that the pattern of intrigue in this type of otherwise efficient drama is so involved that "the mind's eye cannot follow it," and he opined that the public is more likely to notice the skill of the playwright than the substance of the play.

Undoubtedly it would be pleasant to be able to supplement the text of *Play-making* with a sympathetic chapter on poetic drama, especially verse drama, to which T. S. Eliot and other men of letters have brought much thought. And such a chapter would have to be supplied by a radically different temperament than Archer's; there is no possibility of ignoring the fact that Archer was antipoetic, even if it is possible to appreciate his impatience with artificial efforts to beautify the drama and his contempt for pinchbeck dramatic literature whether imitative of Elizabethan poetic drama or Restoration drama of wit.

Most men of letters in England would have hesitated long before ceasing to genuflect before fine literature, but Archer made himself vulnerable to the charge of a philistine bias with his plain-speaking on the subject of poetry. And criticism of his views was surely made inevitable by the fact that modern prose drama tended to become a desiccated, bloodless and colorless thing, already evoking Synge's celebrated protest a year or so before the appearance of *Play-making,* that "on the stage one must have reality and one must have joy" and that a good play should consist of speech "as fully flavored as a nut or apple." But what would we wish to amend in Archer's treatment of dialogue? His declaration that English verse drama from 1700 to 1900 was a dreary failure and that the worship of the minor Elizabethans was deleterious? The same opinions were expressed no less forcefully by his friend, the arch-enemy of philistinism, Bernard Shaw, who referred to John Webster as a "Tussaud laureate." Shall we take exception to Archer's contention that the use of blank verse had ceased to have any value for the theatre, that "for the mere rhetorical 'elevation' of blank verse we have no use whatever"? T. S. Eliot, who proposed a revival of verse drama less than a quarter of a century later, adopted the same view.

Who, besides, can object to Archer's exclamation, "Better no style at all than style thus plastered on"? Insofar as he rejected the substitution of rhetoric for drama, he was only repeating an ancient complaint. Rossini made it constantly when he used to tell a poor librettist, "You have given me verses but you haven't given me situations"—*Tu mi hai data versi, ma non sitzuandi.* Nor could Archer have been in disagreement with Synge when he himself said so plainly that "Style, in prose drama, is the sifting of common speech" and concluded that the idea that poetry of drama is to be sought specifically in verse had been exploded by Maeterlinck and Synge. Even his objection to resorting to soliloquy as a dramaturgical crutch would receive hearty endorsement from anyone familiar with the absurdities of nineteenth-century melodrama. Only a certain coolness toward manifestations of ecstasy and spirituality on the part of a confirmed rationalist shows Archer to be wary of poetry as the highroad to modern dramatic art, and it is significant, in fact, that many a poetic dramatist (one thinks of Claudel, Eliot, and Fry) has had a penchant for religion. Leonardo da Vinci declared that "Every good artist has two subjects: Man and the hopes of his soul." Archer had only one subject, Man.

It would seem that an amendment of Archer must rest on foundations more solid than a watery-eyed defense of the fair maid Poetry against a starched-collar ogre named Archer. The basis for a revision rests, rather, in Alexander Bakshy's point (expressed in *The Theatre Unbound,* a work published less than a dozen years after the appearance of *Play-making*) that there are actually two types of theatre, the "representational" and the "presentational." The former, historically a latecomer, since dramatic realism did not take hold until about the middle of the last century, should not be allowed to preempt the entire world of the theatre. A niggling "fourth-wall" convention of stage illusion did not exist during the centuries that produced Aeschylus and Sophocles, Marlowe and Shakespeare, Molière and Racine, Goethe and Schiller. And in "presentational" theatre, the imagination which invents and orders scenes in time and space can be as unbound and varied as the poetic spirit.

By their fruits, finally, shall ye know them. A play is good or bad not because of its observance of this or that theatrical convention, but because it commends itself to us by the quality of its sympathies and antipathies, by its wit or its passion, and by its illuminations. Archer cared for truth even if he did not care for "presentational" drama. *We* care, if our theatre is not to be unnecessarily cramped or defensively given over to musical entertainments, which by their very nature are always "presentational." (Even antiromantic musicals filled with sordid detail such as *Pal Joey* and *The Threepenny Opera* are not actually "representational" in style.) The point to bear in mind is that Archer, involved with revolutionary late-nineteenth-century realism, had discovered "representationalism," while we have had to *rediscover* "presentationalism." He was aided in making his discovery by such leaders of the modern theatre as Ibsen, Antoine, Hauptmann, and even Pinero and Henry Arthur Jones. We have been aided in our discovery by such leaders of the modernistic theatre as Strindberg, Cocteau, Jouvet, Wilder, and Brecht. He had his lessons to learn, we have ours. But in learning ours we would do well to assimilate his. Isolated miracles *can* happen in art; now and then, the grace of God does descend upon us, the jongleurs and innocents of the world of play. But, in all reason, we should not expect to achieve a vital kind of drama without regard for truth, grasp of character, sense of crisis, and attention to dramatic progression. It is better to put some trust in "Archer" rather than in theatrical airs and airy pretensions. I would merely add, at the same time, Shaw's half-truth that nothing succeeds like excess. A plodding approach by the playwright will beget a plodding play. *"On trouve d'abord, on cherche après"*—there is much truth in the axiom that one finds first and searches afterward.

Bibliographical Note

Archer was a prolific writer on a variety of subjects. His writings on the theatre include the following books: *English Dramatists of Today* (1882), *Henry Irving, Actor and Manager: A Critical Study* (1883), *About the Theatre: Essays and Studies* (1886), *Masks or Faces? A Study in the Psychology of Acting* (1888), *William Charles Macready* (1890–91), *Study and Stage: A Yearbook of Criticism* (1899), *A National Theatre: Scheme and Estimates* (with H. Granville-Barker, 1907), *Playmaking* (1912), and *The Old Drama and the New: An Essay in Revaluation* (1923). Two volumes of his plays were also published: *The Green Goddess* (1921) and *Three Plays: Martha Washington, Beatriz-Juana, Lidia* (1927).

Archer, like his colleague Shaw and other contemporary British men-of-letters, also wrote extensively on social, educational, and political issues, traveling far and doing patient research on journalistic assignments. Among his books and pamphlets were *America Today: Observations and Reflections* (1900), *Let Youth But Know: A Plea for Reason in Education* (1905), *Thro' Afro-America: An English Reading of the Race Problem* (1910), a temperate study of racial tensions in the South, *The Life, Trial, and Death of Francisco Ferrer* (1910), a vindication of the Spanish progressive educator and philosophical anarchist, which won the admiration of Shaw and Pinero, and *The Great Analysis: A Plea for a Rational World-Order* (1912), published anonymously with a Preface by Gilbert Murray.

Posthumously published, in addition to *Three Plays* (1927), were *William Archer as Rationalist: A Collection of His Heterodox Writings* (1921) and *The Religion of To-Morrow: Correspondence between W. Archer and H. H. Powers* (1925), a seventy two-page pamphlet. Like many distinguished Victorians, Archer was much concerned with religion, toward which he took a strictly rationalistic, "Liberal," view, and he entertained a high opinion and optimistic view of science. In his brother Lieutenant-Colonel Charles Archer's biography, *William Archer: Life, Work, and Friendships* (New Haven, Yale University Press, 1931) will be found a fragment of verse he scribbled in pencil on the night before his fatal operation. He is grateful to the discoverers of anesthetics or "balsams anodyne" for reducing the amount of pain in the world and anything but complimentary to the Deity for the long postponement of the discovery:

> My brother-men I praise, those men divine
> Who fought with Pain and hurled it back to Hell,
> From Nature wrung her balsams anodyne
> And told the secrets God forgot to tell.

And he is even more grateful to the intellectual leaders who liberated him from the "spiritual bugbears" that haunted men and made them cower beneath "a fancied curse" as they approached Death:

> If I with brow serene can face to-night
>   The Great Perhaps, whose praise shall be my theme?
> The men's, God wot, who said: "Let there be Light!"
>   Where God left Ignorance and Fear supreme . . .

But Archer was a man of his times rather than a profound religious philosopher. Even in dramatic criticism he was not usually to be found among those who develop timeless perspectives. His judgment was distinctly time-conditioned and he would not have wanted it to be otherwise. His evaluations of the theatre of his day were mainly relativistic, if not indeed opportunistic. He leaned backward to praise and encourage even glimmerings of merit: "The worst sort of criticism," he declared at a Club dinner in 1902, "is sterilizing criticism." I would rather see columns of fatuous gush about a foolish play, than a brilliant but discouragaging and sterilizing criticism of a play with any germs of good in it." This helps to explain why Shaw outdistanced him as a critic. Archer did not quite appreciate the helpfulness of destructive criticism, and he was bent upon being helpful above all else. And if Shaw's description of him as a man endowed with a sense of humor is accepted as correct, though exaggerated, it is equally true that he kept his humor in check; for he had a strong sense of duty and felt obliged by his position as an influential drama critic to be "serious." Since a new generation, impatient with the work of the old, is usually several steps ahead of an "encouraging" and "constructive" critic, Archer's reputation in dramatic criticism started declining even before his death while Shaw's "discouraging" and "destructive" criticism, written back in the 1890's, has continued to gain admirers.

PLAYWRIGHTS AND PLAYWRITING*

I

It is no secret to anyone familiar with the theatre that modern playwrights have been a self-conscious breed. Anyone whose wares are so conspicuously on display and make such excellent targets for critical marksmanship is bound to be self-conscious. Modern playwriting, moreover, came into being during the latter half of the nineteenth century when intellectual conflict was making itself felt in the theatre and writers were even becoming oracular. Old dispensations in the arts were being challenged; new dispensations were being explained and defended. The age of literary criticism was moving toward high noon. Critics were becoming playwrights, play producers, or stage directors; and it followed that the playwright could turn critic if the critic could turn playwright. Imbued with new intellectualism and estheticism, showmanship itself—once a simple, if not indeed simple-minded, activity—began to buzz with theories supplied by scenic artists such as Appia and Craig and directors such as Antoine and Stanislavsky. Objectives were constantly affirmed or revised in a theatrical world from which improvisation and intellectual innocence had departed while ideas and ideologies multiplied. The modern theatre, it would seem, was born with a program, and it will probably end with one.

From the abundant literature on the modern drama written by the playwrights themselves, Toby Cole has compiled a volume rich in matter and provocative in manner. To read the discourse of intelligent writers on their principles and problems is to observe the modern drama in the making. We merely allow for the fact that there is always a breach between ambition and attainment, and especially so in an art so utterly dependent upon stage production and the intervention of the actor. The danger of succumbing to "the intentional fallacy" need not deter us from attending to the playwrights' objectives once it is understood that we shall judge the play rather than the authors' intentions. It is not likely, moreover, that their pronouncements will make bigoted converts of us and limit our horizons or so bewilder us with their variety as to make us incapable of judgment. We live in an eclectic age, are unlikely to be

* Introduction to *Playwrights on Playwriting,* ed. by Toby Cole (New York: Hill and Wang, 1961).

seduced into exclusive dramatic theory, and have been inured to contradictions.

Fortunately, too, the playwrights afford a relatively simple perspective. We find them engaged to two kinds of theatre—the *modern* and the *modernistic*. The first sought realism of content, style, and form; the second aspired toward poetic and imaginative art. The first began to expel romantic and pseudorealistic drama from the theatre by the 1870's, the second to challenge, modify, and supplant realism by the 1890's. But romantic drama was never conclusively routed by the realists, and realistic drama has not been substantially displaced by neoromanticists, symbolists, expressionists, and other proponents of poetic or imaginative drama. Styles of dramatic composition have jostled each other and contracted marriages throughout our century.

It is surely true, besides, that realism is as much a "style" as any nonrealistic fashion of playwriting. Style in the latter case is merely so conspicuous as to give an impression of stylization, whereas style in realism is concealed to such a degree as to afford the illusion of naturalness. We are concerned with theatrical reality whether we erect or banish an imaginary "fourth wall" between the actor and the audience. The realists endeavored to make the theatre less theatrical after it had been meretriciously "theatricalized," while their usually younger opponents, the antirealists, wanted to make the theatre more theatrical after it had been "detheatricalized." The culprits in the first instance had been mediocre romanticists *and* show-business operators; the culprits in the second instance, mediocre realists *and* show-business operators. Whether distinguished playwrights spoke for or against realism, then, they were equally aiming for distinguished theatre.

It does not of course follow that they were invariably successful, or that they were superior to error in their respective procedures. Scientism trapped naturalists and partiality for the commonplace mired realists, while an overfondness for subjectivity made symbolists turn poetry into mist and expressionists transform dreams into nightmares. It follows only that we do not have to take irreversible sides in an ideological war when different playwrights offer conflicting opinions or programs. The playwrights themselves set us an example: Maeterlinck, for instance, acclaims Ibsen as a great symbolist writer while Shaw honors him as the supreme dramatist of ideas. Synge avows himself the enemy of Ibsen and Zola whereas he could have convincingly contended that he was making it possible for creative realism to thrive in Ireland. O'Neill is at one point convinced that naturalism is insolvent but is not deterred from composing naturalistic tragedy in *Desire Under the Elms* or from bringing his latter-day career to a climax with *The Iceman Cometh* and *Long Day's Journey into Night*. Most of the important modern playwrights, from Ibsen and Strindberg to O'Neill and O'Casey, did not actually make exclusive commitments to any philosophy or style of theatre, although they sometimes wrote as if they were making them.

In reading *Playwrights on Playwriting* it is well to realize that the authors' most fervent generalizations usually proclaim a departure from convention that may no longer seem necessary or urgent. To appreciate the force of their pronouncements we should possess some knowledge of the practices they rejected; or else we should be capable of imaginatively identifying these practices, which current malpractice or the insidious return of discredited practices (humdrum realism, pretentious symbolism, or morbid expressionism) will make discouragingly easy. Thus Shaw had a certain vapid kind of contrived playwriting in mind when he struck at "Sardoodledom," and Strindberg was not tilting at a paper dragon when he fought for multidimensional characterization. In his polemical essays he had in mind the nineteenth-century practice, present alike in Boucicault's plays and Dickens' fiction, of reducing the individual to a type and the type to a trait; character-drawing became caricature. We must realize the extent of the provocation when Strindberg declares that "a character on the stage came to signify a gentleman who was fixed and finished—nothing was required but some bodily defect—a club foot, a wooden leg, a red nose. . . ."

It should be apparent that the playwrights speak to us most effectively when they have in view the problems and principles with which they were involved as *creators* rather than as theoreticians. We turn to their essays for an introduction to their collective and individual aims and practices. We must agree with Brooks Atkinson when he reminds us that "rules are only a by-product of creation, which is the sole business of art." It is not in search of "rules" that we seek out a playwright's commentary. We still want to read it because it may cast some light on his personal effort and achievement, as well as because it may rouse us from the torpor of standardized expectations and responses. It is not absolute principle, for example, but stimulation (including the stimulation of dissent) that we derive from Bernard Shaw's declaration that "A play with a discussion is a modern play; a play with only an emotional situation is an old-fashioned one."

It is evident, too, that the effectiveness of a prescription depends partly on the patient. Shaw could safely assume that old-fashioned playwrights would not write discussion plays, but he must have known better than any of his readers that a discussion play would be dull if written by a dullard and old-fashioned if written by an old-fashioned thinker, or by no thinker at all but a Philistine—however new-fangled the chatter that constitutes the outer garment of his thought. Conversely, it is also possible to be distinctly "modern" while discoursing not at all skeptically on such "old-fashioned" matters as morality and manners—when the discourse, let us say, is by Lionel Trilling rather than by Bruce Barton or some publicist of "positive living." It may also happen that the prescription does wonders for the patient at one time and very little for him at another: "discussion drama" yielded *Man and Superman* at one time and *Fanny's First Play* at another. We cannot escape the conclusion that playwrights writing on playwriting are worth heeding in so far as they are provocative and suggestive rather than prescriptive.

It is not even certain that they always know exactly what they have accomplished or that they accomplished what they intended—it is even possible for a writer to have deviated into something remarkable by *missing* his predetermined target. But it does not follow either that a playwright's understanding or even misunderstanding of his work is without significance. That Chekhov thought he had written *The Cherry Orchard* as a "comedy" is important to our understanding of the play, particularly in a translation, even if we should be convinced—and grateful (as I am) —that he did not. Shaw's prefaces are gratifying and revealing even when they bear only a faint relation to the play they introduce. They may represent the mental climate in which the play came to life—and the mental climate is a significant quality of Shavian playwriting.

In the case of a specific program, indeed, the direct result may matter less than the indirect. Yeats, for example, dreamed of furthering the cause of poetic drama in establishing the Irish national theatre, but there was only one Yeats in Ireland. He got noteworthy drama from his colleagues of the Abbey Theatre almost exclusively in prose plays of peasant life such as Synge's *Riders to the Sea* and *The Playboy of the Western World*. He wanted, above all, *romantic* drama from the Irish theatre; even Maeterlinck was not romantic enough for him. He did get the somewhat unfinished *Deirdre of the Sorrows* from Synge in 1910, but it was not romanticism drawn from the glorious Celtic past but a clamorous realism wrung out of the inglorious present that saved his declining Abbey Theatre when O'Casey rescued it with *Juno and the Paycock* and *The Plough and the Stars*. Nevertheless, Yeats found and fostered "poetic drama," too, in the very realism of the young O'Casey; the paradoxes of creation never cease. It is a paradox, too, that when, after 1917, Yeats came to the peak of his personal effort to create poetic drama, he wrote not for his Irish national theatre but for private drawing-room performances and took for his model not a native but an exotic, Japanese form of drama.

The case of Maurice Maeterlinck is equally instructive. When the Belgian symbolist wrote his celebrated essay on *The Tragic in Daily Life* in 1896 he proposed plotless, static drama as the ideal form for the modern theatre, and his program won considerable support. Subsequently he revised his eloquently expressed views, revoked them indeed as a youthful extravagance (in a letter to the late Barrett Clark), and wrote "active," more or less melodramatic, plays. Nevertheless, Miss Cole exercised exemplary judgment in reprinting the essay in which he advocated "static drama." He was at the height of his powers as a playwright when he wrote this apologia, and it defended his practice in such poetic one-acters as *The Intruder, Interior,* and *The Blind* which won the admiration of the modern theatre's arch-realist, the great Stanislavsky, himself. Synge's related practice in the virtually plotless *Riders to the Sea,* produced in Dublin eight years after Maeterlinck's essay, resulted in the greatest one-act tragedy in the English language. Maeterlinck had his finger on the pulse of modern drama in expressing a widely felt dissatisfaction with plotty playwriting which resulted in attacks on the "well-made play" from such different schools of writing as those represented by Strindberg, Shaw, Yeats (in the very same essay in which he asserts romantic ideals), and Andreyev, who proclaimed—I should say, rather prematurely—that life in the modern world had moved inward. For better or worse, plot and external action did lose status in the modern drama, as they did, more thoroughly, in fiction. The Zolaist naturalistic "slice of life," the Shavian discussion-play, subjective and psychological drama—these and other types of dramatic writing have reflected the same tendency. Well-regarded plays such as *The Glass Menagerie* and Carson McCullers' *Member of the Wedding* (as well as present-day *avant-garde* works by Beckett, Ionesco, and others) continue to exemplify the vitality of a principle Maeterlinck laid down, too romantically and dogmatically yet by no means absurdly, more than half a century before.

II

In one respect or another, then, the effort to create a modern theatre receives support and personal interpretation from every playwright represented in the present collection. The strivings for such a theatre have been manifold, and it is risky to predicate unity in diversity for the main pursuit of modern dramatic theory and practice. One would have to allow too many exceptions to the rule for the rule to have any validity. But paramount in the modern experiments and achievements is the determination to express some aspect of reality, some measure of experience, some vision or conviction. This is the organizing principle of Ibsen's work when he develops modern realism and of Brecht's when the latter promulgates his antinaturalistic "epic realism"; and it appears alike in the social optimism of Shaw's and O'Casey's plays and the nihilism of Beckett's and Ionesco's.

The search for truth of experience comes into view when Ibsen declares as early as 1874 that "All that I have written these last ten years I have lived through spiritually"; it reappears when Zola declares: "I am waiting for someone to rid us of fictitious characters, of these symbols of virtue and vice which have no worth as human data. . . . I am waiting for everyone to throw out the tricks of the trade, the contrived formulas, the tears and superficial laughs." The errors of Zola-sponsored naturalism have been aired often enough; they need not discredit the ambition to give dimension to character, a degree of meaningful determinacy to behavior, and fluidity to dramatic action. Nor is Strindberg to be ignored when he makes a necessary distinction between microscopic or "little" naturalism that sees only the minutiae of reality and the naturalism that provides the wide prospect of, let us say, Hauptmann's *The Weavers* rather than the same author's *Lonely Lives* or *Before Sunrise,* with its doctrinaire genetics and small-souled sociology.

Nothing perhaps corrects false perspectives better than Strindberg's distinctions, set down in 1889 and still indispensable to theatre, in the great essay "On Modern Drama and Modern Theatre" Miss Cole has so ably edited for inclusion in *Playwrights on Playwriting.* On one hand, we find in the theatre "the little art that does not see the forest for the trees," the "misunderstood naturalism" that photographs everything but actually reveals nothing. On the other hand, we have the possibility of *"the great naturalism"* (that of *The Power of Darkness* and *The Plough and the Stars,* for example) which, Strindberg says, seeks out "the great battles" and takes delight in the conflict of powerful human forces. And Strindberg adds the one requirement least likely to occur to the "little naturalists"—he expects playwrights to see reality through a *temperament.* When he rejects a reflection of life devoid of temperament as inadequate because "soul-less" he does something momentous, whether he does so knowingly or unknowingly; he invites not only passion but poetry into the modern theatre. Once these are present in a play, along with what

Strindberg calls "significant motif," the differences between realistic and imaginative, naturalistic and poetic drama become technical and, in the main, superficial.

Once this is understood, we do not have to feel that we are either pushed back from the modern theatre or thrust out of it whenever the poets and the advocates of "the theatre theatrical" speak their piece. We are moving in the right direction of the expressive dramatist rather than the juggler when Maeterlinck asks the playwright to deal with an essential life "beyond the life of every day" and calls for an "atmosphere of the soul" in the theatre, although we may well prefer Chekhov's "atmosphere" to Maeterlinck's. We can appreciate Maeterlinck's point when, in calling for "sorcery" in the drama, he finds "sorcery" in *The Master Builder,* even if we suspect pinchbeck mysticism when he writes such puerile sentences as "It is this sorcery that imposes action or the power of the beyond. And we have to yield to it. Whether we want to or not." We can also agree with Yeats and Synge when they want the theatre to be rich in language. "On the stage we must have reality, and we must have joy," Synge's famous sentence in the Preface to *The Playboy of the Western World,* does not order playwrights to leap out of time and space by means of mystical rocketry. Synge, whose beautiful dialogue comes from the Irish peasantry, is not so far removed as we might expect from John Galsworthy, the confirmed naturalist of the English stage. In "Some Platitudes Concerning Drama" Galsworthy praises *The Playboy of the Western World* for its natural matching of matter and poetic style. He objects only to an "ill-mating of forms" (in plays, I take it, where verbal poetry and the subject matter are at odds) and warns that the poetry in ordinary naturalistic drama "can only be that of perfect rightness of proportion, rhythm, shape—the poetry, in fact, that lies in all vital things."

In this brief introduction it is impossible to dwell upon the various ways in which modern playwrights have tried to make the best of the two possible worlds of "reality" and "poetry," or endeavored to treat them as identical or interchangeable. But it is also true of course that a number of modern playwrights (Yeats, Lorca, Giraudoux, and Ionesco—to mention just a few) have, at one time or another, proposed imaginative flights that would whisk us out of the orbit of everyday life. I do not believe that they have usually realized their program without botching their plays or even at times "realizing" themselves right out of the theatre. It would appear, too, that the reality of everyday life often seeped right back into their more or less successful plays. Giraudoux's characters are often piquantly mundane in the midst of the fantastic and supernatural action of such plays as *Amphitryon 38, Intermezzo,* and *Ondine.* Cocteau's return to the Oedipus legend in *The Infernal Machine* is spiced with many an intentionally anachronistic detail more native to the Parisian boulevard theatres than to the classic theatre of austere tragic vision.

In spite of these qualifications, however, it is gratifying to observe that the flight of the modernistic playwright has often been *into the theatre* —where all good playwrights belong—rather than into the blue inane. This has been evident in the practice of Giraudoux, Anouilh, Ionesco, Wilder, and other twentieth-century playwrights. The necessity of landing in the theatre was understood by them all, as their comments show. Moreover, their "flight into the theatre"—that is, the "theatricalization" or distinctly theatrical realization of the subject matter of the play—could actually result in an intensification and highlighting of reality, as in Brecht's *Mother Courage* and Wilder's *The Skin of Our Teeth.* It became certain in our time that the "theatre theatrical" did not necessarily conflict with the playwright's engagement to modern life. He could use the theatre as show-window, pillory, or rostrum as, for instance, Brecht did in different plays. These and other expressive uses of the theatre have been widely recognized by contemporary playwrights; and at least in its best practice, the modernists' flight from illusionism into imaginative theatricality has advanced, rather than retarded, the contemporary theatre.

How well contemporary reality is presented or projected, how soundly appraised, how conclusively judged—these questions must, of course, receive answers that will fit the individual case. Fortunately, Miss Cole has devoted the second part of her compilation to notations by playwrights on the specific plays they have written—from *A Doll's House* in 1879 to Ionesco's *The Bald Soprano* and *The Chairs* in our own time. These essays, which are concerned with individual creation, are illuminating in themselves, and they are instructive when read in conjunction with the plays to which they pertain. They take us into the creator's workshop. The notes are not offered as a passport to the heart of the mystery of creation, and they cannot of course take the place of the final work, which will probably differ from the author's best-laid original plans. The insights afforded by the notes are, nevertheless, important additions to the *Credos and Concepts* of the first section of the book, exemplifying or confirming them, fixing them in a specific context, and perhaps, when read in conjunction with the play itself, illustrating the difference between the aim and the fulfilment. In all respects, then, *Playwrights on Playwriting* is an important theatrical and literary document; and more than that, it is a collection of opinion and data that should have practical value to playwrights in our time and in the foreseeable future. Looking into this book, we may not be able to tell which grain of an idea or principle will grow, but we have much to choose from in the data Toby Cole and her publishers have so generously made available.*

* [As an addendum, Professor Gassner planned to mention Horst Frenz's book, *American Playwrights on Drama* (New York: Hill & Wang, 1965), and several other more recent works, identified in a marginal note as "etc., etc." *Ed.*]

A CHALLENGE TO WRITERS*

I should like to talk briefly about the *life of letters* and *the life of theatre,* but realize in the same breath of desire that one cannot talk *briefly* about either subject, let alone both. Nevertheless, this is a proper occasion—I know of none *more* proper—for considering both subjects. I shall therefore speak, if only at random, about *some* aspects of the writers' situation in literature and in the theatre.

Young writers should know—I believe they usually do know—that the pursuit of their career will bring them into a special world. They usually start their work or discover their impulse to create in schools and colleges, and they invariably belong, as well, to an ordinary, nonliterary and nontheatrical world.

They will not be able to step out of it entirely. Nor should they want to abandon the source of their original experience and inspiration. But there awaits them an exigent objective world of publishing and of theatre in which they will have to effectuate themselves as writers and playwrights if writing is to be their vocation rather than merely their avocation.

Of the market in literary and theatrical wares I shall not speak directly, except to say that the professional writer soon becomes aware of it—to his *profit* and to his *peril.* To his profit, because he cannot follow his profession successfully, except for a fluke success once in a lifetime, without having some knowledge or "sense" of the market. To his peril, because he cannot pander to the market, he cannot trail after its motley and contradictory requirements and seductions, without mortal risk to his talent. More often than not, he will quickly lose the spontaneity and the personal expressiveness which are the necessity of the true artist, and the bouquet, if not indeed also the essence, of his work.

But even if I should be so impractical as to disregard the market as a vulgar circumstance, I should still have to call attention to the world of publishing and the world of theatre. Writing may be in the first instance a lonely life; but it becomes a public one soon enough when the article or book has to be published and the play has to be presented before an audience. In the final sense, creativity is a public act, and creation in a vacuum is a sheer impossibility.

There is a contagiousness about such public activity. In every period,

* An address delivered at Queens College, May 23, 1956.

186

a tone or attitude prevails. Only very remarkable writers, extremely sturdy creators, escape (and escape only to a degree) the influence of a style, a technique, an attitude, and a subject matter that has proved effective in certain books or plays. Ibsen had his followers as T. S. Eliot now has his. In the 1920's there was a bull market in a commodity called "debunking" —that is, of showing-up everything and everybody. Sinclair Lewis, the debunker of *Main Street* and the creator of Babbitt, was a leader of the movement, and his followers were legion in the literary world. A skeptical attitude gave rise to the George S. Kaufman clan of wisecracking iconoclasts who made Broadway breezy, gay, and impudent. Even the aristocrats, Pound and Eliot, made literary capital of the fashionable negations of the period. Many writers who made a quick reputation out of following fashion—Maxwell Bodenheim was merely the most notorious of these—quickly went out of fashion and failed to develop by contrast to the few who survived the fashion and developed their perceptions and skill. In the 1930's, the vogue of so-called social significance was resisted by few novelists and playwrights. Zeal for social protest seized even those writers who had no talent for protest and did not know what to protest against except their own futility. In the thirties, scores of playwrights endeavored to write like Clifford Odets. Toward the end of the decade it became distressingly evident that even Odets was trying to write like Odets; his manner, having lost a clear objective, was becoming a mannerism.

The period was bedeviled by fascism and by the imminence of war. The times, no doubt, demanded seriousness. But many writers confused seriousness with solemnity, and the responsible mind with the single-tracked one. In the embattled 1930's it almost became necessary to apologize for humor before one could be accepted or one could accept oneself as an artist and citizen. I am often deeply pained by the memory of the many ardent writers, mostly playwrights, who worked with me and who have been lost to literature and theatre in the past fifteen years. The fashion they followed to their detriment confused art with politics; it made the right opinions a substitute for the right art or craft.

In the past decade or so, the pendulum has swung from social protest to the cultivation of private sensibility. The loud voices of the literary demagogues have also been followed by the sussuration of literary mystagogues. The sharp and unyielding outlines of themes and challenges have been succeeded by the misty outlines of impressionism and symbolism.

But it is hardly necessary to continue this review to make the point that, first of all, there is considerable pressure for conformity in writing for publication and for the stage, and not all of that pressure is commercial at all. Even writers who are wary of market pressures may succumb to ideological ones or to pressures from critics, clans, and claques. It is a mistake to assume that a reputable publishing firm seeks only standardized products from its authors. The diversity of a publisher's list, such as Knopf's or Viking's, will usually refute such an assumption. If there is any standardization in these quarters, it arises from the taste and thought of a publisher's editors, themselves men of letters who help to make up the literary world. In the theatrical world, which is less aristocratic and necessarily more commercial than publishing, it is also generally true that there is no such thing as a single standard imposed by the mercenary will of Broadway producers. The contrary prevalence of extreme eclecticism is much more evident in show business—which is more speculation than business anyhow.

Mr. John Golden himself provided an example of the catholic spirit of our theatrical enterprise. The man who had made a fortune out of producing plays before 1920 that nowadays we are apt to consider old-fashioned had no hesitation in producing, and all with his own money, such a variety of pieces as Rose Franken's *Claudia*, Rachael Crother's *Susan and God*, Sidney Howard's *They Knew What They Wanted*, J. B. Priestley's Fabian social allegory *An Inspector Calls,* and the Nugent and Thurber satire *The Male Animal*, which remains the theatre's liveliest contribution to the defense of academic freedom. The producing records of The Playwrights' Company and the Theatre Guild are also remarkable for diversity rather than conformity to a single idea, style, or technique. The truth is that many of the fashions and conformities of the literary world are compounded and more or less willingly accepted by well-intentioned writers rather than by malign and calculating publishers and producers.

The greatest danger from publishers and producers comes from their overzealous partiality for literary polish, neat construction, and tidy ideas. This partiality benefits the mediocre and may even promote the public success of the talented author. But it tends to strangle genius and sometimes enfeebles and distorts highly original or profoundly truthful work.

There is, however, no easy answer to this problem. It is not easy for the writer to resist the reasoning of his editors. It is even harder for a playwright to resist the pressures that come from the director of the play —a pressure usually supported by the producer, the leading actor, and seemingly the out-of-town tryout public and the reviewers of the out-of-town press. Every stage production is, in a sense, a battle that tries the author's mind and spirit. Whether he writes primarily for print or for the stage, however, it is plain that he must cultivate his individuality without losing touch with humanity in general, with the currents of the life of his own times, with the character of his medium, and the conditions of work and the means of communicability the medium usually imposes on him.

Journalism is not to be scorned, and much journalism, in fact, is superior in literary value as well as human interest to a great many purely literary productions—hothouse products consisting mainly of the tender tendrils of private sensation. But it is precisely because of the competence as well as the rewards of journalism that the writer must be wary. He must know when he is writing journalism and when he is not. He must not muddle intentions and accomplishments; he must learn to make distinctions here, just as he must make the distinction between prose and verse, and between the prose of critical writing, which has one function, and poetic prose, which has a different function.

The writer must understand his objectives. It is a romantic, or perhaps only pseudoromantic, fallacy to assume that a creative writer needs to be less clear-headed than his fellow men. Precisely because he is a maker of magic, among other things, he must be more clear-headed than most of them. It is *not* the magician who must be spellbound, but his public!

However, there are many practical considerations that arise from the nature of literary and theatrical enterprise. Here are a few.

How, for example, shall the young writer begin his career? If it is true that the rule of fashion endangers the writer's art even when it furthers his material success and even enhances his prestige, shall not a conscientious beginner consider himself talentless and renounce his career when he discovers how imitative he is? And he is bound to make that discovery, in time, if he has the perception of a good writer. Nothing I have said was intended to deny a certain inevitability of imitativeness in a young writer's work. Or even the value of some degree of imitativeness. A writer develops, indeed, in two stages—in assimilating an influence and in transcending it, or in adopting an object for imitation and then leaving it behind. There are no absolutely original *good* writers; there are only absolutely original *bad* writers—a goodly number of whom will be found in institutions for the mentally disturbed.

Beginners are inclined to mistake novelty for originality. They may forget that literature is ultimately a texture woven out of strands of common feeling, thought, and insight; and that literature and theatre are founded upon constructive conventions. One may, indeed, depart from these. But the point of departure, the convention from which one deviates, is usually quite apparent in the deviation; and the point of arrival is only another convention. In many respects Emerson was altogether right when he declared that "the greatest genius is the most indebted man."

Much depends, however, on the models one adopts. To follow false idols and not abandon them in time may prove fatal. And it is in this connection that the taste-makers of any period and country play an important, and not necessarily beneficial, role. It is probable, for example, that the overvaluation of blank verse as a dramatic medium during the last century virtually to our own day proved injurious to the development of modern poetic drama in English.

Ibsen has not been altogether a good influence in the twentieth-century theatre. Chekhov's influence in the British theatre after 1914 was generally unfortunate; I know of only two examples distinctly to the contrary: *Heartbreak House* in 1916, and *The Chalk Garden* in 1956. The problem play and the propaganda play were unquestionably poor models for American playwrights in the 1930's, and led them to compose sterile harangues. In the same period before World War II, the tradition of British drawing-room comedy proved stultifying to English writers. They became ridiculous babblers in a political situation charged with thunder.

Nor are the idols of the contemporary advance guard to be followed without considerable risk. The current worship of Henry James may well prove confining to novelists. It may cause them to sacrifice the breadth of life for the carefully circumscribed point of view and fastidious moral analysis that may soon make the novel as esoteric a form of reading as modernistic poetry.

A few decades ago the stream-of-consciousness technique led novelists and the expressionist technique led playwrights into mazes of confusion from which hardly a handful emerged into the light of clarity and intelligibility. It is unnecessary, however, to multiply examples. It is surely apparent that imitation may be the first stage of creative endeavor but can hardly be recommended as the final stage. It is one thing to imitate while one is learning; it is another to make a career of playing the sedulous ape.

The world of letters tends to be so self-contained that it is altogether too easy to develop cult-heroes. The latter's function should come to an end when they cease to prove educative to the individual and become proscriptive and restrictive. What the writer has to learn is, of course, a vast subject, and one about which nobody can say the last word. I should like to conclude, however, with some general reflections.

The writer must get to know his medium, of course. Craftsmanship must be learned by study and practice—largely, I believe, by trial and error. This is a subject I must evade here because even separate semester-long courses devoted to poetry, fiction, and drama barely scratch the surface of the subject. But I would remind the young writer and his instructors that the cult of craftsmanship, as in popular writing courses, can prove inhibiting and debilitating. It can become an end in itself rather than the means to an end. The result may well be *virtuosity in a vacuum*.

Some of the worst plays I have encountered are those written by show people who know all the "ins and outs" of theatre. The most arid students in my professional playwriting seminars came directly from the theatre as actors, stage managers, and amateur directors. They were always working for effects, never allowing an effect to come of itself without calculations that rarely attained fruition in anything better than a gag or wisecrack of the order of, "This gal is a nice kid," to which the rejoinder is, "She won't be after she knows you long." (Broadway)

At the other extreme, of course, we can find numerous writers who came to literature and the theatre not from the craft or the business but from some other art or from some other profession, such as medicine or law.

Moreover, there is little feasibility in fostering a single narrow kind of craftsmanship except for some special market such as the pulp magazines; and even their requirements may change. Indeed, the erosion of boundaries between the genres of writing has been so extensive during the past two centuries, and especially in our own century, that the novel that is merely a competent feat of narration often seems considerably more dated and academic today than a novel in which the narrative element is a secondary ingredient, as in Virginia Woolf's *To the Lighthouse*. Thus, the play in which the maneuvers of plot are dominant often proves less entrancing even on Broadway and wins considerably less esteem from Broadway reviewers than nearly plotless plays such as *The Member of the Wedding* and *The Glass Menagerie,* not to mention *The Cherry Orchard* and *Uncle Vanya*.

It would be a grave error, of course, to conclude that the lack of conventional craftsmanship is tantamount to an actual lack of skill. I have in mind here mostly a difference between a machine-made product and a hand-made one. It usually takes a highly refined and sensitive craftsmanship to transcend the mass producing of an article.

Nor should the writer allow himself to be intimidated by literary history and definitions of literature. It is the work, not the label one can put on it, that matters. Terms such as "romanticism," "realism," and "symbolism," for all their currency in the literary world, should not give him much pause in his writing. Nor should he feel himself particularly committed to observing rules for the so-called types of literature such as farce, comedy, and tragedy. It is a distressing fact that one can make a muddle of creation in any form. There are bad tragedies as well as good farces. It is more important to produce a lively farce or a gripping melodrama than a dull tragedy, even if we grant the supremacy of tragic art at its best. It is false artistry to try to lift oneself up into the empyrean of tragic art or poetic drama by means of a willed and forced exaltation.

It is also erroneous to conclude that because a certain type of literature was produced very well in one age, it must be produced as well, if produced at all, in another age. There is always the danger of straining for an effect.

There is danger for the writer even in the concern with genres that often produces considerable agitation in academic and high critical circles. Such agitation may yield stimulating literary criticism but does not necessarily produce good poems, novels, and plays. After all, is it so certain that we know *what* a novel or a play is until we have experienced the effect of it. Excellent novels were written long before Henry James and Percy Lubbock laid down principles for sound novel-writing. The last great Greek tragedies were produced a full three-quarters of a century before Aristotle discoursed on tragedy in his *Poetics*.

Not to labor these considerations, however, I should go on, I believe, to another point in the learning process—a point that always seems obvious to everybody except to the person to whom it matters most—namely, the beginning writer. Just as he must get to know both the importance and unimportance of craftsmanship, so he must come to understand the importance and unimportance of success. In the first place, success has different gradations in the different fields of writing. One must understand the law of probabilities in each case in order to avoid undue disappointment and irritation. An American poet who expected to turn out best-sellers in the year 1956 would probably need the ministrations of a psychiatrist, if not the restraining influence of a straight jacket. But the number of novelists who have expected to sell a vast number of copies of their books has been large, and these writers are mad only north-northwest.

They are simply unfamiliar with publishers' statistics while being only too familiar with the best-seller lists. The truth is that few books of fiction, especially by new writers, have more than a very modest sale. If I am not mistaken, two thousand copies sold in a nation of 160 million people is about par for all but fairly well-known novelists.

The injunction that is in order here for the young writer, if he is resolved to be a novelist, is to keep on writing novels, and not even to wait for the results to come in from one novel before starting a second one. The same advice is appropriate for playwrights, too.

Important as well is some sense of proportion in assessing the nature of success and failure—especially, failure. Thus, the good reviews that novels receive are rarely instructive to the author. Reviewers of fiction in all but a handful of critical journals that ignore most books are so perfunctory in praise and blame that neither the praise nor the blame usually signifies much. Usually the novelist doesn't know how bad his performance was because he isn't kicked hard enough.

In the theatre, on the other hand, the fate that generally awaits the playwright is a corrective to complacency and a powerful solvent for vanity. Dramatic criticism is likely to be savage, whereas the criticism of fiction tends to be at worst diffident. One reason is that the play reviewer is stuck in his aisle seat, which he rarely ventures to leave in the middle of the performance—unless he happens to be George Jean Nathan. I have longed for the same retreat from time to time, but usually I have endured my agony until the end of the act. The book critic is more good-natured because he can lay the book aside without embarrassment and inconvenience to anyone.

By the same token, however, a playwright who wakes up after the opening night to find himself treated in the press worse than a moral leper and criminal learns that life is still worth living and people still speak to him on Broadway. He may even be pointed out with envy as that rare individual who actually got his play produced on Broadway—no mean achievement, at that, since sixty or a hundred thousand dollars' worth of faith had been invested in his work. Moreover, he may be singled out by Hollywood for a contract. Thus, Hollywood offered one of our John Golden contestants a weekly salary of $350 after his play had had a two-week run at the Theatre de Lys in Greenwich Village. Had his play failed *uptown,* there is no knowing what a scramble there might have been for his services. One thing is certain: both success and failure are immensely exaggerated on Broadway. The playwright must take care not to be overelated by success, which in any case he owes not only to himself but to his producer, director, scene designer, and actors.

He must take equal care not to be depressed by failure into a total loss of nerve and into retreat from the theatre. The case of Oscar Hammerstein should hearten the falterers. He had a record of continual failures in the theatre for about a decade before Miss Helburn of the Theatre Guild, with a little indirect help from your speaker, married him successfully to Richard Rodgers for the production of *Oklahoma!* in 1944. . . . And by way of contrast look at those who allowed themselves to be driven into exile. Many of them were to be found until recently rolling in wealth as screenwriters and weeping copiously for a wasted talent amid the alien corn of Hollywood—pun intended! And one of the most promising playwrights of the thirties has been the postmaster of a New England village for the past fifteen years!

First and last, the writer must learn to acquire courage and wear the triple plate of esteem for his art—if not for himself, for armor. He should not expect to be unacquainted with grief in the line of duty. But he may even glory a little in his vulnerability—for scientists bury their mistakes in the laboratory as physicians bury theirs in the cemetery, while the writer offers his errors to public view. There may be vanity and folly in doing that; but there is also courage in the act of self-exposure. And if he is neither a quack nor a hack, he may surely take a certain pride in a career that sets him rather apart as a Nazarene, however imperfect, of the humanistic spirit. For literature, whether intended to be read or performed, is a product of that spirit. And if the writer's career is not actually as glorious in practice, the true writer may well aspire to make it so.

As an artist he will have to make a total commitment of both heart and mind. Society and circumstances usually conspire to divide the modern writer and to rend him with inner conflicts as well as conflicts of external allegiance. His effort must be to make himself *whole* for his own sake as well as for humanity's. He can begin by respecting his vocation—the power of the word and the glory of design.

LITERATURE AND THE GARDEN
OF EPICURUS*

I would prove myself an ingrate after your welcome if I did not perform a service to the young writers of Queens College. And the service not likely to be often enough performed for young American writers is that of seducing them from the ways of respectability and sensibleness constantly pointed out to them today. I mean the ways of vocationalism, mass communication, flexibility, and practicality, on the one hand, and narrow academicism, on the other.

Our writers are beset today by two kinds of Philistinism—the Philistinism of the market place and the Philistinism of the academy. The former requires conformity in the name of practicality, the latter in the name of impracticality—that is, in the name of traditions whose cultural basis vanished long ago. The former demands too much flexibility from the writer, the latter too much inflexibility. If he is *flexible* enough, he will be able to bend to all the breezes wafted from the offices of television and movie studios, sponsoring agencies, Trendex operators, and the like. If he is *inflexible* enough, he will be able to resist the ideals of the democratic world, the hopes of liberalism, the incitements of social conscience, and the conflicts of our time. Unlimited flexibility and inflexibility are equally bad for creative writing and literary criticism. What the writer truly needs is to adopt an attitude which can be described, in Colley Cibber's terms, as *"resistant flexibility."*

The market place is the stronghold of a specious and vulgar democracy; its antithesis, the academy, tends to become the outpost of a phony and baseless aristocracy. And the young writer who is not drawn to the one is usually drawn to the other. In effect, and in the long run, however, both schools militate against real individuality and true generosity of spirit. Both tend to be fundamentally mean-spirited, joyless, and prissy. And both schools are essentially corrupted by "vocationalism," the vocationalism of the market place and the academy respectively; jobs in the mass-communication media and jobs in the teaching profession respectively are the material rewards that await the faithful acolytes of pulp or preciosity.

The alternative is a nihilistic revolt against both schools, as in the

* Based on an address delivered at Queens College, Spring, 1957.

recent case of "beatnik" San Francisco vorticism. But when we look at this neo-Bohemianism we are apt to find it equally arid and, for all its noise and fury, equally joyless. Since the neo-Bohemians cannot drown out the voice of the world, they are condemned to shout themselves hoarse in their cafés and literature. Since their glorification of sensuality does not invalidate the young Ezra Pound's reminder that "the twitching of three abdominal nerves is incapable of affording a lasting Nirvana," the neo-Bohemians are condemned to a career of repeating their orgiastic endeavors or pretenses. Above all, it is apparent that conformity to Bohemianism is no different than conformity to anything else. What we are apt to encounter there is inverted Philistinism rather than the self-realization attainable in genuine art. The rowdy self-publicizing practitioners are simply turning rebellion into a vocation.

And so one kind of Philistinism, vocationalism or utilitarianism, follows another or is contiguous with it in our society. In one way or another, the voice of the market is loud in the land, and one kind of commerce only invites or incites another kind. Commercialism, snobbish academicism, and anarchic Bohemianism seem to be manifestations of the same disease of pharisaism and spiritual vacuity.

It is evident, however, that the most widespread and insidious form of the disease is that which manifests itself particularly as the occupational theory of writing—namely, that literature is to be pursued as a job. Opportunities in pulp fiction, trade magazines, motion pictures, radio, and television have popularized this view in America. Writing for a job is to be distinguished from the writing of plays, stories, novels, and poems as ends in themselves. This is writing *to order,* in conformity with market requirements and by assignment.

I have no objection, of course, to a writer's earning a living with his talent. But I believe that the cultivation of talent should come first, and that this cannot properly take place in servitude to a job or an assignment. Moreover, the young writer must be made aware of some facts generally overlooked in the zeal for professionalism that prevails on many campuses. One such fact is that writing as an occupation produces not only an artistically harmful kind of specialization, but a specialization that may prove useless after a while. In the first place, the market in literary commodities changes with disconcerting rapidity. In a mass-communication medium—and television is a prime example today!—there is no telling what the customer or the sponsor may approve from year to year. The specialist in suspense melodrama one year may have to make room for the specialist in gag-writing for comics the next year. The character of the whole industry, too, may change overnight. Most of the dramatic shows that may have provided an occupation for dozens of writers one year will be off the air the next year. The plight of the motion-picture writer is even greater. He became an expert for a business now largely bankrupt or drastically curtailed. Hundreds of scenarists use to be under yearly contract to the Hollywood studios. Now that many of them have reduced the production of films by more than half, have ground to a halt altogether, or have been taken over by television producers, there are—with very few exceptions—no longer any regular jobs for scenarists. The scenarist may be writing for television now on a short-term contract or under a contract for only a single piece of work. He may even be in the position of the novelist or playwright who writes on speculation, a mode of operation for which he is unprepared. In the United States, it was long considered possible and feasible to write on order, to work under contract, to perform a job—that is, to be "practical." It is now becoming increasingly impractical to be practical.

The state of the writer who was stalemated by vocationalism of this sort was bad enough. He earned a lot of money year in and year out on his job, but he felt frustrated as an artist and a person; he developed neuroses, and he made desperate promises to himself to write a novel or a play—which he rarely kept. Today he no longer earns a lot of money —often he barely earns a living; but he retains his sense of frustration and his neuroses. As for the novels and plays he was going to write once he escaped from golden captivity in the motion-picture studios, which maintained writers' buildings very much as the state maintains workhouses for prisoners, there is little sign of these. A rare individual has gone to Hollywood and emerged to write a good novel or play. Recently, Dore Schary, the scenarist and former production head of MGM, emerged with the Franklin Delano Roosevelt drama *Sunrise at Campobello,* which has been thriving on Broadway under Theatre Guild auspices. But one Schary does not make a summer. Most of his colleagues continue to vie for the diminishing screenwriting assignments on the West Coast, and in the winter of their discontent nearly all of them try to sell television scripts. And with the market for these also beginning to diminish, one wonders what they will do next. Certainly very few of them—after periods of professional writing ranging from ten to thirty years—will produce a distinguished or successful novel or play. They worked on jobs too long. They learned a craft, a skill; and when the demand for that skill dropped, they had few resources left. As employees who produced on order, they no longer owned, they no longer had, themselves; and the creative writer's natural resources, of course, lie in himself. These writers had cultivated a job; they had not cultivated themselves.

Ironically, then, their practicality had proved impractical, whereas "impractical" novelists and playwrights still manage to make small fortunes from time to time in publishing and in the theatre. In sum, there are practical as well as cultural reasons for warning young writers and their teachers against putting their trust in narrow craft-training and leaning on the broken reed of Mammon-art. There is every reason for holding fast to the humanistic tradition of writing as an art, as a dedication, and as the emanation of the personality of the writer who belongs entirely to himself.

To the long-cherished false Eden of vocational training for the writer I would therefore oppose the Garden of Epicurus as a symbol. I would stress self-development rather than opportunism. I would even go so far as to stress writing for pleasure rather than for use, confident as I am that the pleasure of the free artist will prove to be the pleasure and profit of humanity as a whole. And I make antivocational recommendations to the writer all the more readily because vocational training has been absurdly overrated, if not in fact grossly exploited.

The enticements of so-called schools of writing that promise a fortune or a steady living from writing once the appropriate techniques have been mastered are perhaps not as familiar as the promises of other merchandizers, but they are familiar enough. If many would-be writers resist these allurements consciously, they nevertheless succumb to the popular American notion that technique or "know-how" enables one to solve every problem. The belief prevails that if only the writer knew how to satisfy the demands of the market in stories, plays, scenarios, and television dramas, success would inevitably follow. It is unnecessary to labor the point that this expectation is as illusory as it is demoralizing. The fact is, there is so little to learn in the way of external technique that what needs to be known can be learned in hardly any time at all.

Obvious examples can be drawn from the fields of motion-picture and television writing. If you bear in mind that the picture on a screen must move continually in order to command continued interest you need to know little else. Nearly everything else follows—the numerous brief scenes, and the varied visual images. Does the machinery of moving scenes or camera shots overwhelm you with craft-mysteries? If so, remember that anybody can write the shooting directions, but it is only the director who makes the decision to use them. The writer's directions are considered of small consequence in motion pictures and television. Usually it is enough for television writers to divide the page into halves, and to leave the left-hand half empty, so that the director may write in the camera and stage directions. Do the elaborate directions—the camera angles, dissolves, "fade ins" and "fade outs" in a movie scenario intimidate you? You, too, can write them in—just apply your imagination and take courage from the fact that in the finished script, it is the director's directions that count and that most of these merely record on-the-spot decisions made during the shooting of the movie; moreover, a good many of these are half-improvisatory in character. As for the placement and the technical jargon of the directions, it is perhaps insufficiently known that the external form of the scenario can vary greatly, and Hollywood has paid fabulous sums of money for literary properties in any form rather than for original shooting-scripts. The latter are created in the motion-picture studios, not bought in the literary market. Hollywood has sought suitable situations, plots, notions, backgrounds, characterizations and, occasionally, ideas, and has bought these in almost any form of presentation —that is, in articles, synopses, short stories, novels, plays, biographies, autobiographies, histories, and so on. The technical know-how is the last thing one sells as a writer to the mass media. This is not to deny, of course, the value of mastering modes and styles of narrative and dramatic artistry, and especially the art of joining words together and putting the right words in the right order. But these are organic matters that involve the total sensibility of the writer.

Closely associated with the delusion of technique, let me add, is the delusion of knowing the market—or, rather, of teaching the writer to know the market. This is tantamount to trying to anticipate the buyer's demand when those demands are frequently not even known to the buyer himself. Everywhere in the buyer's market there is instability— the story editors' and the producers' needs are constantly changing and they are not even clearly understood. Yet writers are encouraged to fritter away their time and energy trying to guess what the customer will want.

Even if you have guessed right, it is probable that the customer has changed his mind or has had it changed for him by the time you have your work in presentable shape. And so, year after year may pass without your having come nearer to the goal of becoming a professional writer. You have sought a false stability while you should have spent the years growing yourself, increasing your awareness, sensibility, and expressiveness. You have sold yourself for a rapidly cooling mess of pottage often whisked away from you before you have tasted more than a spoonful.

It will now be clearer, I trust, why I have suggested resistance to the seductions of vocationalism and merchandizing in the field of letters. It will be clear why I oppose the Garden of Epicurus to the Eden of Utility, desiderated and invented by a puritanically anticreative, anxiety-ridden consciousness that passes for practicality in our land. I propose that the writer create for the greater gratification of a developing personality that he can call his own.

I would especially stress the ideal of pleasure. Writing well entails taking pains and is fraught with many pains, and the writer should write for pleasure if only in order to abreact painful tensions. If he takes no pleasure in his art, besides, how can he reasonably expect that it will give pleasure to others? All his experience must undergo an intensification, transformation, or transcendence. All his geese must become swans on the written page.

Epicurus went to Athens in 306 B.C., bought himself a garden, and established a hedonistic school of philosophy there. The Garden of Epicurus became famous for wise and good living, which combined a decent respect for individuality with a goodly feeling of companionship. The cultivation of the self cannot, of course, take place in a vacuum, and the creative writer to whom I recommend a greater regard for himself than is encouraged in our world cannot live productively unto himself alone. He must combine individuality with relatedness. It is not neurotic isolationism that I recommend when I commend individuality. I count, rather, on individuality to give the writer his position as an acknowledged artist and a person in the community of man. Epicurus spoke well when he wrote, "We ought to look around for people to eat and drink with, before we look for something to eat and drink; to feed without a friend is the life of a lion and a wolf."

The hedonism I recommend is the Epicurean one of pleasure under restraint and of individuality under discipline. Gross self-indulgence is no more likely to produce pleasurable art than pleasurable life. At the same time, I must insist that restraint and discipline are valueless if they produce crabbed and dreary poetry, fiction, drama, or criticism. The morality of art should remain Epicurean in essence. As Robert Louis Stevenson said, "If your morals make you dreary, depend upon it they are wrong." I would recommend a little feeling for leisure, too. We have too many young men in a hurry to "make good." Suffering from occupational hypomania, they move so fast that they leave themselves behind and have no leisure for nature and humanity.

We also have too many writers who try to live only in the head. D. H. Lawrence acutely denoted one such manifestation as "sex in the head." We must avoid such transpositions. Both greater wisdom and art —and art is a form of wisdom—will be ensured by a regard for the senses as a source of pleasure. I would like to commend to our ultracerebral symbol-hunters in literary art and criticism the practice of a seventeenth-century Chinese critic who set himself the problem of adding up thirty-three moments of happiness when he was confined indoors by ten days of rainy weather. And I would call special attention to one of these moments—namely, to the gratification of cutting "with a sharp knife a bright green watermelon on a big scarlet plate on a summer afternoon."

To continue, I would recommend the effort to make life more vivid, lively, and varied as an end in view for the writer, who is most creative when he makes the most of life he can. He should avoid making sharp distinctions between the flesh and the spirit; he should resist the tendency to overintellectualize sensations and feelings whether in response to religious or academic puritanism, whether in the name of the saintly T. S. Eliot or the unsaintly Sigmund Freud. In America, in particular, we draw too sharp a line between the physical and the spiritual. We worry about it, as we also worry about the possibility that our impulses may not be normal. We become intellectual and at once try to dissect our feelings. We desiccate ourselves as persons and writers with so-called psychology until we write "psychology" instead of writing poems, plays, and novels. The young American could listen with profit to the Chinese sage, Lin Yutang, who writes in *The Importance of Living:* "Just as it is impossible for me to say whether I love my children physically or spiritually when I hear their chattering voices or when I see their plump legs, so I am totally unable to distinguish between the joys of the flesh and the joys of the spirit." He reminds us that "the partition separating our flesh from our spirit is extremely thin, and the world of spirit, with its finest emotions and greatest appreciations of spiritual beauty, cannot be reached except with our senses."

And with this in mind, especially in our present disenchantment, the young writer may escape from the feeling of boredom and apathy to which only his experienced elders are entitled. They may have earned their inertia or disillusion, whereas the young writer still has to earn it—with his life. If he arrives at this dubious sort of maturity too soon, he will have no life with which to make his art. He will have slept before the sleep; he will have been in deep freeze from the start. Between the older "lost generation" and the "beat generation" of the present, we are in danger of arriving at a state of affairs described by Byron in his couplet,

> Society is now one polished horde,
> Formed of two mighty tribes, the Bores and the Bored.

For effective writing, we need bravura and élan; we need to ride the crest of a wave of enthusiasm or at least curiosity of interest. For "literature," as Pound has said, "is news." So very much so, in fact, that it is "news that stays news." It is necessary for us to attain awareness as much as possible, whereas ennui closes the very portals of the senses and the intellect, diminishing access to both sensibility and thought. A morning freshness, a fresh prospect, is always needed by the writer. Thoreau put it well when he said "Follow your genius closely enough and it will not fail to show you a fresh prospect every hour." And he spoke well for every developing writer, too, when he declared, "I love a broad margin to my life."

Finally, as for the élan, which in the young artist is pardonable, perhaps even valuable, even when it becomes bravura, there is no reason to fear that it will destroy art. It used to be said that a Hollywood studio needed two men for success, a genius and a sleeve-puller. The former dared all, while the latter caught his sleeve and pulled him back. The writer as artist is also two men—except that, since the sense of life and the sense of form or order are ideally the same in his case, the artist is both genius and sleeve-puller. Likewise, the artist-writer is both democratic and aristocratic in his make-up, and he commands empathy and sympathy, on the one hand, and judgment or esthetic distance, on the other. He creates with his individual temperament and he creates with his sense of order. Neither must be neglected in the conservation and development of the writer as artist.

Finally, I would caution the young American against getting fixed in a mold too soon. We have too many writers who do the same thing over and over again. They are always writing the same novel and play. They have the same little observation to make, the same little thing to say, the same little private ego to make public.

Moreover, too many American writers actually desire this state of affairs or invite it, while the conditions of publishing, play production, and mass-media entertainment encourage such type-casting in the field of letters. This tendency is part of the overall drive for security in a shifting world, the cultivation of moral and artistic sloth as the first and last of the cardinal virtues—the Alpha and Omega of "Adjustment," "Practicality," "Good Citizenship," and Rotarian running with the herd. It is essential to disturb rather than to stabilize the writer, and one can do worse than refer him to Unamuno's concluding remarks to readers of his famous book, *The Tragic Sense of Life:* "Forgive me if I have troubled you more than was needful and inevitable. . . . And may God deny you peace, but give you glory!" It is that special glory in the case of the writer that Mallarmé called *"la gloire ardente du métier"*—the blazing glory of the profession of the artist—which the latter identified with the *life* of the artist, *"Magnifique, total, et solitaire"*—magnificent, total, and solitary.

THEORY AND PRACTICE FOR
THE PLAYWRIGHT*

Most playwrights are college-bred or soon will be, since nearly every reasonably intelligent and assiduous young person is going, or is about to go, to college. I address myself therefore to the young author who is likely to have his apprenticeship to writing advanced or protracted by the academic world; that is to say, by exposure to literary study, criticism, categories of drama, and conceptual thinking.

My general view is that the writer must learn to benefit from this experience, to be enlightened by it and liberated for creativity, rather than to be circumscribed and inhibited by it. I have encountered (although not exclusively in academic circles) altogether too many instances of educated or, shall we say, half-educated writers who try to cut their cloth to academic theory, who worry too much about ideas of writing rather than the writing itself. They usually talk a good play or book, instead of writing or rewriting it. This is particularly the case today, in an age of distinguished criticism rather than of creative vitality.

In the 1930's the young writer related himself to his times; today he relates himself either to an abstraction known as the "human condition," by which is meant the absurdity and hopelessness of the human estate, or to esthetic concepts and dramatic theory. In either case he gives primacy to concepts rather than to human experience, from which useful concepts arise; and he *defines* things before *experiencing* them. There is such a thing as becoming too bright and self-conscious for creativity.

In the 1930's the playwright was wont to ask himself how vigorously he could write, with how much anger at injustice and with how much sympathy for its victims. His self-esteem was dependent on how well he could engage himself to social conflict, rise above and escape from morbid subjectivity, and avoid esthetic isolationism or nihilistic despair and so-called defeatism. Today, the young writer is apt to concern himself with how many levels of meaning he can attain or how well he can convert reality into symbol, dropping the substance of reality and retaining only the shadow.

If the young writer is particularly "bright," moreover, he may endeavor to give point to his anemic playwriting with travesties of common

* From *First Stage* (Spring, 1962).

life and despair of any future for men. He may dedicate himself to an ardent pursuit of stalemate and pointlessness that will dictate stasis as the end of drama, and circularity—a *da capo* return to the beginning, as in *Waiting for Godot,* rather than progression with an Aristotelian beginning, middle, and end—as its structural pattern. With contemporary examples by Beckett, Ionesco, or Genet in mind, he may proceed to depersonalize his characters (if he has any) and refine his action (if he started with any) out of existence. It may become a point of honor with him in the end to produce a nonplay with noncharacters and nonaction. Or, if you will, to do without life in a play as a principled avoidance of life or as a convenient defense against it!

It is difficult for the teacher or the critic, or the producer in the event that such a play is submitted to him, to cope with this type of nondramaturgy. To decry it will usually prove futile if this is the only kind of play the author can or wants to write. Outraged cries of "decadence" will be met by the young author's no less outraged protest that contempt is what contemporary life deserves, that despair is an exact description of the human situation today, and that the nonplay merely matches the nonexistence toward which we are heading. And in the age of runaway nuclear fission it is not easy to come up with refutations not based upon banal optimism or unsupported faith. Moreover, the young rebel against Aristotle and Ibsen cannot be crushed with professional or professional frowns, because he is not without support from a modern dramatic tradition that starts with the nihilistic spoof *Ubu Roi* of the 1890's and courses through expressionism, dadaism, and surrealism. Nor is he likely to be dissuaded by any prospect of failure with which one may threaten him. For one thing, he knows that there is always the chance he may win the esteem of a like-minded *avant-garde* audience; and small as that public is apt to be, the production may draw attention to him and give his burgeoning ego the support it needs from his green peers and perhaps some charitable critic even more than he needs an overflowing box office and a fat movie sale. There is always the possibility, too, that he will strike a note of dramatic originality or attain a lyrical intensity that is worth more to him, as well as to many a jaded Broadway playgoer or reviewer, than the formula-made and star-studded staples of show business. The possibility is brought vividly to his mind by the genuine accomplishment and the high, if perhaps fleeting, reputation of a Beckett or Ionesco especially in more or less short plays that can be sufficiently sustained by a notion or a mood. And finally, one has to reckon with the fact that the nonplay may be the only kind of work the young writer can bring to completion at a particular stage in his career; one would rather have him write a nonplay than no play at all if he aspires to work in the theatre. He is, besides, in understandable revolt against tired middle-class realism, and the revolt of a would-be creative individual should be respected whenever his iconoclasm is well directed—and sometimes even when it seems ill-directed.

The only help, aside from patience, we can extend to him is to accept his intentions and go on to show him where he has not realized them or spur him into realizing them more fully and effectively. One may perhaps help him, or he can help himself, by closely examining some of the work that has won an audience of some size as well as his regard. I am willing to bet that his scrutiny will disclose one fact about the particular work: he will discover that its substructure is more "conventional" than would seem—that the play does have a beginning, a middle and an end; and that it does convey a feeling, if not necessarily an "idea," and an attitude, if not necessarily an argument. For a start, I would direct his attention to *Waiting for Godot,* by comparison with the same author's less satisfactory *Endgame,* and Ionesco's *The Chairs* and *The Lesson,* by comparison with, let us say, the same author's *Jack, or The Submission.* And if the substructure does not prove to be "conventional" but convoluted, as in Beckett's *Krapp's Last Tape,* or even turns out to be virtually nonexistent—that is, utterly "free" or "spontaneous," as in the case of Edward Albee's *American Dream*—let the novice consider what the work in question does accomplish. He is likely to find that when the play is successful the spinning indirectness, the corkscrew twistings, or the improvisatory features of the work also "add up" to a point. The addition has merely taken place *in flux* (comparable, I should think, to the calculus by which one determines the trajectory of a moving bullet) rather than in static terms, and that a form-giving imagination has shaped the work. The "shape" of the play has been merely worked out, so to speak, in non-Euclidean, rather than Euclidean, terms because of indifferent space and time relationships—as when the depersonalized son of Philistine parents in Albee's play appears on the stage in the person of an adopted son. In brief, "play analysis"—if the young writer needs it as a corrective for his tendency toward fragmented and confused artistry—is a remedy not to be overlooked by him and whoever ventures to instruct or guide him. And at this point the author of this article has reached the limit of his resources.

There is, however, another hurdle to be overcome, a very considerable one in the case of the academically educated, even if it concerns the radically simpler problem of working within the more or less established categories. The playwrights I have in mind allow themselves to be bedeviled by classifications of comedy, tragedy, and other types of plays, and by what these classifications are supposed to imply about the writer's attitude toward his world. Here I propose to touch upon only a few matters, and briefly at that.

We may start with comedy as a presumably simple subject for consideration in a nation in which every right-thinking person is supposed to possess a sense of humor. There is no problem for those writers who take an uncomplicated view of things; they will find human foibles or contradictions an ample source of innocent merriment and employ the medium of comedy for restorative rather than corrective purpose. Theirs is the kingdom of Broadway or, at least, of television if they have an eye for detail and are skilled in contriving situations. But trouble darkens the prospects of a writer who for various reasons, such as academic conditioning, vanity, or genuine taste, resolves to write *high* comedy. Occasionally, owing to social background, he finds a proper milieu for charming persons and witty discourse; the only difficulty is that he becomes self-conscious in our aggressively democratic environment, so that his writing shows strain, or the society he cherishes for its comic possibilities seems tenuous and remote from reality. Worst of all, in the relatively classless world or the adulterated "social register" society of the United States with which he deals he seems to be beating a dead dog whenever he ventures into satire, which is the leaven without which "high comedy" rarely rises.

Rarely, in fact, does it really rise these days, the ferment having seemingly evaporated since the lavish use Behrman and Barry made of it in the 1920's and the 1930's. When a "comedy of manners" succeeds nowadays, it is likely to be sustained by "bad manners" or by the antics of a roguish *bon vivant* who overthrows the apple cart of respectability, as in *The Pleasure of His Company* a few seasons ago; and this is no great feat since the cart is already half empty and the apples in it look rather sickly anyhow. Usually, therefore, the new writer avoids high comedy, and this, along with the attendant loss of verve and taste, is surely regrettable. An important area of theatre tends to be neglected, except in the rare instances when satire infiltrates musical comedy and musical revues, as in the current season's musical travesty *How to Succeed in Business without Really Trying* and the Chicago revue *From the Second City*. (It is interesting to observe, incidentally, that the current off-Broadway season has been enlivened with musicalizations of high comedy classics such as Sheridan's *The Rivals* and Goldsmith's *She Stoops to Conquer*.)

To my way of thinking, however, a young playwright should consider two matters above all else: he should not swallow the frequently parroted notion that high comedy cannot be created without being based on a more or less stable upper class, and he should not assume that there is one absolute or unchanging pattern to be followed in creating comedy.

(Let him observe how different is high comedy by Jonson and high comedy by Shakespeare, for instance.) Not only should he refuse to be deterred from high comedy because of the leveling character of American society, but he should not hesitate to stretch the form or style to suit his intention. And there is no lack of example to encourage an original approach to modern comedy when the playwright turns to such writers as Becque, Strindberg (*Comrades,* and *Crimes and Crimes*), Shaw, Wedekind, and Brecht. I don't believe that it is too much to say, in fact, that contemporary American playwrights still have far to go before they exhaust the possibilities of high comedy in contemporary terms. What Shaw, for example, accomplished with *Pygmalion* and *Major Barbara* (not to mention *Heartbreak House*) before the end of the First World War should serve as an example in that extension of high comedy that has been described more or less correctly as "comedy of ideas." It is an immensely fruitful field, which he started cultivating as early as 1892 with his very first play, *Widowers' Houses*. It has been cultivated assiduously ever since (with annexation of much territory once given over exclusively to social drama, fantasy, melodrama, and tragedy) in the case of such divergent works as O'Casey's *Juno and the Paycock* and *Cock-a-Doodle Dandy,* Pirandello's *Six Characters in Search of an Author,* Giraudoux's *The Madwoman of Chaillot* and *Tiger at the Gates* (*The Trojan War Will Not Take Place*), and Brecht's *The Caucasian Chalk Circle.* I know of no interdict in the theatre or elsewhere against cultivating the possibilities still further in order to express one's mind or one's times. For this one does of course need a mind, an awareness of one's times, some integrity—and a modicum of dramatic talent, along with the will to stretch it. But the educated young writer today simply must not allow himself to be hobbled by the labels, categories, definitions or generalizations of literary and dramatic criticism.

Finally, I would like my admonitions concerning the writing of comedy to apply doubly to the writing of tragedy because *obiter dicta* on the impossibility of writing tragedy in our century have been dinned into our ears incessantly. If the student listens to some erudite writers, he will be told that there has been no tragedy written since Racine died in 1699, a piece of information which will probably encourage him to enlist his pen in the service of television. Anybody who reads the present article is sure to be familiar with the argument, as well as specifically with its application to *Death of a Salesman*. Whether Miller's play is a tragedy has been debated over and over again, and there is no secret about Miller's defense of the work as *bona fide* tragedy on the grounds that a man of low degree like Willy Loman ("the low man") qualifies as a tragic hero.

Although there is room for disagreement on this point, and although I would be the last person in the world to dissuade young writers from exploring the possibilities of democratic tragedy, I would suggest less concern with the label than with the realities of character, situation, and milieu. What if the work does not turn out to be a tragedy in any accepted sense of the term? The important thing is to turn out a good *play,* and it is obviously possible to write one without inditing a high tragedy. Moreover, who is to decree what requirements must be met because the play is certified as such. Playwrights can only be misled by assertions that tragedy cannot be written at present, that it can be written only if certain standardized requirements are met, that it is the one exalted art to which the dramatist should aspire, or that there are no alternative ways of writing seriously, passionately, and provocatively.

The alternatives do exist, and one of these is *comedy.* Even farce may be an acceptable alternative if the farcical approach, as in both *The Beggar's Opera* by Gay and *The Threepenny Opera* by Brecht, best serves the serious purpose. And an important alternative to tragedy remains in that indefinable genre called "drama" or *"drame"* in which comedy and tragedy meet and mingle; in which an admixture of comedy and tragedy that is neither the one nor the other is the proper solvent for reality. There is only one requirement here, imposed by the conditions of human concern, that can be entirely validated: the character and his situation should be arresting and meaningful. Beyond meeting that requirement, which is an obligation to the audience, the writer need not go; he has no obligation to the theorist inside the academic world or outside it. In a time of the breaking up and the transformation of genres (paralleling upheavals and transitions in society) the playwright's allegiance should be to his substance and to his vision.

THE AMBIGUITY OF DRAMA
AND THEATRE[1]

The topic of ambiguity in poetry has been well aired. But ambiguity in the theatre has usually been either indulgently overlooked or dogmatically deplored. Nevertheless, it is of paramount importance in the practice of playwriting and play production as well as dramatic criticism.

Far from being a meager subject it is an almost overwhelmingly rich and complicated one, and this is perhaps the main reason why we have avoided it. Another reason may be the gratitude usually felt by persons concerned with play-production for even a modicum of success and a reluctance in that case to play the precisionist concerning the play's meaning. Rarely does the author rush into print, as did William Gibson in *The Seesaw Log,* to protest that success was won at the expense of his original intentions. Rarely does he make public, as Tennessee Williams did in the case of *Cat on a Hot Tin Roof,* two versions of the same work.

In Williams' case, it was clear that he considered the original third act of *Cat on a Hot Tin Roof* superior to the one that opened in New York under Elia Kazan's direction. He published both third acts and allowed me to reproduce them in one of my American play collections, although I must confess that neither version made the author's professed theme of so-called "mendacity" particularly clear. But William Inge was less certain that he had made a mistake, under the suasion of the play's director, in the case of *Picnic* when the conclusion was altered in the Joshua Logan production. This was a case of converting an originally "down-beat" drama of small-town frustration into a more romantic one which sent its young heroine in search of her ne'er-do-well athlete lover who had found it expedient to leave town. Inge hesitated to commit himself to his original pessimistic ending when I wrote a Sunday article for the *New York Times* on the influence of stage directors. Later I offered him an opportunity to publish that ending. Although Mr. Inge initially responded to the proposal with alacrity, he ultimately turned it down. He wanted to give the ending more thought and to consider making adjustments in other parts of the text. A few years later he supervised a

[1] The Theodore Spencer Memorial Lecture at Harvard University, December 3, 1965.

210

production in the Midwest which restored his original ending. He appeared very satisfied with it.

Inge's honest waverings are perfectly understandable. I have known instances of playwriting in which the author started with one point of view and arrived at a distinctly different one by the time his play opened in New York; of a playwright actually finding out what he meant, or thought he meant, in the course of the stage production; of a playwright apparently accepting as his own original intention some interpretations proposed by his producer—or producing company—and the stage director.

In two versions of Odets' *Awake and Sing!* I read before its historic 1935 Group Theatre production, I found no "awaking" and no "singing." The play was then merely a family drama of lower-middle-class frustrations and restiveness. The title the play bore then was not *Awake and Sing!* but *I've Got the Blues.* By the time the play had had its successful Group Theatre presentation, it would have been difficult for its author to believe that he had ever harbored any other intentions for the play's principal characters than for them to "awake and sing."

In 1931, Paul Green was persuaded by the Group Theatre to replace the tragic ending of his drama of social transition in the South, *The House of Connelly,* with an optimistic conclusion. In a period that sorely needed faith in social progress, it was plainly difficult for the author to insist on preserving his original ending. At my suggestion, Paul Green restored it in a collection of plays I recently edited. It took nearly thirty years for the play to recover its tragic form. When I think of my experiences in the theatre over a period longer than Shakespeare's entire career, I can only marvel at the confidence with which some scholars have arrived at interpretations of intention in the case of plays published centuries ago.

In view of the conditions of writing for the stage and the nature of the dramatic medium itself, I am diffident about offering any single analysis of dramatic ambiguity. It has so many aspects and sources that I could almost be content to say that the ambiguity is just *there,* without speculating too strenuously on any theoretical basis or readily definable esthetic justification for it. I am also diffident about propounding solutions for even those ambiguities which we tend to deprecate. And this is something of a concession on the part of one who, in starting out as a drama critic some thirty years ago, once announced confidently in a theatre magazine that "A play lives by its logic and reality. Conceptual confusion is the disease that halts its pace, dulls its edge, and disturbs its balance."

John Howard Lawson sufficiently approved of this generalization to

212 *Dramatic Theory and Practice*

make it the topic sentence of one of the central chapters of his *Theory and Technique of Playwriting,* published in 1936. Without renouncing this statement as arrant nonsense, I am no longer sure that I couldn't reverse it with equanimity and maintain that a play does *not* live by its logic and extra-dramatic reality. And I could further reverse myself so far as to say that conceptual confusion can be the disease that *quickens* the pulse of some plays and *sharpens* their edge. By grace of some overleaping imaginative association of emotions and perceptions, the ambiguity may actually secure a rewarding complexity unlikely to be derived from the operation of discursive reason.

A simple example is the case of *Awake and Sing!* in the form it had acquired when it reached Broadway. It could be shown that the young Odets had made a bit of a muddle of his play. I contended that this was so when I spoke to a large group of young authors, directors, actors, and would-be critics plainly in sympathy with the author. And when my analysis was reported to him by one of the faithful, Odets astonished him by writing that "John Gassner is right," which was enough to make me reflect that "Gassner" was possibly wrong—at least partly wrong. I had declared that Odets had not convinced me of his implicit argument, that the frustration of the characters was directly attributable to the evils of capitalism. I was anything but convinced that one of the two principal characters, Hennie Berger, who had got herself an illegitimate child and foisted it on a devoted immigrant husband, was exactly a victim of frustration. I saw no reason for rejoicing in heaven when she subsequently left her child to run off to the West Indies with the petty racketeer who had been her first clandestine lover. I could not applaud their flight as a glowing act of liberation, as did her brother Ralph, who had been ostensibly awakened to the cause of social justice by his grandfather's suicide.

Nevertheless, I could not deny that *Awake and Sing!* was one of the most moving plays of the 1930's; that an intense sympathy suffused the work; and that if Odets muddled his argument, his very muddlement achieved something worth realizing on the stage—namely, a vivid family drama of restless and troubled individuals seeking outlets for inchoate desires and dreams. Joseph Wood Krutch described this theme as "the persistent and many-sided rebellion of human nature against everything that thwarts it."[2]

Another, more recent, example would be *Look Back in Anger,* the successful play which brought John Osborne into the English theatre. It

[2] *The American Drama Since 1918* (New York: Braziller, 1957), p. 260.

would be difficult to prove the worth, let alone the consistency, of its young hero's rebellion. This invalidated the play for me as a work of genuine importance. Nevertheless, I could not deny that the play lived vividly on the stage, and there could be little doubt about the talent it revealed. And it may well be that in this case, as in the case of *Awake and Sing!*, the author might have given us a weaker play, one less rich in both nuance and truth of character, if he had adhered to the logic of his theme with greater consistency.

With respect to many classics from Sophocles' time to our own, we would do well to pursue a similar inquest concerning aborted themes, divided feelings, or unclarities of motivation. It may be essential to defend the vitality of a play against a narrow zeal for ironing out all ambiguities or for forcing it into a strait-jacket of a hypothetical overriding idea or unitary scheme. The dramatic medium naturally provides temptations to adept explicators since, unlike novelists, playwrights can seldom talk themselves out of contradictions, explain away an inconsistency, or recon-cile ambivalences. Dramatic characters ostensibly speak for themselves rather than for their authors; when they do and are to be caught at it, as allegedly in some of Shaw's plays, they are derogatorily called mouth-pieces rather than characters. Dramatic characters' asservations are supposed to be personal; their reactions subjective; their explanations of motive partial and, on occasion, as in the case of Iago, disingenuous. Antigone and Haimon in Sophocles' tragedy do not fully divulge their feelings in their dialogue; and Creon, in Anouilh's *Antigone,* makes out an excellent case for himself which may have impressed the German command in Occupied Paris during the Second World War, but which must have left—and was intended to leave—freedom-loving Frenchmen unimpressed.

The dramatic vitality of a play is the paramount consideration, and nothing, not even consistency or unity of idea, is quite as important. To adhere exclusively, for instance, to the Battenhouse morality-play interpretation of *Measure for Measure,* one would have to content oneself with a diminished and partial picture of the play from which one may be happy to return to a view of it as a comedy made up of a variety of elements that do not necessarily crystalize into a perfect but arid whole.

If we leap forward to the modern drama, we would have no difficulty in making similar observations even in the case of playwrights who first acquired international reputations on ideological grounds. To acclaim or denounce *A Doll's House* as a feminist tract is an absurd oversimplification that has long been out of fashion. But undeniably the one unitary theme of the play is the need for women to leave sheltered lives which keep them in a state of ignorance and dependency. Yet little of this has as much cogency as the shattering of Nora's romantic expectation that, rushing to her defense when she is accused of having forged her deceased father's signature to a promisory note, her husband would prove himself a Launcelot in mufti by claiming her guilt as his own. It is his failure to live up to this role that is decisive in her disillusionment and her resolve to leave him. Victorian criticism was not altogether benighted in refusing to be convinced by the play as an argument for feminine emancipation. Whatever dramatic vitality *A Doll's House* can possess for us is closely associated with the disparity of the elements that entered into its composition, including the contradictions in Nora herself and the haziness of her expectations not only of her marriage but also of what she thinks she can learn and attain in the outside world.

The creative ambiguities in the plays that followed *A Doll's House* are many. They are present in the entire texture of *The Wild Duck,* though masterfully held together too by Ibsen's rejection of moral absolutism. They form the substance of the conflicts in *Rosmersholm,* the confusions of motive in *The Master Builder,* and the tensions of the title role of *Hedda Gabler.* A rich awareness of contradiction or a sense of the ironic many-sidedness of human drama was, in fact, habitual with Ibsen, whose last spoken words are reported to have been: "On the contrary."

It is possible to conclude that the range and depth of procreant ambiguity in the drama actually grew rather than diminished with the advent of modern theatre, which scorned both the simplistic fare of nineteenth-century melodrama and farce and the generalized postures of poetic romanticism, even if clothed in verbal splendors. The major realists were concerned with character in depth with social tensions and transitions. The greater the specificity of Ibsen, Strindberg, Chekhov, or O'Neill in social and psychological drama, the greater the complexities and configurations of motive. Examples will be easily found among the best modern dramas such as *Rosmersholm, Miss Julie, The Cherry Orchard,* and O'Neill's *Long Day's Journey into Night;* and among the best individual scenes of these and other plays, such as the aborted proposal scene played by Lopakhin and Varya in *The Cherry Orchard* and the drunk scene played by the James O'Neill character and his sons in Eugene O'Neill's autobiographical drama. The reflection of these complexities in modern realistic acting or Stanislavskian character creation is well known. Character in such cases is not established by definition or convention, as in idealized and rhetorical performances, but by organic means involving involuntary, or but dimly apprehended, behavior on the part of a character or actor.

A noteworthy example in modern playwriting would be the valet Jean's reaction to the unseen arrival of his master, the Count, in *Miss Julie*. Jean has just cohabited with the latter's daughter and begun to strut about as her manly master, but the mere presence of the Count in the house has made him feel like a valet again. A noteworthy example in modern acting would be the marvelously apt maundering and bumbling of Amanda, the mother in *The Glass Menagerie,* as played by Laurette Taylor in the original 1945 Broadway production.

Neither social nor psychological certainties have been so thoroughly operative as to eliminate ambiguities, for better or worse, even in realistic or naturalistic drama. Many pressures or factors involving the playwright's complex orientation to his subject matter make themselves felt, quite against the will of the author, or of his producers and mentors. I was deeply distressed when Tennessee Williams' first produced play, *Battle of Angels,* written in one of my playwrights' seminars in New York, had to close in Boston in 1940, before being risked on Broadway. Several years later, Mr. Williams published a version in a now defunct periodical, *Phaidon,* and more than a decade later, still another version appeared at last on Broadway, under a new title: *Orpheus Descending.* But a fundamental problem in the play was never solved. It consisted of a fusion in the audience's mind and sensibility of two themes—those of sexual and social frustration—the very themes he amalgamated more or less successfully in *A Streetcar Named Desire,* and completely failed to fuse convincingly in a later play, *Sweet Bird of Youth.* The same fusions that gave the author much success also brought him failure. Nor could he resolve ambivalences, seemingly ingrained, with respect to woman, to masculinity—alternatively viewed with attraction and revulsion, and to the artist as outcast—fascinating and perverse. And none of the psychology he, William Inge, and others who drew upon psychoanalysis and psychotherapy have used has solved the knotty problems of dramatic clarity and conviction automatically. Realism in itself has often muddled as well as at times deepened dramatic work.

In the modern theatre and drama there have been, besides, other avenues than realism and naturalism for ambiguities of motive, feeling, and argument. These were, in fact, deliberately cultivated in the symbolist movement represented in the drama by Maeterlinck and Andreyev, and developed on the stage by Gordon Craig and his followers in scene design and stage lighting. Perhaps the greatest fault to be found with even well-written symbolist pieces is not that they were too complex, but too simple; not that they were too deep for understanding, but too superficial in their morality-play reductiveness of character-dimension and motivation.

Thus, revolution is too abstract and fleshless in the Belgian post-playwright Verhaeren's *Les Aubes* (translated as *The Dawn*); the search for happiness has a fairy-tale simplicity in Maeterlinck's *The Blue Bird;* and man's unequal struggle with fate under the shadow of personified death verges on rhetorical banality in Andreyev's lugubrious allegory, *The Life of Man.* Since plays such as these consist almost entirely of merely conceptualized figures and events, there is actually no genuinely dramatic, rather than thinly spread poetical, ambiguity in them. Where there are no objects there can be no shadows.

The most gratifying dramatic manifestations of ambiguity in symbolist drama have appeared not in verbal mystifications or atmospheric suggestiveness but in those works in which human contradiction is the realized theme, as in Ibsen's late plays, *The Lady from the Sea, Little Eyolf,* and *When We Dead Awaken;* in Strindberg's mordant comedy, *Crimes and Crimes;* in Hauptmann's *The Sunken Bell* (in which the tragic hero is destroyed by the call of earthly life and conscience), in Lorca's poetic dramas (especially *Blood Wedding*); or in William Butler Yeats's *A Full Moon in March, Calvary,* and *Purgatory.*

Much the same thing has been apparent in the vogue of expressionistic drama that followed that of symbolism. In so far as extreme abstraction and depersonalization prevailed in expressionism, this modern style was apt to be arid; and expressionist frenzy was a poor substitute for life in the work. In so far as a play or scene conveyed human perturbations and anxieties, there was apt to be dramatic power in the writing.

But expressionism often introduced psychic disorder into the structure and form of a play to such a degree as to vitiate it as intelligible communication. It is to this debilitating subjectivity, and not to presentations of inner conflict or ideological divisions, that proponents of epic theatre such as Piscator and Brecht objected when they broke with expressionism or endeavored to correct its morbid manifestations, as Piscator did in his Berlin production of Ernst Toller's political drama of disenchantment with the Weimar Republic, *Hoppla, wir leben!*

One way of putting this is to say that expressionist confusion has been in art and not merely in the life expressionism purported to reflect or express. When it is virtually impossible to distinguish between what is dream and fantasy and what is supposed to be reality in a play we are apt to be merely confused, which is anything but the case, let us say, in *The Tempest,* despite Prospero's "We are such stuff as dreams are made on" meditation. In *A Midsummer Night's Dream,* demarcations between waking and sleeping states are clearly observed; objective and subjective states of being are plainly distinguished. By contrast, some of the most noteworthy modern expressionist plays, such as Kaiser's drama of a lowly cashier's revolt against society, *From Morn to Midnight;* Ernst Toller's drama of revolution, *Man and the Masses (Masse-Mensch); The Hairy Ape,* and *The Adding Machine,* are more or less flawed by formal confusion.

Epic theatre endeavored to overcome this defect that afflicted expressionist social as well as psychological drama between 1914 and 1924, or to cool off, with satire and dialectical demonstration, the theatre that expressionism had overheated. Since ideological clarity was a prime objective, formal and stylistic ambiguity was strictly banished; or it was displaced by irony, as in the Brecht-Weill musical collaborations *The Threepenny Opera* and *Mahoganny,* Piscator's dramatization of Hašek's World War I satirical novel *The Good Soldier Schweik,* and Brecht's *A Man's a Man (Mann ist Mann).* Realistic or Stanislavskian character-creation in depth also had to be renounced as a disturbing factor in *Lehrstück* productions, intended for instruction. The desire to demonstrate an idea could lead, in fact, to drastic reduction of complexities of character and circumstance, and to formulaic playwriting and stage production. It could become a habit of mind or an automatic response to a problem to reach for a handy Marxian or moral cliché such as the class struggle or the injustice of society. I recall how desperately Erwin Piscator struggled to disentangle the tangled strands of fate when I got him to stage a dramatization of Richard Hughes's novel *The Innocent Voyage,* or *High Wind in Jamaica,* in which a child's fear dooms a pirate-captain to the gallows for a murder not he but a little girl had committed. Piscator's proposed solution, when the play didn't seem to work, was to turn it into a drama of social injustice, whereas the actual theme concerned children's primal amorality.

Simplification was both the intrinsic virtue and defect of epic theatre, and it is to Brecht's credit that he was often able to overcome or minimize the defect. He accomplished this with his lyrics and music in his early plays, with irony throughout his career, and with protagonists whose dividedness enhanced a play or scene as its root idea or root action. This is particularly observable on the biographical plane in Brecht's *Galileo,* who is presented by Brecht as anything but a romantic martyr-hero; on the level of character drama in *Mother Courage,* and on the folk-tale, theatricalist level of *The Caucasian Chalk Circle, Puntilla,* and *The Good Woman of Setzuan.* In the last-mentioned piece, Brecht even divided his protagonist into two *personae:* Shen-Te, the kind-hearted prostitute, and her pretended cousin and hard-headed alter-ego, Shui-Ta. The latter is the personality and, literally, the mask she assumes for self-defense. It may be said, in this instance, that Brecht dealt with ambivalence or the ambiguity of the human will by objectifying it in separate persons, instead of presenting it in unitary characterization as Ibsen did in his Hedda Gabler and his "master-builder" Solness. (O'Neill resorted to the same device in *The Great God Brown* and *Days without End* to denote the divided personality of his protagonists.) But then Ibsen in the 1880's and 1890's employed an integrative realistic technique. Brecht's (as well as O'Neill's) morality-play division of characters into separate *personae* was possible only by means of a highly stylized theatricalized technique borrowed from the Chinese theatre.

Theatricalist stylization has been, in fact, an important general means of avoiding confusion in presenting two or more sides of the same person or situation. In theatricalist technique, there is no problem of clarity or unclarity regarding these matters for the simple reason that in theatricalist theory the sole reality is theatrical reality rather than realistic illusion. The illusion of reality is not categorically driven out of the theatre; it can even take over an entire scene, though probably only in some stylistically heightened manner. But the audience and the reader are not deluded into believing that they are seeing anything but a play; and the playwright does not feel restricted to mere replication of reality. He can employ comment freely. He or his character may step out of the frame, so to speak, and address the audience. He can certainly resort to arbitrary fantastication, if he finds it desirable to do so.

In such instances, it should be noted, the burden on the critic and the public is, inevitably, one of comprehending the theatricalist premises of the work. And it must be observed that this is not always sufficiently understood—even, as I discovered, in the case of such a simple play as Molnar's *Liliom.* Earnest colleagues once expressed confusion as to what justification there was in the transition from early naturalistic scenes to the fantastic scenes that followed Molnar's hero's stabbing himself in the heart in order to escape arrest. Liliom finds himself in a police-court anteroom of heaven, and is later given an opportunity to return to earth under the watchful eyes of other-worldly police agents, only to ruin his chance to express the longing he feels for the daughter he never lived to see born. Was all this a dream or delirium on the dying Liliom's part? How were my colleagues to explain this part of the play to their students? The question would not have occurred to them, of course, if the play had been an opera or musical comedy, because everyone is accustomed to accepting theatricalist assumptions automatically with respect to these media. But a little theatrical sophistication was needed to explain that the fantasy in Molnar's play was not the character's death-bed illusion, but the author's way of commenting on a chronically unlucky and inept individual by means of a ruefully entertained hypothesis. Molnar was saying in effect that his hero Liliom was the sort of person who if he entered another world would find himself in a police-court, and if he ever got a chance to return to earth would mess up his opportunity.

In plays employing more distinctly theatricalist machinery than *Liliom,* such as Yeats's *Full Moon in March,* with two Attendants constituting a chorus, dramatic ambiguity is removed by stylized theatrical commentary. Yeats's Attendants avow from the beginning that they are playing parts in a play. One Attendant announces the theme when he sings the lines, "What cares love for this or that? . . . Crown of gold or dung of the swine," and the other explicitly closes the play, which dwells on love's need to defile itself with the flesh, with the thought that the very saints must descend from their "emblematic niches" in quest of what they lack—namely, "Their desecration and the lover's night."

Still more elaborate theatrical machinery appears in Giraudoux's *Electra,* in which the author deplores Electra's neurotic obsession with revenge. To enforce his commentary theatrically, Giraudoux invented soliloquies by an ironic Zeus masquerading as a beggar and by a peasant gardener, who congratulates himself on not having to marry Electra in an address to the audience. Giraudoux also invented a small chorus of Furies. They start out as little girls and grow throughout the play until Electra gets her revenge, at which point they have become as tall as Electra herself. After such straining for clarification of theme and character analysis, there can be little room in the play for any mystery or uncertainty (except for charges and countercharges by Electra and her mother): provided, of course, that we accept the play not as a transcript of life, but as a theatricalist *tour de force*. Not ambiguity, then, but irony is the real fabric of Giraudoux's play.

The other remaining distinct modes using ambiguity creatively in our time have appeared in surrealist theatre and in the so-called Theatre of the Absurd. In surrealistic drama, we are concerned with "subliminal experience" or, as in Cocteau's *Orphée,* a sort of fantasia of the unconscious. And in Theatre of the Absurd, both verbal ambiguity and ambiguous experiences have been used to express the absurdity of the so-called human condition, the inadequacy of language (as in *The Bald Soprano*), the folly of trying to find a meaning in life (as in Ionesco's *The Chairs*), the sense of doom for the human race to be found in Beckett's *Endgame,* and other indications that man is in a sempiternal pickle from which he cannot extricate himself with reason or social activism. It is this belief that became the basis of Ionesco's avowed hostility to Brecht.

In all these experiments the ambiguity of existence is assimilated into the form—that is, into both the texture and structure of the work. This accounts for the difference between ordinary pessimistic representations of failure and Theatre of the Absurd treatments of the same theme. The difference is apparent when we compare Camus' realistic treatment of the absurdity of human fate in *Le Malentendu* (dubiously translated into English as *Cross-Purpose*) and Ionesco's nonrealistic treatment of the absurity of man in *The Chairs*, which is as bizarre as in its multiplication of empty chairs on the stage as in the author's view of the incoherence of existence.

And now it is imperative to conclude this discourse, which could go on interminably since it implicates virtually all of the world's drama and theatre. It must be apparent, for instance, that we have not yet touched upon the ambiguity of genres, a topic of importance since the time of Euripides, when classic tragedy underwent transformations into romance. In our own times unambiguous tragedy has rarely been produced. There has been, instead, a considerable mixture of genres for which the term "tragi-comedy" would be appropriate but for its special Jacobean connotation. Lionel Abel has recently called it "metatheatre."

In pursuing this subject, we would be led into a thicket of critical controversy from which we would not soon emerge. Consider only the arguments that arose in 1949 over *Death of a Salesman*. Is Arthur Miller's hero Willy Loman capable of sustaining a tragedy? London and Broadway divided sharply on this question, as did the American literary Establishment and our so-called "Broadway intelligentsia." For Miller himself the question was of practical importance since he went to some trouble to defend the play as a tragedy of the common man. With characteristic determination he returned to the problem of writing one both in *The Crucible* and *A View from the Bridge*. In the case of Elizabethan and Jacobean drama, we have the problem of distinguishing between the tragic and melodramatic elements; in the case of modern drama, of distinguishing between tragic and pathetic elements—if not, in fact, between *p*athetic and *b*athetic ones. Ambiguousness of genre has also been apparent in contemporary Theatre of the Absurd fantasy, as in *The Chairs,* and in Genet's *The Balcony* and *The Blacks,* and in a modish type of play called "black comedy" in England.

Also, even if I had the time, I would not have the temerity to deal with the ambiguity of *poetry* in the drama. That it has served to deepen dramatic as well as poetic effect has been evident since the time of Aeschylus, who made superb use of it in the *Agamemnon* when the Chorus refers to the events that led to the sacrifice of Iphigenia at Aulis. This is also true, of course, in the use of song, familiar in the plays of Shakespeare and his contemporaries, Goethe and Schiller, and Brecht, who, unlike them, undercut his lyricism with irony. An excellent use of lyric poetry for dramatic purposes appeared in Arnold Wesker's recent play, *Chips with Everything*. Pip, the recalcitrant Air Force recruit, leads his fellow-soldiers in the singing of "The Cutty Wren,"[3] an old peasant revolt song, at the Christmas Eve party attended by their condescending upper-class officers. It starts with the stanzas:

> "Where are you going?" said Milder to Malder.
> "We may not tell," said Festle to Fose.
> "We're off to the woods," said John the Red Nose,
> "We're off to the woods," said John the Red Rose.
>
> "What will you do there?" said Milder to Malder.
> "We may not tell you," said Festle to Fose.
> "We'll shoot the cutty wren," said John the Red Nose,
> "We'll shoot the cutty wren," said John the Red Nose.

The deliberate ambiguity of the lines, combined with the insinuating rhythm and cadence, rising to a menacing climax, accounted for one of the most powerful scenes of the play.

Good prose can, of course, also supply poetic effects, and an insinuating ambiguity can accompany even ostensibly direct and lucid assertions, particularly when the author has Strindberg's subjective intensity, or Shaw's apostolic fervor and rhetorical powers.

Finally, I realize that I have barely touched upon the vast area of ambiguity present in theatrical production at any time and in any place, both in the case of old plays and new. And I am not even concerned with questions of expediency that arise in the case of productions that must somehow or other avoid offending a particular government or particular political or religious interests. (I am not thinking of enforced ambiguity, such as appear in, let us say, Molière's *Don Juan*, which the critic Lemaître described as devilishly obscure—*obscure en diable*). Whenever an actor steps into an important role, he introduces personally determined impressions into a play, as does also each stage director. If you have seen many Hamlets or Heddas, you will agree that you never saw the same

---

[3] "Cutty" is Scots for "short."

one twice. It is impossible to discuss this matter here, although it is obviously an extremely important problem to playwrights and producers, who must cope with it continually.

It is a problem for working critics, too, while reviewing specific productions. I recall that when I saw the burly Lee Cobb fighting for self-respect and for the esteem of his eldest son in the role of Willy at the premiere of *Death of a Salesman,* the play possessed tragic dimensions for me. But when Thomas Mitchell took over the role and projected the image of a representative *little* man, I saw only a middle-class drama. It is also well to realize how much may elude the critic as well as the public even after one has made a strong effort to qualify a point with a textual underpinning, as I did in adapting Stefan Zweig's drama *Jeremiah* for the Theatre Guild in 1938. I went to great pains to avert possible criticism that the pacificism of the play was too absolute and too naïve. I drew a distinction several times in the play between wars of aggression and a people's laudable defence of its liberty against aggressors, a point well worth making when Nazi Germany was on the march. The qualification was ignored. In watching Jeremiah oppose war in Jerusalem, the reviewers saw a Jeremiah occupied with the sole task of trying to oppose an alliance that would precipitate a war. Both the *Times* and the *Daily Worker* attacked the play as too naïvely pacificistic.

Regardless of where we look, then, we cannot escape the conclusion that the theatre bristles with uncertainties and other incommensurable factors. And its most stable element, the text of a play, has also been conducive to every sort of ambiguity. Even attempts at clarification can introduce obscurities into the text, unconvincing transitions, dubious motivations, inconsistencies, and infirm conclusions. Because of the delicate balance that must be maintained in dramatic writing, a change of circumstance or of mere pressure in one part of a play requires a balancing and compensating factor elsewhere. Important aspects of the medium work against exactness of communication, chiefly the relative absence of description, analysis or explanation, and the speed required of dramatic development if the play is not to bog down in expository stalemate. The great problem in all aspects of the theatre has been and will always be how to turn a disadvantage into an advantage, a danger into a potency.

Miraculously, of course, the ambiguousness of drama *can* turn into an advantage rather than a disadvantage—with an enhancement, rather than an impoverishment, of the dramatic experience, and with a deepening or intensification of emotion rather than mere confusion. It is the business of the dramatist, as well as his collaborators in a stage production, to make this miracle happen. When it occurs, and when the drama operates in conjunction with poetry, then the theatre can impress us as a very great art; when this does not happen, the theatre is apt to seem a decidedly shabby enterprise, and the drama a thin, subliterary medium. Many persons have accepted the challenge to make the miracle happen, and a few have risen nobly to it. Among these have been some of the great poets. And the greatest of these, as Theodore Spencer said in the conclusion to his *Shakespeare and the Nature of Man,* was supreme in expressing the greatest of these ambiguities—namely, "Birth, struggle, death, and renewal."

Part Three

PERSPECTIVES ON AMERICAN THEATRE

■

THEATRE ARTS IN A
FREE SOCIETY[1]

I

In a world of growing tensions, the subject of freedom for the theatre and its related arts necessarily gives us great concern. The subject, considering the state of the world, can be approached only with faith in the strength of American democracy to survive the onslaughts of totalitarianism from abroad; and faith, too, in the common sense and the confidence of the American people to resist intolerance within our own borders. Faith should not be confused, of course, with complacency. It should be accompanied with works; that is, with a constant endeavor to sustain a free theatre in all the communities in which it is threatened or is likely to be threatened.

We shall not be able, however, to retain our faith and to give it the support of policies and action unless we achieve usable perspectives. And for this purpose we must remind ourselves of several salient facts.

The first of these is that the fate of the theatre arts is inextricably associated with the fate of the society in which they exist. As goes society, so goes the theatre. The United States must remain independent and free, if the theatre is to enjoy any freedom at all. Our subject would have had no relevance—it could not even have been raised before this or any other convention—if Hitler's totalitarianism had conquered. And today we can entertain no thought of a free theatre whatsoever without an unqualified rejection of illiberal dogma and without giving complete support to intelligent efforts to oppose aggressive totalitarianism in the world. I have no hesitation in saying that anyone of good faith who does not fully sub-

[1] From *Educational Theatre Journal* (October, 1954). [NOTE: Less than a decade after the end of a global war that was believed to have secured liberty for the peoples of the world, intimidation or suppression of thought and art was widespread. Stalinism in one hemisphere and McCarthyism in the other were the two manifestations that gave the greatest concern to defenders of the arts.

The following address at a national convention of the American Educational Theatre Association held in Chicago in December 1953, represented an effort to define some issues of particular interest to leaders of the community and university theatres in the United States. This address was intended to be cautionary, and for this purpose I took into account various facets of American cultural and commercial enterprise. I wish I could believe that it was no longer necessary to resuscitate the admonitions expressed here. *J. G.*]

scribe to this premise is living in a Never-Never-Land of such woeful ignorance and pathetic naïveté that he can be of no more use to the theatre than to his country. Stalinist totalitarianism is inimical to a free theatre because it is inimical to a free society.

Nor should we allow ourselves to be deluded today when we read that a Soviet composer or a man of letters such as Ilya Ehrenburg is attacking the narrow censorship of his craft to which he paid a full measure of tribute only a week or a month ago. Liberty that is at the mercy of shifting lines of political strategy is not liberty. Freedom that exists on temporary sufferance is not freedom. Liberty must be ingrained in a society and in the traditions of a people if it is to have any reliable existence.

Moreover, it would be a gross error to assume that in such a society one craft or one aspect of the craft can go free while another remains enslaved. One of the first arts to be controlled in a dictatorship—once speech is controlled—is the stage. The theatre is considered dangerous because it communicates directly with a people, and because theatre is necessarily a public activity and does not exist in the privacy or the secrecy of a man's library. But before long, as experience has demonstrated, the less specific, or less public, arts also fall into a state of slavery.

In the theatre, too, the first art to be shackled is the playwright's, because he employs words, and words have a high degree of specificity. The first men of the theatre to be restrained in Russia were the playwrights, whether they had their plays removed from the theatre or were denied access to it; whether they were deprived of a livelihood or of life itself; or whether they were tethered semivoluntarily or by prescript to the wheel of utilitarian playwriting. But before long, the controls were extended to cover not just the words and subject matter of the play, but the very style and dramatic form. At first, in 1934, Soviet writers were merely *lectured* on the desirability of favoring a "constructive" style of so-called Socialist Realism. But the recommendation quickly turned into an order. Whereas realism has been and still is an acceptable style when left to the discretion of a playwright, Socialist Realism, a narrow style fostered by intimidation, is tyranny. Stalinism established the dictatorship of a single style in the theatre.

Before long, finally, this dictatorship was foisted not merely on playwriting, but on styles of play production. Meyerhold, the great if eccentric Russian director, was discredited and removed from his position in 1937 as an alleged purveyor of foreign ideologies because he employed nonrealistic styles of stage production, and was arrested after protesting against criticism of his art. He has never been heard of since that day. Henceforth it was expedient for nonmusical stage directors to follow the blueprint of humdrum Socialist Realism, and a theatre that had once won the interest and admiration of foreign visitors without regard to politics was entirely subdued to a policy of narrow and literal showmanship.

The history of the enslavement of the Russian theatre is given in devastating detail by Juri Jelagin in his book *Taming of the Arts*.[2] But even my present brief summary is sufficient to show us the "shape of things to come" if our theatre were to fall into the hands of the totalitarian state. That state can alluringly offer the security of employment so greatly desired by all who work in our theatre. It can provide, if so disposed, magnificent theatre buildings, expensive scenery, and financial rewards to favored artists. But sooner or later, the theatre must pay for such security with a complete sacrifice of integrity and freedom.

II

My second point derives from the first. If ideological strangulation of the theatre is repugnant to us when it occurs in a foreign and totalitarian country, it certainly cannot be accepted at home, in the country we want to cherish as the one strong bastion of democracy left in the world. So long as the American way of life remains substantially unaltered, thought-control in the theatre cannot be considered even tolerable by most Americans.

That there are fears for that way of life in general, however, and fears for the continued freedom of the theatre, is no deep secret to any of us. They are intensified whenever a vocal minority exerts pressures against a play, an author, or a player. These pressures have been most strongly exerted in the mass media, but they have also been felt in the theatre, especially in communities where the commercial stage leads a marginal existence, and where the noncommercial stage depends on the support of subscribers and sponsors.

The active members of the American Educational Theatre Association are in a better position than I to determine how great or how small these pressures actually are at present in their communities. And they will have to search their own hearts to determine how far their policies have undergone any change in consequence, and to what degree they have been intimidated into conformities to which their minds cannot give a true consent. For myself, I can only say that the consequences of hysterical repressiveness and of submission to such repressiveness would set back the noncommercial theatre by half a century and subvert the purpose for

[2] New York: E. P. Dutton & Co., 1951.

which the "Little Theatre" movement was created—namely, the presentation of stimulating art in American communities. I know of very few distinguished plays written since the advent of *A Doll's House* in 1879 to which fanaticism or timidity could not point a censorious finger if it tried. For that matter, I am not sure that many of the older classics could not also be assailed. If Robin Hood is not conducive to public safety, why should Falstaff be! We cannot pretend that he was a paragon of morality, and his record as a recruiting officer was distinctly below par.

If I refrain from exhuming more Shakespeariana, foraging among the minor Elizabethans and the romantic playwrights, looking too closely at Molière and the Restoration wits, and browsing in the Loeb Library of Greek and Roman classics, I, too, am following the paths of caution that in the theatre lead but to Cain's Warehouse for discarded scenery. I might be taken seriously! I recall a luncheon conversation in the twenties at which Senator King declared his intention of reducing a wave of censorship to absurdity by offering a bill requiring the Library of Congress to put all the classics under lock and key. He was instantly dissuaded by a veteran editor, who warned the Senator that his bill might be passed! I cannot, however, refrain from reporting that my research into recent world theatre uncovered the information that *Hamlet* was banned in Japan a short time before Pearl Harbor on the ground that the treatment of Claudius was conducive to disloyalty.

To return to serious business, it is obvious that a community theatre for adults reduced solely to a diet of absolutely safe *Charley's Aunt* and *What a Life* theatricals would avail little in securing national safety and avail a good deal in securing the demoralization of the theatre.

The logic of refraining from the production of good and approvable plays solely because the author happens to be in our bad graces, of course, also escapes me. And perhaps the last word on this delicate subject was said recently in a bulletin of the College English Association. An article on "Book Lists" concluded as follows:

> Nearly two hundred years ago we sent Benjamin Franklin to Paris and there was a good deal of evidence that while there he broke at least one of the Ten Commandments several times. But his fellow citizens at home did not on that account tell their children they must not read *Poor Richard's Almanac*.

It is obvious that reason and good judgment are necessary if we are to continue the high enterprise of theatre in times of understandable anxiety and irritation. And we should assume that a theatrical producer can count on the reason and sound judgment of a majority of the community to support his honorable decisions against submitting to the idiosyncrasies or malevolence of anybody who takes it into his head to censor his endeavors.

Before the producer, however, can act upon this assumption—to me the only one that expresses any faith in the American people and the strength of our institutions—he must give some further thought to the realities of theatre in a free society. If he expects millennial conditions for his enterprise, he is likely to move from disappointment and chagrin into desperation, a desperation of inactivity or an equally unfortunate desperation of cynical opportunism.

III

We must realize that the freedom of theatre has not been unlimited even in a free society except at rare intervals. When we do realize this we are less likely to be overwhelmed with terror upon encountering opposition or angrily to conclude from such opposition, however unreasonable, that ours is an *unfree* society, and that its defense need not, therefore, be our very first consideration.

The decisive difference between a society such as ours and the Stalinist totalitarian state is that in the latter the artist can work only for the state, that the theatre can subsist only on the bounty of the state, and that artistic policy is determined only by the state. In a free society, the artist works for himself or for other individuals. And if, as in the case of the Comédie Française, his enterprise receives government subsidy, it does not take orders from the government in those matters which are vital to art— namely, choice of material and mode of execution.

An important distinction, too, lies in the fact that the theatre arts in a free society are not tethered to any officially sanctioned or imposed style of writing and performance. Our theatre artists today are not mechanics on an ant heap, despite the tremendous development of machinery and mass-production methods for which our industry is celebrated and by means of which the American standard of living is the highest ever achieved in human history. The individuality of our theatre, indeed, is so pronounced as to be sometimes indistinguishable from a plain case of anarchy. And I may say from direct experience that even in our mass-communication media there is more individuality than would appear on the surface. There is considerable flexibility in dramatic structure and style. Our motion-picture, radio, and television writers and directors, not to mention performers, bring a personal equation into their work regardless of its merit, and often leave their personal imprint upon that work.

Stereotypes there are, of course, especially in the most popular types of entertainment. These, in the opinion of a mature and independent intelligence, may even be patently absurd in Grade B pictures and in soap opera. They are fostered by showmen who try to pyramid entertainment on the broadest base, on the lowest common denominator of taste and mentality. From the point of view of literary and dramatic criticism there is no excuse for such stereotypes and clichés. But a distinction must be made between totalitarian dictatorship of the arts and the commercialism of a private enterprise. The one presumes to *rule* the public, the other to *reflect* it. The one permits no violation of policy, the other allows it; is, in fact, always subject to correction by competition. Stereotyped entertainment has even been travestied, as it was for years by Henry Morgan, and so long as it has captured the interest of the public, the travesty has even enjoyed lavish sponsorship.

Above all, however, we must realize that stereotypes are present in every national art. There is nothing more stereotyped in my opinion, indeed, than the risqué boulevard comedies on which the Parisian stage has nourished generations of Parisians, presumably the most individualistic and intelligent public in the world. And the stereotypes of folk humor among *all* nationalities, as well as the theatrical cultivation of English superciliousness, rustic Irish charm, and Latin fervor, are too well known to require comment. We are correct in deploring tendencies to "mass produce" taste and thought. They are inconsistent with good art, intellectually debilitating, and unwholesome for a free people. But there is no tyranny where alternatives exist or can be created because they are not forbidden by government policy.

Another decisive consideration is the distinction that normally exists between censorship and private opposition. Censorship is official action enforcable by every means available to the state. It is also *a priori* action. The censor reads the script in advance and decides against its publication or production. Censorship thus described is dictatorship, and it is not only especially associated with a totalitarian philosophy of government but is intrinsic to that philosophy. I am unable to make a blanket statement to the effect that there are absolutely no elements in this or any other free society that favor this kind of censorship and that try to impose it. But this tendency is aberrant in, not characteristic of, a free society. And I believe that the point needs to be borne in mind, in order that we may, on one hand, distinguish between democratic and totalitarian rule even when intolerance does flare up in a democracy; and in order that we may, on the other hand, detect and oppose any tendency to destroy the distinction. It tends to vanish when plays or other books are taken from library shelves before anyone has read them simply because some individual or group has decided that they are harmful to the reader, or when productions are forbidden in the same manner. This is not the same thing as simply expressing and urging disapproval, a move which is the prerogative of any person or group in a free society; and without which, for example, dramatic criticism would cease to be a profession. One of the many casualties of Stalinist totalitarianism was, indeed, the disappearance of independent dramatic criticism. Critics became mouthpieces for the Stalinist bureaucracy.

In a *free* society, many things are possible because human beings are not invariably models of discretion and integrity. Groups have tried to exert their pressures again and again, and have succeeded or been thwarted. In France and Ireland, where tempers have often been inflammable, there have been riots over plays and concerts. The battle of *Hernani* and the patriotic demonstrations against *The Playboy of the Western World* and *The Plough and the Stars* made theatrical history. But the distinction between censorship and unofficial pressures remains. And as long as the distinction is maintained, the theatre arts are fundamentally free. The theatre arts can be harassed in a democracy, as in any other society, and patronage of them can be withheld or made conditional. But there remains a distinction between impediments to free creativity in a free society and strangulation in a totalitarian state.

A free society does not and could never guarantee the artist against the criticism or even the censoriousness of individuals and groups. It is, in fact, contrary to the spirit of a free society to abolish the right of individuals and groups to endeavor to influence an artistic enterprise. The right of free association *against* an enterprise is as inviolable as the right of free association in its behalf.

An issue is properly joined and the freedom of art is endangered only when such free associations acquire the power to legislate against an artistically valid enterprise. Yet even in this case there is a difference between totalitarianism and a democracy. In the former, there are no alternatives once such legislation is in force. In a democracy, the alternatives are always present. For example, such legislation may be local, in which case it can be appealed, repealed, or evaded by transfer of the stage production beyond the reach of local power, as was the case when the city fathers of Boston banned the production of *Strange Interlude* in 1929. In a totalitarian country, the law is inflexible and nation-wide. In a free society, it is entirely possible for municipalities to be agitated over actual or imagined affronts, and take suitable action. This does not, however, mean that it is impossible and unsuitable for citizens to take counter-action, to try to exert persuasion, or to challenge the legality of an edict.

Nor are inconsistencies in human attitudes or opinions automatically eliminated by the mere existence of a democratic form of government. The fact that we had drafted the Declaration of Independence and the Bill of Rights and had concluded the Revolutionary War did not automatically open every community to the theatre. It was still necessary after 1776 to present Sheridan's *School for Scandal* as a "Comic Lecture in Five Parts on the Pernicious Vice of Scandal" rather than as a play. And lest we begin to contemplate the benightedness of late-eighteenth- and early-nineteenth-century America, we would do well to look at England, the cradle of liberty, where the Lord Chancellor still licenses plays for non-subscription performance and was able to keep Shaw's *Mrs. Warren's Profession* from the public stage for decades. Nor can a free society always escape detraction by fear or self-interest. Especially in an age of uncertainty, although it is especially then that we ought to mind John Donne's words "What almsman of any foreign state can do so much harm as a detractor ... !" Freedom, we must conclude, does not come into existence, does not indeed exist, to an equal degree on all levels of human activity, in all parts of a country, and among all segments of the population.

In a nontotalitarian society, moreover, the ownership of a radio or television station and the support of its program are generally in private hands. We cannot expect to order owners or sponsors to accept or support a production they deem to be injurious to their best interests.

And these interests are likely to be large and based on calculations that the producers must be allowed to compute themselves. If they make the wrong computation, they will injure themselves. We must assume therefore that we cannot in principle compel them to grant every privilege of free expression in the case of productions for which sponsors pay the entire cost. The air is free and belongs to all of us. The production is *theirs* in so far as it is their own operation and is paid for by themselves. All we can do is to hope that they are properly imbued with the democratic spirit, that they are reasonable persons, and that they have the good sense not to make judgments in fields in which they have no competence.

If the professional stage centered in New York has enjoyed a much greater measure of freedom than any of the mass-communication media, an important reason is that it is relatively a small business enterprise. It also depends entirely on the support of individuals, dozens of so-called backers or angels, who band together on a basis of common taste or, as frequently happens, common indifference to the matter of the play. And once the play opens, it is on view to a public that may attend the performances or stay away from them, that may like or dislike them without affecting any other product than the stage production itself.

In the case of the media of radio and television, we have only one recourse, the full implications of which are a tangled mass of legalities. The government which issues licenses to the stations may be reasonably expected to require equitable policies from them. But the very fact that the government's role in regulating these media involves areas of cloudy indeterminacy points to an important difference between a free society and the totalitarian state. In the latter, there is never any doubt as to what the state may do: it may do anything it pleases.

IV

It does not, however, follow from what I have said that our free society is one which guarantees individuals, groups, cities, or states the liberty of withholding liberty from those who wish to exercise it in the theatre arts or, for that matter, in any art.

In the first place, there are constitutional guarantees, born of this nation's original belief in freedom, forbidding those infringements of freedom of speech and assembly which are manifest and decisive. Folly, fear, or power lust may endeavor to infringe upon these rights, or to expunge them. But the law of the land and its strongest traditions are on the side of those who desire to preserve them. Fundamental freedoms in a free society cannot be lost. They can only be surrendered.

Only apathy on the part of the theatre's leaders and supporters can result in surrender. No free society ever came into being on the premise that liberties once achieved could be left unguarded. The theatrical profession, along with its public, would be unworthy of freedom if it failed to make every effort to defend constitutional rights and to strengthen American traditions. And I may say with gratification and pride in the profession that I have found no indication of negligence or carelessness in the one region of our country which I have had occasion to visit three times within a period of eighteen months. That region is our old-new South and the groups I have in mind belong to the educational theatre.

First at Shreveport, where I had the honor to address the Southwest Theatre Conference headed by John Wray Young, then at Chapel Hill where I addressed the Southeastern Theatre Conference, and still more recently during a tour of the open-air theatres in Virginia and North Carolina under the tutelage of Samuel Selden, I saw heartening indications of every resolve to sustain and advance those values which have kept

Americans free. And I did not visit a single outdoor production, attended by a thousand or more citizens at each performance, from which any man could not derive an education in the history of our struggle for freedom and justice. The American dream seemed firmly enshrined in these summer productions which have enjoyed the encouragement of their communities and states and the patronage of hundreds of thousands of Americans every year since the projects were established.

From Roanoke Island, the seat of the first English settlement on the Atlantic Coast, to Cherokee, in the Smoky Mountains near the border between the Carolinas and Tennessee, I saw a fervent dedication to national tradition and heard ringing words on behalf of freedom such as I have not heard on Broadway since the production of Robert Sherwood's *Abe Lincoln in Illinois* some fifteen years ago. [One could wish then, and even more so now, a decade or more later, that the liberalism manifested in these open-air festival theatres could have had a more direct bearing on the civil rights problems affecting the Negro population. *J. G.*]

I have spoken of the South because, in this instance, I can speak from experience. I have no reason, however, to believe that the theatre in other regions is less devoted to democratic principles. Nor was it my intention to content myself solely with a tribute to Southern colleagues. The main point I have wanted to propose is that the theatre has, in some measure, its own correctives for intolerance—in the cooperation without which no theatre can exist, in the humanist tradition which it has inherited from its long history, and in the educational possibilities of the stage. The theatre can educate for democracy, and in doing so help to assure freedom for itself, as well as for our other institutions.

In the second place, let us reflect that only in a totalitarian state can pressures be exerted from a single direction. In a free society, there are no irreversible equations. If those who are disposed to impose restraints upon the arts and its artists are free to make their influence felt, so are those who oppose those restraints.

It is one of the cardinal principles of a free society that the channels of public opinion are open to all. In practice, this is not always the case, for many of these channels are *owned* and others can be *bought* if not already owned. But nobody's vote is owned in a democracy, nor voice either. It follows then that if only antidemocratic clamors are allegedly heard in any marked proportion, and if these fill the conference rooms of the mass-communication media to such an extent that restraints on freedom multiply, there must be considerable torpor on the part of the professed believers in freedom. Concerning failure to oppose well-organized pressure groups articulate well beyond their actual numbers, we may say with Shakespeare:

> And why should Caesar be a tyrant then?
> Poor man! I know he would not be a wolf
> But that he sees the Romans are but sheep:
> He were no lion, were not Romans hinds.[3]

And with respect to this matter of staging countermoves—that is, of making opinion effective—surely, again, it is the theatre's practitioners who should have the edge. The art of showmanship, of vivid presentation, belongs to them. If they do not choose to use it, they waive their advantage. And in doing so, they fail to exercise not merely a privilege but an obligation in a free society—that of making a forceful presentation of an honestly held and openly maintained case. A free society does not offer sanctuaries for anyone from the vigorously driven arguments of the other side, as every election year demonstrates anew. A free society merely allows the traffic to be a two-way affair. But for this to be the case, the drivers must *use* the roadway.

In the theatre, moreover, my metaphor may be applied in another way than that of expressing a demand that the channels of communication be kept open. Even in these days of high production costs, it is still possible to present stage productions representative of divergent opinions and taste. That is how an art theatre came to be born in the United States between 1910 and 1920, a period when a few managements virtually preempted Broadway and the touring circuits. If there is one institution in which uniformity cannot be imposed except by totalitarian rule or a reign of terror, it is the stage. Professional producers and off-Broadway theatre groups are constantly cropping up in our society with no more regulation than that which comes from building and fire-prevention rules.

Nor is individual enterprise entirely closed even in the case of the more expensive mass media. The range of private enterprise in the field of broadcasting has been wide, and the networks are not in absolute control. Time can also be bought from stations for radio and television programs. Motion pictures have been produced outside the orbit of Hollywood industry, and some of these have won esteem and a public. The financial fiascos of Hollywood in recent years may indeed have beneficial results in one respect. Film production with a view to reaching every available spectator has been an important factor in imposing intellectual conformity and a common banality on studio-made products. When more

[3] *Julius Caesar*, I, 3, ll. 103–106.

motion pictures are made with reduced budgets for different types of audiences, there is a likelihood that there will be less self-decapitation by movie-makers. Hollywood's golden dream of pleasing everyone is coming to an end now that its mass audience has been whittled down for most of its offerings. It may not be the 3 D's but the three R's that will revive motion-picture production.

I would conclude, then, that in a free society the theatre arts do not necessarily give rise to imperishable masterpieces, do not necessarily attain distinction or infallibility in performance. Nor are they able to operate without impediments to honest and worthy creativeness at one time or another or in one place or another. But the range of possibilities for the exercise and public enjoyment of creativity remains large and varied. And the degree of freedom enjoyed by these arts is proportionate to the will of the majority of people to grant and preserve that freedom.

V

The question that cannot be answered so as to cover every exigency is what freedom invariably consists of in the theatre arts. But on that score I do not hesitate to say that our demands, as a rule, have surely not been excessive. No responsible representative of the legitimate stage has broken any lances in behalf of obscenity and of any candor that cannot be justified to the adult mind. A reasonable area of disagreement arises only in the case of the mass-communication media to which children and impressionable adolescents have easy access. I do not know what solutions there are for radio and television theatre except the scheduling of certain programs past the bed-time hours of the young. In the case of motion pictures, the best solution may well be the restriction of certain films to theatres where attendance by the young is unlikely and can be restrained by regulations, preferably voluntary. There is no sense, however, in depriving adults of the gratifications of wit and intelligent observation, and the dangers of a widening and spiraling dictatorship of the arts are considerable in any effort to do so.

In the case of the legitimate stage, of course, the question of safeguarding the morals of the young hardly ever enters. Commercial productions are well beyond the price range of adolescent attendance, and attendance in the case of the comparatively small communities in which our noncommercial theatres flourish can be regulated easily enough by the parents themselves. As for efforts by any group of citizens to safeguard the morals of adults who are likely to want to see a play of any intellectual caliber, the case is a clear-cut one. Such efforts will be defeated, I trust, by their very impertinence so long as our society remains intact. It is not a principle of democracy that the bias of the uneducated or the bigoted is sacrosanct even when they constitute a majority. A free society guarantees fundamental rights to an educated minority no less than to the uneducated, the half-educated, or the miseducated. A free society, secured by constitutional guarantees, differs from a totalitarian society in securing its citizens against a legalized leveling of taste and thought. Such leveling is public policy only where it is public policy to establish uniformity in the interests of tyranny.

The problem of restriction is more complicated in the case of motion-picture licensing, since a board of censors, unlike a pressure group, is vested with legal authority. Lines are drawn fine in making distinctions between turpitude and genuine art in cases of censorship. In such instances, persuasion and a resort to the courts of the land decide the particular issue, whereas in a totalitarian country attempts at persuasion are construed as disloyalty and a resort to the courts is impossible. It does not follow, of course, that errors and injustices cannot be committed in a free society; we should never confuse the City of Man with the City of God, as some naïve liberals have tended to do. But in a free society men are at liberty to combat the errors and injustices; and labeling their effort treasonable is the real treason we must guard against.

Beyond flagrant and commercialized depravity, against which laws are in force, we are left only with the question of subversive propaganda, alleged or actual. This question, however, brings us back to the problem with which I started. And I have no further views to offer on that subject other than the belief that our free and strong society has little to fear from the assaults of subversive propaganda via the theatre arts and much to fear from the suppression of anything on which opinion can be honestly divided. Men and women who understand the nature of a free society and want to keep it free will, if anything, be inclined to err on the side of laxity rather than rigor. And on this subject there are still no sounder words than Milton's when he wrote "I cannot praise a fugitive and cloistered virtue, unexercised and unbreathed, that never sallies out and sees her adversary, but slinks out of the race," or our own Benjamin Franklin's ringing reproof: "They that can give up essential liberty to obtain a little temporary safety deserve neither liberty nor safety."

[POSTSCRIPT: After the rhetoric of the above-printed conclusion, it is regrettable to have to add that the American theatre proceeded to succumb to other factors of debilitation, against which it was impossible to defend it in the nineteen fifties and sixties with anything as simple as tolerance, freedom, and good will. The economics of the commercial theatre was one such factor and the ineptness of those who endeavored to establish an "uncommercial" theatre was another. Freedom is a condition that does not automatically assure creativity. It does not insure against the stupidity of the talentless, the chaos of "free enterprise," and the far greater chaos of inner demoralization evident in the Theatre of the Absurd excesses and crudities, a general loss of good taste and sense of form, and the failure of nerve evident in bohemian or "antibourgeois" theatre, on the one hand, and the sentimentalities and banalities of the "bourgeois" theatre, on the other. And it could be said ironically but also, accurately that the solution for both kinds of theatre was "entertainment." (Even Brecht made "entertainment" the central tenet of his "organon.") The question is chiefly one of determining exactly what is meant by "entertainment." For the antibourgeois theatre, it often seemed to me a more or less juvenile form of nose-thumbing. For the bourgeois theatre, it appeared to hover between a passive sensuous enjoyment of dazzling and deafening musical comedies and theatre-party communion of matronly audiences on a level of interest that rarely transcended domestic felicities and infelicities. And I incline to the opinion that the complacency of that audience and those who serve it is more deplorable than the militant crudity of unlicked proponents of avant-garde theatre. As between middle-aged stasis and youthful pyrotechnics, I would choose the latter. There is even a chance that the young may grow up, although there is little assurance that they won't merely resemble their elders and succumb to a comfortable *embourgeoisement*. J. G.]

A HUNDRED YEARS OF
AMERICAN THEATRE*

It would take a man endowed with greater temerity than I possess to venture upon my subject without apology, and it is obvious of course that this assembly does not expect me to review a hundred years of American theatre in a single hour. But I welcome this opportunty to have my say about certain features of the American theatre and to propose some perspectives on its capacities and shortcomings.

In 1863 the American nation and, with it, the American theatre were in great peril; the situation is not substantially different today, a hundred years later. Nevertheless, an account of the intervening period cannot be wholly dispiriting with respect to the nation or the theatre. It is not a period of stasis but one of much effort and marked development, so that it is possible, I trust, to engage in rational discourse rather than fruitless lamentation as we approach our subject. In some respects, with respect to the disorderly world of the theatre, it is even possible to take an orderly view of the period.

Several perspectives suggest themselves. We may view our theatre, for one thing, as an organism sensitive to the world around it. It is not at all true that our theatre remained provincial after its eighteenth-century beginnings. In point of fact, it was never provincial, if for no other reason than the influence of eighteenth-century British comedy already apparent in Royall Tyler's *The Contrast,* in 1787, and the vogue of European melodrama in a large number of imitations or adaptations. When provincialism appeared in our hundred-year period it was usually a deliberate effort to satirize pretensions to European culture (as in *Fashion*), to tap native resources of rustic humor as evidence of Yankee shrewdness (as in Winchell Smith and Frank Bacon's *Lightnin'* in 1918), or to extract entertainment from the American melting pot of races and nationalities, as in the minstrel shows and the Harrigan and Hart farces of the 1880's. Later, provincialism took the benign form of the so-called regionalism to which we owe such sophisticated productions as *The Green Pastures, Porgy and Bess* (which may be called regionalized Puccini), *Green Grow*

* An address delivered at the Centenary Theatre Festival Boston College, May, 1963.

241

the Lilacs, and *Oklahoma!,* by such urbane cosmopolites as Richard Rodgers, Oscar Hammerstein II, and the Theatre Guild.

In recent decades, especially in the 1930's, we took pride, when we did not find displeasure, in the so-called social consciousness of the American theatre. Until the vogue of Britain's angry young men, responsible for such explosions as Osborne's *Look Back in Anger* and Wesker's *Chips with Everything,* England's social drama was tame by comparison with ours. But there was drama of social consciousness in the nineteenth-century theatre abroad, and both romantic and realistic variants were by no means absent on the American stage during the very decades that we customarily write off as premodern. I have in mind the latter half of the past century, although it is well to remember that even topical drama was plainly present in the eighteenth century when *Androboros,* satirizing the Trinity Church parish in New York, was privately performed in 1714, and when General Warren's plucky wife, Mrs. Mercy Warren, denounced the Tory faction as a "swarm of court sycophants, hungry harpies, and unprincipled danglers" in *The Group,* a play printed a day before the Battle of Lexington. I have in mind two late-nineteenth-century developments. One is the drama of liberal sentiment, as one could call it, represented by Boucicault's *The Octoroon,* which reached the stage on the eve of the Civil War in December, 1859, and had been preceded by the popular dramatization of *Uncle Tom's Cabin* in 1852; the other is the emergence of the "problem play."

Historians have no difficulty in locating an interest in problem plays on the part of American playwrights before World War I. We find Bronson Howard writing on the conflict between capital and labor in *Baron Rudolph* in 1881, and on Wall Street speculation in *The Henrietta* in 1887. We find Steele MacKaye treating class conflict with considerable concern the same year in *Paul Kauvar, or Anarchy.* We find other playwrights during the next three decades concerning themselves with the depredations of monopolistic business (Charles Klein's *The Lion and the Mouse*), with corruption in city politics (Edward Sheldon's *The Boss*), with slum conditions, and with racial conflict.

Our playwrights were sensitive to the existence of social problems and to the European theatre's concern with them well before the outgrowth of World War I. But the relative inadequacy of the plays cannot be denied; they impress us today as ludicrously unoriginal and tepid by comparison with the work of Ibsen, Shaw, Hauptmann, and other major European writers. Our sobriety and penchant for *moral* reform since Puritan times, combined with the country's optimistic frame of mind and the promises of the expanding frontier, reduced the intensity of social tensions in our drama; life in America disposed playwrights toward sentimentality and to such congenial resolutions as the reformation of a corrupt politician by his noble wife in Edward Sheldon's *The Boss*. The naturalistic fiber and the revolutionary fire of European plays were not in evidence in our theatre until it responded to the temper of the 1930's and produced that period's dramas of protest. The European masters' ironic viewpoint, sultry in the case of Ibsen and jaunty in the case of Shaw, was virtually foreign to our theatre until it responded to the sophistication of the prosperous 1920's and produced that period's comedies of irreverence.

Similar observations may be made about another important manifestation of modern drama—the development of "character drama," with or without reference to environmental factors. An interest in character, colored by concern with moral attitude and environmental factors, began to appear in our theatre in 1890 with the production of James A. Herne's *Margaret Fleming*. Interest in psychological phenomena made an impression when Augustus Thomas employed mental suggestion in resolving his trial drama *The Witching Hour* in 1907, and when William Vaughn Moody made discreet overtures to the subject of sexual inhibition in *The Great Divide* and *The Faith Healer*. Tentative ventures such as these pale into insignificance, however, when compared with such European treatments of character and psychological conflict as *The Master Builder, Hedda Gabler, The Father,* and *Miss Julie*. It was with the advent of the 1920's that our playwrights began to explore character even as mildly as in George Kelly's *Craig's Wife* and Sidney Howard's *The Silver Cord*, not to mention the grim procession of dramas headed by such studies of human desolation as *Desire under the Elms, Strange Interlude, Mourning Becomes Electra, Long Day's Journey into Night, The Children's Hour, Toys in the Attic,* and *A Streetcar Named Desire*.

For a considerable time, progress in the direction of true realism was delayed not only by the vestigial Victorianism of our cultural life but by the delusion that realism was a mere matter of verisimilitude. Pictorial realism, applied mainly to melodramas, came into vogue in the second half of the nineteenth century. Along with developments in the mechanics of scenic illusion, this surface realism grew in spectacularity. This penchant for sensational naturalism, later the chief commodity of the motion-picture industry, spilled over into the twentieth century. It became the naturalism for which David Belasco was first noted and ultimately notorious—until the term "Belascoism" became the last word in scenic deception and dramatic charlatanism.

It soon became necessary to liberate our theatre from this kind of surface naturalism, and ever since World War I dramatic interest has fluctuated on our stage from realistic to antirealistic substance and style. Our playwrights have evinced divided loyalties, as exemplified by O'Neill's, Elmer Rice's, Tennessee Williams', and Arthur Miller's wavering between one extreme and another.

Whether they wrote *Anna Christie* or *The Emperor Jones* and *The Hairy Ape, Desire under the Elms* or *The Great God Brown, All My Sons* or *Death of a Salesman, A Streetcar Named Desire* or *Camino Real,* they felt justified in thinking of themselves as modern or "advanced" writers. And it is also noteworthy that fusions of realistic and poetic style, reconciliations of naturalistic and imaginative drama, have appeared significantly in our theatre. Syntheses of dramatic styles appeared impressively in many a noteworthy play whether it was social or psychological in interest: in the Elmer Rice and the Kaufman satires *The Adding Machine* and *Beggar on Horseback;* in the Clifford Odets and Irwin Shaw social protests of *Waiting for Lefty* and *Bury the Dead;* in *Strange Interlude* with its blending of realistic portraiture and interior monologue, *The Glass Menagerie* with its combination of authentic characterization and direct address to the audience, and in *Death of a Salesman* with its alternation of realistic and memory scenes.

In these and other respects, American playwrights became notably eclectic, acquiring imaginative features without losing connection with American life or foregoing a degree of rough-hewn realism. It was possible for O'Neill to be at once colloquial and imaginative, and to embrace both naturalistic detail and symbolic nuance in *Anna Christie* and *The Iceman Cometh* toward the beginning and end of his career. Tennessee Williams could combine poetic imagination and naturalistic sensationalism in a number of successful works. Arthur Miller was moved to break out of the Sardoodledom and early Ibsenite realism of *All My Sons* without renouncing, in *Death of a Salesman* and other plays, his distinctive leanings toward social drama and Ibsenite social moralism. And most recently, Edward Albee is seen alternating between the realism of *The Zoo Story* and the surrealism of *The American Dream;* and a somewhat fruity naturalism in *Who's Afraid of Virginia Woolf?* vies in that controversial drama with elements of the imagination that border on the *surreal.*

An historical overview may project this picture I have drawn on a larger screen than I have used thus far. It is possible to maintain, for example, that our most distinguished dramatic writing belongs to one of two major dispensations—namely, the Ibsenite and sociological, as in the case of Arthur Miller, or the Strindbergian and psychological, as in the case of Tennessee Williams. But a more comprehensive description would maintain that the coalescence of two modern styles of theatre has accounted for all the progress there has been on the American stage.

Progress was *first* assured in Europe by the rise and growing influence of the so-called Independent or Free theatres such as Antoine's Théâtre Libre in Paris, founded in 1887—theatres that established naturalism. But hardly had these theatres attained their objectives when the countermovement of the Art theatres under Copeau, Reinhardt, and other directors dedicated to imaginative drama and theatrical stylization asserted itself. All this occurred several decades before the American stage had divested itself of its Victorian harness. When this happened, therefore, there occurred in America a simultaneous pronaturalistic and antirealistic revolution—an assimilation of both Independent and Art Theatre esthetics.

An organization like the Theatre Guild stood for progress whether it produced Tolstoy's naturalistic peasant tragedy *The Power of Darkness* of the year 1886 or Ernst Toller's contemporary expressionist political drama of the early twenties *Masse-Mensch* under the title of *Man and the Masses*. The earlier experimental Little Theatres, such as O'Neill's theatre group, *The Provincetown Players,* and the Theatre Guild's predecessor, "The Washington Square Players," elected for progress whether they produced O'Neill's naturalistic *Bound East for Cardiff* or Edna St. Vincent Millay's *commedia dell'arte* piece *Aria da Capo*.

Progress in the American theatre has had two faces; eclecticism, as illustrated by these different examples of playwriting and by the different styles of staging associated with them, is perhaps the most noteworthy feature of the American theatre after World War I. And what has come of this duality of focus is undoubtedly a prime question in any assessment of the last five decades.

The simplest answer is that we got out of this development one playwright of major importance in the history of the Western theatre—Eugene O'Neill. We also got at least three other playwrights who attained international repute—Wilder, Williams, and Miller—in addition to a number of more or less distinguished individual plays by other authors. I should judge that we have acquitted ourselves fairly well—but less and less so recently—by comparison with France, Germany, England, and the rest of Europe since 1918. France alone, I think, has done somewhat better during the latter half of this period—the period of our dramatic maturity—with its succession of playwrights of varied origins such as Giraudoux, Anouilh, Sartre, Genet, Ionesco, and Beckett.

One way of arriving at a proper evaluation of our theatre, however, is to ascertain what we did not get from half a century's strivings.

We did not get a distinctive *American* style of drama and theatre or achieve a great deal with it whenever we got it. We got a cosmopolitan, nervous and loud, for the most part jerry-built, theatre whose most successful product proved to be in the main the American musical. We acquired musical comedy and music drama for the legitimate stage, replacing nineteenth-century grand opera with such relatively informal musical works as *Porgy and Bess, Street Scene, Lost in the Stars,* and *The Medium,* and replacing Central European operetta with such lighter and keener entertainments as *Pal Joey, Oklahoma!, Guys and Dolls,* and *How to Succeed in Business without Really Trying.*

As for the nonmusical stage, its genuine comedies have had no particular coloration or accent that would distinguish them from European comedy of manners. Literate entertainments like Behrman's *The Second Man,* Sherwood's *Reunion in Vienna,* and Barry's *The Philadelphia Story,* with the possible but inconclusive exceptions of *What Price Glory?* and *Born Yesterday,* could have been written for almost any other theatrical capital in Western Europe. It is mainly on the lower levels of farce-comedy that our playwrights did their writing across the American grain of humor and manners, as in *The Front Page, The Show-Off,* and *Boy Meets Girl.* And it is hardly established that American farces and farce-comedies have possessed a more than temporary liveliness and relevance. It is certainly doubtful that a national theatre can be founded on them. They have rarely been revived on the professional stage with any success; most of them have become dated most unconscionably, as have indeed most of the high comedies as well, almost as if they had been written a century earlier but for differences in manners and in idioms.

Regional theatre promised a rich harvest in the 1920's; it now looks like a very lean one. For one thing, American regionalism began to vanish as a social reality almost as soon as it began to assert itself in the theatre; regionalism had no future in an age of rapidly developing communications and space-annihilating radio and television information, instruction, and entertainment. Regionalism tended to restrict the intellectual reach and the emotional range, as well as to limit the nonlocal articulateness, of the drama. The success of our regional drama, but for plays by Paul Green, E. P. Conkle, and Lynn Riggs, became indirect rather than direct. It has lived on chiefly with the help of universalization by music, in *Porgy and Bess* rather than in the original *Porgy,* or in *Oklahoma!* rather than in the original *Green Grow the Lilacs.* There is vastly more valid regionalism to be found today in the outdoor pageant-plays turned out by Paul

Green and his Southern colleagues since the production of *The Lost Colony* on Roanoke Island in 1937 than in anything produced in the American professional theatre anywhere.

We have a multifarious theatre, which accommodates foreign and home-made plays in almost any style, but we do not have a distinctly American theatre in any positive sense. It can be maintained at most that acting, directing, and playwriting have favored a stronger thrust and realism in the United States than in most European countries.

A further test concerns the question of whether, given good repertory companies, we could establish a national theatre based on native plays. I daresay we could, but the repertoire would be subject to constant challenge, if not total rejection, by a new generation. This was, in fact, the case a scant dozen years ago when the young blades of Eric Bentley's generation of critics were inclined to cast O'Neill, not to mention the less impressive members of O'Neill's generation, into the dustbin of history. And it may as well be admitted that our theatre has thus far produced few, if any, plays invulnerable to racing time and changeable taste. If the test of a national repertoire is unfair to the American drama on the grounds that it is younger by several centuries than the English drama or the French, it is nonetheless true that we have accumulated considerably less dramatic literature of distinction than England did in the twenty-eight years that elapsed between *Tamburlaine* and the death of Shakespeare or the twenty-eight year interval in Scandinavia between *A Doll's House* and *The Ghost Sonata*.

We are alas confronted with the salient fact that another thing we did not get was a *literary* theatre. It was one of the things we sought and expected to achieve in the formative postwar years. One of the leading exponents of the period, Joseph Wood Krutch, made this expectation a major distinction between the prewar and postwar periods. But our theatre never became notably literary, whether in verse or prose. With barely an individual exception here and there, we failed to develop verse drama of any but derivative, quasi-Elizabethan, quality as turned out by Maxwell Anderson; and the inadequacies of O'Neill's prose dialogue have been bruited about by his friends as well as enemies. I know of few exceptions such as *The Glass Menagerie* and *A Streetcar Named Desire*, and I am not at all sure that their author's writing is not most distinguished when it is least poetical. The dialogue in Southern regional drama is the most authentically poetic, but is often encased in a weak dramatic structure. The poetry in the American drama has been *poésie de théâtre* rather than strictly verbal poetry, which does not give the plays themselves distinction as dramatic literature. There has been a dearth of tragedy in our theatre, which is, however, a shortcoming of the entire modern theatre. This can nevertheless be deplored insofar as it entails a want of elevation in our theatre, and this deficiency in our case must be attributed to a want of language no less than to the deterministic philosophy of naturalism that first whittled down the characters on the modern stage. A low-grade sensibility, of course, is also reductive in the theatre; it reduces potentially tragic characters and situations to pathetic, if not actually *bathetic,* ones. Whatever the reason or the circumstance, the modern American drama has been subliterary in the main, though often pungently and excitingly so.

This condition, if we are to judge by results here and abroad, is veritably preferable to the derivativeness, preciosity, and dubious formalism of many a self-consciously literary or poetic effort. The latter is sometimes mistakenly recommended by theatre-shy academicians and considerably overrated by their students. We have seen how the attempt to force literature on the theatre removed the latter-day Yeats of the pseudo-Noh plays from the public theatre and propelled him into esoteric drawing-room dramatics. And it is noteworthy how brief was the career of Eliot-inspired verse-drama in contemporary England, how its recent promise was nipped in the bud and its vogue quickly overshadowed by the present vogue of England's angry literary generation. And it does not follow that because high tragedy gave distinction to some premodern periods of Western theatre history, it can do so again under radically different conditions. There is no evidence whatsoever that twentieth-century high tragedies have proved superior to "subtragic" American dramas such as *The Glass Menagerie, Death of a Salesman, A Streetcar Named Desire, The Iceman Cometh,* and *Long Day's Journey into Night*—plays not often equaled in the recent British and European theatre.

The main historical reason for disappointment for our failure to produce an ample body of literary drama is that we expected the American theatre to do so when it began to distinguish itself from the pragmatic older American theatre, which did not, in the main, consider the produced drama as literature at all. Another purpose of the striving to give our plays literary status was, however, achieved when playwrights acquired the status and privileges or rights nondramatic writers already possessed, so that the American stage finally became more of a playwrights' theatre than ever before in its history, affording incentives to the playwright not to truckle to popular taste, giving him some necessary measure of control over his playscript, and encouraging him to use modern content, argument, and ideas into his work. Not the least of the attractions to be found in an O'Neill play of the twenties and early thirties was the playwright's traffic with modern ideas; and his experiments in dramatic structure and stylization reflected new views of human character and motivation. Those who had hoped that the American drama could acquire literary worth also expected it to be intellectual, serious-minded, passionate, and daring in content, style, and dramatic structure. That the American drama at its best after World War I became all that but usually without attaining literary distinction is another characteristic of the American drama, comprising at once its strength and its weakness —the strength deriving from directness and candor, the weakness consisting of cumbersomeness, commonplaceness, and redundancy. In their eagerness to achieve intellectual or ideological ends, our dramatists have more often than not employed a bludgeon rather than a rapier in their contest with mediocrity or quarrel with pharisaism; our playwrights consecrated themselves to the literary flicker rather than the flame of literary distinction. The twentieth-century American drama may come to be known as the greatest *subliterary* drama in the history of the Western theatre.

This is not said, however, in total derogation of our stage, and should not be considered a blanket invitation to reject the American drama, as do academicians who tend to judge the plays solely by reading them. The purely verbal element in O'Neill's play does not at all convey the depth and power of the plays as theatre. The frequently subliterary character of many plays that have succeeded on the stage does not rule them out as effective dramas or works of the theatre. When read with theatrical imagination they may even reveal qualities that belong to good literature—namely, insight, sympathy, sensitivity, judgment, and that awareness of reality and capacity for judgment which was perhaps best summed up by Matthew Arnold when he called poetry itself a "criticism of life."

Any relaxation of literary standards is apt to have—has had, indeed —a deleterious effect on the play as theatre evidenced by such defects as careless dramatic structure, arbitrary or superficial portraiture, illogicality, lack of cohesiveness, and arid or sloppy dialogue accompanying emotional aridity and mental sloppiness. The danger of degeneration became evident after the two exciting decades of the 1920's and 1930's, though it has been halted by the emergence of such new talent as that of Miller and Williams. Moreover, it was possible for us to draw upon resources abroad or resources and stimuli not confined to a single nation—in our 1920's from European wit and sophistication, in our thirties from the pervasive rage for social protest, and since 1945 in a widespread disillusionment, and a feeling of impasse or doom, and a general sense of despair in the atom-splitting and missile-spewing age that produced the "theatre of cruelty" or "theatre of the absurd" in France and has already accounted for some provocative new writing for the American stage by Albee, Gelber, and other young playwrights.

This reflection induces another one. If I were asked for some term under which one could subsume the overall character of our hundred years of American theatre, both for better and worse, I would call it Rousseauism—the exaltation of the common to the very extreme of underwriting the commonplace as a viable form of dramatic vision, the adulation of the raw material and the raw expression of life that the critic Philip Rahv once called our "cult of experience," and the infiltration of the democratic field into our modes of feeling and conduct to such a degree that it has infiltrated areas of sensibility and art where there is a scale, or hierarchy, of moral and esthetic values, and where superiority is the constant ideal and equality is not a viable ideal—where, for example, Homer, Pindar, and Sappho, all proponents of aristocracy in early Greece, are immeasurably superior to more democratic poets like Edgar Guest some 2,500 years later.

Rousseauism established itself early in the American theatre, about as early as Rousseauism in American life and democracy in American politics. It assumed such forms as the cult of nature, and regard for the natural man of simple manners, undevious conduct, and plain speech. These virtues were apt to be contrasted favorably with dandyism and pretentions to upper-class European culture. The contrast appeared in the very first true American comedy of manners, Royall Tyler's *The Contrast,* a few years after the war for independence, and was agreeably present some fifty years later in Mrs. Mowatt's *Fashion.* Rousseauism sparked the vogue of the stage Yankee bearing such apt comic names as Nathan Yank and Deuteronomy Dutiful, of the noble savage in plays about the American Indian, and of later immigrant and regional plays.

The simple common man has continued to be a focal point in our theatre and this democratic interest characteristic of American society has also been characteristic of our theatre and drama. It may account for the strength and weakness of characteristic American acting, as in the Group Theatre performances in the thirties and subsequently in realistic acting justly or unjustly designated as Method or Actor's Studio acting. And since the release from puritanical restraints in the drama signalized by reproductions of *Anna Christie* in the early 1920's, our theatre has had a succession of unprettified and unfumigated dramas of common life of varying merit. *Anna Christie, What Price Glory?, Street Scene, Awake and Sing, Our Town,* and *Death of a Salesman* have been among the best of these. Miller's strong affirmation of the possibility of making tragedy with lowly characters such as Willy Loman was more than a defense of the last-mentioned play: it was good democratic American doctrine.

But Rousseauism has its pitfalls as well as potentialities. It is conducive to dramatic sentimentality and glorification of the commonplace, to an uncritical cult of the little man and the slovenly life, and to making tragic mountains out of pathetic molehills. It must be considered a factor in keeping good and honorably intentioned American playwriting on the plateaus of dramatic art and dissuading playwrights from climbing to its peaks. This has also been the case in American theatrical production; we have had many excellently conceived and executed productions of new plays and some old masterpieces, we have experimented commendably with documentary forms such as the New Deal "Living Newspapers" confected by the Federal Theatre of the late thirties (noteworthily so in the case of *Power* and *One-third-of-a-nation*), with varieties of arena theatre or "theatre-in-the-round," and with outdoor pageant-drama. But acting in the elevated and passionate style of Judith Anderson's performance as Medea has been exceedingly rare, and a strong "high" style of staging, such as the Olivier production of *Oedipus Rex* in 1947, is something I cannot recall encountering in Broadway productions during a period of forty years of steady playgoing. In this respect, our acting and production triumphs have been chiefly on the plateaus rather than the peaks of dramatic art, though I would by no means wish to underrate our plateaus. And for all I know the plateaus may be more habitable by modern art than the peaks.

A closing topic must inevitably involve the conditions of the American theatre that affect its content and artistry, its quality and also its amplitude. One of the things we struggled but failed to achieve was a theatre consistently favorable to creativity on a professional and more than coterie basis. The struggle was ever present during the past hundred years, especially during the past fifty, and the impediments to victory have not only been numerous but have grown with the years. This is a large subject and I cannot give it the attention it deserves. This much, however, must be said. Late-nineteenth- and early-twentieth-century efforts took the form of progressive efforts on the part of managers, a number of whom were actor-managers such as M. James Herne and Mrs. Fiske, to bring modern drama, mostly European and mostly realistic, to the American stage. These were followed by efforts to augment realism with imaginative styles of production and win a public for them during the first twenty-five years of our century—attempts observable in the distinguished managerial and artistic careers of Winthrop Ames and Arthur Hopkins, and the importation of Granville-Barker by our theatre. A fiercely fought battle broke the old business monopoly of the Theatre Syndicate, leaving more room in our theatre for progressive individual enterprise such as that of Ames or Hopkins. Then came the Little Theatre movement of the 1910's that challenged the commercial theatre and within a decade reformed it sufficiently to make Broadway reasonably daring, hospitable toward a variety of modern styles such as expressionism and even surrealism (as in the case of *Beggar on Horseback, Lady in the Dark,* and *Four Saints in Three Acts*), and favorable to experimentation, as in the case of *The Glass Menagerie* produced by a former song-and-dance entertainer, Mr. Eddie Dowling, and a real estate operator, Mr. Louis Singer. Out of these Little Theatre groups, moreover, arose the professional Theatre Guild in the 1920's that revolutionized Broadway or at least moderated commercialism on the Main Stem, and out of which came the Group Theatre of the 1930's, the best ensemble company of its time, whose influence on American playwriting and acting has continued to be a force in our theatre. It is to be noted especially that several off-Broadway groups and their supporters accounted for the emergence of several generations of playwrights, from O'Neill in the twenties to Albee in the sixties, without whom the American stage would have little distinctiveness and hardly any distinction.

Nevertheless, the Art Theatre dream of the 1910's and 1920's, and the "peoples' theatre" dream of the embattled 1930's did not materialize —and perhaps could not have materialized without nationally and locally subsidized repertory companies for which there was very little precedent aside from the abortive turn-of-the-century repertory of Mrs. Fiske, Eva Le Gallienne's short-lived Civic Repertory Company in the twenties, and the W.P.A.'s Federal Theatre of the 1930's, out of President Roosevelt's budgets by economy-minded legislators. In time, a new off-Broadway movement, the current one, came to the rescue with debatable results and an uncertain future, owing to the riskiness and growing expensiveness of stage production. In the meantime, the commercial theatre itself has shrunk in size and increased in expense, and in the process corrupted the public, which nowadays patronizes "hits" rather than plays and undermines creativity with quick failures and inordinate requirements for success the theatre has never before had to face, so that playwrights and stage directors, too, concern themselves more with turning out "hits" than plays. The American theatre, in brief, has faced shipwreck on the granite facts of economics. Miracles, however, are events that occur in defiance of evident facts. These have occurred in the past, and they may occur in the future, especially because the theatre has not lived and will not live by bread alone; and this reflection introduces us, of course, to the growing role of the university theatres, which should and will concern us before the Boston College conference is over.

EUGENE O'NEILL*

When Eugene O'Neill received the Nobel Prize in 1936 he was in his forty-ninth year and appeared to have concluded his career. More than thirty-five short and long plays by him had been produced in the United States, and they had won him important awards in his own country and an international reputation. But a long period of absence from the theatre followed *Days without End,* which had opened in New York on January 8, 1934, and O'Neill did not return with a new play until the Theatre Guild production of *The Iceman Cometh* in 1946. Another decade of absence from the New York stage then ensued when his next play, *A Moon for the Misbegotten,* was withdrawn from a trial tour in the Midwest by O'Neill and the Theatre Guild management. Not until 1956 did another new play by him, *Long Day's Journey into Night,* reach New York. In the meantime, O'Neill had died in Boston on November 27, 1953, so that his renewed career as a dramatist, concluded by this more or less autobiographical drama and three other new pieces (*A Touch of the Poet, More Stately Mansions,* and the one-act play *Hughie*), was mainly posthumous. It may be said that O'Neill, who performed many other feats of endurance in the theatre, happened to have two careers in it rather than the customary single one.

O'Neill also attracted attention with two styles of theatre rather than one, being equally adept in the styles of realism and expressionism, and with two radically disproportionate types of drama, since he was equally effective in one-act plays and in cyclopean dramas twice the normal length of modern plays. His search for expressive form, in his case a combination of private compulsions and public ambitions to incorporate modern ideas and notions about life and dramatic art, led him to undertake numerous experiments with symbolic figures, masks, interior monologues, split personalities, choruses, scenic effects, rhythms, and schematizations. In O'Neill's work there is a veritable *summa* of the modern theatre's aspirations and achievements as well as its more or less inevitable limitations and failures. It is largely this multifarious engagement with the possibilities of dramatic art, combined with an endeavor to apply them to significant as well as very personally felt subject matter, that made O'Neill a playwright of international importance.

* University of Minnesota Pamphlets on American Writers, No. 45 (Minneapolis, University of Minnesota Press, 1965).

In all his major work O'Neill traced the course of a modern dramatist in search of an esthetic and spiritual center. It is not certain that he found it often, if ever, but the labor involved in the effort was usually impressive and sometimes notably rewarding. His plays embodied the ideas and conflicts of the first half of the twentieth century, assimilated its advances in dramatic art and theatrical technique, and expressed its uneasy aspirations toward tragic insights and dramatic vision. His impressiveness as a dramatist is ultimately, in fact, the result of his determined effort to trace a thread of meaning in the universe virtually emptied of meaning by a century of scientific and sociological thought. He did not, it is true, find any comforting assurances in the world, but he had the integrity to acknowledge his failure and the persistence to dramatize it with much penetration into human nature. O'Neill's experiments were not undertaken to suit the whims of a volatile trifler or the calculations of a theatrical opportunist bent on following the latest fashion; they manifest, rather, a unity of high purpose rarely exhibited by modern playwrights.

Eugene Gladstone O'Neill was born on October 16, 1888, in a hotel room in the very heart of New York's theatrical district applauded and derided as "Broadway." He was the son of the matinee idol and successful actor-manager James O'Neill, who amassed a fortune touring in a melodrama based on Alexandre Dumas' famous romantic novel *The Count of Monte Cristo*. The playwright who took so many successful liberties with dramatic form was entirely at home in the theatre, and later also acted in his father's theatrical company. But it early became distressingly evident to his parent that the young O'Neill was a rebel who would be more inclined to revolt against the romantic tradition than to preserve it. O'Neill was born into a tragically disturbed family (his mother suffered from drug addiction and his elder brother was a confirmed alcoholic) and had an unstable childhood, touring the United States with his parents and receiving an irregular education in different private boarding schools. "Usually," O'Neill declared to a reporter in 1932, "a child has a regular, fixed home, but you might say I started as a trouper. I knew only actors and the stage. My mother nursed me in the wings and in dressing rooms." Encouraged by his irresponsible actor-brother James, he was inducted into the Bohemian life of the theatrical world at a tender age. After a year at Princeton University, he was suspended in 1907 for a student prank. In 1909 he entered into a secret marriage, later dissolved. That same year he went prospecting for gold in Central America with a mining engineer. Having contracted malaria in the course of this fruitless expedition, he returned to his parents and joined his father's company as an actor and assistant manager for a brief period.

Growing restless again, he shipped to Buenos Aires on a Norwegian vessel and found employment for a time with American companies located in the area—an electric company, a packing plant, the Singer Sewing Machine Company. Tiring of clerical employment, he took a job on a cattle boat, tending mules while voyaging from Buenos Aires to South Africa. On his return to Argentina, he found himself unemployed and fell into a state of destitution which came to a close when he joined a British vessel bound for New York; but he promptly relapsed into a life of dissipation on the New York waterfront, frequenting a disreputable tavern, "Jimmy-the-Priest's," which he was to re-create in the milieu of two of his best-known plays, *Anna Christie* and *The Iceman Cometh.* Still attracted to the sea, however, he became an able seaman on the American Line and made a voyage to Southampton, England, before deciding to settle down to a less adventurous mode of life.

After joining his father's company again and playing a small part in *Monte Cristo,* followed by several months of intemperate living, he went to New London in Connecticut, where the family had its summer home, and joined the staff of the local newspaper, the *New London Telegraph,* as a reporter. He had begun to publish humorous poetry in a column of that newspaper when his journalistic career was abruptly terminated by a blow O'Neill could only consider ironic fate. His health undermined by his profligate mode of life, he succumbed to tuberculosis and had to be hospitalized in 1912. A term of six months in a sanatorium, however, proved to be doubly beneficial: it arrested the disease and made an avid reader and introspective artist of O'Neill. He read widely during his convalescence, falling under the influence of the Greek tragic poets and Strindberg. He began to write plays in 1913, and in 1914 enrolled in a course in playwriting given at Harvard University by the famous Professor George Pierce Baker.

The next year he moved to Greenwich Village, then regarded as the progressive "Left Bank" of New York, and in 1916 joined an *avant-garde* group of writers and artists who had established an amateur theatrical company. The first season in the summer of 1915 had been presented on an abandoned wharf in the artists' colony of Provincetown, on Cape Cod, Massachusetts, and they came to call themselves the Provincetown Players. O'Neill began to write short plays for them and soon became their foremost playwright as well as one of their directors when they moved to a small theatre in Greenwich Village on Macdougal Street, where theatrical experiments continued to be unfolded long after the dissolution of this company. (The best known of these have been Samuel Beckett's *Krapp's Last Tape* and Edward Albee's *The Zoo Story*.) O'Neill and his associates, the critic Kenneth Macgowan and the great American scenic artist Robert Edmond Jones, also ran a second enterprise, the Greenwich Village Theatre, from 1923 to 1927. In these years, at one or the other of the theatres were produced such varied plays as Strindberg's exotic *The Spook Sonata,* O'Neill's own expressionist race-drama *All God's Chillun Got Wings,* and his naturalistic New England variant on the Phaedra-Hippolytus theme, *Desire under the Elms.* Both the Provincetown and the Greenwich Village ventures were among the most influential of groups in the seminal Little Theatre movement, which gained momentum after 1912 and succeeded in modernizing the American theatre in the 1920's by bringing it abreast of European developments in dramatic art and at the same time discovering American backgrounds and rhythms.

The importance of O'Neill's early association with "the Provincetown" can hardly be exaggerated. He found an acceptable channel for his dramatic talent and theatrical interest because he also had an outlet for his personal rebellion in associating himself with an enterprise created by Bohemian rebels against materialistic American society and the commercialism of the professional theatre. In writing for the Provincetown Players and having his early plays performed before a small public of artists and intellectuals, he escaped the necessity of conforming to the popular taste to which his father had catered all his life with old-fashioned romantic theatricality. The prodigal son could deal with the life he had come to know during his years of wandering, poverty, dissipation, and desperation among common men and fellow-exiles from respectable society. As a result, O'Neill made himself, in his early short plays about the seafaring life (especially those collected under the title of *S. S. Glencairn*), the first American "naturalist" in a period when the general public in America was still expecting from its playwrights discreet pictures of reality that would give no offense. At the same time, his early plays evoked a vigorous poetry of naturalism compounded of the atmosphere of the sea and the moods of the men for whom their life on ships and on the waterfront was both an occupation and an occasion for romantic escape. For O'Neill himself, the sea was a symbol of the lostness of mankind in a hostile or indifferent universe, of a conspiracy of Nature against Man. Had he started his career thirty years later—say, in 1945 rather than 1915—he might indeed have been enrolled in the ranks of existentialist writers, and another decade later in the company of the "theatre of the absurd" playwrights.

It would appear that O'Neill became a significant figure in America because his early work was a natural synthesis of both the naturalistic and the poetic strivings of the modern theatre. He combined realism of characterization with a sensitive regard for the romantic longings of characters, a naturalist's concern for environmental detail with a metaphysical flight from the particular to the general, and plodding realistic prose with a poetic flair for imagery, atmosphere, and scenic imagination; it could be said of him that he was one of the least poetic and at the same time one of the most poetic of modern dramatists.

This synthesis was apparent virtually from the beginning of his work, in the one-act plays that first drew attention to him. The cultivation of one-act drama was characteristic of the entire *avant-garde* movement of the period. The Provincetown Players, along with other progressive Little Theatres, favored this genre for a variety of reasons. One-act plays required less professional experience to write than full-length dramas, and these novices of the theatre found one-act playwriting especially congenial because it enabled them to dispense with the complicated contrivances of plot they despised as unauthentic and artificial. One-act plays were also inexpensive to produce and easy to perform by the amateurs of the Little Theatre movement. (The same tendency to favor the one-act drama had been marked among *avant-garde* writers for Antoine's Théâtre Libre between 1887 and 1890, and for the Irish national theatre, the Abbey in Dublin, before 1914.) With his decisive success in this genre, O'Neill emerged as the foremost product of the Little Theatre in America, and its major justification.

O'Neill started with short "slice-of-life" dramas dealing with the miseries, delusions, and obsessions of men adrift in the world. With the appearance of the *S. S. Glencairn* cycle of sea-pieces, beginning with the Provincetown Players' production of his atmospheric drama of the death of a common sailor, *Bound East for Cardiff,* in the summer of 1916, he became the undisputed master of the one-act play form in America. The sharply etched playlets *In the Zone* and *The Long Voyage Home* (1917) and another atmospheric piece, *The Moon of the Caribbees* (1918), along with O'Neill's first Provincetown production, made up the remarkable quartet of one-acters subsequently produced under the collective title of *S. S. Glencairn.* A number of independent pieces such as *Ile* (1917), *The Rope* (1918), and *Where the Cross Is Made* (1918) also enhanced their young author's reputation by the end of World War I. *Ile* is especially representative of his early naturalistic-symbolic style with its mordant treatment of a New England sea captain's obsessive pride in his ability to hunt whales for their "ile" (that is, oil) that drives his lonely wife mad. This little play exemplified O'Neill's taste for tragic irony, his characteristic concern with destructive obsessiveness that resembles the *hybris* of classic tragedy, and his fascination with the sea as a mystery and a seduction, and as a symbol of the malignity of fate.

The same interests soon appeared in a richer and more complicated context when O'Neill began to write his early full-length plays. He gave his sense of tragic irony full scope in the first of these, the saturnine drama of fate and frustration *Beyond the Horizon,* produced in New York in 1920. A country lad who longs to go to sea attracts a farm girl with his dreamy romantic personality and is condemned by an unsuitable marriage to a routine life on the farm for which he is utterly unfit while his practical-minded brother and disappointed rival in love, who was cut out to be a farmer, departs for strange lands and leads a life of adventure for which he has no particular liking. The thwarted romantic man, Robert Mayo, is an absolute failure on the farm and his marriage is destroyed by poverty and domestic recriminations while, ironically, his unromantic brother Andrew actually prospers for a while in his adventuring and amasses a fortune (which he later loses) in romantic surroundings from which the other brother is forever barred. Only death holds the prospect of sailing "beyond the horizon" to the dying Robert Mayo for whom life on the farm had been ensnarement and defeat. Blinded by the sexual instinct, the characters made the wrong choices in life and destroyed their chances of happiness.

In *Anna Christie,* first produced under a different title in 1920 and successfully revived a year later, it is the attraction of the sea that is blamed for the combination of circumstances making a prostitute of the heroine. She had been neglected by her father, a sea captain incapable of resisting the seductions of seafaring life. The captain, unable to understand his own behavior and overwhelmed by his sense of failure as a father, speaks of the sea as a demon and equates it with diabolic fate. And in *Diff'rent,* also produced in 1920, fate plays an ironic trick on a New England girl who broke off her engagement because her seagoing fiancé was not chaste enough to satisfy her puritanical principles; having doomed herself to a life of lonely spinsterhood, she ultimately rebels against frustration by succumbing to a designing rascal many years younger than herself. Whereas *Diff'rent* made crude use of both the irony of fate and the theme of sexual repression attributed by O'Neill's generation to the rigors of New England puritanism, *Anna Christie* moved naturally and smoothly up to its climax, the rejection of Anna by a young Irishman on his discovering her sordid past. Only the ending of the play seemed marred by vaguely promising a reunion between the lovers. (O'Neill himself was apologetic for this concession to sentiment.) But even the concluding scene in which Anna's lover and her father have signed up for a sea voyage after a drinking bout possessed a raffish mordancy that suited the subject and tone of the work, and did not impair the effectiveness of this justifiably popular play. Although O'Neill's dissatisfaction with it arose from a belief that he must write unalloyed tragedies to fulfill his vision of life and his destiny as a significant tragedian, he nevertheless had no reason to be ashamed of what he had accomplished in this play. He had achieved a wry tragicomedy enriched with fully flavored naturalism in dialogue and background that proved satisfying to playgoers in America and abroad, gave the play a good run on Broadway in the theatrical season of 1921–22, and won for its author a second Pulitzer Prize. (He had first received this coveted award the year before with *Beyond the Horizon.*)

In one way or another, the characters in these and other early works were entangled with circumstances which if not tragic in any strict sense of the term were destructive of happiness, and O'Neill was by no means a poor judge of his potentialities as a dramatist in believing that his forte was tragedy. He was least successful when the quality of the characters and their conflicts fell short of tragic dimension or elevation, as was the case in several minor works that followed *Anna Christie.* The earliest of these, *The Straw,* produced in 1921, dealt with the love of two tubercular patients in a sanatorium, one of whom is cured after a few months and leaves behind him the girl, whose situation is hopeless and is alleviated only by the illusion that she will join him some day. In *The First Man* (1922) a scientist, who is deficient in tragic stature, destroys his prospects of happiness by resenting the intrusion of a child into his married life; and in *Welded* (1924), a play clearly written under the influence of Strindberg, although also steeped in personal experience, husband and wife are consumed with resentment while drawn to each other so powerfully by an irrational force that they cannot live apart. But it was not long before O'Neill lifted himself out of the morass of petty and pathetic situations and attained tragic power, when he combined naturalistic drama with fateful characters and atmosphere in *Desire under the Elms,* produced in the fall of 1924.

A tragedy of passion involving the third wife of a New England farmer and his son by his deceased second wife, this work was altogether dynamic and grim. Suffering in this play was produced by strong passions and conflicts of will on the part of determined characters. And over the developing destiny of the fateful lovers, Eben and his stepmother Abbie, drawn irresistibly toward each other despite an initial conflict of interests, brood the trees, symbolic of natural fertility and mystery, of a flourishing New England farm. O'Neill, who belonged to a generation severely critical of Victorian, especially puritan, morality, contrasted the passions of his youthful characters with the hardness and lovelessness of a Calvinist view of life. This is represented by the old farmer who has nothing but contempt for sensitive individuals like his son Eben—whom he takes for one of the world's weaklings—and whose first and last trust is in the Old Testament God who tests men's strength with severe trials. Eben, who betrays his tyrannical father Ephraim Cabot, is engaged in Oedipal conflict with him; and the young stepmother Abbie, who married Ephraim because she sought security and coveted his farm, becomes tragically involved with her stepson when her suppressed hunger for love turns into reckless passion. *Desire under the Elms* held in solution O'Neill's critical view of his milieu and his interest in Freudian psychology as well as his tragic sense of life; and in this intense play he strained the boundaries of naturalistic drama until the play verged on melodrama when Abbie strangled her child in order to convince Eben that she had given herself to him out of love rather than out of a desire to deprive him of his heritage by producing a new heir to his father's farm. And in *Desire under the Elms,* as in earlier naturalistic plays, O'Neill also strained toward the estate of poetry with his symbols of fertility and an enveloping atmosphere of longing, loneliness, and lust. An imagination strengthened by a feeling for primitive severity in tone and characterization pervades this naturalistic treatment of a classic theme in which the Theseus is a lusty elderly farmer, the Hippolytus a mother-fixated son and jealous stepson, and the Phaedra a former household drudge with an ambition to secure her future as the inheritor of a thriving farm. If *Desire under the Elms* lacks the elevation it nevertheless possesses the strength of classic tragedy. If its stream of action is muddied by Freudian details of characterization in the portrayal of Eben, it nevertheless proceeds with mounting energy toward its destination, reflecting in its course the wind-swept landscape of the human soul. In any case, nothing comparable to this work in power derived from a sense of tragic character and situation had been achieved by the American theatre in the hundred and fifty years of its history.

A more complacent playwright than O'Neill would have been content with this achievement and endeavored to repeat it. Not so O'Neill, who did not give the American stage another naturalistic adaptation of classic subject matter until the Theatre Guild production of *Mourning Becomes Electra* in 1931. The plays that followed *Desire under the Elms* were *The Fountain,* unsuccessfully produced in December, 1925, at the Greenwich Village Theatre, and *The Great God Brown,* presented at the same theatre in January, 1926. They represent O'Neill's strivings to enrich the American drama with styles radically different from the naturalistic —namely, the romantic, the symbolist, and the expressionistic.

The effort started earlier, in fact, with the production of *The Emperor Jones* in November, 1920, and some seven months later with *Gold,* an expanded version of the one-acter *Where the Cross Is Made.* The first production was decidedly auspicious, the second inauspicious; the first virtually introduced expressionism into the American theatre, the second inaugurated O'Neill's ventures into symbolist-romantic drama with which he succeeded only once—and but moderately even then—when the Theatre Guild produced *Marco Millions* in 1928. In the contrived and awkwardly written melodrama *Gold,* a sea captain is driven mad by his lust for gold, contracted on a desert island when, crazed by thirst, he thought he found a treasure trove. Its successor in the romantic style, *The Fountain,* fared scarcely better with the overextended story of the legendary search of Ponce de Leon for the Fountain of Youth which becomes obsessive until he finally realizes that "there is no gold but love." Only great dramatic poetry, which O'Neill was never to write, could have fulfilled his intentions, for it was his ambition here to attain exultation and not the "morbid realism" with which he considered himself unduly taxed. He was to return to this striving for verbal ecstasy with somewhat more success in the romantic scenes of *Marco Millions* but with generally turgid results in *Lazarus Laughed,* a boldly and nobly conceived drama in which the resurrected Lazarus teaches man to laugh at death.

Failure in romantic and symbolist drama could not, however, deter the playwright from seeking other means than realism for giving form to his vision of life and his aspirations for significant artistry. O'Neill was determined to enlarge the techniques of his playwriting, and this determination was sustained by a genuine need to find suitable methods for expressing insights and attitudes for which realistic play structure seemed to him patently inadequate. Restiveness was only a secondary motive in O'Neill's case. European example, especially that of Strindberg, was a strong influence; his associates Macgowan and Jones had written enthusiastic and provocative reports on the European *avant-garde* in books and articles. But it was not direct example that influenced him. (He claimed to have had no knowledge of German expressionism when he conceived his first expressionist plays.) It was not theory but a belief in the potentialities of nonnaturalistic drama that motivated O'Neill in the series of expressionistic experiments that started with the Provincetown Players productions of *The Emperor Jones* and *The Hairy Ape* in 1920 and 1922 respectively and continued, with a variety of modifications, in *All God's Chillun Got Wings* in 1924, in *The Great God Brown* in 1926, in *Strange*

Interlude and *Lazarus Laughed* in 1928, and as late as 1934 in *Days without End,* a drama of a split personality played by two different actors. It was a personal pressure that dominated these plays and the statement of principles he set down for playwriting when he drafted the program note on Strindberg for the Provincetown Players production of *The Spook Sonata,* which he co-produced: ". . . it is only by means of some form of 'super-naturalism' that we may express in the theatre what we comprehend intuitively of that self-defeating self-obsession which is the discount we moderns have to pay for the loan of life. The old 'naturalism'—or 'realism' if you prefer . . . —no longer applies. It represents our Fathers' daring aspirations toward self-recognition by holding the family kodak up to ill-nature. But to us their old audacity is blague; we have taken too many snapshots of each other in every graceless position; we have endured too much from the banality of surfaces."

The first product of his reaching out for expressive form was *The Emperor Jones,* in which he dealt with the flight of a Caribbean Negro dictator from his aroused victims, a subject suggested to him by Haitian history, which he transformed into a succession of scenes of panic. In these vignettes, the man fleeing through the jungle is plagued by recollected events from his private past such as his slaying of a prison guard, his meager knowledge of racial history, and his superstitious fears and savage rituals.

Impacted into this drama of a frustrated escape and the influence of atavism was a powerful sense of theatricality that expressed itself most effectively in the incessant beat of tom-toms while the rebellious natives made magic and cast a silver bullet with which to destroy him, since he had fostered the belief that no other sort of bullet could harm him. O'Neill, having read accounts of Congo ritual, was impressed by the suggestive power of relentlessly repeated rhythms of the drum, "how it starts at a normal pulse and is slowly intensified until the heartbeat of everyone present corresponds to the frenzied beat of the drum." He asked himself, "How would this sort of thing work on an audience in a theatre?" The question was quickly answered by the suspense and tension built up in the audience and the conclusive success of the play, which was also revived some years later with the celebrated Paul Robeson filling the role originally created by another gifted Negro actor, Charles Gilpin. (Later, the play was turned into an effective opera by Louis Gruenberg.) O'Neill's success with *The Emperor Jones* was dual: it was an original play—virtually a dramatic monologue without intermissions in which fantasy cut across reality and the subjectivity of the protagonist was converted into objective reality for the mesmerized audience; and it was a play in which the wordless sequences were no less expressive than spoken dialogue.

The Emperor Jones was a tour de force of imaginative theatre. It was followed by an even more exciting and certainly more provocative expressionistic drama, *The Hairy Ape,* which was somewhat baffling in meaning yet also richer and more complex in action and symbolization than *The Emperor Jones.* On the surface, the play was a series of vignettes dramatizing the bewilderment of a powerful stoker, Yank, when his naïve confidence in brute power is shaken, and his desperate efforts to find a place for himself in the world (*"to belong,"* as he puts it); on a more sophisticated level, Yank's fate expressed man's search for the meaning of his life and his alienation in the universe. Its larger, metaphysical and not readily transparent meaning was more clearly defined by O'Neill himself in an interview published in the *New York Herald Tribune* of November 16, 1925. Yank, it was plain, was not merely a portrait based on O'Neill's memory of a rough and powerful stoker whose acquaintance he had made in Jimmy-the-Priest's New York waterfront dive, but an intellectual concept of man's alienation in an indifferent universe. He was a symbol, as O'Neill put it, of man "who has lost his old harmony with nature, the harmony which he used to have as an animal and has not yet acquired in a spiritual way." The public, O'Neill complained, saw only the baffled stoker, not the symbol; yet "the symbol makes the play either important or just another play."

As O'Neill went on to explain, Yank with his narrow spirit and limited intelligence is incapable of achieving any really developed humanity, even though no longer content with his previous animal-like status. He strikes out but blindly and in vain against a reality he cannot affect or even comprehend: "Yank can't go forward, and so he tries to go back," as O'Neill put it. "This is what his shaking hands with the gorilla [in the last scene, set "in the monkey house at the Zoo"] meant. But he can't go back to 'belonging' either. The gorilla kills him.

O'Neill concluded that he had dramatized a universal theme: "The subject here is the same ancient one that always was and always will be the one subject for drama, and that is man and his struggle with his own fate. The struggle used to be with the gods, but is now with himself, his own past, his attempt 'to belong.'" It was to be O'Neill's primary theme in a series of plays that either failed or missed maximum effect to the degree to which in his impatience with realism he reduced characters to abstractions or harnessed them to metaphysical conceptions irreducible to concrete reality. In *The Hairy Ape* he succeeded in producing a powerful dramatic experience through the sheer vigor of the writing and the vibrancy of the action distributed in concise and visually arresting scenes. The fact, acknowledged by the playwright himself, that the public did not grasp the larger symbolic content did not greatly militate against the fascination and direct effect of the play. The ambiguities in it actually whetted the public's curiosity and, at the very least, served to differentiate *The Hairy Ape* from Zolaist "slice-of-life" naturalism.

O'Neill was less fortunate in a third expressionist experiment, *All God's Chillun Got Wings,* involving the marriage of a tarnished white girl and a devoted Negro lover. Here a metaphysical conception of fate seemed somewhat arbitrarily inserted into racial and psychological conflicts sufficiently immediate to make abtruseness a limitation rather than a valid extension of the drama. O'Neill dealt here with the subject of miscegenation and an ensuing Strindbergian duel of the sexes in the course of which the neurotically jealous Ella destroys her Negro husband's chances for a career and then, after going berserk and trying to kill him, lapses into remorseful dependency upon his forgiveness and devotion. Although O'Neill was not aroused especially by racial prejudice as a national problem, and was resolutely disinclined to write problem plays, the story he had chosen in this play committed him to a nonmetaphysical resolution of its tensions. Instead, he dissolved the substance of this provocative drama by placing the burden of guilt on God and fate instead of on society. "Will God forgive me, Jim?" Ella asks plaintively as she sinks into a state of childishness. Jim replies, "Maybe He can forgive what you've done to me; and maybe He can forgive what I've done to you; but I don't see how He's going to forgive—Himself." This rather irrelevant interchange was nevertheless intensely moving, as were Jim's later exclamations, even less relevant to the logic of the play, when he asks God to forgive his blasphemy: "Let this fire of burning suffering purify me of selfishness and make me worthy of the child You send me for the woman You take away!" and his response to his demented wife's plea that he play with her, when he cries out brokenheartedly: "Honey, Honey, I'll play right up to the gates of Heaven with you!" Once more O'Neill's intensity of feeling and uncanny sense of theatre came to the rescue of his dramatic reasoning.

The same talents saved his next expressionistic experiment, *The Great God Brown,* from total disaster, leaving him with a flawed and overworked drama that was nevertheless impressive enough to win respect for his earnestness and his theatrical imagination while disappointing sociological critics. Here, too, O'Neill hit upon a recognizable social fact, which may be defined as the defeat of the artist in a materialistic and unsympathetic society, and here too he concentrated on private psychology and metaphysical intimations rather than sociology. Here, however, far from veering from the logic of his argument he pursued it so persistently that he pushed schematization to extremes of abstraction and weakened credibility and reality of character in the melodramatically snarled action of the drama. In no other play did O'Neill symbolize his theme so intensively. We must remember that his early Greenwich Village associates, especially Robert Edmond Jones, had been affected in their youth by the symbolist school of literature, drama, and scenic design inspired by the semimystical esthetic aims of Gordon Craig. With such *avant-garde* sanctions, O'Neill went confidently ahead in this play, splitting his characters into sharply contrasted personalities and even resorting to masks in order to represent the antinomies of the artistic and the pragmatically bourgeois temperaments. At one point the masks are interchanged for the purpose of dramatizing the seemingly placid bourgeois personality's envy and attempted incorporation of the artist. To effectuate his symbolizing intentions, O'Neill virtually stopped at nothing in *The Great God Brown,* making it one of his boldest as well as most transparent theatrical experiments.

O'Neill had been driven once again to expressionist experiment and formal schematization by something deeper than a penchant for showmanship and a passion for experimentation. His generation, led by such rebels against the complacent materialism of a thriving middle-class society as Van Wyck Brooks, Sinclair Lewis, and H. L. Mencken, was keenly aware of the artist's isolation in such a milieu, which was either hostile or indifferent toward him, and American writers treated the subject variously in both realistic and fanciful novels, poems, and plays. O'Neill endeavored to treat it not farcically like George S. Kaufman and Marc Connelly in their Broadway expressionistic comedy *Beggar on Horseback,* but seriously; not urbanely and fancifully as did James Branch Cabell in *Jurgen* and other novels, but tragically; not realistically like Lewis in *Main Street* and *Babbitt,* but imaginatively. Primarily he was interested, as usual, in inner tensions and the drama of the soul, and it was to this end that he invented the use of masks to accentuate conflicts and changes in individuals and, in the last part of the play, to visualize a *transfer* of personality from one character to another. For some kinds of modern plays, O'Neill, who found it necessary to abandon the use of masks later on (notably in *Mourning Becomes Electra*), was at least temporarily convinced that the mask was the solution for expressing, as he put it in an essay on the subject, "those profound hidden conflicts of the mind which the probings of psychology continue to disclose." What, after all, were the new psychological insights of the age "but a study in masks" or "an exercise in unmasking"?

Troubled by the difficulty of communicating his meaning even with the device of the mask, O'Neill took pains to explicate his play in a newspaper article in the February 13, 1926, issue of the *New York Evening Post.* His chief character, Dion Anthony, represented in his dividedness the conflict between "the creative pagan acceptance of life," symbolized by Dionysus, constantly at war with the "masochistic, life-denying spirit of Christianity," symbolized by St. Anthony. The struggle resulted "in mutual exhaustion—creative joy in life for life's sake frustrated, rendered abortive, distorted by morality [O'Neill had in mind chiefly the puritanical morality of American society] from Pan into Satan, into a Mephistopheles mocking himself in order to feel alive." Perhaps Faust or, rather, Faust-Mephistopheles would have been a better choice of name, because O'Neill's heroine Margaret, Dion Anthony's long-suffering wife, was the playwright's image of the Marguerite of Goethe's *Faust,* "the eternal girl-woman with a virtuous simplicity of instinct, properly oblivious to everything but the means to her end of maintaining the race." Continuing his pattern of analogies, O'Neill made the prostitute Cybel, to whom his hero resorts for comfort and counsel, "the Earth Mother doomed to segregation as a pariah in a world of unnatural laws, but patronized by her segregators, who are thus themselves the first victims of their laws" (O'Neill's direct attack on puritanical hypocrisy); and Dion's friend, rival, and employer Brown stands for "the visionless demi-god of our new materialistic myth," inwardly "empty and resourceless," who builds his life with "exterior things" and moves uncreatively in "superficial preordained social grooves." The peripety at the end which conduces to confusion in the play consists of Brown's theft of the dying Dion's mask, which symbolizes his effort to appropriate the creativity energy he had envied in Dion. But despite believing that in stealing Dion's mask he has gained the power to create, he has actually possessed himself only of "that creative power made self-destructive by complete frustration"; and, says O'Neill, the "devil of mocking doubt makes short work of him"—a provocative idea for which O'Neill unfortunately found an incredibly melodramatic plot rather than a simple objective correlative. Despite this, the play ran nearly a year in 1926. One reason was probably the dramatic fascination of the novel and atmospherically enriched action. Another and simpler reason surely was the intensity of Dion's anguish as man and artist.

The Great God Brown, which exemplifies so much of O'Neill's striving for personal expression that it became his favorite play, was its author's most "successful" failure not merely in practical but also in dramatic and poetic terms. *Marco Millions,* which followed it some two years later, was pallid by comparison. O'Neill's animus against materialistic society led him to write a sardonic comedy on the career of Marco Polo, who turned rapidly into a Philistine impervious to beauty and romance despite his travels in the wondrous East of Kublai Khan and the love of Princess Kukachin, the Khan's granddaughter. The playwright proved to be too heavy-handed and repetitive, making his point long before the conclusion and overextending the play in performance with his quasipoetic rhetoric and requirements of spectacle. A lighter touch and a swifter pace, as well as greater verbal and situational inventiveness, were needed to realize its potentialities as satiric comedy. *Marco Millions* has its felicitous passages and telling moments. It cannot be written off as a total loss in the unfolding of its author's talent. But it cannot be considered a major or consistently absorbing work.

A return to his metaphysical vein in *Lazarus Laughed* led him into the blind alley of reiterative pseudophilosophy from which he emerged too rarely to make this huge and unwieldy drama much more than an enormous spectacle strung upon a slender thread of plot and, despite its abundant rhetoric, a subliterary ritualistic effusion. In any case, this work was more suitable for outdoor pageantry than for the ordinary stage. Its chief interest lies in the variety of theatrical means—masks, choruses, crowds, choreographic movement, and other visual effects—O'Neill's stage-struck imagination could muster in the service of an idea. It could be said that on the level of show business, the son of the star-actor of *Monte Cristo* never quite left the spectacular romantic theatre his father had turned into a livelihood; and that on the level of "art," he remained attached at heart to "Wagnerianism" or the *mélange des genres* esthetic of Richard Wagner that influenced the late-nineteenth- and the early-twentieth-century theatre. Inspiring these esthetic proclivities was an earnest effort in O'Neill to express a tension that all the Bohemian sophistication of the 1920's in America had been unable to allay or repress. It derived from the loss of religious faith that was traumatic in the case of the scion of an American Irish-Catholic family, and he was inwardly compelled to dwell upon the loss very much like his great Irish contemporary James Joyce.

O'Neill was aware of the possibility of pursuing substitutes and dramatized the search for them throughout his career. In *Lazarus Laughed* he temporarily found or thought he found an *ersatz* religion consisting of a mystical denial of death. It provided a doctrine of salvation by affirmation that was vastly more rhetorical than substantial. In *Dynamo,* his next engagement with the problem of faith, which had an unsuccessful though (largely thanks to the scenic genius of Theatre Guild designer Lee Simonson) visually stunning production early in 1929, he dramatized the substitution of machine-worship after his hero's renunciation of the puritanical faith of his fathers. While watching a dynamo in operation turning the energy of Connecticut rivers into electricity, O'Neill had been impressed with it as a veritable image of the new god of the scientific age. In *Dynamo* it became the dominant symbol, a hydroelectric generator described as "huge and black, with something of a massive female idol about it, the exciter set on the main structure like a head with blank oblong eyes above a gross, rounded torso," and it inspired him to undertake the writing of a trilogy on faith he never completed after the failure of *Dynamo* on the professional stage.

The story of the play, more simple than credible, revolved around a Calvinistically reared young American, Reuben Light, who, upon falling in love with an atheistical neighbor's daughter Ada, becomes an atheist himself. In search of a new faith to replace the old, Reuben adopts the electric generator as the symbol of his belief in science, paralleling the "Virgin and the Dynamo" contrast aptly drawn by Henry Adams. He soon finds himself worshipping the new god with the same violence with which his forebears worshipped the Old Testament deity. "O Dynamo, who gives life to things," he cries, "hear my prayer! Grant me the miracle of your love!" Driven mad by his fanaticism, he kills Ada, who made him violate his vow of undivided loyalty to the dynamo, following which he immolates himself on the lethal machine. *Dynamo* was a greater credit to its intrepid author's ambition than to his taste and discretion, and discouraged by the poor reception of the play, O'Neill abandoned his plan to write "a trilogy that will dig at the roots of the sickness of today as I feel it—the death of an old God and the failure of science and materialism to give any satisfying new one for the surviving primitive religious instinct to find a meaning for life in, and to comfort its fears of death with."

Nevertheless, he could not resist his need to return to the subject of faith and the conflict with skepticism, which he described as the "big" subject behind all the little subjects of plays and novels whenever an author is not merely "scribbling around on the surface of things." He returned to the theme but with rather dreary results in *Days without End,* which O'Neill's latter-day producing organization, the Theatre Guild, presented for a short Broadway run in 1934. This play is for the most part a lesson on the need to return to conventional religious faith, but it is doubtful that O'Neill himself ever regained such faith for more than a brief period. (It remains to be noted that in Dublin the play reaped considerably more success than in New York; the conventional religious ending, in which the divided hero John Loving loses his skeptical, diabolical alter ego at the foot of the cross, apparently appealed more strongly to the Irish than to Americans.)

Fortunately, O'Neill had started a return to modified realism and interest in character drama some half a dozen years earlier with *Strange Interlude,* which became a great Theatre Guild success in the year 1928. Instead of dealing with metaphysical content and struggles over faith, O'Neill concerned himself here with character dissection and inner conflict. Whatever means he adopted in this play, his schematizations and his recourse to the Elizabethan device of the "aside" on a scale never before attempted on the stage, served the author's sole objective of portraying a modern woman. O'Neill showed her being driven by the strange life-force in her bloodstream to unconventional relationships, and seeking multiple possession of men's lives before peace descends upon her at the end of the "strange interlude" of her premenopausal life history. With many details drawn from contemporary manners (the mores of the "sophisticated" 1920's, and contemporary psychology (chiefly Freudian), *Strange Interlude* proved engrossing to its New York public throughout the greater part of the long procession of revelations and incidents. The play was in nine acts (in contrast to the usual three-act play), ran from five-thirty P.M. until past eleven save for an eighty-minute dinner interval, and traced the critical relationships of a small number of characters for nearly three decades. Above all the characters stood Nina, the attractive daughter of a possessive university professor, who lost her athlete lover in World War I, regretted not having consummated her love with him, and sought fulfillment in desperate promiscuity. Later, having married a man to whom she would not bear children after being warned by his mother that there was insanity in the family, she gave birth to a son by another man (the neurologist Darrell) but could not bring herself to leave her husband and never could reveal the boy's true parentage. It takes a husband, a lover, a family friend, and an illegitimate son to fill her womanly life while at full tide. Then, as the vital flood recedes, she loses her husband to death, her emotionally drained lover to science, and her athlete son to a girl of his own age. By then, however, a twilight calm is descending on the central figure of this novel in play form, in which a vital modern woman is observed from many angles and in many situations. The resulting portrait was drawn on the stage by the gifted and resourceful Lynn Fontanne with such conviction that no one was likely to look for hidden meanings while she held the stage, which she did most of the time.

As a matter of fact, there were no hidden meanings in the play; if anything, O'Neill was only too explicit in his spoken and especially his supposedly unspoken dialogue—that is, the asides with which the author outlined the true thoughts and sentiments of the characters at the risk of redundancy. There could well be two strongly contradictory opinions about the recourse to asides. The British theatre historian Allardyce Nicoll deplored them as a "somewhat tedious and fundamentally undramatic elaboration of the quite worthy convention of the 'aside' into a pretentious artistic instrument." Others found much to approve in this type of "interior dialogue," which bore considerable resemblance to the stream-of-consciousness James Joyce employed in *Ulysses*. In the excellently paced Theatre Guild production of 1928, staged by the gifted director Philip Moeller with an incredibly apt and able cast, there was little cause for complaint except for the decline of interest in the last two acts. In a highly professional New York revival given about a third of a century later by the Actors Studio Theatre, the negative opinion was more or less vindicated. Even then, however, *Strange Interlude* impressed the majority of reviewers and playgoers as a weighty experiment and, more than that, as a wide-ranging human document. What rigorous criticism was tempted to dismiss in that document as mere cliché overinsistently communicated was redeemed by effective confrontations of the chief characters and by the substantiality of Nina Leeds as a veritable incarnation of *das Ewig-Weibliche*. Nina, whose grosser and more elemental ancestress may be said to be Wedekind's Lulu, is a sort of Social Register earth goddess who encompasses during her "strange interlude" the functions of daughter, wife, mother, mistress, and superwoman whom all men find attractive and whose needs no single man is capable of fulfilling, although it is surmised that the untimely lost lover, Gordon, might have been able to satisfy them. Both as a character study and as a dramatic novel, *Strange Interlude* commanded the interest of a large public grateful for an exacting and unconventional drama. And its augmented realism was sufficiently successful to direct its author back to the paths of realism he had followed rewardingly in the early sea and waterfront plays.

This was notably apparent in his *Mourning Becomes Electra* trilogy, when he domesticated or "naturalized" Greek legend and its various treatments by the Greek tragic poets. This was truly an enormous undertaking worthy of his ambition to treat significant themes and apply to them the insights and idiom of his own age. Although he employed formal elements in this work, such as a truncated chorus and masklike facial expressions, these did not undercut the fundamentally naturalistic character of the work but merely punctuated and magnified it. Turning to the Orestean theme treated by Aeschylus and his successors, O'Neill localized it in New England immediately after the conclusion of the Civil War (instead of the Trojan War) in 1865, and translated and paralleled it in terms of the American environment of that period. The scion of a wealthy mercantile family, General Ezra Mannon, the Agamemnon of *Mourning Becomes Electra,* returns from the Civil War to learn that his alienated wife Christine (the Clytemnestra of O'Neill's treatment) has been unfaithful to him with the seafaring Adam Brant from a rival branch of the family, and to be poisoned by her when he seeks a reconciliation. In the second part of O'Neill's trilogy, as in *The Libation Bearers* of Aeschylus and the *Electra*'s of Sophocles and Euripides, the Electra character, whom O'Neill calls Lavinia, and her brother, O'Neill's Orestes named Orin, avenge their father's death by killing their mother's lover Adam Brant, the Aegisthus of the modern play, whereupon the mother commits suicide. In the third part of the trilogy, the burden of guilt rests heavily on the son, although unlike the Orestes of the Greek plays, he did not directly murder his mother. Orin is virtually mad, and so dependent on his sister Lavinia that he won't allow her to marry anyone. At this point O'Neill whipped up the action into a rather melodramatic frenzy with his Electra driving his Orestes to suicide, following which she is so overwhelmed with remorse that she renounces all possibilities of happiness, shutting herself up forever with her conscience in the mansion of the ill-fated Mannons.

The power of this work communicated itself instantly on the stage in the memorable Philip Moeller production of the year 1931 for the Theatre Guild. It had a neoclassical-colonial setting by Robert Edmond Jones and featured the veteran actress Nazimova in the role of Christine, and Alice Brady (succeeded by Judith Anderson) in the part of Lavinia. But there was more to the play than the transcription of Greek matter into American terms. O'Neill, it is true, did not differ from the Greek tragedians in concerning himself with Fate and the working out of the family curse, the "domestic Ate," in the story of a New England Brahmin family. But it was his intention to go much further and translate fate into modern terms, an enterprise already started before him by the late-nineteenth-century naturalists who found an equivalent for the Greek idea of fate in their rudimentary scientific concepts of determinism by heredity and environment. Locating the determinism more directly in the human psyche, O'Neill adopted the Freudian emphasis upon the sexual instinct, especially the much publicized Oedipus complex. His Clytemnestra had been horrified on her wedding night by her husband's brutal sexuality (a case of the libido welling up from puritanical suppression) and subsequently felt alienated from the fruit of their union, Lavinia, thus alienating her daughter and making the girl excessively attached to her father, Mannon. She had lavished possessive affection, however, on her second child, Orin, during her husband's absence when America waged war with Mexico, thus causing the son to be pathetically fixated on her. It is chiefly Oedipal resentment that pits the Electra of O'Neill's trilogy against his Clytemnestra, and it is Oedipal attachment that makes O'Neill's Orestes the tool of his sister's animosity, which results in his seeking out and killing Captain Adam Brant on his ship. Orin's act and Lavinia's provocation lead step by step to his mother's suicide, his disturbed state of mind, his incestuous dependency on the sister (who has begun to resemble the mother she has destroyed), and his own death.

Schematization was carried too far in the play, but the Freudian interpretation produced intensely dramatic moments, especially in the mother-daughter conflict. Still, in resorting to psychoanalytical explanations and highlighting them in each of the three plays of the trilogy, O'Neill deprived his characters of tragic stature insofar as they became clinical cases, and this invited criticism from some quarters that O'Neill had written a case history rather than a tragedy. One could offer the defense that the characters and events as observed in the Theatre Guild production certainly *felt* tragic—at least until the excrescence of melodramatic action in the last part of the work. A better case could be made against the trilogy by those who noted the poverty of O'Neill's low-grade naturalistic dialogue, so distressingly at variance with the powerful passions and mounting action of the trilogy, so downright flat precisely when the language should have been made to soar, as in the scene in which Orin tells his mother that he has killed her lover:

CHRISTINE. (*stammers*) Orin! What kept you—?

ORIN. We just met Hazel. She said you were terribly frightened at being alone here. That is strange—when you have the memory of Father for company!

CHRISTINE. You—you stayed all this time—at the Bradfords'?

ORIN. We didn't go to the Bradfords'.

CHRISTINE. (*stupidly*) You didn't go—to Blackridge?

ORIN. We took the train there but we decided to stay right on and go to Boston instead.

CHRISTINE (*terrifiedly*) To—Boston—?

ORIN. And in Boston we waited until the evening train got in. We met that train.

CHRISTINE. Ah!

ORIN. We had an idea you would take advantage of our being in Blackridge to be on it—and you were! And we followed you when you called on your lover in his cabin!

CHRISTINE. (*with a pitiful effort at indignation*) Orin! How dare you talk—! (*Then brokenly*) Orin! Don't look at me like that! Tell me—

ORIN. Your lover! Don't lie! You've lied enough, Mother! I was on deck, listening! What would you have done if you had discovered me? Would you have gotten your lover to murder me, Mother? I heard you warning him against me! But your warning was no use!

CHRISTINE. (*chokingly*) What—? Tell me—!

ORIN. I killed him!

CHRISTINE. (*with a cry of terror*) Oh—oh! I knew! (*Then clutching at* Orin) No—Orin! You—you're just telling me that—to punish me, aren't you? You said you loved me—you'd protect me—protect your mother—you couldn't murder—!

One expects less prosaic language from a master tragedian, which O'Neill narrowly missed becoming in this play.

The language and the heavy emphasis on incestuous feelings elicited unfavorable comment at first mostly in England and later in American literary circles, the most considered being perhaps Allardyce Nicoll's conclusion that "This is rather a magnificently presented case-study than a powerful tragic drama." O'Neill resented the allegation that he had borrowed his ideas, claiming that he knew enough about human nature to have written the play without having ever heard of Freud and Jung. But O'Neill had himself imposed restraints on his endeavor to write a modern high tragedy by domesticating the Orestean legend to the point of restricting his dialogue to naturalistic commonplaceness, and by asking himself (in his preparatory notes to *Mourning Becomes Electra*) whether it was possible to "get modern psychological approximation of Greek sense of fate into such a play." His play is an affirmative answer which, nevertheless, leaves unanswered the larger question O'Neill did *not* ask himself—namely, whether modern dramatic vision needs to be limited, or is actually exhausted, by "psychological approximation."

Some necessity of art and personal expression, then, kept O'Neill moving back to realistic drama as the style of writing by which his reputation would stand or fall. This led him to yield to psychopathology and lapse into sunless Gothic melodrama in *Mourning Becomes Electra*. It also led him, two years later, to the pleasant alternative of producing the genial genre painting of *Ah, Wilderness!*, a family comedy set in a small Connecticut city at the beginning of the century. A nostalgic comedy of recollection, it revolves around a bright and spirited adolescent who has his first and luckily harmless fling at low life when jilted by the daughter of a parochial father, who disapproves of the boy's penchant for the "pagan" poet Swinburne. The boy's understanding and ever-smiling father, who is the local newspaper publisher, straightens everything out to his son's satisfaction, and to the gratification of playgoers pleased at meeting O'Neill for once without his tragic mask. The popular star George M. Cohan, playing the newspaper publisher, toured this comedy of reconciliation across the nation without adding substantially to O'Neill's reputation or altering it for admirers, who cherished their memory of him as a singularly sultry dramatist. Today, *Ah, Wilderness!* falls into proper perspective as one of the most attractive of American domestic comedies—nothing less, and nothing more. For the author himself it was only a brief holiday from his most persistent memories, which were normally bleak, and from the contemporary world, about which he never felt particularly cheerful. That it represented only a vacation from a gloomy view of *la condition humaine* was to become evident in his last plays, first brought to the stage many years later while O'Neill was leading a life of mental and physical torment and, in the case of several of his plays (*Long Day's Journey into Night, A Touch of the Poet,* the one-acter *Hughie,* and *More Stately Mansions*), after his death in 1953.

More than a decade—twelve years, to be exact—elapsed between the middle and last periods of O'Neill's career. These were years of isolation during which he planned and wrote plays he withheld from the stage and did not publish. Illness hampered him and depression over the state of the world, which was veering rapidly toward a global war, immobilized him and kept him virtually bedridden at times. As late as 1946, he still felt that it would require strong efforts on his part to recover enough confidence in the worth of literary labor to start writing again. In a press interview he declared that "the war has thrown me completely off base. . . . I have to get back to a sense of writing being worthwhile." Morosely, he added, "In fact, I'd have to pretend." It was not a period to encourage optimism, and there was none forthcoming from O'Neill as he brooded on the past that prepared the way for the dreadful present while at work on a tremendous cycle of plays tracing the tragic history of an American family from colonial times to his own, destroying some of his completed drafts and leaving other planned plays unwritten or unfinished.

Shortly after the conclusion of World War II, it became possible for him to entertain prospects for new productions and to allow the publication of two new plays, *The Iceman Cometh,* written in 1939, and *A Moon for the Misbegotten,* completed in 1943. Both were to a degree memory plays, the first dealing with the period of his waterfront days at Jimmy-the-Priest's dive, the second with the broken life of his alcoholic brother

James. But the mordancy of both plays derived not from memories (the autobiographical elements were thoroughly transformed) but from a strong and vivid sense of man's private and public failure, which the recently concluded holocaust and the growing materialism of the world only served to confirm. In an interview he gave to the press in September, 1946, on the occasion of the Broadway opening of *The Iceman Cometh* by the Theatre Guild, O'Neill held out little hope for man. He included in his indictment his own nation, which had but recently emerged the victor and the champion of humanity from a second world war. "I'm going on the theory," he declared, "that the United States, instead of being the most successful country in the world, is the greatest failure." His country had been given more resources than any other, but while moving ahead rapidly it had not acquired any real roots because its main idea appeared to be "that everlasting game of trying to possess your own soul by the possession of something outside it." He included the rest of the world in his indictment. If the human was so "damned stupid" that in two thousand years it had not learned to heed the Biblical admonition against gaining the whole world but losing one's own soul, then it was time humanity were "dumped down the nearest drain" and the ants were given a chance to succeed where men had failed.

The Iceman Cometh, which the Theatre Guild produced with only moderate success but which was later revived with great success, proved to be one of O'Neill's most powerful as well as most pessimistic plays. Bearing considerable resemblance to Maxim Gorky's turn-of-the-century naturalistic classic *The Lower Depths* (both plays are set in a cheap boardinghouse for the disreputable and the derelict, and both show man trying to subsist on illusory hopes), *The Iceman Cometh* nevertheless presents a radically different view from that entertained by the Russian author who had stood at the dawn of the twentieth century and shared its optimism. O'Neill expressed no hope for men at all, and therefore considered illusion to be the necessary anodyne and death a welcome release for bedeviled mankind. In Harry Hope's saloon, life's exiles and failures lead a besotted and befuddled existence and subsist on hopes of recovering their lost status. Most of them are reasonably happy until their drinking companion, the flashy traveling salesman Hickey, shows up for one of his periodic drinking bouts. Instead of joining in the expected revels, however, he is bent upon making them renounce their illusions and face the truth about themselves, which is that they no longer have anything to hope for. Accepting his challenge, at last, that they leave the saloon and proceed to accomplish the restitution of reputation and position with which they have long deluded themselves, they sally forth, but only to return, one by one, frightened and dispirited. Nothing feels right anymore, and even the liquor in the saloon has lost its savor and has no effect on them. Contentment returns to them only after Hickey's revelation that he has murdered his long-suffering wife who persisted in believing in his eventual reformation as the only way to free her from the misery of loving him, although he has also hated her for her infinite trust and forbearance. ("I couldn't forgive her for forgiving me," says Hickey. "I even caught myself hating her for making me hate myself so much.")

They derive reassurance from the conviction that Hickey, who has given himself up to the police, is stark mad, and relapse into their comforting illusions. The liquor begins to have an effect on them again, and all is well with them once more, so far as they know or care. The one exception is Larry, the disenchanted radical, who also turns out to be the only convert the miserable Hickey made, for Larry is the only one who really grasped Hickey's meaning when Hickey called for the abandonment of illusions as the only way of attaining peace. The death of illusion is the end of life, death, "the Iceman," being the sole possible release. For, as Larry has said earlier about men's dependence on false hopes, "the lie of a pipe dream is what gives life to the whole misbegotten mad lot of us, drunk or sober." Larry, in fact, performs one act of kindness at once; he persuades a miserable youth, who has betrayed his anarchist mother to the police, to put an end to his inner torment by committing suicide.

Rich in detail, complex in contrivance yet seemingly natural, naturalistic in speech and situation yet also somewhat symbolic and grotesque, *The Iceman Cometh* looms large in the O'Neill canon. Even its prolixity has redeeming qualities; Hickey's confessional speech, which lasts some fifteen minutes on the stage, constitutes gripping theatre. Its defects are the corrigible one of repetitiveness, some of which can be removed without injury to the play, the slight but embarrassing one of some banality of expression (as in the overuse of outmoded slang and the jejune phrase "pipe dreams" for false hopes), and the intrinsic one of spiritual torpor that derives from its author's persistent philosophy of negation.

The failure of O'Neill's next production, *A Moon for the Misbegotten,* which was withdrawn after its out-of-town tryout in February and March, 1947, marked the end of its author's active participation in the theatre. *The Iceman Cometh,* which opened in New York on September 2, 1946, was the last of O'Neill's plays to be seen on Broadway in his lifetime.

During his final years O'Neill was stricken with an obscure degenerative disease which made writing and finally even locomotion extremely difficult, although his mind remained clear. His third wife, actress Carlotta Monterey, whom he married in 1929, was his nurse during these years, and for long periods they lived in virtual seclusion, in Marblehead, Massachusetts, and later Boston. He had become wholly estranged from the children, Shane and Oona, of his second marriage, to Agnes Boulton. (O'Neill had been so angered by Oona's marriage, at eighteen, to Charlie Chaplin, who was the same age as O'Neill himself, that he never again— according to his wife Carlotta—mentioned her name.) His older son, Eugene, Jr., born of his short-lived first marriage to Kathleen Jenkins, committed suicide in 1950.

Three years after O'Neill's death, and a decade after *The Iceman Cometh* opened, his posthumous career on Broadway began brilliantly with the José Quintero production of *Long Day's Journey into Night,* which had Fredric March, Florence Eldridge, Jason Robards, Jr., and Bradford Dillman in the main parts. This opening, on November 7, 1956, repeated the earlier triumph of the play's world première in Swedish at the Royal Dramatic Theatre in Stockholm on February 10, 1956. (In 1945, O'Neill had stipulated that *Long Day's Journey into Night,* which has strong autobiographical overtones, should be sealed for twenty-five years after his death. But Carlotta O'Neill, as his literary executrix, released the play for both publication and production, saying that her husband had changed his mind after the death of Eugene, Jr., at whose request O'Neill had originally withheld the play.)

In *Long Day's Journey into Night,* in many respects a simple naturalistic family drama, there were no plot contrivances, no "well-made" play intrigues, but only uncommonly moving revelations of character and human relations. These came in the wake of closely connected tensions and conflicts shattering to the young man, actually the young O'Neill, who is patently the transcriber of the events of the play. Were it not for the prosaic quality of the dialogue and the extreme length of the work, there could be no doubt whatsoever that it is a twentieth-century dramatic masterpiece.

Long Day's Journey into Night brought O'Neill back to his real forte, and that of most American playwrights—plain, honest realism of character and situation. For all that, and despite his laboring of some points (finesse was never one of his virtues), O'Neill could not be charged fairly with commonplace obviousness. He was subtle in his own way in noting the complexity of the young hero's somewhat avaricious and penny-pinching actor-father, his mother too frightened of life to be able to give up the drug habit, and his demon-driven alcoholic brother. *Long Day's Journey into Night* is perhaps the modern theatre's outstanding dramatization of the ambivalences omnipresent in the human species. This alone would have given authenticity and depth to the play, which O'Neill managed to convey with much dramatic skill in a crescendo of revelations and even with some delightful humor, as in the scene in which the father tries to contradict the charge of miserliness by turning on all the lights in the parlor and then cautiously turning them out again. A forgiving spirit hovered over O'Neill when he came to write his *chef-d'oeuvre* (in 1940, sixteen years before its production), and his reward was the favorable response of even those members of the new generation who had found little to praise and much to blame in the playwright's earlier plays. For them, moreover, there could be special merit in the analytical, unsentimental insight that accompanied the compassion. The young O'Neill, who manifests a poet's sensitivity and a literary bent, is shown acquiring a painful understanding of life's ironies, which in the mature O'Neill's own case is not a jaundiced view of humanity but the tragic sense of life for which he becomes noted.*

After *Long Day's Journey into Night,* the New York production of *A Moon for the Misbegotten,* which opened about half a year later (in May, 1957), was bound to seem anticlimactic despite the services of the gifted British actress Wendy Hiller in the role of an oversized farm girl who tries to bestow her love on a guilt-laden alcoholic lacking all capacity to receive, let alone return, it. Faulty in several respects, it was nevertheless another work of considerable depth and compassion, here presented largely in terms of grotesque comedy.

Also weak in some respects, *A Touch of the Poet* (which, although written in 1936, first opened on Broadway on October 2, 1958, about six months after the world première at the Royal Dramatic Theatre) is chiefly noteworthy for giving us an inkling of what its author had in mind for the dramatic cycle he had planned under the title of *A Tale of Possessors Self-Dispossessed* and abandoned. This play, the sole finished survivor of the project, dramatized the beginnings of the American family with which the cycle was to deal. Here, the daughter of an Irish pretender to aristocratic status, Con Melody, reduced to keeping a pub near Boston, resolves to marry the poetical scion of a wealthy Brahmin family despite parental interference. The full significance of the play could not be established without reference to the nonexistent cycle, but its self-sufficient qualities were considerable. They were most evident in the character studies of a man who is dignified by his sense of distinction out of all proportion to his merits (he is a liar and often an inconsiderate one),

---

* [Professor Gassner apparently had second thoughts about this evaluation. In the proof margin beside this sentence, he jotted a single word: "revise." *Ed.*]

his drudge of a wife who in understanding his proud spirit forgives all hurts, and his daughter Sara who scorns his pretensions but mourns for him as one dead when he renounces them.

Another play, *More Stately Mansions,* which was apparently to be the fourth in his eleven-play cycle and was to follow *A Touch of the Poet,* was retrieved from the O'Neill papers in Yale University's O'Neill Collection and produced in considerably shortened form by Dr. Karl Ragnar Gierow, the Royal Dramatic Theatre director who had staged productions of two other posthumous O'Neill works in Stockholm, in November, 1962. The manuscript was revised for publication by Dr. Gierow and Donald 'Gallup, the curator of the O'Neill Collection at Yale. Since this version, released by the Yale University Press in 1964, was prepared from the Swedish acting script, it cannot be judged as an original O'Neill work; the original manuscript is more than twice as long as the published play. Whatever the favorable impression of the Swedish production, the published play may well strike a reader as decidedly scattered in effect. But it is plain that O'Neill wanted to indict the growth of materialism in the modern world. Con Melody's daughter Sara of *A Touch of the Poet* is here married to the young man, Simon Harford, she fancied. But her possessiveness and her rivalry with his equally possessive mother prove to be his undoing; the poet in him dies as he becomes a relentless materialist before breaking down mentally. O'Neill's old feeling for compulsive conflict is once more uppermost in this salvaged but rather inchoate drama, which has yet to be tested on the American stage.

Fortunately, there was one more posthumously published work of the final period that shows no decline or dispersion of O'Neill's power, the short two-character masterpiece *Hughie,* written in 1941 and published in 1959, the first of a projected series grimly entitled *By Way of Obit.* For the most part a monologue spoken by the "Broadway sport" Erie Smith to the night clerk of a shabby New York hotel in the late 1920's, *Hughie* is a tour de force that does not flag for a moment in revealing the emotional vacuity of the narrator and a deceased night clerk, Hughie, whom he used to fill with wonder at his inflated gambling exploits. Marvelously vivid and rhythmic dialogue that seems utterly authentic in its colloquialism and slang in this play recalls O'Neill's early achievements in the best sea-pieces of the *S. S. Glencairn* series. *Hughie* is the last testament to O'Neill's prowess in naturalistic playwriting and to his lingering attachment, despite his success with oversized dramas, to the spare one-act play form with which he had first established his reputation as an authentic American playwright.

Nothing needs to be added, perhaps, to this critical chronicle of the efforts and achievements of the one American playwright whose place in the hierarchy of world dramatists seems as secure as any twentieth-century dramatist's can be. To his critics' justifiable impatience with his laboriousness, the appropriate reply is that O'Neill is the *master* of massive dramatic assault. His power is not often separable from his repetitiveness or even verbosity. His sense of theatre was so strong that more often than not his best plays, when well structured, proved to be considerably more effective on the stage than a literary reading of them could possibly suggest. His sense of drama was so rarely "posture," despite his not always trustworthy flair for theatricality, that much of his work seems wrung from him rather than contrived or calculated. In a very real sense it is a testament to a uniquely tormented spirit that subsumed much of the twentieth century's dividedness and anguish, largely existential rather than topical. And while the penalty for his metaphysical concerns and brooding inwardness was often a quasiphilosophical windiness, the reward for his refusal to settle for small temporary satisfactions is an aura of greatness in the man and his labors, or, at the very least, a dark impressiveness not easily to be dismissed by dwelling on his verbal limitations. This much can be said, without fear of contradiction, of the man who, in the words of his publisher-friend Bennett Cerf, was "the first universally recognized world dramatist America produced" in some two centuries of theatre in the Western Hemisphere.

■

IMPORTS AND INFLUENCES
FROM ABROAD

I. THE INFLUENCE OF STRINDBERG
IN THE UNITED STATES*

My mind goes back to 1940 when William Saroyan, fresh from his success with the Pulitzer Prize play *The Time of Your Life,* visited me at my Theatre Guild office after having just left the dean of American dramatic criticism, George Jean Nathan, who was then presiding over the career of the young playwright. "George wants me to read Strindberg," said Saroyan, distinctly elated with the promise of impending discovery. The same elation appears to have seized the youthful Eugene O'Neill about a quarter of a century earlier when he discovered Strindberg, along with the Greek tragedians, while convalescing in a sanatorium for tubercular patients. Ever since then it has been impossible to certify American playwrights for critical consideration as travelers on the road to modern dramatic art without invoking the name of Strindberg as the trailblazer.

As the present essay is a virtually impromptu tribute to the great Swedish author rather than an academic investigation, I offer neither statistical proof nor a collection of signed testimonials and confessions by our playwrights. It is not even important to be certain how direct Strindberg's influence has been, for the indirect influence—that which appears in conjunction with other factors and is assimilated into the cultural life of a writer may be the most potent and profitable one. In one way or another, American playwrights were bound to become aware of Strindberg's work, which was too powerful to be ignored despite the dearth of adequate productions of his plays in this country. It was simply impossible to turn in any direction, except that of trivial entertainment on the one hand and strictly political drama on the other, without seeing Strindberg on the horizon—either alone or in the company of some other seminal writer, such as Nietzsche, Shaw, or Freud.

It is surely no accident that the two most Strindbergian playwrights of the American stage, O'Neill and Tennessee Williams, should also be the most creative and penetrative. Nor is it surprising that there should

* From *World Theatre* (Spring, 1962).

be a Strindbergian quality of passion and imagination in a large number of plays by the reputable writers such as Robert Sherwood, Philip Barry, George Kelly, Maxwell Anderson, Arthur Laurents, William Inge, and Arthur Miller, and (can irony of fate go further?) several women writers, among whom will be found not only such tart ones as Lillian Hellman and Clare Boothe, but the genteel Rachel Crothers. Judgment here is patently subjective and invites argument, but this does not deter me from saying that I have felt "Strindberg" in such a conglomeration of plays, aside from those written by O'Neill and Williams, as Sherwood's *Reunion in Vienna,* Barry's *The Animal Kingdom,* Maxwell Anderson's *Gypsy,* Kelly's *Craig's Wife,* Miller's *The Crucible* and *A View from the Bridge,* Inge's *Come Back, Little Sheba,* Hellman's *The Little Foxes,* Clare Boothe's *The Women*—and, even Crothers' *Susan and God.* Added to works by O'Neill and Williams (*Desire under the Elms, Strange Interlude, A Streetcar Named Desire, Cat on a Hot Tin Roof,* etc.) the list is obviously an impressive one. It could even be expanded considerably, though not without some risk to Strindberg's reputation, if I yielded to the temptation of citing half-remembered divorce dramas and some fortunately almost forgotten unpleasant plays about harpy wives and their victims, reminiscent of Strindberg's Laura and the Captain. If my memory does not fail me, there were three of those so-called "bitch" plays on Broadway in a single season during the 1940's.

It does not, of course, follow that a play automatically acquires extraordinary merit simply because its author has paid Strindberg the compliment of imitation. As a matter of fact two of O'Neill's poorest plays are *Diff'rent* and *Welded,* in which the Swedish master's influence is most observable. No list of plays, moreover, can tell us what it is that we attribute to Strindberg that makes him specifically an "influence" rather than simply a distinguished dramatist. Perhaps it is enough to say that he is the recognized master of modern psychological drama and that no one writing this type of play could possibly escape indebtedness to Strindberg. Since the very term "psychological drama" implies an important species of realistic drama, the debt becomes even more apparent. It mounts in importance, besides, since in creating psychological drama he set lessons in concentrated dramaturgy and intensification of character-motivated conflict with *Miss Julie* and *The Link* (or *The Bond*), as well as to a lesser degree with *The Father,* that strengthened the entire art of playwriting. The rise of the serious one-act play, as a work distinguishable from trivial curtain-raisers or after-pieces, is largely attributable to this example, and it is noteworthy, in fact, that early efforts to create a genuinely modern theatre in the United States were advanced by the production of one-act dramas such as O'Neill's celebrated sea-pieces. O'Neill, it may be noted, also sedulously followed his master into the field of the dramatic monologue with *Before Breakfast,* a *tour de force* of dramaturgy inferior only to Strindberg's monologue *The Stronger,* until Samuel Beckett's *Krapp's Last Tape* reached the stage. Higher praise is merited only by O'Neill's late one-act play *Hughie,* a posthumously published work that is virtually a long monologue. With *Miss Julie* comprising an overwhelming example, an attempt was also made to dispense with act divisions in the case of full-length plays; O'Neill made it notably in *The Emperor Jones* and Philip Barry in *Hotel Universe.*

It can be argued, nevertheless, that neither intensive realism nor probing psychological drama is the invention of one man or his monopoly; and these terms are, besides, both too vague and too inclusive to be used to define individual creation. Strindberg's legacy of psychological realism was a highly personal creation and, rightly considered, it remains, even after O'Neill, a Strindberg monopoly. The most accessible aspect of this contribution is his subject matter, which concerns the relation of the sexes in general and their conflicts in particular. In the American theatre, his example meant our liberation not merely from long-standing puritanical constraints in the treatment of sex (here popularizations of Freudian psychology were a more potent influence), but from a hardier species of inhibition—namely, American gynolatry. In a country in which cultural and social activities, not to mention "conspicuous consumption," have been delegated preponderantly to women, Strindberg would have found abundant fuel for his dramatic fire. If he protested vigorously against gynolatry in Ibsen's work, it is not difficult to imagine what he would have said about popular American drama and fiction.

Whenever American playwrights departed from the standardized adulation that is actually more condescending to women than complimentary to them, whenever they took note of possessive, predatory, or ruthlessly driving femininity, I can imagine Strindberg's ghost nodding vigorous approval—at least until he detected a disposition to soften the impeachment, albeit for reasons not always meretricious. We are a compassionate people who have been liberal with excuses for notorious females; the heroine of *Craig's Wife* is said to be so possessive because she lacked security in her younger days, and Williams' Blanche Du Bois is so woefully debased because she had the misfortune of marrying a homosexual youth. We have also been an inveterately optimistic people who expect marriages to be saved; it was this latter expectation that apparently prompted the director of Williams' *Cat on a Hot Tin Roof* to ensure its success by persuading the author into providing a so-called "upbeat" ending for the Broadway production. The reconciliation of husband and wife in Inge's *The Dark at the Top of the Stairs* may have been more convincing, but optimistic conclusions with respect to their already traumatized children seemed to me highly dubious.

At the same time, it must also be noted that our playwrights have sometimes succeeded in putting a stamp of genuine individuality on their Strindbergian plays. Thus in *Desire under the Elms,* a "peasant" tragedy rooted in the milieu of puritan New England, O'Neill created one of his most powerful dramas of lust possessiveness in terms of his personal tragic sense of life; O'Neill's treatment of the "war of the sexes" acquired a special perversity and ironic complexity in *The Iceman Cometh;* and the rift in the marriage of the parents in O'Neill's autobiographical masterpiece *Long Day's Journey into Night* is uniquely realized in terms of the self-deceiving father's and the drug-addicted mother's strategies of escape from their sense of failure. In terms of American small-town life, moreover, few contemporary plays have possessed the emotional authenticity of William Inge's drama of a pathetically mismated couple, *Come Back, Little Sheba,* with its cyclic pattern of quiet desperation in the first act, an eruption of alcoholic violence in the second, and a return to passive suffering in the final scene. In brief, there is ample evidence of a genuine assimilation of Strindbergian psychological drama in the American theatre of recent decades. This is apparent despite the fact that Strindberg was welcomed by few American critics (James Huneker, as long ago as 1905 when his *Iconoclasts,* containing an appreciative essay, was published, and George Jean Nathan are the main exceptions) and in spite of a dearth of good productions of his plays.

Psychological realism does not, of course, exhaust the scope of Strindberg's experimentation and the range of his influence, since he made himself the father of Expressionism with his turn-of-century postnaturalistic experiments. O'Neill derived his expressionist technique directly from Strindberg and not from the late central European expressionists, who were themselves indebted to Strindberg. Like his master, indeed, O'Neill built his reputation on two foundations, those of realism and expressionism, rather than one; and he was not alone in the United States to maintain this dual allegiance, as may be observed in the case of Elmer Rice, John Howard Lawson, Arthur Laurents, Williams, Miller, and others. Even the worldly George S. Kaufman, the late prince of Broadway pragmatists, collaborated in *Beggar on Horseback* (with Marc Connelly) on an effective farcical utilization of Strindberg's famous dream technique, and Moss Hart married it successfully to the popular Amer-

ican musical theatre in *Lady in the Dark* by turning the heroine's stream-
of-consciousness on her analyst's couch into a series of musical-comedy
numbers.

Again, as in our use of psychological realism, we have tended to
dilute the Strindbergian soul-medicine, and in popular plays such as the
last-mentioned pieces, we have often favored sedatives rather than purga-
tives. A distinction may also be made between what ultimately belongs
to Strindberg rather than to his Central European imitators. It is *psychological* expressionism alone that comes directly from him; an expressionism of inner tension or division (rather than of social commentary in
the manner of Rice's *The Adding Machine*) is present in such works
as O'Neill's *The Emperor Jones* and Sophie Treadwell's murder-drama
Machinal. An extension of the characters' or the author's private nightmare, however, also produced a metaphysical mode of expressionism—I
call it "metaphysical" because the work dealt with the nature of being—
in some American plays.

It is the whole of life itself that is subsumed under the vision of
O'Neill's *The Hairy Ape* and *The Great God Brown* and Tennessee Williams' *Camino Real* and *Orpheus Descending.* Moreover, there is no
sharp distinction in these works, any more than there is in *The Dream
Play* and *The Ghost Sonata,* between metaphysical and social reality;
the *condition humaine* with which the plays deal is intrinsic not only
to man but to the world in which he lives and for which he is partly
responsible—he exists in man-made society as well as in the universe.
Strindberg's pictures of poverty and social iniquities in *The Dream Play*
and exploitation and hypocrisy in *The Ghost Sonata* have their parallel
in O'Neill's industrial world in *The Hairy Ape* and Williams' fascistic
one in *Camino Real.*

It is evident, then, that it is no narrow technical interest that comprises the Strindbergian ambience of American playwriting. The technique of dream-formation, of rapidly forming and changing episodes,
of uncanny fusions of space and time, and other fantastic distortions of
reality is a means toward an end and, ideally, an expression of the playwright's dramatic vision. Strindberg, it is true, originated some of these
techniques and developed them all; that he did so consciously at least
by the time he came to write *The Dream Play* is made evident by his
preface to that absorbing and influential work, and there can be no doubt
that they were *consciously* adopted by American writers, although it is
apparent that they also followed the example of the stream-of-consciousness technique of twentieth-century fiction, as O'Neill did in elaborating
the interior monologues of *Strange Interlude.* That Strindberg made con-

tributions to our dramatic technique both in the naturalistic and expressionistic vein cannot be disputed. But I should like to conclude this brief essay by declaring that what Strindberg ultimately contributed to dramatic art was himself. I mean his sense of human division and conflict, his intense temperament and his disconcertingly razor-sharp intelligence, and his almost terrifying integrity or faithfulness to that which he observed or felt. The man and the style, the content and the form, were one. When this was more or less the case in American playwriting, as it was in some of O'Neill's work, the results were impressive, while mere imitation of subject matter or method resulted in strain or confusion—and in unmistakable failure.

The most comprehensive statement on Strindberg's role as a catalyst appeared on the playbill of the production of *The Spook Sonata* (the then current title of the great chamber-play *The Ghost Sonata*) on January 3, 1924, by The Provincetown Players, the theatrical company O'Neill had helped to create and that staged most of his early work. O'Neill offered this production "as the most apt" symbol of the Provincetown's intensions to express "a fresh elation and joy in experimental production." Strindberg remained "the most modern of moderns, the greatest interpreter in the theatre of the characteristic spiritual conflicts" of the day. O'Neill rightly concluded that Strindberg "carried naturalism to a logical attainment of such poignant intensity that, if the work of any other playwright is to be called 'naturalism,' we must classify a play like *The Dance of Death* as 'super-naturalism.'" After having intensified the method of naturalism ("the method of his time"), Strindberg, moreover, foreshadowed "the methods to come." The old audacity of the realists, their aspirations toward self-recognition by literalistic drama had become so much "blague." Expressionism, "a new language" of drama, was needed if we were to leave "the banality of surfaces" and pass on to "some as yet unrealized region" where the modern spirit could attain adequate expression. Whether or not expressionism was the solution O'Neill thought it was, one thing is evident: O'Neill understood that Strindberg's example was one of penetrating surfaces regardless of subject matter and that his plays carried dramatic art beyond naturalism even when his methods were naturalistic.

II. EARLY GIRAUDOUX ON THE AMERICAN STAGE*

Amphitryon 38 is Jean Giraudoux's eight-year-old successful play
adapted for the English-speaking stage by S. N. Behrman, himself no
duffer in matters of comedy. According to its author, the play has been
preceded by thirty-seven dramatic versions of the Greek legend. Among
the many playwrights to try their pen on it were Plautus, who was (as
far as we know) the first, Dryden, who was the bawdiest, and Molière,
who—like most Frenchmen—knew how to be witty without being offensive.

The new version is moderately Shavian. Giraudoux plays nimbly
with questions of war and peace, human and divine vanity, love and marriage. Like Shaw, he is an intelligent and sardonic observer of things
mundane. He is a hit-and-run artist over the groggy body of those
blessed idiots who call themselves men and women. It is the cardinal
weakness of Behrman's adaptation that it has fewer sparkling observations than it could use. Perhaps the public must share part of the blame
because it has been discouragingly cool in the past to intelligent conversation. There is such a fear of wordiness among authors that the drama
finds it hard to be literate. Giraudoux's original version was considerably
longer than Behrman's script, and the difference was mostly talk—wonderful talk. To have offered it to the American public would have been
risky. Nevertheless, the history of the theatre shows that if you want brilliant comedy you must be ready to listen to people talking intelligently—
and at length. If you are up on your mythology, you will recall that
Jupiter visited the faithful Alcmena in the shape of her husband. This
story is obviously too anecdotal to last an evening without recourse to
other resources of comedy. That these resources are not tapped more
generously in the Shubert Theatre is a matter of regret. It is the only regret. *Amphitryon 38* has rare distinction for a play of its kind and has
the even rarer good fortune of being presented by the most accomplished
acting team of our time.

The play could have been just another Pullman-car story. But *Amphitryon 38* has, as I once heard Mr. Lunt say, a golden glow. The radiance is partly in the style, partly in the classic setting, partly in the original
source of inspiration, the soul of myth-making Hellas. The cheap glitter

---

* From *One Act Play Magazine* (November, 1937). [A single word, "Revision," is written in the proof margin of this essay. Possibly Professor Gassner would
have added comments about later Giraudoux plays, such as *Tiger at the Gates* and
Judith. Ed.]

of the fashionable bedroom where so many similar anecdotes transpire is mercifully absent here. The air is clear. And it is luminous—luminous with the mind and heart of Alcmena, with the celestial puckishness of Mercury, ever the god of rogues, with the Olympian texture of Jupiter even in situations that are trying to his dignity. There is no strained debunking of divinity in the play, which enjoys the easy playfulness of Greek humanism. The Greeks, while their civilization was still vigorous, did not regard man as a diseased animal. By creating the gods in their own image, they did not therefore degrade them. Bringing the gods closer to themselves, freeing them from their hideous totemistic masks, the myth-making Greeks actually beautified them. The civilizing character of Greek mythology has not always been clearly realized; it exorcised fear. *Amphitryon 38* captures some of this springtime beauty. Those who insist on treating it as just another salesman's joke are under suspicion of being impervious to poetry in comedy. Conservatives and radicals may be equally obtuse to its magic; the former would probably ring the praises of *Amphitryon* if it had a Hollywood setting like *Personal Appearance,* while the latter would no doubt sing hosannas if it appeared under the aegis of the Moscow Art Theatre, in which case it would become a sign of broadening Soviet culture. . . .

It remains to be noted that such a play could have been turned into a cheap romp by a tasteless production. The play is staged with repose and beauty. The costuming and Lee Simonson's lovely settings translate the inner glow into outer color and form. The direction, for which the Lunts are largely responsible, maintains a just balance between liveliness and subtlety, between jest and poetry.

As for the Lunts themselves, comparisons with *The Guardsman* and *The Taming of the Shrew* are superficial and odious. Their performance has new individuality. It is worth considering in some detail as a lesson in acting. Alfred Lunt's self-confidence in the play is not the bravura of Petrucchio; it is Olympian. Toward mankind in general he is the amused father. With Alcmena he is, in the main, a flustered lover who has met his match in a woman's wit, but divinity hedges him even then. You can see him keeping himself in check. When he finally asserts his godhood in the last act, he has dignity without solemnity, tenderness without sentimentality. When he walks in the shape of a god, he is somehow both as old as the world and unaged. Here is virtuosity!

Miss Fontanne's performance is not so new a creation. This is not because her artistry is less, but because what she represents is in effect unchanging. She is the eternal feminine. But she is that more than ever. I can only compare her performance with that of Katherine Cornell's

Candida, with the proviso that Miss Fontanne's requires more virtuosity. There is a compelling simplicity and impulsiveness in her performance. She is constantly discovering herself to her audience and yet always remains the same. There is the wisdom of serpents in her when she regards the foibles of her husband, both the real and the impersonated one. But her cleverness is not a separate thing—it does not war with her genuine feelings. In man, mind and matter are constantly at odds with each other; in Miss Fontanne's complete woman, they are always fused. In her performance, too, there is great virtuosity. Yet basically she is a solvent of the emotions she delineates; being woman, she is somehow greater than the sum total of her experiences.

An analysis of the acting of *Amphitryon* must not, however, conclude without a salute to Richard Whorf's Mercury. Anyone who has watched this actor's last three performances, in *The Taming of the Shrew, Idiot's Delight,* and the present play, must be convinced that we have in Richard Whorf a sterling actor. His Mercury possesses youth, wit, and an imperviousness to morality and conscience which belongs verily to the Homeric Hymn from which he must have sprung. With Sydney Greenstreet, the one-note trumpeter, and Alan Hewitt, the human Amphitryon (a difficult role that is not wholly realized in the text), he accounts for the minor business of the comedy. For light theatre of sheer magic, *Amphitryon* should commend itself to everyone.

III. AN IBSEN REVIVAL: TOO MUCH DOLL*

Considerable courage was displayed during the 1937–38 season by Ruth Gordon and Jed Harris in their revival of Ibsen's classic *A Doll's House*. Perhaps they even rushed in where angels now fear to tread. But anyone who endows this evangelical drama with some semblance of life performs a miracle, and, no matter what one dislikes about the new production, it does perform the miracle. The wonder arises from the excellent ensemble, which is particularly distinguished by Paul Lukas' affecting portrait of Dr. Rank, the chronically dying friend of the family, and Dennis King's Thorwald Helmer, who maintains a just balance between a typical male dynast and a likable person. Sam Jaffe's portrait of a scoundrel may be just a shade too soft, but, within the limits assigned to him by Thornton Wilder, the adapter, he too creates a living characterization. Chiefly, however, the production is a tribute to the increasingly ver-

* From *One Act Play Magazine* (January, 1938).

satile talent of Miss Ruth Gordon. Her interpretation of the lady who slammed the door that rang round the world may not jibe with our notion of the role. And yet a performance as alive, as vibrant and tense as Miss Gordon's leaves one punch-drunk. It is a wonder that she does not leave the stage breathless after her gyrations. There comes a moment in the second act when Miss Gordon's Nora practices the tarantella; it is an unforgettable moment, a brilliant evocation of anxiety developing into hysteria, of fear growing into desperation. The pathos of Miss Gordon's bewilderment at the man-made world which threatens to make her out a criminal because she signed her father's name to a promissory note is indescribably moving. The hurt she sustains when the miracle does not happen—that is, when her husband does not offer to sacrifice himself and take the blame for the forgery on himself—is tellingly present in Miss Gordon's performance. Altogether, Miss Gordon gives the theatre one of the most glowing examples of virtuosity in many a year.

It need only be added that Jed Harris returns to the stage with his old-time directorial power—in his casting of the secondary parts and his staging of such subtle business as Nora's private conversation with her moribund admirer, Dr. Rank, as well as of such dynamic material as Nora's hysteria in the tarantella scene. Only in the finale, when Nora leaves her husband, does the direction seem uncertain. It is also to the credit of the production that Thornton Wilder's adaptation is vivid, sensitive, and idiomatic.

Still, the *Doll's House* currently on view at the Morosco Theatre, although decidedly worth a visit, is basically unsatisfying. It is enlightening and convincing only here and there. The fault resides partly in the play. If it started a new realistic trend in the theatre, Ibsen could then be regarded as wet nurse to modern social drama. But the scrupulous historian may find such claims a trifle exaggerated in view of the fact that realism was in the air, that it had been attempted earlier by Alexandre Dumas *fils*, and already possessed one masterpiece in Hebbel's neglected German play, *Maria Magdalena*, written thirty-four years before. Even granting all claims in favor of *A Doll's House*, the fact remains that its motivations and resolution were never too sound. For a woman to forge her deceased father's note in all innocence argues an immaturity that cannot be laid at the door of any sensible sheltered woman in the middle of the nineteenth century or even earlier. Ibsen's debate with the nineteenth century's attitude toward women could be cogent only if Nora were fundamentally sensible. If you can dismiss Nora as a dimwit there is no argument. Moreover, if Nora had really been as dependent upon her husband as her doll's house existence would warrant, she would probably have confessed her error to her husband; despite her dread of his anger, she would have thrown herself upon his mercy, in which case many of the later complications of the play would never have taken place.

Finally, as has often been noted, Nora's departure at the end gets us nowhere. If she leaves her husband merely because she is disillusioned in him, the resolution of the play is of only minor consequence; and even so, it is not at all certain that a woman as helpless as Nora would not rather hug her disappointment and stick it out with her husband instead of leaving him for an unknown destination. If, however, as Ibsen would have us believe, Nora leaves for the additional reason that she wishes to emerge from her chrysalis into the ever-so-real world, it is never very clear how she will acquire any knowledge. Passive exposure to the world is not much of an education; and Nora's resolve to return to her deceased father's home or estate, without even a suggestion of what she will do there, is decidedly passive. How will she learn there what she expects to learn? We never know! And what will she learn? We never know. Finally, how can one believe that a devoted mother like Nora would leave her two children, who are so affectingly represented in the Jed Harris production? How can one believe that she would leave them at any price, let alone for a wild-goose chase?

The truth of the matter is that Ibsen, like so many evangelists, confused symbols with reality. Nora and her conduct were intended to be symbolic. But realistic symbolism is almost a contradiction in terms. The moment the playwright uses fully rounded characters we expect them to behave in accordance with the dictates of real emotions; we demand convincing motivation. You cannot use real characters and yet demand for them the privilege of leaving the earth on the wings of some dispensation from dramatic logic. (This tendency is peculiarly marked in Odets, and is the real root of his difficulties.) Finally, we may do well to remember that, despite his travels, Ibsen was a provincial Scandinavian in many respects. The type of woman he described in *A Doll's House* was assuredly foreign to a majority of Europe's people. She was not representative of the European upper middle class and aristocracy, whose women were sophisticated. She was not representative of the European working class, whose men could have neither the means nor the inclination, after a hard day's toil, to coddle their women to the point of making nitwits of them. Very much the same thing holds for the lower middle class, which, in fact, often used its wives in petty businesses. Ibsen's Nora, as a real portrait rather than a symbol, had an extremely narrow locus. If she existed at all, she could have only been the wife of a provincial like Thorwald Helmer. It is therefore doubtful whether

Nora was ever sufficiently typical; that she was ever a real problem. I know, of course, that she was regarded as such; otherwise she might not have become the subject of such heated controversy. But it was largely as a symbol that she possessed such representativeness. Today, of course, she is decidedly unrepresentative, and most of us, if we regard her at all, are constrained to take her with some grains of sodium chloride. Does she not resemble some Victorian resuscitation of the Brothers Krimsky?

Ruth Gordon's performance, for all its admirable virtuosity, keeps Nora too childish at the beginning to be representative of the women of even her own time; it is extremely doubtful that Ibsen saw Nora as such a little kitten. She is also too childish to grow up so phenomenally at the conclusion; it is difficult to believe that this particular Nora would leave her husband at the end. One easily tires of her baby ways, and even her frantic efforts at preventing Thorwald from learning the truth become a trifle monotonous. One can acknowledge Miss Gordon's talent and yet question the validity and sureness of her interpretation.

Though Nora, we may conclude, has had many descendants in the theatre, it is doubtful that any of Ibsen's successors ever turned out as naïve a character. But, as was often the case with Ibsen's plays, we must not arrive at judgment without a closer look. Nora was conceived in greater depth by her creator than her impersonators have tended to present on the stage. Her delicacy in not pressing Dr. Rank for financial assistance with which to placate the clerk Krogstad attests her dignity as a woman. So does her persistence in secretly paying off the debt she contracted in borrowing money in order to speed her husband's convalescence by taking him to a southern climate. So does, of course, her refusal to be satisfied with her escape from prosecution for forgery and insistency on a reckoning with her husband, with society's discouragement of woman's progress toward maturity, and with herself as an accomplice in the doll's house convention of middle-class marriage. And at the same time, we must not overlook her avowed disenchantment with her husband because he revealed petty, unheroic selfishness inconsistent with her romantic expectations of him as the master of the doll house and the protector of the presumptive doll in it. (She had expected that instead of behaving like a frightened bourgeois he would save her from prosecution or disgrace for having forged her deceased father's name to a promissory note by taking the guilt on his own shoulders.) And her very willingness to leave her children is a form of self-criticism as well as criticism of her status as the middle-class woman who is not needed in a household in which the children are reared by servants. Ibsen, in sum, created a considerably more complex character and character situation than has been assumed or realized in any productions we have seen. And except for extremely isolated and more arbitrarily contrived treatments such as Shaw's *Candida* and Maugham's *The Constant Wife,* Ibsen was and remains far in advance of his successors and imitators in handling the Nora theme in direct proportion to his capacity for dealing with characters who are infused with the breath of life rather than the gas of specious intellectualism. Ibsen's very realism, seemingly so pedestrian and old-fashioned, ensures this. He started writing *A Doll's House* with a subject as idea and ended with a subject as character-reality, one of the hardest achievements in the theatre (at which he had only two masters, Shakespeare and Racine) even if it now seems one of the easiest and less treasurable ones, retrospectively, because Ibsen got us used to taking it for granted.

IV. ANOUILH'S *VALSE TRISTE:* A MINORITY OPINION*

After having kept Anouilh at arm's length for more than a decade, Broadway appears to have at last taken him to its bosom. Last season's production of *The Lark* was a great success, and Harold Clurman's current production of *The Waltz of the Toreadors* should prove no less successful. There can be no doubt that the tide has turned in favor of the French playwright who captured Paris and London while we repelled him as an exotic foreigner whose cynicism and morbidity had no place on our stage. It is far less certain, however, that our appreciation of these two plays has been sounder than our previous depreciation of Anouilh's work. In the main, we have seen in them only the quality of our own defects rather than, as used to be the case, the defects of his qualities. With the help of an idealistic adaptation and an uplifting performance by Julie Harris, *The Lark,* as mocking a work of disenchantment as is consonant with Anouilh's urbanity, commended itself to us as a heroic drama and high tragedy. And currently, *The Waltz of the Toreadors,* as staged by Mr. Clurman and projected by Ralph Richardson in the leading role of a general who is lugubriously lecherous, and as futile as he is ridiculous, commends itself to Broadway chiefly as a farce, rather than as a work of complex and desolate artistry.

Its hero, General St. Pé, is a pompous roué who dictates his memoirs and makes love to the kitchen maids on his estate while his obnoxious wife,

* From *The New Republic* (February 11, 1957).

the mother of two unbearably ugly daughters, plays the invalid, harasses him continually, and tries to be as unfaithful to him as opportunity will allow. His ludicrous situation reaches its climax when a featherbrained spinster, whom he has idealized but kept at a distance for seventeen years on absurd grounds of marital fidelity, turns up at last brandishing letters by his wife allegedly proposing love to the local physician. But far from liberating the General, the lady's evidence only puts him in the more ridiculous situation of pressing for a showdown with his wife and her physician and of being put to shame by both.

On the surface, *The Waltz of the Toreadors* is so far-fetched that the temptation to treat it as farcical skullduggery is almost irresistible— at least for Broadway. As if realizing that he must not confuse a public, Mr. Clurman gave the first act every possible accent of physical absurdity. At the end of the act, after both women had attempted suicide, he had the General and his secretary swinging the wife and the spinster across their shoulders as if they were bags of extra-heavy flour. Thereafter, the director and Mr. Richardson missed no opportunity to underscore the farcical complications until the final curtain when the General marches his latest conquest off to the bushes.

To do the director and his star full justice it is necessary to concede that they both knew well enough that *The Waltz of the Toreadors* is not a hand-me-down farce. There certainly was never any doubt that that remarkable actress Mildred Natwick played the wife with full aware- ness of its Strindbergian dimensions. The scene in which she stands up in her bed to flagellate her husband with scorn and with a recital of her own infidelities is memorable. At that high moment in the drama, as well as in a few scattered moments elsewhere, Ralph Richardson him- self was only slightly less responsive to the pathos of his part. What he was unable to do—what the production as a whole was unable to do after a strained first act—was to make the play cohere.

It would be easy enough to blame Broadway for this lack of coher- ence. Everything tends to be simplified on Broadway, if for no other reason than that a production is obliged to reach a much larger audience than anywhere else before it can pay. But I believe there is another rea- son, too, which one might call the "either-or" attitude of the American public. An experience has to be either right or wrong, good or bad, funny or sad for that public, for which reason it has difficulty in adjusting itself to many continental plays that abound in ironic ambivalences and mordant ambiguities.

We think we have said a great deal about a work when we say that it is funny, and we rather think it is priggish for anyone to ask for an explanation or to offer one. In the case of the *Waltz,* we do allow ourselves enough leeway to say that it is a work strongly tinged with melancholy. That there is much desolation in *The Waltz of the Toreadors* is true enough, of course, and it is indeed something for our playgoers to be exposed to this sort of "dark comedy," which some will call *civilized* and others *decadent.* To some degree, it would even be good for us to become acquainted with "decadence," as nothing can be more morally debilitating than our present overfamiliarity with wholesomeness: "health" seems to be *our* brand of decadence.

Yet I cannot say that Anouilh's sense of desolation precipitates a completely satisfactory drama. Nihilism stands between the author and a complete dramatic experience. In his plays—*Waltz of the Toreadors* only a little less than in his tragic *Antigone*—the parts are greater than the whole. They are often fascinating, but they don't fit together: this nay-saying writer is too busy thumbing his nose at life to give any genuine significance to its failures, just as he is often brilliant in lighting up elements of human behavior without creating human beings. We do not know Anouilh's principal characters, the General and his wife; we know only the former's amorous animation and the latter's animus against her husband. Nor does the conduct of the characters have any relation to their environment, their status, their past, or their present.

Anouilh is no Chekhov even with the Chekhovian materials of the current work. And apparently he knows his limits—and I rather believe the astute Mr. Clurman knows them, too. For it is evident in this production, as in much else Anouilh has written, that the author relies on his theatricality—here predominantly farcical—to sustain the interest of his work. Such work is sufficient unto the day, but only unto the day. Our belated discovery of Anouilh should not encourage us to overestimate a talent that will always be precarious and will always require the pyrotechnical skill of a harlequin to conceal its aridity.

HEROISM AND THE
AMERICAN THEATRE*

There is travail in the American theatre. The plain fact is that our theatre is endeavoring to foster a type of play which, borrowing a term from the seventeenth century, we may call "heroic drama." For varying reasons of patriotism, art, or expediency, our writers and producers of plays are trying to respond to the heroism that marks the present global struggle. Both the writing and presentation of heroic drama, however, involve special problems in the modern world, especially in America; and this may explain why so many produced and unproduced serious plays fail or prove to be only moderately gratifying.

It may be recalled that the American theatre rose to maturity in the distinctly disillusioned atmosphere of the postwar twenties. For two decades we became accustomed to an essentially antiheroic theatre. Our dramatists deflated the entire business of war and heroism; the very titles of our war plays—*What Price Glory?*, *Ten Million Ghosts*, *Bury the Dead*, and *Idiot's Delight*—bristled with our attitude. Dramatists made much of frivolous, fast-living society people, or sought out the frailties and follies of individuals or groups. Our theatre played at sophistication, and enjoyed pointing the finger at the follies and idiosyncrasies of individuals or classes until the stage was littered with idiotic Babbitts, cheap hustlers, and cheaper purveyors of art. In more serious moments our writers favored unedifying excavations of psychoanalysis or represented people as sorry products of social conditions. The world represented on our stage turned men into the soulless robots of *The Adding Machine* and *Beggar on Horseback;* corrupted them with the brashness, greed, or egolatry of the characters of *The Show-Off, Marco Millions,* and *Merrily We Roll Along;* transformed them into criminals or degenerates of the *Dead End* and *Tobacco Road* variety. And the society that produced them was hardly worth defending when it was not actually eligible for well-merited extinction. It could indeed galvanize man's spirit into heroism by rousing him to revolutionary action, but the antiheroic, negativistic outlook was not materially dissipated by occasional thunder from the left.

* From *Tomorrow* (May, 1943). [Realizing the continuing concern about the nature and quality of our stage heroes and heroics, Professor Gassner intended to update this essay. *Ed.*]

When, therefore, it became imperative for our playwrights to write heroic drama, they found themselves on unfamiliar ground. In the main, S. N. Behrman hit close to the mark when he made the playwright-hero of *No Time for Comedy* fumble pathetically when he tried to be affirmative. A host of well-intended anti-Nazi plays failed ignobly. Our most poetic and spiritual dramatist, Maxwell Anderson, eulogist of many Hamlets and propounder of much Hamlet-philosophy, now dramatized the necessity of taking a stand in *Key Largo,* but with greater verbosity than power; and represented heroic effort in *Candle in the Wind,* but watered it down to a romantic complication. The weather-wise George S. Kaufman abandoned cynicism for a while to produce *The American Way* and *The Land Is Bright,* but, essentially, neither play seemed more than an oblation to show business. Frederick Hazlitt Brennan's *The Wookey* was also stagey, though more ingratiating, while John Steinbeck's *The Moon Is Down* suffered from the opposite defect of understatement on the stage. Only a few efforts had material success. Robert Sherwood, who had read a funeral oration on civilization in the *Petrified Forest* and had stigmatized war as an "idiot's delight," succeeded in *Abe Lincoln in Illinois* by resorting to Lincoln's life and words; and to some extent in *There Shall Be No Night,* although with a specious appraisal of the actual issues that evoked his hero's affirmations. Hemingway, the one-time negativist, turned out a lone tribute to the courage of the Loyalists in *The Fifth Column,* written with the force of a writer long accustomed to dealing with men in action. Lillian Hellman, drawing upon the banked fire of the left-wing theatre, indited an incandescent pæan to antifascist fighters in *The Watch on the Rhine.*

These plays came before our participation in the war, when both authors and audiences had a wider latitude in creating or appreciating the drama of heroism. But since Pearl Harbor our consciousness of heroism has been on a wartime basis, and this has vastly complicated the problem for both dramatists and producers. Some success has been mingled with much failure, and though we have had inspiring moments, we have had few consistently satisfactory plays.

The writer of heroic war drama can bog down in any number of morasses. If he gives precedence to ideas, the necessary action or the heroic spirit may suffer diminution; if to character drama, an audience, geared to wartime feelings and tired of years of costly inaction, may become sensible of a want of action. But if he dispenses with the drama of ideas, or with deeply realized characterization, he runs the risk of melodramatic baldness. Should he maintain that the times *are* violent and melodramatic, he still cannot overcome the feeling on the part of critics and playgoers that melodrama on the grand scale (with the full accompaniment of fighting, shooting, sound effects, and so forth) is something that the theatre has gone beyond. They remember it as the old-fashioned theatre of Sardou and William Gillette that Ibsen, Chekhov, and Shaw decently interred generations ago, and they are acutely conscious of theatrical devices, even though the present struggle is more melodramatic than anything ever seen on the stage.

The clichés and the stereotypes of heroic theatre have been accumulating for centuries, and they cannot be introduced seriously on our stage without great risk. The presence of a traitor, a spy, or a last-minute rescue is immediately suspect behind the proscenium, although the present world is full of traitors, spies, and last-minute rescues. If the heroes are too valiant, they immediately call to mind the countless *chevaliers sans peur et sans reproche* who peopled the thrillers of the past. If, on the contrary, a dramatist endeavors to avoid so-called heroics, his work may seem tepid by comparison with present reality. He is apt to fall into the theatre's most recent cliché of understatement; thus the character who is blasé during an air raid and goes about the ordinary business of life has become a stereotype of English plays, and so has the daring and efficient warrior who is actually very frightened. Finally—if indeed one can write *finis* to the dramatist's worries—he must make a difficult choice between singling out some individual for his hero, in which case his story lacks extension, or dramatizing a group and so saddling himself with too many simultaneously occurring plots or losing his story in a welter of expository detail. It would seem that the playwright cannot win, no matter what course he pursues. That he does win occasionally is the rare miracle that all writers for the theatre expect.

The novelist is obviously more fortunate, as his story of heroic action is less likely to seem melodramatic in the pages of a book, will live comfortably side by side with considerable cogitation and characterization, and can give attention to both an individual and a mass hero, without shortchanging either. No recent play has been so completely realized as novels like Segher's *The Seventh Cross,* Pozner's *The Edge of the Sword* or James Aldridge's *Signed with Their Honour.* But it is the stage that is the most appropriate medium for heroic material, which can have its greatest use when visually projected and publicly shared, a fact realized by the numerous performances of Anderson's *The Eve of St. Mark* in America and of *The Russian People* in the land of the Soviets. The solution therefore is not to give up writing and producing heroic plays, but to find ways and means of skirting the pitfalls or leaping over them.

Recent plays provide exemplary case histories. Three of them—Emlyn Williams' *Morning Star,* Terence Rattigan's *Flare Path,* and Norman Armstrong's *Lifeline*—came from England, where the war was felt sooner and experienced more intensely than here. All three were well received and have enjoyed long runs in Britain, where the audience identifies itself strongly with the material; all three failed on Broadway with a public and critical fraternity that was sufficiently remote from the background to be objective. In the case of *Morning Star,* no one could quarrel with the exposition, though one could detect enough stereotypes and clichés in the author's account of bomb-scarred London to be less than overwhelmed by the data. But the play revolved around the inner conflict of a physician who felt drawn to Hollywood and a blonde Circe— a hero who could hardly arouse our admiration or concern. *Flare Path* exhibited the daily life of the R.A.F., an engrossing subject limited by the impossibility of representing it in action on the stage. The anxieties of the flyers' wives and the gallantry of a Polish count, wedded to a barmaid, provided affecting moments. But the interest centered on a flight officer's wife who renounced a Hollywood lover and a stage career upon realizing that her nerve-strained husband needed her—surely a "stagey" subject for a war. *Lifeline,* a tribute to the merchant marine, was fortunately exempt from theatrical claptrap, but inclined to the other extreme of having no personal complications whatsoever. This substantially reduced our interest, which could have been stimulated only by the epic nature of the material. A more or less factual account of the dangers of keeping embattled England supplied with petrol, the play dramatized the fortunes of a freighter that falls out of convoy, fights a U-boat, is set afire by enemy planes, is abandoned for a time, and is finally brought to an English port with the precious fuel. Normally, an epic theme requires epic extension, whereas the single setting of the play (all the action was confined to the officers' room) actually reduced the picture to microscopic proportions. To English audiences, acutely conscious of the importance of the lifeline of small steamers, the very minuteness of the picture was affecting; it was an excellent frame for the unpretentious heroism of the characters. But the absence of accentuation was a deficiency in America, and Broadway needed a production that would have added some epic extension and excitement to the text. Mr. Gilbert Miller contented himself with a literal rendition. To Americans the play consequently seemed appallingly prosaic and quiescent.

Russia contributed one widely heralded heroic play, Konstantin Simonov's *The Russian People,* in an American version by the gifted Clifford Odets, and its mixed reception reflects the difficulties we have summarized. Its subject was a heroic people, and not an individual; and to those not fully conscious of the collective spirit, the effect seemed divided and diffused. Simonov created believable and noble people, but made their heroism seem almost a matter of course—undoubtedly because the people of the Soviets expect it of themselves. To some Broadway critics, therefore, there was something casual about the play. At the same time, an old soldier dying with words of faith on his lips, women poisoning a sadistic German, a girl scout swimming a river on military missions, a surgeon going to his death deliberately, a town being captured and the girl rescued by the timely arrival of the Red Army—familiar deeds to the Russians—seemed melodramatic to other arbiters of Broadway taste. Nevertheless, the play was not a total loss for our audiences precisely because it combined humanization and action, and external excitement with considerable naturalness. Simonov came close to writing powerful heroic drama. All that *The Russian People* needs is a firmer integration of its story; its spirit is admirable, and some of its scenes are unforgettable.

Our native plays also ran the gamut from bad to tolerably good. *Yankee Point* dramatized the behavior of typical American civilians in relation to a spy hunt and an air raid. Its background of American life was excellent, but its spy plot was routine and its air raid inconsequential. *Cry Havoc* paid evocative tribute to the endurance of the nurses on Bataan, but it was bogged down in exposition for two acts, and lifted into banal spy melodrama in the third act—in addition to dividing the interest among a dozen women. *Winter Soldiers,* written by a new playwright, Dan James, and produced by Piscator's Experimental Studio Theatre, was an inspiring effort because its numerous scenes had epic extension, and were made cumulatively effective by a dynamic idea. The self-sacrificing actions of underground fighters, scattered from Yugoslavia to the Polish-Russian border, delay German armored units headed for Moscow, and this contributes to the defeat of the Nazi hordes when they come up against the spirit of the Russian people. The quality of the play was, however, journalistic; there was no room in a work of this nature for much character realization, and since most of the characters appeared only in single scenes, they could not be revealed as growing in stature.

Maxwell Anderson came through with the best of our war plays in *The Eve of St. Mark.* He descended to shabby, romantic ornamentation in two spurious dream scenes, and to a Fourth-of-July patriotic gesture at the end of the play when the hero's brothers report that they have enlisted in the army. He did succeed, however, in welding individual drama in the person of his young recruit with the American people by dramatizing in simple, affecting terms his relation to his girl and his farmer parents. He drew his hero with delicate and understanding lines, making his heroism grow naturally out of his character. And he had the intelligence to realize that heroic action is most impressive when it is the result of free will and conflicting possibilities. His soldiers have the choice of abandoning a small Philippine base, but choose a delaying action at the cost of their lives when the young recruit makes them conscious of the importance of the sacrifice.

From this review it will be evident that the creation of completely successful heroic drama entails, on the negative side, an avoidance, so far as possible, of clichés and stereotypes—even when they have their bases in fact; and, on the positive side, a sufficient fusion of personal with mass experience, a dramatization of the conscious will in action, and an integration of episodes by a character as in *The Eve of St. Mark,* by an idea as in *Winter Soldiers,* or by a common spirit as in *The Russian People.* But this is hardly all. *The Eve of St. Mark* missed complete realization because its hero was insufficiently conscious of the basic issues involved in the struggle; he never won through to an understanding of what the fighting was for, either in immediate or universal terms, nor did Maxwell Anderson supply any data for the audience to make its own deductions. And this lack was also observable in *Winter Soldiers* and *The Russian People.* Perhaps the authors assumed that the issues were too self-evident to the public they expected to reach, and feared redundancy. Still, no heroic drama will reach anything approximating greatness until it dramatizes the issues, first in immediate terms, and ultimately in terms of man's eternal aspiration and struggle for the good life.

This, it is clear, would require a rare combination of incisive thinking, clearly expressed, and profound feeling, glowingly expressed. That this combination is not impossible in the modern theatre may be seen in Shaw's *St. Joan,* which is still indisputably the best heroic drama of the century. That this may involve subordination of an immediate battlefield to a more universal exposition of the human spirit in historical or imaginative terms is more than possible. But this is not necessarily regrettable, as the data of the war may soon seem repetitious if presented in many more plays. Indeed, the present writer knows that several wellwritten playscripts are already unable to get a production because producers fear the resemblance between their subject and that of war plays already produced. Moreover, as the great Greeks and Shakespeare prove, the universal has generally been the best approach to topical or historical fact. That the thought must already be germinating in dramatists may be deduced from Thornton Wilder's *The Skin of Our Teeth*. Mr. Wilder grew too defensively skittish in his writing, as though he were ashamed of his feelings, and he was guilty of seemingly deliberate obscurities in his last act, which is set in the immediate future; or he simply made inexcusable overtures to "show business," and was just pardonably confused about the future. Nevertheless, *The Skin of Our Teeth,* which dramatizes man's continual struggle with natural and man-made disaster, is genuinely heroic drama. In no current play does the heroic spirit burn so brightly as in the scene in which Mr. Antrobus, the eternal Adam or man of good will, resolves to weather the Ice Age and succors the first masters of song, law, and healing science—despite the behavior of Cain, who drives him to desperation. Possibly, however, completely creative expressions of our present ordeal will come—as Wordsworth, of poetry— only from "emotion recollected in tranquillity." And there can be, there must be, no tranquillity for us as yet.

ANCHORS AWEIGH: MAXWELL ANDERSON AND TENNESSEE WILLIAMS*

Two drama-packed decades separate Maxwell Anderson and Tennessee Williams, the former having emerged in the gilded 1920's with the emergent and growing modern American theatre, while the terrible 1940's were in full swing when they deposited Williams on the narrow beachhead that Broadway has become. They have perhaps only one attribute in common, but it is of such importance that it makes them blood brothers in spite of dissimilarities of temperament, subject matter, and idiom. Neither of them has been satisfied with even the firm ground of journalistic drama or the problem play. Both men have successfully transcended dramatic realism, and they have done so not because they lack social sympathies, an eye for detail, or a strong stomach for indigestible particles in the world of fact. They have envisaged the possibility of a theatre rich in imagination and poetry in an age that has tended to suspect these qualities as gross evasions of reality and social responsibility.

They are not, of course, the only dramatists of our time who have gone on voyages in search of a poetic theatre. The names of Lorca, Yeats, O'Casey, Eliot, Auden, Saroyan, Cocteau, Giraudoux, and Brecht will occur to anyone familiar with the dramatic literature of our times. But Anderson and Williams are particularly important to us as the only playwrights who have not only displayed their cargo in the marketplace of Broadway but have been able to sell it at fancy prices. It is to Williams and Anderson that we have had to look for any sort of assurance that Broadway can be won over to the poetic theatre.

I

Williams' plays present no syntactical or metrical barriers, as they are written in prose. His only published verse play is the inconsequential one-acter *The Purification,* a dance drama that has had no professional production. He belongs to the poetic theatre partly because his dialogue is intensified by imagery and passion, as when Blanche Du Bois responds to the promise of love with the "Sometimes—there's God—so quickly,"

* From *Theatre Time* (Spring, 1949).

304

and partly because he finds expressive adumbrations for his story. The memory pattern of *The Glass Menagerie* is poetic in itself. (It is comparable to the structure of the poetic Noh plays of Japan and Yeats' *Plays for Dancers.*) In *Streetcar,* the poetry lies in such theatrical elements as the subjective music symbolizing Blanche's mental state and the street cries and tenement squabbles in the Latin Quarter that define the environment in which her mind is to be shattered. In *Summer and Smoke,* a good deal of action occurs in front of a statue of "Eternity" in the city square, a symbol of the heroine's spiritual longings. The statue also gives ironic counterpoint to the conclusion when she rebels against the failure of her spirituality and turns to a traveling salesman in desperation. It would be rash to say that every poetic extension of the story or dialogue in a Williams play is immediately perceptible to the average playgoer. But Williams' poetry of theatre is never particularly difficult or esoteric. Not only does it never stand between the playgoer and the elements of plot and characterization that attract the public to any play, but it actually enhances their meaning. The character is rounded out by the atmosphere, and the plot is telegraphed by the mood.

Williams also feels free to avail himself of as much realism as he needs to establish his points. He has never failed to present the pressure of environment upon his characters. In *The Battle of Angels,* small-town curiosity and aridity play a significant part, and the young pagan's destruction is encompassed by a narrow-minded Southern community. Down-at-heels gentility in *The Glass Menagerie* is vividly caught in Amanda's home, and the Latin Quarter of New Orleans is given the weight of an active character in *Streetcar.* Nor has Williams proved in the least queasy about facing sordidness or ugliness when it is part of the data of his drama. Few realistic plays have represented sexual desire and its frustrations so plainly as *Streetcar,* and it is not inconceivable that this most successful of his plays owes some of its continuing popularity to the flagrant sexuality of Stan and Blanche. Williams started his playwriting career with a number of one-act plays in which naturalistic detail is paramount. *The Lady of Larkspur Lotion* is set in a cockroach-ridden boarding house, *The Portrait of a Madonna* gives an almost appallingly vivid description of the fantasies of a woman who imagines herself being raped by a beau of former years, and *Twenty-seven Bales of Cotton* is a miniature "Tobacco Road" account of a lecherous revenge. Like other Southern writers, Williams is attracted to exhibitions of animality and violence.

Unlike an earlier generation of dramatic poets, the so-called *symbolistes* of the 1890's and early 1900's, he has not employed disembodied symbols, hazily suggested backgrounds, and attenuated or bloodless characterizations. He differs from the Maeterlincks, Verhaerens, and Andreyevs of the past, as he differs from the contemporary *surrealistes,* precisely in the density that he gives to reality. If any of his characters are wraithlike, like Laura in *The Glass Menagerie,* or lack the obvious signature of carnality like the heroine of *Summer and Smoke,* or have an unreal component like Blanche du Bois, it is only because this is their character. The playwright has not stylized them out of existence or into a fancied existence. In Gertrude Steinese, they are what they are because they are.

Such "spiritualization" as they receive is, in addition, the essential part of Williams' comment concerning their defeat in life, for he acknowledges in their case a regretful failure of reality. It is not present in the plays because the playwright has exalted a shadowy existence above a substantial one in the name of poetry, or because he prefers weakness. His objectivity is almost callous at times, and it even includes direct observations concerning the social background of his failures. The tragic events of *The Battle of Angels* are produced in part by the sterility and intolerance of the community. Amanda's failure in *The Glass Menagerie* is a projection of her past as a Southern belle, and her son's rebellion is directed against her values and illusions, and against the grubby life of a warehouse employee he will lead by obeying her. His mature outlook in the role of recollector of their home life embraces the inadequacy of that life in the face of the larger catastrophes of fascism and war. His pity for his shy sister and understanding of his bumbling mother includes awareness of the larger failure of the world and the imperativeness of taking some positive stand in the crisis. Even Blanche, in *Streetcar,* who is pathologically confused, is aware of the decay of her planters' world. She is presented as an exile from a society in which her frailties would have been pitied and protected instead of exposed and harried to the breaking point. Her aristocratic pretensions, so out of keeping with her actual situation but so essential to her self-respect, only expose her to further persecution. She is pitted against that vital member of the common people, Stan, whose robustness is both an offense and an attraction to her. Nor is Stan's reaction to Blanche altogether unconditioned by a common man's hostility toward a decayed but still fastidious and arrogant "lady," and it is no small gratification for him to be able to prove that the lady is a whore. A Marxist critic might well say, with some show of reason, that the war between Stan and Blanche is not only a domestic and psychological one but a "class war."

Hunting for a social philosophy in the body of Williams' work to date is likely to be a fruitless endeavor, because it is intuitive, fugitive, and inchoate, even if the evidence of Williams' life and of some of his early writings makes him something of a Depression-period writer. But it is a mistake to overlook signs of some yardstick of social reality and a diffuse critical faculty in him. For the failures Williams has much dissolving and disarming pity, but he does not recommend them to our admiration. Williams, in short, works in the American grain, which is happily a coarse grain. His poetic drama is never over-delicate and never retails moonlight and roses. An effete poetry of the theatre would have met with short shrift on our shores. The playgoer who likes a Williams play may respond warmly to the playwright's sensibility, but only because it is expended upon realities rather than upon figments of fancy or waxworks.

II

In view of Maxwell Anderson's ambitions for himself and the theatre, his problem of winning an audience for poetic drama should have been greater than it turned out to be. Anderson deliberately abandoned prose after scoring such resounding successes in the 1920's as *What Price Glory?* and *Saturday's Children,* and after writing a gripping, if less successful, treatment of the Sacco and Vanzetti case, *Gods of the Lightning.* In the 1930's, he was to return to prose with the Pulitzer Prize-winning, anti-Congressional satire *Both Your Houses,* with *The Star Wagon,* and with more recent, if hardly notable, plays like *Storm Operation* and *Truckline Café.* He turned to the field of poetic drama not because he had no aptitude for prose and even social problem drama (his prose is actually better than his verse), but because of an ambition to scale the altitudes of the theatre, believing it to be, as he says, "a cathedral of the spirit." Prior to becoming a playwright he had been an editorial writer and a college instructor with a partiality for poetry, and evidently the teacher of literature and the versifier exerted stronger claims on him than the journalist. He had also been a militant liberal, who jeopardized several positions on account of his convictions, but the reformer's zeal and optimism had cooled and was giving place to a tragic view of life. Sensible of man's "chance tenure of life," and of his isolation in a universe indifferent to his aspiration and anguish, Anderson elected to write tragedy. The poetic theatre attracted him as the only possible medium for tragic drama. Agreeing, moreover, with Goethe that dramatic poetry is "man's greatest achievement on his earth so far," and convinced that even poetic prose lacked the formal qualities required by the highest art, Anderson decided to write verse dialogue. Since *Elizabeth the Queen* in 1930, his have been the only verse plays to make an impression on the American theatre.

If Anderson has succeeded where failure was most to be expected, the reason is that he is first of all a man of the theatre and a poet and tragedian only secondarily. Realizing that "a certain cleverness in striking a compromise between the world about him and the world within" was indispensable to a playwright, since he is dependent upon his audience, the urbane author of many successes has not ventured wildly. His line structure, which may be described as a free kind of blank verse in the main, is close enough to conversational dialogue to pose no difficulties for the playgoer. Anderson is always crystal-clear in statement, and it is probable that even the prolixity and rhetoric which have been noted to his discredit have been incurred by him less because he is intoxicated with language than because he wants to be fully understood. Also, he entertains a decorative view of poetry, and thus gives his poetic plays a colorfulness of speech that is attractive to a public not particularly dedicated to rigorous standards of poetry.

Anderson also exercised considerable caution by encroaching upon contemporary themes gradually. Having discovered, as he says, that "poetic tragedy had never been successfully written about its own place and time," he started with the historical plays *Elizabeth the Queen* and *Mary of Scotland*. These, along with the latest treatment of a sixteenth-century subject, *Anne of the Thousand Days,* have been his most popular efforts. But it is less the remoteness of the subject matter than its quality and Anderson's treatment of the material that have turned the scales in his favor at the box-office. The fact is that, in spite of injections of a philosophical or social viewpoint, the plays have been robust romances. They have essentially the same attractiveness as the historical novels that publishers find so profitable and that the film industry has consumed so avidly. They are, of course, achieved on a higher plane, owing to the verse form and the presence of Anderson's generally bitter commentary on political chicanery and his tragic attitude. But these only spice the romance for a theatre public that is more selective than the general run of readers and moviegoers. Above all, his romances benefit from a lusty sense of humor and a bravura spirit that rarely fails to be effective on the stage, and he has a special flair for dramatizing the sex duel in costume. Anderson has been able to make successful departures from realism by meeting fairly grownup audiences on their own terms. They are all believers in romance, provided it is not served to them with saccharine. His disenchantment with government and revolution is also not particularly remote from their own outlook, even if, lacking his verbal talent, they could not express it as forcefully.

To leave our report at this point would be, of course, manifestly unfair to Mr. Anderson. He has written verse dramas that have not recommended themselves as easily to the public. The Rudolf of Hapsburg tragedy *The Masque of Kings* contained, it is true, a substantial romance culminating in a double death, but it owed considerable interest to the dilemma of a liberal prince who must choose between a tyrannical status quo and a revolution that might bring in its wake an equally evil state of affairs. Although *Valley Forge* included a rather romantic subplot, it was essentially a political drama. *Joan of Lorraine* posed the problem of compromise in idealistic courses with theatrical ingenuity, by means of the play within the play technique. And Anderson's two most distingushed plays, *Winterset* and *High Tor,* dealt with contemporary themes and characters. In the latter, Anderson conscripted fantasy and poetry into the service of a protest against the predatory industrial world. It contains some of the best satire in English poetic drama since *The Beggar's Opera,* and some of the best poetic fantasy in the language since *The Tempest.* Although a "Romeo and Juliet" story was omnipresent in *Winterset,* it was not of the sort calculated to recommend itself as a romance. A sultry sense of tragedy, of human injustice and of fatefulness, enlarged by the overtones of the Sacco and Vanzetti case, made *Winterset* memorable. With this play, Anderson succeeded in employing poetic tragedy for a contemporary theme perhaps for the first time in the English language. *Winterset* and *High Tor* failed to attain the popularity of his most successful historical romances, but they remain his strongest claims to consideration as a modern dramatic poet.

Still, both plays prevailed on Broadway as far as they did, not so much because they were poetic dramas but because they made good theatre. In *High Tor* Anderson played with theatrical elements quite skillfully. He engaged in amiable horseplay when he hoisted up his real estate prospectors in a basket, and made free use of caricature and oddity. He used theatricality and considerable fancy as a ready solvent for his hero's despair and rebellion against the encroachments of industry and machinery. Nor was the protest anything that would require deep thought or arouse particular public resistance. As for *Winterset,* it may have been high tragedy for its author and for the most discriminating part of the public, but the pattern was, to a degree, the familiar one of standard gangster melodrama. This does not, of course, detract from the merits of *Winterset,* since there is plenty of melodrama in Shakespearian and Greek tragedies. It proves only that here, as in other successful inroads into the poetic theatre, the playwright has had showmanship on his side, and it is precisely practical showmanship that has been absent in much modern poetic drama. Tennessee Williams is the only other American playwright who has combined a sturdy theatrical sense with poetic aspirations.

III

Several questions can be posed concerning the work of both playwrights. How important is it actually? Have they struck out in really new directions, and what can we hope to find at the end of the road they have taken? There is no doubt that they have soared above both commonplace earnestness and clever but hollow entertainment. If we should, however, apply a rigorous standard to their plays, if criticism should rise to the level of their aspirations, I very much fear that we shall not be able to rank Williams and Anderson as high as we should like to. Nor will it be possible to regard them as pioneers in the same sense as an Aeschylus, a Marlowe, an Ibsen, and even an O'Neill stood in the vanguard of a developing theatre. The state of the theatre, in which no new spirit has made itself felt, is partly responsible for this. But so is the quality of Anderson's and Williams' thought and writing.

The small perfection of *The Glass Menagerie,* as well as the charm and rightness of observation in it, should not blind us to its limitations— that is, to its perhaps autobiographical sentimentalization of the Narrator and the lack of resolution in the very conception of the work. It is only a superb fragment of a play. Although *Summer and Smoke* should be, I believe, rated higher than it stands in the opinion of most reviewers, it cannot be considered a fully realized play. Its transitions are either undramatized off-stage developments or arbitrarily imposed events, such as the murder of the young doctor's father. It is a touching story of attrition that emerges partly as a novel and partly as a series of episodes, some of them excellent, from a play fully conceived but only partially written. It is like the drama in a script which consists of scenes in a matrix of summary.

Even *A Streetcar Named Desire* falls short of its possibilities. It aims at tragedy and achieves only pathos, achieving no final meaning beyond a common enough, and futile enough, pity for a victim of delusions and of people's callousness. Since Blanche's condition is attributed to her traumatic marriage to a homosexual who committed suicide, there is something adventitious or special in Blanche's deterioration. Her plight is not a true reflection of her class or of humanity in general. The class attributes are only supplementary in her story and its universality rests on the shaky foundation of private trauma. When you show, for instance, that normal people try to evade reality and are punished by failure, as Chekhov does in *The Cherry Orchard,* you are making a statement of universal application and importance. When you also associate specific class habits and limitations with them, you are, then, also saying something valid about their class or society as Chekhov did. When you say that abnormal people, like Blanche, try to escape reality and are destroyed, you are only being tautological, since neurosis is, by definition, maladjustment to reality and madness is total flight from it. We may still accept your statement that flight spells disaster because we know that to be true from our own observation, but your idea is not established, it is merely symbolized by your story. If you show that the world doesn't get along well with sensitive people, you make a universal and relevant point. But if you show, as in Blanche's case, that the world doesn't get along with neurotics, or that neurotics don't get along with the world, you are again being tautological, since all this is included in the definition of a neurotic or a psychotic.

Nor is there any inevitability in Blanche's seducing schoolboys and turning to prostitution because of the unhappy marriage. Her sorry past and present, including the rape scene which rather piles misfortunes on Blanche as if the author were resolved to give his heroine "the works," makes *Streetcar* more startling than genuinely illuminating. The play, like most of the work of Faulkner, belongs to the school of "Southern Gothic" in which the grotesque seems to be exploited, if not for the sake of creating a sensation, at least for the sake of a hell-vision of life, which is in effect only another form of sensationalism. That is, its creators give you the Inferno without the Purgatorio and Paradiso, thereby retailing a very partial vision of humanity as if it were a complete one.

Williams' individuality has not yet acquired a specific character; it is as yet predominantly intuitive and wayward. It still consists of swirling elements contributed by D. H. Lawrence, Chekhov, and Faulkner; and these, as well as elements singularly his own, have yet to solidify and acquire the cohesion we find in the mature work of a master. Until they do, his work in full-length plays will seem more or less fortuitous and tentative. Its light will be a nimbus around a dark center rather than a searchlight thrown upon human darkness. It will be insufficiently or too uncertainly revealing to possess real significance. Only when Williams gives us as much light as heat, and only if he does so, will he become a major dramatist. And only a major dramatist, upon whom one can place reliance because he doesn't lose his own way, is likely to be followed when he strikes out in a new direction.

IV

Lack of a clear direction, cohesion, or a complete viewpoint cannot be charged against Maxwell Anderson, who is a fully matured dramatist. And there can be no doubt concerning his estimate of his characters, his analysis of their situation, his tracings of cause and effect. Nor can there be any mistake about his pattern. A well-educated man and a thoughtful one, he has defined the nature of tragedy completely to his satisfaction, and he has tried to make his plays conform to it. His aspirations to stature and significance are limited not by formlessness of any sort but by its very opposite—namely, by formalism. It is a quality difficult to define and not easy even to describe in a short essay. All I can say is that, in spite of his air of informality, he tends to maintain a formal attitude toward his matter and toward dramatic art, sometimes even carrying it to the extreme of rhetorical formulation. It is doubtful at times whether he does not dictate formulated conditions to life and history instead of taking dictation from them. Except in *Gods of the Lightning,* the first two acts of *Winterset,* and the first half of *The Eve of St. Mark,* moreover, I have not been sure that the playwright was moving us through the power of his own emotion rather than, more speciously, by a synthetic tragic feeling.

Having set himself the high objective of writing tragedy, Anderson has often created the simulacrum rather than the real article. The formal and synthetic quality, not always apparent while the theatrical spell of a good production is upon us, ultimately reveals itself in a variety of ways. Thus, his traditional philosophy of tragedy makes him take an exalted view of human strivings and gives his leading characters a certain nobility of spirit in a crisis or a denouement. But the character's defiances and affirmations seem less a matter of inner compulsion than of a pose held, an attitude taken. They constitute a sort of rhetoric of the soul rather than the soul itself, I believe, in the third act of *Winterset,* in *Mary of Scotland, Valley Forge, The Wingless Victory,* and *Key Largo.* Often, too, the undoing of a character is the result of a conspiracy (see *Elizabeth the Queen, Mary of Scotland, Anne of the Thousand Days*) rather than the effect of a grave flaw in that character which affords insight into the abysses of human nature. The point of view that emerges concerning the characters, the historical situation, man's destiny or the nature of his world is always forcefully expressed in Anderson's tragedies and yet seems a formal conclusion, like the conclusion in an Euclidean proposition set up for the purpose. (It is only fair to say, however, that *Anne of the Thousand Days* seems blameless in this particular respect, and has more spontaneity than the author's earlier Elizabethan plays.)

Although Maxwell Anderson is a high-minded man, his tragic feeling seems too often prefabricated or imposed by him upon life. And the same sense of something laid on can also be observed in his dramatic verse, since the poetic quality is frequently a polish added to a thought or sentiment rather than compulsive expression or incandescence. A good deal of even his most forceful verse seems less generated by the flame within than acquired by a knowledge of literature and by association with its tradition. In our time, for better and sometimes for worse, O'Neill and O'Casey have often given the impression that their plays were wrung from their entrails. The consecration of art in most of Anderson's work has been, one can suspect, too transparently willed. His poetic drama seems rather academic, an impression also supported by the reminiscent quality of lines and situations. Except to some small degree in *Winterset,* he has staged no more than a palace revolution in our theatre, and, in spite of noble exertions, he is more of an epigone than a trailblazer. If Mr. Anderson has earned our esteem, it is for setting a high valuation on dramatic art and for making literary drama attractive on our tawdry stage.

THE TWO WORLDS OF
THORNTON WILDER*

In recommending a volume of short plays by Thornton Wilder published as long ago as 1931, it is tempting to lean on his subsequently achieved reputation as the author of *Our Town* and *The Skin of Our Teeth,* two of the outstanding American plays of the century, and on the fame of several novels since the publication of *The Bridge of San Luis Rey* in 1927 that contain some of the best writing to be found in contemporary American fiction. But the author of these works is interesting to us not as a reputation but as a living artist, and the pleasure derived from the plays in the present volume is sure to be instant and self-sufficient. I trust it is not a momentary judgment of mine that *The Long Christmas Dinner* is the most beautiful one-act play in English prose; at this writing its only rival in my affections is Synge's radically different masterpiece, *Riders to the Sea.*

If *Pullman Car Hiawatha* is bound to suffer by comparison with *Our Town,* it is questionable whether the comparison should be allowed to carry any weight. Since Wilder did not compose the shorter and earlier play as a mere preparatory exeircse, it has its own distinct substance and style. The presence of an omniscient Stage Manager in both *Pullman Car Hiawatha* and *Our Town* leaves large areas of difference after the technical resemblance has been duly noted. A third experiment in imaginative theatre, *The Happy Journey to Trenton and Camden,* is a deservedly well-known and frequently performed *tour de force.* And even the conventional realistic dramatic structure of the remaining plays, *Queens of France,* an affecting genre painting of social pretensions in old New Orleans, and *Love and How To Cure It,* a nonstagey glance at stage folk, has unique features gratifying to those who know how to read dramatic literature.

Still, it is within the frame of Wilder's total endeavor as playwright and novelist that these short pieces stand out most meaningfully. And, conversely, these little masterworks help to define their author, concerning whom opinions have been frequently divided and rarely cogent despite the attention paid to his writings and the regard in which he is held on

* Introduction to *The Long Christmas Dinner,* by Thornton Wilder (New York: Harper & Row, 1963).

314

two continents. In this collection of early plays we find (not unexpectedly in the case of so disciplined and self-aware an artist) the configurations of a talent that combines sensitivity with a strong awareness of form and embraces both the commonplaces of life and the life of the imagination, which fluctuates between fantasy and philosophy, skepticism and mysticism, playfulness and sobriety. We see him poised between "life" and "theatre," and this not merely as a beguiling technician but as an observer of reality who does not hesitate to throw off the shackles of realistic play construction in order to come closer to reality.

For assembling the scattered endeavors of the author the present collection was extremely well situated in time. When it appeared rather inconspicuously in 1931, its thirty-four-year-old author (Thornton Wilder was born in Madison, Wisconsin, on April 17, 1897) had already published three novels—*The Cabala* in 1926, *The Bridge of San Luis Rey* in 1927, and *The Woman of Andros* in 1930. This early period of his career was marked by considerable fluctuation. *The Cabala,* a Proustian or Jamesian work rich in characterization if not in unity and clarity, was an impressive but hardly successful novel. *The Bridge of San Luis Rey,* a beautifully written philosophical novel, was enthusiastically received as a relief from semidocumentary, naturalistic fiction in America as well as from the pseudosophistication of the literature of the 1920's. One literary critic (Harry Salpeter) wrote that readers "were tired of realistic novels and were rotten ripe for a book like *The Bridge*"; Alexander Woollcott, in the prime of his reputation as an arbiter of taste, called it a novel of "aloof and untruckling beauty," and the book brought its author his first Pulitzer Prize. But the next novel, *The Woman of Andros,* published in 1930, was a failure and, according to his critics, reflected in the most unfavorable light his special limitations of abstruseness, preciosity, and remoteness from the contemporary world. In the fall of that year, in fact, Wilder became the object of a violent assault by the left-wing journalist Michael Gold in the *New Republic,* and although he found so powerful a defender as Edmund Wilson, it was quite evident that the vein of cultivated fiction for which he had evinced a strong affinity was virtually exhausted. It was no longer considered viable art during the "socially conscious" depression period of the 1930's to which volcanic eruptions in Europe were continually adding new challenges.

The Woman of Andros may not be a substantial novel; it is nonetheless an enchanting and affecting book, and it is more satisfying in my opinion than many an acclaimed contemporary novel. But the historical situation was plainly unfavorable to the reflective and tastefully distanced artistry which is one of the two worlds of art Wilder has inhabited in the course of his distinguished literary career. He would have to move into the other world of common reality which he had fastidiously avoided but with which he soon made a successful compromise that accounts for much of his originality and his special genius—the compromise of combining intensive observation of the common world with uncommon transcendence or sublimation of that world. Wilder himself was apparently aware of a limitation in his art when he declared some years later (in 1938) that he had shrunk from describing the modern world and was "alarmed at finding a way of casting into generalization the world of doorbells and telephones." He was ready, he believed, "to accept the twentieth century, not only as a fascinating age to live in, but as assimilable stuff to think with."

He still had to accept the theatre as well. His first plays, published in 1928 under the collective title *The Angel That Troubled the Waters,* were three-minute-long dramatic pieces. They possess some of the features of a literary conversation in the manner of Walter Savage Landor but without Landor's prolixity in prose; there is considerably less dramatic pressure in them than in the miniature verse plays of Pushkin and the short pieces Musset wrote to illustrate proverbs. They are extremely beautiful pieces of writing and I particularly treasure *Now the Servant's Name Was Malchus* in which "Our Lord" in heaven receives the servant of the High Priest whose ear was lopped off by Peter's sword when Christ was arrested. Malchus would like to have his name expunged from the New Testament because the episode makes him look ridiculous. Christ invites him to stay in heaven with Him, saying, "Malchus, will you stay and be ridiculous with me?" Malchus says he will be glad to stay but isn't sure he merits all that attention: "I wasn't even the High Priest's servant; I only held his horse every now and then." Besides, it was his left ear and not his right that was the casualty of that fateful encounter; whereupon "Our Lord" assures him that "the book isn't always true about me, either."

The affirmative counterpart to this rather bitter one-acter is another miniature masterpiece, *The Flight into Egypt,* in which Hepzibah, the talkative donkey that carries the Holy Family fleeing from Herod's massacre of the children, loiters dangerously on the road to Egypt. On being ordered to move ahead, Hepzibah reflects that "it's a queer world where the survival of the Lord is dependent on donkeys," and requesting some answers to the puzzle of faith and reason, is told by Our Lady that there will be an answer perhaps someday, but "For the present just do as I do and bear your master on." A third dramatic capsule, *Hast Thou Considered My Servant Job,* asserts faith in man himself. Wilder's often noted optimistic view of man is expressed with unusual warmth when Judas renounces Satan, who has been awaiting his favorite son, confident that he has defeated Christ, "For I build not on intermittent dreams and timid aspirations, but on the unshakable passions of lust and self-love." The stage direction that answers this boast reads: "Suddenly the thirty pieces of silver are cast upward from the revolted hand of Judas. They hurtle across the stars and continue falling forever through the vast funnel of space." Christ and Judas then "mount upward to their due place and Satan remains to this day, uncomprehending, upon the pavement of Hell."

Still, the world of art that Wilder inhabited with the writing of some forty three-minute plays (and this activity went as far back as 1915, when he wrote the first of these in California) was the same reflective and literary world that had served him in the novels. It was a strong enticement for one who had studied the classics in his youth, written ambitious undergraduate literature, pursued the study of archaeology at the American Academy in Rome after graduation from Yale in 1920, taught from 1921 to 1928 at the Lawrenceville boys' preparatory school near Princeton, and was to teach again for over half a decade, from 1930 to 1936, at the University of Chicago under the classically inspired regime of his former Yale classmate Robert Hutchins. Characteristically, in writing the Foreword to *The Angel That Troubled the Waters* in 1928, Wilder declared that "beauty is the only persuasion." But with the writing of *The Long Christmas Dinner* and the other dramatically active one-act plays in the present volume he was plainly intent on achieving something more than "beauty." He aimed here for the truth of common life, on the one hand, and its theatrical expression, on the other.

Henceforth he was to inhabit two worlds, the real and the imaginary, or to blend the two in the same work. This was apparent in his later fiction—in *Heaven's My Destination,* an amusing yet rueful novel about a moralistic innocent adrift in American society, published in 1935, and in *The Ides of March* (1948), in which he combined a novel of manners in Julius Caesar's times with a penetrating portrait of Caesar and exquisitely reflective prose often intensified with emotion and lightened with humor. (In the invented letters and diary that make up this semi-Shavian novel one comes across well-turned observations such as Caesar's statements that "The Gods hide themselves even in their choice of instruments," that "Hope has never changed tomorrow's weather," and that "wickedness may be the exploration of one's liberty" and "the search for a limit that one can respect.") But it is especially in the plays published after *The Angel That Troubled the Waters* that Wilder effected the reconciliation of reality and imagination which proved so rewarding in *Our Town* in 1938 and *The Skin of Our Teeth* in 1942.*

To the plays in the present volume belongs the distinction of introducing their author as an original and effective playwright, and three of these will introduce the reader to the essence of his craftsmanship. Thus, the omniscient Stage Manager so important to the structure of *Our Town* first appears in *Pullman Car Hiawatha* and serves the same purpose of introducing the dramatic action and functioning within it. He is both the *raisonneur,* or commentator, and, in speaking the lines of several minor figures, a veritable constellation of characters. The Stage Manager is, so to speak, both a one-man chorus and a multiple "second character," or deuteragonist, in the play, which reflects conventions of both Greek and Oriental drama in this respect while the dialogue and the characterizations are unmistakably American.

Time is telescoped in *The Long Christmas Dinner,* so that ninety years of family life flow through the play without interruption in a sequence of merging scenes. Thornton Wilder was to telescope time again on a more historically significant plane in *The Skin of Our Teeth* a decade later. In *The Long Christmas Dinner* the author's imaginative management of time is simple and persuasive. We feel as though we were floating in the flux of life and of time itself, in a broad and never-ending stream which is both "real" and "unreal." We move ahead and are nevertheless becalmed by the sameness of the things that ultimately matter most to us, the quotidian realities that underlie the course of nations and even the ardors and endurances of men and women celebrated in history, saga, and high tragedy. And the marvel is that this effect of simplicity was achieved by the author with some of the most sophisticated strategies of dramaturgy within the competence of modern theatrical art.

The same simplicity of subject and style combined with modernistic structural departures from realism also appears in *The Happy Journey to Trenton and Camden,* in which the author again resorts to a Stage

---

* Mr. Wilder, I should add, has been a more prolific playwright since 1931 than the above reference to his major plays would suggest. *The Merchant of Yonkers,* a Max Reinhardt production in 1938, was revised and entitled *The Matchmaker.* In this version the play was produced at the Edinburgh Festival in 1954 and in New York in 1955. He adapted André Obey's poetic drama *Le Viol de Lucrèce* for Katharine Cornell and *A Doll's House* for a Jed Harris presentation featuring Ruth Gordon as Nora, and he wrote an Alcestis drama, *The Alcestiad,* performed at the Edinburgh Festival of 1955 under the title *A Life in the Sun.* Mr. Wilder is now at work on two cycles of one-act plays, *The Seven Ages of Man* and *The Seven Deadly Sins,* from which three pieces were put together for a Circle-in-the-Square off-Broadway production in 1962. In the best of these, *Childhood,* one finds the same fusion of homely reality and piquant fantasy that characterizes the major stage productions.

Manager who sets up the visible action and participates in the play in several small roles. In *Pullman Car Hiawatha,* moreover, the author's resources of dramatic construction and symbolic visualization even enable him to move into a world of fancy, allowing him to give a speech to a dead woman (Harriet) as affecting as Emily's lines in the last act of *Our Town* and to personify places such a "Grover's Corners" and "The Field" (too archly, perhaps) in the dramatic action. He even feels free to indulge in the playful histrionics of bringing "The Hours" onstage as "beautiful girls dressed like Elihu Vedder's Pleiades," each carrying a great gold Roman numeral; this, after a whimsical introduction by the Stage Manager to the effect that the minutes are "gossips," the hours "philosophers," and the years "theologians." And following this, anticipating a procession of the hours in *The Skin of Our Teeth,* Ten O'Clock, Eleven O'Clock, and Twelve O'Clock quote Plato, Epictetus, and St. Augustine, while "the planets appear on the balcony." Nothing less than a wistful mysticism relating our insignificant species to the universe satisfies Wilder's imagination once he elects for histrionic freedom or "theatricalism."

It is to be noted, finally, that with this roving kind of dramaturgy he brings us to one more paradoxical attribute of his virtuosity. He is at once a radical and a traditionalist in employing a form of stylization that proclaims the theatrical nature of the drama instead of sedulously sustaining the so-called illusion of reality required by the conventions of modern realism. The artificial nature of the theatre was the established convention of classic, Oriental, Renaissance, Elizabethan, neoclassic, and romantic theatre; realistic convention, which became firmly established only in the second half of the nineteenth century, is a very late development. In returning to "theatricalism" or "theatre for theatre's sake" (rather than "theatre for the sake of illusion"), Wilder associated himself with tradition in dramatic art. But returning to tradition in the twentieth century was an innovation, and Wilder's manner of returning to it was personal and unique. It came about not without some dangers, the greatest of these being in his case some frolicsome bookishness and self-conscious skittishness, but it amounted to a minor revolution in the American theatre.

Both its revolutionary character and its risks were, however, minimized by the persuasive humanity, natural tact, and good taste of the well-bred and well-educated author of short and long plays that quickly established themselves as classics of the American theatre in so far as this jittery institution can lay claim to any classics at all. A nearly infallible sense of theatre, moreover, overcame the antidramatic tendencies of Thornton Wilder's temperament, giving liveliness to his reflectiveness and life to his artifices. In a little essay entitled *Some Thoughts on Playwriting,* published in 1941, he set down his creed and awareness of craft succinctly. He declared that "the Stage is a fundamental pretense" and that it thrives on the acceptance of that fact and "in the multiplication of additional pretenses." But he went on to affirm the immediacy of life in the drama despite the pretenses of the stage by writing that "A play is what takes place. A novel is what one person tells us took place. A play visibly represents pure existing." He did not have to defend the paradox as his own plays, beginning with *The Long Christmas Dinner* in 1931, provided sufficient proof of its truth and gratifying results.*

And Thornton Wilder provided conclusive evidence of the compatibility of convention and emotional conviction with an example in *Some Thoughts on Playwriting.* Starting with the statement that the theatre "lives by conventions: a convention is an agreed-upon falsehood, a permitted lie," he cited the case of Euripides' *Medea.* According to an ancient report, the passage in the play where Medea contemplates the murder of her children nearly produced a riot. Yet Medea was "played by a man," "he wore a large mask on his face," "he wore shoes with soles and heels half a foot high," he spoke in metric lines and "all poetry is an 'agreed-upon falsehood' in regard to speech," and "the lines were sung in a kind of recitative"—as in opera, which "involves this 'permitted lie' in regard to speech." Wilder rightly concluded that the mask, the costume, and the mode of declamation were "a series of signs which the spectator interpreted and reassembled in his own mind." That is, "Medea was being re-created within the imagination of each of the spectators."

* Readers curious enough about the nature and justification of this paradox, this dual character of dramatic art, may refer to the following paragraph in John Gassner's *Form and Idea in Modern Theatre* (pp. 141–42):

> The fundamental premise of realism is the Aristotelian one that drama is an imitation of an action; realists held, therefore, that the most desirable theatre is that in which imitation is closest. The fundamental premise of theatricalism is that theatre is not imitation in the narrow sense, which Aristotle never could have held, since the Greek drama upon which he based conclusions in his *Poetics* was not realistically imitative. For the theatricalist, the object of action and of all other "imitative" elements is not imitation but creativeness, and a special kind of creativeness at that. The realists would agree, of course, as to the value of creativeness. But the theatricalist goes one step further, and that step is the truly decisive one for the theory and practice of pure theatricalism. He maintains that there is never any sense in pretending that one is not in the theatre; that no amount of make-believe is reality itself; that in short, theatre is the medium of dramatic art, and that effectiveness in art consists in *using* the medium rather than concealing it.

"THERE IS NO AMERICAN DRAMA"—
A PREMONITION OF DISCONTENT (1952)*

Our young men of letters are beginning to doubt seriously whether we ever had a distinctive American drama, and, even if we did, whether it was or is worthy of our esteem.

Although the American theatre was not exempt from criticism in previous decades, it was badgered rather than written off. Nor did the rebellious groups content themselves with mere rebellion. In the twenties the rebels thought they knew what kind of playwriting they wanted and proceeded to create it—for better or worse. In the thirties the rebels wanted a drama of social significance and proceeded to create it—for better or worse. In recent years the rebels, it would seem, have known only what they don't want—and it happens to be the entire body of American drama since the advent of O'Neill. Or at least that large part of it that succeeded on Broadway and that won the respect of what they contemptuously call "the Broadway intelligentsia."

It seems that for three decades we were totally mistaken in believing that we were creating an American drama. We were deficient in taste and intellect. We were debased by Broadway vulgarity. We were banal, blatant, and shamelessly sentimental. When we evinced sympathy with the common man, we descended to bathos. When we left plain realism, we gave ourselves up to vapid abstractions and to puerile, undergraduate metaphysics.

The indictment has come primarily from comparatively young critics more or less associated with the "New Critics" movement in literary criticism. They are intellectuals, even if they prefer to despise "intellectuals" on Broadway, and write for the small, highbrow magazines. Among other critics, Brooks Atkinson is their special butt, but even Joseph Wood Krutch is assessed with strong reservations. Among the elders of the Drama Critics' Circle, only Stark Young—who has not reviewed for four years—is exempted from some measure of condescension or contempt. And his admiration for O'Neill is already deprecated by his new admirers. Eric Bentley is held in esteem, and when he joins the Circle in the fall as the *New Republic*'s reviewer, it will have a *persona grata* for the first time since Stark Young's resignation. As I am second to none

* From *Theatre Arts* (September, 1952).

321

in my admiration for both Mr. Young and Mr. Bentley, no denigration is intended when I say that both have been the most Europeanized of the critics.

The new "New Critics" also have a more or less European orientation. An American writer is usually favored or disfavored to the degree to which he has approximated some European playwright's talent or has fallen short of it. O'Neill, for example, is apt to be measured against Strindberg and Wedekind—and found painfully wanting. A new play such as *The Fourposter* is apt to be praised, as it is in a brilliantly written *Hudson Review* article by William Becker, because it belongs to an "extremely unBroadwaylike tradition," to the long line of "gay, sentimental but rather exquisite marital farces" of the French theatre. These are "worth having because they tend to keep alive a traditional resource of stage-art." And since Mr. Jan de Hartog, the author, comes from Holland, it is not an American playwright who receives the accolade here at all.

The present European orientation differs from that which made O'Neill one of the most popular playwrights abroad in the 1920's and gave transatlantic reputations to other American plays. It is European *cum* Eliot-sponsored aristocratic traditionalism *cum* erstwhile aristocratic southern agrarianism transposed into the key of so-called New Criticism. It is intellectually more selective, and it is more wary of theatricality (and of social passion, too) than the European intelligentsia was in the twenties. It is certainly more refined. It is intellectually subtler, too. A more complete description would involve the names of Pound the exile, Yeats and the symbolists, and would note that the refinement contains a measure of disgust at the "vulgarity" of Broadway. All this may prejudice them against Broadway, as may the fact that they are attached to universities and tend to be purists in literature. But no one can argue that they lack a perspective denied to those of us who have been close to Broadway.

That Broadway's critics should be assailed is nothing new, even though the reason is no longer that they are too severe but that they are too indulgent. But now the favorite Broadway actors also get a drubbing. Mr. Becker's review, for example, praises Jessica Tandy and Hume Cronyn, but refers to "the cooing drivel endlessly performed by the Lunts." As for José Ferrer's acting in *The Shrike,* for which Broadway critics had the highest praise, Mr. Becker doubts "that there has been a performance in many years as unconstrainedly false, vulgar, and hammy."

It is the playwrights, however, who usually come off worst. They may, indeed, count themselves fortunate when they are granted the possession of elementary craftsmanship and a sense of theatre, if they happen to have succeeded on Broadway. From O'Neill to Arthur Miller our playwrights are said to have bumbled, brazened out their intellectual and artistic insufficiency, pretended—and vulgarized. *The Shrike,* according to Mr. Becker, was "a hopeless turkey, a stupidly written, especially insignificant piece of nothing."

In my latest anthology, *Best American Plays: Third Series of 1945–51,* there is probably not a single play out of the seventeen that would satisfy this latest *avant-garde.* Surely not *The Iceman Cometh,* which Mr. Bentley gently and fairly dissects in the summer issue of the *Kenyon Review.* Since Mr. Bentley has been steadily growing not only as a critic but as a practical man of the theatre ever since the publication of *The Playwright as Thinker,* he is inclined to abandon the holier-than-thou view. But we may be sure that the younger or more academically aloof intellectuals would be more devastating in appraising *The Iceman Cometh.* Tennessee Williams is, of course, vulnerable, especially when he turns symbolist, and Maxwell Anderson has long been considered vulnerable as a would-be tragic poet.

As for Arthur Miller, the diatribe against *Death of a Salesman* contributed by the able Eleanor Clark in the June, 1949, issue of *The Partisan Review* probably represents the views of her less articulate colleagues to perfection:

> The play, with its peculiar hodgepodge of dated materials and facile new ones, is not a tragedy at all but an ambitious piece of confusionism, such as in any other sphere would probably be called a hoax and which has been put across by purely technical skills not unlike those of a magician or an acrobat.

It is at best, she said, nothing more "than the usual operation of the second-rate mind as glamorized by Broadway," and at worst an intellectual muddle and a piece of disingenuous political pleading—the roar of left-wing theatre of the 1930's reduced to a whine. "Very dull business," Miss Clark concluded.

Mr. Frederick Morgan, writing in *The Hudson Review,* concurred in the opinion. He found the play "not surprisingly, a miserable affair," and would not have singled it out for comment from "among the many Broadway productions which are completely devoid of merit," if *Death of a Salesman* had not received so many prizes, plaudits and acclamations. It was "pure Broadway" and, moreover, "Broadway in a self-pitying mood." And when Miller's play is dismissed as tripe, the American drama is surely shown to be worthless.

Before the rout of Broadway's playwrights can be completely

effected, however, their big gun must be silenced, and the big gun is, of course, Eugene O'Neill. But for O'Neill, Mr. Becker contends quite correctly, historians of the American theatre have no focus for their studies. It is unfortunate that he is still "the culture-hero of the Broadway intelligentsia," although the literary intelligentsia have already all but dismissed him from serious consideration. Mr. Becker's view, and he is not alone in his opinion, is that O'Neill has a "mediocre mind with outsize pretensions" and possesses a theatrical talent far beyond his means for employing it profoundly or well.

Many of the particular points Mr. Becker scores against America's foremost playwright are not as new as Mr. Becker may possibly believe. (He does know, I am sure, that Eric Bentley anticipated him in 1946 in *The Playwright as Thinker*.) He is mistaken in believing that to the Broadway critics O'Neill is an unassailable "great," even if he is right in objecting to Brooks Atkinson's insistence on Ibsen's inferiority to the American playwright. Even George Jean Nathan, Brooks Atkinson, and John Mason Brown noted faults in his work a good many years before the publication of the Spring, 1952, issue of *The Hudson Review* in which this indictment appears, and even I set down stringent reservations a round dozen years ago in my *Masters of the Drama*. I even, regretfully, gave offense in one quarter, by referring to him as "an immature and derivative thinker" and accusing him of descending "to incredible banality such as one might expect from a sophomore who has just discovered 'the facts of life.'" But there is this difference between Mr. Becker's views and those we have held. We could accept O'Neill with all his limitations, and we accepted him gratefully. Mr. Becker, using last season's productions of *Anna Christie* and *Desire under the Elms* as a basis, concludes that "the reputation of Eugene O'Neill is possibly the most revealing symptom of the predicament of the American Drama—the predicament being that such a drama scarcely exists."

And Mr. Becker is surely logical. If O'Neill cannot survive scrutiny as a playwright of distinction, what other American writer can? With O'Neill demolished, the entire American drama falls to pieces. We have all wasted our time in trying to create, promote, and support any American theatre above the level of frankly farcical entertainment. And worse still, although Mr. Becker does not quite say so, we have been fools, if not indeed, consciously or unconsciously, knaves in doing so.

Many seasoned men of the Broadway theatre and its environs will be tempted to dismiss both the animadversions and deductions of Mr. Becker and his fellow critics with a snort. But I am equally certain that if the reviews I have singled out as representative of *avant-garde* criticism of the mid-forties and early fifties were read in their entirety, the reader would have to respect the keen intelligence that went into them.

Whatever exceptions I can and will take to certain blasts against the American drama, this much is certain: good taste, knowledge, and understanding are present in the attacks I have noted. One has only to read Mr. Becker's comments on the O'Neill revivals and on the Olivier productions to be convinced that he is an exceptionally keen and educated observer, and a responsible, as well as penetrating, critic. One may object to certain phrases and to the bias he and Miss Clark seem to reveal. But one cannot shrug off their barbs. The charges they make directly and by implication are serious and should be received seriously.

They are important, too, because the attitude they reveal may well pervade the educated members of an entire generation upon which the fate of any significant theatre we may have in the 1950's will largely depend. The attitude of an opinion-making minority is always important to the fortunes of an art. This minority also determines the kind of creativity that appears in a particular period. We saw this happen, for example, in the theatre of the 1920's, created largely by the "lost generation" sophisticates; and in the theatre of the 1930's, influenced by the Depression-bred liberal and radical intellectuals. I believe (although I fervently hope I am wrong) that the stimulus provided by the new critics of the highbrow magazines and their followers will prove quite sterile. Either they will shun the market place, in which case they will exert only a negative influence, or gravitate to the market place and struggle to make the best kind of theatre that is possible under present conditions—in which case they will have descended from their perches and become tainted with some of the muck that is so offensive to them at present. My doubts do not, however, ignore the fact that they are admirably articulate and can often cite chapter and verse to sustain their argument.

The last season on Broadway surely provided both provocation and support to a wholesale indictment. Our playwrights could barely lift themselves above ground and, for that matter, walked only very unsteadily upon it. Even the usually adept purveyors of musical comedy were quite lame. Revivals such as *Kind Lady* and *Of Thee I Sing* gave the impression that the popular theatre of past decades, previously acceptable to even fastidious older reviewers, had little intrinsic value and was outmoded.

Revivals of *Anna Christie* and *Desire under the Elms* proved at least two points: O'Neill's plays, in the main, now belong to a repertory of American "classics," to a nonexistent American equivalent of the repertoire of the Comédie Française. And O'Neill's playwriting cannot serve as a model for a new generation of playwrights. The other playwrights

who came to the fore in the 1920's have virtually shot their bolt, assuming
—most improbably—that they ever had any bolts in the opinion of the
new critics.

The fires of the 1930 dramatists of social protest are extinguished.
Using last season's revival of *Golden Boy* as an example, we may conclude, too, that these playwrights were sustained less by their intellectual
prowess than by their theatrical craftsmanship. A new generation, with
narrower sympathies and less fervor than the generation of the thirties, is
apt to decide that it was not Marx but Sardou who triumphed on the
stage.

Virtually everything seen by discriminating young people who were
not immersed in the theatre of the 1920's and 1930's (and in the overflow
of that theatre in the forties) must make them wonder whether there was
ever any sense in the fuss we made over our drama. Nor will the reading
of older plays change their opinion, since the literary element was never
the strong point of American playwriting.

OUR LOST PLAYWRIGHTS*

What has happened to the lost playwrights of our theatre whose worth and promise were at one time or another manifest? It has been remarked that many American playwrights do not fulfill an early promise. As far back as our golden age of modern-American theatre, the twenties, Mr. Nathan was already lamenting the high incidence of "one-play playwrights," writers who aroused expectations with one of their early pieces but suffered a decline. To speak conservatively, the incidence of "lost playwrights" in this category has not diminished during the past quarter of a century. If it was possible to compile a longer list of names during the twenties, the reason is that a new playwright's chances for production were greater when Broadway produced some two hundred plays per season, rather than approximately sixty. An even larger list could be compiled if we rummaged in the producers' files for the names of playwrights whose work was optioned but not produced on Broadway, or intended for a Broadway showing but withdrawn during the tryout tour.

I hesitate to cite many names because of reluctance to open old wounds upon which scar tissue has mercifully formed. But citations are necessary if the problem is to be presented and some explanations are to be tentatively offered. One type of case history is provided by the playwright who received an auspicious baptism on Broadway at some time or other and even had more than one professional production. Another, by the author whose work was not so favored in spite of vernal promises.

Perhaps we are going too far back to recall the case of Langdon Mitchell, who lived from 1862 to 1933 but is remembered only for the sophisticated piece he wrote in 1906, *The New York Idea,* which may be regarded as a sport in the theatre of its times; or the case of Percy Mac-Kaye, whose poetic fantasy *The Scarecrow,* his best play, belongs to the

---

* From *Theatre Arts* (August, 1954). [This essay had already been revised by Professor Gassner, but the notes which he made for it have not been found. It was apparently his intention to add to the list of playwrights who have shown promise of distinction, only to disappear from the New York production scene, either tersely rejected or voluntarily and dejectedly retired. His concern that poets have not contributed to American drama in an important way was somewhat modified by the success of MacLeish's *J. B.,* not to mention the work of William Alfred, author of *Hogan's Goat,* and Robert Lowell, adaptor of Melville's *Benito Cereno* and translator of Aeschylus' *Prometheus Bound,* among other critically admired poetry for the theatre. His reservations about their work are discussed in "Poetry in the Theatre," in Part Six. *Ed.*]

year 1908. A nearer example is provided by Jesse Lynch Williams, who won the first Pulitzer Prize in 1918 with his comedy on marriage, *Why Marry?*, and wrote a suitable companionpiece on divorce called *Why Not?* in 1922, but was inactive until his death in 1929. An ampler record is supplied by Zoë Akins, whose comedy *The Texas Nightingale,* somewhat uncontrolled but brisk and brightly vivacious, promised in 1922 a brilliant career in comedy after the author's debut three years earlier with the Pinero-like drama *Déclassée,* which had powerful character drawing. Miss Akins won the Pulitzer Prize in 1935 with her adaptation of Edith Wharton's novel *The Old Maid.* But *The Texas Nightingale* remains the author's only truly original piece of playwriting.

Other case histories are those of Edward Childs Carpenter, who wrote *The Cinderella Man* (1915) and *Bab,* the first play in which Helen Hayes starred, in 1920; Martin Flavin, whose *Children of the Moon* (1923) was a striking play, to which *The Criminal Code* six years later was his only impressive Broadway sequel; and Sophie Treadwell, whose *Machinal,* produced by Arthur Hopkins in 1929 and then in Central Europe, has not been equaled by her later work. Who remembers Lewis Beach except for his one-acter *The Clod,* produced by George Pierce Baker's Workshop in 1914, and perhaps for his popular farce *The Goose Hangs High* in the early twenties; or John L. Balderston, except for *Berkeley Square,* which Gilbert Miller staged in 1929; and John Colton, except for *Rain,* which excited us in 1922? And what reputation as playwrights have Harry Wagstaff Gribble except for *March Hares* in 1921, Laurence Stallings except for his collaboration on *What Price Glory?*, Zona Gale except for her Pulitzer Prize dramatization of her novel *Miss Lulu Bett* in 1920, and Dan Totheroh, whose tragedy of young love, *Wild Birds,* produced by the Cherry Lane Players in 1925, was never equaled by the plays he continued to write for more than a decade?

Were the promising plays of authors who had ten, twenty, or more years in which to ripen, bolts from the blue, so to speak? Were they the result of happy conjunctions of subject matter, temperament, the temper of the times and other elusive factors? Each case would have to be studied separately and even then we might not arrive at conclusive answers. Certainly no single explanation can suffice or convince. In some instances, such as that of *The Front Page* (1928) by Ben Hecht and Charles MacArthur, the pleasure we took in breezy acknowledgments of the American scene must have sparked the writing as well as stimulated the public response. Yet the success of their other collaboration, *Twentieth Century,* in the depression year of 1933 and again in 1951, when José Ferrer revived this farce many years after the vogue of the "debunking" style, would suggest that aptitudes developed and tastes in vogue during the twenties are not to be thoroughly discounted. These writers, whether working in collaboration or making solo efforts were least effective when serious; and this was a pity in the case of Hecht's 1937 drama of middle-aged romance, *To Quito and Back,* which revealed considerable incisiveness. Certainly the excitement of lifting taboos or of introducing new material or new modes of treatment stimulated authors and attracted audiences in the twenties. And it may be said as surely that excitement is not the equivalent of a well-planted and nurtured talent. Perhaps the foundations our theatre seemed to be laying generally during that period, as well as those our playwrights appeared to be laying individually, were too blindly placed in the quicksand of fashion and expediency.

Preston Sturges is another case in point. His *Strictly Dishonorable,* which Brock Pemberton produced in 1929, was a bright speakeasy comedy of manners. If it introduced a talent that could have kept pace with the writing of Philip Barry and S. N. Behrman but found a consummation only in Hollywood, the reason cannot be solely Hollywood's allure for writers with the advent of the talkies, since other writers, such as Sherwood and Sidney Howard, left for the "Gold Coast" and returned. It would seem that Sturges preferred an easier way of purveying sophistication because he was not inclined to inquire more deeply into a subject or a character than the hit-and-run technique of Hollywood encouraged.

But it cannot be denied that our motion-picture industry also drained off playwriting talent. The list of writers who departed from the stage for good or for too long a time is a long one, and it is not confined to writers who made a start in the twenties. The economic incentive was particularly strong during the depression of the next decade. It enticed not only Broadway's successful writers but its fledglings, not only a John Wexley or Philip Yordan, who succeeded with a *Last Mile* or *Anna Lucasta* respectively, but a Frank Gabrielson, who had only a Dramatic Workshop, off-Broadway production, and a Daniel Taradash, a protégé of Theresa Helburn's Bureau of New Plays in the late thirties and recently the winner of an "Oscar" for the scenario of *From Here to Eternity*. The question of how Hollywood injured the playwright is a topic for separate consideration. Here I would observe only that the existence of an alternative in screen writing was distinctly not conducive to wrestling with an extremely difficult and usually unrewarding medium of expression such as the legitimate stage. And while we are on this subject, let us not overlook the obtuseness and fallibility of Broadway's producers, critics, and public.

Plays have been ruined by bad productions as well as by bad judgment in requiring revisions that were not merely ineffective but down-right injurious. Nathan has cited the case of Saroyan's *Get Away Old Man,* and my knowledge of the original script leads me to support Nathan's opinion. According to my lights but not according to this senior critic's, Tennessee Williams' *Battle of Angels* was also aborted by bad revisions and a poor production, as well as by some subjective impasse which the author was unable to overcome when he prepared a version independently for publication. It also seems to me that Hollywood and Broadway were accomplices in the stalemate of Edwin Justus Mayer, whose first production, *The Firebrand,* the tart Benvenuto Cellini roman-tic comedy, was a success of the 1924–25 season, but whose superior *Children of Darkness,* produced six years later with Basil Sydney and Mary Ellis in the main roles of an eighteenth-century rake and lady, was inju-diciously slighted. Among critics, only Joseph Wood Krutch, to my knowledge, did it justice. A Davy Crockett chronicle, *Sunrise in My Pocket,* by the same author would have graced Broadway better than many of the hits it has had. Had Hollywood not proved so profitable, Mayer might have developed into an impressive playwright. But had Broadway been more responsive, it is less likely that he would have serv-iced celluloid so exclusively.

Another snare, it seems to me, has been the regional interest of our playwrights, which proved exceedingly attractive in the period between 1914 and 1930. The fruitfulness of that attraction during these formative years need not be underestimated to establish the fact that it ultimately stalemated American playwriting, as well as that it probably made slender talents appear sturdier than they actually were, because attractive local color in these plays also colored our estimate of their worth. Lula Voll-mer's playwriting career took a steadily downward turn after the 1923 production of her mountaineer drama *Sun-Up,* and Hatcher Hughes, who won a disputed Pulitzer Prize in 1924 with the Southern play *Hell Bent for Heaven,* could do no better by the theatre thereafter than *Ruint* and *The Lord Blesses the Bishop.* We expected more of Dorothy and Du Bose Heyward than they delivered after their dramatization of the latter's novel *Porgy,* the play that became Gershwin's *Porgy and Bess* after having been first produced by the Theatre Guild in 1927 as a drama garnished with Negro spirituals. And Marc Connelly's career since *The Green Pastures* has proved disappointing.

A genuine talent has lurked in the writing of Oklahoman Lynn Riggs, but it is more than likely that he will be remembered for the Rodgers and Hammerstein *Oklahoma!* rather than for his short-lived *Green Grow the Lilacs,* upon which the musical comedy is based. Riggs has not displayed any steadiness as a nonregional author. His regional work in *Roadside,* a rip-roaring Texas extravaganza for which Arthur Hopkins had blasted hopes in 1930, and some of the one-acters induce regret that Riggs has not fared better on the Broadway stage. And as much regret may be registered for Midwesterner E. P. Conkle, whose Abe Lincoln play *Prologue to Glory* and sociological play about Alaskan resettlement of indigent Americans, *200 Were Chosen,* received productions in the thirties. A Broadway-oriented playwright who displayed as much talent as one can find in Conkle's work would probably have had a large public.

An especially regrettable loss to our theatre is the Nebraska-born Virgil Geddes, now the postmaster of Brookfield Center, Connecticut, and recently the author of an autobiographical account of his retirement, which is evidently more rewarding than was his struggle with Broadway managements. His talent was acclaimed in 1929 when his farm tragedy *The Earth Between* was produced at the Provincetown Playhouse. He wrote at least eight plays that I know of after this. Three of these made up the Midwestern trilogy *Native Ground,* inadequately produced by the Federal Theatre in 1937 after having been held on option by the Theatre Guild for several years until the author, losing patience, picketed that organization at the première of an English play that first brought Elisabeth Bergner to Broadway.

Another sad case was that of a writer, reputed to be an unfrocked priest working as a messenger boy for Paramount Pictures, who signed himself Roger Flud. He wrote a remarkably eloquent play about the Pennsylvania miners of Irish extraction (the so-called Molly Maguires) whose conflict with mine owners resulted in the hanging of their leaders during the last century. The dialogue impressed some of us as worthy of Synge and O'Casey. Called *The King of the Mountains,* it was recommended by the late Barrett H. Clark, optioned several times by the Theatre Guild in the thirties, greatly favored by Alfred Lunt and admired by Russel Crouse. So far as I have been able to discover, both play and author have disappeared, although Cheryl Crawford expressed interest in the work in the early years of the American National Theatre and Academy.

Although in most instances Broadway cannot be exempted from criticism in failing to make use of the more or less regional plays, the authors themselves cannot be entirely exonerated. Their personal contribution to stalemate ranged from idiosyncrasy to deliberate half-articulateness to "overarticulateness"—in the sense that some of them were addicted to a veritable flood of dialect. In the main, it may be said that they relied

too greatly on more local custom, color, and dialogue than the cosmopolitan stage could assimilate. As the pressures of the economic depression, the threat of fascism in the world and the intensities of World
War II multiplied, the times passed them by. They were frequently
unable to make the transition from provincial to national and international significance; and an insufficiency of professional experience in
the cosmopolitan theatre may well have connived with personal predilec-
tions in depriving New York of their talent.

This diagnosis is patently inapplicable to many playwrights who
aroused some interest during the vogue of the social theatre of the thirties.
Among those who were more or less lost to Broadway, one may list Paul
Peters and George Sklar, who composed the exciting labor melodrama
Stevedore; Albert Bein, whose *Little Ol' Boy* (1933) won attention for
its realistic treatment of reformatory life; Melvin Levy, whose *Gold Eagle
Guy* was produced by the Group Theatre; and Ben Bengal, author of
the trenchant one-acter *Plant in the Sun.* To contend that some of the
writers of social drama were more interested in reform and "class struggle" than in dramatic art may be valid, but does not cover all cases. Some
of the writers were concerned with personal drama, as were Bein in
Little Ol' Boy, Arthur Kober in *Having Wonderful Time,* and Leopold
Atlas in his affecting divorce play *Wednesday's Child.* One may also cite
Irwin Shaw, whose *Bury the Dead* and *The Gentle People* by no means
exhausted his potential. The writers could not quite capitalize on their
initial efforts; they also got tired of the rat-race we call Broadway production. If a generalization concerning the thirties is in order, it is that
the afflatus of social significance proved insufficient for the development
of playwriting even before the zeal for social protest had become exhausted
or had become inexpedient.

There is perhaps no need to prolong this mournful inventory except
to add that accident or luck played some part in determining which playwrights would be "lost." The theatre has been a wasteful institution.
Intelligent younger critics such as William Becker and Theodore Hoff-
man have maintained that many of our best authors have been lost to
Broadway. I believe they had in mind novelists and poets, and this is no
doubt true. The point is particularly relevant in the case of writers such
as Dos Passos, Sinclair Lewis, Farrell, Bromfield, Steinbeck, Irwin Shaw
and other novelists and short story writers who wrote plays or even had
a success on Broadway with one of them, as Steinbeck did with *Of Mice
and Men.* The poets have made the least impact on our stage, and it is
regrettable that poets such as Archibald MacLeish, Robert Penn Warren,
Langston Hughes, George O'Neil, William Carlos Williams and Nor-

man Rosten have not flourished as playwrights, although it is unjust to put all the blame for this on Broadway producers.

But the situation appears to be especially serious when it is possible to record so high a rate of mortality among those writers who were thoroughly devoted to playwriting and had no other creative outlet outside of commercialized art. Will the mortality rate prove to be less for the present generation? It seems unlikely. Broadway has not changed, and if Hollywood is no longer a bonanza for the theatre's expatriates, television has rapidly become an alternative.

■

THE WINTER OF OUR DISCONTENT*

Is the drama a dying form of literature? One might have expected this question to arise with some frequency once critics began to doubt the viability of the novel in our age. If the question has not been asked, the reason is perhaps not so much that literary critics are indifferent to the fate of contemporary drama but that they are accustomed to long, arid periods in the history of the theatre. Bernard Shaw described the situation virtually at the beginning of dramatic modernism in England. "From time to time," he wrote, "dramatic art gets a germinal impulse. There follows in the theatre a spring which flourishes into a glorious summer. This becomes stale almost before its arrival is generally recognized; and the sequel is not a new golden age, but a barren winter that may last any time from fifteen years to a hundred and fifty. Then comes a new impulse; and the cycle begins again." If there is no indication that a new impulse has arisen or is about to arise, there can be little doubt that the rest of Shaw's summary has been demonstrated anew since the thirties.

At the present time, there are only two major playwrights alive in the world. One of these, Sean O'Casey,** has not had a major professional stage production in two decades. The other, Bertolt Brecht,† is the intellectual prisoner of Russian Communism and lives like a chaffinch in a cage in Berlin, alternately praised and scolded, and generally deprived of stage productions behind the Iron Curtain. Jean-Paul Sartre, of whom much was expected a decade ago, has made no progress as a playwright since he wrote *No Exit* and *The Flies* for the Parisian stage. The other French playwrights whose work has recently won more than local interest, Jean Giraudoux and Jean Anouilh, made their mark about two decades ago along with Jean Cocteau, who has ceased to be considered a force even in the Parisian theatre. Spain's last significant playwright, Federico García Lorca, died during the Spanish Civil War. The last Italian dramatist to achieve world-wide importance, Luigi Pirandello, died in the same year, 1936, and resurgent postwar Italy has not yet produced another playwright of comparable international significance. T. S.

* From *Theatre Arts* (August, 1955).
** [O'Casey, who was born in 1884, died after this article was written—in England, in 1964. *Ed.*]
† [Brecht, born in Augsburg, Germany, in 1898, died of a heart attack in East Berlin in 1956. *Ed.*]

Eliot started his professional playwriting career in 1935, and he has yet to equal his success with *Murder in the Cathedral* in advancing the cause of poetic drama in England. That cause has had only one other effective proponent in twenty years—Christopher Fry, who also started his career in the thirties. Now that Eugene O'Neill is dead, the United States has no living playwright with claims to international interest, except possibly Tennessee Williams and Arthur Miller; and these promising writers exemplify rather than surmount the problems of contemporary playwriting.

All in all, the drama has been in a parlous state both in Europe and America even without the agency of the artistically reactionary doctrine of "socialist realism" which has stultified Russian playwriting during the last two decades. The modern theatre generated by Ibsen, Strindberg, Shaw and the other giants before the flood seems to be producing an extraordinary number of pint-sized souls and intellects. The current theatre does not suffer from a lack of competence but from lack of the vitality and significance we have long expected from dramatic modernism.

It is important to arrive at new perspectives or to adjust our old ones even if there is no immediate prospect of a revitalizing force in the world's theatres. All effective writers are instinctively or occupationally concerned with the question of locating their art in its time and place; in England, Eliot and Fry, and in America, Williams and Miller have given much thought to the problems of contemporary playwriting. Nevertheless, most professional playwrights usually confuse a perspective with mere accommodation to fashion. Those who write for the stage are surely more susceptible to the seductions of the moment than to a comprehensive view of their situation, whereas it is of the utmost importance for playwrights to realize that they are standing at the crossroads of modern drama. They are now called upon to choose one of two ways of writing for the stage—the way of the *reporter* and the way of the *creator*. And they must choose the latter if the stage is to survive the competition of the mass-communication media, which has grown enormously and is likely to become even more severe. They can no longer compete against motion pictures and television cameras with facsimile reproductions of human reality.

The playwright often fails to realize that the masters of realistic drama were creators of life *in the drama* rather than sedulous imitators of life *outside the theatre*. The modern masters shaped an experience out of the substance of their passion and intellect, instead of setting up a camera in the streets or the family parlor and letting the camera grind. The new playwright, especially in the American theatre, fails to distinguish sharply enough between an Ibsen or a Chekhov and any of the numerous mediocrities who for a century have taken the name of realism in vain. Nor does he distinguish sufficiently between pseudopoetic artificers and true poets of the theatre. He concludes from *avant-garde* aberrations by Cummings, Cocteau, or Gertrude Stein that these represent the only alternatives to his kind of still-life, or "dead-life," realism. He takes the ersatz article of pseudomodernism at the valuation placed upon it by its obviously partial exponents, whereupon he concludes that there are no satisfactory alternatives to the debased realism which passes for currency in show business. Conversely, antirealists, reacting against pseudorealism, have drawn their own erroneous conclusions. Too many of them, upon observing the commonplace stage, conclude that it is high time to swing from a flying trapeze and thumb noses at the bourgeoisie as a reliable method of creating a new dramatic art. They assume that anything that contravenes realism is *ipso facto* art, thus mistaking ambiguity for profundity and sensationalism for creative potency.

The situation is by no means new, of course. What *is* new is its severity, for today the novelty aspect of both realism and antirealism as technical or stylistic principles of dramatic composition is gone. The so-called realistic playwrights no longer can count on making an impression because he has provided an accurate daguerreotype. Nor can the antirealist expect to startle us into gratitude simply because he has drawn everything topsy-turvy.

Most important to the state of dramatic art, however, is the point that factors that once gave impetus to noteworthy playwriting are no longer sufficiently operative. I have in mind the need of some inner compulsion and strong stimulus for writers who expect to affect a large congregated public. They must be energized by aims and challenges, and by perceptions and ideals other than the mere ambition to write plays for the market place. They need a sense of relatedness.

"Theatre for theatre's sake" may serve not only as a flattering slogan for showmen, but as a deterrent to strictly utilitarian expectations from the stage. It also has been necessary to retheatricalize the modern stage, which had been too detheatricalized by doctrinaire naturalism. But "theatre for theatre's sake" alone has never been able to nourish memorable playwriting. It has never been a substitute for some ruling passion and vision. A sense of *extratheatrical* purpose has been equally marked in the work of such an effective antirealist as Brecht, and in the work of such a great realist as Ibsen; and it has been as decisive in the comic art of a Bernard Shaw as in the tragic sense of an O'Neill or an O'Casey. It is to the weakening of extratheatrical purpose, to the loss of creative incentives which mere show business cannot provide, that we must attribute some of the flatness of contemporary playwriting.

The modern drama was born in rebellion and cradled in criticism. Intelligence, vigor, and vivacity were attendant upon this modern adventure during the last two or three decades of the past century and were its dramatic and aesthetic correlates. The spirit of inquiry provided the aesthetic attributes of the work, whether the author's appraisals of his world were as direct as Ibsen's or as indirect as Chekhov's. One reason why pioneering modern realism was not flaccid, as most realistic plays have been since the forties, is that it was *critical realism*. The critical spirit led to adventurousness in dramatic art itself. Personal passion led to individual style. And the need for making a special view apparent led to the adoption of dramatic structure that carried realistic dramaturgy well beyond the mere adoption of the fourth-wall convention of pretending that actions transpire on the stage exactly as they do off stage without an audience.

Associated with critical realism were, of course, other factors than the adventure of opinion. One of these was the sheer pleasure of intellectualism, most conspicuously seen in Shaw's writing; for intellection was once considered a distinction rather than a detriment. A playwright was expected to have a mind, and he gloried in its possession. Another factor was *principle*. By this I mean the belief that a playwright could not be truly modern if he vulgarized reality with concession to conventional sentiment, which explains the critic Shaw's contemptuous description of Pinero as a playwright who had no idea "beyond that of doing something daring and bringing down the house by running away from the consequences."

Moreover, the playwrights were likely to benefit from the stimulus of visionary optimism closely associated with their humanistic orientation. They had an active faith in man, however greatly scientific or pseudoscientific determinism tended to reduce his dramatic potential. Without that faith there would have been little point in Ibsen's or Shaw's prodding or haranguing him, or in exposing his frustrations in a particular society. It may be argued today that the pioneering playwrights were deluded; that they suffered from the fallacy and pathos of modern liberalism. It cannot be denied, however, that they derived purposefulness, passion, and even exuberance from their belief in reason and reform. Believers in progress may become the dupes, even the victims, of progress, but confidence and a sense of engagement are essential attributes of a vital theatre.

That a disenchantment pervasive in our world should have affected playwrights is hardly surprising. It is understandable, too, that in view of the contemporary situation, playwrights are now wary of social prescriptions that had been popular in the theatre of the thirties. One does not expect writers to *will* themselves into believing untenable postulates for man or society. But our contemporary playwrights have not yet learned to make anything out of their disbelief, and their disenchantment has no substantiality; it is devoid of positive expressiveness, and it is indistinguishable from moral and intellectual sloth. At best, in the work of Anouilh, we get an urbane skepticism that produces little merriment and neither sharpens nor strengthens the mind and spirit. It may be that the alternative to the old critical realism of Ibsen and Shaw, sparked by reformist zeal and optimistic illusion, is a new critical realism sparked by disillusion.

Contemporary playwrights, however, have shown little aptitude for this second—and perhaps more strenuous—kind of realism. For effective iconoclasm we still have to turn, curiously enough, not to exponents of disenchantment such as Anouilh and to professional "sophisticates" such as Noel Coward, but to such believing and affirming playwrights as Miller and O'Casey. The latter's fairly recent sardonic, lyrical, and fantastic *Cock-a-Doodle Dandy,* in which village puritanism is blasted with fantastical humor, possesses the strength of negation so conspicuously absent among the negativists of our day.

The theatre's problem, moreover, does not actually stem solely from the stalemate of present-day realistic drama. Since Western theatre is now eclectic, our playwrights can, of course, elect a nonrealistic style. There is now no reason to assume that estheticism cannot draw upon the resources of modern realism even while discarding realistic dramaturgy and peephole stage conventions. The vital elements of realism remained in force, for example, when Giraudoux wrote plays infused with critical intelligence. There is no essential conflict between the aims of modern realism and of poetic extravaganza in, let us say, *The Madwoman of Chaillot.* The same intellectual strenuousness is present in both Strindberg's late expressionist and early naturalistic dramas. Nor has there been anything but strenuous intellectualism in such antinaturalistic Brecht plays as *The Threepenny Opera* and *The Good Woman of Setzuan.*

There is no intrinsic incompatibility between adventurousness in the domain of opinion and adventurousness in the domain of art. If such incompatibility has often manifested itself, it has been occasioned by the ineptitude of would-be realists and the vacuousness of would-be esthetes.

Modern playwriting is enfeebled today because neither the realistic nor the esthetic legacy retains its pristine potency. Both styles of modern theatre have suffered much deterioration from within—realism because it became too commonplace, estheticism because it became too empty and pretentious. The failings of each mode of modernism, moreover, were inherent in each dramatic style. Bad example stalemated realism and discredited estheticism.

Standing today between realism and antirealistic theatricalism, the contemporary playwright is likely to be cross-ventilated to no particular benefit to his art or his public, especially in the American professional theatre. The above-noted impasse is, nevertheless, neither as inevitable nor as insurmountable as the logic of argument would suggest. A playwright can pursue the way of realism and still reject photography; and whether he adopts the method of direct assault upon reality or some indirect Chekhovian method, he is entirely free to avail himself of an imaginative presentation. Imaginative form sustained by expressive characterization, situation, and dialogue can transfigure subject matter. As Cocteau noted about two decades ago, a playwright can bring into being a "poetry in the theatre" in lieu of dramatic poetry.

The play of ideas, too, need not vanish from the theatre. It is conceivable that the bankruptcy of ideas or of so-called seriousness in the theatre has been, to a degree, a bankruptcy of method, which began when intellection became confused with the vending of specific solutions. That the solutions have not worked out very well is no reason why the intellect must abdicate from the theatre. Nor is there any reason to seek the tether of uncritical traditionalism, by prescript from Eliot or anyone else. Because the relativist, skeptical, and materialistic modes of modernism led the playwright as well as his fellow citizens into error is no reason for replacing inquiry with dogma.

Finally, if the playwright is so inclined, he may endeavor to write poetic drama, whether in prose or verse. There may well be a future for poetic drama, if it serves to illuminate modern life rather than to obscure it with windy exclamations or obscurantist metaphysics. The resources of both realism and antirealistic stylization may have been misspent, but they have not been exhausted. They can sustain a vital drama even today, provided playwriting is not hobbled by insensibility and intellectual cowardice.

THE STAGE AND THE CITY*

When Rodgers and Hammerstein presented us with the least successful of their collaborations, *Allegro,* some of us condemned them for reviving the cliché of the big bad city. So far as the theatre is concerned, however, the cliché did not need reviving; it has been very much with us ever since a "regional theatre" movement started growing in the second decade of our century. The "City," by which was meant New York, was alleged to be so decadent that no fresh vision and dramatic art could be expected from its theatres. The "City" was the infamous bordello whose "harlotry players" would give America nothing but mercenary art, so that the redemption of the American stage would have to occur elsewhere, far from the madding metropolitan crowd and the fleshpots of Broadway.

Unfortunately for the more naïve zealots of rusticity, three of the most mettlesome off-Broadway groups—the Washington Square Players, the Neighborhood Playhouse and the Provincetown Players—entrenched themselves in Manhattan just about this time, while other adventurers in modern art between 1912 and 1916 picked such unrusticated locations as Detroit and Chicago. In due time, moreover, the country met the city; the fields became contiguous with the pavements when the most active regional centers in the Carolinas, the Midwest and the Southwest contributed writers and performers to Broadway. From these regions came Paul Green's *In Abraham's Bosom,* produced by the Greenwich Village bohemians of the Provincetown Playhouse and *The House of Connelly,* the first major production of the Group Theatre, the most pavement-centered and New Yorkish of all American stage companies. From these regions also came *Porgy, Porgy and Bess* and *Oklahoma!* (via Lynn Riggs' *Green Grow the Lilacs*), all presentations of the Theatre Guild, long regarded as the most sophisticated large producing organization in America. Nor may we minimize the fact that *The Green Pastures* and *Our Town,* two of our most "folk-arty" or folk-rooted plays, were written by such ultra-urbane citizens as Marc Connelly and Thornton Wilder, while our folksy musical art has owed considerably less to country bards than to such lads of the city as Jerome Kern (b. New York City), George Gershwin (b. Brooklyn, New York) and Kurt Weill, resident of Berlin, Paris and, beginning in 1935, New York. After the first round of hostilities over the need for so-called native grounds, a feud between country

* From *Theatre Arts* (April, 1956).

town and metropolis simply could not be sustained, and one would have to be a highly professional regionalist to want to sustain it.

Nevertheless, the metropolitan theatre has continued to be an object of suspicion, if not, indeed, derision. The region-slanted attitude reappears healthily in continued efforts to create pageant-drama staged in outdoor theatres, mostly in the South. The latest successful production, Paul Green's *Wilderness Road,* staged by Samuel Selden at Berea College in Kentucky, suggests a rise rather than decline in the kind of theatre which is obviously most suited to the countryside. But there is an implicit and justified reproof of the metropolitan stage in this activity; the pageant theatres are repositories of national tradition, and the Broadway theatres are anything but that. There is also an epic sweep in the pageant-dramas that the typical Broadway play never possesses.

Memories of other lapses from grace also rankle here and there as playwrights or their friends (or for that matter, historians of the stage) recall the ruin, not to mention the neglect of earth-rooted and folk-rooted art by Broadway. A heavy bill of charges can be drawn up against the "City" from the experiences of Paul Green (the misfortunes of his vivid drama *Potter's Field,* produced under the title of *Roll, Sweet Chariot,* is one example), Lynn Riggs, E. P. Conkle, Virgil Geddes and other original and talented country playwrights. Nor are all the actual and potential plaintiffs members of a regional school. Some of the sharpest blasts against city showmanship have come within recent years from a new generation of the intelligentsia, a new *avant-garde,* itself quite citi-fied even when its representatives are occupationally restricted to college towns during the theatrical season. As a result of this agitation, mostly in the literary quarterlies, the terms "Broadway" and "Broadway intelligentsia" have become more opprobrious than they were at any time before—except possibly during the thirties when a left-wing intelligentsia scoffed and snarled at show business as the rancid bloom of bourgeois decadence.

Obloquy, no doubt, will attend any enterprise like Broadway show business that leaves only "crushing failure" as the alternative to "resounding success," and measures the worth of a play by its ability to fill a large theatre for several hundred consecutive performances in a single year. Producers and stage directors who operate in this Babylonian turbulence of hit-consciousness are understandably ruthless in broadening, hustling, and coarsening playwriting and stage performance. Understandably enough, they reap suspicion and contempt, especially from those of us to whom the tactics of a Barnum have brought failure rather than success, or whom the latter-day Barnums have rejected as playwrights and performing artists. For the fastidious man of letters, finally, there must be endless irritations in the slick commonplaceness and pseudo-intellectualism of the cultural context in which Broadway productions germinate as either elephantine hits or skunk-scented failures.

There can be little doubt that the professional theatre's exposure to metropolitan mores and pressures has given it a lamentable reputation. But is it really necessary to take to heart the ill repute of Broadway as some would-be decentralizers do, and are we well advised to deplore the fact that the city is the hive in which the theatrical honey has to be stored, before it can become marketable? I have no consuming desire to defend Broadway, and with respect to the urban professional theatre I am often in the frame of mind expressed in Marianne Moore's line about poetry, of which she is one of the ablest practitioners: "I, too, dislike it; there are things that are more important beyond all this fiddle." But it seems to me that our irritation with metropolitan Broadway can deprive us of a necessary sense of reality. It can only confuse us with an impossible Arcadian ideal or depress us with nostalgia for a pastoral theatre that never actually existed in any mature form.

We must realize that, whatever its country origins in ritual, the theatre always developed as an adjunct to an urban civilization, whether that of Athens, Rome, London, or Paris. And regret as we may the passing of the old stock companies in many American communities, we still must concede that only after the professional theatre became concentrated in New York did our theatrical art undergo genuine modernization. It was in New York, the haven of immigrant populations and of the most restive elements of our older population, that the modern stage found a sufficiently large public interested in unconventional character probing, in the play of ideas and in the wide range of sympathies required by the theatre inaugurated by Ibsen, Strindberg, and Shaw. Smaller communities—homogeneous rather than diversified in background, stilled by a genteel tradition, and settled in their ways rather than skeptical and tensely alert—could not normally have provided a favorable environment for the formative modern theatre.

From the metropolitan centers of Europe to those of America, the course of modern theatre was naturally that of nervousness, social conflict, and fashion-mongering in manners, ideas, and styles of art. To ask for an even-tempered and idyllic art after 1870 was to expect the impossible, and if it had been possible it would not have been worth having in the theatre; a sedate drama is a contradiction in terms. Where but in an unstable, turbulent world could a vibrant new dramatic art have arisen? The great theatres of the past were engendered in other cultural caldrons, just as tumultuous as our own in the opinion of the contemporaries of Euripides, Shakespeare, and Molière, while the conditions of stage production were hardly more relaxed. Nor was the attitude of contemporaries appreciably kinder and more sanguine than it has been in our own times; in the Elizabethan period, indeed, it was decidedly worse. The theatre always was going to the dogs, along with the rest of the world. True art was not to be found within its purlieus, and the unrefined populace was accused of encouraging the worst features of the theatre, which in turn was accused of corrupting the playgoers if not undermining the state. Professional playwrights indeed could be mobbed on occasion and might find it expedient to expatriate themselves as Euripides did. They might run afoul of the authorities whether in Elizabethan England, Nazi Germany or Soviet Russia. Or they might become the victims of some cabal, as did Corneille and Racine. As for professional managements, it would be a miracle if they ever were considered thoroughly honorable, intelligent, or good for the cultural health of a nation while they were alive.

Today, particularly in the United States, the difference between metropolitan and nonmetropolitan life seems to be disappearing rapidly. The mental climate is increasingly uniform. A decentralization of the American theatre is highly desirable, of course, but not because it will enable us to achieve a healthier, purer, or deeper dramatic art. Decentralization will be a good thing for the theatre only because it will give us more professional theatre in more parts of the country. That it will be a different kind of theatre in the main is highly dubious. It would seem, on the contrary, that the areas once considered the hinterland have had a remarkable craving for typical Broadway hits and have been standoffish only toward those plays that Broadway did not embrace wholeheartedly. We may even have cause for concern that a decentralized American stage will favor too many of the metropolitan qualities we deplore, without providing the compensating qualities of mental energy and emotional voltage.

I should not like to conclude these reflections, however, without one qualifying speculation: There may be—there probably is—a difference between a strenuously cosmopolitan context and the *mixed* milieu of city and countryside which characterized Athens and London at the peak of their contribution to the theatre. The mixed milieu was undoubtedly more productive of deeply grounded dramatic art, more favorable to the development of a drama situated, at least for a time, in national traditions and values. This more or less classic theatre (usually only precariously "classic") subordinated topicality to universality, and individualism to a feeling of collective destiny. In the masterpieces of the Attic and Elizabethan age a sense of wholeness prevailed, if only for a time and in rare masterpieces. Tragedy materialized more readily and more fully in such a cultural context. And comedy was likely to attain a greatly encompassing laughter, as in the work of Aristophanes, Shakespeare, or Molière, rather than the nervous cackle or guffaw of most New York comedies or the less than hearty exposés and the troubled, half resolutions of a Behrman or Barry opus. The intensely city-oriented drama has tended to fall short of any exalted view of man when serious, and of any poetic or serene humor when comic.

In having New York for its center, the American professional theatre unquestionably has suffered from limitations, as well as enjoyed advantages. Perhaps our criticism of the professional theatre should be aimed not at show business itself but at our special kind of show business, which has no stability, no sense of continuity, no glimmer of light by which a man may chart his moral course, and in a spiritual as well as practical sense, no "mass basis." It is unlikely that the situation of our theatre will be less unsteady and precarious in the foreseeable future than it has been hitherto. There is "grassroots theatre" in America and I consider myself one of its well-wishers; yet its effect on the professional stage is less now than was the case twenty-five or thirty-five years ago when the familiar plays of Green, Riggs, and the Heywards were surrounded by many other pieces such as Lulu Vollmer's *Sun-Up,* Percy MacKaye's *This Fine-Pretty World* and Hatcher Hughes's *Hell-Bent for Heaven.* Every new Broadway production only confirms the intense and increasing urbanization of the drama, not only in America but also in European theatrical centers. Where are the distinguished new playwrights of today who draw sustenance from the land as Synge, Lady Gregory, Yeats, Masefield, Guimerá, Lorca, and Green did in previous generations? Today the great vogue is for the city dramatist or for the cosmopolite—for Miller, Anouilh, Giraudoux (although he died in 1944, we are still catching up with him in New York), Fry. It is only realism on our part to face the fact that the milieu in which our professionalism flourishes is strenuously metropolitan, and that it is debilitating on the one hand while exhilarating on the other.

When we examine the post-1914 Broadway scene, however, we are unlikely to be fatalistic about the inevitability of a deracinated cosmopolitanism as the sole and unmitigable prospect. The state of mind that passes for cosmopolitanism has not always proved neurotically obsessive. The Babylon of the Western hemisphere has not had exclusive possession of the souls of those who have created theatre on its stony surface, so that Broadway has had more than its theoretically possible measure of "elevated" and "rooted" drama. O'Neill, remaining immune to the city's facile smartness although only too susceptible to its fashions in Freud, managed to approximate tragic art in several plays and also to achieve one sunny, comic epiphany in *Ah, Wilderness!* He was particularly adept in aligning his cosmopolitan dabblings in psychoanalysis with his feeling for the sea, for farmland and for small-town life in such works as his *S.S. Glencairn* series, *Anna Christie,* and his two tragedies *Desire Under the Elms* and *Mourning Becomes Electra.* Moreover, our city playwrights have shown remarkable talent for fashioning a folk drama of the city itself, as O'Casey did so splendidly in *Juno and the Paycock* and *The Plough and the Stars.* No American work has quite equaled these masterpieces but several playwrights, especially Elmer Rice and Sidney Kingsley (with *Street Scene* and *Dead End*), have carved creditable slices of life. And Odets and Miller even succeeded in discovering a source of colloquial poetry in New York, while Miller also has endeavored to turn city drama into high tragedy. He has discovered a faith in the tragic potentialities of the commonplace life of the city and has tried to transfigure it, if not without some conspicuous straining. His latest play, *A View from the Bridge,* may well prove a milestone in this endeavor to make bricks without straw—a metaphor which he is unlikely to approve since he would insist that his vision of tragic dignity in common men is true observation as well as honest democratic doctrine.

AN APPRAISAL OF THE CONTEMPORARY AMERICAN STAGE*

"An Appraisal of the Contemporary American Stage" is the official title of this evening's address, and this instantly introduces a difficult problem: How can one appraise an *enigma?* Moreover, this brings to mind a second problem—namely, by what standards shall we appraise it? This much is certain—our stage is an *enigma* to those who have expected it to become obsolete both as an art and a business ever since the great Depression of 1929; it is in a constant *dilemma* in being continually called upon to decide whether it is an *art* or a *business;* and our appraisals vary because they are bound to be relative to different conceptions and ideals of modern theatre. I say "of *modern* theatre" because classic, Elizabethan, and neoclassic standards have less relevance to our theatrical culture than they have to the theatrical culture of any other Western nation.

The prime characteristic of the contemporary American stage is that it has been for nearly half a century all things to all men. It is the chameleon that changes from season to season. Because it is an opportunistic business, say some commentators—and they are right! Because, others say, it has no inherent sense of direction, no spiritual or intellectual tradition, no classic masterworks to serve the present as a regulative principle from the past; and these diagnosticians are also right! Because, finally, we have no national theatre, say some of us—and this, too, is a valid explanation.

Our theatre is of necessity as mixed or eclectic as it is unregulated, as varied and comprehensive as it is anarchic. This characteristic is, of course, as genuinely American—for better and worse—as is the intensely competitive and individualistic nature of our stage. We have no subsidized national theatre like France and other European countries. We have tended to expect the theatre to pay its way, even, to a limited extent, on campuses where the stage is regarded as an educational institution or, at least, a semi-educational one.

The advantage of a theatre of free enterprise lies mostly in its mobility, resourcefulness, and timeliness; and whenever we resort to the production of classics we present them not reverentially but as just an-

* A lecture given at Johns Hopkins University in 1964.

other enterprise that must compete with nonclassical productions for box-office success. Age bestows no dignity upon the plays we produce professionally, and the historical position of a play gives it no privileges. In our professional theatre there is indeed no such thing as a repertory system dedicated to the recurrent presentation of national and international masterpieces. Each old play is produced separately, as though it were a brand-new work; we do not *present* a classic, we revive it— as if it had been on the point of death until the newest stage production breathed life into it.

As for the limitations and defects of professional theatre in America, these outweigh the advantages to such a degree that the stage is regarded, and regards itself, as a chronic invalid that recovers its strength periodically only to promptly sink back into another comatose condition.

Various questions arise from this condition. Can we count on our somehow being able to create a national theatre that would stabilize the stage? Optimism is strong at the moment in view of the development of the Lincoln Art Center in New York and the rise of more or less subsidized theatres in Washington, Minneapolis, Ann Arbor, and Los Angeles. One thing, however, is plain. In fifty years of continual creative and managerial labor we have not laid down a sound basis for a national theatre in the form of an acting and production style, and we have not been able to accumulate a national literature of classic stature. Yes, we have written good plays since 1915, but relatively few of these have outlasted their initial success. Yes, we have developed a distinctive acting style in New York, but it does not reflect the American North, West, East, or South.

Perhaps no acting style can be described as "American" except a generally quick tempo or a characteristically breezy manner of speaking and moving. We have no official academy of the theatre comparable to the Conservatoire that has prepared actors for the self-renewing acting companies of the Comédie Française—so that we never developed an official or institutional style. This is particularly evident when we consider the characteristic casualness or informality of American theatre, its distinctly imperfect ensemble, the generally poor speaking of our home-trained and home-based actors, and their general inadequacy for Shakespearean and other formal poetic productions.

Even if the New York style of acting—call it the "Method"—were to infiltrate the entire country, as it already seems to have done on a certain professional level, it would still be incapable of providing the necessary basis for a national theatre. It has not been adept thus far at evoking the spirit of our separate regions in rhythm and tonality, on the one hand, and it has been disinclined to relinquish its inner-motivated individuality in favor of the formal patterns of speech and performance that usually sustain a national theatre. This was evident in the 1930's in the celebrated Group Theatre's inability to succeed outside the New York area with some of its best plays, losing money in touring *Awake and Sing!* in 1937 after having thrived with that play in New York.

I hasten to add that American acting has not been without distinction in individual instances (as in the case of the Lunts, Katharine Cornell, or Laurette Taylor) or, for a brief time, in collective performances, as in the case of the Group Theatre during the 1930's. What has passed for distinctively American acting in our age has been a big-city, often rather slummy, type of explosiveness that is neither classical nor representatively American. We have been noted at best for vigor and vivacity rather than for finesse throughout the Western world.

If the above-noted defects in performance, which are to a degree the defects of our virtues, have been unfavorable to the creation of a truly national theatre, this has also been true of our defects in playwriting. For one thing, our plays have been tentative rather than definitive in the vision of life animating them. Frequently, there has been no vision in them at all, but rather a bland skepticism compounded of the mockery and optimism with which our playwrights, chiefly but not exclusively of the gay 1920's, have regarded the world, the flesh, and the devil. I have in mind the mocking comedies of Ben Hecht and Charles McArthur, George Kelly, George S. Kaufman, Moss Hart, and Marc Connelly—and musical comedies such as *Of Thee I Sing, Pal Joey,* and *How to Succeed in Business without Really Trying.* We became past masters at this kind of entertainment in which the wit and the manners were much broader than they had been in social comedy or drawing-room comedy in European countries, especially England. Wit came to be supplanted by the quick jab to the jaw or to the pit of the stomach, the flip brushoff, and the ready jest that came to be called the *wisecrack*.

The visionless play was a huge success in its own day in America and occasionally abroad. It had considerable range, too. This kind of theatre was not confined to light comedy but also comprised more penetrative plays such as *What Price Glory?,* which combines comic buoyancy with pathos and protest, or George Kelly's "dark" comedy *Craig's Wife,* with its strictures against lovelessness and materialism in middle-class marriages. More often than not, the plays hit the mark when they exposed the shortcomings of a society dominated by things rather than values, whether in business, advertising, politics, religion, or mass entertainment. These plays started, as a rule, with acute observation and concluded with pert parody, travesty, and mimicry. The playwrights, representing a lively disrespect for Victorian respectability and prosperous mediocrity, but without any profound probing of our moral state or passionate revolt against our way of life, were among the cleverest but also most superficial of twentieth-century writers.

They were aware of this profitable limitation themselves in so far as George S. Kaufman was representative in denying that he wrote *satire* rather than mere entertainment because, as he put it colloquially, "*satire* is what closes Saturday night." But it remains to be stressed that these comic explosions were harmless fireworks sufficient unto their day but rarely endowed with staying power. Efforts to revive these comedies in the past quarter of a century have been almost consistently unsuccessful. It has been abundantly evident that these comedies or, strictly speaking, farce-comedies, despite their blithe sophistication and their high degree of technical proficiency, cannot provide a basis for an American national theatre. In the long run, *The Man Who Came to Dinner* by Kaufman and Hart may well be the only residue of five decades of popular, socalled "debunking," comedy—with Kanin's *Born Yesterday* or MacArthur and Hecht's *The Front Page* perhaps running a close second.

There is indeed considerably more lasting power in American musical comedy and music-drama. Our successful musical revues, it is true, are out of date owing to their once lively but now moribund topicality. Not so the unified musical comedies and music-dramas since Jerome Kern's *Show-Boat* and especially since the Theatre Guild brought forth Gershwin's *Porgy and Bess* in the mid-thirties and *Oklahoma!* in the early 1940's. Only the purely topical musicals, including *Of Thee I Sing*, a revival which failed on Broadway in the 1950's, have not held up. Revivals of *Oklahoma!*, *Carousel*, *South Pacific*, *The King and I*, *Brigadoon*, *Guys and Dolls*, and perhaps as many as half a dozen other products of the past quarter of a century have continued to be successful. They are, for example, revived periodically by the New York City Center Light Opera Company. The survival of these works, which have also succeeded abroad and have been considered our most original contribution to the theatre, is no great wonder. Theirs is a *survival* of good popular theatre, rather than of distinguished literature; and their success derives from the music, the choreography, the settings, the costumes, and the stage personalities —above all, from song and spectacle—rather than from the original libretto.

This notation need not disturb us, of course, particularly because we are concerned here with the theatre as a whole rather than with the single ingredient of a libretto that may or may not qualify as dramatic literature. What may rightly concern us in an appraisal, however, is the character of the total work we call an American musical comedy. Therefore a few observations on musical comedy are in order. If it isn't primarily literature, it is not to be automatically placed below the salt or given a lower status than works that lack a musical score and are identified as "straight" plays. The derogatory implication in this labeling of plays as either "straight" or "musical" is not of course the supposition that if the entertainment is not straight, it is necessarily *crooked,* but that it is more of an achievement to write the play that does not need a musical score to supplement its dramatic meaning and effect. Perhaps it is, but generalizations are apt to be misleading. The fact is that many a straight play is inferior in dramatic quality as well as in "spectacle" to a musical.

We have had no reason to hang our heads in shame because our theatre has earned a considerable portion of its present reputation abroad owing to our musicals. The greatest contribution to dramatic art made by the Italian theatre until the advent of Pirandello after World War I came in the form of opera, and it was hardly to the discredit of that country in the nineteenth century that it produced the operas of Rossini, Donizetti, Bellini, Verdi, Puccini, and their collaborators. Still, this reflection does not exempt our musicals, especially the musical comedies, from critical scrutiny. One may well conclude, as I do, without attempting to downgrade the American musical as an acceptable form of theatre, that it has tended to substitute noise and spectacle to subtlety and nuance; that very few musical scores have risen above a comfortable mediocrity, that few lyrics have had such true distinction as Richard Wilbur's lyrics for *Candide,* and that few dramatic situations have been thoroughly worked through in our libretti.

The libretto, or "book," has often been the weakest element in the mélange of a musical. The "book" has tended to be slipshod or improvisatory. It is not always devoid of vision (the humanitarian and liberal bent of an Oscar Hammerstein libretto won particular approval in the 1940's and 1950's), but the viewpoint has usually blurred the musical comedy with sentimentality—often to the point of making it maudlin rather than penetratingly amusing. What has most distinguished the American musical is the freedom of form that qualifies it for successful presentation to a nonoperatic audience, and allows inclusion of contemporary, even sociological, material that can give musicals immediacy of interest and direct appeal. This was especially noticeable in *South Pacific, Finian's Rainbow,* and *West Side Story*. Although nostalgic and romantic efforts such as *Brigadoon* have also succeeded in our theatre, our musicals have tended to relate themselves to our times rather than to a remote or imaginary world.

The paramount advantage of our musicals as popular twentieth-century entertainment is contained in the obvious fact that American musical comedy (as represented by such breezy works as *Oklahoma!, Fiorello, Guys and Dolls,* and *How to Succeed in Business without Really Trying*) has been more realistic and vigorous than operetta, which has been Central European and aristocratic in inspiration. And American music-drama (as represented by *Street Scene, Regina, Lost in the Stars, The Medium, Porgy and Bess,* and *West Side Story*) has been lighter in scoring and more limber in action than European "grand opera," for which reason it has more properly qualified for the theatre than the opera house. The relative flexibility or formal freedom of American musical comedy and music-drama, moreover, has enabled us to rely more resourcefully on elements other than standardized choruses, arias, *bel canto,* and pompous *recitative*—that is, on anything from acrobatics to original employment of ballet, as in *Oklahoma!* and *West Side Story*. The memorable ballet Agnes De Mille devised for the first-act ending of *Oklahoma!* would ordinarily have been nothing but a passage of conventional dialogue, a recitative, or an aria awkwardly explaining that the heroine is going to the box-social with the villain of the play, Jud, rather than with her cowboy hero. The realistic ballet technique Jerome Robbins used so excitingly in *West Side Story* endowed that music-drama with much of its suspenseful drama and carried the essential action far more originally and effectively than the pale words of the libretto could. Without the ballet element, *West Side Story* would have been an uninspired and unimaginative Manhattan variant of *Romeo and Juliet.*

With all the aforementioned resources at the disposal of our musical stage it need surprise no one that it seems likely to give us the closest thing to a national repertory we can get—this despite some characteristic addiction to the noise of a loud civilization and the extravagance of an affluent one.

Having taken account of such typical American forms of entertainment as debunking farce-comedy or *"low"* comedy and musicals, we may also glance at American *high* comedy. Here the first question is whether American life has been able to sustain "high comedy" at all. High comedy has ordinarily been "romantic comedy" as in the case of Shakespeare's early plays, "artificial comedy" as in Restoration England, or "comedy of manners" of variable vigor, inventiveness, and style—from Ben Jonson's bludgeoning satire to Somerset Maugham's rapier-like laughter.

How have we fared? The answer, I believe, must be that we have fared well enough but not as frequently as we should have done in order to sustain American comedy on the highest levels of literary excellence. Perhaps to expect more would be unreasonable. We have not had a closed upper-class society with manners so artificial and with privileges and attitudes so stabilized as to provoke criticism from within that society and mockery from the outside. Our greatest successes in this area of dramatic writing came understandably in the prosperous 1920's, when American society became both urbane and self-critical. It is this decade that gave rise to our most distinguished writers of high comedy—Philip Barry, S. N. Behrman, and Robert Sherwood. In that period—say from 1918 to 1931 (which is not, of course, *contemporary* for students young enough to be attending college today)—we produced most of our distinguished comedies of manners, such as Barry's *Holiday,* Behrman's *The Second Man* and *Biography,* and Sherwood's *Reunion in Vienna.* The grain of the humor became rougher after that time—as in Hellman's *The Little Foxes,* Kanin's *Born Yesterday,* and Gore Vidal's *The Best Man.*

The emphasis changed from private to public interest, from drawing-room tensions to social or political conflicts. This, in fact, is the chief characteristic of contemporary American high comedy: it became involved with realities less manageable than drawing-room amenities and hostilities—it became tough-fibered and politically engaged. Other examples than those already cited are Maxwell Anderson's *Both Your Houses,* an attack on Congressional logrolling, and Lindsay and Crouse's *State of the Union.* It is indeed significant that after the decade of the 1920's even the chief practitioners of the comedy of manners veered toward serious drama. Philip Barry dealt with psychological crises or mental shipwreck in *Hotel Universe* and with the conflict of good and evil in his religious allegory *Here Come the Clowns.* S. N. Behrman dealt increasingly in social conflict, beginning with *Biography,* which was followed by *End of Summer, Rain from Heaven,* and *No Time for Comedy* in the tense decade of the thirties. And Sherwood, also in the thirties, moved from the comic urbanities of his first successful plays to the dark antiwar comedy of *Idiot's Delight,* to the despairing melodrama of *The Petrified Forest,* and to his deeply felt paean, *Abe Lincoln in Illinois.* One can only conclude that the climate of American theatre has been favorable to a mixed, so to speak, "impure," type of comedy; and as far as reputation abroad is concerned, it is evident that only our "impure" comedies have made an impression. The examples one may cite range from *The Little Foxes,* with its grim view of avarice and unscrupulousness, and Tennessee Williams' *The Rose Tattoo,* with its psychological tension. At the same time, we cannot consider plays such as these as particularly "American," because many European plays have qualified as "dark comedies" ever since the last quarter of the nineteenth century, when Becque wrote his mordant plays *The Vultures (Les Corbeaux)* and *La Parisienne* and was followed by Strindberg, Hauptmann, Wedekind, Sternheim, and others. Breezy and brash low comedy has grown best in our soil, along with that folksy American regional flavoring or with melting-pot immigrant humor which has been with us since the vogue of the Harrigan and Hart "Mulligan Guard" farces in the 1880's.

Whenever the subject of comedy is raised, the ghost of tragedy rises with it, and it must be confessed that we encounter a rather attenuated ghost in our contemporary theatre. O'Neill aspired to "tragedy" with all his dark view of man's prospects in life, his memories of personal suffering and alienation, and his fierce but futile search for a modern faith to replace the Roman Catholic faith he had lost. Whether or not he wrote true tragedies can be heatedly disputed; he has often been accused of writing melodrama instead. It is certain, nevertheless, that his feelings and aspirations were not those of the man in the street, which ordinary and distinctly nontragic playwrights share. His demands upon life were not demands that could be met with social reforms or psychiatric care. He asked large questions that could not be answered by anything smaller than divine revelation, and his sense of human failure reached cosmic proportions. His frame of mind and his sense of life were impressively tragic even when his prosaic dialogue and his mentally twisted characters interfered with his attaining the elevation and poetic artistry we normally associate with those rare exalted dramas we dignify with the term "tragedy."

Much the same thing can be said for the efforts of other American playwrights, especially Williams and Miller. If they missed tragedy, they nevertheless attained various degrees of tragic mood and tragic attitude. It may be said that more than Maxwell Anderson, who tried to write tragedy in the high Elizabethan manner, employed blank verse, and gave historical settings to his work; O'Neill, Williams, and Miller developed a tragic type of drama that was, paradoxically, at its best when it did not follow any tragic prescriptions but presented realistic views of character and environment. The best parts of such plays as O'Neill's *The Iceman Cometh* and *Long Day's Journey into Night,* Miller's *Death of a Salesman,* and Williams' *Streetcar Named Desire* strayed least from immediate reality and informal, often even colloquial, speech. Contemporary American tragedy, it is not too much to say, has been naturalistic rather than poetic or imaginative, even when the dramatic construction (as in *Death of a Salesman*) has been non-naturalistic.

Mostly, without doubt, the better playwrights, with the exception of Maxwell Anderson, wrote without endeavoring to hew to preconceived lines of tragedy. They wrote as they had to write, with a view to having their say. They wrote serious drama on serious subjects, and let it go at that, achieving, it is true, *subtragic* rather than tragic art but, at the same time, avoiding formal or literary pretensions. They were most effective, in fact, in some fusion of comic and tragic elements, as in O'Neill's *Anna Christie,* Odets' *Awake and Sing,* and Elmer Rice's *Street Scene,* which can be correctly labeled simply as "drama" or as the French would say, *"drame";* in a high order of pathos, achieved realistically and directly, as in *The Iceman Cometh* and *Long Day's Journey into Night;* and, decidedly, in so-called social drama—that is, in plays in which the primary situation is social rather than private, and in which the characters' personal problems have their source in society. Especially in the Depression decade of the 1930's, but also before and after that period, the American theatre produced such works in abundance and with considerable variety. But whether moderate in viewpoint like Hansberry's *Raisin in the Sun* and Kingsley's *Dead End* or radical like Sklar and Peters' *Stevedore,* and regardless of the style in which the plays were written (whether in the realistic manner of *Street Scene* or the expressionistic form of Odets' *Waiting for Lefty* and Irwin Shaw's *Bury the Dead*), American social drama has been distinguished by a special vigor that makes the recent rise of social drama in England, as written by Osborne, Wesker, and other British angry young writers, seem comparatively mild. The same vigor has been noted in "character drama" that may secondarily implicate society, as in George Kelly's *Craig's Wife* and in Lillian Hellman's *Toys in the Attic,* two studies in disastrous possessiveness. And there can be no doubt that, with a few respectable exceptions such as Sidney Howard's early treatment of "Momism" in *The Silver Cord,* our concern with psychological drama has been direct and gross rather than subtle and discreet ever since O'Neill brought Strindberg and Freud into the American theatre.

To conclude this inventory of drama in the American theatre we may say, then, that we have achieved as little in poetic drama as in tragedy but have manifested great strength in presenting social and personal reality. We even made noteworthy strides for a while in *documentary* drama or dramatic journalism. It would appear that no nation has gone as far as we did in the 1930's in developing effective social documentaries, such as the Federal Theatre's Living Newspapers *Power* and *One-third-of-a-nation* on the subjects, respectively, of the Tennessee Valley Administration and slum housing. And perhaps only Germany before the Hitler regime has equaled us in dramatizing morbid manifestations of character with such relentless directness as will be found in the plays of O'Neill, Tennessee Williams, Inge, and others.

We have vitality, I repeat, in our social and psychological dramas; would that we had subtlety and finesse as well. We also try to reproduce reality no matter how far this carries us—even when we adopt non-realistic technical means, as in *Waiting for Lefty* and *Bury the Dead*. Maxwell Anderson even forced gangster slang into the mold of his blank verse in *Winterset;* Sherwood amalgamated an antiwar protest and a "girlie show" in *Idiot's Delight;* and Philip Barry blended an allegory of good and evil with a vaudeville in *Here Come the Clowns.* Occasionally, we have also succeeded in producing plays that combine the commonplace with an awareness and sensibility that is poetic and realistic at the same time, as in Wilder's *Our Town,* Saroyan's *My Heart's in the Highlands,* Williams' *The Glass Menagerie,* and Carson McCullers' *Member of the Wedding,* reflecting the easy, casual way in which Americans have lived themselves into the poetry of common things; thus, Robert Frost has been quite properly regarded as our national poet *par excellence.* Only very rarely have we produced allegory removed from everyday contemporary reality such as the Chapman and Coxe dramatization of Melville's *Billy Budd,* or heroic drama unadulterated by the commonplaces, or religious drama not assimilated into contemporary life, as it is in MacLeish's verse play, *J.B.,* in which Job appears as the American businessman "J.B." For these and other reasons, we cannot but conclude that the American theatre has been virtually the last strong outpost of dramatic realism west of the Iron Curtain. In some fifty years of writing and staging drama we have not established any other style than the predominantly realistic—this despite our frequent desire for relief from commonplaceness that we seek to satisfy, too naïvely as a rule, with oversized musicals.

■

CONTENTIONS

I. FUTILE EDITORIAL: A THEATRE FOR THE PEOPLE*

It seems inevitable at the opening of each theatrical season to revive discussion of the Federal Theatre. Revival of that much debated project seems more remote than ever while our preparedness program piles new burdens on the taxpayer. The cost of giving the United States a national theatre for four years—a mere $46,207,779—seems slight enough.

A short time ago, Miss Hallie Flanagan, the project's national director, could still argue that, after all, the total expense did not exceed the approximate cost of one battleship. Today this answer to sniping legislators would prove a boomerang, although it is hardly Miss Flanagan's fault that one extra battleship in the fleet has become more immediately imperative than four useful seasons in the theatre. It is, nevertheless, a matter of record that of all governmental ventures in the cultural field, the Federal Theatre was the most vital and useful.

When Congress lowered the curtain on hundreds of productions two years ago, a good deal of life departed from the American stage. Good plays are still being written and produced, the present season has excellent prospects, and continued improvement of the "Road" is expected. But hundreds of cities have been left without a theatre by the demise of the Federal project, some valuable forms of production cannot be undertaken without it, the folk spirit will go begging, and large sections of the population will be unable to meet the tariff imposed by the commercial stage.

The Federal Theatre's low-priced productions, which numbered approximately 1,200, reached the millions to whom the portals of the stage are closed by economic and geographical circumstances. A vital theatre goes to the people instead of standing aloof in sumptuous quarters and waiting for cash customers to come to it. Not content with occupying houses on or near Broadway, the project sent its troupers out to hospitals, city streets, parks, village greens, and C.C.C. camps—in fact, wherever an audience could be found. Both the young and the old were reached by them, and audiences were brought together, organized, and educated instead of being left to accumulate by good fortune or accident.

A vital theatre is communal. Drawing its sustenance from the man-

* From *Current History* (October, 1941).

ners and interests of common folk, it explores local customs, finds a common bond in a people's legends and heroes, and celebrates both its labors and its dreams. The humor is home-grown, and it subsists not on the rarefied wit of a sophisticated social set but on the earthly clowning and enjoyment of incongruities that are dear to the farmer and worker. A people's theatre is not afraid to sully its gaudy trappings with the clay underfoot. It is riotous and strong, and does not sacrifice these virtues for the sake of elegance and artificial perfection.

If it turns to problems, it speaks out plainly, as in the Living Newspapers *Triple-A Plowed Under* and *Power,* instead of rationalizing and equivocating under the guise of subtlety. In attacking, it employs a bludgeon instead of a rapier. All this the project did with zest and good nature. Metropolitan critics might make a note of the crudities, and legislators might object to so much plain speaking—but a people's theatre could not have been anything other than a robust, sometimes crude and sometimes bluntly aggressive, enterprise.

It could not, of course, remain only that. Any art worth preserving must ultimately graduate from mere ebullience and hit-or-miss pyrotechnics, just as it must provide other than sociological gratifications. Perhaps the point to be stressed is that this substratum of vitality is the only sound basis for the emergence of an art. Shakespeare came from the haphazard, gross theatricalism of the Elizabethans, and owed much to it; the great Attic drama arose from earthly folk ritual and remained related to it. The leaders of the Federal Theatre knew this, and strove to perfect its artistry. Young actors were schooled, old actors were reconditioned, and the dignity of employment and continuous experience improved their performances. Young talent was given opportunities; Orson Welles, John Houseman, the designer Howard Bay, the lighting genius Feder, and other artists were brought to the fore. Even theatre for children felt the impetus; there has been no production in this field that could stand beside *Pinocchio* as directed by Yascha Frank, an expert who combined uncanny theatricalism with a sensitive understanding of child psychology.

Recognizing, moreover, the importance of cultural continuity in the theatre, the project took an important step long neglected only in the United States when it inaugurated the policy of staging revivals regularly. Its popular-priced O'Neill and Shaw cycles brought these masters of the modern drama to the attention of a vast population that had never seen their work on the stage. For the most part, moreover, the productions were worthy of the plays. Shaw's prophetic *On the Rocks* even gained a dramatic intensity and clarity not greatly apparent in the printed text, and his *Androcles and the Lion,* played by infallible Negro actors, was seen to better advantage than in the Theatre Guild's original production.

It was not long before the Federal Theatre's major productions became outstanding examples of theatrical art. The finest poetic productions of our time were the project's *Murder in the Cathedral,* written by T. S. Eliot, the Haitian *Macbeth,* and the revival of *Dr. Faustus.* The only original and native dramatic form developed in this country, the Living Newspaper, came from this national stage. And it is noteworthy that each artistic triumph was generically related to the rough vigor of the enterprise as a whole. Eliot's liturgical and choral celebration of the martyrdom of St. Thomas à Becket was given folk movement and energy by theatricians who ignored classical inhibitions such as stultified the formal Canterbury Cathedral production of the play. The Negro company's *Macbeth* translated the witchcraft and evil of Shakespeare's drama into racial terms, restoring the violence and eeriness that a thousand classrooms had filtered out of the play. Marlowe's *Dr. Faustus* became a timeless allegory of man's intellectual arrogance and spiritual struggle when the Federal Theatre staged it against empty space and evoked its men and spirits out of the darkness by means of expressionist modern lighting. The Living Newspaper combined the comic strip of Caspar Milquetoast, gusty American journalism, the brash loudspeaker technique of radio advertising, and other native elements into earnest sociological drama in which amusement, excitement, and information were simultaneous.

If all sides of the question are considered it is not true, then, that the people's money was wasted on a worthless enterprise. Nor is it true that the plays were predominently sociological and propagandist. When, moreover, propaganda was evident, as in the Living Newspapers, it was propaganda emanating from the desires of the American people, propaganda that is legitimate in any genuine democracy, propaganda, indeed, for a working democracy. If the project had its failures, so has the best professional theatre, and in this case they were not merely more pardonable but more compensated for by the vitality that emanates from even the rudest art that is close to the pulse of a nation. Doubtless there were communists in the ranks, and union difficulties arose from time to time.

There is, however, no clearer evidence of the essential soundness and moderateness of the Federal Theatre than its program, in which revivals, including Americana, and religious plays far outnumbered the contempopary social dramas that could be questioned by conservative opponents. Nevertheless, it was eliminated by Congressional action on June 30, 1939, under circumstances that reflect no credit on our legislative bodies. Miss Hallie Flanagan tells the sad story and marshals weighty evidence in her notable book, *Arena,* to show the value of the achievement.

Today the record of this great enterprise reposes in Washington, in 222 large press volumes, 749 bound production books, 21 filing cabinets of source material, and 8,860 printed plays and other dramatic material. Its memory is kept alive through the work of the talents it uncovered and developed. There was peculiar irony in the fact that the campaign song of the Republican convention that nominated Wendell Willkie was the *Ballad for Americans* by Earl Robinson and John Latouche. This spirited work had been the closing number of the ill-fated Federal Theatre revue *Sing for Your Supper.* Earl Robinson is at present setting to music Carl Sandburg's democratic pæan *The People, Yes;* John Latouche was a contributor to last season's superb musical fantasy *Cabin in the Sky,* in which Ethel Waters has toured until recently. Orson Welles and John Houseman moved on from their collaboration on the project to the founding of the Mercury Theatre, notable for its famous 1939–40 season of revivals, for the recent production of *Native Son,* and indirectly for the stellar film *Citizen Kane.*

Various local branches have managed to stay alive despite the loss of subsidy. The Theatre Guild is at last resorting to an extensive touring of revivals. A State theatre is being promoted in Virginia by Robert Porterfield, director of the Abingdon Barter Theatre, which has attracted nationwide interest with its policy of accepting produce and hams from rural playgoers. North Carolina now has an annual theatre festival that employs hundreds of actors and attracts many thousand visitors to Roanoke Island, where early settlements in America are dramatized through Paul Green's pageants. The example of a low-priced theatre is being followed by the newly founded Dollar Top Theatre, and was an inspiration to the founding of New York's very successful Labor Stage. An Experimental Theatre was established last year by Broadway to exhibit fresh acting talent and new scripts that would otherwise remain unnoticed. Finally, the need for bringing entertainment to our drafted men has led the government to sponsor theatrical activities that do not differ greatly from what the project attempted in C.C.C. camps.

The Federal Theatre, in short, continues to exert an influence, and will continue to do so. If our theatre is now poorer for having lost this adjunct to the professional field, it would be still poorer today if the project had never existed. Perhaps it is most to be regretted that in the present state of emergency, the government no longer possesses one very potent means of promulgating democratic ideals and educating different racial groups in Americanism. Radio and films decidedly have their uses, but the intimacy and immediacy that prevail exclusively in the theatre have a special potency. It is the Federal Theatre that had historical and Living Newspaper plays and included foreign language branches that could now be serviceable in promoting national unity. It is, however, still not too late to revive certain phases of the project's work that could be rightly charged to national defense. A far-seeing Congress would take this possibility under advisement. After all, a nation's first line of defense against inimical ideologies is at home.

II. CRISIS IN COMMERCIAL THEATRE*

In addressing newspaper writers in New York City it is appropriate, I believe, to speak out frankly on subjects of public interest. One of these subjects is the crisis in our commercial or professional theatre, which has its center in New York, a city more populous and affluent than many a small country.

I want to say, in the first place, that some aspects of the crisis had better be accepted as permanent. Thus, the commercial pay-as-you-go American theatre has been steadily shrinking, a fact so obvious that I shall spare you the statistical proof. And I hasten to add that I, for one, am not totally devastated by this condition. The fact is that the theatre that got reduced during the present century was ripe for a reducing diet. It was overblown and fly-specked with infantile farces, vapid melodramas, and sentimental problem plays. The writing it got, as a rule, was naïve, pompous, largely spurious; the acting it got was more often grandiose and grandiloquent than inspired. What the commercial theatre lost was a great deal of freight that belonged to the nineteenth century.

Before the end of World War I, the theatre was the undisputed purveyor of entertainment to the entire population. Since then a large part of the population has been lost to the films, the radio, and television. The theatre cannot recover this total audience, except by becoming as accommodating to the lowest common denominator of taste and intelligence as the mass-communication media generally are. Even then the commercial theatre would not recover this audience to an appreciable degree, especially in the cosmopolitan areas of the country, for the simple reason that playgoing is costly. In sum, the theatre lost its primal

* Originally a lecture delivered to the Woman's Press Club, New York City, October 29, 1960. Published in *Venture* in June, 1961, as "Crisis in the American Theatre."

Victorian innocence and is extremely unlikely to recover it. It brought its cosmopolitanism at the expense of a mass audience that it recovers only with a few smash-hit musicals. It usually reaches a mass audience only indirectly, when a play is successfully translated into a film or a television spectacular.

But, it can be argued, should a large part of the country, including the younger generation, be deprived of the living theatre and its many cultural benefits? The answer, at first glance, is simple: the country is not being deprived of theatre. Aside from touring companies unfortunately as limited in number as in range—though a few successful tours should not be slighted—we have about 5,000 active theatre groups in the country, and they are continuing to multiply under the auspices of local patronage, colleges, and universities. The fare in plays is no worse than that which will be found on Broadway, and the production setup—consisting of the scenery, lighting, costumes, and even the overall direction —is usually as good as, and sometimes better than, anything normally encountered on Broadway.

I cannot, however, apply this balm to our conscience without reservations. There are a few flies in the ointment, and the biggest fly of all is the general inadequacy of the performances. It would appear that out-of-town audiences get used to the inadequacy just as they get used to the more or less raw, tryout performances of plays heading for Broadway. But it seems doubtful that the audiences get more than a glimpse of the most worthwhile plays from the amateur performance. It has been found profitable indeed to supply this large market with many banal and stereotyped plays and the playlets honestly labeled "amateur." And this is obviously not the exalted art one expects from the theatre when one sets it above the mass media that have cornered the market in entertainment.

It takes a long time to become a trained actor, but the amateur has little time for training; acting, after all, is not his or her métier—as a rule it is a diversion rather than an occupation. In the nonprofessional —or, if you will, uncommercial theatre—the director and the designer and technician work for a salary, but the actor's services are gratuitous. Efforts to solve this problem by bringing in a few paid actors from New York—recently with the help of the Ford Foundation—have been few, and the results have been, so far as I know, inconclusive. It is not at all certain that amateurs and professionals can work well together when mated in this manner, and I doubt that the amateurs or student-actors benefit from the forced marriage.

To transport the thousands of unemployed or rarely employed members of Equity to the thousands of uncommercial theatres is manifestly impossible without subsidy, a subsidy that is unlikely to materialize in our society. Nevertheless, America has not become a wasteland so far as the theatre is concerned; the classics and near-classics, as well as the better plays of recent decades, are revived often enough to compensate us to some degree for the lack of professional repertory companies; and new plays are also being tried out—especially in the university theatres. (Such revivals and tryouts, I should add, are also to be encountered in the summer theatres that augment Broadway professionalism at times perhaps more bucolically than professionally.) The boom in nonprofessional theatre is partly the result of the cultural interests of American communities and the endeavors of our educational institutions. But it is undoubtedly sparked by the relative scarcity of professional productions outside of New York, the limitations of the touring companies, and the disappearance of the old locally situated stock companies. The crisis in our professional theatre has undoubtedly been mitigated by the growing do-it-yourself movement throughout the country.

In recent years, as in the early period of the Provincetown Playhouse, Broadway has also been augmented by the off-Broadway movement in New York City to which drama critics have paid increasing attention. Rightly so, since there have been as many new productions off Broadway as there have been on. The limitations have become increasingly evident. Proportionately as much money is lost by off-Broadway as by Broadway managements; the ratio of success to failure is, in fact, smaller than on Broadway. The facilities have not always been conducive to playgoing for pleasure, and the price scale has become too high for the potential clientele of young people of considerable education and inconsiderable income.

Fortunately, however, there has been little sign of discouragement on the off-Broadway scene, for still they rush eagerly into the breach—the young people with vision and ambition. Their efforts have given New Yorkers more acquaintance with provocative works of the modern and pre-modern stage than any other enterprise in the city since the decease of Eva Le Gallienne's Civic Repertory Theatre in the Depression of the 1930's.

Justice is also being done to meritorious works that suffered defeat or failed to reveal their optimal power on Broadway. I refer in particular to the off-Broadway Circle-in-the-Square revivals of *Children of Darkness, The Iceman Cometh, Summer and Smoke,* and *Camino Real,* and to the other events, such as the successful revival of Paul Osborn's *Morning's at*

Seven and Miller's *The Crucible,* as well as, of course, the fabulous career of *The Threepenny Opera* at the little Theatre de Lys.

Finally, it is especially encouraging to find the off-Broadway theatres offering new plays by new, or relatively new, authors. Last season alone the little off-Broadway theatres introduced new plays by such arresting European playwrights as John Whiting, John Forsythe, Beckett, Genet, and Ionesco, and such native plays as Albee's *The Zoo Story* and Jack Richardson's *The Prodigal,* as well as such original musical pieces as *The Fantasticks, Earnest in Love,* and *Little Mary Sunshine.* If a number of these efforts betrayed some amateurism in the writing or the playing, they provided the compensation of freshness and high spirits. A tired professionalism is not to be accounted superior to inspired amateurism. Abounding minor talent that is not to be slighted became apparent during the past decade at the periphery of the Broadway theatre.

In sum, it has become evident that the grandeur and misery of Broadway show business has become a catalyst, so to speak, of the theatrical ferment that abounds in the country. I must also call attention to the fine exertions of the New York City Center under the leadership of Newbold Morris, Jean Dalrymple, and others that brought New York playgoers the Kabuki players and the improved Lunt production of *The Visit.* And I should mention the growth of Shakespeare in the Park under the leadership of Joseph Papp, and beyond the Hudson the efforts of a "Poet's Theatre" in Boston (actually in Cambridge), the reinvigorated Goodman Little Theatre under John Reich in Chicago, the San Francisco Actors Workshop under Herbert Blau and Jules Irving, the American Shakespeare Festival led by Laurence Langner, and the open-air pageant theatres of the South that grew out of Paul Green's *The Lost Colony* on Roanoke Island.

It looks as if many other communities will exert efforts in behalf of a living, or at least half-living, theatre. Although the prospects for direct Federal subsidy for the stage remains dim, there is some likelihood that more and more communities capable of sustaining the theatre will at least partly sustain it, the national economy and the international situation permitting. Despite the decline of Broadway stage production, it may yet become possible for an historian to entitle a chapter on the contemporary American theatre as *"these full lean years."*

I myself am unlikely to be that generous, I think, and I can be at most only moderate in my expectations, although, as you may have observed, I am not exactly sporting sackcloth and ashes either—chiefly, perhaps, because a state of crisis has been chronic in the case of the theatre here and abroad. And at this point, and before I launch into a coda of disquiet, I must report for the record that we have been, for some time now, the envy of many theatres abroad, especially the English and the Central European. We have been credited with superiority ("vitality") in playwriting and performance, and the plays of such contemporary playwrights as Williams, Miller, Inge, Lillian Hellman, and Wilder, not to mention the only biologically deceased Eugene O'Neill, have been frequently performed in translation. There has been a constant and busy export market in American drama these past fifteen years.

Now as for my personal winter of discontent, let me *begin* and *end* with the frosty reflection that no developments observable today can compensate for failure in the strictly professional theatre. Such theatre, now as virtually throughout the century, has been identified with Broadway— and here the situation is grave and is only thinly concealed by a sprinkling of native and imported hits. The hits, in fact, only call attention to the gravity of the situation. For reasons of real estate, production costs, and the high cost of playgoing, the public supports only a few, usually presold and benefit-party-cushioned, productions, and turns them into supercolossal smash hits. Almost all other productions fail, losing all or most of their investments, leaving actors astray, and making many of the artists of the theatre, including directors and designers, the really underprivileged class in the nation. Unless they find other professions, have private incomes, or get employment in films or television, they are, and have been for the past two decades, worse off than the most economically distressed laborer in the land. This is both a manifestation of our cultural situation and a serious charge against it. Let us not blink this fact.

Let us not blink a few other facts. In the first place, all great theatre of the past, no matter how widespread its activities, has centered in a great cosmopolitan area, such as the Athens of Sophocles, Shakespeare's London, or Molière's Paris. Great theatre is not parochial, and it expresses the vitality of a great society. Failure or deficiency at the center puts the entire theatrical art of a nation in jeopardy. It is in such jeopardy today.

And here I am not weeping for lost investments, and I am less worried than some observers of the contemporary stage that investments, many of them parceled out so that no one who is vulnerable loses much at one throw, will cease to flow into play production. This is *un*likely to happen so long as the government indirectly finances stage production by regarding the loss as a tax-deductible item. This is *un*likely to happen, above all, so long as the gambling instinct persists and there is a chance of making a huge profit with an *Oklahoma!, Life with Father,* or *The Music Man.* And the theatre is, besides, a rather glittering mistress even under rags and will always find accommodating gentlemen. This is not only metaphorically true, by the way, for there have surely been gentle-men among the larger angels of the Broadway scene who have been faced in middle age with the choice of keeping the theatre or keeping a mistress. I leave it to them to decide whether they chose wisely.

A matter of real concern is the *consequence* of the Broadway setup. A condition of starvation or glut dooms most productions to failure from the start, and it tends to undermine the morale and the very integrity of the theatre.

A theatre that has no room for the "in-between" play that is neither deservedly a great hit nor a great flop, a theatre that cannot sustain the in-between play, is bound to be demoralized because just as smash hits like *Suzie Wong* can be meretricious, so in-between plays can be meritori-ous. They can be veracious without being startling, poignant without be-ing overwhelming, and provocative without being sensational. The still small voice of humanity may be heard in its only briefly broken-into susurration of little tensions, contradictions, and climaxes, as in the case of Paul Osborn's *Morning's at Seven,* not to mention an *Uncle Vanya.* Also, the thought, the dramatic form, or the style of the play—in a reflective drama, a poetic one, or a folk-piece—may not recommend itself to a pub-lic capable of filling a large theatre eight times a week for an entire year. Or the author may have an unorthodox mind and a bizarre temperament to express.

Most of the plays that gave the modern stage its claims to distinctive-ness and distinction were in their time in-between plays. I refer to many of the most important contributions of Ibsen, Strindberg, Shaw, Chekhov, O'Casey, Pirandello, and O'Neill. It is virtually safe to say that *without* the in-between play there would have been *no truly modern theatre* in Europe or America. And without the in-between play today there may be little opportunity for original expression in our theatre and little progress, if any.

Occasionally in-between plays have proved successful in our post-World War market place—one thinks of *The Glass Menagerie* and *Mem-ber of the Wedding.* During the past season,* Paddy Chayefsky's *The Tenth Man,* housed in the small Booth Theatre on Forty-fifth Street, could be thought of as an in-between play. But the chances for the suc-cess of such work have grown dimmer with the years, and the temptation to blow up, to sensationalize, or to heat up the little play of intelligence, observation, or fancy has been too strong to be resisted.

Some plays have been *inflated.* I think that Williams' *Sweet Bird of*

* 1959.

Youth became overwrought and labored under the pressure of getting a Broadway hit out of the writing and staging of the work. And some plays have been given happy or so-called affirmative endings, against which Williams rebelled when he published two versions of the third act of his *Cat on a Hot Tin Roof.* Adaptation to the inflationary market in playwriting and play production have been undermining creation. Plays have become patterned. Every play for Broadway must be full length, even though many a play would be far better as a long one-acter. And every play must overwhelm, rather than challenge us—must excite rather than stimulate.

And the chances of the uninflated in-between playwright getting a Broadway production have also grown smaller. I am not at all happy at the necessity of relegating the authors of delicate plays to the off-Broadway theatre. This implies a sort of second-class citizenship for their art, despite the growing reputation of off-Broadway productions, and it involves a very decided reduction of income, so that the author may not be able to give himself up entirely to the writing of his next play.

He has to become an *employee* of the film and television producer rather than an independent artist who has his own say in his own way, and in his own good time.

And the theatre in the rest of the country is also affected by this situation. It must offer its public a certain amount of Broadway-produced drama in order to survive. It has to wait for the smash hits to be released. It is often risky to put on plays that closed rapidly on Broadway, while it is rarely expedient to put on a play whose sole claim to repute is that it had a run in Greenwich Village.

Associated with this situation is the debilitation of professional acting that arises from insufficient employment on the highest levels of professionalism, or insufficient variety of playing in the case of actors lucky enough to be cast in a hit show. The results are likely to be especially deplorable in a country like ours where repertory companies have been virtually nonexistent. If it were not for the fertility of talent in America, our stage performances would be lamentable, indeed. They are not that at all, because we are able to compensate with vigor for the grace we lack.

Even so, however, most of our theatrical performances may be described, to adapt a term from Santayana, as a "theatre of barbarism"—by which I mean a theatre that thrives more or less on raw experience or emotionalism, that (but for the assistance of British actors) rarely does much with Shakespeare's great *music* even in dramatically effective productions, and that avoids or butchers most verse-drama altogether. When high poetry is in order, we fail it too often, and when finesse of wit is needed we are apt to substitute farce for high comedy.

That playwriting is a major casualty of the crisis in American theatre is obvious. I have already implied as much. Trying to make a little fish look like big fish by filling them with stuffing, trying to stretch smallish plays into big ones in order to meet the market requirement of a two-and-a-half-hour show can become as demoralizing as it is likely to be futile.

The reach of the imagination of any author is usually limited by the author's talent, experience, and vision. Inflating a play is not the same thing as creating or re-creating it. Some plays, indeed, should remain little. Carson McCullers' *Member of the Wedding* came into New York a smaller and more successful play than it was during its pre-Broadway tour—minus its externally most exciting scene, but a scene that detracted from the essential simplicity of the work.

The straining or stretching for effect vulgarizes playwriting more often than it improves a playscript, and even the playwright becomes a collaborator with directors and actors in creating or capitulating to a "theatre of barbarism." To which I might add that many of Broadway's favorably received plays are not actually *plays* but shows, musicals, so-called readings, and night-club skits transplanted to a Broadway playhouse. We often seem to be moving toward a nonplay theatre.

Dramatic criticism, or at least play-reviewing, also becomes demoralizing by the glut-or-starve alternatives of the Broadway stage. The reviewer is under inner pressure to abandon criticism's chief prerogatives and obligations—judgment and qualification. The reviewer, if he favors a play, must blow trumpets for it and release a vast volume of superlatives if he is to give it the necessary support. He must write a rave notice when the work deserves only moderate approval. He avoids qualification lest it be construed as defamation. If he is a generous person he may therefore become a publicist rather than a critic. He will publicize much and teach little, and he may fail in providing necessary illuminations or discriminations. At the same time, in his eagerness to help the theatre he may lose a public's confidence by overselling productions of slight merit on Broadway and off Broadway. On off-Broadway especially, we can encounter instances of even good notices failing to bring the public that suspects the reviewer's judgment. I believe it is not too much to say that in our theatre work is either underrated or overrated, but it is rarely properly rated. And no one really wants to be rated; everybody, apparently, wants to be overrated.

Finally, the public itself is demoralized. Playgoers rush pell-mell to a few shows and ignore the rest. The public has become interested in success rather than merit.

To sum up, in this glut-or-starve inflationary situation our professional theatre has been steadily growing smaller without becoming better. Its exclusiveness is based more on the size of our income than the richness of our sensitivity and intelligence. The crisis in our theatre is real and challenges all our effort. To paralyze us with total pessimism would be to be defeated totally. But to accept the present situation as cozy would be willful ignorance and blatant complacency. To say that nothing's the matter with the theatre that genius could not cure is cold comfort. Even great periods of the theatre have had no great abundance of genius. Excellence is rare, and in the theatre even qualified success is infrequent. It is the miracle we wait for. But for an art or an institution to flourish, it must do more than wait.

III. THE PUBLIC IS TO BLAME*

After what may be considered the worst Broadway season since the end of World War II, negative appraisals of the recent past may be superfluous and predictions for the near future may be redundant. Nevertheless, I am going to chance a few appraisals and predictions.

I would observe, to start with, that our audiences have been no more successful than our plays. The public has contracted the habit of falling all over itself to see a few plays, for reasons that have little to do with the essential merit of the work, and of neglecting other productions at least as meritorious, including such plays of the past season as *All the Way Home* and *Big Fish, Little Fish* that the press praised and perhaps even overpraised.

I blame the public, in part, for affording no other alternative to extravagant success than crass failure. This is the rule on Broadway, and it has also begun to be the rule in the off-Broadway theatre, in which *The Blacks* by Genet has been the only unqualified success of the past season. I suspect that something similar to this inequity has been observable in smaller community theatres, and it is certainly true of the big cities toured by Broadway productions prior or subsequent to the Broadway opening. Seldom does a production fail to lose money on tour without at least one of two inducements—*big stars,* whether well cast or ill cast, for the pre-

* An address delivered at the National Catholic Theatre Conference Convention, August 23, 1961, at the Statler-Hilton Hotel, New York City. Reprinted from *Drama Critique* (November, 1961).

Broadway tour, and a big Broadway reputation, whether deserved or un-deserved, for the post-Broadway tour.

This is the American people I am talking about, and not any single segment of it—a people that has admirable qualities but that never learned to support the arts on any large scale. With or without subsidy, this country should have had active professional productions, vigorous civic enterprises in theatre, and a substantial public for outstanding old and new plays (with or without repertory), year in and year out, in at least a dozen large cities.

We say very little when we put the blame on a so-called middle-class public. There is too little evidence that a working-class public is any better. In the first place, it doesn't exist, and it has made at best only picayune efforts to create popular-priced theatre of its own since the 1930's. In the second place, "working-class" values and interests are virtually the same as those of the middle class. Our working-class population adheres to materialistic values to the same degree, and has been just as thoroughly brainwashed by big business, big advertising, big television, and big gov-ernment, as by the little business, little advertising, little television, and little government that follow the same pattern.

We don't really say much either when we talk glibly of the expense-account public. It is very true that this public patronizes the big, brassy musicals, boosting their success. Still, I don't see any harm in this, es-pecially since these musicals are apt to be richer in theatrical qualities than the average nonmusical play that this expense-account public does *not* patronize. The rest of the public does not patronize these plays either—and I am not particularly perturbed by this disinclination to support the humdrum in the name of "serious art" or social obligation. What I care about is the neglect of substantial or provocative or imaginatively charged plays that should not have to depend on any expense-account public, but should have their own public. And I am not thinking of a coterie, a superior "fast set" whose numbers are as small as their pretensions are large. I am thinking rather of the very same public that gives a few pro-ductions extravagant success from time to time and dooms the rest—the so-called "in-between" meritorious plays not geared to smash-hit propor-tions by spectacular and sensational elements—to almost instant extinction by cautiously absenting itself from the theatres.

We cannot of course exempt other factors from responsibility in the crisis of the American theatre highlighted by the failure of the past sea-son. Most of these are indeed distinctly familiar, although they bear more looking into than we think.

The high cost of theatre tickets has undoubtedly been a deterring

factor on Broadway, as has of course the high cost of theatrical production. The same deterrents have begun to operate in the off-Broadway theatre. Real estate is an important consideration here, and the solution is
probably "decentralization" of the theatre, although I do not consider
this a panacea at all. The high cost of playgoing, moreover, is probably a
secondary factor, since the price of nearly everything else has gone up
proportionately. It is extremely doubtful that the theatre would be in a
flourishing condition today even if it had retained its old price scale, assuming that this had been at all possible. The flourishing musicals are
much more costly. Also, the American people, probably the most wasteful
in the world, have not been deterred from paying out vast sums of money
in cocktail-hour drinking, gluttony, gadgetry, and a great variety of other
vapid indulgences and unnecessary purchases; a considerable part of our
economy indeed has been pyramided on the cultivation of waste.

Far more serious, actually, is the high cost of theatrical production
that discourages producers from undertaking the production of original
or controversial plays. These are rerouted to off-Broadway theatres, where
they can languish less expensively if kept running, and where the irre-
trievable investment is bound to be much smaller. Had the Theatre
Guild, my old organization and Harold Clurman's, started on Broadway
in 1949 instead of 1919, it would have been unable to produce without
substantial subsidy the plays by Tolstoy, Turgenev, Strindberg, Ibsen,
Shaw, Werfel, Capek, Benavente, Schnitzler, Molnar, Toller, Kaiser, Rice,
Lawson, Pirandello, Behrman, Barry, and others that gave that organization its eminence between 1919 and the early 1930's. A number of these
plays, I may add, did no better in recent years even when produced in off-
Broadway theatres—not even this year's revival of Denis Johnston's distinguished drama *The Moon in the Yellow River,* originally recommended to the Guild by Harold Clurman, which got an excellent press
last season.

This brings us to the new plays themselves. The average American
plays are now *worse than average;* they are now *banal.* Areas of experience, such as those once represented by regional plays and sociological
dramas upon which Paul Green, Lynn Riggs, Sidney Howard, Elmer
Rice, and others had founded respectable reputations, have apparently
been drained of color and vigor. Domestic problems that once seemed
challenging have become the worn coinage of radio and television drama.
This is also true of political drama, although a little candor still seems
quite fresh to the general public when the play is salted with satire or
irony; as was the case recently in *The Best Man* and *Advise and Consent*

—plays that would have notably advanced the theatre if the younger Dumas had been writing them a full century ago.

Behind these and other kinds of plays, including even poetic dramas, there must lie some particular motion of the spirit and the mind before they can arrest attention. It is ultimately the traffic in banalities and a dearth of creative vision that account for the failure of so many American plays to prevail, on and off Broadway, with dramatic power rather than with accessory sensationalism and sensualism. They express a pervasive mediocrity of mind and spirit. This is less likely to be the case, I think, when the author's position is more or less nihilistic, although it is possible, of course, to be both nihilistic *and* mediocre. At least the gifted nihilist does not try to fob us off with trivial soap-opera concerns and tepid reassurances. His willingness to face an impasse is intelligent and may have a touch of heroism or a defiance in it that amounts to bravura. This, in my opinion, gives the current *avant-garde* in the theatre some measure of distinction. But it is a pinchbeck distinction by comparison with the genuine masterpieces of the past because the nihilistic play tends to be sophomorically elementary; and, above all, because it is antihumanistic, it tends to be *antihuman.* That is, we encounter, in most of these plays, abstractions and symbols rather than people.

We know a great deal more about playwriting than ever before, but we don't know what to say or show with it that is worth the trouble of saying or showing. We contrive muddles of sentiment, high resolves to compose poetic drama, and ambivalent gestures toward the political right and the left. Last season we did not go much beyond the kindly observation of *All the Way Home,* the melodramatic mélange of religious and anticommunist sentiment of *The Devil's Advocate,* and the expertly carpentered but ill-founded drama of political intrigue *Advise and Consent;* ill-founded because the issue upon which the action is founded seems made of quicksilver and the ideological props, insofar as I could see them, are hollow. When the foundations are weak, plays that are less expertly propped up than *Advise and Consent* (which is usually the case), cannot, of course, escape collapse.

Let us not beg the question in one way or another by blaming Broadway conditions exclusively, because experts in the novel make much the same charges against the contemporary novel. We might as well face the fact that we are floundering even without the able assistance of real estate operators, investors, theatre-party operators, and myopic drama critics who see misty mountains where there are only molehills. Let us not beg the question either by complaining about immorality in the theatre when its besetting sin is simply *acedia*—sheer spiritual and mental flabbiness. It is our flaccidity, not our immorality, that has made most contemporary playwriting incapable of sustaining a vital theatre, or of even drawing paying customers to the box office.

There is no sustaining set of values for a generally vital theatre today. Therefore more than ever, we are dependent upon infrequent miracles of private inspiration and special grace in individual jobs of playwriting and play production. The anti-life inhumanism of the extreme *avant-garde* hasn't supplied our deficiency of values either, and is not likely to do so. Nor is the bias of the political right beating the anticommunist drum, the political left beating anticapitalist drum, and the political center blowing the forlorn piccolo of tepid liberalism. The canker is deeply rooted in the world we have made and are obviously not improving.

After saying this, moreover, I have no predictions worth making *in extenso.* I expect special dispensation in the case of individual talent and perhaps even in an individual season "on" and "off" Broadway, but I do not expect a general and reliable improvement. So long as our society holds together somehow, I expect that our theatre will also hold together somehow. I also hope for developments in the Lincoln Center project, municipal, state, and federal assistance, and contined strengthening of individual seasons by the best of off-Broadway enterprise. But my hope is too like despair for me to offer it with any approximation of confidence. I do expect continued growth and improvement in the American theatre that is neither *on* Broadway nor *off* Broadway, but on the general terrain of America—in schools, universities, and communities beyond New York.

But while it is possible for me to be confident in predicting growth, I am inclined to limit my expectations of improvement to stage production rather than to original American playwriting. The latter requires an abundance of life and an amplitude of vision which I simply cannot detect on the horizon. My conclusion is that we shall have to learn to make the most of what we have available from the past and the present, and from Europe as well as the United States. Thus the past season was considerably sustained by plays from Ireland, England, and France.

Of one thing alone am I completely certain. It is that we must and shall continue to create theatre regardless of risk and discouragement—partly because the theatre retains its fascination and partly because nothing is so hard for anyone who has experienced this fascination as not to try to do something about it. Nevertheless, I must close as I began. The root of the problem lies with the American people. How they are *educated* or *miseducated,* and what they accept or reject will determine the normal course of our theatre for good or for ill. Their values and tastes are and will always be quintessential. The more I consider our problem the more I am convinced that in order to have a successful American theatre, the audience too, must be a success.

IV. TOO MANY JUDGES?*

It is high time we took prizes seriously enough in this country to avoid devaluating them with zeal and muddle-headedness, on the one hand, and with timidity and disingenuousness, on the other.

Prize-giving has been getting increasingly out of control in recent years. It has become a springtime ritual presided over by the great national god Publicity. As a social activity among artists and their friends, whether in Greenwich Village or in some more bucolic community, there is no harm in passing out prizes by the dozen. You will find no grim Puritan lurking in me where sport is concerned.

But, organizations aspiring to more than local importance ought to have some sense of the dignity of their office or pretensions instead of making bouquet-giving an end in itself or a mere occasion for jollification. When "everybody" gets a prize, no one gets one.

The chief end of prize-giving is lost sight of, for example, when the genial members of the Outer Circle, an organization of drama critics and reporters outside of New York, over which I have presided, come up with a dozen categories but have to be virtually badgered into making an award in playwriting.

Is it any wonder that categories cease to be meaningful when, late in the proceedings, members are mesmerized into seriously considering *The School for Scandal* for the best "foreign" play category that got side-tracked in a jumble of assiduously thought-up prizes? (Someone, reluctant to see an award go to Brecht's *Mother Courage,* ingeniously proposed Sheridan's eighteenth-century play as an alternative. When the absurdity of making such an award finally became evident, the entire "foreign play" category was abolished, and as a result a major dramatist was forgotten while someone in a musical-comedy production received a citation for excellence in a supporting role.)

That this is not an atypical situation wherever decisions are made by a large number of judges instead of a small committee should not surprise anyone. For years the New York Drama Critics Circle had a Best Foreign Play citation. How it is that this category disappeared last spring I do not know.

* From *The New York Times* (July 21, 1963).

Explanations, however, are unimportant by comparison with the fact that there was no citation for *Mother Courage* in one of our least distinguished Broadway seasons. That the production could be considered unsatisfactory is not a valid excuse; if a member of the Circle is wholly incapable of distinguishing between a play and its production he is presumptuous in voting for any play.

It is not surprising that strange oversights should mar the record of even the most distinguished prize-giving bodies. If *Mother Courage* received no recognition from the Drama Critics Circle, which also scanted one of O'Neill's greatest plays, *The Iceman Cometh,* it is also worth noting that Lillian Hellman, who has written some of our most powerful plays since the 1930's, has never received a Pulitzer Prize.

And if Miss Hellman has not fared well on Morningside Heights (even though her *Toys in the Attic* was recommended by the Pulitzer Drama Jury of John Mason Brown and myself in 1960), what shall we say of the Nobel Prize-givers who failed to make awards to Strindberg, who made enemies in Sweden; to Brecht, to whom amends might have been made if he had lived a little longer; and to Sean O'Casey?

Nothing can be done about past oversights, but the Nobel Prize committee could still redeem itself at its next sitting. No error of omission attributable to the Drama Critics Circle or the Pulitzer Prize judges is as deplorable as the failure to honor O'Casey, that mighty torrent of talent and humanity, who is now in his ninth surging decade.

That there are hazards in anyone's filling the role of judge everyone knows, and at some time or other even the best of critics have been grossly mistaken. And these hazards are surely egregious in the case of the country's most influential body of prize-givers consisting of the Pulitzer Prize Advisory Board and the Columbia University trustees.

Experts (who are too experienced, I trust, to consider themselves experts) are hired to "advise" the Board, which in turn "advises" the trustees. The Advisory Board has the power to overrule the jury of experts, and the Board of Trustees may overrule the Advisory Board. It is a wonder that any awards can be made at all under these circumstances. But somehow or other awards are made, and they are not usually as absurdly safe as this year's posthumous ones in the categories of fiction and poetry.*

Only when considerations of expediency or moralism alert members

---

* [To refer to the awards given to William Faulkner, for *The Reivers,* and to William Carlos Williams, for *Pictures from Breughel,* as "absurdly safe" may be a species of Gassnerian irony. While few would dispute the claims of Faulkner and Williams to literary honors—hence "safe"—some might quarrel about the merit of the particular works in the context of each writer's complete production. *Ed.*]

of the Board or the Trustees, is any "overruling" likely to take place. This was apparently the case in 1962 when the trustees rejected the Advisory Board's choice of *Citizen Hearst* as the best biography, and in 1963 when the Advisory Board turned down the Drama Jury's selection of *Who's Afraid of Virginia Woolf?*

I doubt the wisdom of applying such checks and balances to judging works of literature and art. More than that, the Pulitzer Prize procedure provides no opportunity for appeal or argument on the part of the advisers. John Mason Brown and myself simply sent in recommendations, and there the case rested until such a time, a month or so later, when the Advisory Board held its annual meeting in New York. Mr. Brown and I did not meet with the board, and I never knew whether our recommendations had been accepted or rejected until the Columbia trustees announced the awards at a public ceremony.

I shall not go into the embarrassing question of who is qualified to pass judgment in a particular area of literature and art, especially since the experts' names are supposed to be kept secret. But delicacy does not disallow my questioning the competence of an Advisory Board endowed with veto power that doesn't include a single critic, especially in judging plays produced in New York. All except two of the fourteen men who make up the Pulitzer Advisory Board are editors or owners of newspapers published in areas as remote from Broadway as Ohio, Illinois, Kentucky, Missouri, Iowa, and California.

I am not against the giving of prizes; I have been glad to receive them myself and been pleased to be able to hand them out to others. But let us stop behaving like children on a romp so that we may maintain some sense of values; let us not overlook important works while falling all over ourselves looking for laurels for popular entertainments that will flourish well enough without our prizes, and let us not bestow awards with blithe indifference to the nature of the accomplishment. Let us also get rid of cumbersome procedures intended to guard against impetuosity and error that are worse in their effect than even indiscriminate enthusiasm. In the case of the Pulitzer awards in the arts an intelligent start could be made by abolishing the Advisory Board.

V. *ONE* CHEER FOR THE NEW YORK STAGE*

In describing his love, the seventeenth-century poet Andrew Marvell declared that "It was begotten by Despair upon Impossibility." I believe

---

* Written for *Theatre Arts*, 1964, but never printed because that magazine suspended publication.

this is a good description of the devotion that many of us, not excluding frequently disappointed producers and playgoers, have manifested for the American stage. I include some formidable critics among our theatre's quixotic addicts, and it is their addiction especially that invites the suspicion that the object of all this loyalty has some attractions to which only those who stay away from the theatre can be wholly impervious.

What has kept us loyal and even absurdly hopeful when the noxious experiences we accumulated season after season should have caused us to be hospitalized long ago? What indeed kept such intelligent men as George Jean Nathan, Stark Young, and Joseph Wood Krutch trudging down to Times Square decade after decade? It isn't that they had to do it for a living or that they lacked competence in other fields. What, I ask myself, coming down to the level of personal discourse, has kept the present writer hobbling into the uncommodious temples of greasepaint for a period of four decades, writing about their exhibitions with irrational assiduity, reading thousands of new plays intended for the stage, and actually helping in a small way to produce perhaps a hundred of them?

Surely we could have retained few illusions about the institution, if indeed it may be called an institution, that held us in durance vile. Accident and good fortune, as well as the American enterprise of a Morris Gest and a Sol Hurok, account for a good deal of our hardihood. Our theatre has been enriched by European example, personnel, and play material ever since the Provincetown Players, the Neighborhood Playhouse, the Washington Square Players, and the young Theatre Guild looked yearningly in the direction of the European stage. Year after year we have produced plays written and usually first staged abroad. The early distinction of the Theatre Guild, in the 1920's, was won chiefly with productions of foreign plays; and Broadway continues to be bailed out of the doldrums today by British and European pieces. Our theatrical seasons have also been augmented quite regularly by visiting companies. Since World War I the New York *aficionado* has had his interest in the theatre sustained by the Moscow Art Theatre, the Mei-Lan-Fang company from China, a Japanese Kabuki company, the Hebrew-speaking "Habima," the Abbey Theatre of Dublin, the Old Vic, the Comédie Française, and many another, if often only briefly, distinguished company. If I am not mistaken we have had to forego only one great theatrical company, the Berliner Ensemble. It is certainly no exaggeration to say that assiduous playgoers have had samplings of the world's greatest individual and ensemble performances.

If it is chiefly the wealth of America that has brought them to New York (and in some instances the other American cities) we have nonetheless been the beneficiaries, just as we have also been the beneficiaries of European political upheavals in acquiring talented artists. New York has had the most cosmopolitan theatre in the world. An unearned achievement? Perhaps not so unearned, after all, since it has been paid for with appreciative reviews, the cooperation of American managements, and the support of the public in the highest-priced theatre on the planet. For a nation of materialists and Philistines we have certainly behaved generously as patrons of these visits. It is uncertain only whether we have absorbed the lessons brought by the visitors. Had we done so, the New York stage might have deserved two cheers instead of only one.

In the final analysis, of course, it is not the theatre we purchase but the theatre we ourselves create that should matter most to us. It is on this question that we are most often required to render a verdict, and it would seem unnecessary to review the case since the prisoner has already been indicted, tried, condemned to death, and pronounced dead. But it is more remarkable that he has returned from the grave so often, and there is probably more point in taking note of his stubborn survival.

I can only explain this persistence on the basis of a natural vitality as extraordinary as it is paradoxical. Ridiculous as a business, the American theatre has nevertheless managed to lure many into surrealistic roles as producers and "backers," and resulted in extravagant rewards as well as absurd failures. The rewards of stage production have not been purely monetary any more than the penalties have been. For one thing, I believe we have had over the years uncommonly fine performances from the Lunts, Helen Hayes, Katharine Cornell, Judith Anderson, Uta Hagen, Kim Stanley, Betty Field, Nan Martin, Aline MacMahon, Eileen Heckart, Jo Van Fleet, Colleen Dewhurst, George C. Scott, Morris Carnovsky, Arthur Hill, Jason Robards, Jr., Zero Mostel, Eli Wallach, Christopher Plummer, and others too numerous to mention.

Too haphazard an enterprise to sustain repertory companies thus far* or even to provide steady and diversified employment for performers, our stage has nevertheless maintained a steady flow of superb performances. Actors have either managed to acquire considerable training (except in

* [This essay was written in 1964, before the Lincoln Center Repertory Company had shown what it could and could not do. Professor Gassner planned to add a post-script to these remarks, dealing with the problems and prospects of the Lincoln Center group. His judgments can be found, instead, in the edited extracts of his later criticism for the *Educational Theatre Journal,* which follow this section. Though he did not note it at the time, he would surely have wanted to mention the Association of Producing Artists (APA-Phoenix), under the leadership of Ellis Rabb; the American Conservatory Theatre, headed by William Ball; and the increasing number of regional repertory companies. *Ed.*]

the speaking of verse, alas) or compensated for an insufficiency of training with a sufficiency of talent. Even without the important agency of repertory companies, our theatre has somehow produced noteworthy examples of ensemble playing, sometimes in productions in which hardly any of the actors had worked together before. Collective effort, moreover, has appeared on our stage in combination with strong individuality of performance. Less than in any theatre I have observed, except in the Moscow Art Theatre of the 1920's, has collectivity been attained at the sacrifice of so little individuality.

Part of the credit for what we might call "fortuitous ensemble" belongs to the remarkable *esprit de corps* of our actors, and part to the partiality of American stage directors for a unifying dramatic conception or impulse. Although American stage direction can be distressingly uneven and sometimes strains too much, it usually possesses an electrifying earnestness of purpose and communicates a sense of direct involvement. With a few exceptions, sternly noted by those who have criticized the Messrs. Logan and Kazan, our directors also follow a mean between unimaginative realism and extravagant theatricalism, which they favor only in justifiable cases of musical-comedy stylization. Yet they can also be genuinely resourceful and imaginative, and their production associates in scenery, music, and dance have been invariably reliable and often inspired.

I do not believe it is extreme to say that our practice of the arts of scenic design, stage lighting, and costuming has been second to none anywhere across the Atlantic, whenever our artists are not constrained by the mediocre requirements of commonplace realism. It must be at least thirty years since I heard the great and eloquent scene designer Lee Simonson complain that scenic artists were being increasingly transformed into interior decorators by the legitimate theatre. I would conclude, however, that even the faults of routine in our stage productions have been moderate by comparison with the same faults in European production. Realism in our stage presentations has tended to be more original, certainly more vivid and vigorous than comparable realism in many European theatres.

Moreover, those who accuse a Kazan or a Logan of invigorating plays beyond the call of duty and riding herd on their authors would certainly lower their voices if they considered the liberties taken for better or worse across the Atlantic by a Reinhardt, Jessner, Meyerhold, or Piscator. If we have lacked the art of detachment, variously manifested in British comedy-of-manners production, Brechtian "epic" staging, and Jean Vilar's "cool" or "disengaged" Théâtre National Populaire style of staging the classics, we have often splendidly exemplified the potency of "engagement," empathy, and sympathy. Here I would cite Harold Clurman's Group Theatre productions of *Awake and Sing, Paradise Lost,* and *Golden Boy.* They cut nearer the bone than many a British or continental European production, however polished and provocative, that I have seen. (The actors in Clurman's productions, of course, deserve credit for this along with their director.) This talent for humanization did not end with the humanitarian idealism of the 1930's. Clurman, for example, was just as effective with *A Member of the Wedding* and *Bus Stop,* Kazan with *Death of a Salesman* and *Streetcar Named Desire,* Quintero with *The Iceman Cometh* and *Long Day's Journey into Night,* and Alan Schneider with *Who's Afraid of Virginia Woolf?* I would myself willingly forego all the self-conscious theatricality I have seen anywhere and at any time, no matter how estimable, for the aforementioned productions, to which I believe I could add many more if I jogged my memory ever so slightly. Without jogging it at all, in fact, I would cite Dudley Digges' Actor's Theatre production of *The Wild Duck* with Blanche Yurka and Helen Chandler, the Provincetown Playhouse's *Desire under the Elms* with Walter Huston and Mary Morris, the Theatre Guild productions of *They Knew What They Wanted, Strange Interlude, Mourning Becomes Electra,* and *The Time of Your Life,* and Herman Shumlin's productions of *The Children's Hour* and *The Little Foxes.* None of these productions were *clever* in the sense of being conspicuously ingenious, though many of them were intelligent; none fanciful, though imaginative; none "knowing," though replete with understanding.*

I believe, in fact, that our theatre has been touched with greatness from time to time, and that this greatness usually came without forcing, without playing to the audience, and without attitudinizing. The real trouble with our theatre's performance has been its inconsistency. Except for some eight or nine years of the Group Theatre's checkered career on Broadway, and but for a dozen years of the Living Theatre's recent off-Broadway career, there has been virtually no history of endeavor to maintain a style and program of production for any length of time in our professional theatre. This haphazardness of effort is but a reflection of our entire laissez-faire orientation, and there is no denying that the

---

* [Here Professor Gassner noted the name of Peter Brook in the margin, justifiably intending to add him to the list of directors who deal in "engagement." Elsewhere in this book he has referred to the Broadway production of *Marat/Sade* as "one of the high points of theatrical excitement in our century." But Brook, Professor Gassner reported, was "not above resorting to a considerable degree to expressionistic hysteria and showy *kitsch,*" so the charge of "invigorating plays beyond the call of duty" might have some merit in this case. *Ed.*]

results have been felt. Except in the case of the aforementioned Group
Theatre and Living Theatre ventures, there has been too little opportunity for critics and audiences to make an effective connection with
theatrical art in New York.

A public, in acting upon the theatre with its expectations and
responses, invariably participates in a stage production. But it does not
participate or function reliably when it is bewildered or passive, as it
is bound to be after years of characterless, indiscriminate playgoing and
not knowing what to expect or what the discriminating playgoer is
entitled to receive from any particular production group. It is not surprising then that our reviewers and our amateur critics should be deficient in a reliable basis for judgment; there can be no such basis without
crystallized expectations and opportunities for making comparisons. Every
production in New York seems a brand-new thing or a fresh start,
instead of a portion of a continuum of exploration of artistic potentialities and attainments. Not even the producer knows what he wants of a
production other than that it shall be a hit. Every production is a surprise to those engaged in it; lacking a strongly founded aim and a reliable standard of excellence, not knowing what the results should be
(other than an accommodation to the public and to the conditions of
show business) they cannot of course know what the result *will* be.
Everything in the artistic endeavor then becomes guesswork, and the
artistic result hoped and sought for becomes a mélange, a compound of
satisfactions for different customers—a bit of humor for some and a bit
of sentiment for others, a touch of color and a dash of austerity, an
intellectual abrasive one moment and a salve of Philistinism or inane
good will the next.

Of course, I still have the American playwright to account for, and
the reader will have already noted my reluctance to touch upon this
sensitive subject. I have not even a single cheer for the American playwright today, but it is not merely an evasion of criticism to reflect that
the harvest of playwriting has always been a fluctuating one in other
countries as well as our own. The reflection is worth stressing at least
insofar as it can serve to allay our fears that we are simply doomed to
lag behind the European nations and that nothing can be done about
it. At present, for example, we are impressed with the productivity of
the British theatre, and the French drama has been regarded with envy
by us for nearly twenty years. Assuming the validity of our admiration
(and it is an assumption I cannot myself make without some reservations), it is well to realize that decades of low productivity have not

been spared any nation. Lean years have been more frequent than fat ones everywhere. Promises have been nipped in the bud again and again. What happened, for example, to the poetic revival in England, the existentialist drama in France, Pirandellian drama in Italy (Ugo Betti was surely but a faint reflection of Pirandello), Spanish drama after the execution of Lorca during the Civil War in Spain about a quarter of a century ago? Except for the work of Brecht, whose best work was done before 1945, what has the German drama of the past third of a century amounted to? And the Russian drama since about 1920? And the Irish drama since 1925? And would it be very indiscreet to bring up the fate of the Scandinavian drama since Strindberg, who died in 1912? If explanations for this situation are easy to find, explanations are also near at hand for the plight of American playwriting and for the failure of our own promises.

Without going into this familiar subject or into the matter of invidious comparisons, we may, on the contrary, count our blessings—however dubious or short-lived these may have been or are likely to be. It can be argued with some show of reason that a considerable number of our plays since World War I have been more or less effective. American plays have attained insight informally, provocativeness unintellectually, eloquence colloquially, and poetry unverbally to be sufficient unto the day and perhaps unto the next day. American comedy has had a pleasantly contagious raciness ever since Kaufman and his brethren began their reign in the twenties. A briskly scattered skepticism or irreverence has even lent the theatre at times a semblance of incisiveness, an apparition of critical intelligence. Even our musical theatre, once the repository of Victorian sentiment and now of liberal Rodgers and Hammerstein philanthropism, has appeared sharpened and burnished in such pieces as *Pal Joey, Kiss Me Kate, Finian's Rainbow, How to Succeed in Business without Really Trying,* and the inevitable *Guys and Dolls.* Our tragic or semitragic efforts while lumbering in prose and plot have at least had the impact of blows with a blunt instrument instead of the titillation of slaps on the wrist more usual in the supposedly sophisticated foreign theatres. Not infrequently, in fact, American plays have had the effect of broadsides and heavy gunfire because their dramatic attack has spread over considerable territory involving God, Nature, and Society. O'Neill supplied much of the evidence for these claims, whether in the early period of *Anna Christie, The Hairy Ape,* and *Desire Under the Elms,* the middle period of *Strange Interlude* and *Mourning Becomes Electra,* or the late period of *The Iceman Cometh* and *Long Day's Journey into Night.* But the concentrated artillery of Odets in the thirties and Miller and Williams after 1945 patently strengthened the case for our dramatic firing power. And additional scattered evidence has been available ever since the early 1920's in some of the work of Elmer Rice, Sidney Howard, Paul Green, Sidney Kingsley, Lillian Hellman, Robert Sherwood, and William Inge.

Since much of the ammunition in our theatre was provided by social observation and protest, as well as by individual discontent (individualistic discontent has been one of our oldest American traditions), heavy gunnery has been decidedly intermittent in the present period of political caution, economic contentment, and social complacency. We have had brief intermissions before the present time as well. But the tendency of serious American playwriting to be vigorous, if not indeed explosive, has been one of its most familiar features. There has really been nothing like it elsewhere since World War I except for brief bursts of German expressionism and French existentialism and the very recent and largely inconclusive diatribes of England's angry young men.

To conclude, I would not go so far as the London *Times Literary Supplement* editorial of November, 1962, which declared that "the flowering of American imagination has been the chief event in the sphere of living art since the end of the First World War." I would be more inclined to subscribe to virtually every criticism of American drama that has been made since the forties. I would add some criticisms of my own. I would, for example, commend our fine feeling for the familiar, but wish that we communicated more frequently what Wallace Stevens has called "the way a look or a touch reveals its unexpected magnitude," and also that we did a little more "voyaging out of and beyond the familiar." But to balance the defects I would approve a single cheer for our often lusty realism and those marriages with the bizarre imagination that have continued to take place, as in *The Connection* and *Who's Afraid of Virginia Woolf?* Europe since World War I has rarely attained equivalents for the dramatic vigor of O'Neill, Odets, Williams, and Miller except in the best work of O'Casey and Brecht. And I would give a cheer for our democratic, if rather uncritical, sensibility that tries to admit even a Willy Loman to the tragic pantheon.

Critics, needless to say, are justified in playing the gadfly to our stage. It is an obligation of the critical intelligence not to spare the inadequacy of any single production or of any season such as the last quite appalling one, on the grounds of past cumulative merit in our theatre. But to sell the American theatre since World War I short is to fail, in abreacting our current disappointments, to see the forest because of the trees in the immediate foreground. Thomas Mann, who urged the long view in criticism, quoted Goethe to good effect on this subject: "In a progressive activity and productivity the point is hardly what particular work is worthy of praise or blame . . . but rather what direction has been taken as a whole." I am not at all convinced that we have attained a clear direction. But it is surely the cumulative effect of our theatre, in addition to the little partial miracles we have experienced while waiting for total miracle, that explains our stage-struck loyalty—which is itself no small miracle. Unsubdued intellectuals will always wonder at it; and, to be sure, we often uneasily wonder at it ourselves.

Part Four

THE THIRTIES: DEPRESSION AND REACTION

[Rarely defensive about his judgments, especially those which were strongly challenged by younger colleagues and students, Professor Gassner often would listen with real interest and no little amusement to vigorous attacks on playwrights or productions he had praised. The interest was characteristic of his customary courtesy and his eagerness to examine other points of view. He realized that there is a generation gap in the theatre, as elsewhere today, and he was anxious to understand why younger critics and playgoers turned away from writers and dramas which had once been so much admired. The amusement, on the other hand, was a bonus that comes with wisdom, maturity, and a genuine fondness for the exuberance of praise and blame—if occasionally misguided—he encountered in class and in conversation with fledgling playwrights, actors, reviewers, and scholars. He once pointed out that what seems stale and dated today may have become that way because its original freshness and imaginativeness inspired too many imitations. In time, he suggested, we might again admire the work for its very "datedness"—as a period piece.

Perhaps it was with such considerations in mind that he made a notation of the proofs of the following collection of essays and reviews on the American theatre of the 1930's: "Introduce—why it is worth touching on the period. A watershed!" Though some of the material may now seem rather distant from the concerns and agonies of contemporary theatre, its influence on the development of American drama in script and production in the three decades following the Great Depression cannot be denied. If anything, these essays help to clarify trends in thought and action in our theatre. The initial survey was part of a *Theatre Arts* special issue on the thirties. *Ed.*]

PLAYWRIGHTS OF THE THIRTIES*

The theatre of the thirties will be remembered for its playwrights not because they produced masterpieces for the ages, but because they responded to the challenge of their times vigorously and excitingly. They had the defects of their virtues, of course, and they left few examples of distinguished artistry. But they were faulty and *alive* instead of perfect and dead, or meticulous and tepid. Of late it has become increasingly apparent that the past decade needed their verve, and could have used their passion for engaging themselves to a cause, an ideal, or even a delusion.

By "playwrights of the thirties" I do not, of course, mean everybody who wrote plays during the decade, but only those who had the impulse and will to express the age. It is advisable, moreover, to divide the playwrights of the period into two main groups: those who first arrived in the theatre during the thirties (Clifford Odets, Lillian Hellman, Irwin Shaw, Victor Wolfson, Sidney Kingsley, William Saroyan, and others) and those who brought with them a reputation achieved in the previous decade. I refer in this latter case to such writers as Elmer Rice, John Howard Lawson, S. N. Behrman, Philip Barry, Robert E. Sherwood, Paul Green, and Maxwell Anderson. To those two groups I would add a third, consisting of very young playwrights (Arthur Miller and Tennessee Williams are the most distinguished of them) whose work first arrived on the professional stage in the 1940's, but whose youth and early writings were formed in the decade of the depression.

The first group was, on the whole, the most militant in urging a social conscience upon the theatre, and in proclaiming social protest. The second was, with a few exceptions, more conservative. But it is to be further observed that Lawson, Rice, Green and others entered the turbulent decade with a record of radical or liberal militancy acquired during the previous decade. And others, notably Behrman and Sherwood, whose specialty had been the fabled sophistication of the twenties, saw the handwriting on the wall as the social crisis deepened. The transformation of the twenties into the thirties was not really complete in the theatre until Sherwood, the barometer playwright of the older generation, produced *Idiot's Delight* and *Abe Lincoln in Illinois*. In so brief a review as this, I cannot take space for more detailed conclusions than the following: the

* From *Theatre Arts* (September, 1960).

387

younger generation suspected the older of evasions and sublimations of "social reality"—and with good reason. But even Maxwell Anderson, who aspired to the empyrean of poetic tragedy, reflected the tensions of his time, as in the political satire of *Both Your Houses,* or refracted them, as in the oblique dramaturgy of *Winterset* and *High Tor.* Conversely, the older generation suspected the younger of an addiction to oversimplification and propaganda—and with good reason. But the callow purveyors of leftist ideology were not invariably talentless; at times, poignant realizations of character and feeling were evident. And in a number of plays, most notably in Odets' *Awake and Sing,* it was possible to remove the dramatic grain from the sociological husk.

We may conclude that the characteristic playwriting of the decade was not the exclusive contribution of any single group. The younger generation tended to preempt "social drama," which it made synonymous with Truth, Sincerity, Wisdom, Knowledge and, it would seem, Holiness itself. And the older generation sometimes showed a disposition to cede "social drama" to the younger—or, more specifically, to the young rebels associated with the Group Theatre, the American Repertory troupe, the Theatre Union, and the New Theatre League. But the lengthening perspective of history brings the two playwriting generations of the thirties closer to each other. They were *jointly* responsible for what was good and bad in the dramatic art of the times—for its passionateness and sentimentality, its genuine feeling for common humanity and its *kitsch* or banality, its moral vigor and its didactic crudity.

In fine, the playwriting of the thirties was not a cult but simply playwriting leavened by the authors' engagement to life in the midst of economic and political crisis. Both the leftist *avant-garde* and the political center were, in fact, doggedly optimistic. Even at the worst, the sense of disaster was apt to be qualified by some stubborn confidence in the human spirit.

Various other misconceptions need to be corrected, one of the most prevalent being the view that the period was inimical to humor and light entertainment. Nothing could be further from the truth, even if zealots of "social drama" seemed to think that humor betrayed the high cause of social justice while their opponents seemed to imply that seriousness undermined the American way of life. George Kaufman and his collaborators assimilated the economic struggle quite successfully in their comedies of the depression, *Stage Door* and *You Can't Take It with You,* as did Arthur Kober in *Having a Wonderful Time,* and Saroyan in *My Heart's in the Highlands* and *The Time of Your Life.* And political tension was also successfully translated into comedy by Maxwell Anderson in *Both Your Houses* and *High Tor,* by James Thurber and Elliott Nugent in *The Male Animal,* and by Behrman in *Biography* and *End of Summer.* Even the more or less embattled playwrights of the new generation were not at all monopolized by solemnity; there was a distinct comic strain in the work of Odets, Hellman, Robert Ardrey, Marc Blitzstein, and others. Nor did social tension prevent authors from contriving varied entertainment without social or political animus. No other conclusion may be drawn from the records of the period, which include *The Women, Life with Father,* and *The Man Who Came to Dinner,* than that the vigor of the thirties sustained a frolic as well as a political commitment.

Neither the new puritanism of the "left" nor a residual puritanism of the "right" from previous decades could smother the natural exuberance of American playwriting. And since the period was also enlivened by vivid folk romance of the order of *Porgy and Bess* or *The Green Pastures,* and by fantasies of the caliber of *Father Malachy's Miracle, Lady in the Dark* and *On Borrowed Time,* as well as by impassioned dramas of social conscience, we cannot but agree with John Mason Brown's description of this depression period of our theatre as "these full lean years."

How full these lean years actually were becomes evident when we go into the question of dramatic form and style. We must free ourselves of the notion that the characteristic plays of the period were standardized works of sociological realism. A period that boasts of such plays as *Our Town, The Green Pastures* and *Porgy and Bess* was by no means tethered to realism. But there is a great deal more to be put into the record, without reading into it an inventory of folk plays, quasi-operatic works, romantic dramas, and fantasies.

We may readily grant that most plays suffered from the prosy and unimaginative realism that has afflicted most American plays regardless of period. But at its best the distinctive realism of the thirties was something else. We must distinguish it from merely descriptive realism because it brought factual detail into focus by means of some perspective of thought and feeling. We must distinguish the playwrights' realism from naturalism because they did not carry objectivity to the point of neutralism, or determinism to the point of fatalism. But we must also distinguish their type of social drama from the ordinary "problem play" because they did not offer specific solutions to specific problems so much as they challenged an entire way of life.

If anything, their plays tended to be revolutionary in spirit rather than ploddingly reformatory, and their realism was characterized by intensity and explosiveness. But if they tended to filter reality through a more or less common ideology, they also filtered it through a personal temperament. The pathos and fury in the plays of Odets and the sympathy and scorn in those of Lillian Hellman were anything but impersonal qualities born of ideology or introduced into the work by ideological suasion.

The characteristic social dramas of the decade brought much resolve and not a little bravura into theatre. It is not surprising therefore that poetry should have been stirred and imagination fired by the dramatic afflatus of the period. The colloquial eloquence of Odets and others, the verse dialogue of Maxwell Anderson in such plays as *Winterset* and *High Tor,* and the fine atmospheric writing of Paul Green, which became charged with lambent irony in *Johnny Johnson* and *Hymn to the Rising Sun,* were intrinsic to their authors rather than accidental embellishments. The able playwrights of the thirties were rarely caught in the net of Freudian subjectivity, and only Maxwell Anderson among them made a direct effort to elevate the tone of the drama. But they sought maximum expressiveness for their protest, conviction and compassion. And to expressive language they added an energetic search for expressive form.

It is a major paradox of the full lean years that social realism should have led playwrights to abandon or modify realistic play structure, but the search for forceful dramaturgy had precisely that result. Imaginative dramaturgy appeared variously during the period. Thus Odets combined realistic vignettes with overall expressionist technique in *Waiting for Lefty.* The union delegates who favored a strike of the taxicab drivers in that play moved into a circle of light with other characters to enact a scene from the past that illustrated social evil and the need to combat it. In addition, Odets used the "epic theatre" technique of demonstrating an idea to the audience; he involved it in the dramatic action, and violated the fourth-wall convention of consistent realism. Irwin Shaw followed suit in his antiwar fantasy *Bury the Dead.* Expressionistic pace and eeriness characterized scenes in which dead soldiers refused to be buried, despite the commands and entreaties of their officers, and demanded a chance to really live their lives before consenting to die.

Motion-picture montage was used to strong effect in the short harangue *Newsboy,* and Marc Blitzstein borrowed the techniques of the minstrel show and the revue to produce his satirical music-drama protest *The Cradle Will Rock.* In *Johnny Johnson,* Paul Green made memorable use of Central European epic-theatre satire in the manner of *The Good Soldier Schweik* while tracing the descent of his World War I hero from Wilsonian idealism. Associates of the Federal Theatre headed by Hallie

Flanagan Davis created the most original dramatic style ever developed in America. They produced the "Living Newspapers" *Power* and *One-third-of-a-nation* between 1937 and 1938 by compounding film and lecture technique, minstrel show, revue and other dramatic elements into documentary drama in support of the New Deal. It is not too much to say, then, that, contrary to what one might have expected, there was almost as much esthetic experimentation as social awareness in the theatre of the thirties.

I would conclude by pointing to a final paradox. For a period full of collectivist idealism, the thirties were curiously rich in individuality— very much richer than the fifties, when socialistic idealism had virtually vanished from our theatre. The "social" dramatists who seemed to share so much anticapitalist animus and prosocialist faith were distinct individuals. Their artistry, good and bad, was their own, even if their "ideas" were not. The singularity of the young Odets, poignant and gauche, was often marked. By way of contrast, the young Sidney Kingsley was meticulous and logical. Lillian Hellman was sharp, severe, and as keen-minded as she was keen-spirited. Paul Green was a "regional" yet "universal," realistic yet poetic, earnest yet congenial writer. Sidney Howard, William Saroyan, Victor Wolfson, Irwin Shaw, Paul Peters, George Sklar, Albert Bein, Virgil Geddes, E. P. Conkle, Robert Ardrey, John Wexley, the poet of the Southwest Lynn Riggs, Leopold Atlas, the novelist-turned-playwright John Steinbeck, the poets George O'Neil and Archibald MacLeish (who made his New York stage debut in 1935 with the imaginative depression drama *Panic,* and then gave American broadcasting one of its few masterpieces of radio drama, *The Fall of the City,* in the spring of 1937)—these and other writers possessed more individuality than we can possibly deduce from their subject matter, social sympathies, or political attitudes. I knew most of them, and could not confuse their separate personalities if I were blindfolded.

I cannot close this review, however, without observing that there was one serious fault in the playwriting of the period. Many a playwright used social faith as a crutch, very much as recent playwrights have used psychopathology. When the crutch slipped from under the armpit, the playwright stumbled. Even Odets' considerable dramatic talent could not consistently sustain him, and less gifted social dramatists crumbled. Lillian Hellman alone continued to create with unabated power, but it can hardly be said that she ever really relied on anything but her own strong mind and will. Sentiment dissolved the marrow of many a playwright whose social sympathies made him live for a while above his artistic and intellectual resources. It was also as fashionable in the thirties to avow an interest in social justice as it became fashionable in the middle fifties to disavow it, and the punishment for artistic opportunism is apt to be artistic sterility. Some writers of social drama also came to rely too greatly on indignation as an incentive to playwriting and an enzyme for talent. Once they lost their indignation, they lost their talent. There was a high rate of mortality among the playwrights of the thirties.

ETHAN FROME AND THE
THEATRE OF FATE*

Perhaps more nonsense has been written about the role of fate in the drama than about any other subject. If the question were merely an academic conundrum, one could relegate it to the publications of the Modern Language Association. But the situation is otherwise: the treatment of fate is basic in dramatic writing, which is vastly more conditioned by the principle of causality than, for instance, by the epic or the novel.

The Owen and Donald Davis dramatization of *Ethan Frome* brings the question to the fore all the more forcibly because it is one of the most arresting productions of this or any other year in the American theatre. In a small farming community in northern New England live Ethan Frome and his hypochondriacal wife, Zenobia, whom he had married after she had nursed his mentally diseased mother. One day, under the influence of her hypochondria, she arranges to have her distant relative, the young Mattie Silver, whose health has broken down in the factory, come and live with them and help with the housework. Mattie recovers her health in the salubrious country air, and her uncomplaining buoyancy brings a little sunshine into the otherwise drab and arid home of the Fromes—until Frome falls in love with her in his characteristically undemonstrative manner. His wife's eyes, sharpened by her natural suspiciousness, detect the situation even before it is crystal-clear to the two pathetically inarticulate lovers. Mattie is sent packing, though she has absolutely nowhere to go. After some vain verbal resistance and a daring, but quickly smothered, dream of abandoning his wife, Frome resigns himself to his fate. But the parting hour is too dreadful to be borne. For him it means a lifetime with an impossible woman; for Mattie, parting means not only lovelessness but homelessness, and a return to the dreaded factory for which she was so pathetically unsuited. Recklessness, like passion, flares suddenly, without much preliminary cogitation, on the snow-covered New England soil, and the lovers go coasting down a hill together seeking their death. But instead of dying, Frome is lamed and Mattie is paralyzed for life. Twenty years later they are still alive, the two of them and Frome's wife, whom the tragedy and its ensuing responsibilities seem to have cured of her hypochondria. The poverty, as well as the monotony

* From *New Theatre* (March, 1936).

393

of the household is greater than ever, Mattie's love for Ethan has turned to irrational hate, and hope has vanished utterly for the three people now saddled with each other for life.

This tale makes a bitter story of frustration and puritanic inhibitions. There is further tragedy, for those who understand it, in the abysmal poverty of its people, and in the harshness of the encroaching factory system which is throwing its shadow across their fields. Those who concentrate on the love-tragedy in *Ethan Frome* see only half of the play, only one plane of action, only one collection of protagonists. One cannot separate Zenobia Frome's hypochondria, Ethan's suppressed spirit, and Mattie's birdlike pecking at a few crumbs of life from the bleak poverty that has cradled these characters and has hounded them throughout their existence. The tragedy that ensues arises to a considerable degree from these circumstances, which might have been underscored, perhaps, less ambiguously. The grim effectiveness of *Ethan Frome* is produced by a compound picture of man and environment.

Faced with the necessity of abridging the material of Edith Wharton's novel and of hastening its pace, Owen and Donald Davis have strung together a series of clipped episodes, and it cannot be said that the play flows with any ease and freedom. One could wish for more eloquent transitions, especially in the epilogue, which does not explain why Frome's wife allowed her crippled rival to live with them after the accident, and fails to indicate how this hypochondriacal woman became hale and active thereafter. This has indeed given rise to the complaint that the playwrights suffered from the fact that they were hewing a play out of a novel.

Frankly, I haven't the slightest patience with the view that one cannot dramatize a novel or that a dramatization is necessarily inadequate theatre. This seems to me pure poppy-cock retailed for the consumption of spiritless and unresourceful playwrights. The classic dramatists, who exploited the fertile narrative field of the Homeric and Cyclic narratives, and the Elizabethans who pilfered Italian story books, are evidence to the contrary. Instead of racking their brains for some attenuated and artificial plot, many of our playwrights might do everyone, including themselves, a favor if they resorted to some honest and substantial narrative, remembering only to expect no quarter if they fail to measure up to the job they have set themselves. The playwrights responsible for *Ethan Frome* have been comparatively fortunate. Not only have they found rich resources in Edith Wharton's most distinguished novel, but their relative lack of dramatic ingenuity does not in this instance detract greatly from their effectiveness. Their episodic, sometimes well-nigh creaky construction harmonizes with the inarticulate stiffness of the characters, the wintry season and unlovely environment. The construction of the play reflects the mood of the story.

One of the most completely realized productions of the American theatre is a valuable ally to the play. The play could not have been realized on the stage at all without sterling acting, sensitive direction and ingenious staging in the scenic department. Once again Guthrie McClintic proves himself a very talented director with a practically infallible sense of timing. No one who has watched the tense restraint and sudden explosiveness of the scenes between Ethan and Mattie can fail to appreciate the sensitiveness of the production. Raymond Massey's Ethan Frome realizes to the full the hard-pressed character whose inarticulateness suffuses his entire lean body. Pauline Lord, holding her own as his wife, plays the hypochondriac with silken stubbornness, though with a trace of whimsicality that is out of character except in relation to the epilogue, which reveals a healthier strain in her personality. At the same time, this seeming incongruity in the portrait of Zenobia Frome supports the view that this woman is not naturally a hypochondriac. She is at least partly the victim of a frustrating environment that poisons people by denying them self-realization in the external world, turning them inward. Ruth Gordon's Mattie is literally heart-rending. Her youthfulness beating ever so apologetically against the blank wall of her poverty and helplessness lingers as an epitome of all the eager life that flickers so vainly in the isolated downtrodden. Place these people in Jo Mielziner's steely snow-covered exteriors and cramped interiors, and you have a production not easily forgotten.

Still, there is a definite lack, a constitutional weakness, so to speak, in *Ethan Frome,* which must not remain unnoticed. Fatalism, as defined by the classic Greeks, was originally a revolt against the naïve anthropomorphic philosophy that made human destiny dependent upon the whim or law of some deity or spirit. Fatalism, instead, assigned tragic events to inexplicable chance or destiny and eliminated the gods as causative factors in human life. This fatalism made Aeschylus formulate a rational theory of heredity and morality, and led Sophocles to focus attention on human responsibility and reason. Nevertheless, this originally progressive respect for fate became antiquated and reactionary with the dawn of the Renaissance. The passionate individuality and "will to power" of the Renaissance merchant and prince could brook no external interference. Destiny became "self-made," and tragic fate, though never eliminated from the theatre, ceased to be a major dramatic factor.

Today, though we have come to distrust and disavow the Renaissance type of individualism, fatalism in the theatre has become even more reactionary and stultifying. If despite its unquestioned merits *Ethan Frome* seems unsatisfying, it is because it accepts so much without protest or criticism. Quite obviously, to blame the hypochondriacal wife would be flaying the wrong dog. At first glance, the blame descends upon the will of the characters, chiefly upon Ethan Frome's and Mattie's resignation to the frustration of their lives. They are creatures of tradition, products of a stultifying environment. Therefore, in a fundamental sense, it is this environment and its inadequacies that must be brought to the bar of criticism. Confining themselves to an aloof, uncritical projection of their story, the authors of *Ethan Frome* deprive themselves of the high art of tragic evaluation. They have set down a case history, from which we may draw certain social deductions, but these are not dramatized. In a very real sense they have not wholly mastered their material. The tragedy becomes cramping and somewhat purposeless, almost guignol in a rustic setting. It becomes wearing on the nerves instead of exhilarating, like all true tragedy—for tragedy, rightly understood, is release not merely through the catharsis of watching someone suffer but through creative judgment. Chiefly for this reason one can grant *Ethan Frome* almost every merit except that of greatness. A marvellous case history, it falls somewhat short of tragedy.

PARADISE LOST AND THE THEATRE
OF FRUSTRATION*

It is historically significant that the theatre of frustration should be the special province of modern times. There was wailing and gnashing of teeth or subdued grief in the theatre long before the middle of the last century, but the antiheroic or nonheroic type of tragedy seems to be the prerogative of the middle class. And it is not surprising that the drama of frustration should be the expression of the lower middle class, which is not high enough to escape frustration or low enough in the social scale to have its plight taken for granted and regarded as inevitable. Nearly every generation for more than three quarters of a century has given theatric expression to its doldrums, and one need only mention Ibsen, Strindberg, Turgenev, Ostrovsky, Chekhov, Gorki, Brieux, Hauptmann, Kaiser, and O'Neill in confirmation of this analysis. It was not to be expected that our own economically "depressed" and spiritually stalemated generation should fail to contribute to the harvest of dramatized defeat and stagnation. . . .

It should be noted that in general the theatre of frustration is also a theatre of protest. Airing one's discontents is a patent form of rebellion, and dramatization of frustration is already a form of acting out; exposing a situation is criticism and often a challenge to action. This seems to have been sensed by those who have welcomed the work of Lawson, Kingsley, Geddes, Green, Odets, and others, partly or wholly, into the camp of revolutionary drama. Sometimes the flame of revolt is quickly smothered by general pessimism and passiveness, as in *Beyond the Horizon, Juno and the Paycock,* and Andreyev's *The Life of Man.* You can see the victim writhing, but there is practically nothing you can do for him. On the other extreme, the theatre of frustration flares into open revolt, and defeat becomes a springboard for action. The evils of *A Doll's House* and *Ghosts* were eradicable. Drama of this order presupposes a program.

A third intermediary type of drama unrolls a situation without either

---

* From *New Theatre* (January, 1936). [Professor Gassner intended to introduce this essay with a re-appraisal of *Paradise Lost* in relation to Odets' later difficulties as a dramatist and thinker. His succinct jottings give an economical but pungent evaluation: "Beginning of troubles of Odets? He weakens—yes! The poetry that did not grow . . ." *Ed.*]

accepting it as inevitable or flourishing a reform plank. Actually it presents an impasse from which one may gather that the status quo is impossible, that things cannot go on as they have been going, but the playwright, remaining strictly true to his characters, confines himself to their confusions and gropings. To the classic example of *The Cherry Orchard* one would add such dramas as *The Lower Depths, The Moon in the Yellow River, Tobacco Road* and, most recently, Clifford Odets' *Paradise Lost,* which, however, does at least imply a program, if ever so subtly.

The honesty of dramas of this order commands respect, but their tight-rope walking exposes them to perpetual danger. Because they do not editorialize and fail to point to the road ahead with the definiteness of a partisan, they are apt to be denounced as confused and obscure. Because their preface to victory is infinitesimal in comparison with the long-endured suffering and bewilderment of the characters, such plays are likely to be reprimanded as exaggerated and unreal—witness the reception of *Paradise Lost.* If the playwright seeks to avoid this danger by means of understatement, like Virgil Geddes in his published plays, he is charged with incoherence. If, on the other hand, the dramatist allows his characters to express their doldrums openly and makes them symbols in the flesh by moving from photographic reality to caricature, compression and poetic intensification, he becomes guilty of every conceivable crime against dramaturgy in the eyes of those who are bound to a plodding, prosaic kind of realism. Let him fall short of perfect technique here and there, and he will face a determined firing squad.

All these problems appear to have swooped down upon Clifford Odets with the persistence of an anemic vulture when he wrote and launched his latest, and to date most comprehensive, drama. Turning from the relatively simple terms of his powerful shorter plays, Odets undertook the ungrateful task of holding up a mirror to the times that would reflect its deformity. He had already attempted this in his decidedly less mature first full-length play, *Awake and Sing.* But this play could be, and was generally, taken as a realistic picture of life in the Bronx—that is, as simple *"genre* painting"—with a detachable revolutionary peroration. Nothing can be detached from *Paradise Lost,* no matter how hard one tries, and it cannot be accorded the faint praise of being considered a fluid picture of family life in a rather "unique" environment.

Regarded as simply another ploddingly realistic family picture the play would become the jumble of troubles it has been accused of being. A kindly and idealistic pocket-book manufacturer has financial difficulties. One of his sons has had an attack of encephalitis and loses his reason at the end of the play. Another son, an Olympic champion, develops heart trouble, contracts an unhappy marriage, tries to sell toys on the corner when the Wall Street bubble bursts, and allows himself to be killed in a holdup upon learning that his wife and his best friend have betrayed him. The daughter of the family loses her lover, a violinist with an unenviable future, in a period of depression, when he leaves town in search of employment. The manufacturer's partner, an unhappy impotent man whose frantic viciousness is that of an animal at bay, finally embezzles the firm's money. Bankruptcy and eviction from the two-family home follow. And throughout this tragic tale three outsiders fill the stage from time to time with their private sufferings and confusions—a lonely young gangster with tangled emotions, a native radical nursing his hatred for those who sent his sons to their death in the last war, and a senile old family friend.

That is all one sees in the play, if that is all one wishes to see. Then criticisms rush to one's lips. This is not reality, one says; too many catastrophes in one family, too much trouble in one package! (According to this indictment, *Oedipus Rex, Antigone,* and the *Agamemnon* trilogy of Aeschylus should have received no-star ratings from the Athenian critics!) Moreover, this is not the middle class, one protests. Surely, this estate does not abound in cases of encephalitis, and even if this were so it would still fail to be a strictly social or economic or political issue. Surely, members of the middle class do not go about cheating their partners because of genital impairment. Surely, this class is not preponderantly composed of such helpless, dying, and inchoate individuals as the characters of the play. One grants that there are special cases, but one denies that the characters are representative.

Such an approach to *Paradise Lost* is the method of obdurate Philistinism. It does not catch the intent of the play as bodied forth in its flow of characters and events, as expressed in its tone (or "feeling-tone," to lift a good word from the psychiatrists), as circumscribed by its economic picture and social viewpoint. Since when has dramatic art been a statistical graph to be tested by the mathematical method, instead of a mode of dealing with the essence of things in tangible terms of flesh and blood! *Paradise Lost* brings together a group of people and a set of circumstances in the arbitrary manner of all art. Statistically speaking, you will find few middle-class families in which this combination is duplicated, but the dramatic complications of this drama represent the quintessence of a social tragedy—that of the disintegration of the middle class in our self-confessedly stalled social order. This stalemate is indicated in the play on two intimately connected levels: a general economic plane, the living presence of the depression with its accompaniment of financial pressure, foreclosure, evictions, homelessness, and artificial demagogic reassurances ("prosperity block-parties"); and a private, personal plane. The play is basically a *condensation* of a historic process.

In one compact and crowded picture, Odets *expresses* the morbid state of society as he sees it. His is the method of realistic symbolism rather than realistic *representation,* which would be inadequate for his purpose. You cannot "represent" a complex social phenomenon in the limited form of a single play. The impotence of much that seems hard-boiled about the small-time merchant and manufacturer finds rich exemplification in the character of Marcus Katz. He may rage and fume but he is unable to perpetuate himself, and with all his shrewdness he cannot cope with a relentless economic order. He may intimidate and exploit his handful of employees, but he is himself a pawn in the larger game which he does not run. His life's achievements are a woefully inadequate private life, economic insecurity, fruitless exploitation of the under-under-dog, and a petty embezzlement, the consequences of which are bankruptcy. The iron men of the middle class in an era of economic gigantism are mostly straw. The other putative heroes of the family group are likewise duds. The handsome Olympic runner lives on the thin air of promises and goes downgrade in a society which he helped to "glorify." His friend Kewpie is a pathetic caricature of the tough-minded individualists who run the world and are aped on a slightly higher scale by the petty owning class of which Katz is a member. Only the radical furnace man and the shop delegates possess some real positiveness insofar as they are floating or being driven down to the clear and bracing sea of social responsibility instead of stagnating in a private puddle like the Gordon family.

But the middle class is not composed solely of professed materialists. Contrary to the opinion of some embattled persons it has its dreamers too, men of great inner refinement and idealism. Their tragedy can be the most appealing, and Leo Gordon's failure provides a sound and incisive analysis. His soul has been almost continually insulted by the sordid details of business enterprise, and he has even been an unconscious accomplice in the exploitation of his employees who are living on a starvation level. He has tried to escape these and other realities, but they close in on him. Then comes the final débâcle, with his home and business lost. He does not quite realize it yet, but he has become a worker, and an unemployed one at that; he is an example of "the proletarianization of the middle class." He is left only with his least material possession, his spirit that tells him that there must be something beyond the impasse which he has reached, that the spirit of man must leap over it, for a fruit tree does not wear a lock and chain.

A play that presents all this in flowing language and characterization is obviously a significant and deeply moving achievement. Its symbolism, much more potent than that of the *Within the Gates* which received last season's plaudits (undeservedly in our opinion!), falters here and there. Thus one could have wished for a better exposition of the radical's and the working-class delegates' positive attitude. This might have clarified Leo Gordon's own vision at the end. The play would have also profited from the inclusion of a more robust and resilient member of the middle class who would speak for whatever real stamina it still possesses. The middle class may be dying according to Odets, but only an unrealistic optimism or pessimism will deny it a certain degree of vitality. The symbolism is a trifle misleading in this respect. We might, moreover, dispense with a few gratuitous speeches on decay and bewilderment particularly in evidence at the end of the first act, and with the encephalitic son, whose corroboration of the playwright's testimony is unnecessary and not quite clear. One would prefer a little less of the old family friend and his oblique action and statement. And finally, this reviewer could wish for a more native idiom and characterization at times. Still, with all its minor shortcomings, *Paradise Lost* is not only a notable advance in Odets' craftsmanship but one of the most thoughtful and moving plays of the American theatre. It is certainly the outstanding play of the season to date.

The Group Theatre, facing the best test of its art of collective acting, gives *Paradise Lost* the flow and studied *ensemble* which alone could do justice to the play. Not since the visiting Moscow Art Theatre's production of *The Cherry Orchard* and *The Lower Depths* has this reviewer seen such a richly human and sensitive collective performance. Harold Clurman's direction is sensitive and forceful; his handling of the final act gives it a tension and rising power essential to the production. A swifter pace in the second part of the first act, a smoothing out and additional clarification of Luther Adler's tense performance, and excision of Stella Adler's mannerisms at the beginning of an otherwise even performance would have made the production perfect in its kind. This reviewer would have also preferred a somewhat more native idiom in the acting of several parts, which would have strengthened the representativeness and credibility of a few of the characters.

PAUL GREEN: PLAYWRIGHT ON NATIVE GROUND*

It is not too much to say that Paul Green is the only playwright, with the uncertain exception of Eugene O'Neill, who belongs notably to both the American land and the American theatre. He came to the latter as the natural poet of the Old South. The depth of his commitment to his people, which was from the beginning a commitment to the human race, also made him the laureate of the *New* South aborning not without labor and turbulence. He started in the 1920's as a writer of short plays of local color, moved into a professional Broadway theatre with full-length dramas of the South, and after 1937 started extending his horizons with the writing of epics that encompass historical events for which ordinary playhouses and the resources of realistic plays are patently inadequate. At one time he could have chosen to become one of Broadway's and Hollywood's journeymen, and, since he is a resourceful playwright, there can be little doubt that he would have had a thriving career.

He chose instead to return to the original source of his observation and sensibility, to dwell among the people he had always known, and to make only a few excursions into Shubertland or Disneyland, usually justified by securing for the South some proper representation on the stage or the screen. It is evident, moreover, that attachments and temperament made this course of conduct the only one he could have elected for a lifetime pattern, and that, nevertheless, he was one of those rare individuals whom loyalty to a region would not subjugate to provincialism. Living among his people has not dissuaded him from being critical of them, and devotion has not tethered him to Chapel Hill, North Carolina. He has traveled extensively and acquired a catholic taste in theatre that has made him one of the rare champions of modernist and oriental stylization on the American scene. Curiosity about other parts of the world in his case has been a projection of lively concern for his own time and place. He appears to be at home in other worlds to no small degree because he is at home in his own.

Paul Green was born on March 17, 1894, the descendant of prominent Southern families on both sides, but also the son of a less than affluent

* Introduction to *Paul Green: Five Plays of the South* (New York: Hill and Wang, 1963).

402

farmer. He has remembered his early environment in Harnett County with mingled compassion and repugnance as "one of the dark spots of the commonwealth—a place of sandy roads, crude and cruel doctors, maladjusted and lonely children, weary housewives, ignorance, pain, and cheap religion." And a champion cotton-picker at one time, he has touched upon the sources of his inspiration with as much humility as truth: "By forced laboring in the fields, association with plants, animals, and birds and long experience with wind and weather I gradually grew to love the earth and sky for themselves alone and thereby finally ceased to be afraid or apprehensive," he wrote. "No doubt, through the long summer days of working with Negro field hands, living in and out of their cabins as it were, wrastling, playing, fighting with them, I developed some fellow feeling for people who have to bear the brunt of things."

To acquire some resources for college, he taught country school for several years after graduation from the Buies Creek Academy (he even became principal of the school, which had three other teachers and about 125 students) and augmented his earnings by pitching sand-lot baseball during the summer. In 1914 he entered the University of North Carolina at the somewhat advanced age of twenty. A year later, during the First World War, after winning a prize with a short play produced at the university, he enlisted in the Army and served in it, partly in Belgium and France, until 1919, when he returned to his studies. Completing them at Chapel Hill and adding two years of graduate work in philosophy at Cornell University, he arrived at last at the foothills of a career as an instructor in the aforementioned subject at the State University, by which time he married Elizabeth Lay, a former fellow-student, playwright, and collaborator with her husband. He continued to write plays, however, and even went to Hollywood on screen assignments between teaching— all this with a minimum of fuss and without uprooting himself. The usually separable worlds of schoolteacher, cotton-picker, ballplayer, professor, playwright, and screenwriter were plainly one world to this remarkably vital person, who has been more nearly a philosopher than a teacher of philosophy.

Paul Green, who has also written a considerable body of fiction and criticism, elected the theatre as his favorite profession and, at the beginning, experimented with dramatic writing in its tightest form—namely, the one-act play, which he first wrote under the late Professor Frederick Koch, teacher of dramatics at the university and founder of the Carolina Playmakers. On these regional grounds—on which the young Thomas Wolfe also tried to effectuate himself as a playwright before succeeding as a novelist—Green formed his early dramatic style, combining a keen eye for detail with deep sympathy for the failures and victims of society. His early plays fill three volumes, *The Lord's Will and Other Carolina Plays, The Lonesome Road: Six Plays for the Negro Theatre,* and *In the Valley,* published respectively in 1925, 1926, and 1928. One would be hard put to determine which of these collections is the richest. They all reflect a keen spirit and fine dramatic instinct at work on elemental feelings, folk material, and social realities without sharply distinguishing one category from another, but rather encompassing everything pertaining to nature and man. And this includes farce, as in the little comedy of religious fanaticism, *Unto this Glory,* from *In the Valley,* poetry of dreamfulness and native buoyancy, as in the delightful, if slight, *No 'Count Boy* from *The Lord's Will,* and compressed pathos, as in *White Dresses* from *The Lonesome Road.*

But if there are short masterpieces in these collections of folk drama, such as *White Dresses,* they are equaled by plays that emanate less from their author's regional feeling than from his deep-seated social conscience. The passionate yet powerfully poetic one-act chain-gang drama, *Hymn to the Rising Sun,* comes from this source. At the time of its original production in New York City during the 1930's, what we usually had was more partisanship than poetry in the work of social critics. If the exhibition of sadism and chain-gang conditions is plainly horrifying in *Hymn to the Rising Sun,* the ultimate effect is one of pity, irony, and anger so finely commingled that the writing amounts to poetry of the theatre and verbal music. In this and other works it has been Paul Green's unique gift to aim for message and musicality, exposé and compassion, and reality and wonder all at the same time. And if his success in this enterprise has at times been almost unavoidably dubious, even Paul Green's unsuccessful efforts have been more valuable both as literature and theatre than most American playwrights' easy and oversimple Broadway successes.

In coalescing a number of one-act plays of Negro life into the Pulitzer Prize drama *In Abraham's Bosom,* in 1927, Paul Green enlarged his dramatic scope impressively. Full-length plays of varying magnitude succeeded this memorable and still timely chronicle of a Negro youth's struggle for self-realization and enlightenment in the Old South. *The Field God* was a rural tragedy that resembled some of O'Neill's early efforts, and one may well consider its failure on Broadway less important than the fact that its atmosphere of doom and some of its scenes of gloomy passion and guilt can still haunt us. This is no less true of the turbulent semisymbolistic drama of racial tension *Potter's Field,* published in 1931 and produced in an amputated version on Broadway under the title of

Roll, Sweet Chariot in 1934. *The House of Connelly,* the play with which The Group Theatre opened its momentous career in the 1930's, remains the most poignant drama of the postbellum South, and *Johnny Johnson,* given another Group Theatre production in 1936, is by far the most imaginative and affecting antiwar full-length play in the American theatre. And although vivid plays of Negro life have continued to appear in the New York theatre during the thirty-five years that have elapsed since *In Abraham's Bosom,* it was Paul Green himself who contributed the most powerful of these productions when Orson Welles produced his dramatization of Richard Wright's novel, *Native Son,* in 1941.

There could never be any doubt about the genuineness of this playwright's sympathies. One is reminded of the moving sentences with which he concluded his account of a childhood experience of seeing a Negro teacher struck in the face with a walking stick for asking an innocent question of a train engineer: "The school teacher of that spring morning long ago still lives—a very old man. [This was written in 1948 or 1949.] A bad scar still shows on his face, running from his forehead down across his chin. And there must be a scar in his heart, too. There is in mine, and always will be."

That these are not this playwright's only memories, however, has been abundantly evident for nearly forty years. The other side of regret and protest has been love for America and pride in its history of achievements and promises. His pageant-plays have expressed these sentiments ever since the summer of 1937 when *The Lost Colony* was first produced on the open stage on Roanoke Island, North Carolina, approximately the site of the first English settlement in the New World. With this annually presented work Paul Green started a career that was to bring his love of country to multitudes unknown to Broadway. *The Common Glory* (a chronicle of the American Revolution in Virginia under Thomas Jefferson's leadership), *Faith of Our Fathers* (a drama about George Washington), *Wilderness Road, The Founders, The Confederacy, The Stephen Foster Story*—these and other pageant dramas produced under summer skies mostly in the South add up to the most ambitious effort of the American theatre to review the nation's past. It is impossible to judge these symphonic spectacles by ordinary literary and dramatic standards. They have to be *seen* to be felt, and they have to be *felt* to be understood. The printed page cannot do justice to the experience, to which star-studded skies and breezes redolent of field, forest, and mountain lend enchantment and give refreshment. And Paul Green, to be sure, would have it so. His generous spirit cannot brook confinement in the stuffy playhouses of show business; it needs fresh air and a wide expanse of landscape; and it seeks communion with fellow Americans. The plays contained in the present small volume convey only a limited reach of his talent, but that reach would have been impossible without the further range of his sympathies implicit in his smallest one-act drama and explicit in his most expansive pageantry.

■

SAROYAN'S *THE TIME OF*
*YOUR LIFE**

No play demonstrates the potential vitality of our stage at the end of
the 1930's more convincingly than William Saroyan's fugue, *The Time
of Your Life*. In most countries his first effort, *My Heart's in the Highlands,* would have been hooted off the stage as the work of a charlatan.
Here it was recognized by most critics as a thing of beauty, even if its
charm was found to defy analysis. It was not the masterpiece some commentators thought it was; its thinking was decidedly muddled and its
assault on the penumbral regions of the mind grew somewhat wearying.
Nevertheless, few of us failed to respond to the advent of a fine talent,
and within a few months his new play, *The Time of Your Life,* had been
jointly acquired by Eddie Dowling, for whom the central character had
been written, and by the veteran Theatre Guild. Disaster seemed imminent at its Boston showing, and so discouraging seemed its prospects
that it might have normally been discarded as hopeless. Instead, however,
the author, Mr. Dowling, Miss Theresa Helburn, and Mr. Lawrence
Langner refused to accept defeat, and their New York production is at
present one of the outstanding plays of the season.

Theoretically, the play should have been a disastrous failure, and
purists must exclaim that it is not a play at all. So must writers, young
and old, who have gone to the trouble of learning the rudiments of
dramatic technique only to find that their efforts are unrewarded or are
less rewarded than the seemingly scrambled lucubrations of a short-story
writer who does not hesitate to proclaim himself a genius. What they
fail to see is that there may be direction in indirection, and that the
theatre which lives by nuances of acting has always been grateful for
nuances in the drama except in the most embattled episodes of its history. Moreover, there is a lasting power in obliquity, in leaving implications to the audience, in asking it to participate in an experience instead
of driving the spectator to an acceptance of a philosophy of action that
he will very probably forget the moment he leaves the theatre unless he
is preconvinced. It is generally safer to steep him in the substance of the
life of his times and to let him try to make sense and purpose out of it.
For the record, it is necessary only to go back to Shakespeare, whose dis-

* *One Act Play Magazine* (February, 1940).

approval of both feudalism and Renaissance Machiavellism was so implicit that it could be more explicit than any preachment—and far more
persuasive. Even Euripides practiced this art, as did Ibsen at his best,
not to speak of Chekhov and other moderns. Odets, in our own day, has
employed the same means in *Golden Boy, Rocket to the Moon,* and in
portions of both *Awake and Sing* and *Paradise Lost;* so has Paul Green
in *Johnny Johnson,* and even in *The House of Connelly* and *Hymn to
the Rising Sun.*

Most of these examples have been chosen with malice prepense, since
they have been recognized as "social plays," and since there is much to
be said for those who maintain that all significant plays of our day must
have social implications. (Actually, there never was a time when most
meritorious serious plays and many comedies were not socially oriented.
The proponents of social drama are therefore frequently thinking merely
of degrees of social meaning rather than of the mere presence of this
attribute.) The truth about *The Time of Your Life* is that its uniqueness
resides in its form rather than in its content or meaning, and even the
form departs from convention only by a greater degree of obliquity and
by a more persistent employment of nuances than we have found customary. If the play is to be measured by the yardstick of social criticism,
it is not likely to be as exasperatingly negligible as some young critics are
inclined to believe. If it is to be measured by the yardstick of conventional
dramaturgy, it is also not to be dismissed as a hopeless object of curves
and angles. Only those who believe that social drama must be hortatory,
or that a good play must adhere to the rules of Freytag, will not know
how to measure it. It may also be argued with some validity that we
need not measure a work of art at all; it is necessary only to feel its
magic. That too is criticism or a form of judgment, and the trouble with
this absolutely valid approach is only that one cannot argue about it.

The Time of Your Life is a genre picture with a wealth of chiaroscuro,
the latter being intellectual or critical as well as sensory. Packed into a
"honky-tonk," a saloon that supplies entertainment as well as hard liquor,
are a number of people. They are, superficially considered, hopelessly
miscellaneous. But they have one thing in common—their burden of
aspiration or of frustration or of both. The young marble-game addict,
the melancholy comedian, the Negro who collapses of hunger and plays
divinely when he is revived, the overzealous comedian, the ludicrously
love-sick swain who telephones a nurse in vain until she finally appears
and gives him more than he dared to expect, the prostitute who veils her
past in dreams, the sensation-seeking wealthy woman married to a comically strait-laced husband, the policeman who detests his job—who are

these and others but waifs of the world, impressing upon us the fact that we are all waifs of one kind or another!

Nor is this all. Those who want more cohesion in the drama will find it, if they have unimpaired eyes, in the presence of Joe, a shiftless young man with money at his disposal. Everything, every event or presence in the play, impinges upon him, so that he becomes the sensitive film and focus of the episodes, and many of the events are directly or indirectly inspired by him. He is many things in one, this man who acquired money and sickened of it, who is alone and inscrutably so, as so often happens if not to the same extent. Out of his loneliness and sensitivity he has developed a pity for all mankind and a feeling of brotherhood; and having money and time at his disposal, he has made himself a paraclete or comforter of his fellow creatures, giving understanding where it is needed and material help where it is imperative. He is not a wise legislator or a sound philanthropist, and a course of socially integrated action is foreign to him, for he is mysteriously wrapped up in himself and in his loneliness. One cannot attribute supernatural or social leadership to this figure. But as a very human person, he is the catalytic agent of a large portion of the play. He has a mystic prototype in the Paraclete of Evreinov's *The Chief Thing,* and a realistic one in the interfering Luka of Gorky's *Night's Lodging.* There is, in short, a subtle integration in the play.

Those who want more social pertinence than has been indicated thus far will also find it. To the implicit reference of frustration in our life must be added the hardly irrelevant idea of human brotherhood; all mankind is to be pitied, a doctrine that needs some reaffirmation at this time. "All," is, however, too large a prescription, and for practical purposes a dangerous one. All mankind is pitiful, indeed; even the sadistic vigilante who bullies the prostitute and maltreats the Negro who comes to her defense is a pitiful specimen. Still, Saroyan realizes, at least fugaciously, that there is a degree of evil that can be overcome only by the application of force. Joe wants to give his gun to "a good man who can use it," and the fantastic relic of the frontier, Kit Carson, who claims the honor of having killed the vigilante is received with approval by Joe; it is to him that he bequeathes the pistol. As a course of social action, this assassination is of course deplorable, when approached literally; apprehended symbolically or suggestively, it is only too pertinent today when men of good will are called upon to cope with international bullies. And if we must labor the point, it is also possible to call attention to the fact that the casually introduced characters suggest the actual social scene. Surely the hungry work-hunting Negro represents something more than an isolated case; does he not remind us of a certain pressing problem that all the New Dealers have been unable to solve in eight long years, as well as of the richness of talent or spirit that goes begging in the streets! The seedy comedian who fails to amuse because he has nothing to laugh about represents a shrewd appraisal of reality by the playwright; and there is much satiric comment inherent in the moronically hopeful lad at the slot machine whose Jobian patience is finally rewarded with a collection of nickels and a display of three American flags. Beyond the confines of the saloon, moreover, there are no brass bands but picket lines, and the proletarian dock workers are ready to lock horns with the proletarian police.

Compassion and perception, and laughter and pity, are fused in Saroyan's play into one of the richest experiences provided by the American theatre in many years. Nothing is basically vague, although everything is fugitive, in this play. If it does not come to a single point (and there is no reason why any play must, provided it is richly alive), all its separate points are vividly realized. Only a certain sentimentality attenuates them, particularly in a bedroom scene. The prime condition of dramatic structure is not actually the principle that everything in a play must be tied up in a knot (*vide King Lear, Henry IV, Peer Gynt,* etc.) but that there should be no inconsistencies in the development of character and plot. A writer who keeps us in one groove and then suddenly jolts us out of it is far more culpable than a Saroyan.

An analysis of the production is impossible within the limits of this article, which has stressed the playwriting problem because it is uppermost in the discussions of the play. There has been some debate on the question of style, and it has been maintained with some show of reason that the original direction by Robert Lewis, who treated the play as fantasy, was more appropriate to the spirit of Saroyan's work. The fact is, however, that the author did not think so, and that the production supplied by Messrs. Saroyan, Dowling, Langner, and Miss Helburn is both affecting and amusing. This does not of course settle the larger problem of form, and I trust I shall have the opportunity to return to it. One may, however, ponder the question whether this play is a fantasy; I do not think it is— one does not consider Brueghel's crowded canvases or Igor Stravinsky's *Sacre du Printemps* fantastic. The assumption that anything not completely integrated constitutes fantasy is an illusion of reason-inebriated members of the intelligentsia; to them we recommend the platitude that a good deal of private and social life is unintegrated and illogical.

DRAMA VERSUS MELODRAMA: AN EXPERIENCE OF THE THIRTIES*

By one of those coincidences not rare in a theatrical season, most of the substantial plays of the spring of 1936 revolved around highly melodramatic situations. *The Case of Clyde Griffiths* was based on Theodore Dreiser's notable treatment of a notorious murder in *An American Tragedy*. *Love on the Dole,* an English import, culminated in the stock situation of young people getting into trouble in the time-honored manner. *The Crime,* the left-wing Theatre of Action's one-hour play about a labor leader, could easily have become the regulation melodrama of betrayal and retribution. Dan Totheroh's *Searching for the Sun* involves its characters in illegitimate parenthood and an aborted holdup. Not to be outdone by any of the aforementioned pieces, *The Postman Always Rings Twice* was on view with two eerie auto accidents and jingled the familiar tunes of crime, detection, and retribution. In every instance except *The Crime,* the surface formula was the familiar one of "Boy goes wrong— girl goes wrong."

However, it is pleasant to reflect that plays that would have chugged along once to a consistently melodramatic finish could give new significance to stock situations and order them into a meaningful design. With the exception of one "un-reconstructed" melodrama, the aforementioned dramas justified themselves largely on the ground that they compelled thought. Melodrama, like romanticism, has of course never been routed from the stage. But the efforts of the pioneering realists, with Ibsen leading the charge, did force this debased form of tragedy to take a subordinate position. The later social theatre now prevailing has renewed the attack through its unconditional demand that a play have purpose and meaning.

Under the old dispensation, a dramatization of *An American Tragedy* would normally have been (and actually was, in the late Patrick Kearney's version of the 1920's) a crime thriller rather than a social analysis like the Group Theatre's *The Case of Clyde Griffiths.* In this new dramatization by Erwin Piscator and Lena Goldschmidt, the tables are turned: Society indicted Clyde Griffiths of murder in the first degree. His counsel, voicing the collective conscience, hurls the charge back against society

* Adapted from *New Theatre* (April, 1936).

411

in more ways than one. Clyde is not exonerated. It is a mistake to say that the social determinism of the play relieves him of responsibility to the girl he betrayed or overlooks his weakness of character. The Time and again he is sharply criticized by the Speaker, or commentator, of the drama, as well as by its working-class people, who disclaim him. But while rich and poor alike disown Clyde, and even when his behavior sets him down as a cad, the Speaker viewing the tragedy under the aspect of social conditioning, understands and pities him.

Was Clyde Griffiths' longing for the conveniences and amenities of the rich a symptom of perversity, an expression of sinfulness? It was nothing of the sort. Why should he not have nursed these desires? In what way were his wealthy cousins superior to him that they should be living on the fat of the land while he sweated out his guts in the shrinking room of his wealthy uncle's collar factory? Who is to order the human soul to cast out its longing for the brightness it too might possess? To make such desire sinful is the way of the master and the first condition of slavery. The temptation became overwhelming when Clyde was given an opportunity to rise in the world under the aegis of the society girl who loved him. But in the way of happiness stood the factory girl who had been his mistress and who was bearing his child. Against the temptation he could muster few resources. Had not the society, which decrees poverty for the millions of Clyde Griffiths, cradled him in the gospel of personal ambition? Was a simple, untutored lad to deny the validity of its teachings? Would the tub-thumping evangelism of his parents, with its doctrine of individual salvation, the only system of ethics to which the lad had been exposed, inoculate him against the bacillus of individual escape, of rising above the others—if need be at the expense of others? Would this evangelism be potent enough to oppose his thoughts when they applied themselves to the problem of eliminating the girl who stood between him and the only paradise he could conceive? In the critical moment his inhibitions, if not his reserves of common decency, prevented him from committing the murder, but an accident arising from his homicidal plans did the dirty work for him, and he swung for a crime he had not committed but had nevertheless intended.

The analysis of Clyde's tragedy is airtight. Its soundness can be questioned only by those who doubt the fatality of man-made conditions that cradle the individual from birth to death. Its logic may be a bitter pill to swallow, but it must nevertheless be downed. Clyde Griffiths, it has been seen, is not whitewashed; whatever whitewashing he could receive would more probably emanate from the melodramatists who might plead his youth and immaturity, who would be least inclined to scorn him as a so-called traitor to his class, as the Group's play does quite stridently. But neither is society whitewashed or relieved of its responsibility for tolerating flagrant social inequalities and failing to crystallize an adequate order in which the young may live and reach fruition. On this score, the play makes no compromises, from the first words of the Speaker when he calls "money" the root of evil to his closing statement that society is on trial.

The total effect is absorbing. *The Case of Clyde Griffiths* is one of the most stirring, as well as unique, plays of the season. The bewilderment of the youth plumbs the depths of an experience which must be immediate to most people. The pathos of the abandoned factory girl is compelling. The scenes in the factory are filled with excitement, and even more forceful is the grotesque picture of Clyde buying a dress suit and being confronted by workers who have been "locked-out" by his uncle. To single out individual members of the Group Theatre for their performance would be unfair, as they all fit into Lee Strasberg's frequently brilliant pattern with uncanny precision. Much of the play's impact is due to their collective organization and training.

However, a proper appreciation of the play is inseparable from a consideration of its style—its most troublesome feature. Consisting of brittle cinematic flashes, fragments of scenes unified by a commentator who addresses both the actors and the audience, the play does not follow the usual lines of exposition and development. Its expressionism is further complicated by the fact that it is a didactic instrument; *The Case of Clyde Griffiths* is "a learning play" much in the manner of Brecht's *Mother*. Much has been accomplished by this technique. Its novelty and crass directness can provide a tonic to jaded theatre-going nerves, and any procedure which will shake the average spectator's complacency deserves a blue ribbon. Expressionism is also, in this instance, a ready means of condensing the vast bulk of Dreiser's novel, of achieving condensation without emasculation. The novel's melodramatic surface action lends itself to conventional dramatization, but the larger implications of Dreiser's work would be of necessity a sealed book to the traditional dramaturgist. It is not easy to compress a social system into the so-called "well-made play." To a great extent, then, "learning play" expressionism is the technical device that transforms the play's potential melodrama into social tragedy.

Still, the fact must be faced that expressionism, particularly of the Brecht-Piscator variety, is a double-edged weapon. If it attracts, it also repels. In too many instances it comes up against the inertia of the spectator. He must adjust himself to a relatively new theatric convention, and this adjustment is further hampered by the harangues and explications basic in the style. To sneer at these exhortations as soap-box business rather than theatre is to beg the question. The lengthiest and most straight-forward harangues of the theatre are to be found in the choruses of classic Greek tragedy and comedy. But the fact remains that harangues can be tiresome; the preconvinced part of the audience finds much repetition in them, while the stiff-necked tribe of unbelievers is not apt to humble itself in dust and ashes before a direct assault. There are therefore serious im-pediments in *The Case of Clyde Griffiths*. The Speaker's interruptions of the flow of the drama are sometimes discouraging, and his explanations occasionally superfluous and bald; it is not surprising that some people should even find them blatant. But for Morris Carnovsky's persuasiveness, the Speaker would have been a downright bore part of the time.

Equally distracting is the abbreviation and kaleidescopic scattering of the scenes. Sometimes the condensation of an event goes to the heart of its meaning and reaps gratifying results. The scenes in the tailor shop and in the street, when Clyde is cornered by the unemployed, are a case in point. On the other hand, the truncation of other scenes results in flatness. I refer especially to the rather wooden Christmas party at the rich girl's home, and the automatic exit of the factory girls, leaving Roberta alone with Clyde. It is also tantalizing to watch the freezing of some actor in his tracks. Alexander Kirkland, who performed so appealingly when he was permitted to act, was called upon to assume a dozen or more spotlighted poses reminiscent of the artificial, often pretentious, close-ups of the flick-ers. Momentary immobility on the part of a character can be effective in the theatre, but only when properly related to the other stage business. The problems of stylization are among the most difficult in any art, and those inherent in *The Case of Clyde Griffiths* are still far from settled. When they are least in evidence, the play is powerful drama; when they are most apparent the effect is sometimes forthright and exciting but much more frequently uneven and disconcerting. . . .

TOWARD A ONE-ACT THEATRE*

Perhaps the most striking phenomenon of our recent theatre has been the resurgence of the one-act play. Broadway playgoers have been made aware of it by that exciting trio—*Waiting for Lefty, Till the Day I Die,* and *Bury the Dead.* But these pieces have been no more than the apex of a broad pyramid consisting of the work of many young organizations and playwrights whose upward climb became noticeable in 1934. For practically a decade the one-act form had lain under a cloud of commercial and esthetic disapproval. You couldn't make money with it—a serious consideration at a time when everybody in the theatre expected to become enriched. At the same time one was eager to forget the Little Theatre days as a kindergarten period which, though fun while it had lasted, was something a grown man puts behind him. At best the form was held to be a finger exercise for the aspiring amateur. The few exceptions that a scrupulous historian might wish to record are revivals of O'Neill's sea-pieces, Schnitzler's *Anatol,* and a few others, and the Theatre Guild's production of George O'Neil's *American Dream,* a brilliant work which was in effect a trilogy of one-act plays, even if not conceived as such.

The years that followed the collapse of the Wall Street bubble in 1929 saw the fat of the theatre transformed into leanness. Darkness fell upon many of Broadway's theatres, productions became fewer and more risky, and the great wide "road" became a mere footpath at the end of which there was a headache instead of a bonanza. At the same time most of the topics that had exercised the theatre of the twenties had become pretty much exhausted. The time was ripe for a new movement, which under the stress would be aggressively social in outlook.

It was almost axiomatic that the new movement should express itself to a great extent in the shorter form. Beginnings in the theatre are often punctuated by the one-act play. It is less expensive to produce and requires less expertness of the performers; and it is more adapted to the simple expression of a thought or impression. European drama itself, began with the short forms—the trope or churchly dialogue, the miracle or "mystery" plays, and the moralities. Molière's theatre also started unambitiously; early pieces like *Les Précieuses Ridicules* utilize his satiric mode with less circumlocution than many of his longer works. The birth of the Irish theatre is inseparable from the history of the one-act play; W. B.

* From *New Theatre* (July, 1936).

Yeats, Lady Gregory, Synge, and their colleagues caught the spirit of Celtic fantasy and the hard realities of peasant life equally well in their short pieces, and managed at the same time to add iron to the resolution of Irish nationalism in the struggle against imperial Britain. The American Little Theatre movement was likewise a predominantly one-act venture, impressed in the service of a cause. Despite formal bows to art for the sake of art, the Provincetown and the Washington Square Players ground an axe quite unabashedly, except that the word "propaganda" was not applied. The object was the enlightenment and emancipation of the younger middle class that was cutting loose from the ascetic fare of its pioneer ancestors whom thrift and hard application, including ruthless business practice, had enabled to swallow the country. Determined to enrich their lives they imported European sophistication, broadened their own horizon, and fought for sexual liberty and fuller experience even if this included obscenity and naturalistic descriptions of common life in the early O'Neill manner. In the early thirties the task of emancipation and protest devolved upon a new theatre born of direct economic pressure.

The new one-act theatre was born kicking; it was topical, haranguing, strident—agitation first, drama only secondarily. Since these beginnings, the plays have become increasingly finished and complex, but it is well to remember their origins in order to understand their possibilities and present defects.

That the return of the one-act play is vastly encouraging is due not merely to the fact that its appearance is a symptom of freshening forces in the theatre. The shorter form makes experimentation economically feasible and it is more suitable for distribution over the country and participation by larger segments of the people. It increases the number of productions, and adds variety to a theatre that is, for the most part, monotonously devoted to a three-act pattern. It is, finally, admirably suited to the expression of ideas and the exposition of significant situations which have been giving new vitality to the stage. An idea stretched out for three acts sometimes becomes as attentuated as Europe's unpaid war debt. I have read at least a score of unproduced plays that elaborated upon the causes and consequences of war, the depression, the class struggle and so on with anæsthetic detail, whereas a single well-chosen episode would have been exciting and sufficient. The theatre as a whole stands to gain when playwrights no longer feel compelled to write full-length plays when the subject range calls for only one act.

The time has, however, come for a little truth-telling or, if you please, blood-letting to counteract unconsidered adulation and self-satisfaction, and ensure the progress of the movement. The situation of the present one-act theatre is far from satisfactory. Though the plays deal with pressing realities, are conceived in sincerity and written honestly, they are distressingly uneven. A scattering of superlative pieces like *Waiting for Lefty, Till the Day I Die, Hymn to the Rising Sun,* and *Bury the Dead* is supplemented by a host of second-rate efforts, some of them abysmally primitive and naïve. I shall endeavor to illustrate this situation in some detail, though it is only fair to state beforehand that all the plays mentioned in this paper are better than the average.

At present the plays, except for a small body of innocuous pieces extraneous to the general movement, fall into two classes: those that have and those that have not outgrown the elementary agitational form. In the latter category the piece dramatizes some single instance of social injustice, grinds close to the issue, and comes to rest with a bang on some definite act of protest—a strike, generally triumphant, or a conversion symbolic of the worker becoming class conscious. If plays of this brand are deliberately keyed to meet certain practical needs, such as to convert certain workers to unionization, they are *ipso facto* utilitarian, and standards of art are largely inapplicable to them. If on the other hand the plays are intended to be works of art, they must be considered, in a distressingly large number of instances, well-intentioned failures. In most instances it is evident that a serious effort to achieve artistic merit has been made.

It cannot be stressed too strongly that these pieces do not fail because they serve a definite direction and point of view. Plays have not been known to die because they possessed definiteness and clarity. That agitational drama is not necessarily doomed to failure is shown by many of the world's great plays, and has been proven again, in the one-act form, by the work of Odets, Green and Shaw. Nor can one quarrel with the militancy of the dramas. Intensity of conviction, vehemence and passion, are not faults in the theatre. Where, in fact, the militancy is lacking in a play about conditions literally crying for a definite reaction, the piece may well lose incisiveness and dramatic resolution. In *His Jewels,* a play in the New Theatre League's repertory, a sharecropper is not only evicted from his home but driven out of the church in which he has sheltered his children, one of whom is dying of tuberculosis. The drama is based on an actual occurrence, in which the victim maintained possession of the church with his rifle. The real situation is obviously the mo dramatic one: the passiveness of the hounded sharecropper muffles the impact of the play.

That action requires reaction, charge demands discharge, is the "pleasure principle" of art as well as of life, and militancy that produces a satisfactory discharge of tension is an asset, not a liability, in the theatre.

But cause and effect must be powerful and equal. Thus in *Waiting for Lefty* the provocation producing resentment and action was established in a series of searing scenes; the tension simply clamored for discharge. Similarly, after the horrors of war, the callousness of the generals and the emptiness of the lives of the poor have been burned into the mind, we cannot but want those killed and mangled soldiers of *Bury the Dead* to rise up and march. In contrast, there is the routine militancy of the average piece, in which the plant goes on strike, the vacillating worker joins the pickets, the clerk returns to his class (*Take My Stand*), and so on. Here cause and effect are equally undistinguished. Generally the effect in these plays—the striking back of the oppressed—is meant to be signally powerful. But first of all it cannot be effective unless the provocation is sufficiently realized to make us desire a heroic consummation. Secondly, a stock situation rarely impresses. One may have the highest respect for the strike as a weapon in labor struggles and still fail to thrill to every scene in which workers lay down their tools.

Furthermore, not everything that is a correct and logical resolution of the action is necessarily exciting. If one swallow doesn't make a summer, neither does one person's conversation or the distribution of a dozen leaflets make a social upheaval. Here we have the case of a powerful cause and a disproportionately tame effect. It comprises the deadly sin of anticlimax. There is the classic example of the chap who warns his relentless enemy: "You have stolen my cow, you have robbed my home, you have slain my grandmother and now you are assaulting my wife. If you try my patience any further I shall have you arrested!" A related danger is that of allowing the excitement to run down hill. In *Private Hicks* the national guardsman's initial refusal to fire upon the pickets is the real climax. Everything that follows is merely an explanation and confirmation of an already established fact.

In other instances a major difficulty is the delaying of the climax due to unnecessary preparation. In the first scene of *Trouble with the Angels,* an "angel" of the cast of *Green Pastures* learns that members of his race are not allowed into the theatre and determines to challenge the Jim Crow ruling. In the third or final scene the entire cast with the exception of "De Lawd," refuses to perform unless the theatre alters its policy. The middle scene shows the "angel" persuading his fellow actors to take this course of action. Would not the play be more exciting and the final scene considerably more effective if we didn't already know what the angels were going to do? A delayed climax is also a basic weakness of Michael Blankfort's *The Crime* and of *Bury the Dead*. In the former play the vacillation of the labor leader does not provide sufficient driving interest in itself while the culminating tragic situation—namely, the loss of the strike—has been imminent so long that it fails to be electrifying when it finally comes. In *Bury the Dead,* fortunately, the macabre power of the initial situation, the pressure of several minor crises and the galvanic strength of the conversations between the dead men and their women are all sufficiently exciting to compensate the long delay between the rising of the men and their marching back into life. Indeed, despite its success and the fine example of effective fantasy it presents, *Bury the Dead* is a dangerous pattern to follow. It strains a single assumption immoderately. It is given to piling a Pelion of gratuitous humor and naturalistic horror upon its Ossa of social indictment and challenge. It is too long to completely hold the tension of the dead rising, and much too concerned with incidental detail such as the stench of the risen, the mockery of the whores and the idiosyncrasies of the general to maintain the illusion. The drive of its singular idea, its trenchant irony, its pity and passion set it to rights. But few playwrights can count upon the extraordinary endowment of talent that went into the making of Shaw's play.

Percival Wilde, in what is probably the best book on the subject, *The Craftsmanship of the One-Act Play* (Little, Brown and Co., 1923), differentiates the one-act play from the full-length form by pointing out that "it is superior in unity and economy, playable in a comparatively short space of time, and intended to be assimilated as a whole without the aid of intermissions," that it is not just an abbreviated play—a point that authors would do well to remember. Writing a short play simply because one lacks the patience to write a long one is poor economy. The effects of the two forms are different. The one-act play pursues a single effect and demands "an instantaneous arrest of attention, a continued grasp, and relinquishment only after the curtain has fallen." Character must be likewise quickly established. With the above definition it is impossible to quarrel; it is not an *obiter dictum* but a description of effective writing in the one-act form.

Playwrights sometimes show a rash disregard of the limitations of the medium. They forget that the shorter form requires briefer preparation, quicker attack, and more unified development; that terseness of expression necessarily accompanies such an approach to play material; that, finally, characterization must be swiftly realized and sharply etched. The result is spineless and flabby drama, a play lacking in distinction. Observe by way of contrast how everything in Paul Green's *Hymn to the Rising Sun* is precipitated around the fact that today is the Fourth of July. The Captain makes a speech that becomes a devastating satire on the chain-gang system, at the same time that it fixes the blame upon the legislature of the state and illuminates his own character. A prisoner is brutally flogged—on Independence Day! Another is freed in honor of the day, only to be found dead in the sweat box! The drama of the entire penal system of the South is thus realized by means of a few well-considered strokes. One also notes the dispatch with which the character of the Captain has been established. The sadist, the egomaniac, the vestige of a human being under the tyrant's mask, and finally the cynic whose mockery is partly hate and partly defense—these facets of a personality are flashed before us in rapid succession. *Hymn to the Rising Sun* is a fine example of dramatic compression.

On the other hand, playwrights fumble just as often by failing to exploit the richness of their medium. There is a shrug of the shoulder in their attitude: "After all what can you expect? This is only a one-act play!" The point does not have to be argued in view of the existence of plays that are incontestable evidence of the rich possibilities of the art. A whole devil's kingdom is bounded in a nutshell in *Hymn to the Rising Sun*. Synge's *Riders to the Sea* captures the strange hard life of the Aran Islanders, as well as the whole tragedy of motherhood, in a few pages of dialogue. Allowing themselves more space, Odets and Irwin Shaw have painted extraordinarily rich canvasses in their plays. It is well to remember that the playwright is free to employ as many scenes as he pleases provided they comprise a closely woven and inevitable pattern. The more of life he can pack into his plays the nearer he may bring it to significance. At the same time, of course, length itself will not guarantee richness. *The Crime* lasts an hour without achieving a commensurate affluence of characterization and situation. Much depends upon an eye for detail, for differences and nuances of character, for dramatic situations. A good deal also depends on a feeling for contrast and variety in every phase of the writing. It distinguishes the natural playwright from the camp-followers. Percival Wilde, in one of the brilliant introductions of his extremely interesting compilation, *Contemporary One-Act Plays* (Little, Brown and Co., 1936), writes of *Till the Day I Die:* "His [Odets'] swift alternations of light and shade are remarkable."

There remains one general problem of variety about which it is not always easy to speak to young playwrights. A complaint to the effect that their themes duplicate themselves, that they are always assailing us with the same tale of woe, is sure to draw fire. The complainant is a reactionary or at least a compromiser. Doesn't he realize that the world is full of wrong, that mankind is in the grip of a great struggle? Unfortunately, the barrier of human receptivity is a fact of nature. If a man tells you that his grandmother has died you may be exceedingly sorry. But if a hundred men report the same event you may find yourself approving the high rate of mortality and wishing that it also applied to the bereaved. My quarrel is not with the topic of injustice. The fault lies in a tendency to follow a more or less rigid pattern of economic or racial struggle, the same didactic resolution of the conflict, the same situations, the same characters, and the same sombre tone.

Without greater variety of situation, tone and character the well-springs of the one-act theatre may dry up sooner than its adherents imagine. And this would be a pity, for the possibilities are almost infinite and close at hand. There is, for instance, the wide field of satire, so brilliantly utilized by Molière in short pieces like *Les Précieuses Ridicules* and *Georges Dandin,* and so slightly explored by the new movement. (The single exception seems to be Philip Stevenson, whose *God's in His Heaven* and *You Can't Change Human Nature* have been efforts in this direction.) There is the field of humor that should not be despised even by a theatre that has a sizeable chip on its shoulder. There is the domain of fantasy which, as *Bury the Dead* shows, is not compelled to consort with leprechauns and Celtic mist to be richly imaginative. There is, finally, the poetic drama, in which MacLeish, Auden, Kreymborg and Humbert Wolfe have been leading the way. Here indeed is an extremely suitable medium for one-act writing. As for topics for investigation, current one-act writers have as yet made little use of history, folklore and folkways, private relations and the drama of character. Malnutrition, let us remember, is a fatal disease in, as well as outside, the theatre. Incidentally, the righteous who fear that their theatre will suffer dilution from the infiltration of private matters and character studies have no real cause for worry. A majority of the tragedies of the people take place in the home; the full impact of economics is felt there. A majority of actual conflicts, visible on the stage, must take place between characters rather than impersonal forces.

It is not inconceivable that this running fire of comment could be continued indefinitely by multiplying special instances. There is no point, however, in going beyond a general appraisal. If it serves as a purgative and tonic it will have accomplished everything that was intended, and a good deal more than was hoped. It has seemed necessary because after several years of activity the one-act theatre at last stands some chance of becoming as permanent a factor as the full-length variety. If the average in the one-act theatre can be raised sufficiently it can be made to flourish on our stage. Its immediate future lies in the hands of all theatre workers who are capable of rigorous self-criticism and are not content to look upon the one-act play as a mere stopgap.

THE ONE-ACT PLAY IN THE REVOLUTIONARY THEATRE*

I

INTRODUCTION

Pascal once wrote, "I have no time for a short letter. Therefore I am writing you a long one." When the theatre does not take time to deal with essential matters and to deal with them cogently, it is content to ramble, hoping that the sum of its irrelevancies will somehow assume relevance, that many things poorly said will become one thing well said. It is then that some alert idealists, generally young and rebellious, take time to write a short letter. A one-act theatre comes into existence, ready to excise the hypertrophic tissues of the established full-length theatre. Although not all new movements begin with shorter forms—witness the birth of European realism in Ibsen—the Irish renaissance, the Little Theatre movement in America, and left-wing insurgency in the thirties favored the one-acter.

The history of the revolutionary theatre had many points in common with the earlier movements. It returned to the "people," it expressed the leaven of new forces in the social and political sphere, it broke with commercialism, and it attracted a new generation of theatre folk. Like the earlier movements, it produced a large body of half-realized drama and an impressive number of short masterpieces.

Again, moreover, the shorter form was not dictated solely by esthetic considerations. It is more economical to produce a one-acter than a full-length play, and new movements are notoriously short of cash. Their proponents are also short of time. They earn their living by means of some concession to Mammon, and what leisure they have is sometimes divided between art and politics or some form of social activity. The young men of the thirties earned their living as best they could in offices and factories, acted in professional companies, or wrote for the radio. Their rehearsals or wrestlings with the muse would have to give precedence also to party meetings, protest meetings, picketings, and other so-called "dress rehearsals" for revolution.

* From *The One-Act Play Today,* ed. by William Kozlenko (New York: Harcourt, Brace and Company, 1938).

Many of the playwrights were impatient with extended and arduous writing. Art struck them as an anachronism in a world cracking in the joints and falling to pieces, a bourgeois luxury, and a sign of decadence. The theatre they held to be a weapon in the class struggle, in the war against poverty, unemployment, and class and racial oppression. What they wanted to say had to be said simply and directly, had to be addressed to agricultural and industrial workers who had rarely been inside a theatre. Subtleties of characterization and development did not seem to matter when larger issues were at stake, nor would such refinements avail much in galvanizing an audience into indignation or inculcating the principles of mass action. Many of the playwrights were, moreover, unprepared to cope with larger forms, even if they had been inclined to favor them. Their apprenticeship to the theatre had been of short duration, they were young, and some of them were primarily sociologists rather than natural-born artists.

If their selection of the shorter forms was partly dictated by the deficiencies of their talent and the limitations of their audiences, there is a difference between the halting steps of childhood and doddering old age. Childhood is a promise and a capacity for growth, and the new movement began to grow in talent, as well as in numbers. Moreover, even its inadequacies possessed a certain attractiveness, just as childhood has a charm all its own. The crude early efforts of the playwrights may have been negligible as drama, the early productions may have fallen short of the fine art of theatre, but their enthusiasm and vigor were attractive by comparison with the tired sophistication of many Broadway cream puffs. They were also indirectly useful to the theatre as a whole. A new audience was being won for the theatre, an audience that had been hitherto regaled solely by the films. This became evident when the Theatre Union began to muster a working-class audience to its support; when the principle of a low-priced theatre culminated in the Federal Theatre; when amateur organizations sponsored by the New Theatre League began to recruit an audience in the hinterland after the "road" had collapsed as a result of the depression and of competition with the motion pictures.

New writing talent was developed in the political theatre ushered in by the one-act movement—one need only list the names of Clifford Odets, Irwin Shaw, Albert Bein, Victor Wolfson, Marc Blitzstein, Paul Peters, George Sklar, Albert Maltz, and Michael Blankfort, who made their mark in the professional theatre. Older writers like Paul Green, Claire and Paul Sifton, John Howard Lawson, and John Wexley found a new place in the theatre. Not merely did they find a new theatre hospitable to their outlook, but they could only feel encouraged by the work of the novices who were exciting audiences. Other playwrights must have been brushed with the wings of the new spirit: Elmer Rice turned from profitable ventures in the general theatre to the field of social drama in which he had won his spurs; Sidney Kingsley turned to vigorous playwriting with *Dead End;* Maxwell Anderson's *Both Your Houses* and *Winterset* bowed to the time spirit which was being so insistently promoted by the young apostles; *Idiot's Delight* was a new departure for the author of *Reunion in Vienna.*

New, important producing units were either born of the movement (the Theatre Union and the Actors Repertory Company) or affected by it, as in the case of the Group Theatre and the Mercury Theatre, not to speak of the Federal Theatre and its inclination toward social drama. New dramatic forms were either created or disseminated by the ferment—the "Living Newspaper" form, the epic theatre and its variants, and the mass recitation. Even the musical revue was subjected to the new influence— in the Theatre Guild's *Parade* and Labor Stage's widely heralded *Pins and Needles.* It is incontestable that, with all its errors and blanks, the revolutionary one-act movement wrote a significant chapter in American theatre history. In fact, it is still writing it,[1] though it seems to have passed its peak in the season of 1936–37.

II

THE WORKER AND THE THEATRE

In the gilded twenties, when the Little Theatre movement ripened into the progressive professional theatre, a purely working-class theatre was almost unthinkable. A benevolent capitalism was the order of the day; organized labor, dazzled by high wages, tended to identify its interests with the capitalistic economy; and the progressives of the theatre were far more concerned with the dangers of mechanization and the vulgarities of successful business, popularly known as Babbittism, than in class conflicts. Moreover, the struggles and problems of the working class were incorporated somewhat in the so-called middle-class theatre. O'Neill described the homelessness of the proletariat in his sea pieces and symbolized its rebellion in *The Hairy Ape.* Elmer Rice dramatized the mechanization of the worker in *The Adding Machine* and the life of the slums in *Street Scene.* Imported dramas like Toller's *Man and the Masses,* Kaiser's *From Morn to Midnight* and Werfel's *Goat Song* variously represented the worker's insurgency. Associated causes, such as peace and the

[1] In 1938.

rights of the Negro people, were expressed in *What Price Glory?*, *In Abraham's Bosom*, *All God's Chillun*, and other plays. None of the above-mentioned plays would have satisfied the demands of the revolutionary theatre of the thirties, but they went as far as most professional playwrights could go and sometimes further than their audiences would follow them.

Efforts to create a workers' theatre that would toe the class line and avoid the mixed sympathies of the more established playwrights were sporadic. Foreign language groups arose from time to time, but their work was not always clearly defined, and the linguistic barrier was too great to be overcome. A Workers Drama League, founded in 1926, had no language problems but lasted only two years. It provided a leaven, however, for the one considerable radical theatre of the twenties. In 1927, a group which called itself the New Playwrights Theatre prevailed upon the unfailingly generous Otto Kahn to grant it a subsidy of one hundred thousand dollars. It enlisted the services of the insurgent writers John Dos Passos, John Howard Lawson, Francis Faragoh, Paul Sifton, Emjo Basshe, and Michael Gold. Though some of the plays seemed foggy enough in execution, a number of them confronted working-class problems more single-heartedly than had been hitherto the case. Lawson's *The International* dramatized aspects of American imperialism; *The Belt* by Sifton described the struggle against the Taylor system and Fordism; Upton Sinclair's *Singing Jailbirds* dealt with the framing of a labor organizer, a subject perhaps inspired by the Mooney-Billings case. In spite of its peregrinations from Greenwich Village to Broadway the New Playwrights' group remained a small patch of revolutionary theatre without a mass basis and failed to make an impression on the country as a whole. It was not even, strictly speaking, a workers' theatre; it was *for* the workers but was hardly *of* them. After three seasons the New Playwrights Theatre called it a day.

Consequently, the workers' theatre of the thirties started almost from scratch. Fired it must have been by the New Playwrights' effort and by the early experiences of the Little Theatre movement, which had proved that it was possible to begin on a small scale and reach new audiences with a minimum of expense. The experiences of foreign language groups and of the workers' theatre groups in Germany also contributed an impetus. The immediate inspiration of the movement, however, came from conditions outside of the theatre.

The movement arose as a response to the terrifying conditions of the Depression. The stock-market crash left about thirteen million people unemployed, the wages of those fortunate enough to remain employed were slashed mercilessly, labor unions were helpless in the grip of economic circumstance, unemployment relief was still in the apple-selling stage; and everywhere, including the circles of the rich, there was talk of the imminent collapse of the social order. Banker and worker alike expected a death struggle for domination. And abroad there was Soviet Russia making giant strides, a visible symbol of what could be accomplished by successful revolution. "Theatre is a weapon in the class struggle," the motto of the John Reed Group Theatre of Philadelphia, expressed the objectives of the new movement, which took as its twofold aim the spreading of the communist gospel and the agitation for specific palliatives, which could be, and were as a matter of fact, slowly adopted by the American people without commitment to revolution.

Two theatre groups, working at first independently, became the spearhead of the movement—the Prolet-Buehne, a German-speaking unit, and the Workers Laboratory Theatre of New York. The former, founded in 1925, and strongly influenced by the workers' theatre movement in Germany, adopted a militant policy. By the fall of 1930, under the vigorous leadership of John Bonn and Anne Howe, Prolet-Buehne was appearing at a variety of mass meetings, on improvised stages, with few props, and inexpensive facilities. Its plays, stylized, rhythmical, and adapted to chanting, called "agit-prop" because their object was agitation and propaganda, frankly dispensed with characterization and developed situations. To the student of dramatic literature they are worthless. Whatever artistic merit they could claim lay entirely in production. Prolet-Buehne depended on a theatre of slogans, denunciations, and caricature held together by rhythmic movement and songlike expression. Its characters were broad types, easily distinguished and symbolic; thus, the capitalist wore a top hat and the worker an open shirt, the employer was a mealy-mouthed oppressor, the employee a downtrodden worm until he turned. The subjects ranged from the speed-up in industry to the Scottsboro case. In its typing, stylization, and popular style, "agit-prop" was almost a species of *commedia dell'arte,* which has never been judged by literary standards. This drama also marked a return to folk theatre, in which the common people voice their resentments by satirizing their masters and parasites. The frontal satire of "agit-prop" spared no one, not even socialists and labor leaders, who were accused of misleading the working class.

This style was adopted and extended by the English-speaking organization that paralleled the work of the Prolet-Buehne, the Workers Laboratory Theatre, founded in 1929. Its members were possessed of all the enthusiasm of youth, but they had little use for collegiate high jinks. Many of their actors and writers had grown up in poverty and had worked in factories. Few of them had gained practical experience in the theatre; their ablest director, Alfred Saxe, a fiery and gifted young man, had only a year of acting to his credit.

By 1931 the group was actively engaged in propaganda, appearing at mass meetings in New York and elsewhere. Its first production, in the winter of 1930–31, a skit entitled *Unemployed,* had for its lesson the necessity of organizing the unemployed to demand humane treatment and work when this could be managed. The group participated in political campaigns. Its contribution to the 1932 election was a skit, *The Sell-Out,* attacking ameliorative liberalism and socialism because they deflected the struggle for a collectivist society. An auctioneer selling "Civil Librolax" offered the workers "A cure for unemployment, A cure for corns and bunions," and assured them that "Our laxatives are gentle, mild. . . . They do not pinch, they do not gripe." Another political burlesque, *The Great Show,* had for its characters a Worker, a Speaker, a Capitalist, and a political charlatan named "Chameleon," described as "a reptile possessing the power of changing its color."

Resolved to spread its type of drama over the country, the Workers Laboratory Theatre encouraged the creation of similar units elsewhere, until even Canada had its "agit-prop." Los Angeles had its "Rebel Players," Chicago its "Blue Blouses" and Boston its "Solidarity Players." Contacts with these and other groups were maintained largely by means of a new publication, *Workers Theatre,* which grew from two hundred mimeographed copies in April, 1931, to one thousand printed ones by the beginning of the next year. In April, 1932, the movement had grown to proportions that warranted the holding of a national festival and conference, the so-called Workers Theatre Spartakiade and Conference, in New York City. Ben Blake, the left-wing theatre's first chronicler,[2] notes with some pride that this was "the very spring when for the first time since its initiation in 1923, the National Little Theatre Conference Tournament annually staged by Walter Hartwig was unable to take place." The conference made it evident that the theatre had given birth to a lusty infant inclined to strangle serpents in its cradle and bent upon keeping the neighborhood awake with its howling. Its Dramatic Bureau, which had been created in the middle of 1931, now had twenty-three short plays in its repertory. A central organization, the League of Workers Theatre, abbreviated in New Deal fashion as the LOWT, was established, and *Workers Theatre* magazine was adopted as its official organ.

[2] Ben Blake, *The Awakening of the American Theatre* (New York: Tomorrow Publishers, 1935).

The Conference was a landmark in more than an organizational sense. The "agit-prop" groups surrendered much of their brash certainty and self-assurance, and a commendable capacity for self-criticism became apparent. Hitherto they had scorned the professional stage as a fen of stagnant waters and an abomination in the sight of the deified proletariat. They had behaved as if there had been no theatre before them, as if everything "bourgeois" was simply waiting for the harvester, Death. Some respect for the continuity of culture, a principle recognized by Marx and Engels, even if forgotten by their more or less recent converts, became apparent. A healthy concern with theatre technique became manifest, training schools were established, and appeals for assistance were sent to the professional theatre and the Little Theatres. Attracted by the sincerity and enthusiasm of the new groups and by an opportunity to exercise talents lying fallow in the depressed theatre, professionals soon responded in increasing numbers. Their effect upon the movement was eminently salutary, and the movement amply discharged its indebtedness by providing them with a new stimulus.

At first, direct agitation was not greatly abated, and it is a matter of record that it was never wholly abandoned. The first signs of growth were felt in the efficiency of the new productions. As late as November, 1934, the Workers Laboratory Theatre, whose most active members lived for a time in a collectively run apartment, reaffirmed the ideals of its inception, by establishing a "shock troupe" prepared to perform at a moment's notice wherever agitational drama was urgently needed. Collectively, the shock troupe created a topical *montage, Newsboy,* which was vibrantly directed by Alfred Saxe. Technically, *Newsboy* was a unique fusion of suggestions from *Merry-Go-Round* and the Jooss Ballet that would interest the student of esthetic forms without respect to political sympathies. But the form was primed for agitational effectiveness. Later, when it was temporarily included in the Theatre Guild's *Parade* in Boston, it was still sufficiently point-blank to shock the Governor of Massachusetts out of his seat with the query, "Do you remember Sacco and Vanzetti?" A powerful *montage, Free Thaelman,* which made an impression on students of the theatre, agitated for the release of the German radical leader then languishing in a concentration camp. For elementary agitation, the group also established a puppet department devoted to such topical titles as *Mr. Morgan's Nightmare* and *N.R.A. and Blue Eagle,* in which the President of the United States was made to say: "If the workers are striking, we'll give them the *bird*," and Punch, the Worker, declared:

My stomach often rubs my spine
And now it's started shrinking.
And though my head is made of wood
I've lately started thinking.

III

THE NEW THEATRE MOVEMENT

The natural processes of growth and the influx of professional people nevertheless operated increasingly against the "agit-prop" drama. The principle of "a theatre greater than the labor movement but drawing its inspiration from the latter and continuing the new social outlook on a broader scale," to which the movement had committed itself, was beginning to be realized both organizationally and artistically. In response to this trend, *Workers Theatre* magazine changed its name to *New Theatre* in September, 1933. The magazine ushered in the new policy by distributing a questionnaire on the social relations of the theatre among prominent playwrights, producers, and craftsmen. Among the many to respond to *New Theatre*'s appeal were Paul Green, Philip Barry, Sidney Howard, Sherwood Anderson, and Hallie Flanagan. In September, 1934, the magazine, which acquired an exceptionally gifted editor in Herbert Kline, of Davenport, Iowa, announced flatly that "the day of the cliché and mechanical statement has gone by for the workers' theatre." Another factor in the broadening realism of a movement that had begun by specializing in dramatized poems, expressionistic satires, and mass recitations (of which Alfred Kreymborg's *America, America* remains the finest example) was the success of the Theatre Union in full-length social drama of the type of *Stevedore* and *Black Pit*. This institutional radical theatre, which owed its inception to the spadework of the League of Workers Theatres, repaid its debt by setting the one-act movement an example in rounded characterization and dramatic development.

In response to the new trend, which would have been regarded earlier as perniciously compromising, the League of Workers Theatres changed its name in January, 1935, to the New Theatre League, with Mark Marvin, another immigrant from Iowa, as its executive secretary. Eligibility to membership was construed along the broad lines of opposition to war, fascism, and censorship—a policy that left the door wide open to writers, actors, and directors who would have otherwise remained aloof. (The precise formulation of the program was: "For a mass development of the American theatre to its highest artistic and social level; for a theatre

dedicated to the struggle against war, fascism, and censorship.") Almost
at once New Theatre affiliates sprang up in approximately one hundred
and fifty communities. Little Theatre groups became increasing hospitable to New Theatre plays; and the "road," which had been largely
lost to the professional theatre, showed recovered vitality. The repertory
department became an active play bureau and play publisher, stimulating
production throughout the country; and the New Theatre School, which
attracted a vigorous student body and an advanced faculty, became a
major institution of its kind. *New Theatre,* which became increasingly
hospitable to writers of different shades of opinion without sacrificing
its social critique, grew rapidly in circulation, which at one time reached
the high-water mark of twenty-three thousand. Soon recognized as the
most vital publication in the theatre even by those who still found many
of its policies unacceptable, it gave impetus to the composition of distinguished one-acters. Its annual contests, given in conjunction with the New
Theatre League and other organizations, netted numerous playlets of
variable quality, and made such notable discoveries as *Waiting for Lefty*
and *Bury the Dead.* Under these auspices, "New Theatre Nights" became
a regular feature, attended by large audiences and respected by the press.
It was at one of these special performances, in January, 1935, that the
prize-winning play, Clifford Odets' *Waiting for Lefty* received its first
production. Another New Theatre Night unveiled Irwin Shaw's *Bury
the Dead,* written for another annual contest. A third evening saw the
production of Paul Green's *Hymn to the Rising Sun,* considered one of
the short masterpieces of the American theatre and subsequently revived
by the Federal Theatre. Albert Maltz's *Private Hicks,* though a less distinguished work, achieved another respectable success. In each instance,
moreover, production in New York was followed by performances
throughout the country.

The Workers Laboratory Theatre veered to realism in Peter Martin's
Daughter, a dramatization of a short story by Erskine Caldwell, in January, 1935, and in Michael Blankfort's *The Crime,* in the spring of 1936.
Changing its name to The Theatre of Action the group also turned to
full-length drama in *The Young Go First,* a collaboration by three young
writers which represented conditions in the C.C.C. camps. But the honor
of shaking down the ripened fruit of the revolutionary one-act movement
was reserved for groups that had started less militantly—the Group
Theatre and the "Let Freedom Ring" Company, later known as the
Actors Repertory. Both were professional units, drilled in the technique
of realism, though not impervious to the influence of "agit-prop." It is

significant, too, that both companies had been producing full-length plays before turning to one-acters, a reversal of tradition.

The Group Theatre, which had begun as an affiliate of the venerable Theatre Guild, was an actors' company that had been a collective since 1930, after germinating in the minds of its leading spirits, Harold Clurman, Cheryl Crawford, and Lee Strasberg. From an ideal of collective acting it was a short step to a more or less collectivist social ideal. The Group, according to Clurman, would eschew doing merely "amusing things." In 1931 he wrote to the Directors of the Theatre Guild:

> We are passionately devoted to the theatre because only through it can we most successfully say the things we have to say. We believe that men cannot live without giving themselves completely to some force outside themselves and that this must have a concrete object and form which can absorb the activities of men in their daily lives. The generations before us seemed to have been strenuously individualistic without believing very steadily in any particular good for their individuals. We, on the contrary, feel that the individualism of self-assertion which made of the ego the sole and final reality of life is self-destructive, and we believe that the individual can realize himself only by seeking his spiritual kindred and by making of their common aspirations and problems the object of his active devotion. We believe that the individual can achieve his fullest stature only through the identification of his own good with the good of his group, a group which he himself must help to create.

The Group's productions strove to realize these ideals, both in technique and choice of plays.

In the fall of 1931, while still functioning under the Guild's directorate, the Group had given a memorable production of Paul Green's *The House of Connelly,* a sensitive study of decayed Southern aristocracy. Its next production, the Siftons' *1931,* also owned by the parent organization, proved to be the first full-length study of the actual effects of the depression. After a brief excursion into romanticism with Maxwell Anderson's *Night over Taos,* the first independent venture, this organization returned to the social theatre with John Howard Lawson's *Success Story* in the fall of 1932. *Big Night,* which followed it, was only mildly satirical and died a-borning, but the socially insignificant *Men in White,* produced in association with Broadway managers, proved a bonanza and won the Pulitzer Prize. With its next two plays, Lawson's *Gentlewoman* and Melvin Levy's *Gold Eagle Guy,* the Group returned to social drama but in a muddled and inconclusive manner which bespoke neither commercial nor artistic success. The Group was stumped. It possessed a play, *Awake and Sing,* by a member of the company, but seemed disinclined to risk it after two failures.

It was at this point that *New Theatre* came to the rescue. It had offered a prize for the best one-act play, and Clifford Odets, locking himself in a hotel room, set his nose to the grindstone. After three days he completed *Waiting for Lefty,* a playlet revolving around a recent taxi strike, which won first prize. Members of the Group Theatre accepted the magazine's invitation to perform the play at a special showing as a kind of extracurricular performance. The opening night at the old Civic Repertory Theatre, then occupied by the Theatre Union, proved memorable. The audience wept and refused to leave the theatre. The enthusiastic reception became the making of the most promising playwright to be discovered in years. The Group resolved to give the play a professional run, and to fill out the evening at the Longacre the wildly acclaimed young author prepared another short play, *Till the Day I Die,* less enthusiastically received but regarded by such authorities as Richard Watts, Jr., and Percival Wilde as the most distinguished of his shorter pieces. Convinced that it had a full-fledged playwright in its ranks, the Group looked again at *Awake and Sing* and produced Odets' first full-length drama with uncommon success. Thus the New Theatre movement had given birth to a new and important playwright.

The two short plays, which opened on March 25, 1935, enjoyed an excellent press and a respectable run; with the exception of George O'Neil's *American Dream,* which was presented by the Theatre Guild as a single play, Odets' one-acters were the first in a decade to be successful in the professional theatre. But the history of *Waiting for Lefty* went far beyond the limelight of Broadway, which was as the folk-minded New Theatre movement would have it. Six months after its première, this one-acter was being played from coast to coast in twenty cities by twenty different companies. Eventually, more than a hundred cities saw the play. Even conservative England played host to it in London, Durham, Newcastle, and other places. The Unity Players who produced it in New Haven won the much-coveted George Pierce Baker cup at the Yale Dramatic Tournament and gained the right to present the piece throughout the state in spite of opposition from the police department and sundry irate elements. Numerous efforts to suppress *Waiting for Lefty* made the one-acter a *cause célèbre,* and the New Theatre League soon had a censorship fight on its hands, which it fought to a successful conclusion with the aid of divers liberal and theatre-loving friends. Not all of its enemies, however, were in the ranks of capital. Some of the most indignant protests came from labor itself—more precisely, from its conservative leadership, which was angered by the charge of racketeering within unions. Thus, *Labor Chronicle,* organ of Joseph P. Ryan, old-line leader of the Longshoremen's Union, complained that the play held "legitimate unionism up to obloquy."

The Group's other ventures in the one-act field were less overwhelmingly successful. *Till the Day I Die,* which dealt with foreign fascism, was less calculated to attract American audiences, although in point of distance its productions outranked *Waiting for Lefty* when the play was given in Perth, West Australia. *Dmitroff,* an early play, written by two other members of the Group, Elia Kazan and Art Smith, and the latter's *The Tide Rises,* a picture of the San Francisco waterfront strike, won attention on a smaller scale.

Less eminent in full-length production, but the Group's peer in the one-act field, proved the "Let Freedom Ring" Company, originally assembled by Albert Bein for the production of his full-length drama of the Southern mills, *Let Freedom Ring.* Ultimately organized along collective lines, and keenly alive to the struggles of the day, this company contributed its services to a number of New Theatre Nights. After giving two short pieces at the first Night, in November, 1935, the company was allowed to present the prize play of the year, *Private Hicks,* on January 11, 1936. This playlet proved eminently successful in its numerous productions throughout the country, perhaps largely because it voiced labor's opposition to the use of militia in strike areas.

It was not long before the company's impressive showing attracted new players, as well as plays that were to excel *Private Hicks.* In their next appearance on a New Theatre Night, also in January, 1936, they unfolded Paul Green's *Hymn to the Rising Sun,* an exposure of the Southern chain-gang system, which had been first published in *New Theatre.* With Charles Dingle in the role of the sadomasochistic chain-gang boss and an effective cast of prisoners and guards, the playlet made a profound impression upon audiences and critics. Supplementing it, the company revived the same author's satire on evangelism, *Unto Such Glory,* a folk piece that was invested with new relevance by the players, among whom the excellent actor Will Geer was most impressive.

Paul Green did not of course need to be "discovered." At most it can be assumed that the New Theatre movement gave him renewed impetus and an audience which his earlier dramas had barely scratched. Irwin Shaw's antiwar drama *Bury the Dead* was, however, a real discovery, and the honor of presenting it for the first time under New Theatre League auspices devolved upon the group, which soon constituted itself as a collective known as the Actors Repertory Company. When this long-acter narrowly missed becoming the prize-winner of a New Theatre contest, Irwin Shaw, who had seen the actors at work, selected them to perform his play. It was instantly acclaimed at the Forty-sixth Street Theatre, and the press was so favorable that a commercial manager, Alex Yokel, whose current success was far removed from the social drama, undertook to finance it for a Broadway run. Directed by Worthington Miner, it opened in May, 1936, at the Ethel Barrymore Theatre, with a curtain raiser collectively composed by the actors. Although *Bury the Dead* did not prove a bonanza to its angel, it had a respectable run and was a success of esteem having few equals in the contemporary theatre. And again, as in the case of Odets' one-acter, the triumph of the play can only be measured by its dispersion over the country. A most colorful moment in its history occurred in Hollywood at a preview arranged to stimulate interest in its forthcoming production by the Contemporary Theatre of Los Angeles. The occasion took the form of a public reading by Frederic March and Florence Eldridge. Among other notables who participated were James Cagney, Francis Lederer, Donald Ogden Stewart, and Arthur Kober; and Lewis Milestone, the film director, who was subsequently to take Odets under his wing in pictures, telegraphed the audience, "Let there be more of these plays for the sake of humanity."

When *Bury the Dead* closed in New York, the Actors Repertory Company returned to full-length production with a high-minded drama of unemployment rehabilitation, E. P. Conkle's *Two Hundred Were Chosen,* but it was unable to match its previous triumph. The group, however, continued to have faith in the one-act form. It was prepared to present another New Theatre winner, Marc Blitzstein's music drama *The Cradle Will Rock,* when it was prevented by the financial failure of its full-length play. It remained for the Mercury Theatre, an off-shoot of the Federal Theatre and an organization not uninfluenced by the New Theatre movement, to salvage *The Cradle Will Rock* from the Federal Theatre's scrap heap, to which it had been relegated in the summer of 1937. The Actors Repertory Company is still interested in one-acters;[3] recently it contributed an enchanting musical skit, *A Town and Country Jig,* which should commend itself to many amateur groups.

The early work of the Prolet-Buehne and the Workers Laboratory Theatre and the later accomplishments of the Group Theatre and the "Let Freedom Ring" Company comprise the most colorful aspects of the movement. But by no means do they exhaust it. Thus, The Theatre Collective of New York produced numerous social playlets and launched

---

[3] This was the case in 1938. The Actors Repertory Theatre became defunct a year or so later.

another able, if less widely recognized, writer, Philip Stevenson. The Collective made an impressive showing with his satire on lukewarm liberalism during the American Revolution, *You Can't Change Human Nature*. One of the directors of the Collective, Brett Warren, subsequently made theatrical history with an admirable production of the Federal Theatre's Living Newspaper, *Power*. It is in fact impossible to record the work of groups like the Collective individually. At the peak, the New Theatre movement could boast of more than three hundred affiliated groups throughout the country.

To their activities, moreover, must be added the work of independent organizations like The Vassar Experimental Theatre under Hallie Flanagan, soon to become national director of the Federal Theatre Project, which produced a militant farm drama, *Can You Hear Their Voices?* an adaptation of Whittaker Chambers' story by Mrs. Flanagan and her student Margaret Clifford as early as 1931. (This play and W. H. Auden's *Dance of Death,* produced first at Vassar, are classified as full-length plays. Actually, they are long one-acters, as a glance at their structure would reveal.) Independent, but allied in spirit, were also the Brookfield Players, who held forth in a converted tobacco barn on the Pittsfield Post Road near Danbury and presented the work of Virgil Geddes. Though his plays were listed by their author as full-length dramas forming a tetralogy, *From the Life of George Emery Blum,* they were individually long one-acters in structure. The Rebel Arts Group of New York, another independent unit of Socialist inspiration, offered a number of short plays, the most recent and impressive being Michael Blankfort's drama of the Spanish civil war, *The Brave and the Blind,* given in the spring of 1937. Noteworthy, too, was the annual tour of the Brookwood Labor College Players, who at one time covered as many as one hundred and fifty cities with short labor plays and mass recitations given mostly in union halls under union auspices. "Economics without tears, and history with footlights instead of notes," the motto of this training center for labor organizers was scrupulously adhered to, although the writing talent available to it was meager. For the record it must also be noted that the Theatre Guild's trilogy of one-acters, George O'Neil's *American Dream,* consisting of episodes in the American struggle for freedom, had much in common with the revolutionary one-act movement, as did the better skits of the Guild's musical revue *Parade,* a costly failure, to which many a Theatre Unionite contributed.

Finally, there is a phase of the movement to which this historian cannot do justice. Its active proponents can paint a vivid picture of participation in vital industrial conflicts. When relief workers in Madison,

Wisconsin, took possession of a courthouse, it was a theatrical unit that kept up their morale. *Private Hicks* was based on the Auto-Lite strike, during which a number of strikers were killed in a clash with the State militia in Toledo, Ohio; it was not surprising, therefore, that this playlet should have been presented wherever its protest seemed called for. From the General Motors strike a number of embattled actors still retain souvenirs—blackjacks with which the strikers are said to have armed themselves for defense against hired thugs. Actors played to rubber strikers in Akron during freezing weather. The Mass Action Theatre played to the steel strikers' picket line the day after a "Memorial Day Massacre" in Chicago. When the civil war broke out in Spain there was no dearth of anti-Franco actors who went to the front to fight or to entertain the fighters, some, like John Lenthier, to lay down their lives in the struggle against their archenemy, fascism. Units of the one-act movement not only expressed the ardors of the industrial conflicts that were to culminate in the birth of the C.I.O., but participated in them. Whether all this activity enhanced or detracted from the quality of the plays and performances is a debatable subject, although there was no intrinsic merit and little, if any, evidence of talent in the writing; one thing is certain—the New Theatre movement would have had to forgo its inspiration if it had maintained a lofty neutrality in social and political conflicts.

IV

THE RECESSION

In 1936 the New Theatre movement entered a period of recession, as well as of transition. As a result of the decline, as well as of a necessary cleansing of the stables and concentration of the work, it has shrunk considerably in size and activity. Among a variety of causes perhaps the prime one was the development of a subsidized Federal Theatre offering many of the movement's workers a livelihood, however meager, and also an opportunity to carry their ideals into an institution that bore the seeds of a full-grown national people's theatre. The assimilation of their objectives, to some extent, in the Federal project and, to a slighter degree, in the general theatre did away with the uniqueness of their stage for audiences that might have otherwise supported it. A temporary lifting of the heavier clouds of the Depression in 1936 disposed an increasing number of regular playgoers in favor of light entertainment. The suspension of *New Theatre* magazine (which became *New Theatre and Film* for the two last issues) deprived the movement of a valuable organ in the spring of 1937. Debts resulting from the bankruptcy of its commercial distributor undermined this publication at a time when the need for its influence was greater than ever, leaving *Theatre Workshop,* a technical, nonpolitical quarterly, as the sole publication of the New Theatre League. Support from sympathetic sources also declined; perhaps chiefly because other causes, like Spanish loyalism, were regarded as more immediate.

Intrinsic weaknesses also contributed to the recession. Although the movement afforded opportunities for young and talented directors, its collective ideals did not suffice to encourage the emergence of a directorial personality or magnetic *régisseur* sufficiently potent to create a solidly grounded one-act theatre. Theoretical hair splitting has always been the bane of a semipolitical movement; if the Irish theatre once suffered from such disadvantages, the New Theatre League's energies were even more decidedly depleted by them. Moreover, the emphasis upon economic struggles tended to produce monotony of treatment. It is perhaps not so curious that the libido should be able to endure countless regurgitations in the theatre while the repetition of social problems in unsublimated form should try the patience of audiences. Playgoers bring a variety of resistances to anything that does not titillate them. "Escapism," a much overworked charge, may be more inherent in the theatre than the movement could realize. It failed to sublimate much of its depressing and strident material. That there is an essential difference between escape and isolation is something the theatre of social purpose had yet to learn and apply. The weaknesses of this type of theatre were inherent in its strength, and once the physical energies and novelty of the movement suffered depletion, its shortcomings became apparent even to sympathizers.

At the same time, the recession was hardly an adequate reason for a funeral oration. It was difficult to believe that a theatre so rooted in contemporary realities could end in the morgue so long as those realities continued to exist. In fact, there was much evidence of continued activity and of some very respectable achievement after the 1935–36 peak. Preeminent was Marc Blitzstein's music drama *The Cradle Will Rock,* another New Theatre League prize-winner, which had a checkered history in the Federal Theatre until it was given special performances by the Mercury Theatre beginning on December 12, 1937, and set for a regular run by the commercial producer Sam H. Grisman on January 4, 1938. This long one-acter was promptly hailed as a major *tour de force* and considered the equal of practically anything discovered by the New Theatre League. The first half of 1937 also saw productions of Michael Blankfort's *The Brave and the Blind,* a moving drama of civil war in Spain, by the Rebels Arts Group and by the Current Theatre of New York.

Another impressive event was the appearance of William Kozlenko's indictment of unscrupulous utility corporations, *This Earth Is Ours,* produced by a New Theatre League group in February, 1937, to much acclaim, cited as one of the best one-act plays of 1937, and included in four general anthologies of short plays. Productions of this piece took place in Chicago, Pittsburgh, New Haven, Boston, London, Prague, and Melbourne. The nonpartisan *One-Act Play Magazine,* founded by Kozlenko in May, 1937, continued to reveal a number of respectable one-acters of social purpose, such as Percival Wilde's *Blood of the Martyrs,* a dramatization of Stephen Vincent Benét's antifascist short story, which should rank as one of the most gripping of contemporary one-acters, and Philip Stevenson's *Transit,* a dramatization of Albert Maltz's novelette *Season of Celebration,* which is even more deserving. Somewhat later, the New Theatre League revealed a touching and colorful short sit-down play, Ben Bengal's *Plant in the Sun,* and the Actors Repertory Company produced the earlier mentioned satirical skit, *A Town and Country Jig.*

Also significant was the progress made in the broadcasting field, largely owing to the interest of Irving Reis, former director of the Columbia Broadcasting Company's Workshop. Marc Blitzstein's *I've Got the Tune,* a radio music-drama, was an interesting accomplishment, and Archibald MacLeish's highly imaginative poetic drama, *The Fall of the City,* was universally regarded as the most significant event in radio theatre. In *The Fall of the City,* broadcast on April 11, 1937, the New Theatre movement, which supported this poet's first appearance in the theatre in *Panic* and found him one of its most ardent champions, could properly take credit for a short American masterpiece. A second MacLeish drama, *Air Raid,* dealing with the bombing and terrorization of towns like Guernica in the Spanish Civil War, was another in tense protest.

It is evident, then, that the aforementioned recession has not been followed by anything describable as *rigor mortis.* At the peak of the development it was possible for Sheldon Cheney, one of the fathers of the Little Theatre movement, to report that he "felt the surge of a new theatre life in the workers' theatres: that the leftist stage has afforded me, personally, the most poignant theatrical emotion born out of the clash of modern living that I have experienced." Turning to the older movement which he had sponsored, he mourned, perhaps a trifle exaggeratedly, "We were thinking of the theatre only on the esthetic side; thought to perfect it as a form of art expression . . . , not recognizing that there must be significant life-content—the play, and this in turn vibrating to the deepest life-consciousness of the audience."[4] As late as December, 1936, Archibald MacLeish could write: "No man who has had the experience of presenting plays first before Broadway audiences and thereafter before such audiences as the radical theatres would ever of his own choice return to the Broadway audience."

V

SOCIOLOGY AND PLAYWRITING

Ultimately, of course, the movement would have to be judged by the plays it left to posterity, as productions are too elusive to withstand the erosion of time and memory. Although it is impossible to consider all or even a large portion of the plays, the chronicler must give some brief consideration to the body of dramatic literature available to us. Misrepresentations and misunderstandings have, however, abounded in all considerations of this drama. Friends, as well as enemies, have laid down a smoke screen which must be dissipated before a just evaluation is possible.

The plays have frequently been referred to as brutally realistic. A blanket charge of unmitigated propaganda has also been their lot. They have also been referred to as an absolutely new phenomenon in the theatre. Like most generalizations, these are at best only partially true. The margin of error comes, in part, from the fact that art rarely toes the mark of a prescribed formula. Art has its own momentum, and the personality of the writer is highly individual even when it owes much to the general environment. The playwrights were individuals differing in temperament, politics, and social background. Not all of them were revolutionaries, and, strictly speaking, not many of them emanated from the working class. Even those who did could not always claim a patent of proletarian royalty, for nearly every artist in a variously stratified society embraces in his imagination, education, and taste the other classes. As a matter of fact, many of the playwrights were charter members of the middle class who may or may not have been temporarily in bad standing, though perhaps no more so than most artists from time immemorial. Man, being a mammal, is an umbilical-minded animal—which is perhaps all to the good, since art owes its depth and scope to the fact that it possesses a multifarious root system. Nevertheless, few of the playwrights could avoid acceptance of the principle of class conflict and of revolutionary philosophy.

[4] Sheldon Cheney, "The Art Theatre—Twenty Years After," *The New Caravan*, (New York: W. W. Norton, 1936), pp. 426–445.

Some of the plays were unmistakably revolutionary; others, like *Hymn to the Rising Sun,* were reformist. Still others were both. In describing them as a group, it is therefore perhaps nearer to the truth to call them "sociological" rather than "revolutionary" or even "left." They may be called "revolutionary" in a strict sense only in deference to their formative period. If they were revolutionary, in a wider sense, they were so because the abuses they described struck most of the leaders of the movement as remediable only by the inauguration of a new collective social order.

To say that the movement was unmitigatedly realistic is also an exaggeration. Omitting the early "agit-prop" forms, which were completely stylized and made scant use of realistic modes, we must still note that the expressionistic technique was apparent more or less in the flashbacks of *Waiting for Lefty* and in the warp and woof of *Bury the Dead. The Fall of the City* is altogether a feat of the imagination rather than of documentation and realistic development.

I would go further and claim considerable romanticism for many of the formally realistic pieces. Propaganda ("agit-prop") plays romanticized the worker, who was frequently a Bayard in overalls, while his capitalistic antagonist could trace his descent from the mustachioed Mephistos of early American melodrama, if not from *Die Räuber.* Greatly in favor for a time were conversion endings; Michael Blankfort referred to such pieces, whose object was to "show a worker or intellectual swing from a conservative position . . . to a militant class-position by the final curtain," as "pendulum plays."[5] Apologists for "pendulum plays" liked their conclusiveness and found them realistically justified by the fact that many workers and intellectuals did undergo conversion. In practice, however, the conversion was frequently effected too rapidly and unconvincingly in a short play. It looked like wish fulfillment, and stood suspiciously close to romantic hero-worship. Conversion endings, in fact, often made the play puerile, although they sometimes infused better-written pieces like *Waiting for Lefty* and *Bury the Dead* with poetic fire.

A cynic might even say that the entire movement, often so all-fired proud of its tough-minded realistic outlook, was cut from the cloth of romanticism. And if one holds that faith in human nature, in the possibilities of changing mankind for the better, is a major delusion, the cynic would be undoubtedly right. Short of such a view, however, one must allow the movement its claim to a modified realism, a realism with a purpose, sometimes described as "socialist realism." This is in fact the

[5] Michael Blankfort, "Facing the New Audience," *New Theatre* (November, 1934).

only sense in which the revolutionary one-acters could be freely regarded as a new phenomenon in American playwriting, since realism was nothing new on our stage.

What was the nature of this new realism? On the one hand, it shrank from nothing sordid, horrible, and painful. The horrors of poverty, of industrial conflicts, or life in the chain gang were set down with resolute fidelity. Still, they were not set down with an eye to sensationalism or simply for the record. They were intended to inculcate a lesson, agitate for the elimination of abuses, and indict a social order that tolerated them. They were not recorded pessimistically, but in the belief that society could be transformed, that in fact it was already being changed. They were set down in hope rather than in despair, and their ultimate object, though sometimes honored only in the breach, was to exhilarate. They aimed at the catharsis that comes with recognizing an evil and endeavoring to remove it. In every event, they saw symbols of a vast struggle between the owning classes and the workers, between the servants of injustice and justice, between *Ahriman* and *Ormuzd*. Theirs was the drama of dynamic processes affecting society and its individuals.

Not only was such a viewpoint relatively new in the American theatre, but it frequently expressed itself in new forms—new at least on the American stage. The earliest form, "agit-prop," was essentially an expression of conflict, in which the two sides were sharply and arbitrarily divided, the viewpoint was stated as baldly as possible, and the lesson was pressed home beyond all possibility of misunderstanding by means of caricature, insinuating rhythm, and broad acting, as well as verbally. The mass recitation, a secondary form, broke up a recitation into its dramatic components and underscored them by means of appropriate gesture and movement, using different voices for different characters or groups, in an effort to present a lesson as tellingly as possible.

When, later in its history, the movement turned to fully developed plays, these frequently retained "agit-prop" elements in solution. They were primed for a rousingly militant ending that frequently propelled the characters, as well as the audience, out of the immediate situation into the world of larger social conflicts. Thus, the strike situation of *Waiting for Lefty* is only a springboard to a call for action on all fronts for the overthrow of the old order and the creation of the new. Thus, the soldiers who come to life in *Bury the Dead* march out of the grave not merely because they have renounced imperialistic war but because they intend to set the world to rights—the world that cheated them as much back home as when it sent them to their death on the battlefield.

Technically, moreover, the plays tended to be inclusive and frequently even, as in the case of *Waiting for Lefty, The Tide Rises,* and *Bury the Dead,* kaleidoscopic. Although *Waiting for Lefty* deals primarily with the calling of a taxi strike, it is largely composed of vignettes describing an assortment of lives and a series of indictments of the social order in such varied fields as medicine, industrial chemistry, and the theatre. Although *Bury the Dead* has for its central situation the revolt of a group of soldiers against death it moves far afield in dramatizing their individual frustrations in society. *Till the Day I Die* alternates between scenes of the National Socialist terror and the underground movement in Germany. Despite extreme concentration, *Hymn to the Rising Sun* manages to bring Southern legislation within the compass of a chain-gang drama. *The Fall of the City* shifts its camera eye constantly in the effort to describe a mass drama. Even the less ambitious plays strove for scope and mass. The objectives of the movement expressed themselves technically in considerable extension of the one-act form. The one-acter became generally longer and more varied, favoring many scenes, the use of blackouts and flashbacks, and large casts. In this respect, the movement blazed new possibilities of expression in the short play.

VI

THE PLAYS

A descriptive account of the hundreds of short plays written between 1930 and 1937 would make a small volume. Fortunately this is not necessary, not merely because many of them would be thrown out of court by any discriminating judge, but because so many of them fall into a few convenient classifications. Trade unionism occupied the foreground of a great many of them; the most notable perhaps were *Waiting for Lefty, The Tide Rises, Plant in the Sun, The Crime,* and *I Take my Stand.* Militarism and war were the subjects of *Bury the Dead, Private Hicks, The Trumpets of Wrath* by Kozlenko, and a number of less distinguished pieces. Sharecroppers and the submerged farmer received attention in *His Jewels* (Bernice Kelly Harris), *This Earth Is Ours, Mighty Wind A'Blowing* (Alice Holdship Ware), *Daughter,* and *Can You Hear Their Voices?* Problems of the Negro race were treated by several of the aforementioned plays and by *Trouble with the Angels.* Poverty and city life found expression in Virgil Geddes' *In the Tradition,* A. B. Shiffrin's *Kids Learn Fast* and *Return at Sunset,* and Stevenson's *Transit.* Fascism was excoriated in *Till the Day I Die, The Fall of the City, The Brave and the Blind,* and *Blood of the Martyrs.* Sundry abuses filled other plays and served as secondary motifs in a number of the aforementioned one-acters.

A considerable percentage of the play crop was, as noted, rank and worthless, which is perhaps no great indictment of the movement when we consider the mortality rate on Broadway. Many of the playwrights were unskilled, and their philosophy of art was too sophomoric to promote good work. Gradually, however, some of them grew in power and their ranks were augmented by respectable and in a few instances superlative talents.

The gifts of satire and humor were underdeveloped in them at first, perhaps because few of the playwrights were disposed to find anything amusing in the world about them. But the blanket charge that the movement lacked humor is a rank libel. One of the first to disprove the indictment was Philip Stevenson, whose *God's in His Heaven* and the more fully rounded *What It Takes* satirized the complacencies of average Americans. The last-mentioned play, in particular, revealed a fine feeling for characterization and wry pathos. Another play of his, *You Can't Change Human Nature,* owed much of its power to its humorous treatment of fence-straddling elements in the American Revolution. Particularly apt seemed his parallels between 1776 and 1936, and especially pointed was the implication that the American fathers had been revolutionists. Later, in dramatizing Albert Maltz's novelette, Stevenson also uncovered a talent for stark realism rarely associated with a humorist; *Transit* is a profoundly moving transcription of life among society's outcasts that comes close to the spirit of Gorky's *The Lower Depths.*

Stevenson's comrade in arms was A. B. Shiffrin, who moved from a brutal exposure of slum life in *Kids Learn Fast,* a play in which a number of white children lynch a Negro boy in jest, to one of the most amusing comedies of the movement, *Return at Sunset.* How poverty grinds the faces of the poor into the dust is not a naturally entertaining subject. Shiffrin makes it both entertaining and moving in his rather diffuse one-acter by virtue of some keen observation of shanty-Jewish life, by the accumulation of tragicomic errors which approach the fantastic. Pithy folk humor studs its family scene in which the paterfamilias loses his horse, the son gets a broken head for listening to a street-corner speaker, and the daughter leaves a position because her employer has made advances to her. A real jewel of a humorist is Wassermann, the boarder, who had a nervous stomach and was told to go to a farm. "So what happened? I got sick. I had to go back to the city again. I couldn't stand the fresh air." He tried to join the army, when his trade was eliminated, but he was rejected. "I wasn't healthy enough for them. To get killed in a war you first got to be healthy."

In time, too, there appeared considerable talent for musical comedy and the composition of satiric skits dear to our musical revues. One of the earliest examples was the collection of sketches by Paul Peters, George Sklar, Alan Baxter, Frank Gabrielson, and David Lesan in the Theatre Guild's ill-fated revue, *Parade*. Harold J. Rome, who composed most of the skits, lyrics, and music for the highly entertaining Labor Stage revue *Pins and Needles,* is an impressive craftsman in the musical comedy form.

A curious, mordant type of humor also makes itself felt in some of the work of Virgil Geddes, whose *Native Ground* is no criterion of the range of his talents. A macabre and savage humor pervades *In the Tradition,* which dramatizes the economic plight of an undertaker—almost unbearably for some tastes. A bizarre feeling for the tragicomedy of human relationships in *I Have Seen Myself Before* underscores the same character's search for a job.

The undisputed master of them all in a satiric vein is, however, Marc Blitzstein, who uses the resources of both music and drama to send his points home. *I've Got the Tune,* his radio play, produces incisive and bitter effects with the device of propelling a composer who has the tune out into the world to look for the words; he finds them at last after surveying the social scene. *The Cradle Will Rock,* a rich satire on respectability and an excoriation of the professional men and artists who sell their souls to Mammon, proved a major event in the season of 1937–38. Blitzstein has a biting feeling for lines and music; he is a caricaturist who transmutes the clichés of the old agit-prop into artistry. In a more realistic genre he is equalled only by George O'Neil, whose third one-acter in *American Dream,* entitled *1933,* is a vigorous satire on the decadence of upper-class society. Though it ends tragically, with the suicide of the last of the Pengree dynasty, its force resides in its vitriolic treatment of social parasites and futilitarians.

Less abundant than humor is, as a matter of fact, imaginative drama, the relative absence of which is, however, characteristic of our entire theatre. Moreover, the movement did produce two of the rare imaginative works of the thirties, against which we can set only one example from the full-length nonpolitical stage—namely, Anderson's *High Tor.* Irwin Shaw's *Bury the Dead* possesses pathos and indignation in its diatribe against war and frustration; much of its uniqueness resides in its fantasy of dead soldiers coming to life, an idea used before in the Theatre Guild's *Miracle at Verdun* but expressed by Shaw more dynamically and with a spare economy which guards against operatic fireworks. MacLeish's

The Fall of the City went even further in its claim upon the imagination with its use of mass effects and adaptation to the demands of the non-visual medium of radio drama. That so distinguished a poet should have added the imaginative qualities of the most forceful verse written for the American theatre goes without saying. In comparison with MacLeish's poetry, most of Maxwell Anderson's sounds epigonal, an echo from the past. The theme, within the small compass of a thirty-minute play, is epic.

> The city of masterless men
> Will take a master,

When the dictator before whom the populace bends in adoration and submission appears,

> The helmet is hollow!
> The metal is empty! The armor is empty! . . .
> The push of a stiff pole at the nipple would topple it.

But,

> . . . they don't see! They lie on the paving. They lie in
> Burnt spears: the ashes of arrows. They lie there.
> They don't see or they won't see. They are silent. . . .
> The city of masterless men has found a master!
> The city has fallen!
> The city has fallen!

Confronted with the uncanny power of imaginative drama, however, realism has no reason to turn away abashed when it is deeply and excitingly realized. The bulk of the plays were realistic, and although many of them were pedestrian, their militancy stood them in good stead, ensuring them excitement and vigor. The least successful plays were naturally those which lacked these attributes. Folk drama like Alice Holdship Ware's *Mighty Wind A'Blowing* and Bernice Kelly Harris's *His Jewels* is distinguished in dialogue and native characterization. In the first, the rapprochement between Negro and white sharecroppers is treated with verisimilitude and charm. *His Jewels* possesses an unusual central situation—the eviction of a sharecropper and his daughters from the church in which they have sought shelter—which lends itself to much pathos and irony. The Siftons' *Give All Thy Terrors to the Wind* is an admirably rounded drama of a ship disaster caused by the greed of the shipping interests. Michael Blankfort, one of the leaders of the Theatre Union, contributed a searching, if somewhat static, study of a vacillating but honest labor organizer in a flavorsome long one-acter, *The Crime*. His drama of the siege of the Alcazar or some similar fortress in the

Spanish civil war, *The Brave and the Blind,* is likewise distinguished by its just appraisal of men and their motives. Although it is characteristic of Blankfort that his psychological insight and molding of character are not always equaled by his dramatic feeling, his work possesses rare persuasiveness. William Kozlenko, another exponent of the long one-act form, shows a stronger feeling for drama with very much the same talent for characterization in *This Earth Is Ours.* The persecution of an obdurate farmer by a power company that wants the right of way for its lines makes an affecting short play, one of the strongest in the movement's realistic repertory. Finally, there are the three acknowledged masterpieces *Waiting for Lefty, Till the Day I Die,* and *Hymn to the Rising Sun.*

The first mentioned remains the most exciting of the trio. A panoramic study of suffering and injustice in society, it draws its lines together in a terrific onslaught on the whole social fabric and fulfills Odets' requirement that "art must be about something. It must be hot and spiteful." Anybody, however, can be hot and spiteful. In *Waiting for Lefty* Odets revealed an uncanny sense of showmanship, which is not so easily encompassed. Three strike scenes, well placed at the beginning, center, and conclusion of the play, provide an exciting framework for flashbacks into the lives of the strike committee, each of which forms a brief history of a man driven to militant action by poverty, frustration, and injustices covering a wide range of abuses. Suspense is the keynote of the play from the moment it begins in the hall where a strike vote is being taken. It is resolved at the end when we learn that the leader of the militant faction has been murdered, presumably by the racketeer who runs the union for his own profit. Dialogue of rare vigor, sensitively attuned to living speech, flavors the drama and reflects its drive. The passions are involved in the struggle against the racketeer, who is imaginatively treated in successive scenes as an incarnation of predatory society. Pathos is distilled from several pictures of suffering and humiliation. Occasional lapses into sophomoric or cheap dialogue and some exaggerated stridency vitiate the little drama but do not destroy its total effect, which is pure theatre. Even those who disagree with its viewpoint must pay tribute to its power. If *Waiting for Lefty* did not leave one with reservations regarding the easy way in which it sees only one aspect of human experience, it could be unhesitatingly set down as a little masterpiece of the theatre.

This playwright's second short play, *Till the Day I Die,* uses a plummet that sinks deeper into human drama and contains an even more affecting theme, compounded of pity and terror, in the tale of a German revolutionist who asked his brother to kill him before he revealed the secrets of his party and betrayed his comrades under torture. It overreaches itself in its satirization of the fascist tormentors, suffers from some arbitrary theatricalism, and some of its details ring untrue. But for all its unevenness, *Till the Day I Die* compresses its ardors and endurances into something very close to a masterpiece. It is "hot and spiteful" in a finer sense than these words would indicate; it is heroic. In both plays Odets, who loves music passionately, is a symphonic artist, with a fine mastery of crescendo and decrescendo, of the development and weaving of themes, and of climactic force. They are youthful works, and their flaws could only become more conspicuous when their author turned to full-length drama. But without the *élan* of young manhood, which found inspiration in the revolutionary leaven of the movement, they could not have been written.

For maturity we must turn to the last of the trio of realistic master-pieces, Paul Green's *Hymn to the Rising Sun.* In anguish and irony there is perhaps no short play in the theatre's treasury to excel this masterly description of chain-gang horrors,—which take place on Independence Day! Dedicated to "Tom Thumb, the brave legislator who, in the con-fines of the little black bag, declaims of liberty," *Hymn to the Rising Sun* is a lambent protest against a long-standing blot on the American scutch-eon. To wish to erase it, it is not necessary to accept the First, Third, or Fourth International, it is necessary only to be human. It is the distinction of the play that it abates nothing of its proper indignation and yet meets its audience on the lowest common denominator of humanity. This beau-tifully compressed and poignant work may serve as a fitting conclusion to the survey of a movement that began as partisan agitation and ended as art.[6]

[6] Most of the material in this chapter is based on information contained in *Workers Theatre, New Theatre,* and *New Theatre and Film.* Two pamphlets, *Audience Organization,* edited by Mark Marvin, and *Censored,* by Richard Pack and Mark Marvin, contain helpful information. For other aid, the author wishes to express his gratitude to: Emanuel Eisenberg, press representative of the Group Theatre, John O'Shaughnessy, of the Actors Repertory Company, Ben Irwin and Mark Marvin, of the New York Theatre League.

■

POLITICS AND THEATRE*

Since *Drama Was a Weapon* is a thoroughly scholarly work, it is sufficient unto itself. It presents the self-contained thesis that the communist movement of the 1930's endeavored but failed to win control of the American theatre. Morgan Himelstein, the author of this work, argues cogently and documents his contentions so well that he does not need the support of any "on-the-spot" observer like myself. But it is one of the merits of this study that it propels the reader into areas of interest adjacent to the author's central argument, and the more one enters these the more one arrives at a just picture of an exciting period in the theatre. Mr. Himelstein is himself quite aware of the total reality of what was the theatre of the thirties, for he supplies much detailed data on the subject. The larger the base of his investigation, however, the more provocatively he invites me into considerations into which he himself cannot deviate without blunting the edge of his argument.

It is important to realize that the leftism of the theatre of the period was many things at the same time, if it was not indeed many different things to many different people. Depending upon the way one looked at it, it was Marxist and non-Marxist, foreign to American culture and native, large in compass and small, influential and uninfluential, productive and sterile. It started with the economic depression or it started long before. It ended with the end of the Depression and the start of World War II or it never died. Something can be said for each of these contentions, and the continuity of creative work by graduates of the social theatre (Odets, Hellman, Kingsley, MacLeish, Blitzstein, Kazan, Clurman, Bobbie Lewis, Cheryl Crawford, Strasberg, and others) and the influence on Williams, Miller, and others in the next two decades should certainly make one hesitate to write *finis* to a chapter on the thirties without some qualifications. One may, finally, consider the esthetic problems highlighted, although hardly resolved, by the leftist theatre movement. Where, for example, does propaganda start or stop in a dramatic work? And how is it to be served best? By fiat or example, directly or indirectly, with dramatic realism or with nonrealistic stylization? Debate raged over these and related questions, and over the question of whether politics was swallowing up esthetics or esthetics was undercutting politics. Patently, there

* Introduction to *Drama Was a Weapon,* by Morgan Himelstein (New Brunswick: Rutgers University Press, 1963).

448

is sufficient material here for a supplementary book on the period's socially oriented theatre. But while a necessarily brief Introduction is not a substitute for such a book, it can perhaps suggest the further range of the subject brought to our attention by Mr. Himelstein's study.

For one thing, it is to be observed that the social orientation of our theatre goes back a long while. The American stage was consciously political and social virtually from the beginnings of the Republic when the Tories and the Revolutionists exchanged insults in their amateur stage productions. Then ensued the considerable vogue of comedies like *The Contrast* and *Fashion,* favorable to our frontier virtues and democratic ideals. In the middle of the nineteenth century, abolitionism found its greatest popular expression in an immensely successful stage dramatization of *Uncle Tom's Cabin;* and when the late-nineteenth and early-twentieth-century period of social reform set in, there was no lack of dramatic writing about the issues of the day in workmanlike exercises such as Steele MacKaye's labor play *Paul Kauvar,* or *Anarchy,* Charles Klein's antitrust drama *The Lion and the Mouse,* and Sheldon's *Salvation Nell, The Nigger,* and *The Boss.* In the theatre of the prosperous 1920's, the light-minded comedies of Kaufman and his collaborators riddled our mass culture with laughter, while a heavier assault was launched by O'Neill, George Kelly, Elmer Rice, Paul Green, and a New Playwrights' Company that included Mike Gold, John Howard Lawson, and John Dos Passos. The socially slanted theatre of the thirties had a long background of journalistic topicality and democratic sentiment, although both friends and foes tended to overlook this fact, the friends acclaiming leftist social drama as a whole Marxist invention while the foes called it an alien abomination. Only a special species of plays and productions could be designated as "leftist" in any precise sense. But they were influential for a time and could be distinguished from other plays because their authors implemented their social sympathies with revolutionary Marxist visions of the overthrow of the capitalistic system in the course of an apocalytic "final" conflict between capital and labor.

That this point of view made only a small dent in our theatre is well established by Mr. Himelstein. Yet the label of "leftism" got attached to the entire serious-minded stage in America, which even included the work of such strongly anticommunist authors as the late Maxwell Anderson. And the label of "leftism" was not used pejoratively, as it came to be used in the 1950's, but in a vaguely complimentary sense by proponents of liberalism and radicalism. "Leftism," for them, was the banner under which one fought *against* fascism and Naziism and *for* human decency, justice, and social reforms soon to be incorporated in the law of the land without commitment to the overthrow of capitalism and the establishment of a "dictatorship of the proletariat." Men of good will, and I venture to say, sound (if politically limited) intelligence ranged themselves around this banner, and what they had in common may be lumped together as a sentiment, or a collection of sentiments, important politically because sentiments affect politics, and important *theatrically* since feelings and attitudes are of the essence in the theatre.

A moderate optimism, consisting of a belief that social evil could be destroyed, injustices eliminated, inequities eradicated, humanity saved, and the "good society" erected, was shared by all contributors to leftist theatre. There can be no doubt, of course, that communist leaders endorsed this view and fostered it, with expected, perhaps even calculated, advantages to their cause. But if this optimism was derived in the case of Marxist bellwethers from the gospel of dialectical materialism, it came, in the main, from distinctly different sources to the majority of the theatre's liberals and radicals. It came from the sanguine American temperament, from native movements of reform, from the spacious tradition of the frontier, and, ultimately no doubt, from the eighteenth-century liberal Enlightenment that had sustained American life from the very beginnings of the Republic. The history of the country was viewed as a sustained struggle between materialism and idealism, specifically between vested property interests defended by Hamiltonian conservatives and the democratic spirit championed by Jeffersonian liberals, Jacksonian frontier egalitarians, and Emersonian moralists or mystics. The native roots of this liberalism and radicalism were everywhere apparent. I, personally, never encountered so many people in the theatre with populist, frontier, "hobo," or rustic backgrounds before or after the thirties. (Both the leader of the militant New Theatre League in the mid-thirties and the editor of *New Theatre* magazine were recent arrivals from Davenport, Iowa; and some of the most politically articulate and active performers were corn-fed confederates.) Finally, I should not like to underestimate the very simple factor that optimism was also the other side of despair and the alternative to a passiveness disgraced by the appeasement policies of the governments. A great fear of social acedia, of evading or having evaded, one's social responsibility, pervaded the world of the artist and the intellectual as the depression grew deeper and the fortunes of fascism in Italy, Spain, and Germany rose higher. The one thing the artist and the intellectual feared most from an embattled leftist critic was the charge of "escapism" frequently thundered at them from the doctrinaire left. Engagement to a cause became a guilt-enforced virtue which was to lead to some kind of activism such as signing a petition or a protest, marching in a parade, and writing a story, poem, or play of so-called social consciousness. Thus *enthusiasm,* an important factor in the practice of the arts, became a ferment in the depressed 1930's just as depression concerning humanity's condition and prospects became *de rigeur* for the intelligentsia of the prosperous 1950's. Some of the most effective plays and stage productions of the thirties were inspired by confidence and enthusiasm, just as some of the most impressive works after 1950 were sparked by disillusion. A veritable longing for heroism or the heroic gesture was apparent in circles which in the blasé 1920's would have brazened things out a modish skepticism and diffidence. The generation of the thirties were determined to avoid the opprobrium of having it said of them, as Eliot said of the previous slothful generation, that

> . . . Here were decent godless people,
> Their only monument the asphalt road
> And a thousand lost golf-balls.

This is not to say, of course, that communism did not exist in the thirties and make converts among the neophytes of the stage, or that Marxism did not exert an influence on the leftist theatre of the thirties. But the uninitiated majority of playwrights, actors, producers, and directors manifested the aforementioned larger and less definable promptings. Even when they adopted the political catchwords of the period, the heart and mind of the artist belonged not to a "Party" but to the human race. If Marxism was an element in the more or less uncommitted thinking of the sympathizers of the left, it was frequently parroted rather than understood by them; had its implications been grasped, Marxism would have frightened them off perhaps almost as much as fascism did. Marxist theory was just one more attractive piece of driftwood afloat in the current of fashionable intellectualism, along with amateur Freudianism and hazy, antibourgeois romanticism.

It was, in fact, this inchoate radicalism that infuriated communist spokesmen and led them to charge the playwrights with the cardinal sin of "confusion." What troubled them most was the "political unreliability" of men of good will and democratic sentiment who contributed most of the dramatic substance of the theatre of the thirties. These writers and artists rarely offered any effective intellectual defense against such accusations, but they had a built-in defense, so to speak, in their "innocence"; for they could create only as their talents, temperament, and conditioning dictated. They couldn't have followed blueprints from Union Square headquarters successfully even if they had thought they should do so in a time of social crisis. S. N. Behrman was self-consciously moved to offer an apologia in *No Time for Comedy* when he showed a successful writer of comedies allowing himself to be talked into writing weighty dramas such as the age presumably demanded, but returning to the craft of comedy after badly fumbling as a would-be writer of "serious" plays.

I must not, for that matter, be too moderate in my qualifications of leftism lest we overestimate the orthodoxy of the talented young who actually tried to adhere to Marxist doctrine or to some segment of a "Party Line." Their deepest desire was to relate their work to the tensions and aspirations of their times, and however public these may have been on the surface, their protests and hopes were personally rooted and usually private. Not the least of their motivations, besides, was a search for stability in a period of uncertainty veering toward chaos, for a means of overcoming their sense of frustration and isolation in a society in which the need for artistic fulfillment seemed inconsequential beside simple economic necessity, and for giving meaning and a sense of direction to their lives. If they lashed out at existing society with some ferocity, they did not—and by temperament probably *could not*—launch a planned assault. "Society" was often an abstraction in their work, and it was the very last thing they actually saw and knew; they were apt to confuse it indeed with their close relatives and neighbors whom they knew a great deal better than they knew the so-called System. Nothing, I believe, is more ridiculous than to envision them as the well-trained, cool, and consistent cadres of "the revolution." Their worst vice (and perhaps also greatest virtue) from a detached point of view was an excess of zeal, just as the chief vice of the later cold-war generation was an excess of caution.

Except for the ending artificially grafted on *Awake and Sing,* Odets' first and best full-length play was a strongly localized family drama replete with lower-middle-class manners and sensibilities. If vaguely stirring in the final version of that work was the notion that the family is the breeding ground of rebels against the capitalist world, it was the plenitude of pathetic and humorous and slightly bizarre characters and life situations rather than Marxist ideology that made *Awake and Sing* an appealing drama and drew attention to the author's talent. If the ideological content of the same young author's *Waiting for Lefty* was based on the Marxist prescript that labor strikes should be viewed as "dress rehearsals" for the revolution, it was certainly no such idea but the overall dramatic rhythm and imaginative dramaturgy of the play and the vibrancy of life in its individual episodes that distinguished this one-acter from the routine propaganda-pieces of the political left. It was not the author's fleeting membership in a communist cell tucked away in the Group Theatre but personal associations, attachments and rejections that gave life to the work.

It is doubtful that a single play for which one could claim some modicum of life was significantly a demonstration of ideology, or was exempt from criticism by the communist press. Only the nondramatists who invaded the theatre with propagandist designs upon it hewed to a straight line, and the greater the propaganda the less the effect except on a small politically minded and preconvinced coterie.

If the drama was expected to be a "weapon," its edge was soon blunted when realistic plays with dimensioned characters displaced the original leftist plays. Short hortatory pieces, called "agit-prop," these plays lost their vogue early in the thirties because of their transparent crudity. The blunting must have come, in part, from what I shall call the blessed confusedness of writers which prevented them from following a Party line in any work dealing with human beings rather than with mere puppets. Once characterization and individual motivation became important, as they were bound to do in realistic playwriting, discrepancies between apparent intention and actual execution began to appear—often to the advantage, rather than the disadvantage, of the individual play. Propagandist clarity became supplanted or obfuscated by humanity. Thus, working-class characters were no longer simon-pure heroes nobly ranged against capitalist villains; *Waiting for Lefty* even had a couple of proletarian villains, a corrupt labor leader and his stooge. Conversely, middle-aged characters could be made sympathetic and diversified human beings, as in the case of an entire family in *Paradise Lost* and the dentist-hero in *Rocket to the Moon*. From these plays and the earlier *Awake and Sing,* it was abundantly evident that their author, Clifford Odets, the white hope of the thirties and of the left-wing theatre, was a middle-class, rather than "proletarian," writer. He was perhaps the most authentic American author of *drame-bourgeois,* a form of literature advocated nearly two centuries before by the eighteenth-century philosopher Diderot.

Leftist orthodoxy required "conversion endings" for plays; that is, the principal characters were expected to acquire awareness of the class struggle and to actively participate in it. Action carrying the characters of a play from a state of ignorance to recognition or knowledge (Aristotle's dramatic element of *anagnorisis*) has been considered an honorable and effective mode of progression ever since the age of Sophocles; it is described in Aristotle's *Poetics* as a highly desirable plot element. But the brisk conversions of "agit-prop" drama became discredited. The conversion element either vanished in leftist drama altogether (there is no conversion, for example, in *Golden Boy*) or was fumbled when appended to plays of private life written with predominantly realistic observation. Thus, the boy-hero of Odets' first full-length play, called *I've Got the*

Blues before it acquired a "positive" conversion ending under the title of
Awake and Sing, decides to ask for "steam-heat" in the factory, and his
sister, the heroine of this drama, is converted to love without benefit of
clergy when she runs away from her husband and child with the family's
star boarder! It is a wonder that orthodox leftist critics did not rise up
in arms and accuse the author of having perpetrated a travesty. So far as
I know, they did not; though I would judge from their press notices that
they felt somewhat embarrassed.

One tendency that did not greatly abate during the period was that
of attributing individual failure to society ("the System") rather than to
character, probably because social determinism had had a vogue in literature ever since Taine and Zola. But the most flagrant tendencies to refer
every private distress to social causation were modified. The character had
to bear at least part of the responsibility for failure because the decisions
were his own, as when the violin-playing prizefighter Joe Bonaparte, in
Golden Boy, abandoned the fiddle for the fist. In one way or another,
even the doctrinarism of the rebellious young writers, the hard core of the
leftist theatre, underwent considerable softening. So far as absolutist Marxist drama is concerned, it remained pretty much a formula in an unwritten handbook once creativity rather than creed asserted itself on the
professional stage.

The decade proved far more fruitful than one could have expected
from the deepening of the economic depression, the unresisted spread of
fascism, the imminence of a second war, and the profusion of poor dramatic criticism—flabbily impressionistic on the right and dogmatic, almost
formulaic, on the left. To the theatre of the thirties, notably augmented
by non-leftist producers (such as The Theatre Guild, Guthrie McClintic,
and Gilbert Miller) and playwrights (O'Neill, Wilder, Barry, Behrman,
Anderson, Sherwood, Saroyan, and Sidney Howard), social fervor and
compassion gave an indisputable vitality found nowhere else in the world
during the decade—a vitality thus far not yet recovered in some twenty
New York seasons. This was, moreover, the case with noteworthy variety,
with considerable use of both realism and imaginative stylization, and
with advances in several genres. The social ferment of the decade leavened
quite a number of the period's and the nation's most effective comedies,
such as *The Male Animal* and Lillian Hellman's "dark comedy" *The Little Foxes;* poetic plays such as *Winterset* and *High Tor;* biographies, notably *Abe Lincoln in Illinois;* and works of social realism embracing
group drama (*The Time of Your Life*), satirical protest (Sherwood's
Idiot's Delight), sociological studies (*Dead End*), and documentary works
such as the celebrated Living Newspapers *Power* and *One-third-of-a-na-*

tion. Since the period, moreover, placed no interdict on plays of such general interest as *Mourning Becomes Electra, Our Town, The Man Who Came to Dinner,* and *Life with Father,* it cannot be argued that the social drama overran the theatre and stifled all other growth. A proper understanding of its complex character can win considerable respect for the theatre of the thirties. To that understanding, Mr. Himelstein's book brings objectively accumulated data and an historical account that students of both social history and theatre will no doubt find enlightening.

SOCIAL REALISM AND
IMAGINATIVE THEATRE*

It has long been customary to deal with the social theatre of the 1930's in terms of explicit content; I shall deal with it in terms of theatrical style.

The first point that needs to be made is that realism was not a discovery of the social theatre of the 1930's. Both as an ideal and as a practice, realism was strongly in evidence in the 1920's, if not indeed in the successful Belascoism of earlier decades. The producer-director Arthur Hopkins, whose Shakespearian productions in association with his distinguished designer Robert Edmond Jones were notably symbolistic, had perhaps his greatest success with his naturalistic production of *What Price Glory?* in 1924. The nascent Theatre Guild, which was about to collapse after its initial production in 1919 of Benavente's symbolist *commedia dell'arte, The Bonds of Interest,* was launched upon a successful career with its next, ultrarealistic, production of St. John Ervine's *John Ferguson.*

It is also significant that the Group Theatre, with whose career we associate the socially directed realism of the 1930's, was born in the bosom of the Theatre Guild. Actually, the break between the two organizations in the 1930–31 period has been exaggerated. One fact has been public knowledge ever since 1945 when Harold Clurman published an important acknowledgment of indebtedness in *The Fervent Years.* The infant Group had wanted the Theatre Guild to subsidize it as a so-called Studio. Harold Clurman reports as follows: "When Cheryl Crawford asked the [Theatre Guild] board to release a play they held an option on—Paul Green's *The House of Connelly*—they were prompt to do so. More than that, they allowed us to engage Franchot Tone and Morris Carnovsky, who were then under contract to them, and they added the gift of a thousand dollars toward our expenses in rehearsing the play that summer."[1]

It is less well known that several years later, even after succeeding with its notably realistic production of Sidney Kingsley's *Men in White,* a director of the Group Theatre submitted Clifford Odets's *Awake and*

---

* From *Theatre Survey,* 1962. Reprinted in *Theatre and Drama in the Making,* by Gassner and Allen (Boston: Houghton Mifflin Co., 1964), pp. 992–1007.

[1] Harold Clurman, *The Fervent Years* (New York: Alfred A. Knopf, 1945), p. 36.

Sing, then (in 1934) still titled *I Got the Blues,* to the Theatre Guild for production.[2] It was not felt by those who knew the Theatre Guild intimately that realistic productions were the exclusive province of the "social theatre" vanguard of the 1930's. Weren't there, however, distinctions between the realistic style of the twenties and the thirties? Naturally, the friends and associates of the social theatre of the thirties liked to think so, and they were not altogether mistaken. There can be no doubt that there was greater militancy in the new plays of social protest. Even in domestic dramas, such as *Awake and Sing,* the emphasis was on economic pressures or on the effects of economic insecurity on little people. As for the stage productions, some differences can certainly be noted.

On the one hand, there was the predominantly psychological realism of Group Theatre productions, representative of so-called inner realism for which no other theatrical organization of the 1930's, no matter how earnestly "social" in philosophy or sociological in interest, showed any consistent aptitude. The Group's aptitude was the result of a happy coincidence of talent and training. On the other hand, there was the nonpsychological style of realism of *propaganda.* A characteristic outwardly-directed production such as the Theatre Union's *Stevedore* might be described as rapid-fire realism specially suited to themes of social rather than psychological conflict. As a rule, the only inner conflict pinpointed by the productions and projected by individual performers, was apt to be one of divided loyalties. In *Stevedore,* both the cast and the audience were whipped into a frenzy by the physical encounter between Negro stevedores and armed company hirelings which reached a dramatic as well as ideological climax when the hitherto temporizing white workers joined their Negro fellow-workers. This brought the house down on the opening night, for the audience did its part on this occasion at the former headquarters of the Civic Repertory Theatre on West Fourteenth Street.

It remains to be added that scenic design also contributed a sense of mobility and conflict through effective arrangements of space. The Theatre Union's *Stevedore* was one of a number of productions of the thirties in which, despite an abundance of realistic detail in costuming, furniture, and sets, space was organized and action was localized dynamically in relation to the social conflict rather than as a mere effort to photograph an

---

[2] The play was turned down by me as the Guild's playreader because the version I read (it lacked the "Awake and Sing" theme and conclusion) struck me as depressing and maudlin. It is my impression that Miss Theresa Helburn, the Guild's executive director, had a similar reaction, for it was she who officially returned the play to the Group.

environment, as in the 1929 production of Elmer Rice's *Street Scene* with its impressive but static tenement façade. In the *Stevedore* production one was aware of locations for action rather than of an environment *per se;* the sets comprised areas for planning action, arguing, and fighting rather than for private living. The master of this type of dynamic realism was Mordecai Gorelik, who designed memorable settings for both the Group Theatre and the Theatre Union and who had previously, in 1925, created the stunning theatricalist setting for the Theatre Guild production of John Howard Lawson's jazz vaudeville of American life, *Processional.* He has described some of his procedures and given us indications of his thinking in the chapter he contributed to *Producing the Play.*[3]

In an early essay called "Scenery: The Visual Machine,"[4] Gorelik summarized the principles underlying this style of dynamic realism rather simply but tellingly. The designer, he wrote, should "seek out the basic conflict around which the action revolves"; and he should analyze it, scene by scene, in order to make sure "that in each scene some separate phase of the struggle comes to the foreground." While warning against "the cult of abstract symbolism," which he deplored as "vague, unhistorical and meaningless," he wanted the setting to become symbolic of the play. And his description of the scenic idea to be arrived at as "the designer's conception of the battleground," a term he uses twice in the same paragraph, is perhaps the best definition of dynamic realism in the social theatre of the 1930's. Life was not conceived as an unchallenged status quo, as in passive realism or as a mystical or desperate stasis, as we find it in the turn-of-the-century plays of Maeterlinck or, for that matter, in the plays of Beckett, Pinter, and other playwrights of the present-day *avant-garde.* It is, rather, life conceived as a battleground—and a battleground on which battles could be *won*—that sparked the dynamic realism of the period under review.

It is, finally, on those grounds chiefly that critics of productions by politically neutral producers took their stand. Thus, even the Theatre Guild's production of *They Shall Not Die,* in which the Scottsboro case lawyer delivers a fiery harangue at the end, was criticized as being too bland, too detached, and essentially too passive in view of the explosive character of the subject matter. An uncommissioned setting designed by Gorelik contrasted sharply with the Theatre Guild's setting by Lee Simonson; Gorelik's evoked a struggle over the Scottsboro case that involved the outside world in visual images and in possibilities of movement,

---

[3] "Designing the Play," *Producing the Play* by John Gassner (New York: Dryden Press, 1941, 1953), pp. 301–52.
[4] In *New Theatre* (January, 1934), 9–10.

whereas the Guild's setting concentrated on the Negro youths who were being tried on trumped-up charges, on the patently witless Southern white jury that was going to convict them, and on the judge, the prosecutor, and attorney for the defense. The treatment closed in on the private persons involved in the drama. The dynamic realism envisioned in Gorelik's plan concentrated on the forces involved in the case. The Guild located the play in a specific sector of the South. Mr. Gorelik wanted to locate it in the world at large, wherever injustice and oppression prevailed or was denounced.

A comparison of the Gorelik and the Simonson courtroom settings for *They Shall Not Die* can be conclusive. The Simonson set for the Theatre Guild production is a simple realistic one and is on a single level except for the elevation of the judge's seat or dais and the witnesses' chair. The Gorelik design is animated and agitated. It is crowded with busy figures distributed on two levels connected by a staircase with a backdrop providing a third level projecting crowd scenes in unidentified cities with the figure of the Goddess of Justice holding the traditional scales in the center and with signs at one side featuring slogans. The caption under the *New Theatre* reproduction reads as follows:

> This design projects the play by John Wexley frankly as a propagandist medium. Making no effort to appear "impartial," it places the bullying prosecutor and terrorized witnesses directly below a silhouette of abstract justice. Above this silhouette is a space in which is mirrored by means of projected photographs, the ever-widening impact of the Scottsboro case upon the masses of the American people. Instead of working inward toward an introspective mood of passive sympathy, the design explodes toward panoramic facts and the need for public action.

The review of the Theatre Guild's production which appeared in the April, 1934, issue of *New Theatre* magazine (pp. 18–19) complimented the Guild for doing "a courageous thing, from the commercial viewpoint, to stage the play at all" and for producing it handsomely. But the reviewer, Ben Blake, complained that the Guild gave a revolutionary play the same kind of treatment, stylistically, that it gives to a drawing-room comedy or a *Strange Interlude:* " 'Realism,' the production board, with Philip Moeller directing, decided. And to them realism means literal faithfulness in the representation of characters, locale, tempo, and so forth." The reviewer called for an entirely different production such as Piscator would have provided. Such a production, the reviewer concluded, "would have abounded in dynamically staged clashes. The action would have shifted rapidly from locale to locale on sets with several playing levels, with rapid mass actions on the upper ones, alternating with the action below in the courtroom."

I do not intend to cast doubt on the integrity of Philip Moeller's Theatre Guild production—the realism was actually too much for some of the Guild's subscribers, who staggered out of the theatre after the first scene. My object in calling attention to contrasting approaches of realism is merely an attempt to differentiate between two applications or interpretations of realism. The dynamic realism I have outlined here—and its vivacity is a quality that defies description by generalization—carries us, moreover, *beyond realism,* too.

The fact is that the social theatre of the thirties was fundamentally ambivalent toward realism and settled for it chiefly because it simply worked out better as a rule, on the American stage, because it could be glorified as both propaganda *and* art, and, not least, because it could be modified when necessary or fused with nonrealistic style in a variety of ways.

If realism was not a discovery of the socially conscious twenties, neither was *theatricalism*—a term I use here as a catchall for nonrealistic stylization of all types from symbolism to surrealism, and, if you will, from expressionism to the style of "epic theatre" realism associated with the German director Erwin Piscator and the playwright-director Bertolt Brecht. Virtually all these styles had been sampled before by the American theatre, in the 1920's.

It must also be observed that theatricalist stylization in the previous decade was, to a large degree, social commentary rather than psychological analysis. This was transparently the case in the Theatre Guild's production of *The Adding Machine* in 1923, and in its vaudevillian production of Lawson's *Processional* as designed by Mordecai Gorelik in 1925. When the play was revived by the Negro Unit of the Federal Theatre it still seemed as advanced in theatrical style as almost any play of the 1930's, and the production was actually tamer than the 1925 production. The Guild, in the twenties, was obviously fascinated with the social expressionism of the Central European writers and staged a number of their works such a Karel Capek's *R.U.R.,* Kaiser's *From Morn to Midnight,* Toller's *Man and the Masses.* In the case of the Toller drama of revolt, Lee Simonson, who both directed and designed *Man and the Masses,* duplicated as far as possible the original Berlin production of Jürgen Fehling, with its steep gradient in the turbulent key scene in which masses are whipped into frenzied violence.

Social elements were also unmistakably present in the Provincetown Players' expressionistic O'Neill productions, *The Emperor Jones, The Hairy Ape, All God's Chillun Got Wings,* and *The Great God Brown* despite O'Neill's psychological and metaphysical leanings. It should be observed, finally, that the productions of the short-lived New Playwrights' Company, made up entirely of writers in revolt against American middle-class society such as John Dos Passos, the communist journalist Mike Gold, and John Howard Lawson were generally theatricalist. Even the commercial theatre of the 1920's was attracted to this kind of experimentation and actually succeeded with it twice; once in 1928, when Arthur Hopkins produced Sophie Treadwell's expressionist murder-drama *Machinal,* a play soon transferred to the Russian stage by the famous theatricalist producer-director Tairov, and once earlier in 1924, when such Broadway personalities as George S. Kaufman and Marc Connelly collaborated on *Beggar on Horseback* and Winthrop Ames produced this dream-satire on big business and "babbitry" with Broadway breeziness.

As for the social theatre of the 1930's, it started early to employ various degrees and kinds of theatrical stylization and never renounced its use even after the concept of "Socialist Realism" became dogma for the Soviet theatre and "party-line" doctrine elsewhere. Many short plays were produced early in the thirties with no other end in view than to attack some abuse and agitate for some reform during the economic depression in the United States and the spread of fascism abroad. These productions called for more or less expressionistic techniques of playwriting and staging. The professional outpost of the left-wing, the Theatre Union, started its career with a production of the antiwar drama *Peace on Earth* by George Sklar and Paul Peters in which the rapidly changing episodes had an affinity to expressionism even though the principal episodes were objectively rendered rather than subjectively modified or transformed. The Theatre Union's later staging of *The Sailors of Cataro* combined realistic acting with semiconstructivist settings by Mordecai Gorelik. The Theatre Union's most artistically ambitious and controversial offering was its 1935 presentational production of Bertolt Brecht's *The Mother.* The play was staged in strictly "epic style" (as epic style was understood then), with the lighting equipment of the production (designed by Mr. Gorelik) in full view of the audience, and with periodic interruptions of the story presented episodically on the stage by hortatory so-called mass chants delivered to the audience by a shabbily dressed, throaty chorus that clambered on the stage from the auditorium. The Group Theatre production of *The Case of Clyde Griffiths,* Piscator's dramatization of *An American Tragedy,* was also primarily presentational. Dreiser's story, given epic-theatre treat-

ment, was presented in flashback scenes of evidence, argument, and demonstration by the attorney for the defense at Clyde's trial for murder. Set
up on platforms distributed on different parts and on different levels of the
stage, the scenes of the dramatization started and ended abruptly while
the attorney down front to the left faced the audience as if it were the jury
and pointed to the episodes as proof of his contention that society with
its false values was the real villain. The Orson Welles production of Paul
Green's dramatization of *Native Son* in 1941 employed the same narrative
frame and, less obtrusively, somewhat the same formal device of presenting chapters from the story as demonstrated pieces of evidence tending to
vindicate the murderer, or at least to offer extenuating circumstances for
his crime.

The Group's most ambitious production, Paul Green's antimilitaristic
satire *Johnny Johnson,* staged by Lee Strasberg in 1936, bore some resemblance to Erwin Piscator's epic-style production in Berlin of another
antimilitaristic extravaganza, *The Good Soldier Schweik,* in 1928. A noteworthy parallel appears in scenes of interrogation by a psychiatrist. In the
Piscator production, the crippled little Czech soldier about to be inducted
into the service of the Austrian-Hungarian Empire at the start of the
First World War faces a medical examiner represented by a projection of
a huge face with an enormous cigar stuck in its mouth. This impersonal
apparition, drawn by the great cartoonist George Grosz, completely overshadowed the little conscript Schweik standing humanly frail before the
screen. In *Johnny Johnson,* Paul Green's hero, having upset the war machine and the whole earnest business of war between the nations with
laughing gas, is brought to an alienist. In Lee Strasberg's Group Theatre
production, the examining psychiatrist was barricaded behind an enormous, crazily-aslant table and, as played by Carnovsky with deliberately
jerky and angular gestures and body movements, seemed decidedly crazier
than the patient, who was played with characteristic gentleness by that
most gentle of Group Theatre actors Russell Collins.

But the Group's most exciting production was, of course, *Waiting for
Lefty,* in which the realistic episodes were flashbacks held together by a
frame as each prostrike delegate explained his position or the manner in
which a life experience influenced him toward militancy. In brief, an expressionistic technique constituted the groundwork, and it was effectuated
on an almost bare stage by the rapid succession of episodes, the suggestive
darkness in which the sinister labor boss hovered over the action, the explosive appearance of Elia Kazan out of the auditorium in the role of
a cab driver seized with revolutionary fervor, and the shadows out of
which each prostrike delegate successively emerged in an area of light to

address the audience here treated as an assembly of taxicab drivers gathered in a union hall to vote on a proposal to call a strike against the taxicab owners.

A year later, in 1936, came the next New Theatre prize play, *Bury the Dead,* Irwin Shaw's antiwar fantasy, in which dead soldiers in some future war refuse to lie passively in the grave. This play also received modified expressionist treatment on the stage, though without direct address to the audience in the Worthington Miner production on Broadway. The individual scenes of this multiple-action long one-acter were presented with hardly any localization. This production provided a characteristically expressionist rapid-fire succession of fragmentary scenes on a space-stage. By placing the action on different levels, moreover, the director achieved a dramatic separation of politicians and war lords from the recalcitrant dead soldiers who refused to be buried because they had never really tasted life before dying. A sultry eeriness suffused the action, which had the effect of a dream or a nightmare.

We must also call attention, of course, to the presence of much non-realistic stylization in the work of the government-subsidized Federal Theatre Project. It was particularly successful with its turbulent, voodoo-inspired West Indian *Macbeth,* staged by Orson Welles; its enchanting children's production, *Pinocchio;* and several "Living Newspapers."

Two of its productions, *Power,* dealing with utilities and the TVA, and *One-third-of-a-nation,* dealing with the problem of slum housing, won the admiration of the press and public support to such a degree that it seemed for a while that America had given birth to a new style of drama uniquely suited to the pragmatic interests of the American people. Briefly, the Living Newspapers style can be described as an amalgam of motion-picture, epic-theatre, *commedia dell'arte,* and American minstrel-show techniques kept within the framework of a question asked, usually by a puzzled little man who represents the public, and answers supplied by a series of presentational devices consisting of scenes, demonstrations, slides, lectures, and arguments. Symbolism was not excluded from this technique; one of the high moments of *Power* was the scene in which the legality of the New Deal effort to initiate public ownership of utilities is argued before a hostile Supreme Court consisting of nine imperturbable masks on a covered table. Pageantry was also not foreign to the medium; another high point in *Power,* indeed the climax, consisted of an exuberant procession celebrating the TVA in song and dance. Naturalism could also be assimilated into the medium, when this was deemed theatrically feasible. Particularly effective were a bleak tenement house background in

One-third-of-a-nation and the climactic conflagration that broke out in this fire-trap.

Finally one may offer in evidence the case of the Mercury Theatre operated by John Houseman and Orson Welles from 1937 to 1938. Having distinguished themselves with theatricalist productions under Federal Theatre auspices, they continued to do so with their antifascist modern-dress *Caesar* and then gave New Yorkers their finest non-Shakespearean Elizabethan production when they staged *The Shoemaker's Holiday*. Their *Heartbreak House* was dreary, and their *Danton's Death* some-what muddled, although the menacingly high backdrop stuck full of plaster heads to represent the French Assembly while Danton and his associates faced trial amounted to a stroke of theatrical genius.

Both the Federal Theatre in New York and the Mercury Theatre, moreover, ended their respective careers, with a theatricalist work that came closest to the specially stripped theatricality of propaganda and agi-tation, known as agit-prop,[5] with which the decade of social theatre in the 1930's had started. The play was Marc Blitzstein's *The Cradle Will Rock*, a New Theatre prize play dedicated by the author to "Bert Brecht." This work was compounded of razor-keen sketches and songs in a matrix of plot involving an attempt to stamp out a strike, discourage pro-labor agitation, and encourage soporific mass culture. The play was to be pro-

[5] Since "agit-prop" drama and its outgrowths are difficult to locate, I would direct the reader to examples available in the files of *Workers Theatre* (June–July, 1932, pp. 11–19; August, 1932, pp. 9–11, 14–15, 21–22; September–October, 1932, pp. 11–16; April, 1933, pp. 9–10; May–June, 1933, pp. 7–8 and p. 18; July–August, 1933, pp. 10–13); and *New Theatre*, July–August, 1934, pp. 20–24, *Dmitroff: A Play of Mass Pressure*, by two Group Theatre actors, Art Smith and Elia Kazan. "Agit-prop" drama started shading off into *illustrative* personal (rather than exclusively hortatory and declamatory) one-act plays in 1934, and early examples of this traditional type of drama were published as pamphlets. One of the best was *Can You Hear Their Voices?*, adapted by Hallie Flanagan, then professor of dramatics at Vassar College, from a story by Whittaker Chambers, originally published in the *New Masses*.
    Particularly useful in illustrating the "agit-prop" production are the articles "Di-recting the Agit-prop Play" in *Workers Theatre*, May–June, 1933, pp. 3–4, *"Newsboy* —From Script to Performance," *New Theatre*, July–August, 1934, pp. 12–13 and 29 by Alfred Saxe. Problems related to "agit-prop" were treated by the old-time director Frank Merlin in an article "Crowded Scene," *New Theatre*, May, 1934, pp. 9–10. Theory for the theatre of agitation was well formulated in print by John Howard Law-son in an article "Towards a Revolutionary Theatre," subtitled "The Artist Must Take Sides," in *New Theatre*, June, 1934, pp. 6–7, and Michael Blankfort in "Facing the New Audience," in the same issue of *New Theatre*, pp. 11–12 and continued in the July–August issue, pp. 14–15 and in the November, 1934, issue, pp. 25–27. Also illus-trative of the season for nonrealistic theatre is Stephen Karnot's article "From a Direc-tor's Notebook," *New Theatre*, September, 1934, pp. 12–13. Criticism of "agit-prop" appeared perhaps most directly in the present writer's article, "A Playreader on Play-wrights," *New Theatre*, October, 1934, pp. 9–11, especially p. 10.

duced by the Federal Theatre, then under severe harassment from legislators who opposed the Federal Government's support of the arts. *The
Cradle Will Rock* was considered too inflammatory to be risked by the
Federal Theatre. It was therefore produced by Orson Welles under the
auspices of the Mercury Theatre, and for reasons of economy presented
without scenery. The space-stage treatment proved to be the most theatrically effective style that could have been chosen for this lively yet
austere work in which the actors were types bearing such nicknames as
Mr. Mister, Mrs. Mister, Junior Mister, Sister Mister, Editor Daily, and
Reverend Salvation.

The Cradle Will Rock was "agit-prop" that had found its artistic fulfilment in the musical form most natural to it. It was indeed only the
starkest and sharpest example of a trend to infiltrate and modify the musical theatre with social satire and protest.

The period, then, was rich in theatricalist efforts. They also differed,
on the whole, from all but some previously mentioned experiments of
the 1920's. It can be noted, for instance, that the expressionism of the
social theatre of the thirties tended to be *exclusively* social, whereas previous expressionism had been largely concerned with individual disorientation or depersonalization. Actually, the social critics of the thirties and the
epic-theatre advocates Piscator and Brecht tended to dismiss expressionism as too bourgeois, too subjective, and too devoid of an objective critique
of society. In the pages of *New Theatre* magazine, both O'Neill and Toller
came in for much criticism on the grounds that their imaginative subjectivity tended to obfuscate social realities and dissolve conflicts.[6] It
should also be noted that expressionistic technique often appeared in the
framework and transitional moments of the play and its production, while
the episodes themselves were realistic. *Waiting for Lefty* offered an almost
classical case; while establishing and sustaining the premise that the auditorium was filled with taxicab drivers, the scenes dealing with individual
prostrike delegates were projections and dramatized versions of the
speeches with which they were addressing the cabbies, and these scenes
were thoroughly realistic.

At most, one would have to differentiate their style from the leisurely
realism of domestic life. The theatricalism of the thirties, moreover, assumed two extreme forms both distinctly removed from merely esthetic
theatricalism—namely, hortatory so-called "agit-prop" theatre replete with
caricature, harangues, and slogans, and didactic theatre ranging from
epic-theatre to Living Newspaper productions.

[6] See especially Charmion von Wiegand's "The Quest of Eugene O'Neill," *New
Theatre* (September, 1935), pp. 12–17, 30–32.

The genres of epic-theatre didacticism and Living Newspaper documentary argument both violated the fourth-wall convention of realistic illusionism in order to serve a more significant and dynamic realism of analysis. These genres generally used a presentational style and a horizontally episodic form of dramatic structure, which the stage production did not conceal or compensate with efforts at unification by the stage setting. In the exceptional case of the omnipresent tenement of *One-third-of-a-nation,* the setting did not unify the separate scenes, but stood at the back of the acting area of the stage as a hulking reminder or symbol, if you wish, of the problem of slum clearance. The sole unity of these plays was unity of point of view or argument.

Also, if there was no marked progression in the plot, there was certainly progression in the idea and the situation. A case *was* proven in *The Case of Clyde Griffiths;* an argument for slum clearance *was* advanced in *One-third-of-a-nation* and brought to a stunning visual climax with the tenement fire; and an action *was* completed in that other Federal Theatre Living Newspaper *Power* in which the Tennessee Valley Administration victory was consummated and celebrated. After all, the social theatre was in different ways "waiting for *Lefty*" and not for "Godot." A mood of depression and stalemate, so often favored in the present *avant-garde* theatre, was therefore absent in the productions. The settings were not submerged in gloom, and the lighting was usually bright rather than misty or mystical. Even the stock characters of the Living Newspapers, not to mention the caricatures of "agit-prop," possessed considerable bounce in performance.

All this, however, takes me to the last important question that needs to be raised in this paper. If nonrealistic stylization manifested so much variety and inventiveness during the period, why didn't it prevail? Why has the social theatre of the period been identified primarily with realism and why did the American theatre continue to be preponderantly realistic? We are familiar with a few generalizations. America is alleged to be too young and too materialistic a country to sustain the refinements of stylization and imaginative artistry. I am not impressed with these generalizations, but it is not my intention to refute them here. It is my intention, rather, to stick to the specific realities of the period of the thirties in proposing an explanation or, rather, several explanations.

One of these is that theatrical stylization was strongly discredited by the crudity of the "agit-prop" plays and their productions.[7] Articles and

---

[7] Even *The Cradle Will Rock* was somewhat resisted by some leaders of the New Theatre and had to share the New Theatre annual prize with a realistic play by Philip Stevenson in 1937. It was my vote—from the outside, so to speak (that is from the

discussions proposing the displacement of "agit-prop" by realistic drama and rounded characterization abounded. One article, believed to have been somewhat influential, was indeed written by myself quite early in *New Theatre* magazine.[8]

Another reason was the enthusiasm with which Group Theatre realism, whether or not understood, was greeted in New York. Every effort by the Group to venture into nonrealistic stylization was met with resistance by the public and the press, and failed on the stage. The most crushing failure the Theatre Union encountered came with its production of Brecht's *The Mother* in 1936, and the reaction of the left-wing press and of the Theatre Union's audiences, many of them members of sympathetic trade unions, was in the main unfavorable. So far as I know, only Archibald MacLeish and I gave public support to the play. And when we gave our favorable views of the play's early epic-theatre style at a symposium held by the baffled directors of the Theatre Union, we were severely admonished by a lady representing the International Ladies Garment Workers Union. The playgoing public was simply not ready for nonrealistic stylization except when it was enabled to focus on empathic realistic scenes as in *Waiting for Lefty* or on topical matters, as in the best Living Newspapers.

Lastly, we may observe that the theatrical groups themselves were not ready to carry out stylization successfully. The productions of *The Mother, Johnny Johnson,* and *The Case of Clyde Griffiths* left a great deal to be desired. Even at their best they were overshadowed by such realistic Theatre Union and Group Theatre productions as *Stevedore, Awake and Sing,* and *Golden Boy.* Sidney Kingsley had three of his plays produced during the prewar period. Two of these, his realistic hospital drama *Men in White* and his naturalistic slum drama *Dead End,* got superb productions; the third, his study of profiteering by cartels in World War I, *Ten Million Ghosts,* failed dismally in a diffuse and tepid pseudo-epic-theatre type of production.

Sidney Kingsley was certainly not unique among the writers of social drama who sought a more ample theatricalism than even the best realistic techniques of acting and stage production could provide; and he was not the only playwright to have his theatricalist intention frustrated by inadequacy of execution. A case in point is the experience of Sklar and Peters during the rehearsals of *Peace on Earth.* Molly Day Thacher, now better known as Mrs. Elia Kazan, reported on the problem in the 1934 July—

relatively conservative Theatre Guild), that broke a tied verdict and got *The Cradle Will Rock* a favorable decision.

[8] "A Playreader Looks at Playwrights," *New Theatre* (October, 1934), pp. 9–11.

August issue of *New Theatre* magazine,[9] in an article that reflected an aim editorially endorsed in the previous issue to create, as the editors put it, "not only revolutionary drama but revolutionary staging." Introduced to stylized stage production at the Vassar Experimental Theatre, Molly Thacher criticized the Theatre Union for giving the multiscened anti-war play a realistic rather than imaginative production, but admitted that the Theatre Union could not have provided the latter. *"Who* would have attempted it?" she asked. "The form of the last act, with its rapid flashes from scene to scene, as provided by the authors, invited a strong distortion, an element of caricature and comment upon the characters. . . . How can this sort of comment be arrived at? It is easy to talk about . . . but we have no experience in doing, or even seeing, it." The fact is, as Molly Thacher noted, that the authors of *Peace on Earth* had originally required a fantastic treatment of their third act and provided specifications for securing such a treatment in their stage directions. For instance, they had wanted the policeman in Act Three to float down from the flies wearing a gigantic policeman's badge. When the attempt was made during the rehearsal period to carry out the authors' suggestions, however, the theatricalist details seemed merely absurd and had to be scrapped. Only a song-and-dance act by, among others, a college president and a settlement worker was retained in the production.

The reason for failure was not, however, necessarily ignorance and consequent incompetence. On the contrary, the Group Theatre's artist-leaders Harold Clurman and Lee Strasberg knew a good deal about stylization and had a high regard for its possibilities. Clurman had actually studied in Paris with Jacques Copeau, and served him as an intermediary or interpreter in New York when Copeau directed his own dramatization of *The Brothers Karamazov* for the Theatre Guild. Lee Strasberg and he were impressed, but, writes Clurman, "We believed we were on the road to learning a sounder technique for the actor . . . that of the Moscow Art Theatre, the so-called Stanislavsky 'system.' "[10]

Strasberg himself was intensely interested in Vakhtangov's imaginative use of realism (sometimes called "fantastic realism"), and communicated his knowledge to the Group actors who trained under him. Strasberg was also familiar with the latter-day theatricalist experiments of Meyerhold and wrote an interesting article about them in *New Theatre* magazine in 1934.

Without being able to go into details in the short article derived from

[9] "Revolutionary Staging for Revolutionary Plays," *New Theatre* (July–August, 1934), p. 16.
[10] Clurman, *op. cit.,* p. 17.

observation of the Meyerhold productions of *The Forest* and *Camille* in Moscow, Strasberg nevertheless revealed a keen awareness and appreciation of Meyerholdian theatricalism developed since 1910 and not yet extinguished in Russia in 1934. Among the features Strasberg listed in his *New Theatre* summary were Meyerhold's utilization of the forestage and restoration of the Molière technique of "proscenium acting," his strongly marked dynamic rhythms (as in the use of large swings in *The Forest* for a love scene), omission of a stage curtain, lighting the auditorium as well as the stage, employment of bizarre details (such as a "masque of death" in a party scene in *Camille*), marked playing with objects, and "prevalence of movement and gesture over the word." Strasberg also noted Meyerhold's dispensing with "psychological motivation of action," "easy transitions from the lofty-heroic to the base and the ugly-misshapen and comical," "spontaneous combination of ardent rhetoric with exaggerated buffonade," sharp singling out of some feature of the character "leading thus to the creation of conventional theatrical figures," and, as Strasberg put it so well, "coalescence of the actor with the acrobat, jongleur, clown, juggler, mountebank, songster, fool," and "the universal technique of acting conditioned by this versatility, built upon the mastery of one's own body, upon an innate rhythmicality, upon an expeditious and economical use of movements."[11]

For all that, however, neither the directors nor the actors of the Group Theatre ever gave themselves up wholly to stylization once they became the acknowledged masters of realistic art in the thirties. The one successful sally into poetic stylization, which might be freely called surrealist, came in 1939 when the Group produced William Saroyan's tenderly bizarre piece *My Heart's in the Highlands*. Here, however, the slightly fantastic action was anchored in one superb realistic characterization—that of an impecunious and rejected yet undefeated poet. The production, staged for the Group by the gifted director Robert Lewis, aimed at both realism and stylization. The director, who worked in full consciousness of this dual objective, expressed this problem succinctly when he wrote in *Producing the Play* (pp. 297 and 300) that "In addition to the usual work on the psychological meaning and development," it was necessary to find the "poetic expression of the content" and "to arrive at an *image*" to convey the feeling of the work. This was particularly apparent in the memorable scene in which a trumpet-playing refugee from an old peoples' home entrances the villagers, who bring him and the poet sheltering him food in token of their appreciation. The image that came to the direc-

---

[11] "The Magic of Meyerhold," *New Theatre* (September, 1934), pp. 14–15, 30.

tor's mind was, as he puts it, *"a plant flowering as it is watered."* Robert
Lewis achieved this image brilliantly with his crowd of villagers tightly
grouped below the hoary trumpet-player in different positions and holding aloft their offerings, "as if these were growing out of the branches
of a large tree." (p. 300)

With this possible exception, and it is a moderate one since the focus
remained on the poet and the stout-hearted little boy who played his son,
the Group's directors moved very hesitantly and inconclusively toward
theatricalism. Unlike recent *avant-gard*ists, they were disinclined to dismiss environment and characterization in-the-round. Environment, in
particular, was too much of a reality of their times to be loftily ignored
by them, and reality of character was something too painstakingly achieved
by Group acting to be airily dismissed, as if art lay only in producing
patterns and postures.

An extra surge of imagination or even exaggeration and a stepped
up vivacity were needed to push plays such as *Johnny Johnson* and *The
Case of Clyde Griffiths* across the borderline between realistic illusion
and fully established theatricalism. I believe this is what Lee Strasberg
had in mind a day or so after his return from a visit to the Berliner
Ensemble, when I asked him how he would stage *Johnny Johnson* today
—a quarter of a century later. He replied that he would stage it the same
way, *only more so!* I take it, then, that he would increase the tempo,
accentuate the satirical touches, sharpen the outlines of each action, give
more pattern to the stage movement, and improve the singing and choreography. In other words, he would enable the play to escape from the
indeterminate No-Man's Land between realism and theatricalism, where
the credibility of the former is weakened and the verve of the other style
is subdued, so that both realism and theatricality are simultaneously
weakened.

Whether out-and-out theatricalism can succeed today in our professional theatre, however, is a question that must remain moot.[12] The
Broadway playgoer continues to limit his theatricalist gratifications mainly
to musical comedy. Moreover, it is not at all clear at what point a fully

----

[12] The transfer of conspicuously theatricalist productions from London to New
York has been more or less unsuccessful, and the failure of such offerings as the charm-
ing Peter Brook's production of the Anouilh-Fry *Ring 'Round the Moon* in 1951 and
N. F. Simpson's *One Way Pendulum* in 1961 does not bode well for imported the-
atricalism. Only the partial success of Brendan Behan's *The Hostage* provides some
evidence to the contrary. Revived and refurbished famous French farces like Noel
Coward's *Look After Lulu,* two or three seasons ago, got short shrift in New York.
The last time we had the ubiquitous farce *The Italian Straw Hat* in the vicinity of
Broadway was when Orson Welles staged an unsuccessful adaptation under the title of
Horse Eats Hat for the Federal Theatre in 1936.

theatricalized *Johnny Johnson* would be distinguishable from musical comedy any more than is the Greenwich Village production of *The Threepenny Opera,* which got a foothold here fully thirty years after its phenomenal success in Central Europe. Perhaps a significant American theatricalist theatre distinguishable from musical comedy like *Of Thee I Sing* or *Fiorello* is something that has yet to come. One thing is certain: it failed to materialize in the 1930's when the conditions for its success seemed most favorable.[13]

---

[13] [A note indicates Professor Gassner's intention to revise and enlarge this final paragraph. He surely would have corrected the previous footnote, now that Joan Littlewood's *Oh What a Lovely War* and Peter Brook's *Marat/Sade,* both from London, have shown theatricalism, even at an unexpectedly high pitch of violence or of satire, to be successful on Broadway. *Ed.*]

THE GROUP THEATRE*

Celebrations are inappropriate in the desperate world in which we are living, and there will probably be no extraordinary festivities in November when the Group Theatre begins its tenth year. But this fact should not disturb that valiant organization, since the meetings that launched it on its notable career took place in another dreary and desperate year, twelve months after the historic stock-market disaster. After a difficult, financially unstable decade, it is nonetheless generally recognized that the Group Theatre's history constitutes one of the brightest chapters in our theatre.

The Group has not been particularly successful in finding a critical understanding of its approach and its problems; it has been subjected to uncritical rhapsodies, on the one hand, and deprecatory, vague skepticism, on the other. Actually, however, the truth is simple and clear: namely, that the Group's work was grounded in the principle of collectivism in art and life, with due respect, at the same time, for individual self-realization and democratic procedure.

In the middle twenties, a number of young people who appeared in various Theatre Guild productions discovered that they had common interests. The "new art" in the theatre propounded variously by Gordon Craig and Stanislavski, which had by now spread to this country, had one aim in common—namely, that all the arts of the theatre must be completely integrated in a production. Artists worth their salt subscribed to this principle, and many extended it in practice by striving for community theatres and permanent acting companies. It was not extraordinary then that Harold Clurman, fresh from Paris, should have been fired by Jacques Copeau's community theories of acting, and that Lee Strasberg should have immersed himself in the "Stanislavski system."

* This anniversary article was written for *Theatre Arts* (October, 1940). [There is something decidedly anachronistic about reading a topical appraisal of a company that has now passed into theatrical history, if not into limbo. Professor Gassner was well aware of this, and he planned to preface his account of the Group Theatre with an introduction which would emphasize the importance of its contribution, not only to the theatre of its period, but to contemporary theory and practice. Even though the Group was not able to live up to its high ideals or even to survive, various members have nonetheless made valuable, if controversial, contributions in training, criticism, direction, acting, playwrighting, and designing. It was obviously Professor Gassner's intention to discuss these talents and their achievements as a post-script to the essay. *Ed.*]

In the winter of 1928 these progressive young artists and their associates began a seventeen-week rehearsal period on two strongly stylized, uncommercial plays, and a number of the actors were actually included in a short-lived experimental Theatre Guild studio which aroused interest with its production of the Soviet play *Red Rust*. By then, however, collectivism in the theatre reached a clearer definition, probably under the stimulus of the social idealism of the period, and the upshot of a series of meetings that began in the fall of 1930 was a resolve to establish a true "group theatre" which would embrace a great deal more than the idea of simply acting together.

In April, 1931, Harold Clurman drew up a provocative program for submission to the Theatre Guild's Board of Directors, in the hope that the Guild would give his company the permanent status of a First Studio. This was not to be, and the Group became an independent organization. Clurman's "Plans for a First Studio," however, remains a classic statement of first principles. The theatre, if it is to be an art, must have "singleness of meaning and direction." It "must create from the chaos which is the common experience of its members an expression that will have . . . an identity and a significance with which people, sharing the common experience, may sense their kinship and to which they can attach themselves." Its artists must be "confident all the time that the thing that binds them togeher must be a reflection of a sentiment that animates many people in the world about them." This "thing," it was evident from both Clurman's statement and the Group's later history, was to be the collective way of life and of art: "The generations before us seemed to have been strenuously individualistic without believing very steadily in any particular good for their individuals. . . . We believe that the individual can achieve his fullest stature only through the identification of his own good with the good of his group, a group which he himself must help to create." It would be difficult to find a more comprehensive definition of the Group's subsequent policy as exemplified by its close unity, its partiality for plays that had reference to social realities, and its persistent discovery or underscoring of such meanings in every script selected for production.

Clurman's program, moreover, recognized the importance of the individual in the collective enterprise. The actor was expected to develop himself continually, instead of contenting himself with superficial success. The actors spent their summers together, engaged in mutual criticism, and participated in special productions not intended for Broadway or in experimentation with scenes from plays. In order to make such an enterprise possible, the Group kept its actors on an annual salary basis for six years, even adjusting the scale in accordance with the needs of its individuals. Nor did actors have to prove their adequacy at their first reading of a part, as is customary on Broadway; instead, they were enabled to grow into their roles under sympathetic guidance, and for the early education of the group, Lee Strasberg, in particular, proved himself an accomplished teacher. It is not surprising then that the Group developed many young actors of sterling quality, as well as directors like Harold Clurman, Robert Lewis, and Elia Kazan, and that its ensemble received unstinted acclaim; it was not unusual for critics to refer to the Group as the best acting company in America. Incidentally, too, the same painstaking "group" approach was contemplated for the playwright in the 1931 program, which held that the organization "should not confine itself to doctoring his plays but criticize them, not simply criticize them but come to grips with him on fundamentals—in other words, actually collaborate with him." It was precisely such collaboration that Odets received.

The Group has been chary of calling its methods the "Stanislavski system." Nevertheless, no other theatre has adhered so closely to Stanislavski's approach to acting. The Group actor realizes, among other things, that he must re-create a given situation in terms of his personal associations, and that he must perfect sense memory, as when that superb actor Morris Carnovsky acquired his gait in *Golden Boy,* in which he played the old Italian father, by striving to realize what would happen to a body shoving a fruit wagon for years. The actor must develop to the highest degree his ability to find inner justification for his conduct, to believe what he is saying or doing; he must master the kernel or spine of his role until it assumes a distinctness that is the acme of individuality or personality. He is expected to place himself in a "circle" which keeps him real to himself, at the same time making sure that he is responding to the other characters on the stage instead of merely addressing their ears. Characteristic of this approach are Clurman's recorded injunctions during rehearsals of *Rocket to the Moon:* "The spine of the character should be found by the actor himself. What's the simplest thing an actor can do today? He knows immediately he's talking about his [own] life." To encourage a maximum realization of each role in terms of the actor's personal experience, Clurman exhorted them to express themselves freely: "If you feel the impulse to do something, to do more than is called for, do it. If you are doing too much, I'll stop you."

It is necessary only to add one cardinal element to the Group's production procedure—namely, the realization of the social significance of the play and of its parts. No one must regard the play or the role as an isolated experience, but virtually as a social one. Thus, the larger content of the dentist's love story in *Rocket to the Moon* was for its director, Mr. Clurman, the thesis "that the free exercise of the passion of love is impossible in middle-class life today." Clurman's introductions to Odets' published plays teem with such references to the purport of the play-wright's fable. *Golden Boy,* according to its director, was "the picture of a great fight—a fight in which we are all involved, whatever our profession or craft. What the golden boy of this allegory is fighting for is a place in the world as an individual; what he wants is to free his ego from the scorn that attaches to 'nobodies' in a society in which every activity is viewed in the light of a competition."

Any evaluation of the Group Theatre is impossible without at least this fractional analysis of its approach, which has made it not only a redoubtable producing organization and a repository of impressive acting talent but also the only theatre consistently concerned with social tensions that has refused to content itself with presenting elementary, one-dimensional conflicts. Clurman, for example, criticized the Theatre Union because it thought that "one aspect of the whole thing which is the art of the theatre is enough." Whatever the future of the Group may prove to be at a time when we can only regard the future of all civilization with a shudder, its past has been honorable and fruitful. Confirmation of this fact, regardless of any esoteric contribution that the Group or its friends may claim, is abundantly present. It developed the most important new playwright of the thirties, Odets; it introduced Saroyan to the theatre; it produced such notable experimental plays as *The Case of Clyde Griffiths, Johnny Johnson,* and *My Heart's in the Highlands;* and it was largely, if not wholly, responsible for the rise of such outstanding actors as Franchot Tone, Morris Carnovsky, John Garfield, Lee Cobb, and Luther Adler. However, every enterprise suffers from the limitations or problems imposed upon it by its approach, and a survey of the Group's record must take account of some understandable shortcomings.

Although comedy is one of the potent forms of social drama, this theatre has thus far found few occasions to exploit its actors' impressive comic talent. Perhaps, too, the Group would be in a sounder financial condition today if it had successfully tapped the resources of comedy. Its immersion in social significances also left that organization vulnerable when the social situation no longer held out any direct hope of social change for the better. Almost unavoidably, in presenting social plays devoid of simple and direct militancy—that is, in favoring allegories, or oblique social commentaries—the Group Theatre often favored weighty but foggy dramas. This was conspicuously the case in such productions as *Gentlewoman, Gold Eagle Guy, Weep for the Virgins, Casey Jones, Thunder Rock,* and *Night Music.* At the same time, the Group's insistence on discovering social significance in everything it touched led to occasional straining of effect without actual achievement of clarification. A supposedly significant but fugitive detail, such as a minor character's longing for window curtains in *Night Music,* may too often elude attention; it may not be safely expected to exemplify the central meaning of a play. Symbolism or allegory often possesses an esoteric character, and to communicate it to an audience it is not sufficient to assume an air of profundity. When the actors perform certain movements or scenes slowly and with high seriousness, they do not actually convey any meanings that the playwright has failed to clarify in his script. Moreover, such emphases may labor the point unnecessarily, retarding its tempo and giving it a lumbering pretentiousness like that which prevailed in such a frequently beautiful play and production as *Night Music.* Lightness of touch, in fact, has not been one of the Group's virtues.

High tragedy has not been conspicuous in its repertory, which has favored little people and their problems, consequently keeping Group audiences on the plains and in the valleys instead of lifting them to the heights, as the theatre must do at least now and then. Nor has this organization given sufficient scope to the imagination. That the company is abundantly endowed with this desirable faculty was apparent in Saroyan's *My Heart's in the Highlands* and Paul Green's *Johnny Johnson.* But the realism that has dominated the Group's approach to acting appears to have inhibited freedom of treatment. A certain heaviness was apparent in the production of *Johnny Johnson,* and despite the fine fantastication of Lee Strasberg's production idea many of the performances seemed slack and pedestrian. Although the productions of Robert Ardrey's *Thunder Rock* and Clifford Odets' *Night Music* were effective whenever some actor evoked that veracity of characterization which is the Group's crowning achievement in acting, they somehow lacked the free flow of imaginative beauty. The treatment tended to be solemn rather than inspired.

The staging of Ardrey's *Casey Jones* should have evoked folk poetry and theatrical opulence, instead of contenting itself with a flatly realistic presentation of a drab plot. In all such instances the scenic designer, Mordecai Gorelik, was sufficiently creative, but other elements of the production fell short of his achievement, due perhaps to the company's realistic orientation. It may also be noted that enthusiasm for the "little man" has encouraged a certain sentimentalization of the weak and foolish in Group productions; this was evident in the casting and direction of the heroines in *Rocket to the Moon* and *Gentle People,* as well as in the text of the plays. These characters were far less appealing and "significant" than its directors seem to have believed; it was only too easy to dismiss them as trite and unwise virgins.

Regrettable, too, has been the Group Theatre's avoidance of revivals to which many of its actors and so brilliant a director as Clurman could have brought new values. Nor has the acting company been efficacious in enacting other than proletarian or lower-middle-class types, most of them markedly and specially metropolitan. A notable example was the otherwise sensitive production of Odets' *Paradise Lost,* which nevertheless failed to convey the representative qualities of the American middle-class beyond certain, seemingly exotic, areas of New York City. Its predecessor *Awake and Sing,* on the other hand, was plainly a realistic play about the Bronx, apart from its larger significance as a call for a more abundant life than life constrained by economic interests and middle-class respectability, and Clurman's staging came as close to perfection as anything in the American theatre. It may be no accident that the Group Theatre has rarely invaded the road successfully; and its influence, too, might have been greater if its productions could have been less local in color and tone.

In its tenth year, this gallant company is at the crossroads; it is contemplating some reorganization, and it is considering a broader program, possibly based on a more popular price scale. It intends to interest itself in anything that is simply good theatre. More than ever, too, it disclaims being a cult or "mystery," pointing to the fact that even such arrivals from Hollywood as Frances Farmer and Jane Wyatt found no difficulty in working harmoniously with the regular members. Owing to its admirable combination of social awareness and respect for individuality, it is capable of becoming even more distinctly a theatre for varied, broadly acceptable, and nationally pervasive dramatic experience. It has gone far; now it may be expected, if external circumstances permit any growth, to go further.

P.S. The Group Theatre, succumbing to inevitable economic pressure, dissolved in 1941 after the failure of a last desperate bid for Broadway success with an Irwin Shaw comedy. The Group dispersed, and Hollywood became the temporary haven for Harold Clurman, Morris Carnovsky, Lee Cobb. [This post-script was never finished, but Professor Gassner's brief notation indicates that he also meant to discuss the limitations of the Method. *Ed.*]

Part Five

BROADWAY IN REVIEW:
PRODUCTIONS OF THE SIXTIES*

* The following excerpts are taken from the author's regular column in the *Educational Theatre Journal;* dates are as indicated.

Section One*

■

LILLIAN HELLMAN'S *TOYS IN*
THE ATTIC (MAY, 1960)

Only the peal of thunder from Miss Hellman's quarter dissipated the torpor of the 1959–1960 season on Broadway. At that, some critics, whose interest wavered until the second act, found the thunder somewhat slow in arriving. But arrive it did, and most of us could agree that the detonation had been worth waiting for. At the conclusion of a decade of depleted energy, moreover, the arrival of Miss Hellman's first original play in nine years was as significant as it was welcome. At the beginning of the decade, in *The Autumn Garden,* this unmistakably powerful playwright, too, had displayed symptoms of enervation (mild ones indeed when compared with the tepidity of most playwriting), but it was now apparent that neither time nor *Zeitgeist* had got the best of one of the contemporary theatre's most invigorating practitioners. It is difficult for me to refrain from rejoicing, almost as if I had scored a personal victory, that Miss Hellman should have prevailed once more in a theatre so largely given over to mental and moral flabbiness since the advent of *A Streetcar Named Desire* in 1947, except for the chance appearance of *Death of a Salesman* and *The Crucible.* And it was apparent that by comparison with the authors of these plays, the writer of *Toys in the Attic* (as well as of *The Children's Hour, The Little Foxes,* and *Watch on the Rhine*) remained a paragon of classic soundness and unpathological penetration.

Toys in the Attic is one of Miss Hellman's most hard-driving plays. Among her earlier works, only *The Little Foxes,* her masterpiece of the strenuous thirties, possesses as much penetration and dramatic vitality; and rarely before has Miss Hellman written dialogue with such vigor and virtuosity. It is apparent that at least one American playwright has

* [The unfortunately limited space available for reviews in the *Educational Theatre Journal* often required Professor Gassner to write "omnibus" critiques in order to cover the number of plays he had seen in any one quarter. When he could do so conveniently, or when he felt a major new work had been staged, he would write at length on it. The reviews in the first section, selected by Professor Gassner as important comments on the early sixties, are thus a mixture of omnibus and single commentaries. *Ed.*]

kept her sword of judgment unblunted in the damp mental climate. She brought to the task of adapting Emmanuel Robles' *Monserrat* early in the fifties an existentialist concern with decisions that test man's stamina. In adapting Anouilh's Joan of Arc drama, *The Lark,* she invigorated the play by counteracting the French author's sophisticated skepticism. The loss of dramatic voltage in *The Autumn Garden* at the beginning of the decade was apparently a temporary loss and a compensated one. It accompanied experimentation with a loose form of dramaturgy for the purpose of giving a rueful account of the erosion of lives in a drifting society.

In *Toys in the Attic,* Miss Hellman has picked up the sword of judgment many playwrights of the period have laid aside and wields it with renewed vigor. But this time, compassion guides her hand so that she performs surgery on her characters instead of summarily decapitating them, and she gives some heed, too, to the pathos of misunderstanding and the power of circumstance. The reach of compassion in the play extends even to an unseen character, a woman whose hatred for an unscrupulous husband and desire to get away from him at all costs lead her into a shoddy scheme for mulcting him of a small fortune in exchange for a piece of swamp land he needs for one of his speculations. This woman, who never appears on the stage although she is in league with the young hero of the play, Julian, is made as real as any character on the stage. When we learn that she has been mutilated along with Julian by her racketeering husband's henchmen because he has been led to believe she is running away with Julian as her lover, our pity for her can be as considerable as if we had always known her. Her story, moreover, acquires intense reality from the action she unknowingly precipitates. Her young collaborator Julian, who has pocketed $75,000 from his deal with her, upsets his sisters with the possibility that he may become independent of them, and his neurotic wife suspects him of infidelity.

There is indeed a profound pathos as well as an ironic judgment of petty lives in the misunderstandings and entanglements that produce the catastrophe. In *Toys in the Attic,* a young man's life is ruined by his overprotective spinster sisters, one of whom has desired him incestuously. And the catastrophe that results in his disfigurement is brought about by his frantically jealous child-wife, who also wrecks her mother's life.

Miss Hellman's play has proved to be distinctly superior to the other new plays of the 1959–60 theatrical season, and the decisive factors that give the play its superiority are many indeed. Miss Hellman displays controlled artistry in this work. It contains excellent dialogue, incisive characterization, and a mature understanding of human attitudes, relationships, and drives. Even the faults of the play seemed contributive to its powerful effect. The first act is undoubtedly somewhat slow and meandering, but Miss Hellman has prepared us suspensively with this act for the mounting passions and the tightly coiled spring of doom to be found in the rest of the play. Only a nagging feeling that the author was dangling the characters on the strings of contrived plotting as if they were puppets (which they really aren't) kept on interfering with my submission to the drive of the play; the author even used the familiar device of letting one of the sisters overhear a conversation and then use it to prevent her brother's escape from the danger that threatens to destroy him.

It is the special merit of Lillian Hellman's work that dreadful things are done by the onstage characters out of affectionate possessiveness, rather than out of ingrained villainy. Although the author's corresponding view of life is ironic and is trenchantly expressed, there is no gloating over human misery, no horror-mongering, no traffic with sensationalism in *Toys in the Attic*. And, unlike some well-known contemporary playwrights here and abroad, Miss Hellman has proved once more that she can deal with human failure without falling in love with it herself. She remains admirably sane in the midst of the ugliness and confusion she so unerringly exposes. Although she looks at life steadily and unsentimentally, she does not advertise herself as a flinty cynic or hopeless nihilist. She is, on the contrary, remarkably understanding in her treatment of the scapegrace brother's affectionate but awkwardly expressed feelings for his sisters (he unloads extravagant presents upon them the moment he acquires money) and she is as poignant as she is restrained in her fine treatment of a Negro lover's attachment to the wealthy white woman so attractively played by Irene Worth. Miss Hellmann demonstrates that for people to behave monstrously it is not necessary for them to be monstrous, it is sufficient only to be unthinkingly possessive or "loving." *Toys in the Attic* is mordant rather than morbid drama.

The Broadway production directed with distinction by Arthur Penn proved itself altogether worthy of Miss Hellman's craft. But it was altogether apparent that the playwright was directly responsible for the excellence of the presentation. For one thing, Miss Hellman contributed an absorbing story that translated itself into vivid stage action. For another, she supplied her actors with multidimensional characters. Maureen Stapleton especially had a full range of emotions to convey as the younger spinster sister in her destructively possessive love of her brother, her jealousy of his child-wife, her dependency on her older sister Anna, and her resentment of the latter's penetration into her secret incestuous passion. That apparently infallible actress Anne Revere had a truly gratifying role as the older sister who combines an affectionate nature with a forbidding exterior. The appealing British actress Irene Worth (it is difficult to forget her Celia Copplestone in *The Cocktail Party*) also had a role of some substance when called upon to play a woman who is burdened with a chronically childish and troublesome daughter. Rochelle Oliver, making her first appearance, is overpoweringly dynamic as the terrifying neurotic daughter, but the role is, of course, Miss Hellman's creation, and hardly anyone else except Tennessee Williams could have created it. And the immensely rich role of Julian, the well-intentioned but ill-starred brother, was as beneficial to the superb acting of Jason Robards, Jr., as his talent was to the role.

Not the least of Miss Hellman's durable talents is her ability to write for actors. Her art of characterization is insight exercised in the theatre and completes itself in performance. With such talent at her disposal and a vigorous mind and temperament as her natural endowments, Miss Hellman is one of the very few playwrights who could be expected to stop the escape of vitality from the decade's theatre. At the end of the 1950–60 decade, it is apparent that she has successfully resisted the seductions of fashionable enervation and negativism to which her frequently jaundiced view of men and women might have disposed her. But there are unfortunately too few playwrights in America who can follow her example of mastering melancholy views and visions instead of being mastered by them.

FABLES ON BROADWAY
(MAY, 1960)

Weight and regrettable failure could be noted in a Broadway effort to produce the late Albert Camus' youthful play *Caligula*. A bleak drama about the awareness of the absurdity of life that drives Caligula into a career of insolvent crime with a view to exposing the worthlessness of men, *Caligula* is both slightly sophomoric and considerably engrossing drama. In the Broadway presentation, the sophomoric element took precedence; it got inflated into grand opera by the directional ambition to make a big Broadway production out of the work for both artistic (that is, *bad* artistic) and commercial (*unsuccessfully* commercial) purposes. A more inappropriate approach to Camus' philosophical play could hardly be imagined; although it is understandable that a director might be tempted to view *Caligula* as an historical pageant, he would have to be singularly dense not to realize that the play is the very opposite of "costume drama." Since the director Sidney Lumet is not at all dense, we may only conclude that his hand was forced by a producer who saw no other way of "selling" the play to the public. This, however, may be a charitable conclusion, for it is equally likely that the director succumbed to the chronic bad taste of Broadway that also gives us our usually successful mammoth musical comedies.

Overpackaging and overproducing plays is the habitual response of show business, and so it seems to follow in the thinking of our movie and TV addicted directors that a "big" idea needs a "big" production; it is deemed less necessary to understand a play and enable the public to understand it than it is to attract the eye and (in the big musicals) deafen the ear. The results of this inflationary misdirection were regrettable because Caligula was well played by Kenneth Haigh, who derived good support from such able performers as Philip Bourneuf, Frederic Tozere, and Colleen Dewhurst. It is a pity, of course, that *Caligula* should have failed on Broadway, which kept us waiting some fifteen years for this flawed but arresting play that ran two years in Paris with Gérard Philipe in the main role. Behind the production it was possible to discern an original intelligence at work on such elusive but provocative subjects as Caligula's rebellion against death or the limitations of the human condition. Camus stressed the madness of inhuman logicality, which leads

485

the young emperor to conclude that if life is absurd, a man may do anything to himself and everybody else, or, as Dostoevsky put it, that if God doesn't exist everything is permissible. Apparent, too, is the ruinousness of any passion for absolutes when accompanied by absolute power such as the Roman emperor possessed. To which Camus added the idea that "Caligula accepts death through the realization that no one can save himself all alone and that one cannot be free at the expense of others."

It is too late in the day to lecture Camus on the faults in his dramaturgy of the year 1944, and it is more important to deplore the fact that Broadway displayed all the defects, especially the lack of sustained development, and hardly any of the virtues of this early existentialist work, the chief of which is the simultaneous representation and discrediting of a nihilist attitude toward existence. An off-Broadway production of *Time of Vengeance* did better by Ugo Betti's hardly less taxing drama of contradiction in the human condition. Revolving around the mysterious presence of evil in an Italian mountain village, *Time of Vengeance* combines melodrama with ironic penetration. Betti exposes the high degree of involvement in guilt that pervades society even when that society punishes the evil upon which it gluts its desire. In *Time of Vengeance,* the community persecutes a petty official and his family only to evince the greatest reluctance to let the family depart. It needs especially the official's crippled and cretinous daughter as an object of its lust, and both the official and the daughter as scapegoats. The villagers turn on the policeman for whom it had sent to purge the village of its evil. The fascination is not unaccompanied by confusion in this blend of mystification, mleodrama, and mysticism. But David Metcalf's clear and carefully paced production of Charles Wassermann's adaptation of this play (it was originally presented in Italy in 1950) provided the first relatively successful introduction of Ugo Betti's work in our professional theatre. Our playgoers could at last understand how it has been possible for the Italian public to rank this playwriting magistrate as Pirandello's legitimate successor. Betti, who was born in 1892 and died in 1953 in Rome as one of Italy's chief jurists, had established a notable reputation in Europe. But his American admirers had only the failure of his *Island of Goats, The Gambler,* and *The Queen and the Rebels* for their pains until the production of *Time of Vengeance.*

IMAGINATION AND STYLIZATION
IN NEW YORK (OCTOBER, 1960)

I

On Broadway during the 1959–60 season, the hopeful playgoer could briefly encounter one work of true distinction, and several valid experiments in stylization. It was Giraudoux's last play, *Pour Lucrèce,* very literately translated and more or less adequately adapted by Christopher Fry under the title of *Duel of Angels.* The Roger L. Stevens and S. Hurok production staged by Robert Helpmann had lovely costuming by Christian Dior and attractive provincial settings by the English scene designer Roger Furse. The casting was gilt edged, with Vivien Leigh and Mary Ure, the "Lucretia" of this Gallic *Rape of Lucrece* variant, providing most of the gilt. This was certainly the sort of production that only years of experience with décor and cosmopolitan sophistication, preferably Parisian, could supply. This was certainly not an off-Broadway presentation, despite the penchant for European culture and sophistication that now prevails in Greenwich Village circles almost as much, though far less meaningfully, as during the twenties. And the production reaped the expected plaudits from the press. One reviewer considered Vivian Leigh and Mary Ure "two of the most alluring women speaking on the stage today" and considered it a delight to spend an evening with them; another pronounced their charm irresistible; and a third found Vivian Leigh, the antiheroine who punished the virtuous heroine's offensive righteousness with a trumped-up rape, "viperishly desirable" and her victim Mary Ure "gloriously glacial." Brooks Atkinson considered the entire production "a splendid demonstration of high style," and he was anything but isolated in proferring this opinion, while Richard Watts of the *New York Post* thought that the war between the angels of light (Mary Ure) and darkness (Vivian Leigh playing an elegant Frenchwoman) was "carried on with a dramatic forcefulness that is arresting and absorbing." *I* found the play drearily dull and the production just as drearily labored, and could not but consider the play and the production the unfortunate product of the combined laboriousness of the American and European commercial theatres, which are only superficially distinguishable.

All the ironies at the expense of overly righteous virtue were laid on with a gilded trowel. And the ironies of the text were made more obvious, I suspect, by Mary Ure's expert but obvious playing of the Lucretia part, assumed in London, I understand more felicitously, by Claire Bloom. It is permissible to wonder why the scanty theme needed so much dressed-up verbiage and such dressed-up marionettes. The town bawd summarized the content as well as anyone can when she solemnly declared that "Purity is not for this world"—concerning which Brooks Atkinson's comment was a classic understatement when he wrote that "As a thought it is not remarkable." He would have also had my assent when he added that the theme was an occasion for "a dainty conversation piece in terms of playful cynicism" if I had found the play dainty and playful in the "big" Broadway production. I would have preferred a stripped production, as well as fewer words and lighter phrases by Giraudoux and Fry. The thought that "Broadwayism" of writing as well as of playing is not a strictly Times Square monopoly suggested itself to me when I came across *Variety*'s report on the earlier, April, 1958, London production starring Claire Bloom and Vivien Leigh: "If *Duel of Angels* is to succeed," wrote *Variety,* "it will be a triumph of marquee talent over matter." In New York, fortunately, the "marquee talent" was also superbly genuine talent in the case of Vivien Leigh. Her performance had beauty and grace, superb professional command and aplomb. I wish I could say something half so complimentary about Robert Helpmann's direction, which New York newspaper reviewers found so charming; I thought it modishly ornate and pictorially mannered.

II

The serious side of the theatre was better represented on the off-Broadway stages, although not without disasters, disappointments, and inadequacies as representative of trying to make do with too little as the defects of Broadway production are representative of trying to overwhelm the public with too much—even with too much weight in the wrong plays and on the wrong occasions. Fuzziness of thought is not, of course, the monopoly of any one kind of theatre any more than is fuzziness of style. Both kinds were lamentably present in the case of *Between Two Thieves,* a discussion-piece presented as "a trial of Jesus" type of drama with the ostensible purpose of relieving Biblical Jewry of responsibility for the crucifixion, a worthy effort no doubt, since it is made with a view to depriving anti-Semitism of some of its fuel. Delivered with argumentative passion and considerable pathos, *Between Two Thieves* now and then proved engrossing but in the long run rather futile since the convoluted argument, like a scorpion with its tail in its mouth, actually got nowhere. The "play within the play" device, that of a narrator presenting a "trial of Jesus" demonstration, amplified by the planting of actors in the audience, lacked order and definition. It appears to be assumed by advanced off-Broadway groups that they can achieve theatrical vitality and depth rather automatically by adopting "Pirandellism" more than a quarter of a century after Pirandello started imitating himself unsuccessfully. We tend to forget that he won his perdurable place in the theatre with keen intelligence and wry compassion rather than with theatrical legerdemain. There was less resolution than ingenuity in *Between Two Thieves,* more conflict of attitudes than realization of a point of view. When the argument, moreover, deteriorates into the nonresolution of a symposium with actors planted in the audience, the point of view dissolved the play's very reason for being. There is no doubt, nevertheless, that most spectators, probably moved by the subject, found the play replete with interest and that this sultry work made most Broadway plays seem trivial.

Confusion also hounded *Program One,* the tripartite offering of a young company whose ambitions exceeded its talents and apparently beclouded its judgment. As performed, the first part of the program, E. E. Cummings' *Santa Claus,* made sense only at the cost of much tortuous mummery and trumpery while Death impersonates Santa Claus and *vice versa.* The second item was Yeats' Noh play on the Crucifixion, *Calvary,* which is two-thirds successful in text (a sufficient reason for wanting to stage it) and was only half-successful in the staging, being completely effective only in the moving appearance of Lazarus, who complains that Christ robbed him of his death, and in the use of some remarkable masks. And the third item, the grand guignol *Escurial* by the Belgian *avant-gard*ist Michel de Ghelderode, might well have provided an exciting rather than enervating experience if the play had been acted rather than shouted. Yet two-thirds of *Program One* could have introduced the New York public to work distinctly superior to a majority of the plays Broadway managers presume to expose before reasonably intelligent audiences.

Confusion proved devastating in the case of Lionel Abel's *The Pretender,* a well-written drama of a Negro intellectual's error of judgment and domestic complications. That confusion was an essential part of the meaning of this character study is entirely true, and the author should have received more credit for insight and intelligent, ironic, intention than the press gave him. The hero, a northern novelist residing in the deep South, was conceived with commendable originality as a romantically inclined individual who tries to adopt old chivalric codes as a means of putting himself on a par with the white race and believes that the way to maintain racial dignity is to stage an old-fashioned lynching bee when his wife, irritated by his lofty diffidence, pretends that she was violated by a white Southerner. As the plot thickened, good things were said, especially by a colored leader, and the muddle-headedness of the central character was ably exposed by the production, which was staged well enough by Herbert Machiz. But the Negro novelist-hero's desperate confusions infected the entire play with locomotor ataxia, and the author's irony was largely wasted since this inept character simply became unendurable. The author escaped the Scylla of conventional social drama only to become the prey of the Charybdis of intellectual gyrations of plot and character assassination—two of the three besetting sins of advanced off-Broadway writing: the third is the *hybris* of cleverness, which often results in the author's or director's outsmarting himself.

Nearly the same victimization of playwriting by mind (by intellectual *hybris,* if you will) appeared in Ionesco's *The Killer,* and the production—an impressive if uneven one, graced by one of Hiram Sherman's beautifully modulated performances—was punished for overreaching itself when it had to be withdrawn after a distressingly short run. Yet I would have gladly dispensed with several dozen Broadway productions in favor of the "Theatre 1960" production of *The Killer* presented by Richard Barr and H. B. Lutz at the tasteful little Seven Arts Theatre located on Madison Avenue. A decade or two ago a playgoer or reviewer would have been contented to commend the play quite flatly as an antifascist or antitotalitarian fantasy. Nowadays, the tendency is to talk around the subject, for you don't allow yourself to be an advanced intellectual without avoiding a commitment that so "simple" a fellow as a liberal might make and a man of average education could comprehend. The director, who is called the Interpreter of the play, talked Zen mysticism in a program note while the action talked antitotalitarianism. Perhaps the latter's simplicism is a form of critical resistance to an overwrought piece of work, and perhaps the director's questionable metaphysics was a means of swallowing the veritable camel of a turgid third act, hump and all. Who knows? And Ionesco, who has his own penchant for double talk and triple velleity, is himself apt to speak portentously of "the unreal transparency of the world and its opacity. . . ." But, in the main, *The*

Killer revealed itself as a work of creative and reflective playwriting. The present reviewer was stirred to recognition and rage by this expressionist-surrealist improvisation. I was only moderately put off by the transparencies and obscurities, and by the repetitions and seeming elisions, whether of the production or the playwriting (both seemed culpable), that cropped up. Diffusion in the second act and superfluity in the third could not cancel out Ionesco's imaginative projection of a world made convenient and impossible by modern science, and of a society of deluded and driven goose-steppers. The author was particularly vigorous in lampooning humanity in a characteristic state of wavering between feverish activity and bumbling apathy while the corrupters and destroyers ride herd on it. Realization of the destructiveness loose in the world and the poignantly inept pursuit of "the killer" in a sequence of surrealistically incohesive actions kept the play generally engrossing.

A desperate view of contemporary life, of life in the machine age, was also expressed in an ingeniously staged revival of Sophie Treadwell's expressionistic drama of the twenties, *Machinal*. Miss Treadwell's play has integrity of treatment but also a good deal of aridity. Desiccation of the soul is the theme of this bleak chronicle of an unhappily married woman who murders her husband and goes to the electric chair, and desiccation is what we are apt to get on the stage in any reliable production. Gene Frankel's direction provided the play with a colorful and mobile framework, stylizing the scene-shifting and employing a sort of *bullet méchanique* choreographed by Sophie Maslow with fine expressive lighting. The effect of the action was internally still arid except for moments of genuinely pathetic characterization of the heroine Helen Jones by Dolores Sutton. But *Machinal* could have extraordinary impact on spectators not so lofty as to be impervious to compassion for the inarticulate Helen and not so time-conscious as to be eager to "date" the work.

For a time, indeed, it seemed as if some special providence attended the fall of every downtown sparrow when nearly every potential fiasco somehow ended with at least some shred of honor while Broadway productions, which often started with distinct advantages, collapsed ignominiously. This was specially apparent in the "theatre of chance" program of that venturesome off-Broadway organization The Living Theatre that had already won high repute with *Tonight We Improvise* and *The Connection*. The first part of the program, a nondescript work called *The Marrying Maiden,* could have capsized almost any other enterprise. I omit a description partly because I could not offer one with any confidence, and partly because to say how the "play" could be made intelligible would be to propose revisions that would give it a beginning, a middle, and an end. This would require *dramaturgy,* the one quality that the author of this experiment in haphazard invention would repudiate as a betrayal of his "theatre of chance." He is apparently one of those advanced authors, the present epigones of the French surrealists of the twenties, for whom dramatic construction amounts to original sin. But the second part of The Living Theatre program consisted of Ezra Pound's free rendering of Sophocles' *The Women of Trachis* (the *Trachiniae*), beautifully staged by Julian Beck, poignantly played by Judith Malina in the role of Sophocles' love-destroyed heroine, and impressively performed by the physically imposing and immensely dignified Leonard Hicks in the role of Herakles. Except for some unsuccessful colloquialism, the Pound version is fluent, vivid, and effectively direct; it carries no excess baggage of words and sentiments. It went directly to its mark, and it ascended from pathos to tragic dignity at The Living Theatre. The production of this choral drama could have been a mess; it became superb as it proceeded relentlessly from exposition to resolution.

Finally, if the off-Broadway theatre is to receive its proper measure of regard, some observers are sure to point with gratification at the two parts of *Henry IV* and virtually all would add the production of *A Country Scandal,* a version of Chekhov's discarded early drama *That Worthless Fellow Platonov* excellently translated, trimmed, and adapted by Alex Szogy and no less expertly staged by Amnon Kabatchnik. Both men were inducted into the theatre at the Yale University School of Drama and the former is now a professor of French at Wesleyan University. But theirs was the least "academic" job on view in New York. It was Chekhovian without effort and without confusion after the first scene, which was muddled by the presence of too many fuzzily identified characters. It would have constituted a gratifying production in any season; in the 1959–60 season, so rich an experience was as welcome as it was rare. To describe the play in detail would be a wasted effort after it is noted that the action revolves around a Byronic provincial schoolteacher or, if you will, a middle-class Hamlet whose moody appearance and air of disenchantment attracts a succession of bored women. Comedy and farce, but also pathos and near-tragedy, come into view as they light on him with designs that partially succeed despite the fact that he is married to a woman who cherishes him. The life of the work is in the characters and most of the persons in the play elude definition to the degree that they are uniquely alive.

III

For many playgoers, however, the climax of the season was reached with the appearance of the Grand Kabuki Players from Japan under the auspices of the New York City Center. Enough has been written about Kabuki style to make comment from my corner superfluous. Anyone who attended at least one of the three programs of one-acters presented at the City Center could generally endorse the favorable views that promptly appeared in print. The present reviewer feels compelled to offer two unoriginal qualifications. One is that the style is entirely unsuited for "Western," especially American, theatre, and is at its best when that is the case. A sedulous imitation would be without reason, too. When we talk so freely about the need for stylization, let us avoid the mistake of assuming that "style" may be created in a vacuum and the equally fatuous error of thinking that that which is remarkable in one language and milieu must also be remarkable in another. There will not be any style or any strongly marked stylization in our theatre until we acquire new dramatic horizons, which is an unlikely eventuality in our lifetime. My other qualification concerns the Kabuki plays themselves. Those on view at the City Center were no worse or better than those we are likely to encounter in our reading. They are taken from large and loosely organized chronicle cycles. These are pastiche at best, and most of the individual plays, equivalent in extent to substantial one-acters, are quite trite or banal, whether fantasies based on native superstition, domestic dramas, or accounts of the extravagant feudal loyalties of vassal to master, of ronin to lord. The exceptions I have noted in my reading and playgoing are episodes closely linked to medieval tradition, plays that carry the live-wire charge of a high style both in art and belief. Then the masked, highly costumed, and intensely conventionalized art of Kabuki, which nevertheless employs modern theatre engineering and lighting, becomes truly imposing. It acquires an obdurate nobility that contrasts sharply with the middle-class complacency and modern flaccidity of most Western plays. It stands at the opposite pole from realism in order to attain the most intense reality of spirit. It is aloof but not without a degree of understandable desperation. It conveys or, rather, projects, if one may use Pascal's famous phrase, the grandeur and misery of man.

Of such a nature was the Grand Kabuki presentation of *Kanjincho* (The Subscription List) on its first program of one-acters, a dramatization of a vassal warrior's great trial in smuggling his prince across the mountains in the disguise of a monk. And here, translated not merely into text but into the most broadly and expressively stylized action, Kabuki art was truly impressive. Chiefly, moreover, it was the stylized acting of a truly great actor, Onoe Shoroku II, that brought a rare glory into our theatre with intonations, symbolic foot-stomping movements, gestures, and postures that transcend literature at the same time that they transfigure life. Some of this magnificence fortunately transferred itself on occasions in the other Kabuki plays that varied from fantasy and heroic melodrama to domestic comedy, the latter achieving its own grace with a knowing realism curiously strengthened rather than weakened by stylization. Part of the art lies, I might add, in a style of being partly inside the role and partly outside it, as if one *persona* of the actor were observing and directing another *persona*. It appears to be essentially the technique advocated by Brecht, who turned to the Orient for his theory and practice of stylization. I doubt, however, that this technique can be safely entrusted to American-trained actors, and I would take special precautions against student-actors' tendency to interpret the style as license to feel self-conscious or to register coyness. Unimaginative—and for me this means *impersonal*—intellectualism is apt to accomplish even less than our wonted sloppy emotionalism. The former, as Heine said so well of a certain contemporary writer's poetry, resembles Bayard's horse: "It has every conceivable virtue, but it is dead. . . ."

BROADWAY VERSUS OFF-BROADWAY
ENDEAVORS (DECEMBER, 1960)

In 1960, Broadway and off-Broadway managements tried as many dodges as possible to avoid having to trust themselves to plays and the failure of all but a few that appeared on the scene in the early fall made me sympathize with the managers' desperate efforts to bet on something less risky than a drama. Even on a well-tried one like the fiasco *Farewell, Farewell, Eugene,* which flourished in England for reasons that entirely eluded New York. Nevertheless, off-Broadway soon endeavored to supply the longed-for article of a play in its characteristic "revivalist" manner. It revived Philip Barry's 1958 somber allegory of good and evil *Here Come the Clowns,* Strindberg's saturnine sex-war drama *The Dance of Death,* Shaw's lively *Man and Superman,* and one of the strongest "social" plays of the 1940's, *Deep Are the Roots,* D'Usseau and Gow's drama about the roots of racial prejudice. But somehow there was no discernible excitement on the periphery of Broadway even when reviewers dutifully applauded the worthy efforts. A little more curiosity was engendered when a dramatization of Dostoevsky's great novel *The Idiot* by Boris Tumarin and Jack Sydow, very ably staged by the former, opened downtown and got a favorable press. The first of the two acts of the dramatization actually sustained the vague praise of the daily papers, the adapters having exercised considerable skill in maneuvering the bulky matter into dramatic shape. Unfortunately, the second and more important half of the dramatization fell apart, and it was evident that even this latest of many efforts to dramatize *The Idiot* had not succeeded in reducing the turbulent and multileveled novel to the dimensions of a stage play, or even in making the conduct of the characters conclusively comprehensible. Another off-Broadway venture, the Donald Goldman presentation of Guenter Rutenborn's *The Sign of Jonah,* only briefly seen before in New York, promised a great deal, too. This play by a German pastor deals directly with the question of war guilt and Nazi brutality. But even in the American adaptation used in the downtown production, *The Sign of Jonah* seemed much more suitable for German than American audiences. The style was hortatory and the form fragmentary, and the play rattled with the frantic didacticism and vehement expressionism that has long been characteristic of "seriousness" on the modern

German stage. One could reluctantly conclude that even with so impressive a harangue as *The Sign of Jonah,* a play was still not available on the off-Broadway scene. It remained chiefly for Broadway to come to the rescue of the drama-starved minority, and for once Broadway did—with three imported pieces, *The Hostage, Becket,* and *A Taste of Honey,* for which high expectations could be entertained on the strength of their success across the sea. Once they were successfully launched on the Broadway stage, it was apparent, however, that unanimity of appreciation could be earned only for *A Taste of Honey,* the least ambitiously conceived of the three works. It was once more evident that nowadays Europe's playwrights are no more adept than ours in engaging large issues with concentrated intelligence and energy.

The Hostage is Brendan Behan's second play to be seen in New York. The first was his deeply felt, if limited, prison drama *The Quare Fellow,* and José Quintero's "Circle-in-the-Square" production of this work introduced us not only to an immensely talented new Irish playwright but also to a colorful personality who can deflect us from considering the play itself. Looking at both plays together, however, we can form an estimate of his talent far more relevant to dramatic art than newspaper accounts of the author's penchant for pubs and publicity. It is plain that he is a superb "scene-wright" and an indifferent "playwright." In the *Hostage,* it is evident that his forte is theatrical improvisation rather than dramatic construction. Once he glimpses the ruling idea for a play he seems perfectly content to make it the basis for a series of variations. The result in *The Hostage* is more variety show than play.

With the same fundamental idea of the wastefulness of civil war, O'Casey wrote a masterpiece in *The Plough and the Stars* by concentrating on the tension and confusion of his characters, wheras Behan concentrates on their theatrics. A young English soldier has been kidnapped by Irish I.R.A. patriots and held as a hostage for one of their number who is to be hanged in Belfast for some act of violence against the British government. Kept hidden in a brothel owned by another patriot, the life-loving English lad is killed at the end during a scuffle with the patriots after an affectionate Irish peasant girl has brought the police to the hideout in order to save him from retaliatory execution. *The Hostage,* however, consists mainly of quips, songs and dances, often addressed to the audience directly—the quips as asides, the songs as divertissements. Even the death of the young English soldier turns out to be a mere vaudeville incident when he rises from the floor to lilt a song the gist of which is "Death where is thy sting-a-ling-a-ling-a-ling." The Joan Littlewood production brought over from London cooperates unreluctantly, though in a somewhat genteel manner, with the author's irreverent attitude toward Church, State, Politics, and Theatre (especially "fourth-wall" theatre), capitalizing on the author's merits of lively caricature and raffish detachment.

For all its faults, *The Hostage* is *alive,* and my reading of the play inclines me to believe it is even more alive than I found it to be in the production. The life of the work emanates from the assorted characters and cartoons (and it is not at all certain that the latter are less vital on the stage than the former), and from the author's personal buoyancy as manifested in dialogue, song, and a blithe scorn for self-inflationary idealism. His very irreverence is a form of piety, a regard for the preciousness of life. A considerable compassion, secured against sentimentality by Behan's ebullient writing, wells up from the cross-currents of the wayward action when young life is put in jeopardy by ideological righteousness. If *The Hostage* is, so to speak, "antiplay" it is fortunately also anticant. One could develop considerable affection and a rather amused respect for its author. And one could feel honestly indebted to him for being almost the only Irish writer since Joyce and the young O'Casey to spare us Celtic mist and windy heroics while treating the subject of nationalist conflict. Yet it must be admitted that Behan's success in engaging a "big" theme lay mainly in ignoring his plot and dissolving his theme. And in this respect so highly individual a writer as the author of *The Hostage* appears to have much in common with other contemporary writers whose commendable success in picturing life is associated with a reprehensible success in reducing it to insignificance.

This was evident in Jean Anouilh's *Becket,* which opened at the St. James Theatre with considerable éclat in a resplendent Peter Glenville production. With Laurence Olivier adding a fine finish of intelligence and spirit to Becket and with Anthony Quinn conveying a genuine animality and a cumbersome pathos to Henry II (although neither actor seemed entirely comfortable in his role), the production was punctuated by dramatically intense scenes. The lengthy and somewhat lagging chronicle proceeds with interest as we follow Henry's infatuation with the brightly inscrutable Becket, the King's disappointment in the worldling he made Archbishop of Canterbury, and his deadly duel with the now intensely zealous churchman over the respective claims of Church and State. In the arid young season, the *Becket* production was a welcome arrival as a glossy and spectacular boulevard bonanza for the playgoer, offering him pageantry and "information," a sense of "history," and a sense of personal "drama." It was decidedly "theatre," the text was "literate," and the treatment was knowingly modern in combining sympathy with irony as well as some cynicism. It is the sort of entertainment that in personalizing history (and considerably altering it) offers culture and sophistication to its playgoers whether it collects them on the boulevards of Paris or on Times Square. It is, in brief, the sort of play that the journalists who review plays invariably call "impressive." I was considerably impressed myself.

I refrain from poking easy fun at Peter Glenville's use of hobby horses on which the actors were mounted part of the time, but deplore the procedure as an unnecessary expense. The hokum was efficiently managed. I desist from protesting against the author's historical inaccuracies since they don't greatly matter, and he is no more guilty in this respect than all the other little Schillers of the stage. I am not particularly exercised over the author's failure to make Becket's position wholly understandable. Becket, according to Anouilh, has been looking for a way of recovering his self-respect or honor, which he forfeited by passing from his low estate into the favor of Norman royalty, and he finds it at last in the cause of the Church that he identifies with the honor of God. This explanation will do as well as any other (so long as I don't look up the historical facts), and it has the merit of being integrated into the play in several small scenes. As for Henry II, if Anouilh, Peter Glenville, and Anthony Quinn want to present him as a rough lout rather than as an intelligent ruler, that is their privilege, and Henry's reputation is of no particular importance to me or any other unspecialized playgoer. Even the cloudy nature of the issue does not in itself trouble me, although a scene between the Pope and a Cardinal in Rome does because it is vaudeville Italian at its worst in a tasteless performance.

Somehow the adept French playwright and his British director succeeded in maintaining the interest of most scenes and in relating most of them externally, but without actually relating them inwardly. The chief defect of the play is that the whole is very much smaller than the sum of its parts would suggest. With the issue tenuous and the motivations vague, and with a great scattering of historical or pseudohistorical detail, we are ultimately left with nothing more meaningful than regret that the friendship of Becket and Henry II should have broken up. It is even a question whether we are obliged to feel this regret very deeply since Becket remains an enigma and Henry's affections border on the ludicrous—and not so much because they are apparently homosexual (as I think his jealous Queen implies) but because he is so stupidly irritable and monomaniacal in the Broadway production. Ultimately, the Glenville production proves to be a penetrable façade, and behind it will be found hardly anything that is not merely cloudy history, shallow biography, and out-of-focus sentiment. Only a point of view could have made the history and biography meaningful, and transformed sentiment into conviction. I suspect it was there in the play—in the dramatically submerged though baldly stated idea that the deracinated Becket needed to attach himself to a cause that would give him a high purpose and self-respect. Sartre would have made some such point the center and justification of his play. But if Anouilh brought a point of view to *Becket,* he was apparently unwilling or unable to entrust himself to it sufficiently. In *Becket,* as in so much else he has written, Anouilh stands at the fringes of feeling and thought, trains romantically colored lights on the realities of alienation or failure, and sprinkles the human scene with irony as a substitute for conviction. And, I might add, as a solace and confirmation for the sense of defeat rather than as a stimulus or challenge. The difference between *Becket* and some earlier plays by Anouilh is that the large dimensions of costume drama and spectacle simply smother any subtle and oblique artistry of which he has proved capable in other plays, while the huge labor of a history play promises the playgoer a work of epic stature which Anouilh, the suave Parisian, does not provide and may be constitutionally incapable of providing. If nothing else, *Becket* is useful as a means of measuring the talent of one of the most highly regarded playwrights of our time.

Fortunately, the early fall theatre had one radically different, a modest and essentially fulfilled piece of writing to display on its counter when the indefatigable David Merrick presented *A Taste of Honey* by Shelagh Delaney. Miss Delaney was nineteen years old when she wrote the play, which won instant and well-merited acclaim in England. The American production, a virtual duplication of the British with Angela Lansbury and Joan Plowright in the principal parts of a flighty mother and her neglected daughter, met with an equally warm reception on Broadway. It is a little play made big as life by the sensitiveness of the writing, a sensitiveness without the slightest evasion of reality and with hardly any concession to sentimentality.

The locale is a dreary factory town, the family story is tawdry, and the mother's self-indulgence sends her lonely daughter to seek solace in a brief affair with a handsome Negro sailor who does not keep his promise to return within six months and marry her. The girl, who is now carrying his child, is saved from despair only by the watchfulness of a homosexual friend affectingly played by Andrew Ray. He is a lad whose gauche attempts to behave in a manly manner and whose feminine talents in keeping the home tidy and preparing it for the arrival of the baby dignify his relationship with the sloppy and bewildered girl. The mother, after having lost her playboy lover to a buxom rival, returns just when the young man has everything under control. Sentimentally she proposes to take charge of her daughter and drives the boy away, but makes herself scarce again once the girl tells her the child she is carrying may be a black baby. The girl goes into labor a moment after she has been left alone.

That is about all there is to the play, and I suppose it would be accurate to call it a slice-of-life. But commonplace realism is surmounted by the setting, which combines an outdoor scene with a skeletal rendition of the apartment in which most of the action transpires; and the production includes on the stage a small jazz band, which accompanies some of the action and provides incidental jazz music for the blackouts that separate one scene from another. A wry and poignant piece of poetic realism on stage, *A Taste of Honey* provided the early season's most gratifying Broadway production even if the character of the neglectful mother was somewhat ambiguously presented, perhaps as a sop to Broadway's queasy stomach, as well as a result of Angela Lansbury's overly farcical playing in contrast to Joan Plowright's flawless portrait of a lost but vital young person. Especially noteworthy was the tact without evasiveness that appeared in the treatment of the homosexual youth, proving that Miss Delaney is one new playwright who can avoid sensationalism without avoiding reality. Moreover, the gift of multiple characterization never failed the observant young author. In her work, characters that could have become stereotypes assert an individuality that makes persons of them; even the trollop of a mother is given qualifying moods and extenuating intentions. And a tale of woe that could easily have resembled old-fashioned laments for the seduced daughters of the lower orders acquires vitality and freshness because instead of prating about sin, guilt, and forgiveness, the author relied on detached observation rather than sentiment. There are no stereotypes when the pregnant girl feels interest in her condition rather than maudlin fear or remorse, and there is no possibility of embarrassment in the audience when her homosexual friend takes over the running of the fearfully untidy house as a matter of course. It will be interesting to see what Miss Delaney will be able to do with more comprehensive and challenging matter as her talent matures and her horizons widen.

AVANT-GARDE DRAMA (MAY, 1961)

It would be gratifying to find a play of some seriousness on Broadway about which it could be said that the whole is the sum of all its parts. Nor is it parenthetical to remark that it would be pleasant, too, to encounter plays in which the seeker after spiritual reality is himself a human embodiment of the search instead of a bloodless or more or less abstruse figure. Pinchbeck religiosity comes into vogue occasionally when true religiousness ceases to be a way of life or, failing that, at least a passion—as, for example, in Claudel's best work. The ultimate defect of religion-mongering in contemporary drama or fiction is not that there is too much religion in it, but that there is too little. If romanticism can be called "spilt religion," willed religiosity should be recognized as "spilt romanticism."

A larger symptomatology is to be noted here than some critics are inclined to charge against Broadway showmanship. The *avant-garde* is no less given to tensions and inconclusive writing, if not indeed to furtive and futile skirmishing, than Broadway is. One would imagine that this is not the case when the leader of the *avant-garde* delivers himself of a rare full-length play such as *Rhinoceros* that is received almost as sacred writ in European capitals and then crosses the Atlantic and gets a respectful reception in New York. It is a notion of this advanced continental writer that the growing conformity and brutalization of the world can be best conveyed by the idea of men unaccountably (or, rather, only too accountably) turning into rhinoceri. It is a fine notion, and it is a pity that Ionesco thought he could, and had to, make a full-length play with it. It is also his good luck, as well as to some degree the public's, that he thought so; otherwise, *Rhinoceros* might not have reached a larger public than that which his shorter pieces have reached. But the pity of it is that invention fails Ionesco and the play he has written is essentially a long one-act piece unconsciously padded and kept from falling apart on Broadway by three performances—namely, Anne Jackson's playing of a young woman's deterioration into the shrewishness that begins her transformation into a pachyderm, Zero Mostel's sublimely skillful burlesque that turns the character John from an irascible stuffed shirt into a trumpeting rhinoceros before the very eyes of the public, and Eli Wallach's serio-comic idealist and fuzzy little man who becomes the only surviving human being in a bestial world.

These performances, as well as Morris Carnovsky's droll impersonation of a fulsomely futile "philosopher," alone deserve the patronage of the Broadway playgoer, as does the general production staged by Joseph Anthony and designed by the play's gifted New York producer Leo Kerz. Without going so far as to say that this presentation is the best conceivable (Miss Jackson and Mr. Wallach are less sharply defined than one might desire) or the one that most fully conveys Ionesco's intention (he has been reported as feuding with the producer), one should not hesitate to list the production as one of the few gratifications of the Great White Way. The play itself offers good scenes and moments; the coming of the off-stage rhinoceri fills the first act with effective tension and the animal transformation of Zero Mostel is a memorable scene.

All the praise in the world cannot, however, make out a convincing case for considering *Rhinoceros* a full-length play that does not wear exceedingly thin. Even Ionesco's redoubtable talent for inventing farcial scenes and dialogue cannot counteract the aridity that afflicts the play when the author turns allegorist with a solemn message. It is possible to interpret various details in such a manner as to suggest layers of meaning and richness of observation, but these have not actually become a dynamic part of his fable; they are not the substance of the action or of the character-realization. Ultimately, then, *Rhinoceros* must be set down as the inevitably abortionate product of a talent suffering, like most original contemporary talent, from hemophilia.

In drama, as in fiction, the sign of this debilitation is currently an unwillingness (arising, I suspect, from an incapacity) to create character. A certain antihumanism is connected with this quality, and one may sense its presence even in a work that presents a concern over the dehumanization of mankind as explicitly as *Rhinoceros* does. At the same time, it must be noted that *Rhinoceros* does not have to be a very vital play in characterization to benefit from the vitality of its subject or ruling conception. It communicates a sense of importance, and almost urgency, in terms that are successful, if not dramatically, at least theatrically (except for the pace) and histrionically. Playgoers so often trapped in a quagmire of humdrum realism are apt to feel that their imagination has been stimulated and their minds stretched by Ionesco, and for this relief they are likely to express understandable gratitude. No playgoers with any regard for "serious" theatre will want to miss *Rhinoceros* just as no lover of the art of acting should deprive himself of the opportunity of seeing Zero Mostel's supreme performance.

FORAY INTO THE ABSURD
(DECEMBER, 1961)

The 1960's seemed dedicated to a variety of adventures in the new theatre of the so-called Absurd, started in the 1950's by gifted new writers such as Eugene Ionesco and Samuel Beckett who were located in Paris though of different national origins. In the new decade, England and even America joined the movement, if movement it could be called in view of its variety. And it *could* be considered a movement on at least the grounds that its leading playwrights thrust stalemate and confusion in the foreground of the dramatic scene and employed imaginative styles of farce and fantasy to enforce their meaning or, if you will, *non*meaning on audiences. Several plays on view in Manhattan in the fall of 1961 illustrated the range of the effort.

It appeared in an exemplary farcical display in Samuel Beckett's weirdly elegiac *Happy Days* and Harold Pinter's *The Caretaker,* for which the *New Yorker* description of "mysterious, frightening, funny and altogether remarkable" was entirely apt. Both plays provided a concentration of mature feeling with worthy skill and control that set them apart from other new plays as products of a virtually different world of theatre than the customary commercial product.

In the Beckett drama, a middle-aged woman called Winnie chatters incessantly while entrapped up to her bosom in a mound of seemingly scorched earth. Seeking to fill in the interminable day, she addresses trivia of all sorts to her mate, who spends much of his time in a narrow hole behind the mound. Above all, she assures him, without getting any particular response, that all's well, that she has had a grand life, and that this is one of her really "happy days" when it is evident that her situation is hopeless. A certain jauntiness is also evident in the way her mate sitting behind her with his back to the audience, adjusts his straw hat over his broken head, to which he applies a handkerchief now and then. So ends the first part of *Happy Days*. In the second part, after a long lapse of time, Winnie still rattles on and still insists that this is one of her happy days, although she is now buried up to her neck. She cannot even get to the revolver she took out of her purse and placed on the mound in the first act. Her mate's condition has also deteriorated; we see him as an old man who is unable to walk erect. His human determination is manifest by his wearing formal clothes, his creeping up the mound in an effort to reach her face—or is it to reach the pistol on the mound with which to put an end to it all? But he has not the strength to carry out his design, and rolls off the mound when he is almost in reach of the revolver.

Happy Days is another Beckett threnody on the sorry lot of mankind reduced to an absurd stalemate from which man can only decline into a worse one on a planet plainly doomed to devastation. In *Happy Days,* at the same time, one encounters another tribute to human endurance and the determination to shore up inner defenses of faith or delusion against failure. Never yielding an inch to sentimentality, against which the writing defends itself with sustained irony, so that human heroism also appears to be a ridiculous capacity for self-delusion, *Happy Days* is compact and self-contained. It is a "whole" as few recent full-length plays have been. In this, however, also lies the limitation of the work, which appears on the stage, as well as in print, as an extended metaphor. And since what it provides is a kind of *summa* of the "human condition" rather than a story or an unfolding action, Beckett's metaphor is not merely extended but *overextended.* It is that at least for the stage, on which it seems unduly prolonged, because the playgoer can "get the idea" faster than it is given to him by the playwright's dialogue, so that as work written for the stage it seems rather redundant.

It is indeed one of the apparent limitations of much of our *avantgarde* dramatic writing that it quickly *runs out of development.* Depending upon mood or metaphor, the playwright produces full-length plays that are one-act plays in dramatic outlines and substance. Sometimes, as in the case of a number of Ionesco one-acters (especially *The Chairs*) and in Beckett's dramatic monologue, *Krapp's Last Tape,* the author actually writes a one-act play, and the results can be marvelous within the narrow compass of the work. There are occasions, however, when the author needs more than a single episode along with an indefinite lapse of time between episodes, as in *Happy Days* when the characters' situation appears —I think necessarily so—in two stages, first a bad situation and then a worse one. In a case like *Happy Days,* the author cannot then crystallize his theme very well in a one-act play and writes a full-length one instead which, nevertheless, doesn't sustain itself as such on the stage. A relatively closed situation, conveying a quickly established mood and a rapidly completed point, is the one thing offered instead. *Happy Days* cannot escape the integrity of its theme of stasis without itself suffering from stasis.

Happily, this condition was overcome to a degree by Ruth White's superb performance rich with the quiver of life in the rhythm and inflection of her speech. And the stalemate was further counteracted to some degree by Alan Schneider's production with its focus on the fateful mound in a full blaze of light that provides simultaneous relief and ironic contrast. One does not have to blink at the limitations of the work in order to respect it. With a little sensitivity and some regard for the drama as art rather than as an exercise in pay-dirt *kitsch*, it should not be difficult to do so.

The "negativism" of the work is a large subject that cannot be explored here (as is the question of whether Beckett hasn't shot his bolt as a playwright by now if he cannot get on to another and richer subject), but it also applies to Pinter's *The Caretaker*, a more active play than *Happy Days* but also a more elusive one. In the New York production, staged by Donald McWhinnie with a fine three-man British cast, *The Caretaker* proved its power to fascinate audiences as well as to tantalize them.

The surface action is a piece of macabre realism, and it is accurate to say that the author insists on our keeping only the liberal substance of the play in view. A gentle and curiously muted and ineffectual young man brings home a seedy tramp for no particular reason other than his habit of collecting almost anything. Yet it is an act of compassion all the same and it is compounded as such by the host's deferring to his guest and protecting him while a breezy younger brother sadistically badgers the tramp, exposes his shabby lies, and frightens him. Later he offers him a job as caretaker of the run-down tenement. The gentle elder brother reveals that he was once an inmate of a mental hospital and that shock treatments has left him enervated and somewhat addled. Armed with this information, the alternately whining and arrogant tramp begins to lord it over his host, scoffs at his vague hopes of putting the house in order after building a shack in the yard, until the host, unable to endure the persecution or outraged by the mockery of his delusion of accomplishing anything, orders him out of the house. The tramp makes a last effort to reinstate himself with the help of the sadistic younger brother, who leads him on with a show of sympathy only to turn on him suddenly and viciously, and the ungrateful tramp, whose bravura cloaks his insecurity or lostness, loses his shelter and departs helplessly. Amplified with many a farcical, grotesque, or mysterious detail, this is the essential action of the play that scored a great success in London, apparently as a *tour de force* of naturalistic theatricality, suspense, and humor. If there is one talent Pinter obviously possesses, it is the compound one of producing mystery, suspense, and surprise, the latter by means of rapid changes of pace and tone. And on the literal level, he succeeds very well indeed, if not indeed too well; that is, so well that he invites a suspicion of charlatanism.

At the same time, regardless of his denial of symbolic content, Pinter writes with poetic nuance and with what seem to be metaphysical overtones, or at least forces the imagination to look for them in his work. One is inclined to do so, I think, for one simply cannot reconcile oneself to *The Caretaker,* as a literal experience if one happens to like the play strongly or is absorbed by it, as the present reviewer was, because one must feel that one has been "had" by a very clever but hollow contriver. To proceed to formulate an exegesis is to invite trouble, but that is unavoidable. The trouble is minimized, however, if one eschews allegory, as one should because the parts of the play simply won't fit together as allegory and one would be forced to ask questions for which there are no answers in the play. Indeed, the author's disclaimer of any sub-surface reality in his play may have been motivated precisely by an understandable reluctance to have to live up to allegorical expectations. Here we come to the difference between *allegory,* in which everything conforms to a scheme or agrees with a definition or lesson (as *Everyman* or the Hofmannsthal *Jedermann* does) and *symbolism,* in which a viewpoint or conception is hinted at or evoked rather than inflexibly outlined or logically defined.

The Caretaker is a haunting work as well as an exciting one; even the humor is wry and enigmatic. To spell out all that this work suggests to the present writer would be time-consuming without being provable. Here I can only conclude that the experience it provides is portentous as well as comically melodramatic and melodramatically comic, constituting, as it were, a dramatic genre all by itself. In my imagination Pinter's broken-down house is the world, the brother whom people considered crazy enough to confine in a mental institution is a Christ-figure like Dostoevsky's "idiot" Prince Myshkin, and the younger worldly and sadistic brother, who has an ambivalent relationship with him, is a Devil figure. Between them stands the figure of the tramp, so wonderfully realized by the British actor Donald Pleasence that he is completely alive and does not appear to be at all a "symbol" or "type." He is Man himself, ever deserving expulsion from whatever Eden or shelter may be offered him out of the compassion of trustful innocence or the design of skeptical malevolence. Out of my own mouth I impeach myself, and even a detailed defense might not acquit me of the charge of straining for "meaning." But I am trying to convey the one certain fact that *The Caretaker,* regardless of my minor dissatisfactions with the work, coheres for me magically and makes sense as a poetic (though not necessarily "anagogical") realization of a "feeling" about humanity. It is possible, I would conclude, to derive gratifications from Pinter's play on both literal and imaginative, or *reflective,* levels.

One socially directed variant appeared in the race-problem spoof of *Purlie Victorious,* fabricated by the actor Ossie Davis who had turned playwright for the occasion. It was made up of addendums, farce, fantasy, and improvisation pressed into service of a plot in which a young Negro (delightfully played by Ossie Davis himself, and charmingly supported by his wife, Ruby Dee, in the other leading role) makes a dithering fool of a moss-backed racist. For obvious reasons *Purlie Victorious* was a successful play on Broadway. Karl Wittlinger's most sophisticated and very much more complicated fantasy *Do You Know the Milky Way* was not. Its European author, seeking a metaphysical extension instead of using absurdism for purely political ends, provided an ambiguously undertaken synthesis of reality and fantasy, imaginatively staged by Herbert Berghof, and performed with charm and resourcefulness by Hal Holbrook and George Voskovec. (The latter was especially fortunate in acquiring the part of a psychiatrist called upon to play a variety of roles, including that of the devil. The part enabled him to display the great histrionic talent that made him one of the great clowns of the European theatre when he ran a celebrated political cabaret in Prague with his recently deceased partner Werich shortly before the outbreak of World War I.) Interspersed with the wit of disillusion and cynicism, this more or less expressionistic and dadaist extravaganza, which included a marvelous film sequence in the "epic" manner of Brecht and Piscator, was distinctly worth seeing. But its arch showmanship exceeded its imaginativeness, producing a superfluity of comic conceit and fancy. And generous potions of romantic sentimentality, of star worship and other worldly nostalgia, watered down its satire on the culpability of mankind, which could remind one of *The Visit,* and its Kafkaesque farce of man's effort to acquire a satisfactory identity.

ROBERT BOLT'S *A MAN FOR ALL SEASONS* (MARCH, 1962)

By far the most distinguished play on Broadway in 1962, *A Man for All Seasons,* came from England, as did the performers led by Paul Scofield who made this Sir Thomas More biography singularly vital and moving. Nothing that American playgoers knew about the author, Robert Bolt, prepared them for this work. He had been introduced to Broadway a year or two before with a quiet and depressing play about a middle-class mediocrity and failure ironically entitled *Flowering Cherry.* The moral of this is simple: Mr. Bolt was depressed by the subject of the last-mentioned play and exalted by the subject of *A Man for All Seasons.* We have met other cases of everyday mediocrity pushing playwrights below their manifest capacity; Maxwell Anderson, for example, functioned well below par in dealing with the adjustment problems of returning soldiers in *Truckline Café* at the end of World War II. The subject has usually dictated the dramatic form in the case of the commonplace characters (*Death of a Salesman* was a rare exception), thrusting the dramaturgy into the troughs of mimetic realism from which the playwright rises only with the help of rare talent and remarkable sympathy. The reverse, fortunately, also occurs, and subject-matter has been known to inspire rewarding ventures into style and form. This happened in the case of *A Man for All Seasons,* which owes its distinction to something more than the admiration the author felt for Sir Thomas More.

As a matter of fact, the latter's distinction as the author of *Utopia* and a leader of the Humanist movement is virtually ignored in the play, and his exalted role as a Christian martyr resulting from his defiance of Henry VIII in defense of papal authority receives an "antiheroic" rather than conventionally heroic treatment. Like the hero of Brecht's *Galileo,* Sir Thomas More manifests every desire to escape the consequences of his point of view and to avoid martyrdom. That this treatment results in an extraordinarily appealing portrait, that of a lovable man who is all the closer to us for endeavoring to save as long as possible both his skin and his integrity, produces an indirect heroism more attractive today than a directly heroic treatment would be. The *style* of the play is determined by the author's confidence in his hero's ability to win our admiration without rhetoric. The *form* of the play, moreover, supports the style so successfully that it confirms the opinion of those for whom content and form, as well as a style and form, are inseparable in a true work of art. The form is "Brechtian," as is much of the style; that is, the play is "epic." It is epic in the narrow sense of being a chronicle unified by an idea— here, the idea of a humane man trying to retain his integrity in a world of opportunists and hyenas. The play is also epic in the Brechtian mode of compressing events meaningfully by means of an overall presentational type of drama carried out with the help of a narrator, who addresses the audience in blithe violation of the "fourth-wall" convention and unfolds for the audience only the episodes that are germane to the theme. And this procedure further strips down those episodes to their significant features or "form," enabling (indeed *requiring*) the production to dispense with routine realism of detail.

The results are gratifying in the theatre not merely because the play moves with ease and authority, but because the demonstration of Sir Thomas More's drama is not presented in the manner of arch theatrical-ism that revels in its ingenuity and, so to speak, winks to the audience in inviting it to play the game of "make-believe" with the actors. On the contrary, the scenes, as in the best of Brecht, possess all the illusion and all the emotional involvement they need to engross the spectator in the human drama unfolding before him; and the actors are allowed, if not indeed enabled, to display all the vitality of which they are capable. Paul Scofield created a truly memorable impression as More, and many of the other performances had about the same vitality; the playing of Cromwell by Leo McKern, of the young Henry VIII, full of bounce and will, by Keith Baxter, and of the multiple "Common Man" by George Rose in a variety of roles had even more vivacity than Mr. Scofield's performance without forfeiting credibility. By now I suppose it is unnecessary to cor-rect the impression that "illusion" and "emotion" are *verboten* in the theatre of Brecht.

It is not my intention, however, to make the virtue of Britain's Robert Bolt depend upon the virtues of Brecht. *A Man for All Seasons* actually lacks certain Brechtian qualities, gaining as well as losing something— gaining a little in depth or nearness of portraiture while losing historical meaning and muddling the political-moral reality of the work. The most cherishable merits of the play are its own, and the dramaturgic feat that unifies the chronicle, the presence of the Common Man who represents the eternal opportunist or petty egoist who fends for himself in the midst of epochal events (he is More's servant at the beginning and More's exe-cutioner at the end), leaps at us directly from the dramatic imagination of the author. With its various virtues, including its well-placed sympathy for More's family and ironic treatment of secondary characters, *A Man for All Seasons* was without question the most impressive Broadway production of the season, and a patriotic playgoer could only regret that it was not the work of an American playwright and of a predominantly American cast. It is regrettable that native playwrights try so hard to lift themselves up by the bootstraps of their contemporaneity instead of using the past significantly. I do have the one large reservation that the historical meaning of Bolt's play is nebulous while the moral meaning impacted in the characters is generally impressive. The one brief section in which the future is fused with the present (in which the deaths of Cromwell and Henry VIII are forecast) is decidedly inadequate. If Bolt's play missed greatness—and I believe it is a small and uncertain achievement by comparison with Shaw's *Saint Joan*—the limitation is in the "head," rather than the "heart," of the work.*

---

* [Further qualification of this remark was intended. Professor Gassner noted marginally: "Limitations—why!" *Ed.*]

LUMBERING AMERICANS
(MARCH, 1962)

Intrinsically more dynamic [than Williams' *The Night of the Iguana*] by virtue of the subject matter, Paddy Chayefsky's extremely well-received Biblical drama *Gideon* impressed me as a rather self-defeating, almost unavoidably lumbering, attempt to write a philosophical play. This was especially apparent in the last part of the work, while the early scenes composed, on the whole, an unpretentious and entertaining pastiche. That the simple clod Gideon should have been chosen as a divine instrument by the Lord, impressively impersonated by Frederic March as the Old Testament tribal Jehovah, had its amusing features. Mr. Chayefsky made a bizarre entertainment of Gideon's leadership of the Hebrews in their war against Canaanite enemies and polytheistic temptations. It is the second part of the play, where the theme should crystallize out of the solution of folk comedy, that the play lost energy as well as clarity. Gideon's relationship to God becomes increasingly ambivalent, and this is a good subject that Mr. Chayefsky and the actor playing Gideon (the talented Douglas Campbell) handled as well as is possible without the playful intellectualism of a Giraudoux or the mordant irony of a Brecht. The conclusion of the odd relationships between Gideon and God is apparently that Gideon, or Man, will have to go his own way to achieve compassion for the human race since God's ways are inscrutably nonhuman. A truly strong conclusion! But it is obfuscated by the action, and especially spoiled by a strip-tease, belly-dance vulgarization of Gideon's decent impulse to spare the shiekhs of the desert whom the Lord ordered him to kill. In one way or another, the most ambitious American play of the season became lumpy as well as murky. The author's widening talent and intentions came up against the difficulty of his subject; as a result, the unquestionable success of *Gideon* with the playgoing public can be called in question on almost any grounds that carry any force in responsible dramatic criticism. Yet the temptation to respect the play is at least as great as the temptation to invalidate respect for it, for *Gideon* does represent a strong effort to create drama of substance in the market place.

*   *   *

Even Thornton Wilder allowed himself to be trapped into solemnity, in the last play of the one-act program produced by the off-Broadway Circle-in-the-Square theatre under the title of *Plays for Bleecker Street*. This climactic play, *Someone from Assisi*, number 4 (*Lust*) in the sequence called *The Seven Deadly Sins*, presented an encounter between St. Francis and a madwoman whom he had seduced before his renunciation of the worldly life. But whatever poignancy the author achieved was nearly lost by the unrelieved overemphasis of the situation and the overwrought performance of the madwoman. Wilder, however, comes much closer than most of our playwrights to the imaginative agility and theatrical lightness of European playwrights, and this was once more evident in the first two one-acters on the bill, *Infancy* and *Childhood*, numbers 1 and 2 from the series called *The Seven Ages of Man*. But for some excess of mugging on the part of a "policeman" in the Keystone Cops manner, *Infancy* was a delightful comedy about infants and the adults who take care of them; and *Childhood*, except for a little slowness of pace, was both penetrating and beautiful in its evocation of children's fantasies about the death of parents and about unaccompanied adventures in the world. Comedy and anxiety intermingled in Wilder's first two short pieces and the José Quintero production was unstrained and gratifyingly simple. If only the production could have concluded with a third good play from the *Seven Ages of Man* series, the Greenwich Village evening would have been a complete success.

Even then, however, the present reviewer would have found himself somewhat cautious in praise because the rather self-conscious fancifulness of the work is itself bound to be a kind of heaviness. Even the outright didacticism of Brecht in *The Caucasian Chalk Circle*, as staged by Alan Schneider for the Washington Arena Stage (the production was the first in the Arena's spacious new home) seemed to suggest less self-consciousness on the author's part. This was chiefly perhaps because Brecht was ostensibly spinning out a folk tale on the subject of who has the real claim to a child, the woman who merely gave birth to it or the woman who cared for it, and sustained his attitude successfully with suitable verve and stylization. In attending as a guest the formal opening of the new Arena playhouse under Zelda Fichandler's management, I was, in fact, pleasantly surprised to find the production free from the portentousness of a lesson. If anything, I was somewhat ungratefully disturbed at finding this Brecht parable "going down" so easily and moving so smoothly in the translation and the production; I wondered whether Brecht hadn't been made too easy and pleasant. This problem may be worth going into, for there is considerable danger that our professional and amateur productions will achieve success at the cost of Brecht's essential mordancy and roughness. It may become too easy to take him into the fold of playwrights who make one comfortable, which is the last thing Brecht would have wanted.

TROUBLE ON BROADWAY
(MAY, 1962)

In the off-Broadway theatre's precincts, we were witnessing in 1961–62 the growth of a "playwright's theatre"—not that there is any dearth of good off-Broadway acting (there is, for example, unmistakably excellent acting on the part of Eli Wallach and Anne Jackson in the dual bill *The Tiger* and *The Typists* at the Orpheum Theatre on Second Avenue), but that you actually need a play of uncommon interest as bait for the public. The play doesn't even have to be very good—critics are kinder to the off-Broadway than to the Broadway play anyhow!—provided it has some substance. And so it happens that the names that matter most in New York's supplementary theatre are the authors' names, and these have recently included Ibsen (a reliable David Ross production with a good cast headed by Richard Waring), Genet (*The Blacks,* still running after a year in Gene Frankel's vivid production), O'Neill (*Desire Under the Elms* at Circle-in-the-Square), Kopit (*Oh Dad* . . . still drawing patrons), the newcomer Oliver Hailey (whose promise has been bruited about town even by those who were not enthusiastic about his Pirandellian fantasy *Hey You, Light Man!*), Pinter (*The Dumbwaiter* and *The Collection* apparently still flourishing at the little old Cherry Lane Theatre), Pirandello (a new and rhapsodically received production of *Six Characters in Search of an Author*), Shakespeare (a vigorous *Taming of the Shrew*), Molière (*The Physician in Spite of Himself* and *The Precious Damsels*), Wilde (what else but *The Importance of Being Earnest?*, Brecht (*A Man's a Man* still holding on), Behan (*The Hostage* still going stronger than it did on Broadway), and even Pinero (*The Magistrate* in an Equity Library Production).

I do not, of course, suggest that all prominent and promising playwrights succeed in off-Broadway houses. The prominent Swiss playwright Max Frisch, for example, had a disaster in the Gene Frankel production of *The Fire Bugs* in a thoroughly commendable Mordecai Gorelik translation. But then, Max Frisch, only a few days before or after this fiasco had an even more crushing experience on Broadway with a Cheryl Crawford production of *Andorra,* an ironic treatment of the irrationalism of race hatred that had won plaudits in about half a dozen European and Near East productions last year. It is also true that most of the playwrights

514

produced on the off-Broadway stage no longer needed to be introduced to the public, but the same thing applied to authors of plays recently presented on Broadway itself. If anything, the noteworthy discoveries were to be found in the off-Broadway theatres, and will probably continue to be encountered there—if for no other reason than the extravagant expensiveness of Broadway production. A Broadway management is more likely to gamble on Shaw than on an unknown writer.

Broadway did gamble on Shaw with a star-studded revival of *Too True to Be Good*. It is, I suppose, too soon to give a meaningful box-office accounting, but there can be no question that for all but the rare purist the production was a success, whereas the play was a failure in New York when first produced by the Theatre Guild. If it has a box-office success, it will only confirm Shaw's genius and the present stage director Albert Marre's abilities, as well as confirm the rightness of my opinion that we are back in an "actor's theatre." *Too True to Be Good* is an improvisation by the master-improviser of the British stage who knew from the start of his career as a dramatic critic and playwright that the most suitable improvisation in the modern theatre was not to be achieved with plot, as many in his time believed, but with a cascade of ideas or notions unloosed upon the audience from all directions until the playgoer doesn't know what hit him, which is the surest way of keeping him alert and interested—provided the playwright takes the precaution of not allowing that interest to be preëmpted from the beginning by plot. Shaw, in his post-1930 period, took this precaution somewhat too recklessly, confusing and therefore alienating his potential audience. But it is amazing how well *Too True to Be Good* gets along on talk alone, and it soars at the end into a speech more stimulating than any passage in many a better—that is, many a more credibly and soundly constructed—play.

The revival succeeded better than the original Broadway production partly because its apocalyptic sense of doom fits in with the *Zeitgeist* that has also produced Samuel Beckett and Ionesco, and partly because the play has been staged as a sort of nonmusical revue. Albert Marre assembled a cast of virtuosi and trusted each performer's individuality instead of subordinating it to the requirements of a unified production—rightly so, since the only unity worth bothering about here is Shaw's gamboling Aristophanic mind. The Aristophanic character of the work would have been better established from the start if the producers of this revival had not cut the first act so deeply and eradicated the fantastic role of "The Monster," a human-sized microbe that blames the heroine for having given it the German measles ("a poor innocent microbe that never did her any harm") and that informs the audience candidly at the end of the act that the play is now virtually over, but that "the characters will discuss it at great length for two acts more." Not all the performances live up to the reputation of the performers, it is true—Sir Cedric Hardwicke is certainly not at his best in this production—but the combination of Lillian Gish, Eileen Heckart, Glynis Johns, Ray Middleton, Robert Preston, Cyril Ritchard, and David Wayne amounts to a massive assault to which it is difficult not to yield. And when Robert Preston launches into the ex-clergyman and present thief Aubrey's final oration in the play, we hear some of the best speaking on the contemporary stage.

Success for the Shaw revival was, in any case, greatly to be desired by Broadway since it looked as if it would have to rely a good deal on an older generation of playwrights than the generation that seemed to be established as a reliable source of American drama after World War II. Arthur Miller was not heard from, but his fellow playwrights had their worst season this year. William Inge's new play, *Natural Affection,* was buried under an avalanche of protest and abuse despite the ministrations of a powerful cast headed by Kim Stanley; and Tennessee Williams' *The Milk Train Doesn't Stop Here Any More,* while more mercifully dealt with in the press, managed to survive only fitfully. A proper balance in criticism cannot be attained easily at this date while the grumblings are still going on. In the case of *Natural Affection,* the blame should have alighted mostly on the director of the production, which was unnecessarily lumpy and obvious, rather than on the playwright. To a degree, the latter was doing in *Natural Affection* what he had done previously with greater facility. That is, he was providing a modestly limited study of confused ordinary people who head into extraordinary troubles. In the play, a boy who had been neglected by his mother and sent to an orphan asylum by her after she had been abandoned by her husband returns home after having spent a period in a reform school. But his mother, first making a strong effort to give him her love and affection, loses control when her lover walks out on her, and the unhappy lad, resenting his rejection, murders a lustful young woman who unintentionally reminds him of his mother. Somehow, from the very moment on stage when the mother was shown fondling her lover's chest as they awaken in the morning, the accent of the Broadway production fell neither on the case history of the rejected lad, which was the main current of the play, nor on the existentialist despair that gave the work its best scene, in which a middle-aged man cursed with bisexual inclinations and a tart of a wife, expresses his overriding sense of failure. The emphasis fell instead on the presumptive lustfulness of the mother when the author must have intended it to fall instead on her desperate loneliness, which is reflected in the boy and by the middle-aged character.

Mr. Inge became the object of a moral indignation that one would least expect from supposedly sophisticated Broadway, and the play could not survive this unwonted reaction. And this was unfortunate because it did not allow either the public or the author to form a proper estimate of his past and present achievements or any comprehension of the impasse in which he has found himself in recent years. It is essentially an impasse in art rather than morals. It may be said generally that Mr. Inge's addiction to naturalistic drama has been paying him diminishing returns. Thus far, in practice, his allegiance has been more noteworthy for its fidelity than its range or depth. I have reason to believe that he has been striving for another mode of expressing his nature, which I know to be notably sensitive and mutedly poetic, and conveying his insights into the isolation of the individual in our time, which I know to be deep and have felt to be poignant. Expressionism and formal poetry, however, are probably foreign to his taste and temperament; and he is too honest a man, although too easily influenced by stage directors, to force himself to move in these directions with a grand flourish of experimental idealism. His honesty and therapeutic discoveries have, at the same time, pushed the sexual aspects of human bedevilment to the foreground in his recent plays, in an insufficiently imaginative manner, and in language that lacks the necessary transcendence of crude social and clinical fact. He will, I suspect, find it more natural as well as more expedient to return to an earlier vein of realism present in his youthful work and most evident in his first Broadway (Theatre Guild) production, *Come Back, Little Sheba,* more than a dozen years ago. That this vein has not yet been exhausted by any means will be apparent to him, I think, as soon as he discovers that he is not a show-business prodigy, a social worker, or a psychiatrist, but a poet who has been more than commonly attuned to the still, small voice of humanity; and that he moves best when he seems to stand still with the deprived and feebly, sometimes comically, aspiring souls of the people he knows with uncommon perception and sympathy. It is not certain, despite his three big Broadway successes, that Broadway's paltry sophistications provide a favorable environment for Inge's particular kind of talent.

■

OTHER BROADWAYS*
(OCTOBER, 1962)

I

A four-month holiday from Broadway and its environs gives the reviewer an opportunity to consider the theatre in some sectors of Europe and the Middle East. I would be less than candid in suppressing my impression that, *with* state subsidy or *without,* the theatre across the Atlantic did not prove radically different from the theatre at home. When I cast up my accounts I felt, in fact, that I was still "covering" Broadway when I covered theatre in such diverse locations as Dublin, Athens, Istanbul, Tel Aviv, Vienna, Berlin, Stockholm, The Hague and London. Perhaps this is so because the traveler brought with him a mind and taste conditioned by our Broadway, off-Broadway, community and educational theatres. But I doubt that this consideration needs to carry much weight in view of the availability of objective evidence ranging from such secondary matters as actors swallowing final syllables and killing lines everywhere to the very serious dearth of new playwriting of any real consequence. The age of the great modern dramatists (O'Casey is the last survivor) seems to have vanished, and when we nowadays acclaim this man's sparkle or that man's ingenuity (Anouilh's or Duerrenmatt's, or Ionesco's for instance) we "consecrate the flicker, not the flame." Moreover, the same uncertainties and problems, whether intellectual or esthetic, prevail on both shores of the Atlantic—and pretty much the same likes and dislikes appear.

In summary, I must declare that wherever I went people associated with the stage were concerned about the state of the theatre. So were people *not* of the theatre—university professors and educators in general; the mayor of West Berlin, who recently empowered Erwin Piscator to create a new *Volksbühne* to compete with East Berlin's famed Ensemble; De Gaulle's minister, André Malraux, variously involved with the ad-

* [Although Professor Gassner customarily concentrated on the New York theatre scene, he maintained a lively interest in the regional theatre and that of other nations. When his schedule permitted him to travel, he made a point of viewing as much production as he could and reporting on it if it seemed significant. The critique which follows chronicles an extended journey in search of theatrical tradition and novelty in the Old World. The review was found among his papers with a note that it be included in the present collection. *Ed.*]

518

ministration of the Comédie Française and with "decentralization" or growth of theatre beyond Paris; and the eminent U.N. diplomat, Mr. Abba Eban, now minister of education in Israel, who conferred with me about the state and potentialities of Israeli theatre after my semi-official two weeks' visit to his country. Everywhere, also, the major concern was with the need to develop good new playwrights along with good productions and good audiences. And strong interest appeared even in distant Finland in departures from commonplace realistic production. There was much buzzing about experimental modes of presentation such as "theatre in the round." (Laurence Olivier's thrust-stage theatre at Chichester, in particular, publicized the issue of "theatre-in-the-round" in England quite intensively.) And "epic theatre" stylization has plainly gained much ground in Europe, primarily from the growing prestige of Brechtian drama and the prowess of the late poet-playwright's "Ensemble" under the leadership of his gifted widow, Frau Helene Brecht-Weigel. And this I could not but consider a victory not only for Brecht but for Erwin Piscator, whose contribution to "epic theatre" has been curiously overlooked by its latter-day advocates. For all that, however, it was a "bourgeois" nineteenth-century realistic theatre that I encountered, with or without disguise, in most plays and productions, as well as in the general public taste. It is not surprising then that intelligent observers should have gone overboard in acclaiming a discursive and incomplete but imaginative play by the poet Paul Valéry, *Mon Faust,* as the one distinguished play of the past season in Paris. And one thing more I encountered—*musical comedy* in more or less the American mode. It seemed ubiquitous except in East Berlin, where operetta did however have a great vogue due to the genius of Walter Felsenstein, director of the Comic Opera.

II

Paying a brief preliminary visit to London, this fugitive from Broadway immediately encountered the two current productions that respectively express the best in "old" and "new" English theatre. The old gracious theatre of wit could not have been represented more vividly and vitally than by *The School for Scandal,* staged by John Gielgud with a well-drilled cast headed by Sir Ralph Richardson, whose Sir Peter Teazle kept his human pathos as an elderly husband and his stock comicality as a nearly betrayed one in admirable balance. "Well drilled" is not the word indeed for several other actors, and is strictly applicable only to John Neville's indifferently individualized Joseph Surface and Anna Massey's external Lady Teazle until the reconciliation scene with her husband. Both individuality and spontaneity were present in the lively playing of Lawrence Naismith in the role of the returning nabob Sir Oliver Surface. And "artificial comedy" found an irresistible combination of "artificiality" and "characterization" in Margaret Rutherford's gossip-mongering Mistress Candour; Thomas Rowlandson, whose drawings must have been consulted by her director and herself, would have been proud of this impersonation. London's *School for Scandal* impressed me as a superb example of that balance between artifice and art which stands for viable English stage artistry. It is of course a trifle late to compliment Sheridan for having written the very best English comedy-of-manners in the pre-modern style and on lines such as Snake's "I live by the badness of my character" that are as good on the stage as they are on the page.

At the opposite extreme stood the impressive production by John Dexter of Arnold Wesker's "new-wave" drama *Chips with Everything*. After its successful presentation by the English Stage Company at the Royal Court Theatre, the equivalent of an off-Broadway production, the play was transferred to the West End. In *Chips with Everything,* Wesker continued his protest against class distinctions in England covered by the currently ubiquitous term "the Establishment." The protest was effectively conveyed by Wesker's picture of a basic-training camp of the Royal Air Force, featuring the snobbery of the officers and the futile revolt of an upper-class rebel, who leads two small but theatrically vivid insurrections against the "Establishment" in the camp. *Chips with Everything* was successfully compounded of apt naturalism, irony, and a quite remarkable flair for theatre. British playgoers felt the impact of the assault on their social and theatrical awareness to such a degree that they may have overrated the play; they apparently overlooked the vagueness of the transition that turned the rebellious hero into a conformist at the end. But they assuredly could not praise too highly half a dozen remarkable performances, especially the inexorable parade-ground and bayonet-drill scenes supervised by Frank Finlay. No amount of stylization, usually described as the opposite of naturalism, was more dramatic anywhere for the present traveler, who was forced to admit (not for the first time indeed) that naturalism can possess all the "punch" and "point" of stylization so long as it projects a pertinent point of view and expresses a passionate involvement with experience. I could only compliment myself on my singular good fortune in being able to observe in London two antithetical styles—those of the Sheridan and Wesker plays and productions within a single week—and to find both equally theatrical and, so far as the theatre is concerned, equally real.

III

r

After London, a visit to Dublin proved a rather depressing experience except for a pleasant Trinity College lecture engagement and reception. Dublin theatre was meager and seemed poverty-stricken, and the situation was well exemplified by the state in which I found the Abbey Theatre Company last April. Still awaiting transfer to a rebuilt home, the famous old playhouse having burned down, the Abbey company performed in unattractive temporary quarters. The play was a comedy, *They Got What They Wanted,* which its author, Louis D'Alton, called an "improbable" one. Actually it was less improbable than inconsequential, and there was no harm in it; it was simply unworthy of the Abbey's once prepotent ideal of a theatre capable of satisfying modern as well as national needs. Only in entertaining the playgoer with a few odd Irish types whose stock qualities were infused with vitality by the actors did the production possess some vitality, and this much could be expected of such excellent performers as Eileen Crowe and Harry Brogan, veterans of the Abbey Company. It was the expectedness of the humor and the demirealism of both the play and the production that made for disappointment. The unexpected was the *afterpiece,* a pleasant enough one-act play in Gaelic (*An Fear Óg Umhal Malde,* which I construed to mean "The Humble Gentle Young Man"), a work after the Japanese by Betty Barr and Gould Stevens and staged more or less in the Kabuki manner. The synopsis generously supplied by the management tells all one needs to know. "The good and obedient young man is thrown into excessive grief by the death of his revered father. His wife advises him to go to the city of Kioto for a little holiday." While there he acquires a mirror which causes much domestic misunderstanding because the wife, who has never seen herself in a mirror before, thinks he has brought home the picture of a mistress. There were actually two surprises in this occasion for this roving reviewer. One was the fact that a piece intended to promote national culture by being given in Gaelic should be *oriental* both in subject matter and style (Yeats's Noh Play experiments, written in *English,* at least had Irish subject matter). And even greater was the surprise of seeing the audience pouring out of the theatre after *They Got What They Wanted* as if they were fleeing the play in Gaelic—this in a city where all the street signs are printed in both English and Gaelic. Perhaps a bus strike contributed the incentive for the mass exit, but all I can say is that my wife, whose arithmetic is usually reliable, counted twenty-one persons in the auditorium exclusive of ourselves.

Distinctly more encouraging was the amateur Orion Productions Company's presentation at the little Eblana Theatre of *Cat on a Hot Tin Roof.* The play was ably staged by Monica Brophy, a great Tennessee Williams fan who has apparently done very well by several of his other plays. Brick and Maggie were completely convincing in this well-paced production. Without even approximating Burl Ives's girth, the mainstay of the Orion Productions Company, Martin Dempsey, did more than justice to Big Daddy, the playwright's most successful character. Except for the fact that Big Mama had been confused with a steam-calliope by a hard-working actress in the company, this production was, somewhat incongruously, the best theatre I saw in Dublin.

IV

Southern journeying, off seasonal and rapid, disclosed nothing to excite me in Italy, and there were not even rumors of any successors to Pirandello and Betti on the horizon. Interest in the theatre was reflected chiefly at Spoleto, where Gian-Carlo Menotti (now fondly dubbed the Duke of Spoleto by the natives) organizes an annual festival. The festival included a revue partly written by Menotti himself and the world première, in English, of a Tennessee Williams play about a rich and much-married former beauty dying of cancer and remembering her past. This work, *The Milk Train Doesn't Stop Here,* was a dramatization of one of the playwright's early stories; it was considered unready for presentation in the United States. In Rome, nothing of moment except for addicts of over-blown open-air productions of opera in the baths of Caracalla; the last time I sat there the *coup de théâtre* was a procession of mounted picadors and matadors in *Carmen* under the Italian moonlight.

V

A great deal more concern with theatre was manifest in Athens: one could find there high dreams of a theatre for the masses rather than for boulevardiers, and there were preparations for the annual open-air classic productions. The *pièce de résistance* was to be Euripides' masterpiece, *The Bacchae,* at Epidaurus, the best preserved ancient theatre, about 110 miles from Athens, attended by some 14,000 persons. This year the subsidized festival, started in 1955, was to consist of ten weekend open-air performances. In Athens in the spring, the playgoer could see operetta,

ballet (Polish!), Greek folk-dances and a Greek revue, two native comedies and one John Van Druten play *(Spring Song)* for which no special
enthusiasm was registered within my hearing, and two plays that have
been getting around a bit in Europe—Pirandello's *Tonight We Improvise,*
for which I have less than the usual regard, and Brendan Behan's *The
Hostage,* for which I have considerable esteem. Also on view was a
memorable production of Ionesco's *Rhinoceros,* staged in the round by
the gifted and progressive director Karolos Koun. Masks were used freely
in this production, with the half-human rhinoceri visible now and then
up to the shoulders in a wooden enclosure behind the audience. It was
as if the playgoers were themselves being caught up by the contagion of
bestiality. Although there was no Zero Mostel in the cast, the production
was, on the whole, more telling than last season's Broadway presentation,
and George Lazaris, changing color, wriggling or slithering like an animal, and growing a real horn, gave the metamorphosis of Jean an insidious, painful, reality. Much of the padding of *Rhinoceros* seemed to have
been taken out of Ionesco's first successful full-length play in this production.

VI

I found Istanbul also straining for vital modern theatre, but also apparently forced to rely largely on imported drama. Vivid in the memory
of the theatrical profession in Turkey was the recent poetic drama, known
to me in translation, György Dilman's *The Ears of Midas,* a symbolic
treatment of the theme of conformism; it was considered the best modern
play written in the Turkish language. It is a thoughtful and sensitive
work, but it is unlikely to form the basis for a *modern* movement in
theatre. It seems significant that one of the two plays available to me at
the end of the past Istanbul season should have been a production of
South Pacific in Turkish (staged by the young American-trained actor-
director Holdun Dormen with commendable vigor, despite blank intervals between curtains that better stage facilities could have shortened).
The other production, *Magara,* was a translation of Anouilh's *La Grotte,*
the melodrama of upstairs-downstairs class relations in turn-of-the-century
Paris that failed in Paris earlier in the year after being criticized as
reactionary. (Anouilh is not reactionary, of course—just *romantic,* though
like most post-Hugo dramatists, he uses a smoke-screen of sophisticated
irony.) The production, followed with the French text in hand and an
interpreter at my side, impressed me as quite a successful piece of the-

atricality infused with a mixture of human sympathy and characteristic French *Kitsch*—that phony awe in the face of sexual passion which I cannot bring myself to believe the hard-headed French really credit except in Racine, whose Jansenist realism about the emotions is antiromantic even in a romantic context. But Anouilh's theatricality was realized with noteworthy control by the director, Sirin Devrim, who also played the leading role—that of a nobleman's cook and ex-mistress, a vengeful downstairs Medea who kills the coachman who has betrayed her with a servant girl. Miss Devrim's performance was made of steel; it had a cutting edge that might have saved the Paris production. The production was also enlivened by the performance of Nüvit Ozdogru in a busy role and intensified by the earthy playing of Kemâl Ergüveni in the role of the coachman. *La Grotte* seemed to fit into a contemporary Istanbul repertory better than it could in a present-day Parisian, not to say American, repertoire, because it appeared to relate more closely to class distinctions in Turkey.

VII

A distinctly dynamic manifestation of theatre interest, however, first confronted me generally in Israel—specifically in Tel Aviv and Haifa, for Jerusalem has no theatre to speak of except at the University. The eagerness of both the theatrical profession and the public to achieve a genuinely modern Israeli theatre cannot be exaggerated. More important than subsidy for the theatre (and there is that in Israel, within limits imposed by the national economy) is the combination of creative zeal with a vigorous critical spirit. I found opinion rather divided on nearly everything except the importance of developing native playwrights and of treating new subjects instead of old ghetto-themes or of quasi-historical ones set in the pioneering *kibbutz*-building period, although there is still some fascination with these matters. A keen concern with the art of staging plays and acting in them was also apparent, and both the productions and the efforts to train actors at a dramatic school in Tel Aviv confirmed the impression.

The productions included a fluent treatment of the present Israeli world contrasted with the old days of the struggle for survival remembered with nostalgia for a lost heroism and idealism. The play, translatable as *A House in Good Order,* was the work of the successful novelist Moishe Shamir, who recently toured in the United States. Sharp characterizations of a disillusioned idealist and his worldly wife were combined in this work with a tantalizing yet provocative dramaturgic device of having another character appear twice in different guises, once as a reproving figure from the protagonist's heroic past, and once merely as a typical baby-sitter in the present. The play may have troubled the realistically oriented part of the public, it seemed somewhat too discursive, and it was rather arbitrarily and inconsequentially resolved. But the attractive production managed to hold the interest of even the present linguistically hampered reporter. The themes of lost idealism and mediation between past idealism and present practical necessity engaged other writers, too, and seemed the subject most generally available to native playwrights. The last-mentioned subject received deep, if rather snarled, memory treatment in Yehuda Haezrahi's *The Refusal,* staged by Nissan Nativ for the "Ohel" Theatre in Tel Aviv. The play revolved around the difficulty a scientist encounters in yielding to an urgent request from the Minister of Industrial Production and Planning that he accept the executive post of Director-General. Impeding his ultimately positive decision is his reluctance to give up the scientific research which has been the passion of his life and his guilt-trammeled memories of love and friendship on a *kibbutz* or frontier village in his youth. Since the action consisted of memory-sequences that were mostly narrations, *The Refusal* was only moderately successful as drama. And much the same thing would have to be said about a treatment of the early settlement of Israel by the eminent Hebrew poet Natan Alterman, *Kinneret,* produced by the Cameri Theatre company of Tel Aviv. But high praise could be meted out to the production staged by Gershon Plotkin with a strong cast reinforced by the Habima Theatre's Duse, the great veteran actress Hanna Rovina, who brought such rich emotionality to one scene that words seemed superfluous. It was also apparent that the author, whose bent was more literary than theatrical, had provided the actors with poetry of a high order.

At the other extreme, the Israeli playwrights could be seen striving with humor and satire. Most successful in this endeavor was the popular humorist Efraim Kishon, who has published two very amusing books, *Look Back, Mrs. Lot* and *Noah's Ark, Tourist Class.* Kishon's comedy, *Hactuba,* had achieved a record of 270 performances by the time I saw it, and there could be no doubt about its entertaining qualities, especially in the tantrums of an elderly domestic despot, brilliantly clowned by an Israeli Bert Lahr, Meir Margalit, who, it seems, had never completely legalized his marriage. A more incisive kind of humor aimed at political pretensions and intrigue was provided by the famous Habima Theatre. The new play, *The King's Clothes,* written and directed by a brilliant young writer Nissim Aloni, was a vivacious, if rather labored and snarled, antitotalitarian improvisation on Hans Christian Andersen's famous tale "The Emperor's New Clothes." I should have preferred to attend one

of the Habima's classical productions and to have seen the high art of
the company's great actors Meskin and Rovina (I was fortunate, however,
in seeing the powerful S. Finkel in one of the leading roles), but the
production possessed importance not only in its choice of a contemporary
play, but in its style, which approximated epic theatre stylization.

I could nevertheless fully understand the dissatisfaction with native
playwriting in Israel on reflecting that the outstanding Israeli productions
during the spring were Ionesco's *Rhinoceros* and Max Frisch's *Andorra*
in the beautiful up-to-date theatre in Haifa. *Rhinoceros* was staged with
stunning aptitude and power by Robert Postec. Although the Haifa company was a young one, it compensated with vigor for what it lacked in
experience, and the Berenger of Yaacov Bodo and the Jean of the company's leading actor, Haim Topol, were excellently characterized. The
production was especially noteworthy for carrying out Ionesco's intention
of relating the action specifically to the past triumphs of Nazism. One
even heard the off-stage stamping and shouting of the Storm Troopers,
and I found this spelling out of the lesson of the play only momentarily
disturbing. I was more greatly troubled by the largeness of the stage that
almost turned Jean's bedroom into an oversized barn. One thing is certain
—it was not easy to take a detached view of this *Rhinoceros* production,
over which Ionesco had himself exerted an influence *via* the director. The
other Haifa production, *Andorra,* staged by Joseph Milo, the creator and
manager of this remarkable repertory company, was even more effective.
It uses the theme of anti-Semitism and the Nazification of Central Europe
in the 1930's as a springboard for the most penetrating protest against
intolerance in broadly human terms that has yet appeared in any contemporary play known to me. Milo's direction of this work was superb,
as was the playing of the principal actors, with Haim Topol again giving
the most definitive performance in the role of a bestial Soldier and the
very talented young actors, Yosef Karmon and Germaine Unikovsky
achieving genuine pathos in the central roles of a persecuted youth and
the girl who was in love with him.

VIII

Vienna, the traveler's next important stop, had nothing so flagellating
to show except in the non-comic scenes of a Burgtheater production of
Gerhart Hauptmann's *The Rats,* which may well be considered this playwright's last testament to the power of naturalistic theatre. This near-
masterpiece, vitiated somewhat by discursiveness, is imaginatively rein-

forced by the double action maintained on a two-leveled stage. It consists of the comic plot of an old-fashioned stage director in conflict with a pupil and prospective son-in-law who disavows the classical rhetorical ("Schilleresque") style and the naturalistic tragic plot of a woman of the working classes whose obsessive desire for a child implicates her in the murder of an unmarried mother. In the more than adequate cast, Hermann Schomberg excelled as Hauptmann's nonplussed theatre director and Heidemarie Hatheyer as the frantically maternal Frau John. This was, on the whole, a highly impressive production, and one that heralded a belated Hauptmann revival. Another Hauptmann revival, by a less prominent theatrical group, was a production of his *Schluck and Jau,* which was decidedly less well received in Vienna; but, then, this play is plainly a secondary product of Hauptmann's talent. A touring company of the Burgtheater, incidentally, took Hofmannsthal's urbane comedy *Der Schwierige (The Difficult One)* to the Holland Festival of the Arts to which England's Royal Shakespeare Theatre and the Old Vic also brought productions and to which the Piraikon Theatre brought Euripides' *Medea* in modern Greek. I caught the Hofmannsthal production at The Hague a month or so later. This graceful comedy, however, lacked topnotch acting except in the playing of the veteran actress Adrienne Gessner, whom some of us may remember as the spinster in the Broadway production of *I Remember Mama.*

Vienna, with its Festival of Arts in full tilt, had, aside from superb concerts by Richter, Oistrakh and Casadesus, other dramatic attractions, such as a delightful *Cosi fan tutte* given at the Redoutensaal (once made famous by Reinhardt) and the Austrian première of Alban Berg's uncompleted opera *Lulu,* based upon Frank Wedekind's *Erdegeist* and *Die Büchse von Pandora* and every bit as mordant as the best of naturalist drama. There was also, at the Volkstheater, a new *Peer Gynt,* in a fine if abbreviated translation by Christian Morgenstern, but the pauses between the numerous scenes prevented it from achieving total success.

There were two distinctly more gratifying productions on view, both staged by Heinrich Schnitzler at the Theater in der Josefstadt, of which he has been the director ever since he left California. The Johann Nestroy production, a little-known farce, *Die verhängnisvolle Faschingsnacht,* was as delightful as it is indescribable. It was a whirl of idiosyncratic characterization, time-honored farcical misunderstandings, and folksy-comic expressions *("Nestroyaden")* revolving around an amorous maid, Sepherl, pertly played by the Josefstadt company's pretty ingenue Luzi Neudechel. A brief report, moreover, is totally inadequate for any proper appreciation of Heinrich Schnitzler's production of his father's beautiful drama of resignation, *Der einsame Weg*. Only slightly known in the United States, Arthur Schnitzler's *The Lonely Way*, which the Theatre Guild once tried out, is a conversational drama of quiet but compelling depth. It is suffused with feelings invariably expressed with delicacy and with due regard to the sensibility of cultivated characters. The acting of the play requires much strength in its delicacy, and much delicacy in its strength. The play also needs felicitous pacing: If the playgoer's attention is not to wander during the muted but seemingly leisurely conversations (they are, actually, decidedly *charged* conversations), the play must move rapidly but without giving the slightest impression of haste, and there must appear a potentiality of impetuousness in the actors without a trace of vulgar impatience. To say that Heinrich Schnitzler's production met these requirements is to say that he gave one of his father's most characteristic plays as much realization on the stage as anyone could desire. And plaudits were well merited also by the actors, especially by Leopold Rudolf in the role of the dying gentleman, Stephan von Sala, and Nicole Heesters in the part of the young woman who loves him hopelessly and drowns herself on his estate.

IX

After Vienna came Berlin and anticlimax!—at least in the Western Zone which had nothing of moment to show except for a clever political revue, an *Andorra* and a *Saint Joan* at the Schiller-Theatre that aroused little interest, and the ubiquitous *My Fair Lady* in apparently the largest West Berlin theatre, the Theater des Westens. (Better luck in Hamburg: A thoroughly incisive production of Lillian Hellman's *Toys in the Attic* staged by the veteran director Willy Maertens with a superb cast, except for a too robust ingénue.) In the Eastern Zone, there was plentiful theatre. At the Deutsches Theater, once the seat of Otto Brahm and Max Reinhardt, there was an excellent production of *The Cherry Orchard* without an inkling of the "new day" or "come the revolution" type of propaganda one might have expected in the finale. The production was in repertory, of course, and the repertory of this theatre and its small "Kammerspiele" affiliate was impressive indeed, including such noteworthy plays as *Wilhelm Tell, Wallenstein, Minna von Barnhelm, King Lear, The Little Foxes, The Beaver Coat, Professor Mamlock,* and Sternheim's *The Trousers (Die Hose)*.

At the Theater-am-Schiffbauerdamm, the great Berliner Ensemble! Its merits have been widely acknowledged in Western Europe and considerably publicized in the United States by American visitors. I have nothing to add to this except a verification of the genius of Helene Weigel, who may well be the greatest actress in Europe today. It was not my fate to be exposed to any of the great Brecht dramas when *Mother Courage* was struck off the calendar as a result of the illness of a prominent actor. But an evening of Brecht snippets, *Lieder und Gedichte,* a collection of "Songs and Poems" comparable to our off-Broadway *Brecht on Brecht,* abundantly displayed the talents of more than a dozen Ensemble performers. I especially remember Felicitas Ritsch and Hilmar Thate, the former a handsome actress of clean-cut intelligence, the latter an actor of compact strength and easy control. I actually liked our own off-Broadway program better, because it was enriched with dramatic scenes, but the Ensemble production was characterized by an effortlessness, a uniform excellence and a bright cutting edge probably unavailable anywhere else. The performances also possessed an excitement plainly dependent upon overriding conviction; thus, the song of unity, *Einheitsfrontlied,* of the year 1931, almost took the top of my head off.

A unique, if not entirely satisfying experience, was the Ensemble's production of Brecht's mock-epic of the rise of Hitler in terms of an American gangster-melodrama, *Der aufhaltsame Aufstieg des Arturo Ui,* a work of brilliant irony and travesty but of rather uneven and attenuated dramaturgy as well as some dribbling out of scenes and of the play as a whole. (A lot of Brecht is like that and, while "epic" theory may explain this defect away, it cannot make any play, whether by Bertolt Brecht or by Joe Blow, better than it actually is. His recent converts in America may not approve of this aside, but I fear it will have to stand for my considered opinion with respect to all but three or four of the full-length dramas.) As in a *roman à clef,* the impact in this late work depends upon our making the proper identifications, and fortunately they are not difficult to make in the case of the characters or caricatures who stand for Von Papen, Hindenburg, Goebbels, Goering, Roehm, Van Der Lubbe, Dolfuss, and Hitler himself. But it was, above all, the uncanny virtuosity of the performances—especially that of the carpet-chewing Ekkehard Schall as the "gangsterboss" Arturo Ui—that made *The Resistible Rise of Arturo Ui* a more than ordinary theatrical experience, no less grim than amusing, "factual" yet imaginative, "instructive" yet wildly Chaplinesque. One truly stunning episode was the Reichstag Fire Trial episode; another powerful scene was the murder of Roehm, and still another the betrayal of Dolfuss followed by the spirited reaction but ultimate submission of Frau Dolfuss impersonated by Felicitas Ritsch, the Ensemble actress who completely won my admiration in every role she played.

Inevitably, of course, there are younger East Zone writers who try to emulate Brecht, in so far as he can be imitated at all. How far emulation can take anyone who does not possess Brecht's highly personal gifts could be observed in a new work, *Frau Flinz,* a comedy of the early post-1945 period in East Germany by Helmut Baierla, with Helene Weigel giving an utterly delightful characterization of Frau Flinz, the politically "naïve" but privately shrewd woman who refuses to adjust herself to collectivism with a great show of spirit. But the author of this work was unable to weld his episodes into arrestingly developed drama, and his play lacked the obligatory scene that could have given credibility to Frau Flinz's last-minute conversion. Apparently even the nursing of ability in the very bosom of a great acting company (I understood that the author is the Ensemble's playreader) cannot produce new noteworthy dramatic talent, and none was apparent on either side of the Berlin "wall."

X

After my German visit, I entered a near-vacuum for a while, perhaps not wholly explainable by the summer interval. From the Scandinavian countries I could carry away with me only the recollection of a run-through in Stockholm of a pleasant but transparent old comedy by the late Hjalmar Bergman, *The Swedenhelms,* better known to us as *The Nobel Prize.* It was given in English and intended for the tourist trade from the English-speaking world. It is my own fault, however, that I missed several musical productions, including a little known Haydn opera, at the Drottningholm Theatre on the outskirts, visited while rehearsals were on for *Cosi fan tutte,* the delightful Mozart opera which seemed to be following me from country to country. From the Low Countries I retain memories of the aforementioned Hofmannsthal comedy *Der Schwierige* at The Hague Royal Theatre, and of a saucy *comédie-musicale* treatment of the Perils of Pauline, *La Femme Femme,* given by a youthful company in a Brussels basement-theatre (the *Théâtre de Quat' Sous*) that recalled our off-Broadway *Little Mary Sunshine.* At Bruges I also accidentally caught the beginnings of a spectacle, one of the numerous historical pageants called *Son et Lumière* that had come into fashion in various parts of Europe.

XI

Scanty theatrical fare was available in Paris by the time I got there, aside from the usual Comédie Française repertoire devoid of new plays. I can list only the Valéry devil-versus-Faust literary comedy, *Mon Faust;*

a revival of Anouilh's nearly twenty-year-old charade, *L'Invitation au Château* (best known to us in the English version of Christopher Fry under the title of *Ring 'Round the Moon*); Archard's *L'Idiote* (which was our inconsequential little Broadway and Julie Harris success, *A Shot in the Dark*); *Mlle. Julie* (hardly a discovery at this late date); and *La Pensée,* a second-rate piece of Andreyev morbidezza about a "thinker's" catastrophic efforts to unriddle the universe, to which venturesome New York drama students were introduced by Maurice Schwartz at his Second Avenue Art theatre as long ago as the early 1920's. Many new or recent movies were on view, however, including Charles Chaplin's attack on "McCarthyism," *A King in New York* (unavailable in the U.S.), that made me flinch at the impression it gave of American politics; there was no doubt of Mr. Chaplin's anger, although there could be some question about his artistry. It is true enough that *The Bald Soprano* and *The Lesson* were still on view at the Left Bank's pocket-sized Théâtre de la Huchette after five years, but it would appear that the *avant-garde* no longer sustains French theatre. Not even with something as sensational as Genet's *The Blacks,* which failed on the Right Bank after a short run on the Left; the one exception was *Rhinoceros* at the old Odéon, now renamed the Théâtre de France. If any "new wave" has been noted by the experts, it is the revival of the old dream of a *théâtre populaire* harbored since the French Revolution under Robespierre and strongly advocated more than half a century ago by Romain Rolland. A new theatre of the provinces was reported to be germinating in France, and even the energetically touring Théâtre National Populaire under Jean Vilar may be considered too Parisian to suit the new need unless it alters its style in favor of more specific, historically and socially oriented (more or less Brechtian) techniques of presentation.

XII

It was in England, to which the present traveler returned for a five-week storm operation of playgoing, that the theatre proved particularly inviting. Playgoing in London alone would fill an American with envy, and all the more because the summer is no deterrent to new productions. A brief report cannot do justice to the wealth of plays and other high-grade entertainments available to the Londoner. The city was teeming with them in July and August. The sheer sum of theatrical activity in London during the late spring and summer period when New York virtually suspends production is impressive, and it is only appropriate that Britain's great interest in the dramatic arts, should have resulted in subsidies or, rather, guarantees against deficits, after World War II, for experimental production (some of these—such as *The Cocktail Party* and *The Lady's Not for Burning* turned into big commercial successes) and should have brought final approval, in July, for a subsidized National Theatre to be erected on the South Bank of the Thames. The city of London also had a two-week Arts Festival in July in addition to its Ministry-of-Works-supported summer season of Shakespeare in Regent's Park now over thirty years old. London, where opera and especially ballet have a tremendous vogue, offers musical comedies almost as abundantly as New York, and several of these, in fact, are American, most notably *My Fair Lady,* in its fifth year in the West End, I believe. The advent, on July 26, of *The Premise,* concluding a two-year run in Greenwich Village, was also quite remarkable; it was the first time that an off-Broadway musical entertainment had been booked into a West End house. (Minus a Kennedy skit, I should add, due to the British censorship.) This bland four-character satirical revue, which gave Britons a dose of their own urbane mockery with on-the-spot improvisations got as good a press in London as its most confident enthusiasts in New York could have wished. Characteristic of both the "Broadway" and "off-Broadway" equivalents in London are, on the one hand, Lionel Bart's stunning musical spectacle, *Blitz!,* a spirited account of London under bombardment, enriched with raffish folksy East End humor if also sweetened with Abie's Irish Rose sentiment, and, on the other, the immensely clever long-running revue *Beyond the Fringe* production by four remarkably talented young men who possess theatrical virtuosity and critical intelligence in equal measure. The satires on political and religious bores are top-drawer humor and their pantomime in such a number as a men's luncheon meeting equals their verbal wit, which is always a sign of total talent in actors. All facets of their competence, including that of *inventing* their material, come to a triumphant climax in what amounts to the best literary travesty I have seen in forty years of steadfast playgoing, a take-off on Shakespeare's history plays as they must strike the spectator who is more dazed than informed by Elizabethan blank verse.

At the furthest end of the spectrum in London one had, of course, the continued passion for Shakespeare and the Elizabethans—sometimes, alas, routinely pursued as in an Old Vic season that called for considerable improvement if that company was to live up to its past. Fortunately, a distinctly more optimistic report is possible concerning the Royal Shakespeare Theatre which had *three* companies functioning simultaneously—two in London and one, as usual, at Stratford-upon-Avon. Its most conventional operation was, inevitably, the lavish and well-supported one at bristling Stratford. Four plays were on the agenda, with a fifth, *King Lear,* postponed until the fall to ensure the availability of Paul Scofield. My schedule did not permit me to see the Stratford *Macbeth,* and it does not seem that I needed to be inconsolate. I could have also done without the *Measure for Measure,* which had a fluid rather than noteworthy production and lacked an Angelo comparable to Gielgud's. I must refrain from going into the problems of producing *Measure for Measure,* or, for that matter, of appreciating this problematic work. (For W. A. Darlington of the *Daily Telegraph, Measure for Measure* was "a play that takes a good deal of swallowing" but the rewards are great "once the gulp is over.") The play has been sufficiently "discussed" by L. C. Knights and others. I shall content myself with saying, first, that the play was better "unified" by the Stratford production than by any other I have seen, and that this was not entirely a cause for congratulation because the unity was gained at the expense of some vivacity in the production despite a brisk Lucio by Ian Richardson, an authoritative Provost by Paul Hardwick, and an attractive Duke of Vienna by Tom Fleming. The Elizabethans don't seem to have been bent upon achieving "unity," and this is apparent in *Measure for Measure* in spite of the prevailing theological "New Testament" "Pardon's the word for all" interpretation. And, secondly, I believe Shakespearean directors and actors could do with a little less "psychology"; Angelo, who at one point in the Stratford production, flagellated himself in an effort to subjugate his lustful flesh, was a bore to the extent to which he was played as a neurotic. Isn't there enough of the scoundrel in human nature to make misbehavior credible without psychopathological motivation? (Note that Brecht also dispenses with psychological explanations of evil, and after the barbarities in his native Germany and elsewhere who can blame him?) Surely this was the general Shakespearean assumption with a long medieval and Christian ("original sin") history behind it. It would have been far better to have ditched the psychological ballast in favor of the one naturally unifying comico-serious theme of the play so well expressed in the Duke's lines "hence shall we see . . . what our seemers be." I would recommend F. R. Leavis' comments in *The Common Pursuit* (pp. 171–72) "that the point of the play depends upon Angelo's not being a certified criminal-type, capable of a wickedness that marks him off from you and me," and that "if we don't see ourselves in Angelo, we have taken the play very imperfectly."

No complaint could be lodged against Stratford's *Cymbeline,* directed by William Gaskill, with Vanessa Redgrave's Imogen and other unexceptionable performances, including Eric Porter's superb Iacchimo and an almost credible Cymbeline. No one could make that inconsistent gentleman totally credible, but Tom Fleming came close to succeeding by placing the inconsistencies in a matrix of semicomic characterization. The director's slow-motion treatment of the battle-scenes and of the descent of Jove from the flies on something that looked like an oversized bronze chandelier was also comically formal and quizzically stylized. That *A Midsummer Night's Dream,* staged by Peter Hall with a well-chosen cast, should also have been quite successful at Stratford was, needless to say, very much less than a miracle, and requires no particular comment here.

For some of us, however, it was the production of Thomas Middleton's *Women Beware Women* that was the greatest treat and it was given not as Stratford but at the New Arts Theatre Club in London. In addition to the interest of seeing a rarely performed Elizabethan drama, the production afforded the excitement of a varied study of passion and perversity, conducted with truly dramatic pace (no scenic impediments on the skeletal stage) and authority by the principals; and sheer genius in malice and lustfulness was attained by that extraordinary actress Pauline Jameson in her Machiavellian role. As for other rarely seen works, note should be taken of a generally satisfactory production of the Wakefield Mystery Cycle at Westminster Abbey in which oddly enough, however, the celebrated *Second Shepherd's Play* (sadly amputated) was one of the least effective episodes and the discursive *Procession of the Prophets* one of the most effective. I don't believe there was any comparable production elsewhere at the time except a production (first at Coventry) of a medieval liturgical drama, *The Raising of Lazarus,* with musical interpolations.

"Back in London," as "back" in almost any metropolis means, among other things, floundering in many attempts at popular entertainment. But there was more than ordinary merit in a number of the efforts, including a production of Tennessee Williams' *Period of Adjustment* which was generally superior, certainly funnier, than the New York presentation of the 1961–62 season; Peter Ustinov's *Photo Finish,* a lively, if attenuated, chronicle of a famous old writer's confrontation with his earlier selves and mistakes; and the double bill *The Private Ear* and *The Public Eye* by Peter Shaffer who providentially contributed *The Five-Finger Exercise* to a recent New York season. *The Public Eye,* in which Kenneth William excelled as a suave private detective with philosophical pretensions, was a delightful one-hour comedy built around the theme of infidelity and marital conflict written in the Giraudoux vein of *The Apollo of Bellac.*

The deeper matter of the London stage fell into several classes—the *avant-gardiste,* the "psychological" (how quickly "psychology" has vanished from the literary vanguard except perhaps for interest in the subject of pederasty), and the "social." The first-mentioned type of drama was meagerly represented, at the New Arts Theatre Club, with a poorly received elegy on man's loneliness, *The Empire Builders,* translated from the French of Boris Vian. "Psychological drama" had its brief innings with an indifferent production of Strindberg's *Playing with Fire* by the Royal Shakespeare Company at the Aldwych Theatre as the first of a twin bill. The second and distinctly superior hour-length play was Harold Pinter's *The Collection,* also a treatment of jealousy quite probing in the characterization of an upper-class sybarite and his slum-born protégé who makes a somewhat bizarre attempt to liberate himself. It was preponderantly the "social" drama, still somewhat novel to Londoners of the past several decades, that galvanized the theatre, its public, and its critics.

Aside from Wesker's *Chips with Everything,* the London theatres display a number of interesting items. Quite effective was the assault on academic stuffiness and indifference to controversial issues in *The Affair,* the somewhat contrived play adapted from Sir Charles P. Snow's successful novel. Alec Clunes in the role of a liberal barrister defending a radical Cambridge scientist against a wanton act of injustice at his university was particularly persuasive, but the entire cast was sharply individualized. The problem of maintaining the middle path between purblind conservatism and rabid radicalism has rarely had a more considered presentation, and I actually found the writing more distinguished in the play (by Ronald Millar) than in the original novel, which rather sustains Leavis' charge that Snow is "no writer" in a recent overpublicized polemic against the latter. More noteworthy as examples on theatrical art, however, were London's two recent "epic" productions, the visiting Bristol Old Vic Company's *War and Peace,* an adaptation of the novel by Alfred Neumann, Erwin Piscator, and Guntram Prufer (English version by Robert David Macdonald) at the Phoenix Theatre. This free adaptation of the Tolstoy novel was staged by Val May, with a first-rate cast, on several levels, and the action was framed by a passionate anti-war prologue and epilogue that gave point to this work, which Piscator had first presented in a tentative version at his New York Dramatic Workshop of the 1940's. The Old Vic Company formed in 1946 reached the peak of its young career with this generally acclaimed production. Not to be outdone, however, the Royal Shakespeare Company at the Aldwych produced *The Caucasian Chalk Circle.* Neither the translation by John Holmstrom nor the production staged by William Gaskill could command more than moderate approval. Yet the power of the play prevailed, and Patsy Bryne's heroine Gruscha and Roy Dotrice's Simon Chachava, Gruscha's soldier-lover, were uncommonly effective. The prologue and epilogue, which Brecht added to the play for the post-war productions of this work, were unfortunately ineffective and seemed quite expendable.

It was also regrettable that a third "epic drama," *Spring '71*, a translation from the French of Arthur Adamov's panoramic account of the Paris Commune, should have been a poor play and should have received an indifferent production on the whole. Still, even here there were compensations not usually supplied by merely "psychological" dramaturgy—even when it is as generally competent as John Mortimer's *Two Stars for Comfort*, a character-study of arrested development in the case of a sporty individual. (The trouble with *Two Stars for Comfort* was the usual one in the case of contemporary realism. The play had too much "character for character's sake" rather than for the play's sake and was much more attentive to the central character than his intrinsic interest warranted.) The last act of *Spring '71*, in which the Commune fails and the insurgent population is barbarously suppressed by the Thiers republic, proved unexpectedly moving. One could have wished for more success for Adamov's play as well as for John Osborne's twin bill, *Plays for England*. The first of Osborne's hour-length plays, *The Blood of the Bambergs*, scored some neat points against royalty-worship such as prevails in England but was on the whole a downright bore. The second, *Under Plain Cover*, combined a fierce attack on invasions of privacy by the press with an unclear exposure of sado-masochistic practices in the privacy of a presumably happy household. It stirred up anger and pity in about equal measure in the well directed production by Jonathan Miller, and there could be no doubt about the evidences of a strong talent for dramatic representation in the play. But for all that, it remained a muddle; it was not only depressing in many of its details but sharply devided in focus between sex-fantasies and protests against yellow journalism.

XIII

It is perhaps most characteristic of the British theatre that its younger leaders have been making so strong an effort, even when it is a muddled or incomplete one, to compensate for many decades of drawing-room drama, which was strictly an upper-class phenomenon, and to put aside recent aspirations toward verse drama, mostly in a quasi-theological and para-mystical context, which was also mainly an upper-class phenomenon. The inauguration of an O'Casey festival on August 15, at the Mermaid Theatre—with *Purple Dust,* to be followed by *Red Roses for Me* and *The Plough and the Stars*—is another straw in the wind. It was especially appropriate that the festival should have been initiated with so thorough a travesty of British Establishment mentality on holiday as *Purple Dust.* But it is still also characteristic that great excitement should have been stirred up in England by a festival of a radically different kind, the Chichester Festival, which more than any other recent achievement probably brought its founder, Sir Laurence Olivier, the directorship of the newly created National Theatre. In this festival, Olivier's choice of two of the plays (John Ford's *The Broken Heart* and John Fletcher's *The Chances*) and their richly theatrical staging reflected England's continued inclination to revivify its theatrical heritage at every opportunity, while the third play, *Uncle Vanya,* reflected the position of Chekhov in contemporary Britain. Chekhov has had a vogue in England as the poet laureate of its slow-paced and muted country-house decadence.

The style of production had a tricksy rompishness in the John Fletcher play, a baroque magnificence in the Ford tragedy, and a discreetly meted out quantity of comedy tinged with melancholy and restiveness in the case of *Uncle Vanya.* Each play was presented with a cast of more than approvable performers, with the sole exception of Joan Greenwood whose failings, chiefly due to her mannered voice, it is a kindness to note without further comment. The British press was particularly favorable to the *Uncle Vanya* production; by the time I saw it there could be no doubt that this opinion could no longer be sustained, for the first half of *Uncle Vanya* was badly botched, whereas the originally least well received of the three productions, *The Chances,* proved to be a total delight. As for *The Broken Heart,* it had, on the whole, a distinguished, suitably melancholy and baroque, production. There is absolutely nothing to *The Chances,* a comedy of confused identities and absurd mischances revolving around two Spanish gallants who become entangled in the flight of a romantic young woman, Constantia, who has aroused her suspicious brother's wrath. But *The Chances* came fully alive as theatre thanks to its abundant stage movement culminating in an extravagant chase by the lively commedia dell'arte stock characters.

In the *Uncle Vanya* production, however, Olivier was partly defeated (though apparently not so in the opinion of his British reviewers) by his extremely "British," genteel and restrained interpretation of the Chekhov play. And he was hampered by the open stage of the new playhouse. It was the good fortune of the production of *Uncle Vanya* that the play itself gathered enough momentum, and the performance of Michael Redgrave as Vanya gained enough serio-comic energy to overcome the lethargy of the early scenes of stalemate. It was plain, in point of fact, that whatever distractions and diffusion of effect, allegedly the fault of the open stage, could be overcome whenever the play and the performances achieved thorough concentration. This appeared to be the case in Chekhov's quite "active" third and fourth acts (the fused Act II of the Chichester production) and Redgrave's and Olivier's respective "Vanya" and Michail Lvovitch (Dr. Astrov) vividly activated by Olivier's stage direction. Joan Plowright as Sonya, the Professor's daughter by his first wife, was also admirably "activated," although by a principle of youthful resilience that came perilously close at the end to teen-age girlishness.

(As a Harold Hobson *Sunday Times* article put it, "there were times when the piece seemed to be on a parade ground instead of in a theatre; actors who dropped their voices and turned their backs simultaneously could not be heard. . . . The garden looked like a drawing room and the drawing room like a garden; and both were indistinguishable from the dining room." I quote this summary of complaints as a warning to insouciant theatre-in-the-roundists. One can also go along with Kenneth Tynan's feeling that he would have preferred to see *Uncle Vanya* at, say, the Haymarket, although, instructed by such experiments as those achieved by José Quintero at Circle-in-the-Square, I cannot by any means subscribe to Tynan's dictum that "only those forms of theatre in which words are secondary—such as musicals, dance drama and Commedia dell'Arte—have much to gain from exposure to the three-sided stage." I am sure that his positive and negative assertions here are equally wrong.)

The Festival was patently a personal triumph for Olivier who proved himself one of the great men of the contemporary Western theatre as the creator and manager of the theatre, his staging of all three plays, and his playing in two of these. When he was appointed director of the future National Theatre early in August, the official announcement had all the impact of a dramatic climax. It is pleasant to be able to conclude the present report on this optimistic note, and it seems almost ungracious to temper it with the reflection that there was nothing in these and other developments to foreshadow a vital *contemporary* theatre, just as there was nothing in the busy London season except Wesker's *Chips with Everything* to indicate that the new wave of British playwriting had not receded, as its most ardent champion Kenneth Tynan himself had maintained earlier in the year. There was busy and varied theatre in London but little indication of impressive playwriting in a season in which even the chief of the *Sturm und Drang* dramatists, John Osborne, was largely ineffective and such playwrights as John Whiting, Harold Pinter, and Peter Shaffer were represented by very much less than top-drawer work. And "Broadway" patently extended clear across the Atlantic when the London public was looking with a great deal of favor on such Broadway imports as *Period of Adjustment, Come Blow Your Horn,* and American musicals.

THE VICTORIAN AND ANTI-VICTORIAN
BERNARD SHAW (OCTOBER, 1963)

About the 1963 American Festival Theatre production, *Caesar and Cleopatra,* one can render only an "on balance" report if justice is to be a component of judgment. But here an area of considerable divergence must prevail because much depends on one's interpretation of the character of Shaw's comedy. If the reviewer or spectator mistakenly insists on a voluptuous queen and seductive woman,[1] Carrie Nye's impersonation of Cleopatra is bound to seem preposterous. It is that of a wilful teenager who develops a crush on a middle-aged gentleman and at the same time intends to exploit her dubious charms and his possible susceptibility to them, until the second half of the play, when having been somewhat affected by him, she tries to grow up. I don't believe we are justified in taking any exception to this portrait, though I concede that nymphets can be as trying inside an auditorium as outside one. It is my impression that Shaw himself would have been pleased with Miss Nye's playing, although he would probably have criticized her inflections. And George Voskovec is an altogether appealing Caesar, although he can strike us as a rather soft hero. Perhaps Mr. Voskovec cannot be a stronger one by temperament or personality, which is a pity. But his is also a valid interpretation, it would seem, of Shaw's ideal of the statesman as sage rather than as warrior. And if there is sentimentalization in this view of Caesar, it is the author's as much as the actor's, and it provides a justifiably comic view as well. I have, I must confess, seen better performances in the secondary parts as well as in the principal ones, although in the former there are also some very creditable performances.

The main fault with this more than half-successful Shaw revival (and "revival" is precisely the word to use unless one meticulously insists on calling it a "half-revival") was with the staging. It made *Caesar and Cleopatra* a costume drama with a vengeance, and if the ghost of any Victorian actor-manager happened to attend a performance he could have chuckled maliciously at the lavish Victorianism of the Shakespeare Theatre Festival production. And Shaw couldn't have squelched him because

---

[1] In the Prologue of the published version, Shaw makes his spokesman Ra declare, "Hath the name of Cleopatra tempted ye hither? Ye foolish ones; Cleopatra is as yet but a child that is whipped by her nurse."

Victorian spectacle-extravaganza is impacted in the play itself. A truly Shavian director would undoubtedly have played it down, but he would have probably fared worse than Ellis Rabb did in paring down the big scenes on Stratford's immense stage; Shaw's play would have been dwarfed there more than at Covent Garden, and the discursive passages, which are the best in the play as well as the most Shavian, would have contributed to the minification of *Caesar and Cleopatra*. Faced with problems of fitting Shavian discursiveness into a theatre designed for Shakespearian expansiveness, the director of Stratford's *Caesar and Cleopatra* took full advantage of Shaw's own Victorian penchant for spectacularity and extravaganza not without the risk of subverting the Shavian character of the play. It is because of this, perhaps, that one could have legitimately longed for a stronger Caesar than that of Mr. Voskovec, fine and devoted actor though he be—that is, for a Caesar whose dry wit would have laid the ghost of Beerbohm Tree in this production.

In this connection, I take pleasure in being able to refer the reader to a remarkably enlightening study by Martin Meisel of Dartmouth College, *Shaw and the Nineteenth Century,* published this year by Princeton University Press. In it I find a wonderfully apt phrase with which to define the core of *Caesar and Cleopatra*—namely, "a modern heroic drama of ideas," which should not be diminished with Victorian spectacularity whether by Shaw (with half his tongue in half his cheek) or by contemporary stage directors, even when they shape the spectacle as well as it was shaped at Stratford. In Meisel's book will be found ample evidence of Shaw's leanings toward spectacularity (pp. 361–65). In reminding us that Shaw wrote the play in the hope that the Victorian actor-manager Forbes-Robertson would produce it because "he is the classic actor of our day," Professor Meisel cannot but raise the question of what Shaw meant by "classical," and expectedly Shaw is ready with an answer: "What I mean by classical is that he can present a dramatic hero as a man whose passions are those which produced the philosophy, the poetry, the art, and the stagecraft of the world, and not merely those which have produced its weddings, coroners' inquests, and executions." Mr. Voskovec in the Stratford production is certainly not a classical actor in this sense, and not because he couldn't have produced "the philosophy, poetry, art, and stagecraft of the world," but rather because his "passions" are so little in evidence. They are not particularly evident in Shaw's deliberately antiheroic (or, rather "heroic-antiheroic") text either, which is not to say, of course, that Mr. Voskovec and his director shouldn't have tried to provide what Shaw, whatever his intentions, didn't supply. Shaw was right in saying that in a "modern" conception of heroism there is no place for "a monotonous ecstasy of continuous heroism" and that he didn't require that "a hero must always soar, in season and out of season." But Mr. Voskovec, who doesn't entirely fail to suggest a latency of power, goes Shaw one better and doesn't soar at all.

Still, it is possible to suspect that Shaw himself did not altogether find the proper balance between modernity and Victorianism in *Caesar and Cleopatra,* in which he overindulged his flair for theatre. And in this respect he was not so distant from the Victorian theatre as he liked to think, or to tell us. I don't recall his protesting strenuously, as he would have otherwise done, against the Technicolor movie that was made of his play; who knows but he might have even enjoyed the current *Cleopatra* movie with *one part* of his sensibility. He had expressed gratification, in fact, in the very early 1920's that "The Cinema has restored to the stage the dramatic form used by Shakespeare: the story told with utter disregard of the unity of place in a rapid succession of scenes." Professor Meisel does well to remind us that "the tendency of Shaw's histories toward Extravaganza [an outgrowth of Burlesque and justified here as a comic assault on romantic heroic drama] was early observed by critics of *Caesar,*" causing Shaw indeed some irritation, evinced in his writing Forbes-Robertson in 1908 after the London première that "The Press, headed by Walkley, said of Caesar exactly what they said of *Arms and the Man* in 1894—Offenbach and Meilhac and Halèvy—opéra bouffe."

Section Two*

■

THE LINCOLN CENTER
REPERTORY COMPANY
(MAY, 1964)

Undoubtedly the most important event of the first half of the year has been the start of the Lincoln Center Repertory Company with three productions in rapid procession at its temporary home in downtown New York, the new ANTA Washington Square Theatre. The playhouse, for which much official enthusiasm was expressed with its extremely steep auditorium beetling over a sprawling and scattered multi-level stage, was by no means ideal for all the productions. It was most agreeable for *Marco Millions,* which José Quintero properly staged as spectacle and least suitable for S. N. Behrman's drawingroom comedy, *But for Whom Charlie.* It seemed as if it would take some time before stage directors would be able to adapt dramatic traffic to the stage, if this is at all possible, without leaving huge empty spaces around the actors. It is also possible that the new Repertory Company will find a more flexible stage, a stage that can "close in" as well as open up, at its disposal when it moves into its permanent home, so that the structure will give less impression of paranoid delusions of grandeur on the part of the builders.

The company itself still has far to go before it becomes a true and distinguished ensemble; it will need more training and a considerably longer period of working together. It may also need a little more talent than it has shown thus far; although one would be hard put to it to determine how David Wayne's performances in *But for Whom Charlie* could have been bettered, it does not seem that the management extended

* [Had he realized *Dramatic Soundings* would be his last book, Professor Gassner would surely have wished to round out his critiques of the sixties with reviews later than those chosen in 1964–65. Accordingly, representative comments have been selected from more recent issues of the *Educational Theatre Journal.* To avoid the diffusion of impact necessitated by omnibus reviews, portions of the quarterly surveys have been extracted and organized under several categories which may prove useful to the researcher and the recreational reader. Where gaps appear in the obvious chronology of reviews of a playwright or a producing organization, they are owing to one of two factors: 1) Professor Gassner was indisposed at that time, or 2) he allowed the editor, as his collaborator, to review the production in his stead. *Ed.*]

itself much in search of brilliance and virtuosity, and it may be that the company was selected in the main for its long-range potentialities. I think we shall have to be a trifle patient with the Lincoln Center, even if the irritation of embittered young magazine critics is understandable; even the ensemble of the Moscow Art Theatre did not materialize instantly. When the potentialities of the cast are better known, moreover, we may expect more felicitous casting. It would be unnecessarily cruel to cite individual names at this time, but one cannot refrain from noting that all three productions have been marred by transparently wrong choices for some of the parts. The "heavies" have been too heavy, and the ingénues have been too disingenuous, although there have been some good choices, too, and two amazingly excellent ones when the Maggie-Marilyn part was filled by Barbara Loden in Miller's *After the Fall* and the role of the roguish elderly novelist Brock Dunnaway in Behrman's *But for Whom Charlie* by David Wayne.

As for the choice of plays, there can be considerable dispute over some things, but it cannot be fairly charged against the Robert Whitehead and Elia Kazan management that it was woefully and wantonly wrong when it chose three American plays, two of them brand-new and one old one by America's leading playwright, O'Neill. One may regret that *Marco Millions* was chosen; there is certainly better O'Neill to be produced, but *Marco Millions* is not dated and affords opportunities for spectacle which the Washington Square arena stage invited and which José Quintero, the director of this production, used justifiably and well. One may also suggest that the management give the younger generation of playwrights a place in the repertory, and I know that Messrs. Whitehead and Kazan are sympathetic to the suggestion; I happen to know, too, that their Executive Consultant, Harold Clurman, has anticipated it. Thus far, it is true, the Lincoln Repertory Theatre enterprise (except for a number of the actors and the engagement of José Quintero to direct two plays annually) has been a middle-aged venture; and understandably so, despite the expressed resentment of some young critics. But in so far as this continues to be the case there will be cause for resentment, and there will be scope only for the outlook of the nineteen-thirties and nineteen-forties. How soon a vivid and vigorous generation grows middle-aged! And how easily does history make it look foolish! And how understandable the demand of the young to give it elbow-room for its own errors and fatuities!

I. *BUT FOR WHOM CHARLIE*

It cannot be said, however, that there is strong reason for gratification with any of the plays presented thus far. The least culpable, as well as least ambitiously conceived, of the three, *But for Whom Charlie,* is certainly the best written. Neither O'Neill nor Miller matched S. N. Behrman's taste, tact, and verbal felicity. It is a pleasure to hear his dialogue; and behind the dialogue there stands a civilized intelligence and considerable cultivation, even if its accent is not factitiously British like that of some other American aspirants to the estate of "high comedy." Behrman has drawn better characters in his time—better than the principal ones in *But for Whom Charlie,* but not better than the delightful secondary character of the sponging elderly novelist so shrewdly played by David Wayne. The plot, as is usually the case in a Behrman play, is a mild confection and revolves around the conflict between integrity and opportunism. The integrity rests with Seymour Rosenthal, the meek son of a Hollywood tycoon who has established a Foundation that renders assistance to imperious authors, played somewhat diffidently by Jason Robards, Jr., while the opportunism is attributed to his former Yale classmate Charles Taney, the *"Charlie"* of the title (played by Ralph Meeker), who runs the Foundation for Seymour. When Charlie's opportunism proves too gross, the long hesitant Seymour gets rid of him. The cause of this reversal, which is a little too good to be true (an accusation that may be directed also at Seymour himself), involves entanglements with a sexually insatiable blonde harpy (chiefly on the part of Charlie) and a gentle girl who also loves him but is ultimately disenchanted with him.

That she marries instead a breezy bassoon-player who contributes considerably to the humor of the play, that Seymour agrees to subsidize her presumably talented alcoholic brother, that the girl and the brother are the unscrupulous blonde's outraged stepchildren, and that the latter gets into bed with the stepson who tries to strangle her but gets a concussion of the head from the wary stepmother—these complications can only suggest that *But for Whom Charlie* is rather cumbersomely contrived. Ultimately the play was defeated, however, not so much by its contrivances, but by the mildness and slowness of the action as it unfolded on the large curtainless stage better suited to a performance of *Aida,* and by the muted character of the humor which might have been less muted, despite the author's genial moralism, if the performances, usually handicapped by too much space around them, had been livelier. Although one could be favorably inclined to Mr. Behrman's "26th play in a 40-year writing career" (so says the press release), one could not be insensible to its longeurs on an "open stage." It would seem, in fact, that however commendable its desire to attempt a reflective comedy, the Lincoln Center Repertory Company courted trouble when it courted S. N. Behrman without having a proscenium arch and a small auditorium for his type of play.

II. *MARCO MILLIONS*

It also courted trouble, though also honorably, when it selected O'Neill's twenty-six-year-old blend of arsenic and saccharine, satire and romance, *Marco Millions;* and this time for the opposite reason that the play is so suitable for lavish production on this large open stage that the spectacle was bound to overshadow the satire and inflate the romantic character of the work. The fault belongs in the first instance, however, to O'Neill himself, since he made too much of too little when he placed his "Main Street" Marco in the center of his play and then surrounded his Venetian Babbitt with the "romance" and "philosophy" of the East. But it was the vastness of the stage that collaborated in making *Marco Millions* seem so pretentious as well as tendentious, so labored as well as so sincere. And here it may be observed that O'Neill is not the only American author of some significance who turned to the Orient for romantic contrasts to the shallow materialism and repressive puritanism they resented at home. He differed from the greatest of these, Melville, only in the degree of flaccid sentiment associated with his striving for prose poetry, which reached bathetic culmination in *Lazarus Laughed*.

Marco Millions, no less than the production, suffers from the obviousness of its anti-hero's Babbittism, even if in Hal Holbrook's impersonation—I cannot say characterization because Marco is not a character but a caricature—the fool of gold was so conspicuously pilloried that O'Neill didn't need a three-act play to make his point; a single scene would have been sufficient. Princess Kukachin never sounded as foolish in O'Neill's text as in the unmistakably talented Zohra Lampert's whining vocalization of an adolescent infatuation with the supersalesman. If in Miss Lampert's case, as in that of most American actors, voice training is indicated, it would not have solved the entire problem. O'Neill provides an almost insoluble problem in compelling the actress to be beautifully in love with a dolt whom Mr. Holbrook regrettably succeeded in making more doltish. The very talent of this actor, his constitutionally undergraduate external acting displayed here with cheery efficiency, writ Marco large in the chronicle of fools.

The more efficient the acting, indeed, the more difficult to escape the conclusion that *Marco Millions* itself is writ too large for comfort, for the author made a ponderous thing of satire that exhausts itself rapidly and eventuates in runaway romance that expands into acceptable spectacle but contracts into very weary pontification on life, death, and wisdom. Here we encounter (though not at his worst) the "literary" O'Neill, who was the external and overambitious O'Neill, not the O'Neill whom the late George Jean Nathan once bracketed with Theodore Dreiser as writers who "wrote badly" but were "great writers." It was no crime for the Lincoln Center to put *Marco Millions* into its repertory, but it was no great gift to the cultural life of America either, and on the large open stage it ended up as more boring than provocative. It was not that in the old 1928 Theatre Guild proscenium-stage production and in Alfred Lunt's Marco who was captivatingly immature and plucky rather than monotonously aggressive. The present production is most satisfactory, as a species of non-musical opera, when José Quintero's fine esthetic sensibility, visual imagination and command of arena-stage stylization assert themselves with valuable assistance from the stage designer David Hays, whose idea of treating the procession of scenes "theatristically," building and unbuilding the settings before the eyes of the audience, is almost consistently successful because it treats O'Neill's play as a comic fable. The scene changes indicated by a group of actors bearing banners and running across the stage is an especially amusing artifice. There are beautiful effects in the production, sumptuous Eastern scenes, and an ingeniously lit turntable that evokes the Venice of gondolas and the departure of the Chinese boat that will carry the Princess to her husband-to-be in Persia in a scene that is also dramatically effective.

III. *AFTER THE FALL*

The Lincoln Center's most publicized and best-attended production during the first season of 1964 was Arthur Miller's *After the Fall,* and the temptation is to treat it at great length as the opening production of the repertory and Miller's first play in nine years. The alternative is to treat it with modest brevity; this too is a temptation, and one particularly attractive both as a true evaluation of the play and as the way to avoid being enmeshed in matters largely irrelevant to dramatic criticism. Much breath has been wasted and much venom discharged in questioning the author's taste in exposing his private life to public scrutiny, in deploring his portrait of his second wife, Marilyn Monroe, and in asserting that the entire work is a confessional that expresses more hatred than contrition. Variations on these charges with many a verbal flourish will be found in the dramatic reviews written for the literary weeklies and quarterlies, and the present writer's admiration for vivacities of dissection have been mixed with loathing for the egotism displayed by those who upbraid Miller for being egotistical, and the obvious hatred of those who charge Miller with venting hatred. It would seem to be far more just to charge him with ambivalence, a venial sin without which this play or many an arresting work (whether *The City of God* and *The Divine Comedy,* Marlowe's *Doctor Faustus* or Goethe's *Faust,* Ibsen's *Brand* or O'Casey's *The Plough and the Stars*) would not have been written at all, or only thinly written. Miller is as entitled to his ambivalences as any other writer, and also entitled to the complexity of the work arising from them. It is only when the complexity becomes confusion that we have a right to complain, or when the ambivalence betrays the proclaimed objective of the play, which is not seriously the case here. As a matter of fact, the complexity of *After the Fall* expresses a perfectly admirable effort on the author's part to restore to playwriting some of the elbow-room it lost with the advent of realism, and the ambivalence is frankly acknowledged by Miller's *persona,* Quentin, from the start.

The charge of egotism, which may be pressed without impertinence and dignified with examination or refutation only in so far as the style and structure are allegedly involved, *is* invited by the author. This is chiefly because he made himself the center of a lengthy play that exalts, even while criticizing, him as if he were an epic hero; he exemplifies doubts and affirmations concerning humanity on a disproportionately large scale. The portentous style reflects the same tendency and borders at times on solemnity in the treatment of the central figure, "Quentin-Miller." And patently this reflective and self-analytical author is not that big, not that significant. To the defense it may be conceded that it has always been a characteristic of Miller's writing to conduct investigations that constitute for better and worse what Harold Clurman long ago called "Miller's moral jurisprudence." His Keller, Loman, Proctor, and now Miller's own *persona,* Quentin, have all been subjected to it. If there is egotism in trying to project the significance of little lives, then it is more than conceivable that this is a meritorious procedure on the part of an author who is addressing himself to public conscience (both in the current English and French sense of the word) in the theatre rather than to private sensibility in the library.

Only by the results may this procedure be judged, and Miller is not blowing himself up more than he blows up humanity as a whole in resorting to more or less autobiographical data, while on the smaller scale of personal experience Miller is also perfectly entitled both as artist and man to ask himself some ultimate question. He may well ask, as he does, "what price living and loving" or "can I, dare I, make another commitment of love to another woman after having failed with two wives and a friend, after having felt a deficiency of love in myself and others, and after having observed in my own case and in that of others (including a simple-hearted wife and a devoted mother) strong inclinations toward destructiveness in a world ripe with the rot of selfishness and rife with destructive and self-destructive manifestations?"

There is actually magnitude, the very magnitude Miller wanted for his play, in posing these questions, and it is regrettable only that they are considerably reduced by the personalities involved in the story. These suffer from such defects and limitations of characterization as the shadowy nature of Quentin's family, the intrusive ineptitude of the girl played by Zohra Lampert whose life had been allegedly altered for the better by Quentin, the gray figure of the first wife, and the tiringly neurotic character of the second wife, the "Marilyn Monroe" (whether fiction or approximate reality) vividly portrayed by Barbara Loden. (If Miller and Kazan, his director, had not wanted to capitalize on the resemblance, why did they allow Miss Loden to wear a blonde wig? And why did they allow so flagrant a transition between her earlier and later personality in the play, so that it is difficult to believe that she is the same person?)

Magnitude resides also in the key concept of the dramatic structure that distributes action, often in snippets of scenes and quasi-expressionistically, all over the playing areas designed by Jo Mielziner and utilized perhaps as well as could be expected under the circumstances by Elia Kazan and his actors—though not always successfully, and absurdly in one minor instance when Jason Robards, addressing the audience, found a convenient ash-tray on the floor of the forestage. Magnitude in the play structure, however, was regrettably won at the cost of concentration when the numerous scenes of the play were truncated, ill-defined, and trapped in the dim mine field of many dramatic explosions that produced more smoke than light. This was noticeable even in the Oedipal memories of the boy Quentin's relation to his parents and in the grown Quentin's relations with the friends with whom he more or less shared a radical past. And Miller's intention of magnitude of meaning led him to make generalizations from time to time that came off awkwardly and were not always sustained by the surrounding action, inviting attention to defects and pretensions in the language of the play. The magnitude was thus spelled out as *statement* more insistently than it was achieved in the concrete situations. The magnitude, as is frequently the case of plays by far less experienced writers than Miller, was in the *external* form rather than in the characters themselves or in the concretely realized events themselves. This deficiency of drama is apparent even in the ostensibly important political scenes that culminate in the suicide of Quentin's former law professor whom he fails to befriend in his time of need while willing to defend him before the Un-American Activities Committee.

The real dimensions of the play are, then, distinctly smaller than those of the claims thrust forward by the author in his structure and sententious reflections on the events, and by the production that has an extensiveness that would have been suitable rather for staging *The Divine Comedy,* especially without acting personalities that could focus attention on themselves. Even Jason Robards, who was appealing and exercised good control in an exacting, if monotonous, role was not vivid enough to manifest such central heating in the big, cold, and frequently dark abyss of this three-quarter arena stage seemingly several stories high; the young Gielgud or Moissi might have manifested it perhaps in *Hamlet* —with more than a little assistance from Shakespearian verse and melo-drama.

One could only conclude, even after crediting Arthur Miller with the most honorable intentions and ponderable sincerity, that *After the Fall* did not live up to either the author's or his producers' expectations. It may be defined as a little private drama inflated into a large public one or extended into a panorama of little agonies. And perhaps the most charitable view would consider the work as the lumpy raw material for two or three plays exposed on the stage too soon and too immoderately by the author and his producers, probably out of eagerness to start the first subscription season with a bang. For unfriendly critics it started with a magnified whimper.*

IV. *INCIDENT AT VICHY*
(October, 1965)

It is no secret that the Repertory Theatre of Lincoln Center did not [help redeem a mediocre season]; at least not until it was too late to bail out the old management, now displaced by Herbert Blau and Jules Irving from whom much is at this writing expected. There is no doubt that they

---

* [A note shows that Professor Gassner intended to be more specific about this point, using Mary McCarthy's attack on the play as an example. *Ed.*]

will receive every benefit that faith and patience can bestow, whereas the old management of Kazan and Whitehead aroused an immense amount of animosity, especially on the part of young reviewers and theatre buffs. Into the controversy itself I shall not enter, but it is only fair to concede that the last few months of the old management were the best. Ironically, it got little credit for the William Ball *Tartuffe,* in Richard Wilbur's translation, which delighted everyone, and the Harold Clurman production of Arthur Miller's *Incident at Vichy,* an improvement on *After the Fall* that moved audiences without exactly converting the young reviewers who had manifested an unconcealed dislike for Miller. The latter's brand of earnestness, in fact, is unlikely to win them over today; his social conscience does not interest them. For them he is a heavy-handed writer as well as a too solemn moralist; and it is mainly his bursts (or, in some instances, outbursts) of dramatic power that call for a higher valuation than that which the young intelligentsia is willing to accord him.

This is true of *Incident at Vichy*. Although the power is diminished by the static nature of the situation (a number of characters await interrogation before being transported to Nazi concentration camps), the tensions of the prospective victims and of a German officer whip up considerable drama. In the Clurman production of this uninterrupted hour-and-a-half-long play, this was vividly achieved by David Wayne, Joseph Wiseman, and Will Lee. (The latter mimed his part, that of an elderly refugee clinging to his sole possession—a featherbed—to great advantage, since any words that could have been reasonably assigned to him in a realistic prose drama would have been woefully inadequate; and both Clurman and Miller, as well as the actor should be congratulated for their bit of genuine theatre.) The climactic scene, in which a guilt-ridden Austrian aristocrat gives his passport to a Jewish psychoanalyst, is especially forceful, even if somewhat sententiously short on logic and long on fabrication since the psychoanalyst's arguments are specious and the aristocrat's motivation is dubious.

Miller's chief mistake and, given his temperament and ambition, a nearly unavoidable one, is his endeavor to write discussion dramas, for which his mind seems to be insufficiently honed, while his real strength is in his power of feeling. Still, in *Incident at Vichy* one of our very ablest playwrights could be seen moving back to the well-springs of his power, and this with a fortunate, though still insufficient, reduction of his reliance on morbid moralism and guilt-complex psychologicalizing. The question remained unanswered why Miller, and with him other able and assiduous American playwrights including William Inge and Tennessee

Williams have showed so little capacity for growth in recent years. But then I have not been aware of much capacity for growth among our novelists of a decade or so ago either.

V. *DANTON'S DEATH*
(March, 1966)

Only two [theatre immortals] were represented in the proximity of Broadway [in the 1965–66 season], Georg Buechner and William Wycherley and no one attending the Lincoln Center productions of *Danton's Death* and *The Country Wife* could be convinced that these revivals added to their author's posthumous longevity or even justified it.

Many strands of action and explanation do not necessarily add up to a dramatically meaningful action. That could certainly be said about Georg Buechner's early-nineteenth-century Shakespearean drama *Danton's Death,* and the Herbert Blau production at the newly opened Vivian Beaumont Theatre of New York's luxurious Lincoln Center made this pre-expressionistic historical drama seem very much more inchoate than it needs to be. It had been my intention to give considerable attention to the production but the lapse of time between seeing it and writing about it has dulled my impressions, and this is itself a form of criticism. Mr. Blau needed better actors than he had in his company for many of the principal roles (although I rather liked his Robespierre and found a "sick" impressiveness in his St. Just), and he lacked the ensemble for mass effects which it may take him years to develop and detach from embarrassingly crude histrionics. Moreover, the stage of the new theatre is too large and deep. It tempted the director to employ its lavish new facilities with too little restraint and to overproduce the play, as in his unnecessarily naturalistic use of a towering guillotine in the climactic execution scene. For many scenes of private emotion and for the imprisonment of Danton the large empty background was simply disastrous. It was nothing less than a vast cavern opening up monstrously to swallow the neutral and uninterestingly used foreground and all its unfortunate characters.

The pity of it is that if there is one near-masterpiece that is ready-made for the present age of disillusion (the *masterpiece* is, of course, *King Lear*) it is *Danton's Death,* written in 1835, out of disillusion with the French Revolution on the part of a twenty-one-year-old literary genius, while in hiding from the police for his own revolutionary activity in Germany. Unromantically, unidealizingly (*pace* the young Goethe and Schiller who, with Lessing, first gave eminence to the German theatre), Buechner takes the measure of revolutions that betray humanity in the name of humanity. It is a profoundly pessimistic or, if you will, "absurdist" testament of the disenchanted mind. It is distinctly superior in text to the quasi-Brechtian *Marat/Sade,* and the dialogue is an impressively poetic expression of the preter-naturally bright young author's frame of mind. His Danton is destroyed before physical annihilation by corrosion of the confidence in revolution that made him unleash the reign of terror in France, by his growing diffidence toward all forms of action until he is aroused by his friends' danger to defend himself against Robespierre. He dies of "existentialist" nausea and "absurdist" disgust some time before Robespierre, the new but only briefly triumphant would-be purifier of the Revolution, sends him to the guillotine. Buechner's perhaps overly metaphorical dialogue, too rich for Broadway and too difficult for vo-cally untrained American actors, teems with ironic disenchantment. It is a proper matrix for Danton's *acedia.*

"The world is chaos. *'Nothing'* is the world-god waiting to be born," is the outcry of anguish that follows the realization (how often repeated in the interval between Danton's times and our own) that high dreams of *liberté, égalité, fraternité* lead but to the grave. Danton's superb reproof to Robespierre and other inhumane purists of revolutionary integrity needs a better-speaking actor than any the Lincoln Center company con-tains at present: "I should be ashamed of myself, running around for thirty years with the same physiognomy, merely for the shabby satisfac-tion of finding others worse than myself." It is, of course, unnecessary to expatiate upon the merits of *Danton's Death,* merits that shine forth brightly from the crude and hastily mined ore of a talent that barely knew the theatre and had virtually no experience within it. Anybody who can bring a histrionic apprehension to printed dialogue can appreciate it. *But can one speak or act it?* It is extremely difficult to do so, and it is un-fair to heap scorn upon the management of Blau and Irving after the first Lincoln Center production, even if one must strongly deplore the direc-tor's decision to resort to operatic stylization. This was especially unfortu-nate in his opening-scene balletic gambit, which his raw company made almost farcically inept, and the grand-guignol naturalism of the guillotine scene toward the end of the play.

VI. *THE COUNTRY WIFE*
(March, 1966)

The second Lincoln Center production, *The Country Wife,* staged by Robert Symonds, who gave the best performance in *Danton's Death* as Robespierre and then one of the best impersonations in his own production as Sparkish, was an improvement, although an insufficient one, I fear. It is an unnecessary piety to overrate this Restoration comedy, which is considerably less well turned than the best of Congreve, and hangs entirely on threads of fashionable adultery and a rake's pretence of impotence in order to facilitate his adventures. These were singularly flat in the competent and physically extremely beautiful Lincoln Center production designed by James Hart Stearns and lit by Jean Rosenthal. The hue and cry about its disappointing results was absurdly exaggerated and, I suspect, rather disingenuous. You would think that a thoroughly living masterpiece had been dismembered when it was mainly a less than exquisite museum piece, here and there enlivened by a sempiternal appeal of salacious detail, that was left undisclosed. The old comedy did not quite "make the grade" in the Lincoln Center revival, no matter how efficiently performed by the young actors, especially by Stacy Keach as Horner, Michael Granger as the quack physician who conspires with Horner to deceive gullible husbands ripe for cuckoldry, and Elizabeth Huddle in the part of the young wife from the country who is more than ready for the city in Good King Charles' Golden Time. What must be charged most severely against the production is the joylessness of it, and the source of this deficiency is not directorial ineptitude but essentially a want of genuine charm in most of the principals of the cast. Several of them, to be sure, made efforts to attain it, but were either not intrinsically entrancing stage personalities (comedy—especially "high comedy"—simply cannot be played without such personalities in the key roles, and youthfulness alone is not enough, especially when swaddled in costumes) or were defeated by a native American strenuousness usually seen to vastly better advantage, say, in *Three Men on a Horse* or *You Can't Take It With You* or in many of our musicals.

The new Lincoln Center management, one suspects, will do considerably better by the modern plays in its first year's repertory. But even if it does, as one hopes it will, this much has been made abundantly evident even to the most starry-eyed optimist: Repertory *per se* is no panacea; it takes years to develop an entirely effective repertory company, and great things in the theatre cannot be accomplished without extraordinary talent as well as effort.

VII. *THE CONDEMNED OF ALTONA*
(May, 1966)

Problems of both greater and lesser complexity vitiate Jean-Paul Sartre's *The Condemned of Altona* (the translation of *Les Séquestrés d'Al-*

tona chosen by the able adaptor Justin O'Brien) and made the task of the young Lincoln Center Repertory Company under Herbert Blau somewhat difficult. One could cavil at the production, but with little justification in the case of the setting by Robin Wagner, the pacing by Blau, and the at the worst over-subdued impersonation of The Father, a German patrician manufacturer, by the veteran actor George Coulouris. (The latter may be well remembered for his playing of Marc Antony in the famous 1937 Orson Welles Mercury Theatre production, as well as for his performances in Lillian Hellman's *Watch on the Rhine* and *Richard III* in the early 1940's.) And if anything, the New York press seemed to me quite unjust to the young San Francisco Actor's Workshop actor Tom Rosqui in boggling at his vibrant performance of the central character Frantz, the guilt-obsessed son who started as a sensitive youth and ended up as the inhuman torturer of prisoners on the Eastern front while serving as an officer in Hitler's army. It is to the shortcomings of the play itself, over-rated and over-publicized by Howard Taubman when it was first produced in America at the Washington Arena Theatre, that we turn to explain the Lincoln Center's third but honorable failure of the season.

Its subject matter made it worth a production; it is an indictment of the brutalization of man by war not only in Germany but everywhere on the planet, including Algeria which was closest to Sartre's mind when he wrote the play. That Frantz, the agent and original victim of brutalization in Germany, should find his life in seclusion after World War II tolerable only so long as he can maintain the illusion that German postwar recovery has not taken place and that Nazi guilt was being paid for, is the most telling point of the play. And telling, too, is the somewhat less original theme of the brutalization of Frantz after his father's interference with his effort to save the life of a rabbi in the early years of the Nazification of Germany. But *The Condemned of Altona* is betrayed, in the last analysis, by the unoriginality of its form. It is plotty and contrived in the manner of the old-fashioned well-made play and of the gradual unfolding of guilt on the detective-story models of suspense and discovery. The commonplaceness of the form undercuts the author's passionately conceived content in several ways. The play constitutes an odd attempt to mix the most unphilosophical type of drama ever developed in Europe, which Shaw the critic called Sardoodledom, with a moral and philosophical viewpoint that unhappily arouses only intermittent attention. The "philosophy" is too obvious while the plot discoveries preempt the attention. The action, when the discoveries are completed, concludes with ostentatious moralism and with the rather arbitrary expiatory suicide of Frantz and his father.

The conventionality of the dramatic form, moreover, results in two contradictory faults—a strong impression of plottiness while there is actually very little essential plot in the play along the main lines of the theme —that is, Frantz's direct guilt and the contributory guilt of his industrialist father. And the impression of plottiness has a strong basis in the dramatic action that is itself anything but an asset to the play. *The Condemned of Altona* is loaded with the secondary situations of a spinster sister's love for Frantz and their incestuous relations, and of a sister-in-law's effort to seduce him in order to free herself and his brother, her husband, of the necessity of guarding Frantz for the rest of his life while he remains morbidly secluded in an upstairs room. These situations contribute little, if anything, to the theme but keep the plot moving as a vehicle of the argument.

It is possible to advance other criticisms against the overrating of this play, and allegations of symbolism even if acceptable (or applicable to the present adaptation, which I don't think they are) would not mitigate them. In one respect or another, Sartre was trapped into writing a discursive and contrived work or, as his biographer Mr. Cranston calls it, "a highbrow melodrama" in *The Condemned of Altona* that does not actually illuminate the meaning of its hero's inhuman act during World War II and his subsequent expiation of the act, which is the ultimate justification of the play in existentialist terms. Jacques Guicharnaud, in his excellent book *Modern French Theatre,* points out that action of existentialist significance is regarded by Sartre as well by other existentialist writers "as a creation, almost as unique and irreplaceable as a signed work of art, and at the same time, as both a source of drama and drama itself, not only at the moment it is committed—when it implies a struggle and a choice (in part well dramatized in one flashback war scene of *The Condemned of Altona*)—but even afterward, in man's effort to clarify the relationship between it and himself." That, indeed, is the deepest motivating factor in Sartre's play. But one has to care a great deal about a character who tries to clarify this relationship between himself and his deed. And it is extremely difficult to do in the case of Frantz, who must strike us as a self-indulgent and whining psychotic rather than as a tragic hero. Moreover, "clarification" must actually *clarify,* which Sartre does not quite succeed in doing when he attributes the deterioration of Frantz into a Nazi torturer to the fact that his father had betrayed the rabbi illegally sheltered by Frantz in order to save Frantz's skin. Sartre's equivocal success in the play comes from precisely the opposite effect, which is one of making us feel that Frantz does not and, indeed, cannot attain clarification; that he cannot explain his barbarities convincingly and can only expiate them by means of a melodramatic suicide involving his father as well as himself.

Sartre's play, then, provides an instructive example of the risks of writing "drama of ideas." These risks were considerably reduced, after Ibsen and Strindberg, with some frequency only in the work of Shaw and Brecht; and, I believe, by the same solvent (which one does not usually attribute to them as a common possession)—namely, the solvent of humor, ranging from mild mockery to abrasive satire. Sartre is humorless, when he is not indeed solemn. But it still remains to be said that *The Condemned of Altona* helped to enrich an impoverished season in which the substance of most plays was thinner than tissue. Second-grade Sartre is still vastly preferable to first-grade *kitsch*. And at least Sartre did not fob us off with the banalities of mere sentiment in returning to the subject of one of the twentieth century's most traumatic experiences.

VIII. *YERMA*
(March, 1967)

It does not follow, of course, that stylization by itself provides an open sesame to dramatic success, and this fact was exemplified rather conclusively by the latest Lincoln Center honorable fiasco, its production of the poet Lorca's *Yerma*. Although the final touch of authenticity was lacking, the production was, in the main, quite well staged by the Canadian Shakespeare Festival director John Hirsch, and the intense portrayal of a passionate but suppressed young peasant woman by Gloria Foster was impressive. *Yerma* is a poetic drama, and its starkly presented domestic scenes were supplemented by two choral folk scenes of considerable dramatic power and vividness on stage. But Lorca's dramatization of a single state of mind (that of a woman whose languid husband refuses or cannot give her a child, and who is severely virtuous in avoiding adultery, but is driven frantic with desire and becomes ultimately murderous by frustration) proved singularly wearing with reiteration. Transplanted to the alien sophisticated environment of Lincoln Center, *Yerma* seemed strained to the point of parody and rather embarrassingly naïve. Stylization, in the play and the production, did not (and possibly could not) overcome the sense of aridity in the dramatic action and of obviousness in the situation. Instead of being an overpoweringly tragic character, as

Lorca intended her to be, Yerma seemed in the Lincoln Center environment only a pathetically lost female in the end, and somewhat embarrassingly now and then just a woman in heat, or a neurotic with an *idée fixe*. It would have been wiser for the Lincoln Center to avoid the play despite its literary distinction.

THE ACTORS STUDIO

I. *STRANGE INTERLUDE*
(May, 1962)

A histrionic assault was staged by the Actors Studio Theatre when it launched its first production on Broadway with José Quintero directing and some of the Studio's best actors playing leading parts in *Strange Interlude*. Especially effective were Geraldine Page as Nina Leeds, Ben Gazzara as Dr. Darrell, and Betty Field as Sam Evans' mother. It is not that exceptions could not be taken to the production; Franchot Tone was not the best possible choice for the role of Nina's father, which remained ill-defined, while Geraldine Page allowed her voice to dribble out in strongly emotional scenes. She was ravishingly beautiful, and she played a number of important episodes supremely well. But at other times one could wish that Miss Page would concentrate more on speaking than on acting. The two are supposed to be indissolubly united, and that is excellent in theory, but there was such a discrepancy between her proficiency in acting and deficiency in speaking that, so far as I was concerned, theory in her case did not hold, and I could only conclude that this fine actress needed voice lessons more than she needed more acting training. It is a pity to have to lose so many important lines because Miss Page was bent upon acting them out in full. Whether we could afford to lose the lines is, of course, a question often raised in the case of O'Neill's plays. The lines needed to be hurried at times, especially in the interior monologues, but surely not lost. From this production, nevertheless, one could gather the impression that for all its limitations (and there is little point in calling attention to them as fresh discoveries) *Strange Interlude* is decidedly less dated than most plays first produced a third of a century ago; and for this much we may be grateful to the Actors' Studio Theatre.

If we cannot any longer assimilate the naïve "psychology" of Nina's plight in the first two scenes or overlook the intrusions of tedium, O'Neill's work still dignifies the American theatre while many fresh-as-paint plays have only devalued it. It is also instructive to observe that although O'Neill was hardly a master of language (he had himself in mind when he made the young author in *Long Day's Journey into Night* refer to himself as a stammerer), he makes his prolixity count in the key situations. It adds up to considerable fascination and force when Betty Field tells Nina of the hereditary insanity in Sam's family that makes it risky for Nina to have a child by him. And always there is O'Neill's characterization that opens up like a flower in water when good acting is available and left unconfined—by awkward arena-staging or by overmotivation, for example. This was not seriously the case in William Prince's playing of Nina's mother-fixated father-image Charles Marsden, although the direction milked the joke of his mother-fixation too far, and Ben Gazzara's tense impersonation of Dr. Ned Darrell was spare and strong, although even Gazzara could not quite make me swallow the crudity of the scene in which Nina prevails upon him to give her a child. O'Neill wrote for actors, but in working with characters he was usually complex rather than subtle; indeed, perhaps no playwright can be subtle in a nine-act play that lasts five hours and provides a stream of interior monologue to supplement conversation that is usually plain enough without commentary. The trouble with *Strange Interlude* may well be that O'Neill did not rely sufficiently on actors to fill in the spaces between feeling and dialogue. He could have relied on the Studio's actors who do not do as well by the play as the original Theatre Guild company headed by Lynn Fontanne did (the Studio's Nina is too neurotic and feline in the early scenes, Sam's mother too placid, Sam too prematurely middle-aged while trying too hard to be youthful, and Dr. Darrell too professionally stiff) but who give O'Neill's points all the accent O'Neill could have wanted—and then some.

II. *MARATHON 33*
(March, 1964)

A production that might not have reached Broadway but for the prestige of the producing organization, the Actors Studio Theatre, and the tireless virtuosity of Julie Harris in the main role, is *Marathon 33,* a play fashioned from June Havoc's autobiographical recollections of the economic depression of the early thirties when couples made desperate efforts to pick up some money by outlasting other dancers in an arena or on a stage. The naturalism of the presentation by the Actors Studio is appalling. Miss Havoc's grimly antiromantic treatment of the subject is a compliment to her sense of reality and her integrity. But one would have to see this production for oneself to realize how double-edged a naturalistic theatre can be. Briefly, the very quality that recommends the play, its honest "slice of life," operates against the play; the low key of some of the scenes is depressing, as is the general sordidness of the work which can be endured only with distaste or only with a heroic resolve to follow the painful proceedings for the sake of their truth. But, as in facing many another naturalistic work, one feels frustrated rather than strengthened by encountering the truth. The elements of enlightenment, exhilaration and catharsis are absent in such a work; we feel thrust into the dumps and there is nothing we can do about it—we merely feel entrapped. It is no wonder than if the public is reluctant to attend even a production as brimful with talent and energy as *Marathon 33*. The more strenuously theatre of this kind labors to express its stalemate of truth the more self-defeating it becomes, since it fails to go far enough as drama and ends as raw experience rather than art. *Marathon 33,* which "builds" as drama in the second half and earned good will as the strenuous effort of an aspiring acting company, would not quite pull itself out of a situation for which perhaps the best description would be Wordsworth's "fen of stagnant waters" in the famous sonnet on England's need for moral re-armament and Milton.

III. *THE THREE SISTERS*
(October, 1964)

A special challenge to our judgment of performance and staging had to be met in the case of the highly successful Actors Studio production of *The Three Sisters,* as directed by Lee Strasberg and played by several of the Studio's best known actresses in the roles of the three sisters—each of them a "star." (No matter how the Studio and *ETJ* readers may dislike the term, at least two Studio performers, Geraldine Page and Kim Stanley, are precisely that by virtue of personality, idiosyncrasy, and stage presence, although they are more than matched by Daykarhanova, the little old lady who plays the nurse in the family and for whose veteran talents no American studio can claim the slightest credit.) There can be widely varying opinions about the performances and the staging, and not to beg any questions I put myself on record at once to this personal extent: I believe with the majority of reviewers that as Chekhov's Olga, Geraldine Page turned in the best performance of her career since her playing of Tennessee Williams' Alma at Circle-in-the-Square and that Kim Stanley was superb as Masha, the unhappily married sister whose chief suffering she successfully conveyed as pent-up romantic egocentricity and *ennui* in a cultural vacuum. Since Chekhov dealt precisely with this—that is, with the bootless romantic yearnings of well-bred ladies and the cultural vacuum of turn-of-the-century provincial Russia, Miss Stanley was to my mind perfectly suited to the role. And I believe Lee Strasberg was penetrative and profoundly right in having her play *away* from much that occurs in the play including her own love affair with Colonel Vershinin. I also believe that both Strasberg and Kevin Mc-Carthy were absolutely right in presenting the latter as essentially disengaged in idealistic pratings about the great future that lies ahead for humanity, in dismay about his half-mad wife and neglected children, in his aborted "romance" with Masha, and in his elegant departure from the provincial capital. For all his aplomb, Vershinin is as shadowy a man as the sisters' futile brother Andrei. I was less happy with some other performances, with the schoolmaster Kulygin, the Solyony, the febrile yet undefined Natasha, and the youngest sister, Irina, of the production, although it is not difficult to validate a washed-out impersonation in this case; and I was impatient with the pace of the performance, which is perhaps less a matter of judgment than of my conditioning and temperament.

It must be noted here that the last thing the Actors Studio accomplished in *The Three Sisters* was an ensemble production. This was evident in the variety of accents and acting styles as in the frequent disconnectedness of the performances. No doubt the latter criticism is unfair; it would take a year of playing together to achieve an ensemble and this seems rather improbable under our economic conditions and in the absence of year-round repertory. It remains questionable, too, whether in this production it isn't the *good* performances that seem least related to one another, and whether this isn't actually a point of the play. It seems to be the point in the inability of the sisters and the brother to act in concert (the sisters and the brother cannot even talk to each other in the crucial scene) and in the signal case of Luther Adler's performance of the alcoholic doctor Chebutykin, whose separateness is his main attribute and the chief manifestation of his personal failure. Lee Strasberg has studiously avoided head-on conflicts, perhaps out-Chekhoving Chekhov in this respect; the penalty is a certain lassitude in the production, while the gain consists of a poignant integrity in dramatizing stalemate and stagnation.

The Three Sisters is at the end of the line, so to speak, in European naturalism, brought to such refinement that even a play that contains a fire, a fatal duel, actual or intended infidelity by *two* characters (by one of the sisters and by their sister-in-law Natasha), the ousting of two of the sisters from their own home, and at least one off-stage suicide attempt (by Vershinin's wife) barely ripples the waters of dramatic action. And whatever the limitations of this genre, it continues to exert a direct or indirect influence, and a benign one, although only within severe limits.

IV. *BLUES FOR MR. CHARLIE*
(October, 1964)

Blues for Mr. Charlie, James Baldwin's first professionally presented play [staged by the Actors Studio], was both believable and significant as the drama of a young Negro's half-invited death in the deep South, culminating in a trial in which racial conflicts turn into a conflagration of animosities. The acting of the principal parts, Percy Rodriguez's impressive minister who becomes a militant after the murder of his son, Al Freeman's playing of an embittered young Negro, and Diana Sands' flaring performance as his girl was vivid and intense, and Abe Feder's lighting and overall design of the production had a crackling vibrancy about it. But *Blues for Mr. Charlie* was also too crudely clapped together by an inexperienced playwright and an exacerbated partisan to provide a satisfactory work of art or even an entirely sound argument. An excess of partisanship, which actually confused the social issue with allegations of white sexual jealousy and inept conduct on the part of the Negro youth, vitiated this intensely felt work.

■

THE ASSOCIATION OF
PRODUCING ARTISTS

I. *THE LOWER DEPTHS*
(October, 1964)

Almost any naturalistic venture would have been overshadowed by the APA (Association of Producing Artists) production of *The Lower Depths,* as staged by Ellis Rabb, who also played the down-at-heels Baron. Brought to New York's Phoenix Theatre, Gorky's fifty-year-old masterpiece seemed anything but dated, and whatever inadequacies one might have noted in individual characterizations and in the evocation of atmosphere were compensated by the general vitality of the production.

II. *JUDITH* AND OTHERS
(October, 1965)

[Off-Broadway] the APA prevailed with its repertory of *Man and Superman* (given complete with the Don Juan in Hell fantasia which has the best writing), Giraudoux's biblical *tour de force, Judith,* thinned out (I think to advantage) in the Savacool adaptation, and *War and Peace,* the free treatment of Tolstoy's novel by Erwin Piscator and others that has succeeded on both sides of the Atlantic. I find *Judith* plethorically romantic and just as plethorically "sophisticated," qualities that often go together in France's two leading theatrical *petits maîtres,* Giraudoux and Anouilh. But we can still make stronger claims for both of them than for most American playwrights that have appeared since the advent of O'Neill some forty years ago. Produced so well, with exemplary discretion due to Ellis Rabb's directions and the acting of Rosemary Harris as the Apocryphal heroine, the results far exceeded my expectations. (Harold Clurman's London production of a "straight" translation had fared nowhere as well.) In the APA's *Man and Superman,* the Don Juan dream lacked the dramatic force of the Laughton-Boyer-Hardwick-Moorehead production presented by Paul Gregory about a decade ago. But in speeding up the speeches in order to keep the "dream" as an integral part of the play—the Gregory production made a full evening of Tanner's fantasia alone—the APA production could not but achieve a lighter effect. Many would prefer it so, besides, as more suitable for a comedy of manners. It is not, of course, as comedy of manners but as "comedy of ideas" that my generation of Shavians, as well as the author himself, most appreciated the play. But other times, other manners, including manners of judging plays; and it is some time since Shaw was admired or resented for his new ideas or inversion of old ones. One estimable thing the APA did accomplish with this production without the possibility of all but minor reservations—it made Shaw seem livelier, if not more alive, than ever; and this without descending to the level of second-grade farcicality, so that it still qualified as serious art rather than as mere *kitsch*. As for the APA's *War and Peace,* it was weaker as antiwar protest than the Bristol Old Vic production I saw three years ago in London, but the production also dispensed with some Kindergarten epic theatre theatrics in favor of character drama, and once more Rosemary Harris, playing Natasha, provided character-dimension. Good taste and fine ensemble work compensated a want of brilliance in the productions. All things considered, the APA helped a good deal to redeem a mediocre season.

III. *YOU CAN'T TAKE IT WITH YOU*
(March, 1966)

The only successful stage veterans [of the 1965–66 season], with the exception of Abe Burrows hitherto identified with TV and musicals, were two deceased ones—namely, the authors of the attractively revived almost thirty-year-old *You Can't Take It With You,* George S. Kaufman and Moss Hart, who had enlivened the twenties and thirties without exactly enrolling themselves among the immortals.

Without any . . . reservations, [the public] was ecstatic about the APA's thoroughly engaging revival of *You Can't Take It With You.* Presumably a vintage comedy, it seemed as fresh as ever in Ellis Rabb's APA production. It was greatly aided by the able, relatively seasoned, young acting company, thus far considered decidedly superior to the newer Lincoln Center one. Clayton Corzatte and Rosemary Harris were especially charming as the young lovers embarrassed by the antics of the zany Sycamore family. The public even brought the kiddies to the show during the Christmas vacation: *I* brought my granddaughter. For what it is, *You Can't Take It With You* is excellent entertainment. It can also be appreciated, now more than in the arduous Depression year 1936, for what it is *not*—namely, a sick play that passes for comedy in some *avant-garde*

circles. It is healthy Philistine entertainment in its genial, for me somewhat *too* genial, anti-Philistinism.

IV. *RIGHT YOU ARE*
(March, 1967)

The generally fine APA *Right You Are* revival seemed to me to
suffer from lethargy despite the presence of familiar Pirandellian inventiveness and mental nimbleness in Eric Bentley's admirable translation,
which is unclogged by the Victorian verbal clutter of the translation used
for previous productions of the play. The play now seems little more
than an amalgam of drawing-room comedy and a mystery story, given a
philosophical patina by a skeptical raisonneur's comments on the officious
who pry into other people's secrets and whom Pirandello balks and re-
bukes by leaving the mystery completely unsolved. *Right You Are* is a
perfectly well-wrought work, but it is apt to impress at least some of us
as a rather conventional foray into dramatic discussion and exposition.
In producing Pirandello's early play competently, the APA has made no
particular contribution to contemporary theatre just as in staging Sheridan's *School for Scandal* it does not exemplify any noteworthy exertion on
behalf of English classics. If anything, its very competence is also conducive to disappointment because it precluded any originality in presenting Sheridan's comedy of manners and Pirandello's metaphysical comedy.
In the very process of making sympathy for the main object of curiosity,
played by Helen Hayes, it depressed the comic élan at crucial moments
in the progress of the action.

THE INSTITUTE FOR ADVANCED
STUDIES IN THEATRE ARTS

PHÈDRE
(October, 1966)

[A] particularly instructive contrast [with Broadway tastes and methods] was provided, most gratifyingly in this reviewer's opinion, by the Institute for Advanced Studies in the Theatre Arts (IASTA), for which accolades, as well as more substantial encouragement, has been due for some time, but never more so than when it put on a *Phèdre*, in William Packard's effective translation, and presented the long absent but always welcome Beatrice Straight in the title role. Every one of the roles was more than adequately performed, which is saying a great deal, alas, for American production of a classic. To say that this is the first time within memory that New York has had a satisfactory production of a Racine tragedy in English is to say too little. Unfortunately, with the praiseworthy exception of Stanley Kauffmann of the *New York Times,* the newspaper reviewers, by and large, chose to say much less. By all but inapproachable French standards, IASTA's *Phèdre* was excellent—well spoken, generally well staged, and impressively acted. It provided a lesson which we can ill afford not to absorb and put to use. Racine, in English, like the Greek playwrights except in the case of *The Trojan Woman,* has always been considered too formidable for New York audiences. But it has been a blot on our much-blotted scutcheon that this should be the case since our theatre can ill afford to cut itself off from access to dramatic masterpieces by lethargy, no less than by directorial ineptness and want of workable translations.

So it was no small thing to encounter a *Phèdre* one could receive in dignity rather than derision, and with pleasure rather than pain. In large measure this was due to an unexpected event in our theatre—the actors proved themselves capable of speaking verse clearly and naturally. It remains to be seen whether this feat and its attending graces of a sense of style and natural dignity will be bestowed on other works not hitherto accessible to an ostensibly culture-hungry public. The present writer would be happy to find it bestowed in coming seasons on *Andromache, Brittanicus,* and *Bérénice.* (It would be too much to expect it for *Athalie,* unquestionably one of the greatest post-classic dramas, since actors—that is, American actors—would not only have to be able to speak verse but speak it in unison!) No doubt there were subtleties missing in IASTA's production as well as subtleties in it worth pointing out to those attending the performance, mostly related to the excellent use of a small stage and the simple dignity of the setting on it. But however the miracle was achieved, it *was* achieved; and not noting the means by which this minor miracle was accomplished may actually be put down to the credit of the production: there simply was too little opportunity to watch details because the paramount interest was so well, and so appropriately, focused on the broad outlines and noble movement of a great play, from which its seventeenth-century author had already pared everything inessential or potentially distracting. That Racine's Alexandrines could not be exactly translated, that his cadences and rhythms could not be duplicated, goes without saying. That despite this the effect of the presentation proved so satisfactory was not the least miracle of the production. Whoever sensed it in the little "Greenwich Mews" theatre could claim that he had come appreciably closer to some degree of rapport with neo-classic tragedy than had ever been the case for those who have no French.

To continue to talk about this would be an exercise in futility for which even the New Criticism has not prepared us. Naturally, it is necessary to have some opinion concerning the kind of play or plays Racine wrote before staging them. A special result may be expected, given good actors, from a director who adopts Francis Fergusson's view in *The Idea of a Theater* (Chapter 2. "Bérénice: The Action and Theatre of Reason") that Racine "says that the passions must be excited; but they are to be roused only to enter the inimical realm of the mind," or when he goes on to make much of Racine's point that "Phèdre's crime is rather a punishment of the gods rather than a movement of her will." Perhaps the above-given two successive statements suggest an antithesis rather than a synthesis. In that case, the conclusion one would draw from the first statement is that the staging of the play should be as detached as possible, "Brechtian," if you will, or neo-classically formal in the bearing and movement of the characters and forthrightly, though not artificially declamatory. That is the interpretation plainly evident in the IASTA production, with its virtually undecorated stage, its simple costuming, and its unencumbered rather than busy stage movement. Provided the spectator brings a "mind" to the performance rather than a soap-opera mentality or a merely sentimental "human interest" disposition, the playgoer's experience can then be decidedly tragic in witnessing a competently acted and better than just adequately spoken performance; and this was the experience at the Greenwich Mews that drew from the present reviewer the above-rendered favorable verdict on the production. But if a director were to adopt the viewpoint expressed in the second statement—namely, that "Phèdre's crime" (I presume adulterous desire and failure to declare Hippolytus innocent) is a punishment from the gods or from a Jansenist deity unaccountable to man, a rather different production would be needed to convey that Racinian message so well defined by whoever wrote that Racine's heroines were "fair women full of Attic grace but lacking *the grace of God*." In that case, we should get a production in which the swirl of the action is constantly flailing against the restraints of the neo-classic form and style, and in which the heroine trapped by her passion (Phèdre in one play, Hermione in another) is blindly struggling against a fate she cannot comprehend and cannot resist. That, it would seem, was the style of performance of the great nineteenth-century French actresses in these roles, displaying an overlay of romantic feeling on a base of neo-classicism." Could the two approaches meet in the same production? They *could,* one may imagine, in a well-staged production featuring a Duse. The limitation of IASTA's production was an incomplete synthesis of restraint and the turbulence, and of "will" and fatality. But this would be to judge the production and its star by standards quite unattainable in the American theatre.

A MUSICAL SAMPLER

I. *HELLO, DOLLY!*
(March, 1964)

Hello, Dolly! [is] expertly fashioned out of Thornton Wilder's *The Matchmaker* by Michael Stewart, with better than average music and lyrics of Broadway timbre from Jerry Herman. Lavishly produced by David Merrick, beautifully staged and "choreographed" by the almost infallible Gower Champion, and almost irresistibly radiated by Carol Channing, huskily and pulchritudinously ample as Mrs. Dolly Gallagher Levi, the widowed matchmaker bent upon seizing her "merchant of Yonkers" prey, this production simply could not escape popularity. With comic enchantment from the lovely Eileen Brennan, the erstwhile off-Broadway belle of *Little Mary Sunshine,* as Mrs. Molloy, and with sundry bravura performances ranging from the necessarily stereotyped to the fresh and original (especially in the case of Charles Nelson Reilly as the head clerk Cornelius Hackl), *Hello, Dolly!* was everything a Broadway audience could desire. This musical started a career in the third week of the year and is likely to last longer than any production of recent years except *My Fair Lady,* a radically different entertainment.

Bustling with dance movement, parades, and eye-filling costumes and ladies to fill them, and abounding in farcical business and trusty show-business specialities, *Hello, Dolly!* can be viewed, and by the general public heartily welcomed, as "Broadway" at approximately maximum effectiveness. The very things that would be considered blemishes by standards other than Broadway's are somehow transformed into lively entertainment. It is not difficult at all to submit to its tuneful and zany turbulence, its machine-made plot and arbitrary reversals, its stereotypes and clichés, and its genial mindlessness interrupted only here and there with a genial philosophical line from Wilder, such as the analogy he draws between manure and money since both have to be spread around.

II. *THE KING AND I* AND OTHERS
(October, 1964)

What can be said about the New York State Theatre's inaugural production of *The King and I* except obvious things? The production, staged by Edward Greenberg, was altogether superb, but Rise Stevens and Darren McGavin, who probably gained ease and flexibility after the start of their run, inevitably fall short of the original performances of Gertrude Lawrence and Yul Brynner but were good enough in their way and were surrounded by reliable performers. The presentation was enriched by excellent voices. As for *The King and I* itself, it belongs to the best Hammerstein and Rodgers confections, and to define its limitations is to define the furthest limits of Broadway musical theatre as a whole. *The King and I* is so decidedly superior to the usual musical offerings that comparisons with it in the present season would be superfluous, and yet it all seems to belong to a vanishing world. It is too refined for the raucous animal age of culture currently being compounded of the vulgarity of the herd that grows more vulgar by the hour and the barbarism of the new intellectualism that nourishes on its own futility, sucks in the noxious air of decadence and belches it out again augmented with poisons produced internally by ungenerous intellectualism.

At the same time, the genre is itself rather musty with antimaccassar complacencies and liberal sentimentalism. The genre makes us feel virtuous as appreciators of a humanitarianism dispensed with unexacting taste and refinement. And this type of American musical entertainment is but a latter-day version of the musical romanticism of Romberg, Friml and company; a mid-century variant of operetta, with diminished voices and gestures, someday bound to be condescendingly wrapped in mothballs and later unwrapped piously in the name of the bourgeois trinity of Art, Culture, and Entertainment. In its most pleasing incarnations, as in *The King and I,* this art, supposedly the prime American contribution to the theatre, rightly belongs to the good museum pieces of our culture, and the plush 2700-seat New York State Theatre will be a suitable home for it for at least a few decades if our society remains essentially unaltered. And if it is radically altered, I doubt very much that new styles and genres won't come from the slag-heap of devolution, instead of emanating from an evolution of musical comedy and music drama to which I cannot look forward with any glimmer of gratification.

At least I see no signs of new *Threepenny Operas* and *Mahagonnys* (or their American equivalents) taking shape, since there seems to be no incentive to a new mode of expression when we don't possess any passionately held aims or ideas. You may call it "bourgeois sentimentalism," from the left, or starry-eyed liberalism, from the right, of our political spectrum, but it is a fact that Rodgers and Hammerstein harbored a congenial viewpoint capable of sustaining a number of syncretic ideals sanctioned by World War II sentiments. Nothing of the sort made much of an impression this past year except *Anyone Can Whistle,* an original and strongly felt assertion of liberalism that made the wrong kind of impression, chiefly one of excruciating boredom, for reasons that it would require some genius to explain. I myself would have entertained strong hopes for the project before being exposed to the unfortunate final results.

I have left out of our calculations, of course, the benign miracle of performance—Inga Swenson's, for example, in *110 in the Shade;* Beatrice Lillie's in *High Spirits,* the musical adaptation of *Blithe Spirit;* Carol Burnett's in *Fade-In, Fade-Out,* and Barbra Streisand's in *Funny Girl.* "Story," of course, had something to do with it, as it usually has in the case of a full-scale musical entertainment. Thus *Oklahoma!* nourished on *Green Grow the Lilacs* and *Carousel* on *Liliom* in the nineteen-forties; *Hello, Dolly!* had *The Matchmaker, 110 in the Shade* derived some nourishment from *The Rainmaker,* and *Funny Girl* owes a great deal of its popular appeal to the personality and career of the late Fanny Brice. But the trick is decisively turned by a performer, and this was emphatically the case when Barbra Streisand undertook to impersonate Fanny Brice. Whatever the resemblance, the important thing is that this talented young lady is a person in her own right, capable of evoking a sympathy more immediate than the object of her impersonation and somehow touching chords of recognition utterly genuine in the pinch-beck world of Broadway musical entertainment. With Sidney Chaplin presenting a remarkably affecting portrait of an elegant gambler, Nicky Arnstein, as the love-object of the former ugly duckling and child of poverty, and given the expected competence of an expensive Broadway musical production, the results were fabulously disproportionate. An ordinary musical with a good subject and a well-supported central performance became a "smash hit" of tremendous proportions. The success of *Funny Girl* comprised the saga of commercial production won by a hair's breadth that makes show-business akin to betting on horses while taking benzedrine and sharing it with the horses. You have to be an addict to take part in the venture, but if you haven't ever taken part in it, actually or imaginatively, you will have missed an indefinable *élan* and catalyst you cannot acquire from books and lectures or from any amount of lofty critical writing.

In simpler days than ours they used to call it inspiration; you can still call it that, or an inner glow that comes without warning in the course of the struggle against inertia and that often departs as suddenly as it came. If I ever encounter it in a university theatre production (and I do not rule out the possibility) I shall know that a star has been born, and unless stars are born like that every now and then, even good community theatre productions will strike me as dilettante theatricals. This may be considered heresy in some quarters, but I believe I shall hold on to this belief even after the educational theatre has launched a comprehensive actor-training program, bcause I believe in the right ensemble principle of "every actor a star" rather than the wrong ensemble principle of "no actor a star."

III. *FIDDLER ON THE ROOF*
(December, 1964)

I think it is good to remind ourselves from time to time that it is the "show" that matters first before anything else in dramatic art can matter. Playwrights from Aeschylus, the first great director of choruses, to the poet who circumscribed the world with Falstaff's *embonpoint,* to Brecht and Beckett, both partial to clowning, have known this. It is less certain that today's academicians know it. And that is a pity because viable dramatic literature has certainly come more frequently from showmanship than effective showmanship has come from dramatic literature.

This was particularly evident in Broadway's immensely successful Joseph Stein, Jerry Bock, and Sheldon Harnick musical, *Fiddler on the Roof,* carved out of Sholom Aleichem's old stories of Jewish life in the pre-Soviet Russian villages. The stories, already made familiar to New York audiences by two off-Broadway dramatizations within the past decade, concern the trials of the dairyman Tevye, a folk-hero blessed with five unmarried daughters and a heap of other troubles. Several episodes concern his efforts to eke out a living, marry off his daughters, and assimilate their unconventional behavior in choosing their own mates, one of whom is a poor tailor, another a revolutionist ultimately exiled to Siberia by the Czar's government, and another a member of the Greek Orthodox faith. From these situations (watered down, according to Sholom Aleichem's admirers) emanate treasurable moments of humor and considerable pathos which deepens when Tevye and his neighbors are afflicted by pogroms and exile at the climax of each of the musical's two acts. The tone of the work is dual and unresolved since the treatment alternates between the humor of the private episodes and the outrage of the public events. Accommodation to Broadway taste plays its part in the treatment, which does not quite reconcile the comic and sinister elements of the story, and everywhere in the treatment one encounters a softening of the edge of satire and a sweetening of the bitterness of the substratum of the folksy humor. The conventional episodic character of the musical, moreover, flattens out the dramatic effect and, along with some poverty of invention on the part of the adapters, accounts for repetitiousness of action and tone.

Since the lyrics, score, and choreography, are competent rather than inspired, it is evident that the immensely successful *Fiddler on the Roof* must be the beneficiary of some miracle-working ingredient. It is the oldest miracle drug in the theatre that makes the difference—namely, the genius of one performer, Zero Mostel, whose every gesture and bit of facial play can score a point and score it delightfully. Mr. Mostel, round and rubicund and marvellously agile for an obese man, is raffish and pathetic yet also persevering, dignified, and granitic. He is on intimate terms with the Lord, whom he alternately importunes and reproves with a mumble and a rolling of the eyes that it would take thousands of words to match in effectiveness. At the most, the long-suffering Tevye allows himself a few wry remarks, and Mostel mutters them so feelingly that pathos and humor require no more elaboration than the shrug of the shoulder or the flick of a wrist. One can only hope that this performance will be preserved on film for posterity to learn how great an art clowning can be and how fine a substitute it can be for the eloquence usually missing in most of our comic and serious writing for the stage. Even when the gestures and facial play become repetitive in the last half of *Fiddler on the Roof,* the diminution of the pleasure they afford is inconsequential, as in the repetition of phrases of music one doesn't mind hearing again for their own sake rather than for their development of the theme. It is Mostel turning corn into caviar against some fine Chagall-like settings by Boris Aronson that we come to watch primarily, and it is chiefly in playing with or against him that several good performers, such as Beatrice Arthur, as Yente the matchmaker, and Maria Karnilova, as Golde the exasperated wife of the philosophical Tevye, acquire an estimable radiance in this controlled Jerome Robbins production of the human comedy that transpires in Sholom Aleichem's village of Anatevka on the eve of the Russian Revolution of 1905.

IV. *CABARET*
(March, 1967)

In Joe Masteroff's *Cabaret,* based on John Van Druten's play *I Am a Camera* and Christopher Isherwood's Berlin stories about Germany on the eve of Hitler's assumption of political power, we encounter a dramatically rich subject. It is made meaningful with concentration on the decadence of the period and the failure of the main characters to resist the attrition of their decent instincts by the love of luxury or the desire for safety. It is difficult to believe that there will be any Broadway play-goer who will willingly miss *Cabaret,* which is well supplied with music by John Kander, excellently choreographed by Ronald Field, and brilliantly designed by Boris Aronson. One could go on cataloguing the professional virtues of the production for several more lines without exhausting these tired but justified compliments, and that would still leave another sheaf of comments to distribute among members of the large cast led by Lotte Lenya. The whole production is particularly distinguished by the remarkable playing of a cynical German night-club Master of Ceremonies by Joel Grey. Inadequacies in the play and the performance can be easily noted, too—especially, the limitations of the wayward Sally Bowles' heroine in the play as competently but uncompellingly performed by Jill Haworth, who acts with much skill but with little temperament. Still, these are not particularly important. A critical estimate of *Cabaret* would be inconsequential if it rested solely on such details.

It is the story element in the musical that undercuts it—that is, so far as it remains unstylized and thus unprojected. It is understandable that one would be strongly prompted by the seriousness of the subject matter to use as much story as possible but, also, virtually inevitable that this would not amount to much more than novelistic fragments accompanied by a score. It is when the musical-comedy complex of spectacle and dance, particularly in the Berlin night-club "Blue Angel" sequences, and ironic song-numbers such as *Tomorrow Belongs To Me* and *The Money Song,* is paramount that *Cabaret* prevails most consistently and conspicuously as both social documentation and entertainment. *Cabaret,* in short, is most successful when it is most stylized, and least compelling when it approximates realistic drama, in the collapse of Sally Bowles' romance with the hero and her landlady's (Lotte Lenya's) plan to marry an elderly Jewish merchant friend.

■

PROMISES: FULFILLED AND UNFULFILLED

I. JACK GELBER: *THE APPLE* and *SQUARE IN THE EYE*
(March, 1962)

Even so uninhibited a venture in something close to improvisation or "free association" as Jack Gelber's *avant-garde* piece *The Apple* seemed ponderous, in the main, despite a few lively episodes and vigorous direction by Judith Malina. *The Apple* had other faults, including a serious lack of consistency and point, and I doubt that one could truly endorse it as a play. But it would have provided an entertaining and even stimulating evening if the imagination that went into its making had not succumbed to ponderousness. On the whole, *The Apple* promised apocalyptic revelation, which it failed to deliver, instead of concentrating on a playful rendition of human inconsistencies, which it did supply now and then quite satisfactorily.

(October, 1965)

[Satire] is the approach adopted by Jack Gelber after *The Connection*. It failed in *The Apple* because of inchoateness of invention and the frenetic character of the author's imagination, but it succeeded to a considerable degree in the season's *Square in the Eye* because of relatively firmer play construction and control of style. The play was especially effective when it was downright satiric toward middle-class life, and when it employed for this purpose, as well as for the valid pathos of a disoriented couple harassed by a difference of religious origins, moderate expressionistic devices such as the duplication of characters who filled the ostensibly divergent but actually related professions of clergyman and doctor. Some confusion in the play, caused chiefly by cutting back from the scene of the heroine's dying to her getting married, called attention to artifice in the play, but not so disturbingly as to capsize it. What seriously hurt the play (*least,* I suspect, for young people who understandably take the most pleasure in jibes at bourgeois anti-culture while their elders have more or less become habituated to it) is the overall transparency and repetitiveness of the work. Mr. Gelber's capacity for growth since *The Connection* remains as yet questionable. As indicated previously, the problem of growth in the case of playwrights is a general one (George

Jean Nathan was touching upon it more than three decades ago), and it has thus caused concern about virtually all our other young writers. This constitutes a challenge for all of us in the educational theatre.

I myself have been concerned with the problem for three decades in the case of writers I encouraged and not infrequently helped to subsidize as new playwrights who remained *new,* alas, ten, twenty, or thirty years later and evinced, as a rule, less talent than they had started with. As in the case of the many promising actors and actresses who failed to develop, the blame does not lie entirely with the playwrights but with the Zeitgeist or temper of their times and their diminished opportunities in the professional theatre. But we cannot entirely exempt from blame ourselves, too, as educators and critics in so far as we failed to stimulate in them a richer sensibility, an ampler intellectuality, and deeper knowledge of cultural or social reality. The inadequacy has been more apparent, I believe, recently than it was in the twenties and thirties. I have encountered too many would-be young playwrights who are ill-bred and ill-read, and are so absorbed with themselves that they show little understanding of anything or anybody outside themselves. And in the drama, it seems to me, one cannot understand even oneself without understanding others, and one cannot comprehend one's own situation without comprehending others' situations. Our teaching is at fault, too. We tend to indulge the would-be playwright; we do not really challenge him to exert himself as a complete person and artist. We deal with craft problems when we should concern ourselves with human ones; we concentrate on a contriving of situations pompously called "dramaturgy" rather than on writing itself and on its possible theatrical adumbrations.

II. PADDY CHAYEVSKY: *THE PASSION OF JOSEPH D.*
(March, 1964)

Paddy Chayefsky's *The Passion of Joseph D.* can be written off as an out-and-out disaster. This Brechtian chronicle and mordant travesty on the career of Joseph Stalin was a failure of judgment compounded by failure of execution, and this in turn was a failure of experimentation with epic style almost consistently maladroit. The theme was commendably important, but the treatment was crude and inconsistent; Stalin was exposed as a crude and amoral sadist in the first two scenes in the midst of the events of the revolution; the finer motivation of the brute, his transfer of adoration of God as a young seminarist to adoration of Lenin as a revolutionist, came late in the chronicle. Had the play won popularity or been received with critical esteem we should be obliged to dissect the play. Since this was not the case, it is enough to inter it decently as the abortive effort of an intelligent author who had honorable intentions and of a trio of producers who gave the play a first-class production against excellent settings by Will Steven Armstrong and with a good cast headed by Luther Adler. Alvin Epstein was perhaps the star of the inchoate proceedings in the role of Trotsky, but a Trotsky so extravagantly caricatured as to be incredible. As a political drama, a genre in which we have been inept as a rule, *The Passion of Joseph D.* simply could not be taken seriously; and considered as "art" alone, if that is possible, the play was uneven, disorganized, and ineffectual too.

III. FRANK D. GILROY: *THE SUBJECT WAS ROSES*
(October, 1964)

A late play of the 1963–64 season, Frank Gilroy's *The Subject Was Roses,* proved to be both the best and most frustrating serious play of the season. Here the author of the earlier drama of frustration *Who'll Save the Plowboy?* gave us one of the smallest of Broadway plays until it started growing after the first act into a viable human document enriched by its nuances of characterization and unemphatic poignancies.

A boy comes home from a stint in the Army, and becomes the center of revelations of emotional bankruptcy on the part of his parents, until at the end, having arrived at some understanding and maturation, he begins to close the rift between them. With this kind of meager material, Gilroy touched upon a large area of loneliness in American life. This "little" (because emotionally circumscribed) and at the same time "big" (because widely relevant) play was greatly helped by the authenticity of the performances delivered by Jack Alberson's combative Babbitt who tries to conceal inner failure with external pugnacity, Irene Dailey's jittery middle-aged wife and mother, and Martin Sheen's young man caught between the emotional needs of nerve-frayed and frustrated parents. A director new to Broadway, Ulu Grosbard, kept this quietly original (familiar yet original) work under perfect control. To measure this play against Chekhov's masterpieces would be patently unfair. This is work of the order of William Inge's earliest and finest Broadway play, *Come Back, Little Sheba* (normally both plays would have been off-Broadway offerings); better built yet somewhat less dramatically interesting than the earlier "big little" play. After a decade of meager prospects since leaving Yale, Gilroy was instantly acclaimed as the year's most promising new playwright on the American scene.

IV. LORRAINE HANSBERRY:
THE SIGN IN SIDNEY BRUSTEIN'S WINDOW
(December, 1964)

In *The Sign in Sidney Brustein's Window,* Miss Hansberry's talents constantly suggested the making of a play without quite precipitating one. The ingredients of several plays were there. The failure of a bohemian idealist who successfully backs a nascent Greenwich Village politician on a reform ticket in his little newspaper only to learn at the end that he has supported a stooge for the drug-peddling interests is accompanied by a variety of other feints and impasses. The idealist Sidney, converted to activism by the example of Thoreau, nearly loses his wife, whose aspirations to an acting career bring her no closer to her goal than a role in a television commercial. Her moralizing elder sister Mavis ultimately reveals her own marital infelicity, and her younger sister Gloria falls in love with a Negro idealist who cannot bring himself to the point of marrying her on discovering that she has been a high-class prostitute because, like his father, he refuses to accept "the white man's leavings." Gloria commits suicide in Sidney Brustein's apartment. For good measure Sidney, out of the goodness of his heart, has aided a young homosexual playwright, whose scornful cruelty to Gloria helps to drive the distracted girl to suicide. Into each of these situations the author and her cast injected the ferment of drama, but without producing one. The overall action failed to define itself except as portions of an unwritten novel about the life history and harassments of the fictive hero Sidney Brustein. In the role of Mavis, Alice Ghostley performed notably in a loose narrative scene detailing the life of the sisters and their father; Rita Moreno, playing Sidney's wife, provided dramatic pressure with her representation of the character's restlessness and serio-comic desperation; and Alton Scales, in the role of her sister's Negro lover, accounted for an appealing portrait that came into impressive focus with his narrative explanation of why he·cannot forget Gloria's past. Miss Hansberry is partly responsible for these and other felicities, as well as for some infelicitous editorializing. But with the best will in the world one could not help wondering how Miss Hansberry could have allowed herself to be trapped in a second-rate novel while trying to write a significant drama. She is one of the few playwrights of the new generation who can be said to *disappoint* us when she fails.

In her case, moreover, an anatomy of failure is not easy, as it is in the case of playwrights whose case is one of morbidity and vacuousness.

One can even argue in her behalf that she does have a theme, which is what most of her colleagues of the younger generation do not have. But even "theme," in this case the prevalence of "accommodation" and corrupting compromises in our world, works no miracle of cohesion on her scattered story fragments. And if Miss Hansberry fails to cohere, what hope is there for other members of her generation? Especially since getting a stage production, nowadays glibly offered as the panacea for a young writer's defects, apparently provides no insurance against failure, does not enhance command of dramatic art, and does not strengthen a playwright's grasp on his materials. Will anything accomplish this? It is an important question, but I doubt whether the pragmatic American "know-how" kind of answers will do at all. There must be a strong drive in the heart and mind of playwrights which, except in the unique case of personal genius and personal revolt, must derive from, or at least be abetted by, social reality. At the present time, one can locate it apparently only in the racial tension of the age, and thus far the results, rather overrated, have been too narrow and too stereotyped to arouse confidence. It is actually to Miss Hansberry's considerable credit that she rejected the help from this quarter that was within her reach. Resentment of "white man's leavings" in her young Negro's case is an authentic emotion, originally expressed, and intelligently kept under control. She avoided the racial stereotypes and clichés of the 1960's. One could only wish that she had also avoided the homosexual ones, which I found both tasteless and unfair, in her treatment of the young playwright.

V. WILLIAM HANLEY: *MRS. DALLY*
(December, 1965)

In the domain of serious theatre, some case histories [of failure to provide developing action] offered themselves to scrutiny at the very start of the season. An important one, *Mrs. Dally,* was especially intriguing since it was the work of one of the most promising of our young writers, William Hanley, and presented the fetching Arlene Francis in a role that enabled her to display greater virtuosity than she has shown hitherto. Consisting of two loosely connected parts, actually two separate one-act plays, *Mrs. Dally* revolved about the marital infelicities of the middle-aged wife of a brutish husband. In the first part she was shown desperately trying to maintain a furtive love affair with a young man, in the second desperately trying to establish some meeting-ground with her essentially affectionate husband, an irritable taxi driver convincingly played by Ralph

Meeker. In both parts of the work Miss Francis was provided with ample provocation or emotional outbursts and rueful exhibitions of frustration. All this was accomplished with efficiency and with only occasional strain, and Broadway audiences understandably attached to Miss Francis as an attractive television personality seemed altogether gratified by her "live" performance. Certainly she was *in motion,* physically and emotively, throughout the evening's performance.

That the results were, nevertheless, singularly arid could not be blinked at by anyone whose judgment has not been dissolved by exposure to soap-operas. The artificiality of the first part was apparent when Mrs. Dally endeavored to impart culture to her lover by reading Donne's poetry to him when it is difficult enough to believe that she could even read Donne to herself. The motivation of her infidelity with a lover young enough to be her son and her husband's troglodyte behavior is the loss of her three-year-old boy years before. This is believable enough for a sob-story but is a laughable *external* fabrication for all the agonizing Miss Francis is called upon to display with all the conviction of amateur-show histrionics.

Perhaps this is all she can do when called upon to hold the stage for virtually two hours, a merciless requirement in any case. But this could well be a wantonly unfair conclusion. What is there in either part of *Mrs. Dally* to sustain a performance? Despite the variety she tried to bring in it, her role remained obdurately invariable in all essentials because mere misfortune or unhappiness cannot sustain drama; only a developing action can do that. The standard modern excuse for failing to provide this has been the primacy of characterization in reputable playwriting. But surely *dramatic* characterization is itself an "action," inasmuch as it involves a growing revelation of character and of occasions for discovering and understanding it. One may not need "plot" in the conventional sense of the term, but one does need progressive "inner" action and progressive outer provocation. The failure to supply these ingredients of drama is not to be glibly explained away by high-sounding esthetic principles any more than it can be concealed from anyone not a willing victim of the cult of TV personality. This failure is likely to be, as I believe it is in the case of *Mrs. Dally,* an effort to make bricks without straw; that is, reality without an adequate objective action because the author happened to lack the imagination to supply the latter for his enterprise. In the present case, it would appear that the author talked himself, or allowed himself to be talked, into fabricating a full-length drama out of a one-act character-sketch.

The hardest thing for playwrights to find in ages of moral and intellectual stalemate (by contrast, shall we say, with Periclean Athens and Elizabethan England) is an adequate action. "Characters" and "psychology" (like the loss-of-child *motif* in *Mrs. Dally*) can be easily found nowadays by any diligent writer, but not the developing action that provides dramatic substance and sustains interest. And if a substitute appears with some success in deliberate representations of stalemate and the futility of action, as in plays by Samuel Beckett, the best results will be found in relatively short plays in which an action does not have to be sustained very long.

VI. JEAN-CLAUDE VAN ITALLIE: *AMERICA HURRAH*
(March, 1967)

Broadway remains competent but dead, while the *avant-garde* remains incompetent but alive. Neither generalization, however, is entirely correct, for despite its tired professionalism Broadway is by no means unfailingly competent and the *avant-garde* theatre is not invariably interesting. But, then, it can also be maintained that a Broadway that brings a *Marat/Sade* (now back for a second run by a new National Company) isn't altogether dead, and that the theatre peripheral to it, with a Jacques Levy and Joseph Chaikin displaying directorial imagination as noteworthily as they did in *America Hurrah,* isn't invariably incompetent.

We are thrown back, therefore, to particular play-writing and play-production problems. We must look at particulars, for example, in dealing with the Belgian-born Jean-Claude van Itallie's *America Hurrah.* We must consider, first, the grounds for the enthusiastic reception it had from the metropolitan press. This production consists of three one-act plays, each presenting evidence of brassy and pseudodynamic American decadence. The first part is a *mélange* of details concerning desiccation in human relations, whether between prospective employees (interviewers and job applicants) or between hosts and their guests. The play shows expressionistically how our occupations call for desensitized robots rather than fellow-creatures, and how our stress on optimism and amiability requires a woman to feel obliged to apologize for coming late, and for not being the life of the party, so to speak, even though she just died in an accident. "I'm dead. Excuse me, I'm dead. Excuse me," she says. The second play emphasizes the banality of popular television programming, by contrasting its strenuous banalities with the blank indifference of those who are employed to watch the programs and determine their ratings. The third playlet focuses with fantastic exaggeration on the destructiveness of the average American male and female in states of elation, including inebriation and lust.

Here are three vehement moral denunciations that could be called homilies were it not for their theatrical propulsion. After numerous Broadway bedroom comedies and farces essentially complacent in their view of life, love, and lust in our society even in the midst of light mockery or breezy laughter, the thoroughly negativistic and abrasive one-acters of *America Hurrah* were understandably welcomed. Considered as a whole, they constitute a decided relief from Broadway's glossy assent to establishment values and to comic complacencies. The author's theatrical talent is unmistakable, and the severe observations that follow are not at all intended to detract from it. But here is only the beginning rather than the culmination of a new talent, and for its sake, as well as for the progress of anti-establishment drama, we must temper our enthusiasm with strictures concerning matters of craft. In recent years, especially on Broadway, we have been so deficient in satirical skill that we are apt to settle for less effectiveness than we strictly should.

The tendency to overrate the first two parts of *America Hurrah* is a symptom of the poverty of recent American satire. In view of the great frustration we have been feeling in the Great Society, we have started overestimating every Nay, every barbarous yawp on the rooftops of our jerry-built civilization. Our understandably irritated intellectuals do not, apparently, weary of the constant hammering on the same idea or the churning up of the same bile in the treatment of American society, as in the first two one-act satires of *America Hurrah*. Or perhaps we simply don't wish to admit that we weary of it, which is virtually the same thing. We overlook the fact that these playlets are oversized revue skits. In the days of the Grand Street Follies or the Garrick Gaieties, they would have been just that—*skits* that make their point with the brevity that is the proper soul of a revue. It is, in fact, not wit we are after, but spleen—and plenty of it. The first two plays are indifferent playwriting that enthusiasts rationalize as very good playwriting because they are enabled by good productions to discharge their revulsion against vulgarized American society.

Fortunately, moreover, the program as a whole derives much benefit from the fact that the last of the one-acters, *Motel,* is a little masterpiece of *poésie de théâtre*. It is an idea realized entirely in terms of the stage and of expressionistic visualization. The landlady who blatantly announces the comforts of her motel is a huge doll, wired for sound. Her guests, a man and a woman, are oversized doll-like figures whose outrageous conduct, sordidly lustful and bleakly destructive, is the very epitome of Babbittry on the loose. This fact is less funny than terrifying. It is a fierce "Theatre of Cruelty" assault on its audience in the best Antonin Artaud sense, calculated to shock us out of our normative complacency by means of distortions of appearance and action, rather than by means of photographic realism and normal dialogue. The extreme of visual theatricality is reached here when the mechanized figures, going berserk, scrawl obscenities on the walls and demolish everything in the motel including the oversized doll-landlady without uttering a word. Symptomatically, *Motel* was the shortest of the three parts of *America Hurrah,* the one that came closest to skit-dimensions, even if it had a blunt and bulldozer-like rather than pointed, quality and a dramatic pressure no review skit, because of its brevity, could possibly possess.

One technical point, finally, should perhaps be added to the present reviewer's essentially negative reaction to the first two parts of *America Hurrah.* This reaction was not caused solely by the repetitious banality of much of their matter. There was, in addition, considerable disadvantage in the author's very use of *montage,* a theoretically commendable and now and then practically effective device for presenting satire. The best use of such *montage,* in fact, appeared as long ago as the 1920's in Kaufman and Connelly's *Beggar on Horseback,* E. E. Cumming's *him,* and John Howard Lawson's *Processional.* The disadvantage I have in mind is the constant rapid blending of subjects and fragmentary scenes in each of the two first parts of *America Hurrah.* This is especially the case in the first of these, which is very much the richer and the less obvious in subject matter than the second play spoof on television viewing. After the vivid opening in which the interviewers and the interviewer are shown to be frenziedly confused, we are presented with only one other vivid vignette (the cocktail party) that crystalizes as a piece of drama. The rest of the work is an emotional and intellectual blur, a *mélange* of inconsequentially detailed happenings and "hurryings," mostly the latter.

TIME AND TENNESSEE WILLIAMS

I. *CAMINO REAL*
(October, 1960)

The animus of *The Killer,* Ionesco's first full-length play to be presented in New York (a second, *The Rhinoceros,* was being prepared for a 1960–61 production), was also amply present in José Quintero's revival of *Camino Real,* which Tennessee Williams apparently simplified somewhat since its original Elia Kazan production of the early fifties. The revival added interest to the off-Broadway season in the laggardly theatrical month of May. What *Camino Real* did not particularly add to the season was provocativeness, for in indicting so much of the world the author apparently had no opportunity or incitement to strip anything down to the bone; and without provocativeness in the matter of the play there could not be much true excitement in it either. Elia Kazan had tried to supply the excitement externally in the original Broadway production, going so far as to invade the orchestra and the front gallery with frantic actors. Mr. Quintero adopted a distinctly more moderate style of staging, for which I was inclined to be grateful. One could become interested and touched as well as depressed by the play Tennessee Williams wrote, as he recently declared, "in a time of desolation." The finely spun Quintero production offered a corrective reminder to recent critics of Williams' "decadence" and violence that he was not at all subverted to misanthropy and despair even in a work as bleak as *Camino Real.* The interpretation was the director's but the score was the author's. Williams indeed called attention to two sentences that in his opinion are the key speeches of the work. In the first, Don Quixote on his arrival in the plaza ruefully declared that "In a place where so many are lonely, it would be inexcusably selfish to be lonely alone." The other line, which the same character speaks at the end of the final published version, "The violets in the mountain have broken the rocks," also expresses an affirmativeness of sorts insufficiently credited to the author, as does a third speech assigned to Don Quixote, "Life is an unanswered question, but let's still believe in the dignity and importance of the question."

585

II. *PERIOD OF ADJUSTMENT*
(March, 1961)

The most obvious fact about *Period of Adjustment* is that Tennessee Williams has proved with it that he can write an optimistic comedy. The obvious answer to this is that so can other playwrights. He has also demonstrated—I hope to the gratification of Marya Mannes and other moralistic critics of Williams—that he can write "wholesomely," to which I can only add that I prefer his "decadence" to his "health." There have been legions of healthy-minded playwrights available to the American theatre, but I haven't noticed they have done much for our stage. They have certainly done a great deal less for it than such morbid, pessimistic, and antisocial playwrights as O'Neill and Williams and such cantankerous ones as Odets, Hellman, and Miller.

Taken on its own terms and on its own level, *Period of Adjustment* is I suppose entirely acceptable. It "builds" amusingly and with sufficient tension and suspense. It pokes fun at all that a "modern" play is supposed to poke fun at, and it gives stuffy characters or cartoons the drubbing that is their proper due. The author's optimism is not of the blithering variety, for the protagonist who espouses the opinion that things will work out satisfactorily after a "period of adjustment" is himself in trouble. The person he especially tries to enlighten happens to be in even deeper trouble after an embarrassingly unsuccessful honeymoon. This is not a frothy or inanely frolicsome play at all. But it is perfectly evident, too, that *Period of Adjustment* is an advice-to-the-love-lorn and to the about-to-be-divorced type of comedy. It is unlikely that Williams would have contributed anything to the American drama if he had had nothing different from *Period of Adjustment* to give to the theatre during the past fifteen years.

What is perhaps most troublesome to me about *Period of Adjustment* is that if it is without question a comedy, it is a singularly joyless one. Indeed, the entire matter of sex, as expounded by one of the two leading male characters and clinically demonstrated by his trembling war buddy, is reduced to unappetizing details and statements right down to the last salacious line spoken in the dark by the former's wife after reconciliation on the matrimonial bed. It is a singularly flat patent-medicine for happiness that is being offered here in lieu of champagne. If sex is so clinically crude, let's turn it over to the baboons, say I. That, nevertheless, Mr. Williams emerges from this descent as a proficient and controlled playwright, with good timing, planning, and manipulating of discoveries, conflict, climaxes, and "peripities," merely proves that he is as good a craftsman as anyone we have had since Sidney Howard.

Fortunately, too, Mr. Williams has not abandoned a somewhat self-mocking attitude that undercuts the prolix earnestness of his spokesman in the play. Now and then I solaced myself with the impression that I detected a saturnine smile lurking behind the pollyannic greasepaint of the work. If only its author could have refrained from a pedestrian recourse to direct psychologism that translates itself, I suppose quite inevitably, into flat, essentially humorless, references to impotence, homosexuality, frigidity, and other commonplaces. And if only the mating of the characters under the sheltering canopy of banal sentiments after exposure to a barrage of seemingly unavoidable clinical reference were not proferred as right, proper, and inexpressibly—or, rather, only too expressibly—desirable. One does not have to be particularly fastidious to find this strenuously sought-after and talked-over mating repellent rather than desirable. Perhaps Mr. Williams has indeed performed a service to the stage after all; he has surely made the callow crudity of our alleged sophistication—"open" discussion of sexuality and our popular phallic worship—singularly apparent even while also ticking off some genuinely appealing and touching moments. *Period of Adjustment,* precisely because it has been astutely pieced together, makes the banality and the blatancy of our supposed sophistication not only apparent but inescapable. And the more efficient the production, so well staged by George Roy Hill and so well performed by a cast headed by James Daly and Robert Webber, the more obvious the result.

For Mr. Williams, a final word: In his pre-première article for the Sunday *New York Times* theatre section, he implied that with *Period of Adjustment* he had liberated himself from "false intensities" and learned to stop taking a problem "as if it affected the whole future course of the world." It has been intelligent of him to arrive at these conclusions. In the same article, however, he reports that a friend of a famous actress who wanted to retire from the stage told her, "You can retire from a business but not from an art; you can't put your talent away like a key to a house where you don't live any more." I very much hope that he will apply these words to the Tennessee Williams of *The Glass Menagerie, A Streetcar Named Desire,* and *Summer and Smoke.*

III. *THE NIGHT OF THE IGUANA*
(March, 1962)

A distinctly heavier, less limber, and at times even lumbering style of playwriting than in the British imports appeared in most American productions of the 1961–62 season. This was apparent even in the new play by Tennessee Williams, from whom we have come to expect a rather violent kind of dramaturgy ever since the Elia Kazan production of *A Streetcar Named Desire* nearly a dozen years ago. The new play, *The Night of the Iguana,* was well staged, with Margaret Leighton giving an especially affecting portrait of a repressed spinster, to whom Bette Davis provided a vivid foil in the part of an uninhibited widow while Patrick O'Neal, a recent arrival on the Broadway stage, filled the role of a bedevilled tourist guide and former minister with almost every conceivable nuance of anguish. His performance ranged from the quiet desperation of Thoreau's "majority of men" to the explosion of violence which results in his being trussed up like a dangerous animal after he attempts to drown himself. This play is compounded mainly of this character's semicomic but painful conflict with the schoolmarm-tourists to whom he ministers rather ineptly as a guide through Mexico's vaunted scenic splendors, his absurd affair with an hysterical college girl, and his pathetic half-romance with the spinster, who fills the role of nurse and companion to a dying grandfather, an extremely old and forgotten minor poet. The elegiac quality of *The Night of the Iguana,* with its mildly ironic concern with the two species of humanity—the rapacious winners and the pathetic losers in life's race—resulted in a bizarrely moving drama of stalemate. But even an appreciation of the play greater than any that I could register would have to admit that its effect was depressing rather than exalting, and somewhat labored and torpid, or at least empty of challenge. A welcome relief from its author's dramatic turbulence, Mr. Williams' last play, nevertheless, left an impression of spent energy and largely directionless protest against the human condition.

IV. *THE MILK TRAIN DOESN'T STOP HERE ANYMORE*
(May, 1962)

Tennessee Williams' problem is not quite the same [as William Inge's], since he is a thoroughly sophisticated writer whose bent has been "literary" and symbol-haunted from the beginning. It is his forced, hot-house artistry that requires attention if we are to account for the impasse into which he has moved; and it is not likely, though not impossible, that this prolific man will be able to simply write himself out of it. To have written *The Milk Train Doesn't Stop Here Any More* is no calamity. It would be quite a credit to a younger and less experienced man. It was not a crass failure on Broadway either, despite some unfortunate casting in the principal parts and not quite the best staging a prominent author should be able to expect from Broadway. It seems to me that he has to revive an objectivity and critical balance that has been fading in recent years. It was bright in *The Glass Menagerie,* slightly clouded in *A Streetcar Named Desire* (clouded by an ambivalence in the characterization of Stanley Kowalski not generally recognized even by critics), and increasingly blurry in *Cat on a Hot Tin Roof* (hence the two versions of the last act), *Sweet Bird of Youth* as seen on Broadway, and the present season's drama. The question is one of values before becoming a question of a critic's impressions.

Briefly, I think, this greatly gifted and, at heart, vulnerably high-minded and generous man will simply have to stop coddling, if not idolizing, the worthless. I know that he had kind words for the clowning heroine of *The Milk Train.* . . . He saw her as a pathetic clown frantically lost in the valley of the shadow of Death despite the social and topographical elevation on which she is located. But for me and for most people I know, Mr. Williams' latest heroine was not another "lady of larkspur lotion" or waif of life as in *The Portrait of a Madonna* (and certainly not an Amanda, Alma, or Blanche Du Bois), but an offensive, wearisome, and thoroughly unbearable woman upon whom God's pity would not perhaps be wasted but a mortal playwright's definitely is. I fear, too, that Mr. Williams will have to reconsider symbolism in the light of T. S. Eliot's requirement of an "objective correlative" for good poetry—a need even more exigent in the case of good theatre. The roles of a parasitical hanger-on of the idle rich, pathetic poet, "Death" and compassionate Paraclete simply don't fuse into one flesh-and-blood character and have no steadfast meaning in the young hero of *The Milk Train.* . . . Mr. Williams has contrived rather than created him. He has forced a variety of roles on him that have little reality and a considerable degree of pretension. Mr. Williams will be able to avoid at least some of the dangers of this tendency to resort to arbitrary or forced symbols (*Orpheus Descending* also depended on a few), by liberating himself from *fin-de-siècle* French poetry, which has always been a disturbing influence in his writing and has never proved half as effective as his much decried, and sometimes runaway, naturalism.

V. *THE MILK TRAIN DOESN'T STOP HERE ANYMORE*
(March, 1964)

Tennessee Williams' *The Milk Train Doesn't Stop Here Anymore* [quickly failed], commendable as it was for Mr. Williams to revise the play and for its new producer David Merrick to present a restaged version of it with a new cast headed by Tallulah Bankhead as the moribund heroine Flora Goforth and Tab Hunter as the "angel of death," Chris. There is no space here to elaborate upon the merits and defects of the revised play and the new production, but the fiasco (and it was that despite Miss Bankhead's attempts to make her role sympathetic) cannot but serve as a reminder that silk purses simply cannot be made out of sows' ears no matter how fine the stitching. The sow's ear in this case is the appalling female on whom the author wasted his talent and his public's patience, and the fine stitching is the symbolism or poetic nuance with which he expected to enhance the work. To the student of playwriting it would be instructive, incidentally, to observe how even so gifted and experienced a playwright as Mr. Williams could not disentangle himself from the coils of his original conception of the characters— that is, from a worthless heroine intended to be the object of our sympathy and from an amorphous figure who was to be at once poet and gigolo, and a paraclete on top of it all. In the latter case, Mr. Williams renounced mystic claims for Chris and showed him to be something of a four-flusher and a bit of a thief (he took the dying woman's rings off her fingers at the end of the revised version of the play), but the naturalism of the new treatment did not substantially alter the original impression of a half-mystical character and added no particular value to the work. As elsewhere, it might be said that Mr. Williams wavered between his flair for naturalism and his aspirations toward symbolic poetry, and in *The Milk Train* he appeared to have been mired by the former and confused by the latter.

■

EDWARD ALBEE: AN AMERICAN DREAM?

I. THE ONE-ACT PLAYS
(May, 1961)

If criticism cannot spare Ionesco, the master, can it spare the disciples and the newcomers to the theatre of current disillusion? The most hopeful of these in America has been Edward Albee ever since *The Zoo Story* first appeared on the off-Broadway stage on January 14, 1960. Nothing he has shown on the stage since then has had quite the impact of *The Zoo Story*. This applies equally to *The Death of Bessie Smith,* apparently written before, and *The American Dream* written after, it.

The trouble with *The Death of Bessie Smith* is that it is lengthily out of focus. Based on an event of the year 1934, when the celebrated Negro blues singer died of injuries sustained in an auto accident because she was not admitted to a white hospital in Memphis, the play concentrates on the sex-duel between a liberal interne and a rancorously prejudiced Southern admitting nurse. Their overextended quarrel completely scuttles the theme.

The trouble with Albee's acutely original play, *The American Dream,* is that its bizarre Ionesco details don't add up to an experience. This one-hour work has almost everything that fancy can supply but hardly anything that experience can validate. The details, either irrational or so logical as to be extravagant, are amusing as they come at the playgoer with a suddenness and a barrage of nonsequiturs rarely encountered in "real-life" situations. For a dozen minutes or so, the humor keeps the play crackling. Mr. Albee's oblique treatment of the banal tedium of domestic life recalls Ionesco's *The Bald Soprano* yet seems decidedly fresh, and the satire is crisp and bracing. Then, with the entrance of "Grandma," who knows she is considered superfluous by her daughter, the author introduces a note of genuine poignancy into the proceedings, and the pathos of old age soon changes into delight when the cross old woman turns the tables on "Mommy" and gives her more than one jagged piece of her mind. (The segment of the play that features Grandma, incidentally, incorporates the substance of Albee's biting and oddly moving and poetic little piece *The Sandbox,* in which death in the shape of a handsome athlete comes for the moribund old woman who has been dumped into a children's sandbox by "Mommy" and "Daddy." The sketch was given to the great American public in March by an "Omnibus" television show about *avant-garde* theatre.) After the Grandma episode, however, *The American Dream* fell apart by the sheer weight of its rapidly accumulated bright particles. A bright new talent went to pieces here because it was unsustained, so far as I could determine, by a point of view that would provide cohesiveness for Mr. Albee's random scorn and rebelliousness.

Mr. Albee's talents are not in question here. They are abundantly present in both one-hour plays. But they are used injudiciously; they are at times thriftlessly overused, as in *The Death of Bessie Smith,* and at other times just wantonly scattered about, as in *The American Dream.* It seems to me that the New York newspaper reviewers have been doing Mr. Albee a distinct disservice in praising him for his faults as much as for his virtues and in failing to challenge him to develop his potentialities.

II. *WHO'S AFRAID OF VIRGINIA WOOLF?*
(March, 1963)

One doesn't have to blink [in disbelief] at all at the performances of *Who's Afraid of Virginia Woolf?*—at least until one arrives at the revelation at the end of the play that the ostensible cause of the devastating sex-duel between husband and wife that has consumed almost three hours of playing-time is the childlessness of the couple. Logically considered, this should invalidate Edward Albee's first Broadway play. It doesn't! And this is due mainly to an elementary fact that some well-educated (but so far as the theatre is concerned, *wrongly* educated) persons don't sufficiently realize. It is the fact that theatre exists moment by moment (this does not mean, of course, haphazardly), and that, come what may later, an experience is an experience *while* it is being experienced.

Albee's first full-length play, as staged for Broadway by Alan Schneider, affords so much pulsating moment-by-moment drama, so many unreeling facets of character and so many fluctuations of feeling, and one is so continuously knocked down, picked up, and knocked down again in the course of the play, that it takes a massive quantity of resistance to conclude that *Who's Afraid of Virginia Woolf?* is not drama on the grand scale. It reaches the same order of harrowing dramatic power as Elizabethan melodrama which the unfinicky Elizabethans called tragedy. The very same thing can be said indeed of a good many of O'Neill's plays; John Mason Brown may have been the first critic to refer to him as a minor Elizabethan dramatist in modern dress. *For me, in fact, Albee is in the direct line of succession from O'Neill.*[1] Even if he has yet far to go if he is to achieve his predecessor's breadth of interest, variety of tone, or range of compassionate insight, Albee has the same slugging technique and the same strategy of massive assault in thrusting across the footlight area his awareness of human bedevilment. And in their writing they employ the same heavy Mahler scoring with an overplus of *ostinato* markings, although Albee's lines move faster and with more precision than O'Neill's. Interestingly enough, both O'Neill and Albee came to public notice as the authors of undeniably effective one-act plays before winning larger audiences as the authors of notably oversized full-length drama. This fact should give pause to those who see in the larger works mere repetitiveness or verbal incontinence rather than an essential dramatic pulsation and rhythm. The larger works reveal, rather, a similar fascination with the details of feeling and dramatic action, and with the momentum of recurring impulses that characterize behavior in an extensive situation of crisis and constitute its exciting vibration.

All this must, of course, develop toward some goal and amount to something more than dramatic vibration for its own sake. It must become meaningful drama, so to speak—if we are not to tire of the experience or feel suspended in the partial vacuum of inchoate emotionalism. This is the case in O'Neill's major plays, and constitutes their "justification" for both the critic and the public. Whether this is the case in *Who's Afraid of Virginia Woolf?* is debatable. That the play provides the most harrowing sex-duel on the stage since Strindberg's *The Dance of Death* at the beginning of the century is certain. Whether the play goes beyond this demonstration is another matter. If it does not, then we may be permitted to doubt that we have been sufficiently rewarded for more than three hours of concentrated attention. What insight have we won, we may well ask, that we couldn't have had an hour or so earlier? Does not the play move toward a veritable anticlimax, moreover, when cause and effect are so disproportionate; when we learn at the end that they never had a son to whom something terrible had happened? They have been tearing at each other's vitals for a deprivation that does not prevent sane human beings from behaving with decency and consideration toward each other. Can anyone doubt that the final revelation of childlessness is not a convincing, let alone significant, motivation for the perversities of hatred and sado-masochism that leap at the greatly tried spectator wave upon wave? And if this is the case, may we not press a charge of superficiality and speciousness against the protracted suspense so artfully maintained by this remarkably adept young playwright?

[1] [Italics mine. *Ed.*]

If it is not easy to secure acquittal on these and related charges (how, for instance, are we to construe the husband's autobiographical references to his novel and a possible murder?), and if a reading of the published text does not secure acquittal for the author, we may have to settle for the strong dramatic experience *per se,* which has been an overriding consideration for most of us in esteeming the Broadway production, especially when the stage is held by Uta Hagen and Arthur Hill, who play husband and wife in the evening performances. (The roles are so taxing that another cast appears at the matinees.) This is not the place for an essay on Uta Hagen, but if there has been a more gripping performance on the American stage since Judith Anderson played Medea I have not seen it. And Arthur Hill is almost as remarkable in containing the offensives she launches at the husband and in counter-attacking. Yet, a defense or justification is not out of the realm of possibility if one acknowledges a latency of meaning in the play. The author does not define it in the play itself, but it is there; and the author may define it differently in any explanation he cares to offer, but individual variations of opinion are possible—which is all to the good, up to a point, since the play is at its best an organic entity vastly more alive than the author's mechanism of plot, suspense, and discovery.

The play, which also contains a secondary exploration of character in conflict in the case of a second couple, is alive in the *struggle* rather than in the explanation. It takes place under special circumstances; when the antagonists are intoxicated. But their condition does not exonerate the characters or invalidate the reality of past tensions between the couple. It is also apparent that these characters are most alive when they are most savage, and that their savagery toward each other is combined with an emotional dependency that no amount of disappointment has succeeded in diminishing. Their personal situation and their relationship are, so to speak, *existential.*

Beyond the struggle, there is nothing but the commonplace round of occupational and social obligations of the professor-hero and his wife, the daughter of the college president. Beneath the struggle there is nothing at the core except loneliness—and so they are lonely together when they are not in the close contact of hurting each other. Beneath the intense embrace of the hurting, there is the emptiness of their being—and so they are empty together. This, then, is the drama of the "absurd" (which is not at all the same thing as "an absurd drama"), in which cause and effect *are* disproportionate. The childlessness of the couple revealed at the end is hardly a cause or an explanation of their real plight, which is their lostness, their state of being. Our reason does not have to validate it any more than it validates or can (without religious faith, as Pascal understood so well!) invalidate the infinite emptiness of the universe that overcomes the thinking reed that is Man. It is possible to work up a strong resentment toward the play, to be sure, but it is not an easy drama to ignore or forget. Mr. Albee has written a terrifying thing—perhaps *the* negative play to end all negative plays, yet also a curiously compassionate play (I feel plenty of compassion for the driven woman and her long-suffering husband), and exhilarating one (if for no other reason than the passionateness of the characters) and even a wryly affirmative one because of the fighting spirit of the principals whose behavior breathes the fire of protest along with the stench of corruption.

III. *WHO'S AFRAID OF VIRGINIA WOOLF?* ON LP*

One does not have to listen to more than the first side of the Columbia album *Who's Afraid of Virginia Woolf?* to realize that one is on the threshold of an important event in the history of recording. By the time one has heard all eight sides no other conclusion is possible than that the threshold has been crossed. Although Edward Albee's play reaches the listener unavoidably divested of the visual components provided by the Broadway production staged by Alan Schneider, the recording does not fail to project the soul and substance of the play. It comes to life in the throat of the speakers; and in the case of a recording that is the essential thing. One might not consider this possible in the case of *Who's Afraid of Virginia Woolf?* since Albee's play gives an impression of exceptional activity on the part of the characters—an impression that is a major factor in the power of the play to arouse concern and maintain tension. But the fact is that *Who's Afraid of Virginia Woolf?,* despite some repeated expletives involving no particular imagination, has an uncommonly rich verbal texture. And fortunately the cast that speaks the words *acts* them, too. *Acted,* in contrast to merely *spoken,* speech is the most difficult kind to obtain from recording artists. Columbia Records apparently had no difficulty in obtaining it from the principals of the cast, Uta Hagen and Arthur Hill, engaged in a duel of the sexes Strindberg himself would have envied. If anything, the chief actors may be faulted for an excess of "acting" in some of their solo passages and verbal assaults on each other, especially in the third act. They shout at each other now and then beyond the call of duty, and early in that act

* From *Saturday Review* (June 29, 1963).

Miss Hagen even appears to have allowed her emotion to suffocate articulateness for a while. But the merits of the performance vastly outweigh the momentary faults, making it remarkably easy for us to forget that we are listening to a recording, except in infrequent passages when we are uncertain for a few beats who is onstage and who is not.

How decidedly this recording is a triumph for those who have made it can be determined by observing how singularly free it is from the factitious ministrations of sound effects. Only an occasional extra-loud clinking of ice in a glass and the sound of footsteps that could have come from dropped ice cubes interrupt the heavenly relief from phoniness.

It is also a compliment to the author to be able to say to him that listening to his lines seemed sufficient. One reason is that they are often very good lines worth listening to for their shape (they are often so neatly turned) as well as content and for their cadence as well as substance; they are caught up, moreover, in a general stream or rhythm of feeling that makes them an authentic part of the action rather than obtrusive bits of declamation. Entire episodes exist as verbal structures in Albee's play and the phrases mesh with each other not so much as logically connected statements but as spontaneous utterances carrying pertinent moods, attitudes, or intentions. Albee's short phrases and sentences make up a series of musico-dramatic movements perhaps even more distinctly related than they could be in a visual production because the text comes at us naked, so to speak—that is, as pure sound.

In Act III, for example, there are several of these movements. The first is Martha's desperation, expressed in a drunken soliloquy (it has its own unique broken rhythm); the second is her disillusionment with men, starting with a teasing colloquy with her would-be but ultimately inadequate lover Nick and culminating in a monologue the keynote of which is "I am the Earth Mother, and you're all flops. . . . I pass my life in crummy, totally pointless infidelities . . . *would-be* infidelities." A new rhythm is established in a second, rather analytical, conversation with Nick concerning her attitude toward her husband George, "who has made the hideous, the hurting, the insulting mistake of loving me and must be punished for it." It is followed by the teasing rhythms of reducing Nick to the lowly status of a "houseboy" in compelling him to answer the doorbell, and of herself being teased and insulted by the mounting aggressiveness of her nearly cuckolded husband George. Then the beat quickens, the pulse grows uneven, and the voices strain toward a climax of violence as Martha strives to preserve her illusion of motherhood while George endeavors to strip her of it, the struggle culminating in the strong counterpoint of Martha's dramatizing the illusioned son while her husband recites the Latin prayers for the dead—that is, for the son who had never existed except in their imagination and whom he now proposed to "kill." Finally, there is the denouement or "falling action" starting with the ominous quietness of George's "I am afraid our boy isn't coming home for his birthday" and concluding with the fragmented sentences with which Martha reluctantly relinquishes her hitherto fiercely defended illusion. After that episode, when the two guests, Nick and his wife, depart, the lines assigned to the emotionally drained Martha and George rarely exceed two-word speeches of "I'm cold" and "It's late," and the play closes with Martha's dully spoken monosyllabic response to the "Who's Afraid of Virginia Woolf?" ditty sung by her husband "I . . . am . . . George . . . I . . . am. . . ."

From this partial analysis it may be evident why the Columbia recording is so satisfactory. The verbal (should I say "musical?") structure serves the drama so well without recourse to other theatrical elements that, given the effective interpretation of the actor-speakers, the dramatic action emanates powerfully from the recording surface.

Listeners who are affronted by a scattering of pungent words and allow their attention to be deflected from the play itself are not likely to rate the play highly. That is their privilege, although I cannot personally compliment them on exercising it. I would rather urge the fastidious to attend closely to *Romeo and Juliet* when the Nurse and Mercutio are having their say about love and domestic felicity. But I fear I would only insult the intelligence of my readers if I dignified charges of immorality against Albee's play with any sort of defense (it is not often that lust or lasciviousness is presented as joylessly and unattractively); and it is not for what the play isn't but for what it is that a work of art should be recommended.

That Albee's play *is* a work of art is something that the Columbia Records album makes even more abundantly evident than the attractively printed text published last year by Atheneum. After all, the play was written to be spoken and heard, and (as the author points out) many people apparently don't know how to read a play. In the Columbia recording, the original New York production comes alive as few previously recorded performances of plays have done. The voices are authentically the voices of Uta Hagen, Arthur Hill, George Grizzard, and Melinda Dillon, and they render the emotional nuances and rhythms of the text with a very considerable degree of success. I have indicated this in breaking down the verbal structure of one of the acts of the play, and the listener should be able to note or at least *sense* the variety of audible movements in every act. There is one other thing, however, he should be able to do, if not at first hearing then at a second or third—and that is to grasp the highly important over-all structure of this anything but haphazard work. Although space limitations do not allow me to undertake this project in detail for the reader, it is not particularly space-consuming to point out that, in spite of its great length and almost musical fluidity, *Who's Afraid of Virginia Woolf?* is a notably concentrated and carefully constructed drama.

An irritable middle-aged couple, notably articulate but also inebriated, comes home from a party, and before long the husband and wife, George and Martha, are slashing away at each other, mercilessly exposing themselves and two guests, a younger and seemingly happier but actually just as miserable couple. The battle attains sensational intensity because the principals are not only sufficiently aroused but, as Albee declares in the Columbia Records brochure, "intelligent and sensitive enough to build proper weapons for their war with each other." The struggle fluctuates, with dubious victory falling first to one side, then to the other, until the antagonists are sufficiently self-revealed and purged to arrive at a tentative reconciliation. Hosts and their guests in conventional American society (which Albee satirized previously in *The American Dream*) go in for "fun and games," and it is under the pretense of "fun and games" that the action proceeds. One movement is a "Get the Host" game in which Martha is the aggressor against George in the presence of the visitors. A second movement, a "get the guests" game, is directed against the visitors by the humiliated George, who resents the smugness of his guest and university colleague, the biologist Nick, on personal and general grounds. Nick, infuriated by revelations of his own unsatisfactory domestic life, and Martha, who is also out for vengeance, collaborate on the third game, in which Nick supposedly makes a cuckold of George—that is, "gets" the hostess, Martha. In the final movement, George counterattacks with a climactic "bring up baby" game that "brings up" the crucial fact that Martha and he have never had a son and could not have a child. After all the devastating "fun" they have been having and the "games" the history professor George and his wife have been playing from midnight to dawn they are brought to the point of renouncing the game they have been playing privately for some twenty-three years. The time for illusions is over, at last, and the husband and wife will have to make the best of whatever reality there is for them, facing life together, even if the thought of "Just . . . us?" fills Martha with misgivings.

An exegesis on this conclusion, and indeed on the entire play, is a distinct possibility. It is perhaps even a necessity for those who sense that a larger gambit than Martha's and George's "games" is being played and would like to have it spelled out for them once the "fun" (and there is plenty of comedy in the text) becomes grim. Symbol or image hunters can have a field day with the play. Professional and amateur psychologists, with or without benefit of Freud, will surely join the game of elucidation, if they have not already joined it. Some attention may have to be given to the question of whether or not the play belongs to the "Theatre of the Absurd"; and although the question itself may be absurd, it can be serious enough for those who hanker for the power of positive thinking. A veritable library of explication (including the suggested one that George and Martha are George and Martha Washington!) may yet accumulate around this remarkable play, which, in concluding with the revelation that Martha and George have no child, seems headed for an anticlimax, when taken too literally. And somehow it does seem that this third-act discovery fails to fulfill the highest expectations one entertains for *Who's Afraid of Virginia Woolf?*, especially after the harrowing *Walpurgisnacht* movement of the second act; in this work of a still very young author the parts are greater than the whole. But the notable Columbia recording makes abundantly evident the most relevant fact about the play—its dramatic power. The parts are alive and vibrant as experience; the movements are dramatically and even "psychologically" related. The recognition and the implicit criticism of a sterile way of life in our society are firmly established. The importance of facing the truth, no matter how bleak, and of alleviating it with compassion rather than with deception is recognized. And all the dramatic power, as this album demonstrates, is in Albee's *text* rather than in peripheral effects and footnotes by enterprising scholiasts who thrive on the perversities of contemporary literature.

IV. *THE BALLAD OF THE SAD CAFÉ*
(March, 1964)

It is possible to wish that the climate were more favorable somewhere in the land for worthy plays that don't quite overpower the public and yet should attract it. Borderline cases abound . . . a successful one [is] *The Ballad of the Sad Café,* Edward Albee's adaptation of Carson McCullers' novella, effectively staged by Alan Schneider and ably performed by a cast headed by Colleen Dewhurst. Should the reader be surprised at my referring to this Albee adaptation as a borderline drama, it is because it is a seminarrated, only half-dramatized work. Distanced in time as an incompletely remembered story of a hard and unloving woman who fell in love with a dwarf after having driven her handsome husband out of the house, *The Ballad of the Sad Café* might never have reached Broadway without Albee's reputation behind it; and it would not have survived there but for the advantages of a production that manages, under Alan Schneider's direction, to punctuate every dramatizable detail of the action while preserving at the same time the penumbral nondramatic values of a well-spoken narration.

Too little or too much dramatization would have ruined a work that depends for its fascination upon the very incompletion of the play, which remains a minor work not merely because it is low-pulsed but because it is insufficiently revealing. It tells us little more than the story of a bizarre attachment and the irony of its failure when the dwarf who is the object of the woman's helpless affection and has taken full advantage of it, himself becomes helplessly attached to the husband she had driven off immediately after the marriage ceremony. Such is life or such is the irrational course of love, the play says; and while this is enough for a novella (or for a one-acter), it is not quite enough for a fully developed play. Some marvellously realized details erupt wherever the dwarf's half-childish and half-devilish character comes into focus; although he is not the protagonist, he is actually more dramatic a character than the heroine. For all her physical strength, she is the sufferer of the main action in that she is moved by impulses of nature as if she were in a dream. This is well realized in Colleen Dewhurst's impersonation, but it keeps her in a sort of limbo of dramatic art. Thematically acceptable, this portrait nevertheless limits not only the scope but the dramatic force of the play. (To understand the nature of this limitation, we ought to compare her with other female characters victimized by a natural force, such as Hauptmann's Rose Bernd, whose passiveness is consistent in her play, and Mrs. John, whose obsession with the idea of having a child makes her consistently active in *Die Ratten*.) Albee's dramatic contribution is more marked in the dwarf character, in such a detail as the suddenly pampered but still profoundly lonely dwarf's envy of the men in the local chain-gang because *they* at least are "together." Loneliness is something Edward Albee understands very well. Largely due to this bizarre character who, along with the half-mesmerized woman who favored him only to be destroyed by him, exemplifies existential fate and its ironies, *The Ballad of the Sad Café* proved to be a curiously moving work even if less than a satisfactory play.

V. *TINY ALICE*
(October, 1965)

The problem of growth could be seen confronting Edward Albee in *Tiny Alice* this season, a problem that did not actually engage him a year earlier when he dramatized the Carson McCullers novel, *The Ballad of the Sad Café*. One could hardly say that *Tiny Alice* represented "growth" (at least in skill and dramatic power), and it would have been unfair perhaps to expect it here. In *Tiny Alice* the youth playwright attempted to achieve a religious and symbolist type of play, and this without precedent in the American theatre since the production of O'Neill's *Days Without End* in 1935, or of Philip Barry's *Here Come the Clowns* three years later. It happens to be a genre, too, in which both O'Neill and Barry in the prime of their talent met defeat. The faults of *Tiny Alice* are largely faults of a genre that involves creating a fable more or less arbitrarily and making a religious mystery mysterious *à la* Maeterlinck and Andreyev. Not very surprisingly this procedure is apt to invite the charge of obfuscation from critics who make the commonplace error, as they did in the case of *The Cocktail Party,* that ideas in the theatre are possibly difficult. And from more sophisticated critics we are apt to get closer comment such as Stanley Kauffmann's recent reference in *The New Republic* to "the patness of its construction, the tagged symbolism of the characters, the mechanical charade of their action" that vitiates Katherine Anne Porter's filmed novel *The Ship of Fools.* I do not think that *Tiny Alice* is at all difficult or obscure, though it is insufficiently worked out in the conclusion. And I do not think that the play is pat in construction or tagged in its symbolism, yet it does not quite escape adding up to a mechanical charade.

Even so, I could not approve the hue and cry raised against the work by some reviewers of the intellectual élite, and I could not but intensely deplore the tasteless sniping of Philip Roth in the *New York Review,* and the niggling irrelevance of a review that belonged in the pages of *Psychopathia Sexualis* rather than in a journal of literary opinion. If *Tiny Alice* shows a still explorative talent succumbing to characteristic mistakes, it also does credit to the venturesome character of the effort to contribute thoughtful and literate drama to our theatre by expressing an author's anguished uncertainties in imaginative terms. If Mr. Albee couldn't quite succeed in view of the nature of the enterprise, he nevertheless earned my respect and regard. What he least deserved, in my opinion, is the contumely heaped upon him by the very *avant-garde* critics who have clamored most for imaginative theatre. The same point may be made about Alan Schneider's production and the performance of the principal actors, Irene Worth (who did not enunciate well enough) and John Gielgud (who posed too much at times in attitudes of anguish): that the infelicities were inflicted in the main by the genre. The performers were called upon to speak or act beyond their depth, or without sufficient support from the overt action. In this respect they were, in fact, duplicating in a small way the young author's own difficulty in leaning on literary and theatrical invention in an area where even reflection and experience as well as wide reading prove unavailing in so far as solutions rather than simple trust are sought. This is of course too much of a subject to discuss here.

Still, my readers will note, I hope, that I have not made a single reference here to Theatre of the Absurd, and I don't intend to. Neither the defects nor the attractions one is inclined to attribute to *Tiny Alice* have anything to do with it. Playwrights have dealt with the enigmas of life or the futility of trying to explain existence rationally since the beginning of literate theatre. I should not, however, like to give the impression that I entertain extravagant hopes for the type of play represented by *Tiny Alice,* even after granting the desirability of promoting imaginative theatre. It is an abstract and rootless, dubiously "literary" effort that also hobbled O'Neill. The enterprise has had rough sledding even in Cathlic countries such as Spain, France, and Austria, where the concern with faith has had a far richer cultural soil than our own. But then, paradoxically yet quite understandably, the proper concern of their best playwrights involved with religious matter (I have in mind such writers as Calderón, Claudel, Montherlant, and Hofmannsthal) have been with men's and women's human relations rather than with abstract problems. It is manifestly easier for a playwright to be concrete where faith is an unquestioned reality and requires no exegesis from dramatists, so that they are left to attend their own specifically creative business with human concerns, which have been and probably always will be fundamentally moral rather than metaphysical. The "proper study" of a playwright is man or, rather, human behavior and human relations. This can be viewed sardonically as well as solemnly, and I rather think our age will remain favorable to a satiric approach. Mr. Albee, himself, was more successful when he adopted that approach in *The American Dream* and *Who's Afraid of Virginia Woolf?*

VI. *A DELICATE BALANCE*
(December, 1966)

Undoubtedly Edward Albee's *A Delicate Balance* was intended to be the big opening of the 1966–67 season, and it was just that if controversy is any measure of importance. But is it? The controversy was inconsequential, since no particular issue was involved. Some reviewers considered it an extremely poor play while others went so far as to regard it as Albee's best work. Reviewers as far apart on basic matters as Walter Kerr, now ensconced in the seat of judgment at *The New York Times,* and Robert Brustein, of the *New Republic,* brought in a distinctly negative verdict, while the enthusiasts included such strange bedfellows as Richard Watts, of the *New York Post,* and Harold Clurman, who writes on plays in *The Nation* when not staging them on two continents. The public verdict unmistakably supported the "Ayes," and it was instantly evident that the investors in the show had made a good investment.

My own conclusion, if it matters to anyone, is that *A Delicate Balance* is neither a very good play nor a very bad one, an improvement certainly on the Albee plays that followed *Who's Afraid of Virginia Woolf?,* that missed the mark in important respects, and was not particularly distinguished when it seemed to hit it. In *A Delicate Balance,* Mr. Albee has returned to the world of domesticity which gave him his strongest full-length drama, and it is understandable that reviewers should have registered some relief at encountering a sympathetic approach to humanity in the work. He has exorcized the ghost of Strindberg without calling up the ghost of Pollyanna to take its place. In fact, some of the bad writing in the play retains memories of *Virginia Woolf* in the airing of the wife's grievances against her husband, and contains a startlingly tasteless reference to *coitus interruptus.* (One of the most deplorable habits our "advanced" playwrights have picked up from the surface Naturalism of modern drama is the fruitless resort to scatology in season or out.) The main trouble with Albee's "playmaking" in this work is in fact closely related to the interest and the potential strength of the play, which makes me wish he had worked longer on the play and that his director, Mr. Alan Schneider, had been more resistant to the author's theatrical guile and dramatic energy.

There is something, perhaps even a great deal, to be said for the domestic situation that the playwright uses to demonstrate how delicate is the balance that keeps a happiness in the home or a domestic relationship possible, and how easily it is upset by a variety of factors. In the present play, these include an element of accident in the antecedent death of a boy-child that ruined the sexual harmony of the husband and wife many years ago, its effect on the marital life of a much divorced daughter of the household as well as on the hysteria of the bleakly crisp middle-aged wife Agnes, impersonated by Jessica Tandy, and the arid passiveness of the husband Tobias, well, if depressingly, played by Hume Cronyn. It is unfortunate, however, that this theme remains muddily omnipresent in the play except in moments when the wife hurls reproaches at Tobias that seem both unwarranted by the objective realities of the play and *dramatically* irrelevant no matter how relevant they might be in a comparatively well executed novel based on this subject.

A second disruption factor is the presence of the wife's hard-drinking and defiant sister Claire. Rosemary Murphy plays her with a vivacity notably absent in the performances of Jessica Tandy and Hume Cronyn, and Claire's dialogue, a tissue of verbal provocations and cynical remarks in general, contains the best writing in the play. But it is virtually impossible to account for her presence in the drama as a disturbing force. Her presence seems arbitrary and is unconvincingly accounted for. Either she shouldn't be in the play or there should be a good reason for her being there. The wife's thin thread of insinuation that the husband had been unfaithful with Claire simply has no roots in either the present action or the present feelings of the characters that would reflect a past relationship.

A third disturbing factor is the much-married daughter who has just left her last husband. There is much talk on her part about the long-deceased sibling, which could account for something significant only in a painstakingly constructed novel. There is also perfervid talk by mother Agnes that Tobias has failed in his fatherly duty to send her back to her husbands containing an insinuation to the effect that he has always been glad to get her back after her various marriages. But this theme, too, seems arbitrary; it hangs like a Freudian spider's-web from the ceiling of the author's aspirations. The only things we can observe relevantly are that the young woman (in her thirties, I believe) simply loathes her mother and is hysterically averse to having two married house-guests occupy her bedroom when she shows up unexpectedly after her latest marital fiasco. Marian Seldes puts life, or at least drama, into the play with her playing of this daughter, Julia, so intolerable a creature that the audience was vastly relieved when the fine actress Carmen Mathews, playing the female house-guest, calmly slapped her face at one especially irritating point.

Next, I must consider the central situation of the intrusion of the neighboring couple, Harry and Edna, long-time friends of the suburban or, if you will, exurban Agnes and Tobias, who were suddenly overcome by indefinable fear while sitting quietly at home. They request succor from Agnes and Tobias and are politely allowed to occupy daughter Julia's bedroom until the latter raises such a row when she returns from her latest marital failure that it becomes necessary to tell the guests to leave. This duty devolves upon Tobias, or rather it is forced upon him by his wife. Haltingly he carries this out, being aided by Harry (effectively played by Henderson Forsythe) himself, who admits that he would have turned out Tobias from *his* home if the situation had been reversed. This scene, which is also the resolution of the play, accounts for some fifteen minutes of almost gripping and moderately penetrating drama that sums up much of the anguish of human aloneness. It is an anguish intensified in the case of Tobias, by the desire to respect friendship to the uttermost and the realization that he is at bottom neither capable of it nor really free to give it, even if he had it to give. If we do not want to betray a friendship, we do not really want to carry it very far. If we do, the others to whom we are committed by marital and parental relationships will force us to set narrow bourgeois limits to it. We will then have betrayed the one ideal we evidently cherished and thought we could afford, and the painful irony of it is that we were mistaken on both counts. We did not actually cherish it, of course, but merely took it for granted, in the spirit of easy neighborliness and country-club cordiality which costs us little and certainly causes no serious complications; that is, the relationship remains intact only as long as it costs us little and disturbs us less. Well prepared early in the play, actually *twice* prepared, this resolution of the play is reinforced rather than weakened by the fact that the friends' fears are never defined. Late in the play we sense, if we don't exactly know, that they were overcome by the pointlessness of their vaguely comfortable and socially acceptable lives and with the lovelessness of their middle-aged and middle-class marital status. It suddenly "hit" them both simultaneously, as it *should* have also overwhelmed Agnes and Toby, and would probably have done so if they had been left as alone as Harry and Edna were.

Nevertheless, even this central situation is ultimately frustrating, even on not very close inspection. It is "central" but insecurely so; that is, it has to share both the foreground and the background of the play with other, at best tenuously related, dramatic elements contributed by the daughter, the sister-in-law, and the central couple itself. And by the same token, the resolution of the play in the final confrontation between Tobias and Harry, good as it is as a dramatic scene *per se,* is not a resolution for a play that has so many diverse and incompletely realized elements. On the most obvious level, it resolves nothing about the daughter and the sister-in-law; and it is altogether vacuous as a resolution of the fuzzy failure of Agnes and Tobias as either separate individuals or as a married couple. And this leaves only one "delicate balance" to be accounted for, but on this subject the play does not contribute anything that is not obvious and banal.

I have proceeded in this methodical and humdrum fashion in order to explain as much as I can my uneasy reaction to *A Delicate Balance.* And I have played the schoolmaster, the egregiously commonplace schoolmaster, rather than the critic, because I believe that Edward Albee, his loyal associates, and his enthusiastic supporters need patient instruction much more than they need or deserve castigation in this instance. You may call my homiletics a lesson in "how not to write a play" when you are as talented as Edward Albee and could, with patience, write a much better one with virtually the same material and the same point of view.

If I refrain from discussing the staging it is because its defects are integral to the play. The direction is faithful, almost painfully so, to the script, and to the author's faults and defaults. I was not alone in the "second night" audience in finding Jessica Tandy much too high-pitched and irritatingly glittery, which is evidently the dramatic intention, and hard to understand in passages of great volubility. Still, the excess is in the author's lines through which he endeavored to convey a variety of tensions and uneasy pretensions on the part of the character. Presenting these would be tantamount indeed to good characterization if the character of Agnes had any perceptible core rather than a posture, and if it did not try our patience more than it illuminated or, for that matter, defined the individual behind the brittle mask. Moreover, it is a mistake for a principal actress to try to define her role in a long play by irritating the audience, as in Miss Tandy's case, even with a display of energy and virtuosity. Just as it is a mistake for the author to overexpose his own virtuosity in speeches that may be abstrusely bright but have little human context! And, let me add, just as it has been a mistake for the designer of the setting, Mr. William Ritman, to turn out a stage set that is designed to suggest the emptiness of the occupants' lives without considering that an illusionistic setting should not fail to localize the action vividly and suggest a lived-in world for characters who are intended to be more than walking and talking symbols. A negative setting, no matter how metaphorically conceived, is visually vacuum, and it is difficult to find a vacuum interesting. Semi-abstractness in the designing and lighting of the environment, either abetted or condoned by the director, was quite unhelpful to the play, which was rather coreless and abstract to begin with so far as the characters are concerned.

A BRACE OF ENGLISH IMPORTS
(MARCH, 1966)

On Broadway, as has been recently the case with embarrassing frequency, the most distinguished productions were of European, mainly English, provenance—most notably Peter Weiss's *Marat/Sade,* Peter Shaffer's *The Royal Hunt of the Sun,* John Osborne's *Inadmissible Evidence,* and John Whiting's *The Devils.* The only thing one would not have considered "normal" is Broadway's indebtedness to one of the most strenuous of "commercial" producers, Mr. David Merrick, as well as other blithe entrepreneurs, for nearly everything creditable as art as well as enterprise. But on second thought this, too, has been par for the erratic course of "theatre"; this is not the first time, as Shakespeare's and Molière's careers attest, that enterprise has accounted for art, and in recent years David Merrick and the David Merrick Foundation have accustomed us to benefactions, mostly imports, we have not received anywhere as often from producing organizations carrying the *cachet* of distinction or superiority to the vulgar considerations of show business. There is a moral to be drawn from this observation, but I refrain from drawing it in order to spare the sensibilities of academic and unacademic friends of "art" and "idealism." If Mr. Merrick, as has been sometimes alleged, is interested only in money, the public is the beneficiary; he has proved it with all the finished theatre and art he can buy abroad. And if something is lost in transit, there is still enough theatrical life left in the commodity to support Broadway's tottering structure.

I. *THE RIGHT HONOURABLE GENTLEMAN*

Some support was lent by the importation of Michael Dyne's *The Right Honourable Gentleman* without assistance from Mr. Merrick. The play was based on a chapter of late Victorian history or, rather a lurid subchapter, somewhat suggestive of the recent Profumo case. It involved the blasting of a promising political career by a scandal that rocked society in Gladstone's and Victoria's England in the year 1885. *Woman* was the root of the evil, when an unhappily married young wife endeavored to rid herself of an elderly husband by falsely claiming an adulterous connection with the rapidly rising political leader, Sir Charles Dike, who might have ultimately succeeded Gladstone as prime minister and advanced the cause of liberalism in England. *Man* was also culpable, not so much as a result of his amorous inclination, as of his hunger for power, which led to flagrant betrayal of the hero by his best friend, the up-and-coming Joseph Chamberlain who ultimately thrust England headlong into the ruinous career of imperialism. It was evident that an effort was made in the play to serve two ends simultaneously—the contriving of elegant melodrama and also winning regard for the works as historical exposé. Melodrama won out. At the most, the writing could only trumpet the doleful fact that social convention and moral queasiness deprived a country of a valuable servant. The point could be sustained by other cases such as the fall of the Irish leader, Thomas Parnell, through whom Ireland might have obtained home rule without bloodshed and long before the end of the first World War. But the animus of the play was not directed against Victorian society or against pharisism. Only the personal complications and, above all, the successful plot occupied both the foreground and the background of *The Right Honourable Gentleman*. These were sufficiently well organized to provide a conventionally structured work and sufficiently attractive in production to satisfy the conventional penchant for tastefully designed settings and costumes. The production could not be faulted, nor could the play itself by the conventional playgoer who has no objection to a well-contrived or "well-made" drama of intrigue. What the play lacked most may be described as the underpinning of satire and the sparkle of wit Shaw could have brought to its subject. The author's work was well done, and for this much one could be grateful; it is certainly no disgrace that an author should be competent or an audience passably satisfied. But it was evident that neither author nor audience was particularly exhilarated, and playgoers not initially drawn to this production felt no great urgency to patronize it.

Although the play dealt with an "event," it was not itself enough of an event in the theatre at a time when, at least in New York, a modest theatrical success is usually tantamount to a failure. The one thing that could *not* be said for *The Right Honourable Gentleman* is that it advanced the drama with respect to either form or content.

II. *THE ROYAL HUNT OF THE SUN*

The one thing that one would *expect* to say about the other British imports is that they do advance dramatic art or at least make a show of doing so. One play that ostensibly sustained such an expectation is *The*

Royal Hunt of the Sun, an epic play about the conquest of Peru, by Peter Shaffer. We have been conditioned to expect thoughtful and at times moderately original playwriting from the still fairly young author of *The Five Finger Exercise* and the one-act plays *The Private Ear* and *The Public Eye.* Yet his skill has been manifest essentially, as John Russel Taylor *(Anger and After)* put it, as "the usual pruned, heightened realism of traditional stage parlance." In the first part of *The Royal Hunt of the Sun* he is actually a humdrum playwright or, rather, he would be one if he were judged by literary rather than theatrical talent. He afforded every opportunity for theatrical virtuosity to the British director John Dexter and the cast headed by Christopher Plummer, in the role of Francisco Pizarro, and strongly supported by David Carradine, as Atahuallpa, the swarthy young Inca ruler. Merely watching the small band of Spaniards strain up the Andes in search of the Inca capital was a tense theatrical experience. In fact, a good deal of the action was choreographed, or mimed. (Memorable, though not without a touch of balletic pretentiousness, is the cold-blooded massacre of the Indians who have come to welcome Pizarro's marauders at the behest of their too trusting ruler.) But once the conquistador and the Inca meet, and two men, the grizzled and embittered former pigherd Pizarro and the young king, strike up a fateful friendship, drama supplants the preponderance of spectacle.

It is all very well for Peter Shaffer to refer to his play as "total theatre," and no doubt the production "gestural as well as verbal, hallucinatory as well as cerebral—magical," is able to make good this claim down to the last glittering Peruvian mask, colorful bird feather, or wild bird cry. But all this the movies can do even better—and *faster.* Where the drama meets its ultimate test is where the words come into the work along with the revelatory interplay of characters. Peter Shaffer understands this requirement well enough and tries to meet it. He succeeds in conveying the relationship between the conquistador and the young king of twenty-four million Indians who allowed himself to be captured as a result of his belief in the divinity of Pizarro and confidence in his own immortality as a god on earth. Pizarro almost believes it, too, and the failure of the wantonly executed Inca to return to life is a crushing blow to the old cynic; it is his last and greatest disillusionment. Pizarro also fights to save his captive's life from those who want to take it as a political measure for subduing the Inca kingdom with a laughingly small contingent of no more than 167 men. For a while, Pizarro's double-pronged dramatic involvement, his faith and his fear that it cannot be realized, even makes for considerable pathos in the play. Moreover, Shaffer sought to express a larger theme than that of the personal relationship.

He concerned himself with the craving for a tenable belief in immortality and its obvious frustration, and he was but contrasting reality in a vile world, which is divided in the play between two superstitions, the Spaniards and the Indians', and two more or less equally unsatisfactory ways of life, European individual activism as represented by Pizarro's empire-building brigands and the Incas' depersonalizing totalitarian collectivism.

With so much working in favor of *The Royal Hunt of the Sun* why don't the fine intentions of the talented author yield a thoroughly satisfying epic drama? It is perhaps easier to ask the question than to answer it except in niggling terms. It is not enough to say that the first half of the play lags as drama and is successful only as a spectacle. It is also not enough to add that the immortality theme is too tenuous, even if we grant the pathos and the appeal of the friendship of Pizarro and the king. Furthermore, the latter is, for the most part, a dramatic dud; his passiveness deprives the play of the possibility of establishing a true and stirring conflict. If the failure of the natives to withstand the encroachments of the Spaniards at any point is a deterrent to the making of a dynamic play, which we have a right to expect in an "epic drama," the failure of the native rule is an even greater flaw in the play, because his passiveness deprives it of the possibilities of *action* in any meaningful sense of the term. Something else is missing in *The Royal Hunt of the Sun;* I would call it want of involvement, almost as if the author wanted to cry out "a plague on both your houses"—that is, on European rapacity and Indian submissiveness, European individualism and Indian collectivism, Christian hypocrisy and Indian superstition. A sense of impersonality in the author has been noted before this, in England. I do not find it objectionable in view of Shaffer's attitude toward the main events and situations of the present work. But it does limit empathy and therefore effectiveness. The effective alternative would have been still greater detachment— mocking in the manner of Shaw, ironic in the manner of Brecht, or saturnine in the manner of Ionesco, Beckett, and other "Absurdists" or "near Absurdists."

The official management of this production is "The Theatre Guild," here virtually a trade name for several other producers as well—a sort of collective David Merrick. This apparently represents the "wave of the future" so long as theatrical production costs continue to mount even in the case of a play first presented abroad. To the Merrick buccaneering enterprise (and Broadway management has become as much a form of buccaneering as the business of an Elizabethan privateer) we owe both *Inadmissible Evidence* and *Marat/Sade*. Both are intensely negativistic plays, the former by the stormy petrel of the resurgent British dramatist John Osborne, and the latter by Peter Weiss, the German Jewish playwright who resides in Sweden, once his refuge from Nazi persecution.

III. *INADMISSIBLE EVIDENCE*

Concerning *Inadmissible Evidence,* much as one may be grateful for seeing another play by this gifted writer, I can only wonder whether, so to speak, Osborne's ingenious game is worth the candle. The game includes such departures from tight, realistic, and "well-made" structure as starting the action backward, deliberately making the scenes repetitive, depriving the story of a conclusion other than letting the central solicitor-character Bill Maitland drop his tired head on his desk, and requiring one actress to play three different women as if to say tell us that the desperately sated, emotionally drained debauchee and failure Maitland sees all women in the same impersonal way. A related intention reveals itself first in a long monologue that isolates the alienated middle-aged lawyer Maitland for the audience and also makes the play-structure as lopsided as the character's life and as febrile (in a somewhat expressionistic manner) as his state of mind. It is only a slight exaggeration to say that the entire play is a monologue even after the bizarre prologue. The central character is morbidly involved only with his own ego, and so nobody else actually matters to him, neither his wife nor his mistresses nor his employees. He seeks to hold on to an office girl with whom he has had a pallid affair, but he has hurt her too much to be able to repair the relationship. He makes one belated effort to attach his legal associate to himself by offering him a partnership. He makes a lame attempt to win the affection or at least the attention of his long-neglected daughter in one fine scene played by her entirely in pantomime, and he gets not a syllable of response from her. He doesn't even get a good fight out of the mostly cardboard figures with whom he has such unsavory relationships or casual dealings; and this fact, this essential lack of conflict, tells heavily against the play. In the end he is left alone, a fading egotist mired in his own quicksand of unstable relationships, a morbid romanticist *manqué,* a moldy Don Juan with a sharp mind that sputters apt phrases to signalize disillusion with himself and others.

That there is no genuine story after the prologue in which he gives "inadmissible evidence" against himself in the privacy of his chambers is easily apparent. There is only a swirl of rapid recollection and confrontations that occasionally constitute an episode; the visit of a hopelessly homosexual client makes an especially strong scene. That the play supplies a remarkably incisive character portrait is its main, perhaps its *only* virtue. That it gives us not much else is the mark of its intrinsic failure, disguised by its theatricality of the structure and the opportunity it affords the gifted young British actor Nicol Williamson for an unforgettable *tour de force* performance. It would be certainly unforgettable if it were not such a relief for some of us to forget the insufferable character he impersonates. In England, the omnipresence of this "person" on the stage must have been appreciated as an exposé, and the public and the reviewers in London (where *Inadmissible Evidence* ran half an hour longer) could endure even more of him than the New York management dared entrust to the mercies of American playgoers, who evinced no eagerness to storm the box-office. Here it seems to me Bill Maitland is mostly a bore. In portraying a corruptible, if supercilious weakling, John Osborne was far more successful when he collaborated with the actor Anthony Creighton on *Epitaph for George Dillon;* even if this role was much less theatrically striking than that of Maitland, George Dillon was involved in greater depth with other and more richly drawn characters. His failure while less spectacular was also more meaningful because the earlier written play developed a natural process of decline in the case of a character who succumbs to a commonplace marriage and a career of hackwriting after pretensions to superiority. It is, in sum, altogether possible to tire of magnified exposure, no matter how brilliantly accomplished, of a third-rate Hamlet of the professional classes like Maitland even while Osborne remains an admittedly vigorous and fortunately still "angry" man. The very magnification of the presentation of this character by Osborne's showmanship, the very theatricalization of the exposé, calls attention to the waste of effort in exposing him at a greater length than a one-act-play.

Inadmissible Evidence came here with the enthusiastic endorsement of London critics, one of whom acclaimed it as "Mr. Osborne's best play to date." Some New York reviewers were also greatly impressed with it. Henry Hewes, of *The Saturday Review,* wrote that the play was a theatrical statement "naked and shattering yet ultimately soaring above the desperation it so relentlessly presents." I wish I could agree with a former student and a tireless friend of the stage on two continents, instead of agreeing with Robert Brustein, of the *New Republic,* that except in the George Dillon play, "Osborne's writing has always lacked a magnetic core around which particles of insight and feeling might collect"—here especially in the case of a mediocre character whose action, if one can call it such, is from the beginning an exericse in "solipsism."

IV. *MARAT/SADE*

The sense of futility so characteristic of our times reached its peak of theatrical expression in *Marat/Sade,* whose egregiously complete title ("The Persecution and Assassination of Marat as Performed by the Inmates of the Asylum of Charenton under the Direction of the Marquis de Sade") fortunately spares a reviewer pressed for space the necessity of providing a summary. It is necessary only to add that the performance occurs in the early years of the 19th century and deals with events that happened more than a decade previously (in the year 1793) when the revolutionary extremist Marat was assassinated in his bath by Charlotte Corday. This came at a time when he was violently proclaiming the necessity for intensifying the campaign of terror against both counter-revolutionary aristocrats and the Girondin moderate revolutionists. It is a curious fact that the director of the Charenton asylum for the mentally disturbed patients allowed the practice of group therapy there in the form of theatricals, and the Marquis de Sade wrote and directed many of these for the inmates during his own incarceration there between the years 1803 and 1814, the year of his death. The asylum background for the action, a keen comment on the lunacy of political affairs, is superbly realized in the imported Peter Brook production. No one can seriously doubt that it is one of the high points of theatrical excitement in our century. The costuming, lighting, musical accompaniment, and choreography makes this play completely, indeed thrillingly, viable on the stage. So does the acting of the ensembles that explode all over the stage except in one corner close to the wings where the asylum's director Monsieur Coulmier and his wife and daughter are sitting and detachedly observing the frenzied proceedings. The principal characters are excitingly impersonated, Jean-Paul Marat by the resonant Ian Richardson and Charlotte Corday by Glenda Jackson, who alternates fascinatingly between the role of a jittery mad girl and the role of the heroine of the play-within-the-play. Only Patrick Magee is somewhat slack or perhaps only vocally light in his impersonation of the Marquis de Sade with some resultant monotony in his discussions with the Marat character.

In these discussions, the Marquis may be considered as being both inside his own play as well as outside it, since the Marat he is addressing at some length is the Marat in the play-within-the-play impersonated by

Ian Richardson. Outside this role, of course, Richardson is as truly an inmate of the asylum as any of the other characters except the director and his family. But one hardly worries about these questions of identity while watching this brilliantly executed production. It is all theatre, the *total* theatre Peter Shaffer has claimed for *The Royal Hunt of the Sun,* only much more engrossingly so. No doubt, too, some confusion is bound to arise from the manic behavior of the inmates and their convincingly crude theatricality, which they interrupt now and then, as when the satyriast who plays Charlotte Corday's idealistic lover tries to rape the girl who plays Charlotte and has to be kept within the bounds of decency. Their chants and processions, especially toward the end of the performance, are especially turbulent, so that exceptionally keen hearing alone would enable one to make out their words. But this is no great matter; their wild chanting and marching have the right impact, and constitute an apt parody of the excesses of irrationality and the explosions of runaway passion that characterize revolutions originally inspired by idealism and ultimately propagate new injustices and crimes against humanity. The vision of Peter Weiss, an author made particularly aware of this historical fact by recent history, of which he and his family had personal experience in the days of Hitler, is a dreary one. It is especially discouraging to well-meaning liberals and radicals who persist in maintaining an unqualified optimism regarding humanity's prospects.

These being decidedly dim in the nuclear age, it is difficult not to respect this work as the *cri de coeur* of a despairing, if not indeed, outraged generation of intellectuals; and if this makes for "Theatre of the Absurd" it makes it better and more authentically than most ventures into this Nay-saying kind of theatre that often "Nay-says" itself out of communicability and artistic coherence. Certainly this is the case even if the author, as he has told us, no longer wishes to be associated with this viewpoint. (Since writing *Marat/Sade* he has come to repose his trust in Socialism, presumably gradual and peaceable in the manner of Swedish parliamentary reform comparable to welfare-state developments in England and the United States.) The discussions in the play revolving around Marat's appeal to revolutionary violence and De Sade's acceptance of human corruption as an ineluctable fact of nature are, actually, the least gratifying parts of the play. They are the most obvious, lacking as they do any dramatic transformation into action such as one finds in Ernst Toller's expressionistic *Man and the Masses* (*Masse-Mensch*), in the short dramatic fragments of *Danton's Death,* and then in crackling lightning-lit poetry of *King Lear.*

It is the Royal Shakespeare Company production transferred from

London to Broadway that makes unquestioned impact on a playgoer even when the director was not above resorting to a considerable degree to expressionistic hysteria and showy *kitsch*. Only the infernal visions of painters such as Bosch and Goya provide a comparably bizarre and devastating experience. At the same time, the danger in all this adept directorial display is bound to be quite apparent to the thinking part of the audience. The experience is apt to leave one stunned and exhausted rather than stirred and enlightened, for in the last analysis we are confronted here with theatricalism run amok. Only the occasional sallies of humor in the text and the production succeed in "distancing" or cooling the histrionics. This occurs most mordantly when the executioner first pours red paint in a bucket intended to represent the blood of ordinary victims of the French Terror and then pours blue paint into the pail after the guillotining of the aristocrats. This qualification must, in the long run, be recorded by me even while dissenting from *The New Yorker* critic's verdict that *Marat/Sade* is "full of song and fury signifying nothing" or *Time* magazine reviewer's more moderate dismissal of the content as "too stale as intellectual inquiry."

V. *THE DEVILS*

Another potentially interesting import, John Whiting's *The Devils,* based upon a discursive narration by Aldous Huxley titled *The Devils of London,* came to New York under the auspices of another Broadway entrepreneur, the cultivated producer Alexander Cohen, to whom we have been indebted for evenings of intelligent entertainment. With *The Devils* he was less fortunate than with some of his previous enterprises. Several misfortunes afflicted the show, the most obvious being the costly transportation strike, the least expected being little better than adequate performances at best by his stars Anne Bancroft, as a sex-obsessed humpbacked nun, and Jason Robards, as Urbain Grandier, the somewhat supercilious vicar of St. Peter's Church in the town of Loudun who is wantonly accused of witchcraft by her. He is tortured and burnt at the stake as a victim of psychosis and mass-hysteria, superstition, and political intrigue in early-seventeenth-century France under the premiership of the Cardinal Richelieu, whom the priest had once offended. But if the principals leave much to be desired, except in the last act when Jason Robards undergoes extreme torture but refuses (alas, somewhat monotonously) to plead guilty, the fault is only partly theirs. Blame devolves upon the scattered production directed by Michael Cayonnis on Rouben Ter-Arutinian's overextended stage setting. And more blame settles on the late gifted British playwright John Whiting who undertook an extremely difficult job when he accepted an assignment from the Royal Shakespeare Company to dramatize Huxley's book and simply could not condense its wandering action despite his literary flair and intelligent sympathies.

It is perhaps understandable that so well-intentioned a reviewer as Howard Taubman should have acclaimed it twice as a masterpiece, once when it opened at the Washington "Arena Theatre" and again when it opened on Broadway. Mr. Taubman's heart inclined him strongly in favor of a play in which an innocent man is brought to destruction by man's ignorance and barbarity. But it is no use blinking at the fact that the shattering effect felt by some, or perhaps many, playgoers was a considerable degree a shattering of sound judgment in an occasionally well-filled void. A general sympathy with a victim of injustice and considerable bludgeoning by superficial visual effects and a stage filled with busy, if largely inchoate, action could temporarily assuage boredom and pacify one's critical faculties. But this is hardly enough in the case of a work from which much more could, and should, be expended. One could even leave the theatre emotionally drained, yet without a genuine catharsis because the dramatized story lacked coherence.

VI. *SERJEANT MUSGRAVE'S DANCE*
(May, 1966)

At first a failure in London at the Royal Court Theatre, over six years ago, John Arden's *Serjeant Musgrave's Dance* returned triumphantly to the same theatre last December after having been produced with considerable success elsewhere in England and on the European continent. This time there was little doubt in London that this was a work of great imaginativeness and dramatic power. Nevertheless, it was unlikely to duplicate its London success in New York when it opened in March, and the press was respectful rather than enthusiastic. The produciton, by the Establishment Company, could not be blamed, for it was a remarkably vivid and vital one. It was defective only in some stereotyping of the minor characters. Even so, several of the secondary roles were amazingly well drawn, and John Colicos was genuinely impressive as the fanatical anti-imperialist soldier who is bent upon impressing his gospel of peace on the people of England. It is Arden's exacting dramatic *élan* alone that could be blamed for the uncertain effect of the play; the overstrained and seemingly obscure dramatic development of the work was the other side of a rare talent for combining theatrical imagination with naturalistic localization, empathy with critical objectivity, and reflection with almost expressionistic explosiveness.

The trouble starts and ends with a "serjeant" (old British spelling for "sergeant") Musgrave who comes to a north England mining town with three soldiers, all deserters from the British army campaigning somewhere in the British empire where they put down a native rebellion. They bring with them their small arms, a Gatling machine gun, and the skeleton of a fellow-soldier, a local lad who had been assassinated by the patriots of a native uprising. Musgrave is a religiomaniac who intends to teach Englishmen, who condone imperialist wars far from home, a much-needed lesson by hoisting up the skeleton and preaching to the townsmen and, if necessary, forcing them to listen at the point of the Gatling gun. Musgrave and his men pretend to have come to the town for the purpose of recruiting for the Queen's army; the period of the play is approximately the time of the Crimean War, around 1875. They are welcomed by the mayor of the town, who is also the local mine owner who has locked out the miners for threatening to strike for better wages than he is prepared to give. A solution for his labor troubles would be the removal of some of the miners along with their union leader.

Unfortunately, Musgrave's idealistic plans go astray when one of his soldiers is accidentally stabbed in a brawl over a woman and attempts to escape with her, which is construed as an act of desertion by his comrades who are, ironically, deserters themselves; and when Musgrave, driven by his excessive zeal for justice, resolves to take the lives of twenty-five local dignitaries as payment for the twenty-five lives it cost to punish the natives in retaliation for the death of the assassinated British soldier. Musgrave loses the support of one of the two remaining soldiers, a veteran who is sick of killing people; and he has no success in winning the support of the strike leader, who, on reflection, prefers to rely on the principles or strategies of Trade Unionism rather than the maniacal Musgrave's Calvinistic code of "justice." Musgrave and his sole remaining comrade will undoubtedly go to the gallows when the Queen's dragoons arrive to pacify the mining town.

It is not difficult to observe that the play is based on a somewhat far-fetched story and a principal character whose passion for peace is perverted by a psychosis. As a result, the play seems decidedly strained, as well as somewhat obscure in motive and development. But it is also undeniably powerful, exciting, and, in fact, fascinating. The writing, interspersed with biting snatches of song, has flavor, poetry, and authenticity.

One is not likely to forget this play once one has seen it in the Theatre de Lys production.

The key to the play is given in its subtitle "An Un-historical Parable," and only when viewed as such (not quite an easy thing to do) is it entirely cohesive and meaningful. As for the "meaning," it may be well to heed the author's own explanation in the 1960 Methuen and Company British edition of his mordant play: "I have endeavored," he declared, "to write about the violence that is evident in the world, and do so through a story that is partly one of wish-fulfilment. I think that many of us must at some time have felt an overpowering urge to match some particularly outrageous piece of violence with an even greater and more outrageous retaliation. Musgrave tries to do this: and the fact that the sympathies of the play are clearly with him in his original horror (of war and repressive imperialism), and then turn against him and his intended remedy (of murdering the dignitaries of the mining-town), seems to have bewildered many people." And, of course, Arden has only followed the Brechtian pattern of "distancing" the dramatic action and "alienating" the playgoer in order to clarify the parable. He explains his point with becoming personal humility when he writes, in conclusion: "Complete pacifism is a very hard doctrine: and if this play appears to advocate it with perhaps some timidity (that is, in undercutting Musgrave's pacifism with the fact that he is plainly a religiomaniac) it is probably because I am naturally a timid man—and also because I know that if I am hit I very easily hit back; and I do not care to preach too confidently what I cannot be sure I can practise."

Part Six

THE MODERN VISION IN DRAMA

THE PLAYWRIGHT AND THE
CONTEMPORARY WORLD*

A pertinent question is exactly what world it is that we call contemporary. I think it is the world we began to encounter with the start of the First World War in 1914. By comparison with it, the earlier world that cradled the modern theatre—from the 1870's to the outbreak of that war —seemed remarkably stable and peaceful, though, strictly speaking, it was neither. The struggle for women's rights, the striving for political liberalism, the agitations of racialism, and the hopes of Socialism now seem remote and muted. Today's artists and intellectuals are normally unimpressed by Ibsenism as a cause or challenge. No matter how Ibsen and his acolytes might fume about nineteenth-century society, they could assume the continuance of man and the inevitability of a rationally ordered, constantly improving, world. Their attitude toward progress in science was no less sanguine. With science functioning as the hand-maiden of the good society, man could confidently expect not only ever-growing standards of material well-being, but equity in social relations based on a rising economy of surplus rather than scarcity. And in international relations, despite several conflicts such as the Franco-Prussian War of 1870 and the later Russo-Japanese War, it seemed as if it would soon be possible to establish amity and reasonableness among the nations of the world. With respect to advance in applied science of salvation, so to speak, by machinery, men could but echo Lord Alfred Tennyson's confident tribute to the "ringing grooves of change" with which he hailed the advent of the railroad. With respect to the rise of democratic government and the adjudication of national rivalries, it seemed reasonable to endorse this Victorian poet's prediction of a "Parliament of Man and Federation of the World," which was henceforth to be assured by the "common sense of most."

It is a radically different conception of man's failure that rules the world of thoughtful men and the uneasy fraternity of contemporary art —especially the public art of the theatre. In the English-speaking theatre the altered outlook was perhaps most poignantly expressed within a dozen

* An abstract of a lecture commemorating the twenty-fifth anniversary of the Department of Drama of the University of Texas delivered on March 22, 1963. From *Theatre Arts* (January, 1964).

years of the Versailles treaty by that most distinguished of pre-war opti-
mists, Bernard Shaw, the one-time apostle of social progress. In *Too True
to Be Good* in 1932, Shaw made his ex-clergyman hero Aubrey exclaim
that "the Western World is damned beyond the possibility of salvation."
The full peroration of *Too True to Be Good,* the product of Shaw's desperate view which preceded the outbreak of a second world war by a
scant half-dozen years, was even more devastating. Shaw anticipated our
current theatre of desperation, or so-called "Theatre of the Absurd," when
he made Aubrey his spokesman. Comparing the past and the present,
Aubrey declares, "Naked bodies no longer shock us; our sunbathers, grin-
ning at us from every illustrated summer number of our magazines, are
nuder than shorn lambs. But the horror of the naked mind is still more
than we can bear."

Aubrey's question of "how are we to bear the dreadful new nakedness?" became the cardinal question of the vigorous expressionist playwrights of the 1920's, just as it became the prime challenge of the existentialist drama written during and immediately after World War II,
and once more again in the present historical moment. And indeed how
are we to bear with this nakedness and this sense of despair deeper than
Pascal's when the old science was aborning in the seventeenth century—
"the nakedness," says Aubrey, "of the souls who until now have always
disguised themselves from one another in beautiful impossible idealisms
to enable them to bear one another's company."

Assigning the blame to the traumatic effect of the First World War
between 1914 and 1918, Shaw's Aubrey continues prophetically as well
as provocatively: "The iron lightning of war has burnt great rents in
these angelic veils, just as it has smashed great holes in our cathedral roofs
and torn great gashes in our hillsides. Our souls go in rags now; and the
young are spying through the holes and getting glimpses of the reality
that was hidden. And they are not horrified [Shaw is right—the young
of the scornfully sophisticated 1920's were not horrified, their despair was
to come later in our own day of existentialist and nihilist theatre!]: they
exult in having found us out: . . . and when we their elders desperately
try to patch our torn clothes, with scraps of the old material, the young
lay violent hands on us and tear from us even the rags that were left
to us. But [and here comes a second prophecy!] when they have stripped
themselves and us utterly naked, will they be able to bear the spectacle?"
That they have not been able to do so is distressingly evident in imported
plays such as Beckett's and Ionesco's plays and in home-grown ones like
Albee's and Gelber's.

Declaring himself to be the new Ecclesiastes, but an Ecclesiastes deprived of a Bible and a creed, Shaw's Aubrey concluded that we have, as he put it, "outgrown our religion, outgrown our political system, outgrown our strength of mind and character."

Disillusion with the old religious faiths, including faith in life itself and its means of communication, became a staple of the theatre of the 1920's. The concomitant sense of intolerable void appeared in the runaway European negativism that went under the name of "dada"—and appropriately so, since this infantile word conveys the fact that the very language of thought and feeling, of communication between adults, was being dissolved. That the dadaist theatre should not have precipitated any noteworthy dramatic literature cannot surprise the drama critic. In, so to speak, *impure* dadaist drama such as the poet E. E. Cummings' sardonic play *him,* it is the *destructive* element of satire that makes the work communicative in so far as the satirized subject is recognizable and the author's attitude is vividly, if not indeed violently, present.

The disintegrative dadaist impulse was also assimilated into, and blended with, the expressionism fashionable in Central Europe during and immediately after World War I, as in Georg Kaiser's *From Morn to Midnight,* or amalgamated with social protest, as in the celebrated Brecht and Weill musical creations, *The Threepenny Opera* and *Mahagonny.* In incompletely dadaist works such as these, of course, the process of artistic disintegration was halted by the constructive quality of musical structure and the reintegrative moral power of satire, which has been rightly considered a social corrective ever since the classic stage of Aristophanes. But reintegration was not to be the order of the day for long in Europe after the second and greater explosion of World War II. In histories of art and literature, dadaism is usually described as a brief episode and a rapidly discredited aberration. But it is surely dadaism in more or less pure state that we have been encountering since the Second World War in such examples of dramatic anarchy as Picasso's incoherent *Desire Caught by the Tail,* Ionesco's inconsequent travesties on man in society such as *The Bald Soprano,* and Beckett's and Genet's apocalyptic visions of a dissolving world such as *Endgame, The Balcony,* and *The Blacks.*

André Breton's first *Manifesto of Surrealism* provides an instructive example, which the recent Theatre of the Absurd has also provided. Breton wrote: "Surrealism is a pure psychic automatism, by which it is intended to express, verbally, in writing, or by other means, the real process of thought and thought's dictation, in the absence of all control exercised by the reason and outside all esthetic or moral preoccupations. Surrealism rests on the belief in the superior reality of certain forms of association neglected hitherto; in the omnipotence of the dream, and in the disinterested play of thought."

Limping raggedly behind the vehicle of so-called modern "drama of ideas," once so brightly furbished and so dashingly managed by Shaw, contemporary playwrights have arrived at opinions which, even if they were sound would be neither fresh nor exciting. And whether the opinion expressed has been liberal or conservative, the dramatic style has been commonplace. Shaw's dialectical brilliance and free-flowing imagination have rarely been present in the theatre since the 1920's—except in France, and this mainly as a result of the work of Jean Giraudoux. And while liveliness of thought has not been absent in Giraudoux's plays, a feeling for character has rarely been evident. "Strength of mind" has been present at least in some pyrotechnical displays of French intellect. But "strength of character" has been a genuine concern only under the existentialist prescripts of Sartre and his followers. Strength of mind and character has, it is true, been abundantly apparent in the work of Bertolt Brecht, and has often been accompanied by moral strength. But the historical conditions of the post-1918 world reflected in Brecht's work hampered Brecht's intellect and sense of character. Whatever independence and originality we may attribute to Brecht belongs to the poet, the craftsman, and the theatrical virtuoso in his make-up.

It is especially significant that neither the schools of Paris nor those of Central European "epic" have been secure in their hold upon "strength of intellect and strength of character." Thus Giraudoux's most successful successor, Jean Anouilh, has been a watered-down Giraudoux whose essentially romantic talent is conspicuously theatrical rather intellectual; Sartre has been followed by no other existentialist dramatist of consequence; and Brecht, despite the recent advent of the Swiss writers Duerrenmatt and Frisch, has not yet had any successors on either side of the Iron Curtain possessed of either his mental power or his flaring moral passion. East of the Iron Curtain, besides, the critic has been able to observe scarcely any enthusiasm for Brecht in Russia capable of nullifying the sway of Socialist Realism which is, in essence, nothing more than a prescription for flabby and unimaginative problem-play realism and old-fashioned moral uplift.

But a deeper disturbance of the humanism of art has been present in the very nature of the aforementioned schools, and of progressive types of contemporary drama in general. It is the actual subversion or even dissolution of character itself. Character in the drama after 1914 was repeatedly fragmented or exploded by the violent expressionist drama that came into vogue in Germany; it was dissolved, introverted, and also exploded by the dramatic surrealism that followed the dadaist movement, especially in France; it was called into question, mocked, and invalidated by Pirandello and his Italian school of the grotesque; and it was variously subordinated to Marxist and psychological interest, as well as to sophisticated theatricality and formalism.

In a large area of twentieth-century drama, characterization no longer meant the creation of characters but the manipulation of attenuated figures, often suggestive of mere puppetry, so that the question of credibility had lost much of its meaning. The characters in modernist French drama, whether by Giraudoux or Beckett, by Anouilh or Ionesco, are essentially there in the plays for purposes of demonstration or symbolization rather than for revelation. One cannot appraise most *avant-garde* writing by asking the old, classic questions of who is the character and why does he do what he does, feel what he feels, think what he thinks. It is the playwright who decides these matters more or less arbitarily or dismisses them as questions not particularly relevant or perhaps even totally irrelevant to his purpose, which may be to spin out a notion or demonstrate a point which may be esthetic, philosophical, or propagandist.

With the dissolution of character in our century, we come to the true age of decadence. It is not obscenity, morbidity, or undue fascination with death and decay that undermines the drama—these are but concomitant characteristics—but the disappearance of man himself, in the fullness of life, that constitutes decadence in the theatre. Depersonalization has been the gravest threat to our theatre whatever its source, whether it rose from a zeal for social reform or for "pure" art and esthetic formalism, whether from fascination with psychopathology and its theories or with theatre and the theatricality of theatre. From this point of view the reform-minded playwright, the writer in love with "psychology" rather than with man, the prophet of doom for whom doom has already struck in the form of the extinction of individuality, and the formalist trapped by form are just about equally culpable. Their morals may be unimpeachable, but in annihilating the person in the play they strike at the heart of the drama and cut off the circulation of the theatre's life-blood.

The drama can be as inventive as any artistic coterie could possibly desire but contradicts its very nature the moment it uses the living actor to simulate everything but life itself. Sometimes the *avant-garde* not only forces him to become a marionette on the stage but distances him even further from life by disallowing him the privilege that even marionettes have of *pretending* to be real. Conversely, it is possible to put the actor on stilts, smother him in padded clothing, and clap a mask on his face, as in the tragic theatre of classic Greece, and yet establish life intensively and vibrantly in the theatre. Seen in this light, the contemporary theatre is not in danger of being undermined by, let us say, a lurid *Streetcar Named Desire* or a flagellating *Who's Afraid of Virginia Woolf?*, but by pious exercises in estheticism and symbolism such as Eliot's verse drama *The Family Reunion* and Yeats's beautifully written but esoterically abstract one-act plays written under the influence of Japanese Noh plays. And depersonalization is but a first step in the devitalization of the theatre, which ultimately, after virtually abolishing human motivation and suspending the operation of cause and effect in human action, goes on to destroy the first and last outpost of dramatic communication—namely, language itself.*

Having learned to do without characters, we may soon learn to do without language, if by language we mean coherent speech. And after that there can be only one more step, and that is to do without a play altogether in writing a play, or to write something Ionesco correctly designated as an *antiplay*—presumably with noncharacters employing nonspeech!

Nor is it merely negation or anguish that pulverizes our dramatic language, an effect sometimes justified on the grounds of suiting the sound to the sense or the nonsense—as in the character Lucky's primitive jabber-wocky in the first act of Beckett's *Waiting for Godot* or in an Orator's meaningless jabber at the end of Ionesco's symbolic farce *The Chairs*. Affirmations, too, have tended to be bizarrely inchoate when they have not been wearily monotonous. At best, the positive statements have been vaguely comforting as in the "Always spring comes again" speech at the end of O'Neill's *The Great God Brown,* or patently rhetorical in the manner of the inept long blank-verse speech with which Maxwell Anderson concluded *Winterset.* The character Big Foot brings Picasso's play to a conclusion with the following call to action, and presumably those who understand it will be able to rise to it: "Let's wrap the worn-out sheets in the angels' face powder and let's turn the mattress inside out in the brambles," says Big Foot. "Let's light all the lanterns. Let's throw the flights of doves against the bullets with all our might and let's close the houses, that have been demolished by the bombs, with a double lock." Following which, we are informed "a golden sphere as tall as a man" enters. This lights up the stage and blinds the characters on it, who take out pocket handkerchiefs and bandage their eyes, calling out to each other "You! You! You!" while on the big golden sphere appear the letters of the word "Nobody." We are lucky, of course, that it wasn't worse! It

---

* [Here Professor Gassner planned an addition, indicated by a cryptic note: "Reaction in England." *Ed.*]

could have been the one-word vulgarism tapped out by a horse at the close of Cocteau's *Orpheus,* which preceded the Picasso opus by some twenty years in the French theatre during the vogue of the *first* surrealist movement.

I say the "first," because in the Theatre of the Absurd dramaturgy represented by *Desire Caught by the Tail* and in other esoteric pieces like Gelber's *The Apple,* we actually have had a *second* surrealist movement. The wheel has been turning full circle round more than once in the modern theatre without young *avant-garde* enthusiasts realizing it. But then anything is possible in the twentieth century, which has been, for better and worse, the most experimental in the history of the theatre. And anything can happen in a period in which the gap between majority and minority audiences has grown wider and wider without either of the two audiences often attaining much relatedness to the experience of reality and the challenge of contemporary life. Although there have been brief historical moments, especially during the 1920's in Europe and the 1930's in America, when a reorientation and integration of the theatre seemed imminent under an ideal of social drama, and though there have been occasions when the majority and the minority seemed to be drawing together, disorientation and schism in the theatre have been chronic.

It is no wonder, then, that anthologies of significant statements by writers on their intention and their craft bristle perforce with avowals and disavowals. So we hear O'Neill asserting the necessity of finding a unique technique for every new play and meeting this requirement himself by adhering to realistic technique in *Anna Christie, Desire Under the Elms, The Iceman Cometh,* and *Long Day's Journey into Night,* but employing expressionistic style in *The Emperor Jones* and *The Hairy Ape,* resorting to masks for split personalities in *The Great God Brown,* and reviving the Elizabethan device of the "aside" in *Strange Interlude* for psychological revelation and ironic effect. We hear O'Neill calling for "some sort of supernaturalism" to take the place of "the old naturalism," and fulminating against the routine realism he deplored as a "banality of surfaces." We hear Pirandello explaining the blending of comedy and tragedy, and the intermingling of reality and fantasy, in his most celebrated drama: "I wanted to present six characters searching for an author. Their play does not manage to get presented—precisely because the author whom they seek is missing. Presented instead is the comedy of their vain attempt with all that it contains of tragedy by virtue of the fact that the six characters have been rejected." Cocteau tells us that "The poet must bring objects and feelings from behind their veils and their mists," and O'Casey, a master of naturalism in his first three produced plays, concludes in the preface to his fanciful *Cock-a-Doodle-Dandy* in 1958, that "naturalism, or even realism, isn't enough," and that he broke with naturalism after his masterpiece *The Plough and the Stars* because he wanted to capture for the stage "a dance, a laugh, and song." Tennessee Williams, in explaining *Camino Real,* calls for "freedom and mobility of form" along with a flowing use of symbolist imagery; Brecht favors "alienating" devices and disjunctive form in order to make his audience think clearly about social and moral problems rather than feel fuzzily and lose itself in empathic situations; and Ionesco, explaining his one-act satire, *The Bald Soprano,* a comedy of human boredom, resolves to write an antiplay for the purpose of ridiculing ordinary life and theatre. He declares that he desired to produce "a parody of human behavior, and therefore a parody of the theatre, too," since man's drama "is as absurd as it is painful"; and Ionesco expects that by revealing man's absurdity one can actually "achieve a sort of tragedy." There seems to be no end to the partial dramatic visions and themes of craft propounded since World War I.

■

BERNARD SHAW AND THE MAKING
OF THE MODERN MIND*

Shaw *knew* he was one of the creators of modern consciousness and modern conscience. He told us so himself many times, and with perfect seriousness. An apt summary of both Shaw's historical position and self-appreciation is contained in a Max Beerbohm cartoon in which the jaunty young nineteenth-century Shaw offers some old clothes for sale to the great European critic Georg Brandes standing behind the counter as "a merchant of ideas."

"What'll you take for the lot?" asks Brandes.

"Immortality," says Shaw.

Brandes protests: "Come, I've handled those goods before! Coat, Mr. Schopenhauer's; waistcoat, Mr. Ibsen's; Mr. Nietzsche's trousers—"

To which Shaw blandly replies, "Ah, but look at the patches."

It is perfectly apparent that Shaw would not have been nonplussed either if Brandes had also referred to some other articles of clothing such as, shirt belonging to Samuel Butler, shoes borrowed from Karl Marx, and gloves and hat from Lamarck and Bergson. It is my suspicion that Shaw would have resented only an attribution of "cummerbund from Freud," since Shaw preferred moral passion to any other kind (his plays were once called "as unemotional as a mushroom"), and since he placed Economics above Eros as the source of good and evil, happiness and misery. And this reflection reminds me that he would have winced at some such phrase as "collar worn by Darwin" unless assured that the collar symbolized strangulation and was being rightly discarded, for Shaw was the sworn enemy of "Social Darwinism." The Darwinian struggle for existence was anathema to the intensely combative Shaw, who once proposed to revise the rules of tennis and penalize players who hit the ball too hard to be successfully returned by their opponents. The Darwinian doctrine of the "survival of the fittest," so sacred to old-line Victorian Liberals that they frowned on social legislation, was altogether abhorrent to this "fittest of the fit" who was in danger, indeed, of carrying survival to excess until he died of a fall in his ninety-fourth year.

* From *College English* (April, 1962). [Although certain observations and judgments in this essay are similar to ones cited in "Saint George and the Dragons" (in *The Theatre in Our Times,* Crown Publishers, Inc., 1954) and related essays, their effectiveness in the present context is such that they have been left intact. *Ed.*]

631

Considering his virtuosity as a writer of comedies, which he appreciated even more than his audiences did at the time, Shaw declared in an early volume (*Three Plays for Puritans*), "I am a natural-born mountebank"; and Shaw was undoubtedly a born showman and devotee of pyrotechnical displays. But he was also a born preacher, and he was not in the least exaggerating when he declared as early as his 1893 Preface to *Mrs. Warren's Profession,* "I have spared no pains to make known that my plays are built to induce not voluptuous reverie but intellectual interest. . . ." Shaw, however, found it possible to reconcile his pedagogical and histrionic inclinations in the same person and the same works. In this achievement, more perhaps than in any other, lay his power as a literary and dramatic genius. And he did not truly do justice to it when he proclaimed, as he was wont to do, that he merely made Mountebank Shaw serve the sermonizing Preacher Shaw. He could advance this estimate of himself well enough, and sometimes brilliantly, for no one writing English could sustain a half-truth with more verbal skill.

Thirty years later, with the world floundering in the economic depression of the 1930's, we find him insisting, in the Preface to his aptly titled political drama *On the Rocks,* that "All great Art and Literature is propaganda." I say that Shaw did not do justice to himself in representing his art as the handmaiden of preachment, because it was often in his preachment that he found his art, as in *Major Barbara, Heartbreak House,* and *Man and Superman.* It is certainly impossible to say with respect to his plays that one side of him was the reformer and the other side the comedian; or that one side of him was the thinker and the other side the artist. Many of his most memorable lines and effective conceits, on the contrary, were inseparable from his social convictions or hopes, his will to teach and his will to create being often the same thing. What Shaw's "Serpent" says in *Back to Methuselah* applies to his best writing and explains why his work has dated so much less than the plays of his contemporaries from Pinero to John Galsworthy: ". . . imagination," says the Serpent, "is the beginning of creation. You imagine what you desire; you will what you imagine; and at last you create what you will."

Shaw the thinker and Shaw the artist are one and the same person. His tracts, of course, deserve a historian's consideration and can stand examination; and in their turn of phrase they too reflect his lively intelligence and talent for language. But he was not at all unique in grinding out programs of social legislation, denunciations of capitalistic laissez-faire, and unorthodox views on church, state, and economics. In retrospect, the content of the purely sociological and political writings may even seem quite outmoded if for no other reason than that the moderate social program of Shaw and his late-Victorian associates was in large part adopted and made the law of the land. Besides, the program was tame from the start, even if Shaw's rhetoric was often, fortunately, unbridled. At the height of his political career as a stump speaker, London vestryman, and spokesman for the Fabian Society, founded in 1884, Shaw was committed to practical policies distinctly more evolutionary than revolutionary. With Sidney Webb, the tireless civil servant and statistician, Sidney Olivier, later the English Governor of Jamaica and Secretary of State for India, Graham Wallas, and (later) H. G. Wells, Shaw was the representative of a reformist group that picked the right label when it called itself the Fabian Society. Its program for socialization and social reform was growlingly gradualist.

At the height of its prestige the Fabian Society scarcely reached a membership of 1,500, and its policy was wisely one of permeation of established political parties. Bluster as he might, the Shaw who engaged in politics proposed the manna of reform in the middle of the road while thundering Marxism on the left. In old age he once declared, "Karl Marx made a man of me," but in the course of his life he repudiated virtually all of Marx's economics and sociology. The young Shaw, moreover, concurred at least officially with his fellow Fabians when they called for patience with the historical process. Their slogan was, "For the right moment you must wait, as Fabius did, most patiently," earning the ironic retort of a member of the Socialist party who once said to them, "Comrades, we must not allow ourselves to be carried away by patience!"

This account of the Fabian Society hardly accords with our impression of Shaw, who lived on until 1950 and retained a reputation to the end of his days that was anything but suggestive of the temperament and mentality of civil servants, statisticians, and reliable sociologists. The Fabian picture is one thing; the Shaw who upset the applecart of middle-class society and recommended all sorts of public upheavals is another. What to make of Shaw became a problem as early as the 1890's when he distinguished himself as a dynamitard among music and drama critics and as a volatile and incalculable heretic among playwrights. He acquired a formidable reputation for irresponsibility while actually leading an exemplary life as the late-blooming husband of an Irish millionairess and as a hard-driving businessman in his dealings with publishers and stage producers. It was plainly his manner, more than his matter, that brought him both his notoriety and fame.

We may return then to the old clothes-and-patches theory of the Max Beerbohm cartoon, and we may end by endorsing its subject's insistence that the patches make a difference. Very much of a difference, indeed, which is tantamount to saying, as I have already done, that Shaw the thinker or maker of the modern mind is actually Shaw the *artist*. He is Shaw the essayist whose imaginative and satirical prose is the best in English after the prose of Jonathan Swift, and Shaw the playwright, for whom no peer can be found in English unless we return to the spacious stage of Queen Elizabeth and James I.

To the great variety of his interests Shaw added an impressive variety of insights and provocative presentations—the presentations of a master stylist, debater, orator, farceur, comedian, fantasist, and even poet. It is safe to say that he brought more zest to debate than any of his contemporaries in England, more eloquence to oratory, more vitality to farce (with the possible exception of Oscar Wilde), more wit to comedy and more poetry to the "play of ideas" than any of his contemporaries. Moreover, in Shaw's case the manner was the man himself, so that behind all his postures and poses there was a remarkable unity of passion, energy, and levity.

There is no other way to substantiate this contention than to examine the works themselves. A modest start can be made by reviewing in summary form Shaw's treatment of some of the tendencies, problems, and challenges he encountered at the turn of the century. We can set his treatment beside that normally accorded to some particular matter by Shaw's contemporaries and so observe the singularity of his temper.

We may start with Shaw's work as a critic of the drama and theatre, since this brings us to his main form of expression. It is important to observe, in the first place, that unlike many advanced drama critics of the late nineteenth century in Europe, Shaw was not impressed by realistic dialogue, realistic play construction, and realistic theatre convention. He certainly did not write for the Stanislavskian actor and director. The only realism he had any use for was neither structural nor scenic, but intellectual and psychological. He had the astuteness to observe how easy it was to make a show of superficial reality and yet *evade* reality, to make accuracy of detail a substitute for essential truth, to feign boldness by presenting an unconventional subject but scrupulously refrain from examining it. While virtually everyone in England was crowning Arthur Wing Pinero the laureate of dramatic realism on the strength of such "problem plays" as *The Second Mrs. Tanqueray* and *The Notorious Mrs. Ebbsmith,* Shaw was firing away at Pinero's pretensions to realism.

Shaw accused Pinero of presenting modern characters or problems and then employing shameless contrivances to reduce the action to banality and the meaning to commonplaceness. A case in point is *The Second*

Mrs. Tanqueray, in which Pinero was modern enough to start with the marriage of a Victorian gentleman to a woman with a past, and conventional enough to conclude with the failure of that marriage. In order to provide a conclusion so comforting to Victorian audiences, moreover, Pinero drew upon the same contrived plot-making that discredited the so-called well-made, but actually ill-made, plays of the century. No wonder Shaw declared that Pinero's formula for popular success consisted of presenting a situation and then running away from it. This policy was the pseudo-Ibsenism that had such a vogue in the English-speaking theatre. Shaw, who would have none of it and was clever enough to detect it behind all masquerades of verisimilitude, insisted that for a modern sensibility "an interesting play cannot in the nature of things mean anything but a play in which problems of conduct and character of personal importance to the audience are raised and suggestively discussed."

In attacking Pinero's realism at a time when even William Archer considered it a model of "playmaking," Shaw stood in the forefront of modern criticism. Pinero, to whom constant reference is made in Archer's classic manual on playwriting, is virtually forgotten today except for a few farces such as *The Magistrate* that possess theatrical liveliness.

It was plain that while the majority of Shaw's contemporaries were interested in "well-made" plays, Shaw was interested only in alive ones. And for him they could not really be alive unless they were provocative and constituted drama of ideas. This is important to our understanding of Shaw's own plays, too. If they belong to the genre of realism it is by virtue of their engagement to reality, chiefly by comprising a conflict of ideas, principles, ways of thinking, and ways of living. For the sake of reality, Shaw was always prepared to violate realistic structure and verisimilitude, to turn somersaults of the most farcical or fantastic kind, and to be arbitrary with his plot or to discard plot altogether.

He was ever ready to stop the overt action for a good discussion or good lecture, or even step out of the proscenium frame to harangue the audience in behalf of a relevant philosophy or sociology which is beyond, if not indeed antithetical to, the illusion achieved by plodding realists and the designers who provided scenic realism. And to serve the "reality principle" of social criticism Shaw also had no hesitation to curtail characterization, to color situations, and to invent a fantasy such as that of a Last Judgment in *The Simpleton of the Unexpected Isles* in which God removes all useless individuals, or of *Back to Methuselah,* in which the world is ruled by men who have willed themselves in some Lamarckian way into living many centuries, since little sense could be expected from the mere infants of sixty, seventy, or eighty who determine the fate of societies.

Shaw also availed himself of every freedom of comic invention or extravagance to overcome public indifference with provocative reversals of viewpoint, as in *Man and Superman,* in which Don Juan is turned into a paragon of virtue for whom the only passion worth having is "moral passion," and *Major Barbara,* in which Shaw maintained the cold-sober argument that all moral problems had their source in economics. In *Major Barbara,* the real benefactor of mankind, it is bizarrely argued, is none other than the munitions magnate Andrew Undershaft who builds the good society with the well-paid, well-housed, and well-entertained employees of his factory; moreover, Undershaft is perfectly willing to sell his dynamite for peaceful purposes or for the eradication of injustice if humanity should ever have sense enough to make proper use of his product.

Shaw, to sum up, took a view of dramatic art that was essentially theatrical rather than antitheatrical, provided true realism—that is, realism of content or idea—was well served. Mind and spirit carried him far beyond the provinciality of realism, which was already, by 1880, little more than the tired *avant-gard*ism of the nineteenth-century European bourgeoisie. So it happened that Shaw, who greatly enriched the realistic substance of the drama by bringing economics and sociological realities into the theatre and by turning the British drawing room into a forum, actually liberated the stage from the limitations of realism. He recalled the theatre to its classic and Elizabethan heritage of freedom from pica-yune illusionism; in other words, he drew close to the freedom of presentational as against the stringencies of representational art. In his own work, he turned to "musical form" in discussion drama, composing plays in the manner of a theme and variations; and he exercised his flair for opera in never hesitating to stop the action in favor of a verbal aria on some subject, which is a mode of drama, too, when competently managed, as old as Euripides and Aristophanes. Granville-Barker, in staging some of Shaw's early plays in London, was wont to remind the actors indeed that they *were* in an opera.

Shaw was surely in the vanguard of dramatic expression whether he championed a species of dialectical realism in becoming Ibsen's most fervid advocate in the eighties or anticipated the imaginative styles of twentieth-century dramatic art that favor theatricalism. (It is noteworthy that he made himself an ardent champion of O'Casey's expressionist anti-war drama *The Silver Tassie.*) We move backward with him to the theatricalist art of earlier ages and forward with him to the dramatic art of Pirandello, Giraudoux, and Brecht. And lest we be misled by his championship of Ibsen, let us observe that in many pieces on Ibsen and most notably in his Fabian Society Lectures, *The Quintessence of Ibsenism,* Shaw paid little attention to the outward and rather provincial realism of the Scandinavian pioneer. Shaw analyzed each play as early as 1891, when he delivered his lectures, in terms of its challenge and reversal of accepted beliefs, its paradoxes and contradiction of commonplace attitudes. Shaw's Ibsen is a fascinating dialectician and a veritable Robin Goodfellow of the realm of comedy who plays havoc with humdrum opinion and custom. And when Shaw ultimately arrived at a view of Ibsen's real achievement he made him not the father of external realism but of discussion drama or the "play of ideas." Beginning with *A Doll's House,* Ibsen, according to Shaw, created a new form of drama by introducing a new movement into it.

Estheticism was one of the recognized ways of revolting against nineteenth-century laissez-faire industrialism and materialism. The Pre-Raphaelite movement, the agitation of Ruskin and William Morris, and the Yellow Book estheticism of Oscar Wilde, Aubrey Beardsley and others in England, the movement of the "decadents" and "symbolists" across the English Channel—these and other art-for-art's sake phenomena of the turn-of-the-century could not but be noticed and in some way or other reflected by Shaw, who was equally conscious of art and sociology. And for William Morris especially, Shaw always expressed the highest regard. Against Philistine attacks on art and artists Shaw was indeed ever watchful. He was one of the few Englishmen to remain well disposed toward Wilde after his prison sentence. He wrote a vigorous defense of art against the allegations of Max Nordau that modern art was decadent and tended to be a manifestation of disease. Shaw's defense was the brilliant essay *The Sanity of Art.*

Yet Shaw's estheticism was radically different from that of most of his contemporaries or successors, and here too his originality and force are apparent. In the first place, he emphatically rejected the doctrine of art for art's sake. He rejected just as categorically the nihilistic or negativistic tendencies that have characterized estheticism from the 1890's to our own times, from the poet-drunkards and suicides of the turn of the century to the beatniks of the midcentury, from the works of Huysmans to the works of Samuel Beckett. In the very depths of Shaw's disillusionment in 1932, in his play *Too True to Be Good,* in which his clergyman-hero mouthpiece, Aubrey, declared that the Western world was "damned beyond Salvation," Shaw made Aubrey conclude with a ringing disavowal of negativism. "Is No enough?" asks Shaw's desperate clergyman, and replies, "For a boy, yes; for a man never. . . . I must preach and preach no matter how late the hour and how short the day . . ."; to which Shaw the chronic activist added a postscript reading, "The author, though himself a professional talkmaker, does not believe that the world can be saved by talk alone."

For Shaw, art was an act of liberation from materialistic interests, a release of the spirit, and, at the turn of the century, a weapon against Victorian Philistinism in general. He defended the right of free expression fiercely and fought British censorship. He drew that censorship down on himself indeed, most notably in the case of *Mrs. Warren's Profession.* He championed Wagner in England, especially with his pamphlet *The Perfect Wagnerite,* published in 1898. But it was Wagner the social revolutionist, as reconstituted into a semi-Marxist and Shavian artist, that Shaw championed him, interpreting *The Ring of the Nibelungs* as a drama of the overthrow of the old order and the triumph of the heroic human spirit. It was possible then for Shaw to give his allegiance almost equally to Mozart, his favorite composer, and to Wagner, his favorite musical cause. And particularly bracing was Shaw's view of the true artist as an unusually strong and independent, supremely *healthy,* individual even behind a mask of frailty and a cloud of alienation and loneliness. Nothing contrasts more sharply with the romantic idealization of the artist as an easily wilted "blue" flower in vogue during the 1890's and Shaw's portrait of Marchbanks, the boy-artist in *Candida,* written in 1893. Marchbanks may delude others and even himself, for a time, that he is a weakling, but to a perceptive "womanly woman" such as Candida he is compact of strength precisely because he is a poet at heart; he remains unimpressed by domestic felicity, refuses to submit to family authority, and is willing to learn to live without happiness.

Shaw put the matter beautifully in a letter he sent at the turn of the century to the Ibsenite actress Janet Achurch. He wrote her: "I realize the full significance of the singular fate which led me to play with all the serious things of life and to deal seriously with all its plays." To be *oneself* and at the same time labor in full knowledge of the fact that we are all members of each other was Shaw's most insistent thought on the privilege of being an artist in society. I believe that the visionary Mrs. George, speaking in a trance in Shaw's discussion play *Getting Married,* speaks for Shaw himself when she declares: "I've been myself, I've not been afraid of myself. And at last I have *escaped from myself,* and am become a voice for them that are afraid to speak, and a cry for the hearts that break in silence."

Inevitably with Shaw we end up—or nearly end up—with his involvement with the social conflicts and expectations and with the views on numerous specific issues such as feminism and social reform that agitated the world of his youth in the 1880's (Shaw, it may be hard to realize, was born in 1856), of his maturity before World War I, and of his old age. Characteristically, he embraced the fashion in ideas with a difference, and gave these the stamp of his individuality while employing them in some provocative synthesis of contradictions and paradoxes. For Shaw, who was one of the least ambiguous of modern authors, was also one of the most ambivalent, and we have owed much of his provocativeness and artistry to his ambivalences.

For one thing, we have owed to them his capacity for writing comedy that is serious and serious drama that is comic. And the duality of his temperament gave us both his magnificent anger and superb geniality, his zeal for reform and genuine aversion to physical aggression, well expressed in his late revision of Shakespeare's *Cymbeline,* in which Imogen says—in, alas, bad verse—

> Oh, do not make me laugh.
> Laughter dissolves too many resentments,
> Pardons too many sins.

To this Iachimo replies,

> And saves the world
> A many thousand murders.

The He-Ancient in *Back to Methuselah* also recognizes the potency of laughter when he declares, concerning the will to longevity, that "Like all revolutionary truths, it began as a joke." One of the physicians in *The Doctor's Dilemma* also scores well for Shaw in saying, "Life does not cease to be funny when people die any more than it ceases to be serious when people laugh."

In specific cases, moreover, we find Shaw gloriously at work in the fine, and difficult, art of reconciling contradictions. We find him, for example, an ardent feminist, yet a blithe satirist of turn-of-the-century feminist fads and extravagances in so early a piece as *The Philanderer.* We find him urging war on the Victorian ideal of femininity or feminine dependency in the 1890's; and right up to the plays written after 1920, from *Saint Joan* to *The Millionairess,* he persists in glorifying the *unfeminine* woman. Yet how warmly he writes of Joan, and how constantly he

creates characters who are marvelous mother-surrogates while also flourishing as clever and sophisticated women of the world. We need only
glance at the marvellous portrait Shaw gave us in Candida, who is both
mother-image and minx, loyal wife and flirt, housekeeper and sockmender
and yet a supremely intelligent person as well. And how neatly and
perceptively he reverses norms and yet rights them in the long run, so
that Candida remains a loyal wife equally for unconventional and natural (or, if you will, conventional) reasons. Shaw, we may say, was progressive in his espousal of feminism in the 1880's and progressive, too,
in going *beyond* feminism in the 1890's.

Shaw's variations on the themes of love and sex are too many to
consider here. It is especially noteworthy, however, that he protested
equally against the Victorian repressive attitude and the post-Victorian
permissive one. Both seemed to him mere obsessiveness with sex when
the real problem was to avoid all forms of enslavement, including enslavement to sex, and all excuses for the evasion of social reality. Unlike the
run-of-the-mill opponent of Victorian prudery, Shaw endorsed progress
in the relations between the sexes as a means toward achieving freedom
from voluptuousness for the sake of progress in *all* relations. And with
this in mind he undertook to modify evolutionary theory itself. He could
not be satisfied with the established disbelief in the inheritance of acquired
traits any more than he could believe that evolution had come to an
end. Annexing nineteenth-century evolutionary theory to his social idealism and adopting pseudoscientific vitalism as a credo, Shaw endorsed
the Lamarckian theory of the inheritance of acquired characteristics as
a necessary assurance that man could progress as a species; and with that
other philosophical evolutionist Nietzsche, though without the latter's
advocacy of "the will to power" as a dynamic factor. Shaw reposed hope
in the coming of the superman. Humanity, as he came to know it, was
a race made up largely of duffers, and what was especially distressing
to him was man's failure as a political animal. But Shaw consoled himself with the reflection that "We have no reason to believe that we are
the Creator's last word."

Shaw, noting the unreliability of social progress, the failures of
parliamentary democracy to which he devoted two plays after World
War I (*The Apple Cart* and *On the Rocks*), and concluding that "every
technical qualification for doing good is a technical qualification for
doing evil as well"—Shaw growing impatient with the inertia of the
masses and the flabbiness of their elected representatives and misleaders,
tended to pin his hopes more and more on self-propelled leaders in whom

he saw the superior beings who had thus far appeared among men only as sports of nature. Around this faith he was apt to spin some of his most provocative plays and vivid characterizations before and after World War I. The Caesar of *Caesar and Cleopatra* is the superman as political leader; Undershaft is the superman as industrialist; Joan of Arc is the superman (or "superwoman") as saint. The eagerness with which Shaw believed or *wanted to believe* in savior-heroes who overleap the barriers of moral sloth and general mediocrity ultimately deceived him. It betrayed him into a kinder view of Mussolini, Hitler, and Stalin than his intelligence should have permitted. In this respect he was almost pathetically a man of the divided and self-betrayed modern mind. Shaw was touchingly aware in the famous epilogue to *Saint Joan* that simple humanity was not yet ready for its saints. He could not but become aware that simple humanity was not yet ready for any other species of superman. He was less inclined to realize that the supermen who arose in the shape of the Caesars, Napoleons, and Undershafts of the world were not necessarily ready for simple humanity.

Shaw, like so many other intellectuals of his time, was also tripped up in the long run by his faith in collectivism. Apparently, it did not occur to him sufficiently that society might manifest a unified effort at a frightful sacrifice of life and liberty. He also evinced an exaggerated trust in economics as the basis of human happiness and advancement. But we can never be fair to Shaw's creative intelligence by measuring his genius by the errors of the amateur sociologist, errors he shared with many other makers of the modern mind. In speaking of Shaw we must ultimately conclude with a proper acknowledgment of Shaw the "poet" —the visionary who refused to accept limits for the human race, the believer in the possibility of a creative will ideally capable of producing perfect men in a perfected society irradiated by right reason and good will. In this faith there could be no antinomies or conflicts of reason and instinct, rationalism and religiousness, individualism and collectivism, truth and poetry.

Perhaps Shaw speaks best through one of his most attractive masks, that of the unfrocked Irish priest Father Keegan of *John Bull's Other Island*. Asked by the pragmatical Englishman Broadbent "What is it like in your dreams?", Father Keegan declares that he dreams of "a country where the State is the Church and the Church the people; three in one and one in three." This ideal state is "a commonwealth in which work is play and play is life; three in one and one in three. It is a godhead in which all life is human and all humanity divine; three in one and one in three."* And Shaw's heretical mystic reminds the skeptical materialist that "Every dream is a promise in the womb of time." In nothing more is Shaw so notably a man of the twentieth century as in this trust in the desirability and inevitability of progress as well as in his perilous impatience with delay after his initial faith in gradualist reform. For all his brilliant show of hard-headedness, Shaw was also at one with the post-Renaissance Western spirit in sharing its dominantly Rousseauist romanticism, its perfectibility-worship, its "Faustian" restlessness. In virtually all his work he also gave us a distinctively nineteenth- and twentieth-century translation, into by now perhaps overfamiliar social and political terms of the words of Leonardo da Vinci, who, standing brilliantly poised between the modern and the medieval world, concluded that "Every artist has two subjects: Man and the hopes of his soul."†

* [Also quoted in the concluding paragraph of "Fabianism and the British Playwright" (in *The Theatre in Our Times*, p. 432) to point up the weaknesses of Shaw's contemporaries and successors in vitalizing their dramatic dreams and plans for a better world. *Ed.*]

† [Professor Gassner intended to add a postscript to this noble sentiment. His marginal notation reads thus: "P.S. This is lost in modernistic *avant-garde* drama—no wonder Adamov changed. But cf. *Marat/Sade*, etc., & Ionesco protested in *Rhinoceros*." The last comment obviously refers to the stubborn refusal of the elemental antihero of that play to join the throng of humans who gleefully metamorphise into rhinoceri. Berenger's final words: "I'm the last man left, and I'm staying that way till the end. I'm not capitulating." (From *Plays*, London: Calder, 1962, p. 107.)

In *"Avant-garde:* Real or fancied?," also in this section, the reasons for change are explored. *Ed.*]

POETRY IN THE THEATRE*

Everyone concerned with literature and with practical theatre sooner or later talks about poetic drama. Like the weather in Mark Twain's familiar quip, everybody talks about it, but not many people do much of anything about it. There are many reasons for this in our times, particularly in America—and there are many problems.

Among these, two problems are, of course, fundamental. One is a lack of talent for *poetry* on the part of workaday playwrights. The other is a want of talent for theatre on the part of most poets.

And this is patently deplorable for the theatre needs—greatly needs— poetry; and the poet, in view of the tendency of modern poetry to become esoteric or uncommunicable, as well as in view of the smallness of its public, needs the theatre.

What can be done about the matter is a question of mutual concern to playwrights and poets, of leaders of the theatre and of guardians, friends, and practitioners of poetry.

There was a time when there was little or no need to consider this question. It is a familiar fact that, before the modern period, throughout all the great ages there was no strict demarcation between the two genres, poetry and drama. A nation's greatest playwrights were often also its greatest poets—Shakespeare in England, Racine in France, Goethe and Schiller in Germany, not to mention Aeschylus and Sophocles in classic Greece. And, *vice versa,* nearly all poets were powerfully drawn to the dramatic medium. This was often the case whether or not there was a theatre worthy of the poet's efforts. Thus, Milton wrote his great poetic tragedy, *Samson Agonistes,* solely for reading, while the frivolities of Restoration comedy were nearing their peak. Shelley, Keats, and Byron, and later also Tennyson, Swinburne, and Browning wrote poetic drama, while the commercial theatre in nineteenth-century England was mired in melodrama and farce.

The sharp division of poetry and drama—largely a division of sensibility on the part of the public upon which I cannot dilate here—is essentially a middle-class phenomenon. But nobody of any consequence to either poetry or dream has been happy about this divorce except possibly for about a decade toward the end of the late century when Ibsen and

---

* An address delivered before the Poetry Society of America, on January 20, 1966.

643

others bent upon establishing a theatre of mundane realism adopted lean, modern prose as the suitable medium.

One obvious resort, on the part of the poet, was to employ the dramatic form without the practical constraints of the theatre—that is, without expecting a stage production; at least not without considerable adaption, as in the case of Tennyson's *Beckett,* when the Victorian actor-manager Sir Henry Irving adapted it and played it with apparent success.

Thomas Hardy faced this gulf between his soaring imagination and the turn-of-the-century theatre when he published his epic drama *The Dynasts,* in which he attempted to encompass the entire Napoleonic age and the theme of universal destiny. In creating celestial choruses and an entire spirit-world, he hoped he could count, in the words of Coleridge, on "that willing suspension of disbelief for the moment which constitutes poetic faith." But he was certain that he could not count on the theatre to secure that faith, or even to try to do so from its audience in the case of so long, so unwieldy, and so demanding a work as *The Dynasts.* And he was assuredly correct before the age of Max Reinhardt stage pageants and Cecil B. De Mille film spectaculars. Hardy therefore declared *The Dynasts* to be intended simply, as he put it, "for mental performance" and wondered whether mental performance alone may not eventually be the fate of all drama other than that of "contemporary or frivolous life."

In entertaining such a view, he was not altogether at variance from even so experienced a writer for the stage as Ibsen, who first aroused attention with *Peer Gynt, Brand,* and *Emperor and Galilean* as published books rather than as performed plays.

But Hardy's view, like that of other ambitious poets who placed no reliance on the stage as a medium, represents a despair of stage production which unquestionably tended to separate the published from the spoken word. And this separation has been detrimental to both poetry and drama.

An alternative to this defeatest attitude appeared about the same time as *The Dynasts* and was characterized by a resolve to write verse drama for the stage at all costs. The leader of this endeavor in England was Stephen Phillips. His dramatic verse was conventional and slightly archaic, which did not prevent one of his blank-verse plays, *Paolo and Francesca,* published in 1897, from reaching its eighteenth edition of 1905. But so far as the theatre is concerned, the effect was nugatory.

This turn-of-the-century poetic movement in England was a failure; there is no blinking of this fact; and in the American theatre it was worse than a failure. The one small triumph that still holds on the stage is properly Edna St. Vincent's *Aria da Capo.* The results were not particularly abundant elsewhere either. Little came of Yeats's effort to make the Abbey Theatre of Dublin, which he helped to establish, a repository of poetic drama. Instead, the Abbey Theatre turned first toward peasant realism with the chief work of Lady Gregory and Synge; then to urban realism with the early masterpieces of O'Casey in the 1920's.

In Italy, there was D'Annunzio, and all that came to be remembered for signal merit out of his perfervid romantic output is one play, hardly known in the English-speaking world—namely, *The Daughter of Jorio*. And in France the verse drama came to rest on the reputation of a single writer—Edmond Rostand, and on two of his plays *Cyrano de Bergerac* and *L'Aiglon*.

Was the failure of this neoromantic movement justified? To some extent it was—because it represented efforts in the main to turn back the clock and retreat to the past. Moreover, too frequently the poetry was applied (or shall we say "appliquéed"?) on to a standard realistic form. The poetry was not often the *essence* of the work but the *varnish* on it. That was perhaps not the chief source of the difficulty. Poets in English as redoubtable as T. S. Eliot and Archibald MacLeish took note of this defect. They blamed much of the failure on the writers' conventional reliance on blank verse, which had long lost the vitality it had possessed in Shakespeare's and John Webster's time.

For dramatic art, a continual flow of the five-foot measure had a monotony, a soporific regularity, and, worse still, a prettiness not consonant with the high passionateness of memorable drama *and* poetry.

Percy Hammond, a formidable newspaper drama critic of the 1920's and early 1930's, once warned producers of old-fashioned musical comedies that invariably had a chorus line of bare-legged, high-kicking girls to please remember that the knee was a *joint* and not an *ornament*. Would-be writers of verse drama needed to be reminded that poetry in the theatre was also a functional thing and not a glossy decoration.

Nevertheless, so great was the need of the theatre for poetry that even ornamental verse continued to be welcome as a release from the drabness and the inarticulateness of commonplace realism. At least popular success was earned from time to time when the playwright's glossy work had a strong dramatic underpinning.

This was notably the case in the plays of Maxwell Anderson, who may not have been much of a poet, although he published a collection of verse early in his career, but who proved himself a vivid and vigorous playwright in a dozen plays, beginning with his war play *What Price Glory?* in 1924, written in pungent prose dialogue.

Success also attended ornamental verse drama whenever an occasion for the ornamental writing was intrinsic to the theme and tone of the work. This was conspicuously the case when Christopher Fry made an art of comic and serio-comic preciosity in the early post-World War II plays *A Phoenix Too Frequent, The Lady's Not for Burning,* and *Venus Observed.*

It was in his later serious plays that Fry courted the most trouble, when he apparently decided that it was time for a middle-aged playwright to advance mightily beyond the poetic precincts of *Love's Labour's Lost* preciosity if he was to become a significant dramatist.

Anderson's vogue as a poetic playwright came to an end by 1950; Fry's by 1960. Anderson's reputation came under severe critical scrutiny, until he came to be regarded as a neoromanticist whose greatest success was won with resuscitations of Elizabethan drama in rather watery verse. Christopher Fry's stock has also dipped sharply. In fact, the entire movement toward poetic drama in England has waned. It has been supplanted by prose drama, whether realistic in the sociological manner of Arnold Wesker, or somewhat symbolic and Kafkaesque in the manner of Harold Pinter. Once more a high promise has been left blighted and desiccated on the altar of art.

Are the poets likely to be deterred from renewing their efforts for a new harvest? Not a bit! Last season's outstanding new play in the opinion of normally severe critics was Robert Lowell's *The Old Glory,* or rather *Benito Cereno,* the main item of a double bill at the American Place Theatre, subsidized by the Rockefeller Foundation to foster new drama. The present season's outstanding play thus far is the poet William Alfred's folk-drama of Irish life in Brooklyn, *Hogan's Goat,* which contains long passages in verse. And the American Place Theatre has recently announced an *Agamemnon* drama by him, published some years ago by Knopf and refurbished for a production.

Is the criticism leveled earlier in this address really invalidated by these examples of laudable obstinacy on the part of the poets? (And we must not forget in this connection Archibald MacLeish's *J.B.,* which became a hit on Broadway after its Yale Drama School production, and which won the Pulitzer Prize several years ago.)

The answer to this question must be equivocal. Many will question the validity of the success of *J.B.* as poetic drama; and surely the best, the most authentic poetry in the play comes straight out of the King James Version of *The Book of Job.* Everyone will agree that, in the theatre, the least effective passages of *Hogan's Goat* were those in which the verse form was most apparent. Where it was most apparent it seemed most obtrusive—a fact that should make us understand why T. S. Eliot considered that he was making progress as a playwright—after *Murder in the Cathedral*—in proportion to the indistinguishability of his poetry from prose to dialogue, a contradiction in terms, it would seem, and an error in judgment on Eliot's part, in the opinion of literary critics.

But is this niggling report all that can be said for nearly eight decades of a struggle for poetic drama in Europe and the United States? It would be a discouraging prospect if this were so.

Fortunately this is not the case, and the main reason is that the theatre itself—theatre old as well as new, Eastern as well as Western—has given the poets working in the drama lessons and provocations leading to new dramatic forms. To put it briefly: the modern or, if you will, the *modernistic* theatre and the classic exotic theatre of the East have set examples of nonrealistic, strongly stylized kinds of drama for which the poet's imagination and feeling for literary style are ideally suited. In this kind of more or less formal theatre, the poet's talent operates in close articulation with theatre itself—that is, with the theatre's scenic effects, its instrumental music, dance, songs, sound effects, masks, and so on. The cue has been given by the total art of the theatre for the creation or adaptation of poetic forms, so that poetry need not be plastered on to a story, need not be mere ornament but must become functional. The transformation has been proved possible in numerous fascinating ways, and modern poets have availed themselves of these possibilities to a degree. And so have playwrights who are not good poets in verse but were truly poets of the theatrical imagination like Strindberg, O'Neill, Pirandello, O'Casey, and Thornton Wilder.

Jean Cocteau gave a name to this use of theatrical imagination that extends from the most external theatrical stage effects to a radical transformation of dramatic structures. Included among these are cutting back in time from one scene to another and other elements of anematic technique, and the use of choruses, loudspeakers, mime, and dance as means of dramatic accentuation. Cocteau called all this *poésie de théâtre*—"poetry of the theatre"—in contrast to simple verbal poetry.

How does this relate to the poet of language, and particularly to the poet whose medium is verse and not poetic prose, which often accommodates itself more easily to naturalistic dramatic form than does verse, since people don't normally speak metrically?

One may cite the example of William Butler Yeats, who upon coming under the influence of Ezra Pound, adapted the Japanese Noh-play form of mime, dance, and ritual to Celtic myth and legend. The result was a series of remarkable short plays, beginning with his *Four Plays for Dancers,* radically different from those romantic plays of his youth that were more poetical than poetic. The effect is in most cases one of formal ritual, even when the sense of the content is as *modern* as Freudian, if you will, as it is in *A Full Moon in March.*

Another example was set by Bertolt Brecht in his development of so-called "epic" drama, which culminated in half a dozen of the century's most original dramatic works, including the two remarkable parable plays *The Good Woman of Setzuan* and *The Caucasian Chalk Circle.*

In Brecht's work, poetry came to be used as a means of distancing the dramatic events for the purpose of sharpening their significance instead of being conventionally employed to intensify emotion. He called this pro-cedure an "alienation effect," making an experience remote, strange, or alien enough to enable us to stand apart from persons or situations and evaluate or, if need be, judge them. To this end, interpolations of bal-ladry and song, recitatives, and even arias could be used freely, calling for the collaboration of such effective modern composers as Kurt Weill, Hanns Eisler, and Paul Dessau.

This technique has won adherents since the mid-thirties in both the British and American theatre, beginning with W. H. Auden and Stephen Spender in England, and Marc Blitzstein in the United States. A third, and to us, more familiar employment and, shall we say, deployment of poetry has been best represented by T. S. Eliot, beginning with his re-ligious pageant *The Rock* and developing in *Murder in the Cathedral, Family Reunion, The Cocktail Party, The Confidential Clerk,* and *The Elder Statesman.* In the most striking of these plays, Eliot used choruses, such as those of the women of Canterbury in *Murder in the Cathedral* and the sparser recitations of the family in *Family Reunion;* Christian ritual or touches of ritual, notably at the end of the second act of *The Cocktail Party* in the "libation" for Celia heading for martyrdom in Africa as an Anglican nun. They are "the words" for those who go upon a journey, formally spoken by the three mystical guardians, Reilly, Alex, and Julia:

> Protector of travellers
> Bless the Road
>
> Watch over her in the desert
> Watch over her in the Mountain
> Watch over her in the labyrinth
> Watch over her in the quicksand.

In viewpoint, the three men whom I have singled out as leaders of the endeavor to create modern poetic drama in our century—all three now deceased—were radically divergent. Yeats's orientation was essentially pagan, Brecht's Marxist or quasi-Marxist, and Eliot's Christian or, more specifically, Anglo-Catholic.

But they (and others one could mention, notably Lorca) had one important attribute in common—namely a transformation or adaptation of dramatic form in the service of both modern theatre and modern poetry. And, with characteristic differences in each case, they used, if they did not indeed create, modern verse forms rather than regular conventional blank verse, and modern poetic idiom. This is in agreement with T. S. Eliot's conclusion when he wrote: "What we have to do is to bring poetry into the world in which the audience lives, and to which it returns, when it leaves the theatre. . . ."

Poetry for them was not a varnish but an alembic—or, if I may mix metaphors for this occasion, not an *ornament* but a *joint!* This was their way of achieving, whenever they were successful, "that vivid single impression left on the mind" or that "true imaginative unity" perhaps approaching "the unity of lyrical effect" that, as my old friend and your dedicated executive secretary Mr. Charles Wagner reminded me, Walter Pater defined as the ultimate ideal of the poetic drama.[1]

---

[1] *On Shakespeare's English Kings*, 1889.

FORMS OF MODERN DRAMA[1]

Whoever undertakes a brief discussion of the drama must be forgiven if he longs for the relative simplicity of the more autonomous forms of literature. He must take into account the interaction of the literary and theatrical elements in dramatic art. He must acknowledge the contributions of acting and stagecraft to the total effect of the play—an effect that is, moreover, always variable since it is dependent upon the variable character of the performing artists and the audience. The calculus of dramatic criticism must consider how the text of the play is projected and inevitably transmuted by the performance and how the audience responds to it. In considering changes in dramatic style and form—and sensibility is obviously involved in such changes—the total experience is of paramount importance, and this is to be derived from the theatre rather than from the printed plays alone.

Concerning that experience, so immense in its totality that even the detailed chronicles of the stage barely do it justice, we may generalize only to a limited extent. We may observe, first of all, that the relationship of the modern drama and the theatre has been a fluctuating one. Sometimes, as in the case of Becque, Ibsen, and Tolstoy when he composed *The Power of Darkness* in 1886, the playwright was in advance of the theatre, which failed to realize his intentions. The Comédie Française, for example, clung to an antiquated tradition of romantic posturing when it gave its first production of Becque's realistic masterpiece, *La Parisienne,* as late as 1890; and *The Sea Gull* was staged so disastrously in 1896, before the advent of the Moscow Art Theatre, that Chekhov intended to give up playwriting. And Strindberg wrote expressionist drama at least a dozen years before there was any expressionist theatre anywhere in Europe. Sometimes, on the contrary, the real pioneers have been the stage directors and designers; Antoine, Stanislavsky, and Gordon Craig were at first well in advance of most of the playwrights of their time. Still, an adjustment between the drama and the stage occurred soon enough in most instances for us to discuss changes in perspective as though they affected playwriting and play production more or less equally and simultaneously.

Notice may also be taken of the relativity of public response. Different audiences in different countries reacted with different degrees of interest and antipathy to such works as *A Doll's House* and *Ghosts*; and the same

[1] From *Comparative Literature* (Spring, 1955).

public that considered plays such as these too venturesome was likely to find them too staid within a decade or two. Even so, however, distinctions can be validly drawn between dominant public attitudes conducive or not conducive to a coherent view of man's character and situation. It is possible to distinguish Victorian and post-Victorian, nineteenth- and twentieth-century, viewpoints and sensibility in the theatre. And there are strong reasons for identifying conspicuous changes in viewpoint or sensibility with fairly well-defined, indeed altogether familiar, transformations of dramatic form and style.

The perspectives of modern drama can be most conveniently considered under the categories of realistic and antirealistic theatre. This is the case notwithstanding the overlapping of different types of drama in any country's or any season's theatre, and despite the mingling of different styles in the same play, as in Hauptmann's *Hannele* or Miller's *Death of a Salesman*. The realistic and naturalistic drama incorporated one view of reality, and the departures from realistic dramaturgy tended to incorporate or at least reflect a different view. It is not without reason that the realistic drama came to be identified with a positivist and liberal or reformist nineteenth-century *Weltanschauung,* and that the postnaturalistic styles were associated with deterioration of this outlook, with protest or rebellion against its complacencies, and with a general sense of *fin de siècle* and twentieth-century alienation.

A hundred years ago, the realistic drama and theatre were still embryonic, but by the end of the last century dramatic realism had become so firmly crystallized that it is still considered the norm in playwriting and play production. Little more than half a century ago, dramatic realism frightened moralists of every denomination. Today the realistic style is more likely to be considered the placid, if not indeed stodgy, method of presenting a situation and idea. The very nature of representational stage art expressed a concrete world picture and centered the individual in it. It is well known that the rise of dramatic realism was associated with the growth of stage illusionism. Action and scenery retreated behind the proscenium arch, becoming framed by the arch until the drama could be looked at as a picture and, finally, as a photograph. The sensibility of the nineteenth century favored every means of strengthening the illusion of environment; and climaxing the development of realistic scenery, there arose the "fourth-wall" convention, according to which the space enclosed by the proscenium arch was assumed to be a fourth wall separating the actor from the audience. The actor could even turn his back on the audience as if he were merely turning his back to a wall, and furniture might actually be placed against the footlight area. Representationalism became the ruling principle.

The effect on playwriting was inevitable. Prose dialogue became the standard medium of drama, and prose was deprived of all embellishment or rhetoric that could not be realistically motivated. Asides and soliloquies, which had been justifiable conventions in the stylized, nonrealistic theatres of the past, vanished as a convincing mode of providing information and expressing tension. Dramatic structure became less and less flexible as the drama became increasingly representational. The natural habitat of playwrights became the parlor, in which the dramatic action consisted of a few episodes. The use of solid settings also discouraged the multiscened playwriting romanticism had brought into vogue a century before. And dramatic action became especially concentrated in the practice of writers concerned with the conflicts of representative individuals involved in a fully explored and discussed situation. Ibsen became celebrated for starting the dramatic action of his realistic plays near their climax. Neoclassic unities returned to the late-nineteenth-century theatre under a dispensation far from neoclassic.

Significant in this concentration on painstakingly represented reality is the veritable passion for *detheatricalizing* dramatic art that seized the theatre. The realistic drama is the least theatrical form of drama developed in the Western theatre.

The pioneering realists and naturalists after 1870 drew a sharp distinction between uncontrived and contrived dramaturgy which still influences dramatic criticism and playwriting. They zealously distinguished realistic practice from the pseudorealism of the popular theatre even when it was journalistically concerned with "moral" or "social" problems in the manner of Dumas *fils*. They waged war on the so-called "well-made" play technique of Scribe, Dumas, and Sardou on the grounds that intrigue, coincidence, suspenseful situations, and striking exit and curtain lines were inconsistent with truth. "The nearer to theatre the further from life" became the ruling principle. When the naturalists led by Zola actually proposed to reduce form to a mere slice of life, they were being consistent, though without being particularly intelligent. As Malraux has said, "Artists build theories round what they would like to do, but they do what they can." Even the theatre's Zolaist disciples did not actually produce absolute "slices of life." But the *tranche de vie* ideal served as a deterrent to merely contrived dramaturgy and as a reminder that the drama should be brought as close to reality as possible.

Between 1880 and 1890 dramatic realism was fully developed and established on firm foundations of intellectual integrity. The term Ibsenism became synonymous with the modern spirit of inquiry and criticism. And it was, paradoxically, only then that outcries against the modern theatre created the impression that Ibsen and his followers were demoralizing society. That impression has not altogether vanished; a more moderate view, that the realists and naturalists reflected a demoralizing influence in society or culture, was recently well sustained by Joseph Wood Krutch in his Cornell University lectures, *"Modernism" in Modern Drama*.[2] Sociological and psychological presentations of characters and their problems did introduce a disturbing relativism into the modern dramatist's picture of man and society, as well as expose much that was distressing about both man and society. It cannot be denied, indeed, that the new realism of Ibsen, Strindberg, and Shaw did represent a corrosion of traditional certainties.

We should nevertheless refrain from confusing an unstable society with an anarchic one, and a state of flux with a state of disintegration. The new realism did not express a sense of disaster or even disorientation. Its tone was confident; its style, fundamentally lucid and consistent; its form, firm and distinct. And it has been, of course, a postulate of the liberal dispensation that it is possible to question or even destroy a convention without precisely exploding the world.

A large esthetic problem did arise in connection with the new antiheroic view of man's capacities and condition. High tragedy became rare. When tragic art appeared at all without the imitativeness of an *Elizabeth the Queen* or *Mary of Scotland,* it generally manifested itself in a mixed, adulterated form. The tragic sense became diminished by a sense of stalemate or attrition and by an interpretation of failure in terms of social or psychopathological causation. When the doctrine of determinism by nature of environment became fashionable, fate was robbed of its time-honored mystery and man of his traditional eminence.

• High tragedy, however, is not the whole of any vital dramatic enterprise, and the same deflationary sensibility which weakened tragic art favored the development of other, intermediate, forms of drama. We may observe this development in a modern sort of tragicomedy, or "dark" comedy, with as wide a range as that spanned by *Uncle Vanya* and *Juno and the Paycock*; in psychological drama, as exemplified by the realistic plays of Strindberg or by *A Streetcar Named Desire,* where we encounter a mélange of tragedy and pathology; in "group" drama such as *The Plough and the Stars*; and, mainly perhaps, in drama of discussion or the so-called play of ideas. The realistic sensibility of the modern theatre gave

[2] *"Modernism" in Modern Drama: A Definition and an Estimate* (Ithaca: Cornell University Press, 1953).

rise to a drama of the plateaus and valleys where a good deal of the destiny of men and society happens to be enacted.

Realism made the individual dimensional and substantial even while diminishing his stature, and dramatized his environment and milieu in the very process of challenging conventional beliefs and values. Among the major realists only Strindberg actually hewed close with some regularity to naturalistic determinism—this in his treatment of the irrationalism of sexuality and sex duel. But even his obsessed characters have too much vitality and individuality to be considered puppets. They also discuss their problems rather analytically, often very cogently. Ibsen, the most influential realist, actually made a cult of self-expression; and his greatest disciple was Shaw, who made volition the very cornerstone of his Lamarckian evolutionary doctrine. Both Ibsen and Shaw, indeed, had an abiding faith in the extraordinary individual. Ibsen, as Krutch has noted, "never shifts the burden of responsibility from the individual to 'social conditions' or economic pressures."[3] That later realists did shift the burden merely exemplifies the transformation of dramatic realism into an instrument of special pleading which came into vogue precisely at the time when antirealistic and antinaturalistic styles were most strongly challenged by new styles ranging from expressionism to so-called epic theatre. The morally responsible individual's potentialities and defects are the paramount subject of Ibsenism; and that this is the case is still understood by a latter-day Ibsen disciple such as Arthur Miller, although his ambivalence is obvious when he fails to make up his mind in *Death of a Salesman* whether Willy Loman or society is responsible for Loman's failure.[4] As for Shaw, it is generally recognized today that neither his Marxian views nor his Fabian activities deterred him from an ardent pursuit of the singular hero, if not indeed the superman, as political leader, manufacturer, artist, and saint in play after play written between *Man and Superman* and *Saint Joan*.

Not even the naturalist dogma of biological and social determinism could entirely banish the modern theatre's inclination to concentrate on individual situations and on characters shown in the round, as long as the playwrights refrained from symbolist, expressionist, or other modes of for-

---

[3] *Ibid.*, p. 39.

[4] I also find some ambivalence concerning individual and social responsibility in *Ghosts,* since Ibsen makes it plain that Mrs. Alving was conditioned by a "Victorian" education and later influenced by the views of the middle-class "Victorian" community exemplified by Parson Manders. But Ibsen does not allow her to beg the question of personal responsibility and brings her to a climactic rejection of the conventional values she had once accepted. Ibsen gave increasingly more weight to individual responsibility in the plays he wrote after *Ghosts*.

malist stylization; for both realistic playwriting and performance were modes of endowing the stage character with reality. The individual and his world retained some rationality, consistency, and dimension even in such depressing naturalist dramas as Hauptmann's *Drayman Henschel* and Gorky's *The Lower Depths*. In one respect, indeed, realism and naturalism actually enlarged the theatre's humanist orientation; for modern realism added individuality and attributed dignity to commoners to whom the older drama had generally afforded only secondary and comic roles.

Significantly, let me add, the naturalist was not infrequently sustained by a view that was fundamentally optimistic. Yes, society was in a turmoil or was undergoing a process of transformation, but the direction of the change held promise of improvement. Many of the characters in Hauptmann's first and callow naturalistic play, *Vor Sonnenaufgang,* are little better than brutes; but the concern and decision of Hauptmann's hero, Alfred Loth, based upon the dread of hereditary alcoholism, exemplifies a belief in the promise of eugenics. Although the machine-wrecking mob of *The Weavers* is thoroughly conditioned by economics and is blindly destructive, its conduct affirms one of the "four freedoms"—the freedom from want. This affirmation, along with an augury of social justice, was obviously foremost in the reaction of the Deutsches Theatre gallery audience at the première when the Social Democrat August Bebel led it in cheering the play and in singing stanzas of the weavers' song, "Bloody Justice." The affirmative view of *The Lower Depths* is memorable enough to be quoted. Satine attributes the failure of the would-be paraclete Luka to the fact that the well-intentioned pilgrim lied to the derelicts in the depths. "But," he concludes, "the man who is strong, who is his own master, who is free and does not have to suck his neighbors' blood—he needs no lies. Truth is the religion of the free man."[5] It is instructive to observe the contrasting negativism present in important social dramas of the expressionist movement, such as Toller's *Hinkemann* and Werfel's *Bocksgesang*—or, for that matter, present in O'Neill's "lower depths" naturalist-symbolist drama, *The Iceman Cometh,* written in 1919 when naturalism no longer possessed a viable career in the theatre.

Still, as previously noted, there were inherent limitations and contradictions in this essentially bourgeois classicism known as realism. It tended to become narrow, flat, and commonplace. It contradicted the very nature of dramatic art with its antitheatrical bias. And, above all, this classicism began to lose its social and intellectual basis in Western civilization. Inevitably, one antirealistic movement after another arose to offer a substi-

[5] John Gassner, ed., *A Treasury of the Theatre: From Henrik Ibsen to Arthur Miller* (New York: Simon and Schuster, Inc., 1951), p. 252.

tute dispensation. The history of the theatre since 1890 is mainly a history of these movements, of their promises and failures, and of the interest they engendered and the resistance they met. In each case we encounter some special view of reality as well as some special concept of dramatic art; the two parallel and sustain each other.

Realism and even naturalism survived, it is true, in pristine and de-based forms. They owe their survival to the present day partly to the failure of our century to develop a more generally satisfying dramatic form for exhibiting and exposing contemporary reality with some plausi-bility or recognizable particularity, and partly to the adaptability of the realistic and naturalistic styles. Program-making modernists have, in fact, invariably minimized the effectiveness with which realism managed to combine with folk speech to produce a naturalistic poetry—in the theatre of Synge and O'Casey, for example. And the modernists have also over-looked the many ways in which realistic playwriting from Ibsen's day to our own has been able to soften the hard outlines of argument, to avoid naturalistic clutter and utilize "selective realism" as a method, and to make discreet use of atmospheric effects and symbolism of the kind Ibsen was the first to employ in *The Wild Duck, Rosmersholm,* and *John Ga-briel Borkman.* Nevertheless, the progress of dramatic art since the 1890's has been largely identified with the antirealistic schools of theatre, while realism has been continually scorned and dismissed as an outmoded style.

A *fin-de-siècle* sensibility marked by esthetic flight characterized the first of the antirealistic movements. A twilight drama of shadows and symbols was introduced into the theatre by Maeterlinck and his adherents. Flight from the realists' world of social and intellectual conflict, if not in-deed from all worldliness, appeared in plays with medieval backgrounds such as Hofmannstahl's *Jedermann* and the celebrated Max Reinhardt spectacle *The Miracle.* And, finally, when symbolism was accommodated to "show business," it resulted in the composition of fairy-world drama in the manner of *Peter Pan* and *The Blue Bird.* The exacting adult world of an Ibsen, Strindberg, or a Shaw made way for the world of the child and the dreamer.

The Aristotelian conception of drama as the imitation of an action was not actually challenged by realists and naturalists, despite their strenu-ous war against mindless melodramas and specious plays of intrigue. But both the program and practice of symbolism tended to reject the primacy of action in the "symbolist" world they considered more real than work-aday reality because "inner experience" was allegedly suggestive of pro-found absolutes or mysterious universals. Significant are Maeterlinck's and Andreyev's theories of "static drama." For the former, writing in 1896, the ideal drama was to be found in the mind of an old man sitting in his armchair at night "giving unconscious ear to all the eternal laws that reign about his house . . . submitting with bent head to the presence of his soul and his destiny." For Maeterlinck, this notably inactive character represented "a deeper, more human, and more universal life" than the usual characters of the drama. And Andreyev, writing *A Letter on the Theatre* eighteen years later, ironically enough, at the beginning of World War I, declared that the true modern hero represented "human thought." "Life," wrote Andreyev, disregarding the machine age, "has gone within."

The idea of static drama was not achieved, except in very short plays such as *L'Intruse, Les Aveugles,* and *L'Intérieur,* and Maeterlinck himself soon abandoned, and later disavowed, his theory. But the symbolist movement in the theatre did tend to dissolve dramatic action in the very process of trying to deepen and universalize it. The individual became a shadowy figure, a state of mind, sometimes a mere symbol. For a time, Gordon Craig actually entertained the notion of replacing the living actor with a "super-marionette," since the human being—that is, the actor—introduces a disturbing factor in the stage director's and scenic artist's production design. But the "super-marionette" was an ideal upon which Craig and his disciples did not insist. It was sufficient to insist upon rigorous stylization of the actor's movements, speech, and gesture or, as Craig declared in 1911 in his influential book *On the Art of the Theatre,* upon the development of "a new form of acting consisting for the main part of symbolical gesture." The symbolist ideal of acting, although often enough modified in practice and actually fused with Stanislavskian "inner realism" by the great director Copeau, was indeed the first of several attempts to depersonalize acting and subordinate it to design. (An extreme was reached by the Russian director Meyerhold in his Soviet constructivist phase when he conceived acting as "bio-mechanics" and associated it with acrobatics; Parisian *avant-gard*ists led by Cocteau were particularly fascinated with the circus, to which they contributed ballet plays, music, and settings; and the *avant-garde* Russian director Tairov virtually treated stage directing for a time as a form of choreography and favored cubism in design.) Human nature, always a complex and exigent reality in the great ages of Western drama, became attenuated, if not indeed theoretically irrelevant, once the theatre's symbolists concentrated on spiritual essence, "beauty," and the power of design. The sense of environment, so important to the realistic theatre, also became irrelevant. A character was very likely to be lost in a mist of electric-light atmosphere when he was not already lost in a forest of verbal and visual symbols.

Symbolist drama gained great attractiveness from advances in stagecraft promoted by Adolphe Appia and Gordon Craig and their talented disciples. Their imaginative, expressive effects had a distinctive, often memorable, character. Dramatically used space, suggestive backgrounds, vertical and horizontal masses shaped and reshaped by electric light, sculptural forms, and careful design brought beauty and imagination to the stage. By comparison with symbolist scenery, realistic stage design had, indeed, been crude and cluttered. As a result of lessons learned from pioneering symbolism at the turn of the century, scenic design today is highly selective, even for realistic social and psychological plays. In every other respect, too—in costuming and in general production design for which Reinhardt became celebrated, as well as in the poetic quality of the dialogue—the sense of beauty, which naturalists had neglected, was now well served.

At the same time, however, the sense of drama itself became enfeebled, and even dramatic dialogue suffered a decline of vigor and vibrancy except when it was fortunately allied with peasant dialect, notably in Ireland, in the plays of Synge and Lady Gregory. Poetry became primary for such symbolists as Hofmannsthal and the young Yeats, and much of this essentially lyrical and narrative poetry talked or sang about dramatic experience instead of rendering it in action-propelled dialogue. And poetic prose, as employed in many a Maeterlinck tone poem such as *La Mort de Tintagiles* (1894) or an Andreyev drama such as *The Life of Man* (1906), represented an improvement only to the degree that the movement of the play was not impeded by prolixity; the prose tended to be repetitive and portentous, rather than dramatically forceful. Dialogue and action often failed to mesh; there was often too little substantiality of action, character, and milieu for the dialogue to stay in gear. Much symbolist writing for the theatre, therefore, sounded as if the authors and their creations were talking around a subject or were trying to attach themselves to an experience constantly undergoing deliquescence.

The symbolist plays of Maeterlinck, Hofmannsthal, Hauptmann, the young Yeats (from 1892 to 1917), and Alexander Blok variously provide substitutions of fancy, mood, sentiment, and lyric poetry for the substantial characters and well-marked conflicts of realistic drama. Writing of Ibsen in 1893, Henry James could declare, ". . . I feel in him, to the pitch of almost intolerable boredom, the presence and the insistence of life." No such confession could have been wrung from James by the plays of the symbolists. Their elusive and allusive style fingered life through veils. Ronald Peacock, in *The Poet in the Theatre*,[6] refers to Ibsen's "extraordinary sense of precipitated crisis" and adds that Ibsen's situations

[6] New York, 1945, p. 79.

"seem to have been shaped under the compulsion of an acute emotional response to the utmost concentration of conflict and tension." I know of only one notable symbolist dramatist in whom this compulsion could be found—Andreyev. And in Andreyev, the compulsion nearly always borders on hysteria.

Andreyev's name, indeed, can introduce the second and explosive antirealistic phase of the theatre. In some of his plays, such as *King Hunger* and *The Black Maskers,* this gifted hysteric bridged symbolism and expressionism. Strindberg, who became the founder of expressionist theatre when he began to write his "dream plays" at the turn of the century, also had an overdeveloped sense of disorientation. The expressionist style reached a turbulent climax, mainly in Central Europe, between 1910 and 1925, and attracted international recognition especially with the plays of Kaiser and Toller and the stage productions of Leopold Jessner and Jürgen Fehling. Expressionist theatre virtually completed the dissolution into dream and the disintegration into frenzy of the classic world picture of the major realists. With the diffusion of expressionism after 1914, the theatre acquired a dramatic style singularly appropriate for revolution and anarchy. It may be of interest to observe that the first well-received play by a new German writer after World War II was also an expressionist drama—*Draussen vor der Tür,* by Wolfgang Borchert.

Strindberg's description of his expressionist method in the Preface to *The Dream Play* may serve as a summary of the main features of dramatic expressionism:

> . . . the author has tried to imitate the disconnected but seemingly logical form of the dream. Anything may happen; everything is possible and probable. Time and space do not exist. On an insignificant background of reality, imagination designs and embroiders novel patterns; a medley of memories, experience, free fancies, absurdities and improvisations.
>
> The characters split, double, multiply, vanish, solidify, blur, clarify. But one consciousness reigns above them all—that of the dreamer; and before it there are no secrets, no incongruities, no scruples, no laws.[7]

To this description of the dream technique, employed in many expressionist plays even without the formal motivation of a dream subject, we may add the extreme rapidity of action and the swiftly stabbing, stenographic dialogue present in post-Strindbergian expressionism, as exemplified by Toller's *Masse-Mensch* or O'Neill's *The Hairy Ape.*

[7] *Plays by Strindberg,* First Series (New York, 1926), p. 24.

The expressionists reintroduced the soliloquy and the aside, the tirade, and the histrionic prose and verse which the realists and naturalists had banished from their stage as inconsistent with verisimilitude or naturalness and especially with the "fourth-wall" principle of scenic illusion. In endeavoring to *express* reality rather than to *represent* it, they inevitably moved toward theatricalism, and their view of life itself tended to be theatrical as well as generally subjective. For this reason, as well as because environment for them was subjectively volatile or in a state of actual transition (if not, indeed, disintegration), the expressionists brought back into vogue the multiscened type of play structure as well. These changes, also present in other kinds of modernist stylization, could in themselves contribute imagination, ingenuity, and verve to playwriting. And the discreet employment of expressionism, as in O'Neill's *The Emperor Jones* and Elmer Rice's *The Adding Machine,* can be genially credited to the modern theatre's resourcefulness or dramatic ambience. The fact is, however, that the expressionist movement returned to theatricality, in the main, as a mode of expressing a disordered world picture, private disorientation, and a sense of impending or actual social disaster. The dramatic world of expressionism became after 1914 a veritable vortex, and expressionist directors led by Leopold Jessner, staging plays on steep ramps soon to be called *Jessner-treppen,* expected their actors to move at breakneck speed and vehemently to theatricalize their performance in voice and gesture too. We may grant to the best examples of expressionist drama some claim to poetic form and style, as well as to social idealism. But the dramatic effect was generally frenzied and traumatic.

It is less necessary here to dwell on parallel fragmentations of the realists' world picture by the dadaist, *surréaliste,* futurist, and constructivist experiments of our century. The subject belongs mainly to the history of the stage, and only a few of the extremist plays, such as E. E. Cummings' *him* and Cocteau's *Orphée,* have texts that can bear critical scrutiny. In the surrealistic theatre, the individual and his environment were allowed little identity and fixity. The surrealist procedure was to develop action and dialogue very nearly by free association, and to contrive somehow to pulverize the world of stable and logical relationships. To approach "reality" in the surrealist sense of the term was to achieve liberation from action and knowledge precipitated and fixed by consciousness, to give free play to the unconscious self. It was deemed necessary for the artist in the theatre to violate the world of recognizable action and things and to cultivate the absurd in the form of bizarre and often inconsequent theatricality. To Ibsen, the world as reflected, analyzed, and judged in the drama had to make sense in order to be truly real. To a consistent surrealist the world was bound to be least real when the action was most cohesive and the argument most coherent. To reflect the world of reason and action was to peddle a pinchbeck reality; to engage in analysis was tantamount to flogging a dead horse; to make evaluations or arrive at judgments was futile when social reality was discarded as a frame of reference.

The advance of dramatic nihilism in various stylistic guises and programs for dramatic art became particularly marked in *avant-garde* theatres after World War I; and it is as significant as it is regrettable that the progress of nihilism on the stage was impeded chiefly by the Philistinism of the general public rather than by a strong countermovement of neorealism.

If we except the Socialist Realism of the Communist world, which calls for an elementary "boy loves tractor" type of realistic drama garnished with propaganda, two movements in the theatre have tended directly to oppose the nihilist tendencies of postrealistic modernism. One is existentialism; the other, epic realism.

The brief vogue of existentialist drama during the 1940's reintroduced some Ibsenist moral jurisprudence into the theatre by stressing the theme of self-reliance and personal responsibility. But the affirmations in the plays of Sartre and his school usually sounded like counsels of desperation; and the odor of decay was not dispelled by existentialist ethics in the case of some of the best-known plays, such as Sartre's *Huis clos* and Camus' *Caligula*. Moreover, existentialism failed to engender any special dramatic form and style.

A more important countermovement has been the epic theatre developed in Central Europe since the 1920's. Its leaders, Erwin Piscator and Bertolt Brecht, have carried objectivity to the point of developing various kinds of documentary and semidocumentary drama; a somewhat parallel development in the United States, mainly under the impetus supplied by the Federal Theatre of the 1930's, led to the composition of the Living Newspapers, such as Arthur Arent's review of the housing problem in American cities, *One-third-of-a-nation*. With or without characteristic Marxist leanings, the dramatists of the "epic" style have adhered to the positivist orientation which sustained nineteenth-century realism. At the same time, however, they have rejected realistic dramaturgy and style as too confining, just as Brecht and Piscator rejected even socially oriented expressionism as too unrealistic because unobjective.

Instead, the leaders of epic theatre have elected a theatricalist approach to playwriting and stage production. Their very desire to express social reality has led them to create a style of drama, epic in extension and presentational in method. The typical epic play consists of separate episodes, less related by plot than by an idea presented in free theatrical style. Episodes objectively rendered as in a realistic play are supplemented by one or more nonrealistic devices, which usually break the emotional connection, destroy the "illusion," and annihilate the fourth-wall convention. These devices may be narrations, explanations, exhortations (by a Voice, a Narrator, or a Chorus delivering a "mass chant") frankly directed at the audience—also lyrics, demonstrations of an idea, or visual aids such as projected slides, charts, and slogans. The ideal epic play has been largely a lesson play—a *Lehrstück,* or teaching play, as Brecht has called it. Some sort of demonstration dominates each epic-theatre variant, whether it be a comic opera such as the *Threepenny Opera,* a Federal Theatre Living Newspaper, a biographical drama such as Brecht's *Galileo,* or a parable such as his *Good Woman of Setzuan (Der gute Mensch von Setzuan).*

Whether factual or imaginative in subject matter as well as treatment, epic drama is the drama of objective relationships; it constitutes an art of "epic realism," the term Brecht now favors. Nevertheless, epic theatre represents a revolutionary twentieth-century departure from the essentially settled, individual-oriented, emotion-based middle-class world of realistic drama. Dramatic realism aims at a unified style; epic realism tends to be a mélange of styles—narrative, dramatic, and lyrical, descriptive and hortatory at the same time. Dramatic realism favors compact action; epic realism, episodic action. Dramatic realism tends to present the individual as an end in himself; epic realism disclaims any such intention even when the genius or sympathy of the playwright and the actors creates rounded and moving characterization. (Brecht was disturbed, for example, when his Zürich audience identified itself with the "Niobe-heroine" of his *Mutter Courage,* and he made alterations in the text with the object of lowering the emotional charge. The camp-following mother, who loses all her children, was not to be allowed to interpose her suffering humanity between the public and the author's intention to demonstrate in her story *"das rein merkantile Wesen des Kriegs."* See Brecht's *Versuche 20/21,* Frankfurt am Main, 1949.) Brecht has rejected the value of emotional identification and catharsis on the grounds that a play should leave the audience in possession of its critical faculties for the purpose of learning something conducive to social action. For this reason, he has been a strenuous opponent of illusionist stage production and Stanislavskian acting, which is individualistic "inner realism" based upon the actor's thorough identification with the character he plays. Brecht, calling instead for *Verfremdung,* requires the actor to stand outside the part to a degree, so that his performance may constitute a more or less detached comment on the character. Epic theatre is both anti-realistic and anti-Aristotelian; and this cool, rationalistic school of neo-realism has actually jolted the foundations of Western drama more drastically, because very much more effectively, than any of the primarily subjectivist deviations from realism.

We may conclude that in only one general respect have the various antirealistic deviations of our century been essentially constructive in the theatre—and that is in their tendency to retheatricalize the drama. Re-theatricalized dramaturgy, as well as stage art, has resulted in the resurgence of poetic and imaginative playwriting and stage production. The results have been least disturbing and have won the widest public acceptance in the case of a more or less autonomous theatricalism dissociated from any specifically symbolist, expressionist, or surrealist program. We may define this theatricalism as the practice of re-creating life in terms of the theatre. Theatricalism favors the cultivation of the histrionic sensibility of the playwright, the actor, and the public in full recognition of the fact that the medium—namely, *theatre*—should be revealed rather than concealed in the text of the play, and that the theatricality of the stage and drama should be developed rather than suppressed. In the arts of the stage this principle was put into practice after the beginning of the century by such renowned directors as Copeau, Jouvet, Dullin, and Barrault. And in playwriting we may observe the results in the varied artistry of Cocteau's *The Infernal Machine* and Obey's *Noah,* Lorca's *The Love of Don Perlimpín for Belisa in His Garden,* Giraudoux's *Intermezzo,* and Wilder's *The Skin of Our Teeth.* At one extreme, theatricalism has been allied with extreme formalism, as in Yeats's latter-day Noh-theatre styled plays; but it has even been found possible to combine realism and theatricalism in the same popular play, as in the case of *Our Town* and *The Glass Menagerie.*

All dramatic writing can benefit from the increased valuation now placed on the theatre as the medium a playwright should use imaginatively and expressively. And the poetry of theatricalism, a *poésie de théâtre,* as Cocteau called it, may well become the standard twentieth-century substitute for a poetic theatre nourished by verse drama. An imaginative deployment of plot materials and visual effects, a creative shaping of the *mythos* or fable with expressive language and stage movement—this *poésie de théâtre* may provide more original and exemplary dramatic art for our century than the neoromantic, reminiscent though sometimes dazzling, ventures in verse from Rostand's *Cyrano de Bergerac* to Christopher Fry's *The Lady's Not for Burning.*

In all but its mildest manifestation as fantasy or simple poetic drama,

however, even this general theatricalism suggests a distinct shift of sensibility and orientation away from the security of the old life-rooted and
illusion-dispensing theatre of realism. The practicing theatricalist fastidiously or "sophisticatedly" draws attention to "theatre" rather than to
that rather crude and exacting commodity of literature which, for want
of a better word, we call "life." He does this with various formalist procedures such as Yeats used in *A Full Moon in March* and T. S. Eliot
in *The Family Reunion* (with its chorus of the Eumenides); or he actually turns out a charade of sorts such as the Anouilh-Fry *Ring Round the
Moon*. Not infrequently, in fact, the author employs the "play within
the play" device or some variant, the effect ranging from a pleasant entertainment such as Molnar's *The Play's the Thing* to philosophically and
psychologically charged comedy (*Six Characters in Search of an Author*)
or melodrama (Pirandello's *Henry IV*). Sometimes the theatricalist principle appears simply in the distinctly theatrical fantastication of the work,
as in Giraudoux's *La Folle de Chaillot* and *Intermezzo,* and the commin-
gling of wit, poetry, and ingenuity results in a twilight loveliness. This
is the drama of civilized disenchantment that has none of the adolescence
but much of the world weariness of *fin-de-siècle* estheticism. And sometimes the theatrical principle is observed by deliberately addressing the
audience (to remind it that it is in the theatre attending a "show"), or
by intentionally destroying the illusion of reality and violating the fourth-
wall convention. Sometimes there is considerable skittishness, esthetic
pretentiousness, or strain in the endeavor to tell the public what it should
know from the start—that life is life and art is art, or that theatre is
theatre. In the case of dramas of serious import, there is a more or less
disturbing reminder that modern theatricalism, unlike the theatricalism
of the Greek or the Elizabethan drama, is an artificial creation. Not only
is the modern author calling attention to his technique as if to say, "Let's
make theatre" ("Yes, I have tricks in my pocket, I have things up my
sleeve," says Tom, the narrator of *The Glass Menagerie,* as if he spoke
for all theatricalist playwrights), but he is likely to create the impression
that he is being coy or apologetic about his seriousness, as when Cocteau
and Wilder burlesque their dramatic action.

In such conspicuously theatricalist plays of exalted purport as *La
Machine infernale* and *The Skin of Our Teeth* (and here I would add
Giraudoux's *Electre*), one may discern a divided intention and a split
effect. There is an intrinsic conflict between the natural creation of illusion and the performance of a stunt or the cultivation of esthetic pretensions. Early in the first act of *The Skin of Our Teeth,* Sabina, the
skittish housemaid *cum* Lilith of this *Finnegans Wake* history of man

("Mr. Antrobus"), tells the audience, "I don't understand a word of this play." And the audiences in 1942 apparently took their cue from her, dooming the most original American play of the war period to failure. Confusion or irritation (certainly the latter) was inevitable when Sabina cried out, "Stop! Stop! Don't play this scene. . . . Last night you almost strangled him," when Henry, the Cain of Wilder's play, in the midst of the tense third-act quarrel was about to hurl himself against Mr. Antrobus. Playing cat and mouse with one's subject by spoofing it theatrically, as in the second-act Rotarian convention of the Mammals in Atlantic City, may provide entertainment. But playing cat and mouse with the audience by taking it *in* and *out* of the illusion of reality, as in the aforementioned third-act scene, is hardly the way to inspire public confidence in a vision or conviction.

Giraudoux was similarly skittish or performed the same theatricalist legerdemain in so somber a drama as his *Electre*. "The Gardener's Lament," an interlude between the two parts of the play, starts with Electra's ex-fiancé, the gardener, stepping out of his role and saying to the audience, "I'm no longer in the running. [That is, I am no longer Electra's fiancé and no longer a character in Giraudoux's play.] That's why I am free to come and tell you what the play can't tell you. In stories like this, etc." This "willed" and cultivated theatricalism suggests, if it does not invariably succumb to, a schizoid and Alexandrian sensibility.

Entirely at home in "show business" with theatrical charades, musical comedies and revues, the theatricalist playwright gives the impression of being an insecure dramatist whenever he becomes serious.[8] Theatricalism, then, curiously appears to be less at ease in the theatre than the old anti-theatricalist realism ever was. It is remarkable how much sheer "theatre" Ibsen and Strindberg, Chekhov and O'Casey, managed to whip up in their realistic plays by ostensibly ignoring the theatre and looking at humanity instead. The presentation of life "in the form of make-believe," as the critic Alexander Bakshy has called pure theatricalism, has been a fascinating enterprise. But it has been a thoroughly solvent one thus far only as "make-believe"—which has surely been only the means rather than the prime end of great dramatic literature.

---

[8] [Here Professor Gassner wondered whether he should include a discussion of the Theatre of the Absurd, as related to the theme. Because his estimate of its powers and limitations has been given elsewhere in this book, it seems unnecessary to reiterate it. *Ed.*]

THE TWO THEATRES: THE MODERN
AND THE MODERNIST*

In the heat of perennial arguments about the state of the theatre one fact
is usually overlooked It is the significant one that the modern period of
the theatre is quite remarkably old. Counting from the mid-sixties of the
last century when Ibsen became a *modern* playwright with the content
of his great critical plays *Brand* and *Peer Gynt,* the modern drama has
lasted a full century; there is no reason to believe that it will not last at
least another if Western civilization does. The modern period since Ibsen
has already lasted three times as long as the Age of Shakespeare. A theatre
repeatedly pronounced dead has proved to be capable of unusual resilience
and longevity—if not always in one country, at one time, then in another.

Why this should concern us as something other than pollyannic reassurance or mere historical record is not easily apparent while we occupy
ourselves with the day-to-day problems of an art that is trying to survive
as a business, wherever it operates as unsubsidized enterprise—as it does
in the United States. Even when we focus on the quality of the plays and
productions we disregard the question of age as an irrelevancy. We concentrate solely on the merits and defects of the production under immediate review, and we parcel out praise and blame in accordance with the
prevailing taste of a decade or of an even shorter period. Fashions in
theatre change so rapidly that the sophistication of the 1920's in America
loses savor in the 1930's, and the social fervor of the 1930's seems inex-
plicably naïve in the 1950's. We are reluctant to observe, let alone evaluate, the productions of a single theatrical season under a larger perspective,
and chiefly this is so because the precarious state of the current stage
discourages concern with anything other than immediate success or failure, immediate profit or loss.

But age has very much bearing on the character of the contemporary
theatre, accounting for its variety as well as its confusion, its unstable
health, and its not always productive restiveness. Styles of playwriting and
stage production have lost their youthful vigor but we adhere to them
as if they were legacies of recent date that could not possibly become
dated. Easily 75 percent of the successful plays of the period before World
War I—plays by prominent men like Galsworthy in England and An-

* A talk delivered at the University of Richmond, March 16, 1964.

666

dreyev in Russia, once regarded as the *avant-garde*—have lost all freshness, yet remain officially designated as modern drama.

It is charged against the modern theatre that so many of its plays have had no lasting power. This reproof may be softened on reflection that a considerable amount of time has been involved in the decline of the popularity or even viability of once acclaimed works. Galsworthy once set the English-speaking world afire with his drama of an unfortunate weakling's entanglement in the web of legal procedures. Is it any wonder that the play in question, entitled *Justice,* should have passed out of circulation? It is now more than half a century old since its first production in 1914, a period long enough to take the edge off many a situation or attitude. Nor may time be measured only chronologically when we consider the sudden disappearance or aggravation of a problem or an issue produced by political upheavals such as our century has experienced.

A case in point is another Galsworthy play, *Loyalties,* which came as the climax to an honorably successful playwriting career in 1922. Its subject matter was prejudice, surely not a dated theme, nor one likely to be dated in the foreseeable future. But the particulars of the indictment in this carefully constructed drama consisted largely of polite upper-class anti-Semitism in England. It requires no great imagination to understand that the provocativeness of this play was reduced to absurdly small dimensions by Hitler's gas ovens. The time differential between *Loyalties* and Hitler's ascent to power was a mere decade, but European civilization was set back a thousand years and more. The effect on the nobly intended work of a gentlemanly liberal like Galsworthy was inevitably that of an earthquake on a mudhut. And the larger a historical period, of course, the greater the frequency of upheavals that tarnish or destroy reputations. Historical changes eclipsed even Shakespeare's reputation in the seventeenth century—and Galsworthy was no Shakespeare.

It is not, however, the reputation of a single author or playwright that is a main cause for concern here. Reputations come and go. And plays are not actually more vulnerable to the corrosion of time than novels and poems. Where, for example, are the best-sellers of yesteryear? It is the fate of dramatic attitudes, forms, and styles as reflected in plays and stage productions that should give us the greatest concern, and this chiefly because the contemporary theatre owes its character and a large portion of its troubles to the directions taken (or not taken) by its leading playwrights, producers, directors, and acting groups as well as the public that supports or fails to support them. A few such problems of direction, which involve a viewpoint or even a philosophy of art, seem crucial in the course of contemporary playwriting and play production.

That they are not often thought to be so is due to the fact that those of us who produce plays are of necessity forced to concern ourselves with selling them to the public, and with patching up the play and polishing the performance for this purpose. It is a main reason for the hack playwriting to which even intelligent playwrights in America are reduced while the show is being readied for the crucial Broadway opening. The problem of getting the play into proper shape is one of trying to outguess and gratify the public rather than of expressing a viewpoint. And for the usually harassed stage director it is one of composing pictures with his actors and yet keeping the traffic going on the stage rather than of interpreting the content of the play in visual dramatic terms. If the dramatist is in danger of becoming a hack writer, the director is in danger of becoming a traffic cop. As for the public, its problem is usually one of staying awake. And its criterion after many disappointments in the theatre is titillation rather than stimulation. The public gets accustomed to thinking it has been satisfied when it hasn't been bored. Any critic or paying spectator who thinks otherwise is apt to be looked upon as a perfectionist or an intellectual pretender. It is not good form on either side of the auditorium, the producer's or the public's, to ask where we are going as long as we are *moving*.

One example of the problem of *going* rather than just moving, of pursuing a direction and relating oneself significantly to the stage, is provided by the course of social drama. Not exclusively a modern type of play, it nevertheless acquired a paramount position in the theatre with Ibsen and his successors under the banner of literary and dramatic realism. It provided the sense of reality that the modern dramatist and his public considered a major desideratum after 1860, first in the European and later also in the American theatre.

A technique of realistic playwriting was expected to provide this sense of reality; and the presentation of modern political and social situations or conflicts was expected to provide immediacy and significance to reality, so that the cause of realistic theatre was intimately associated with social significance. The sense of life that the theatre is always expected to convey in intensified form was closely associated with productions of social drama during the last quarter of the past century, and this viewpoint has never quite disappeared in the present century even if it has been played down from time to time, as it was in the American theatre of the passive fifties after having been played up in the social-minded theatre of the agitated thirties.

There is no question, however, that a strong attitude of skepticism and wariness has been maintained toward the social drama virtually from its inception; and a hundred years have provided more than a little provocation to dissent concerning the merits of a theatre devoted to social problems. I shall not dwell on the artistic limitations of propaganda beyond pointing to the undercutting of character reality and the contriving of situations and plots that propagandist playwrights have perpetrated even when they have not opportunistically truckled—as in Stalinist Russia—to bureaus of official propaganda. Not all simplifications are necessarily detrimental to dramatic art. But truth of art could not be expected from such simplifications as the habit of dividing characters into spotless heroes and utter villains, or concluding with sudden conversions to morality in the early part of the century (as in Sheldon's *The Boss*) or to class-war ideology during the thirties.

But a large number of social dramas have not been structured as propaganda at all—except in the loose sense in which every effective play is propaganda since it presents a point of view.

The main reasons for the failure of social drama to live up to the promise it held at the beginning of the modern period lies elsewhere. A historical reason is that in a rapidly changing society the social situations and problems lost their force and even their relevance within a few decades, if not sooner. Either they disappeared or they were solved, and the urgency of the play subsided with the urgency of the social issue. Consider all the plays in English on, or related to, the once arresting subject of feminism. I can recall only two or three, such as Maugham's *The Constant Wife,* that still have some little bloom on them, and the bloom consists mainly of the wit rather than the conviction with which they were written. And of all the treatments of capital and labor conflict that filled the European theatre for decades I don't think I can cite more than a single one, Hauptmann's *The Weavers,* a drama dealing with the revolt of the Silesian weavers in 1844, for which I can claim some life today; and, produced in 1892, it was actually a historical play rather than a directly topical one since the events with which Hauptmann dealt had transpired half a century before. Here, the spark of spirit and the drive of passion overcomes the sociological torpor that makes most efforts to write nonpropagandist social drama so tepid. And other dating factors have been the manifold prosiness of sociological writing and the unexciting, *subdramatic,* effort to see all sides of a question. (I wonder how Galsworthy's attempt to be fair in *Strife,* a balanced strike play now fifty-five years old, would fare in today's theatre.)

Only wit and theatrical buoyancy have kept the more durable sociology of Bernard Shaw—in, let us say, *Major Barbara*—fresh; and it doesn't take much perception to observe how much more such Shavian products as *Major Barbara* and *Heartbreak House* actually partake of fantasy rather than sociology. They are improvisations on a social theme rather than social case histories, and they were written by a master charmer whose Fabian earnestness fortunately failed to subdue his anything but Fabian high spirits and histrionic vigor. In Shaw's work it is usually not the bare argument, most apparent in Shaw's prefaces, but the bravura passages of dialogue and monologue that have kept the plays lively both in the theatre and the library. It is the largely comic embroidery, the fine patchwork of verbal and theatrical inventiveness, rather than the drab linsey-woolsey undergarment of his social conscience, that attracts us. It would not be difficult to establish that Shaw himself was aware of this; he appreciated his talents better than anyone else and knew how to apply them to advantage even when he had little plot and less credibility to sustain him on the stage, as in the late plays *The Apple Cart, Too True to Be Good,* and *The Millionairess,* composed after he had passed the Biblical age of four score and ten.

It cannot, however, be said that the theatre of social thought has produced a second Shaw, and the best that it has been able to show for its plodding earnestness has been a succession of commonplace exhibitions and platitudinous arguments saved from oppressive mediocrity by flavorsome dialogue, a vivid occupational or regional background, and now and then a burst of moral passion, as in Odets' *Awake and Sing,* Miller's *All My Sons,* and Wesker's *Chips with Everything.* It would seem, then, that our heritage from the first creative stream of modernity—that of social realism—runs thin even if we still draw upon it and shall continue to do so as long as social issues continue to concern and agitate us.

The realistic theatre, however, has had another main outlet and has irrigated another substantial terrain—that of character drama or the principality of private rather than *public* experience or problem. When the experience or problem is sufficiently inward, complex, and intense, we call it *psychological drama.* Strindberg gave it the status of significant art in 1887 and 1888 with his early masterpieces *The Father* and *Miss Julie,* and Ibsen followed in 1890 with his *Hedda Gabler,* the tragedy of an advanced woman who may be considered the prototype of today's career woman.

In such plays and their many successors, the concern with the problem is apt to be larger than the concern with the person, and only by dint of genius, as in the case of the Strindberg and Ibsen dramas, has the modern playwright escaped the snare of substituting a *problem* for a *character.* Psychological understanding has been abundantly present since the time of Sophocles, and even a fifth-century Athenian stage production with masked actors could not have extinguished the character knowledge that the Greek masters introduced into the action and dialogue of their tragedies. And one does not have to endorse the character-mongering of nineteenth-century Shakespeareans to realize that Shakespeare understood humanity at least as well as modern playwrights. But Shakespeare, like Sophocles, wrote *drama* rather than psychology, whereas the reverse must be said of the moderns who have moved in Strindberg's tracks. "Psychological drama," for better or worse, has been the second stream of our heritage from the realistic theatre.

Its fascination for the twentieth-century public was of course enlarged, if not deepened, by the popularization of psychoanalytical findings. Its application to the problems of present-day tensions has been considerable. And modern psychology has been applied with considerable interest even to ancient themes and characters. We have seen this in Cocteau's variant Freudian treatment of the Oedipus legend, *The Infernal Machine,* and O'Neill's updating of the Oresteian saga, *Mourning Becomes Electra,* which was acclaimed, upon its New York production in 1935, as the high-water mark in the American theatre. Nevertheless, it has long been evident that "psychological realism" has been no more resistant to time's corrosion and corruption than "social realism." We continue to write, produce, and patronize psychological drama, but hardly with any invigorating sense of discovery. The novelty has worn off, and the field of observation has been continually narrowed down to *pathology*—that is, to clinical material that may or may not be trustworthy as science but is unreliable as a source of dramatic interest. The analysis of neuroses in plays usually produced schematized and impoverished versions of tension and character conflict.

One of the most debilitating efforts of the vogue of psychology in the theatre is its reduction of drama to analysis—a static enterprise on the stage since explanations are not action; and many of the explanations are themselves suspect. For example, I have considerable regard for Tennessee Williams' *Streetcar Named Desire,* but I have never been convinced that the explanation of poor Blanche Du Bois's state of mind makes sense. She is said to have become nymphomaniacal after discovering that her sensitive young husband is a homosexual and to have driven him to suicide by taxing him with his deviation. I would sooner conclude that such disenchantment with marriage would have cooled her sexual ardor instead of permanently inflaming it. Even if my contention can be questioned, Mr. Williams' explanation becomes a crude structure when its architect piles the Pelion of extravagant heterosexuality on an Ossa of homosexuality, which ultimately becomes the dramatic basis upon which the author erects the psyche-shattering rape of Blanche by Stanley—and I shall not even stop to consider the subtle question of how a nymphomaniacal lady can, strictly speaking, be violated.

Tennessee Williams, of course, wrote a far better play than an explanation, and my point is that the play would have been just as effective, if not more so, without it. In the work of less gifted writers, we would have had the explanation without the play. Mr. Williams at least gave us the play along with the explanation. And I might add that the fundamental weakness of strictly psychological drama is not that it is too complex, but that it is too simple. A definition is always simpler than a life, just as an intellectual paradox, even by so mighty a prestidigitator as Bernard Shaw is simpler than the customary inconsistencies of human behavior. It is this reflection, in fact, that motivated G. K. Chesterton to accuse Shaw, the strenuous rationalist and logician, of lacking a sense of paradox—of "a blindness to paradox everywhere" that "perplexes his outlook." Psychology, erected as a barrier between a writer and the completely realized human being who is a writer's best subject, certainly perplexes the outlook of the modern playwright precisely when he considers himself most realistic or "scientific."

But subordination to psychology often does worse than that. It narrows the writer's humanity whenever he treats a human character as mere case history; and it narrows his intellect when he is compelled to reduce the richness of an artist's insights to schematization. This makes for obtuseness and vulgarization (vulgarization by mental shortcuts) in art regardless of how useful it may be as a clinical shorthand for professional psychiatrists. Psychological drama, then, has ultimately impoverished rather than enriched, dehumanized rather than deepened, and dulled rather than sharpened; it has even cheapened the realistic theatre. In recent decades, after relying mainly on Oedipal motivations, it has made both a fetish and a commodity of the subjects of homosexuality and inhibited heterosexuality. Whatever we may think of the tastefulness of the display, there can be little question as to the sameness of the case histories and the solemn banality of concluding in a manner worthy of a mental hygienist or a *Kinsey Report* emissary that someone is or isn't having sex, while arousing suspicion that the only kind of sex the author himself is having is, as D. H. Lawrence called it, "sex in the head." It is not surprising, then, that even successful playwrights, like Tennessee Williams and William Inge, enter a blind alley of sexual psychologism at a late point in their career when they have had the bad luck to obtain psychoanalytical instruction with their therapy. The therapy may or may not have been needed; the intellectual instruction is distinctly expendable.

It only substitutes cliché for insight. It affords the unwary author the dangerous contentment of a little knowledge in exchange for the potentially profound wisdom of an active discontent and search for elusive truth.

So ends this venture in psychological realism entered into many decades ago with passion and perspicuity by the genius of Strindberg, Wedekind, and O'Neill. And with the hobbled condition of both social and psychological realism, little has been left of the modern theatre's once considerable trust in realism. And this is all the more regrettable when one considers the heroic efforts of an Antoine or Stanislavsky to develop the arts of stage illusion and authentic characterization. Increasingly, the questions that interpose themselves between the realistic theatre and the observer today are "illusion to what purpose?" and "characterization of what?"—that is, a human being who can be "characterized" or a puppet-character who cannot be, so that the actor has to substitute *himself* for his inadequately dimensioned role?

But, as we all know by now, there is also another kind of theatre than that of modern realism—namely, *modernist* experimentation or non-realistic stylization. It has been with us since the 1890's when symbolist poets of the word and of the visual arts declared realism to be passé. They established poetic "art theatres," designed atmospheric or symbolical scenery, and endeavored to write poetic drama and prose with variable success in the cases of Maeterlinck, Andreyev, and other proponents of the symbolist turn-of-the-century movement. A second type of theatre was born then under the inspiration of those visionaries Gordon Craig and Adolphe Appia, whose exalted Wagnerian dreams for the stage envisioned its conversion into a temple for votaries, a shrine for mystics, and a locus for the practice of magic and mesmerism. The practical upshot of this effort was a theatre of spectacle and so-called *Gesammtkunst,* or total theatre, which had such triumphs as the Max Reinhardt production of *The Miracle* in London and New York. This tendency is still with us, but it has been converted into the art industry of the Broadway and Hollywood musical comedy.

The results are by no means always meretricious, even though the showy and noisy effects of musical *kitsch* are very much with us, and are encouraged by the need for huge earnings to defray the costly spectacularity of the effort. A certain degree of folk poetry and color deepened *Porgy and Bess* and graced *Oklahoma!*; a quantity of social compassion accompanied the balletic marvels of the Jerome Robbins production of *West Side Story.* But, by and large, the contemporary musical comedy amounts to the exploitation of art as a commodity. It is always contrived for a quick profit, and because huge profits as well as great risks are involved in it, it has already taken over a large part of the Broadway theatre and is being emulated in London's West End with such spectacles as *Oliver!* and *Blitz!* The contemporary musical is the monster-child of theatrical idealism, and it is more than likely that its parents among the turn-of-the-century symbolists would want to disavow it. The effort to oppose a theatre of the imagination to the theatre of reality is still with us, indeed; but its major result is pinchbeck magic, vulgarized vision, and merely profitable entertainment. I say nothing against such entertainment except that it represents the transformation of theatre into a species of thinned-out opera rather than the realization of early aspirations to an exalted and spiritualized dramatic art. It is a transformation effected by the necessities of show business and conditioned by a pampered and stupefied middle-class public. This has been the case even in periods of acute social stress and war.

There have been other efforts to supplant dramatic realism. There have been so many, indeed, that the history of the twentieth-century theatre is mainly one of unstable antirealistic experimentation against a background of realism. Something can be said for a number of these experiments, but in the end they were unsustained and the experiments piddled out, leaving the twentieth-century stage with a shadowy afterglow except for a small succession of arresting plays and a few positive lessons in stage productions. Not one of these movements—whether they called themselves dadaism or surrealism—had the character of a reliable new dispensation. Rather, they had the features of a temporary eruption, the qualities of a fresh exhibit in an old market—an exhibit soon sold out or discarded while the market remained the same and always ready for a new display.

In only a single stylistic departure from realistic technique—the "epic theatre" of Erwin Piscator and Bertolt Brecht—were affirmative social attitudes asserted and strategies for affirmation provided. And epic theatre, to which Brecht, its only talented playwright, made his last important contribution some twenty years ago with the writing of *The Caucasian Chalk Circle,* has not yet brought any remarkable new lease on vitality to either the realistic theatre (to which it belongs in spirit) or to the non-realistic theatre (to which it is somewhat adjacent in technique). If it has notably revitalized the theatre of the past two decades, the world of theatre does not know it. The most we can say is that the influence of Brecht is present in plays by Duerrenmatt, the author of *The Visit,* and those of a few others.

We must conclude that among the factors that have accounted for a state of tension in the contemporary theatre is the conflict of two kinds of theatre—the *modern* and the *modernistic*. For about fifty years during the latter part of the nineteenth century, the theatre and its dramatic literature could be found moving toward modernity. And in various ways that amounted to a striving for greater realism we achieved "modernity" under the leadership of Antoine and Stanislavsky in the theatre and Ibsen and Strindberg in the drama.

And so arose the two major types of modern drama: *social drama* by the example of Ibsen, and *psychological drama* under the influence of Strindberg. Stage production and performance followed suit, becoming accurate, authentic, even naturalistically photographic for a time in fostering the illusion of reality on the stage. And some interesting variations on realism developed too, the most noteworthy being the drama of ideas, or "discussion drama," which Bernard Shaw made especially incisive, and naturalism, which ranged from quasidocumentary transcriptions of reality with overtones of sociology or scientism to sensitive renditions of reality with overtones of poetry, as in the plays of Chekhov. This, in brief, is what I call the *modern* tradition in drama and theatre.

But neither the creative artist nor his public was content with realism. As a style it became too familiar to be refreshing. Imaginative writing and staging that resorted to poetic effects, symbolism and allegory, expressionistic explosions and distortions, experiments in distinctly subjective art, fancy and fantasia of the Unconscious became the *avant-garde* in the theatre after 1890. Fashion followed fashion in the theatre, and even the erstwhile founders of the realistic theatre soon opted for more imaginative forms of drama than transcripts of life, representation of problems, and arguments about them.

No single type of nonrealistic dramatic art established itself as the ruling one for more than a decade. And now our twentieth-century theatre has run through greatly publicized phases of symbolism, expressionism, dadaism, surrealism, Pirandellism, theatricalism, epic realism, and our recent theatre of cruelty or theatre of the absurd as represented by such imaginative writers as Genet, Ionesco, Beckett, Pinter, and Albee. This is the *modernist,* by contrast with the *modern* theatre.

And just as the realistic modern phase began to pay reduced dividends to the artist and his public after a dozen years of Ibsen and Strindberg, so the nonrealistic modernist styles have paid reduced dividends. Familiarity became the bane of modern realism. Bizarreness has proved again and again the misfortune, as well as the brief fortune, of modernistic antirealism. If realism tended to suffer from commonplaceness, antirealism has often leaned toward preciosity and strained extravagance.

The precision and clarity of realistic drama favored the superficial and exalted the banal, as in average Broadway and West End, London, productions for half a century. The imprecision or obscurity of ultra-fantastic experiments has proved unsettling at first but also ultimately expected and often banal.

Our twentieth-century theatre, therefore, has been in constant flux. It has reflected states of tension and crisis intensified by political upheavals and war. It has been an unsettled theatre, and the best results have often come from a reconciliation of opposites such as modified realism and discreet theatricalism in dramatic style, and wary optimism and qualified pessimism in content or viewpoint. And perhaps the contemporary theatre has been most representative of the age in this very instability and division. A divided world in the twentieth century has had a divided theatre.

THE MODERN, THE MODERNIST,
AND THE ABSURDIST*

My little essay could perhaps be more appropriately entitled "Experiments in Theatre from Craig and Mist to Beckett and Nullity." And indeed it is a major difficulty of my subject that in discussing it, veterans like me and my elders must ever waver between seriousness and frivolity. We have seen too much heterodoxy in the theatre become orthodoxy within short periods of time to dismiss experiments as merely passing fancies, and we have seen orthodoxy in the theatre become atrophy too often to deny the necessity of experimentation. At the same time, we have encountered too much pretense in the perennial vanguard not to view its evangelical claims with misgivings, and not to follow its gyrations of theory and practice or malpractice with skepticism. We have also been too familiar with old experiments not to suspect the newness of the new. And I suppose we are also accustomed to expecting a little common sense, some degree of direct communication on the level of consciousness, and even a modicum of solace or affirmativeness for the stage to be particularly happy with a species of theatre that extends from, let us say Jarry's *Ubu Roi* in the 1880's to Picasso's *Desire Caught by the Tail* in the 1940's and beyond in the ensuing dire decades.

If we sometimes tolerate ultramodernist extravagances and even allow them to be produced, it is more in the hope of teaching the young by chastening experience than in the expectation that we shall become converted by the productions or discover anything from them that we did not really know before. And I doubt that I am exaggerating the extravagance and pretension of a chronic *avant-garde* since the apostolate of Jarry and Apollinaire that is not less insistent today than it was at any other time except perhaps during the heyday of dadaism: I am sure I am not exaggerating after recently observing the performance of a so-called "theatre of chance" play on the stage of an otherwise meritorious off-Broadway theatre in the course of which I did not understand two consecutive sentences, if indeed they were sentences.

I am certain that the American author of this charade would feel grossly misunderstood if I implied that they *were* sentences. In the face

* From *Drama Critique* (Spring, 1963); based on an address delivered before the American Educational Theatre Association, Idyllwild, California, November 12, 1960.

of such an experiment I think William Blake would hasten to revise his dictum that the road of excess leads to the palace of wisdom.

It is essential to draw a distinction between the "moderns" and the "modernists," even at the risk of incurring a few transparent simplifications. The moderns started staking out claims to public attention with a program of militant realism in the 1870's under a succession of leaders beginning with Ibsen. The modernists started staking out their claims with an antirealistic program in the late 1880's. The modernists expressed a reaction against realism, just as the realists constituted a reaction against romanticism. The moderns have followed a course successively and often also simultaneously that has brought to full bloom in literature realism and naturalism, surface realism and inner realism, the problem play and the Shavian play of ideas, psychological drama and social drama, as well as varieties of the folk play, poetic naturalism, and poetic realism. The modernists have followed a course that has run through the gamut of stylization in dramatic literature from atmospheric symbolism to orgies of symbol-mongering, from psychological expressionism to social expressionism, and from dadaist *nonsense* to surrealistic sub-sense or *sur*-sense.

Since these developments, moreover, have not occurred in a vacuum, both the moderns and the modernists have been affected by the pressure of their times and have reflected the divided, more or less schizophrenic, nature of our era.

In general, the moderns, led by Ibsen and Shaw, have favored a liberal but not licentious outlook in morals and politics, whereas modernists have flouted reason and responsibility in life and art. The moderns have leaned toward optimism, the modernists toward pessimism, or even nihilism. The moderns have held out hope for the individual, the modernists have given him little choice between depersonalization and idiosyncrasy. The moderns have expected a better world, the modernists a worse one and even an end to the world; one of their most recent testaments by Samuel Beckett is characteristically named *Fin de Partie* in French and *Endgame* in English. The moderns have favored evaluation, the modernists denigration.

The moderns have abided by objective reality even in psychological drama ever since Strindberg's *Miss Julie,* the modernists by subjectivity even in taking account of objective reality ever since *The Dream Play* by the same author. And there is an additional lesson to be read from the fact that both plays were written by Strindberg, for it is characteristic of the modern era that the division between the modern and the modernistic may be found within the same playwright as well as between different playwrights. Collective schizophrenia has been paralleled in our modern period by individual schizophrenia. Ambivalent and divided artistry has been apparent since Ibsen and Strindberg, in Hauptmann, O'Casey, O'Neill, and other significant writers. And so it happens that the authors of such considerable works as *Hedda Gabler, Miss Julie, The Weavers, The Plough and the Stars,* and *Desire Under the Elms* abandoned realism for the poetic allurements of *When We Dead Awaken, The Dream Play, The Sunken Bell, Within the Gates,* and *The Great God Brown,* just as it happened that the authors of *The Dream Play* and *The Great God Brown* returned to the realism of *The Dance of Death* and *Long Day's Journey into Night.*

In matters of style and structure, of course, the divergences are quite apparent. Thus the moderns aim for clarity in style, the modernists for ambiguity and esthetic double talk; the moderns opt for conversational dialogue, the modernists for formal speech—unless they happen to prefer no-speech or speech so calculatedly simple as to be downright scatological. It is, of course, well known that the moderns have been partial to prose while the modernists have resorted to poetry or pseudopoetry. In play construction, the moderns abolish the soliloquy and the aside and the modenists recover these devices for use and abuse in old ways and new, as in *Blood Wedding, Strange Interlude,* and *The Hostage.* Inevitably, the moderns abolish the chorus while the modernists restore it. In sum, the modern playwrights try to foster the illusion of reality while the modernists try to destroy it; the former promote identification with the characters, the modernists discourage it; the moderns proffer analysis and knowledge, the modernists obfuscation and magic. The pioneers among moderns worked hard to detheatricalize the drama while the modernists, including advocates of the theatre of the absurd, exerted themselves to retheatricalize it.

The same thing can be said, of course, about the arts of stage production and stage performance, and the same schisms have been apparent in them. The modern leaders of the theatre from Antoine to Stanislavsky and their successors built up the principle and practice of illusion, the modernists decried the principle and rejected the practice. The former built up the "fourth wall," the latter broke it down. The former, believing in theatre for "life's sake," played down theatricality on the stage while the latter, paralleling the "art for art's sake" ideal with a "theatre for theatre's sake," enthroned theatricality. The moderns concentrated on creating an environment with realistic settings, the modernists on abolishing it with the help of electric magic and the new scenic art inspired by Appia and Craig. Symbolists dissolved it in a poetic solution or in a mystique of mist, wrapped it in a reflective fog, or in an access of pessimism concerning the life of man smothered it in a smog of miasmatic menace and fatefulness and created a form of drama in the manner of *Pelléas and Mélisande,* which may be described as "atmospheric tragedy." Formalists abstracted the human environment and constructivists skeletonized it; expressionists made nightmares out of it, and theatricalists turned it into an amusement park. The modern stage directors concentrated on a logic of action and nonaction, the modernists on an illogic, if not indeed a frenzy, of action and a mystique of nonaction. The modern directors made performance a representation, the modernists, a masquerade, a shadow-play, an automaticism, a gymnastic exercise, a race down precipitous Jessner-steps, a dance or demiballet, a demonstration, or just simply a witches' Sabbath.

One party—that of the naturalists—has been witlessly solemn about seriousness, and the other party—that of the absurdists—has been no less solemn about farcicality, both parties challenging with *truth* or with *exaggeration,* respectively, the complacency of the middle-class public. We can at times observe lunacy or a pretension verging on lunacy at both extremes. The terms orthodoxy and heterodoxy have no meaning in this case, for one extreme offers scientism and the other nihilism as the key to the human condition, exalting in the service of its respective ideas either the theatre subtheatrical or the theatre hypertheatrical. In this case, the only sound use of terms is that recommended by the celebrated English humorist, Dr. Sydney Smith—that "orthodoxy is my doxy, heterodoxy is your doxy."

There are, of course, less dubious choices available to us, and these have been made continually by many playwrights, directors, designers, critics, and playgoers who are inclined to make little distinction between life and art, between the world inside and the world outside the theatre. Their greatest pleasure is that of *recognition* rather than shock. They must identify themselves with the character on the stage if they are to take the theatre seriously as an art and an occupation. They usually reject fancy (and even valid imagination) except in operettas, musical comedies, and revues. In attending serious drama, they would rather be bored than disoriented. They distrust brazen cleverness, extravagance, and brash mockery when the subject strikes them as important. They do not mind an unattractive or commonplace realistic appearance; they find it rather reassuring, as if it were a warranty of honesty, very much in the vein of the Slavic proverb, "His face is ugly, but his mind is upright." At least in the professional theatre, they greatly outnumber the playgoers who chronically delight in the rather adolescent game of ridiculing sense and respectability. There is a chronic *avant-gard*ism in our unstable age that takes fire from every new fashion, and it seems to find salvation for art and society in every departure from representationalism and realism. This fluttery *avant-gard*ism renews itself constantly, and may become at one time as sure that salvation for the theatre lies in beatnik echolalia or absurdist non-sense as it was at another time, some thirty-five years ago, that the theatre was about to be rejuvenated when Cocteau's horse in *Orphée* beat out a dirty word with its hooves. But because these neophytes speak brightly or talk loudly, it does not follow that they rule the theatre. They remain, rather, a vociferous minority. They do not provide a broad base for the theatre, such as the theatre needs, even when they influence playwrights. And in view of the persistence of realism that has filled season after season with impressive plays, from *The Three Sisters* in 1901 to *A Taste of Honey* in 1960, the overprincipled detractor of realism who expects to prevail in a noncoterie theatre would do well to proceed with some caution.

Nevertheless, we must guard against thinking that there is no choice between the two extremes except a dull middle ground occupied by a mediocrity of intellect and spirit supported by professional craftsmanship. Something may be said for this kind of mediocrity, of course, for no art has sustained itself on genius alone. But the prevalance of this mediocrity is a sure sign of stagnation, whereas some flagrant excess may point the way to progress or herald a vital dispensation, as did the power-intoxicated and word-inebriated talent of young Marlowe, for example.

There may be times even when it is necessary to defend excess against the Philistines whose self-satisfaction leads them to assume a lofty indifference to all experiment.

I know that I have myself been severely critical of Pound and Eliot but have been irritated into defending them to the death against complacent critics of their poetry. I see red every time a lady I know who writes for the slick magazines adduces another piece of evidence against Eliot—usually at second or third hand. I have also found myself under the necessity of smiting some enemies of Samuel Beckett hip and thigh because the smug provincialism of his critics has offended me more deeply than the desperation and obscurities of this author's *Endgame.*

I would personally err in favor of honest experiment, however extreme, rather than in favor of unproductive mediocrity, however sensible. And since I have not been unique in this respect, you have here one explanation (though I am sure it is not the only one) of why the intelligentsia and even some workaday critics go overboard in acclaiming the esoteric or extreme; why they overrate, let us say, E. E. Cummings' *him* and Jack Gelber's *The Connection,* while being less than just to a good deal of perfectly competent but unprovocative work in the theatre.

Often, enough of this duality of judgment, this double standard, in evaluating stage productions, means, indeed, that we have strained at a gnat but swallowed a camel, for there can be little doubt that many experiments have been quite atrocious and have proved unproductive in the long run. I believe this can be said of the Theatre of the Absurd, just as it has been said in the past about expressionism, dadaism, surrealism, and constructivism even when packaged under such distinguished labels as, let us say, Wedekind and Werfel, Verhaeren and Andreyev, Yeats and Cummings, Jessner and Meyerhold, and so on.

Yet I have rarely regretted my own championship of writers who were in the *avant-garde* of their time and place, and I doubt that I shall have reason to apologize for granting talent—*considerable* talent—to, let us say, Ionesco, Beckett, and Genet—or Pinter, Albee, and Jack Richardson. These men's failures could be, and occasionally have been, more precious to me than the success of commonplace playwrights who never disturbed my equilibrium. If these men of capsized careers were mad, they were mad on the right side of the road. I am anything but regretful, for example, that I invested a great deal of hope and effort in William Saroyan as a young playwright. His improvisatory, undisciplined, mode of creation led him into many a blind alley after 1941, but I retain the opinion that the *fauve* artistry of his early plays—especially *My Heart's in the Highlands* and *The Time of Your Life*—were worth dozens of standardized Main Stem productions. I don't regret, of course, my support of those few writers—chiefly, Williams, Miller, and Inge—who did arrive at thriving careers, but we should not forget that their talent, too, first appeared on the fringes of inspired amateurism. At the early stages of a promising career, it was important not to slight Williams' sensitivity, Miller's moral passion, and Inge's disquietingly quiet desperation.

I would conclude, therefore, that we can afford to be patient with the Theatre of the Absurd school, as with any other that has appeared in the quicksands of modernity. This school will not take over the theatre. Its dross will disappear. At the same time that its follies offend us, we must reflect that considerable talent can sprout out of its morasses side by side with considerable speciousness, although it is not always easy for us to distinguish the one from the other.

■

AVANT-GARDE: REAL OR FANCIED?*

One recent *avant-garde* play, *Waiting for Godot* by Samuel Beckett, has been described as "a despairing study of hope." Another even obscurer and "nonpessimistic" play by the same author has been called "a despairing study of despair." To which a friendly historian or apologist of the school of writing to which these and other plays by Samuel Beckett and other playwrights such as Ionesco, Genet, and Edward Albee have been attached replies that these works express "modern man's endeavor to make him face up to the human condition as it really is." And to this new apologist, another critic adds that "the dignity of man lies in his ability to face reality in all its senselessness, to accept it freely, without fear, without illusions, and to laugh at it."

When the concept *avant-garde* is discussed nowadays with respect to the drama (and to some extent the novel, too), the label given it is the "absurd"—a label, I might add, that Samuel Beckett has resented because the word "absurd" implies judgment, and how can one pass judgment on what Beckett has set out to deal with in novels, radio plays, pantomimes, and stage plays—namely, NOTHING. To reduce his enigmatic meaning to *something* that can be evaluated is to diminish his work. He doesn't deal with *ideas* or *meaning,* he would claim, but with what *is*—the human condition. Intellectuals may have difficulty explaining or explicating *Waiting for Godot.* But the convicts of San Quentin prison, some presumably serving life terms, had none. For them *Waiting for Godot* was about *waiting—waiting* for *Nothing.* The learned Professor William York Tindall merely extends the meaning (from Beckett's stoic point of view) when he says, "Godot is what every man waits for. And what he gets (presumably nothing) for waiting," and that Beckett in writing the play has "created from nothing a formal nothing."

My concern with *avant-gard*ism is personal, since the subject evokes for me ghosts of my own past as that most rolling of rolling stones in my time as in yours—namely, a young man of letters. I believe I must make this fact plain at the start if only to counteract any impression I may give later on of frigid detachment. I intend no supercilious haughtiness in trying to deal objectively with the subject, even if my readers may well be

* Reprinted from *Kenyon Alumni Bulletin* (January–March, 1965). Originally a talk delivered as part of Kenyon's Lectureship program.

683

divided on *avant-gard*ism between seasoned repugnance and youthful enthusiasm.

I myself started out as a young man of letters in the so-called sophisticated 1920's. I must even admit to a precocious teen-age attachment to an *avant-gard*ism of slightly earlier vintage. In the years of my turbid and turbulent adolescence during and immediately after World War I, Swinburnian estheticism vied for my allegiance with bleak realism, Bohemian disengagement with social reform, nihilist pessimism with liberal, Wilsonian optimism. Next, in the prohibition and prosperity era of the 1920's I followed the pied—or should I say pie-eyed—pipers of multiple *avant-garde* hedonism as long as I could afford it—not long enough. Then came the stock-market crash of 1929, and I was seized with all the fervors and anxieties of the 1930's. This period of poverty, fascism, and imminence of war drew all of us young artists and intellectuals to heady and at times misguided ventures in social criticism and socially-oriented art. In the course of my two decades of literary roaming, I also gathered my harvest of labels: left-wing critic, bourgeois (that is, "decadent") intellectual, Freudian disciple, and objectivist poet. And I have continued to be involved, at times quite against my will, with changing fashions and clashing experiments in the arts as an author, critic, editor, Broadway producer, and teacher. By now, I am perhaps even a little tired of trying to maintain a semblance of perpendicularity on the shifting grounds of nearly five decades of contemporaneity.

My conclusions reflect a more than slight suspicion that *avant-gard*ism has been chronic in our century. It started, to be sure, earlier—in the nineteenth century with the tensions of romanticism which in turn started a little earlier in the eighteenth century with the *Sturm und Drang* revolt against neoclassicism. Its cultural history consists of one *avant-garde* movement or outlook coming hard on the heels of another. Except where and when some inhibiting factor has been operative, the split of *avant-gard*ism has time and again challenged, if not actually overthrown, the established order in art, literature, drama, and theatre. And the factor inhibiting *avant-gardes*—namely, dictation to artists—has won scant approval, if any, from our century's independent artists and intellectuals. This much can certainly be said for our century's various *avant-gardes*: art has suffered whenever they were suppressed, forbidden, or officially discouraged. This has been the case whether we think of Nazi, fascist, or Stalinist repression or the sheer inertia of the Philistinism attributed to the Broadway establishment, the West End of London, and the posh boulevard theatres of Paris.

What is this *avant-gard*ism? Can it be defined? Can it be subsumed under some artistically and socially meaningful classifications? At first thought, perhaps not! The mind reels as one tries to keep track of the numerous programs and productions of the various movements, even if one confines oneself to a single art like painting or drama. In the theatre alone (and theatre and the other arts overlap a good deal) we have to account for such things as symbolism, expressionism, dadaism, surrealism, constructivism, Pirandellism, epic theatre, and the current fad of Theatre of the Absurd. And this list is but a simplification of a very tangled skein of notions and practices. Somewhere or other I have lost futurism, vorticism, action painting, pop art and, I fear, much else. Some order does, however, become apparent once we ask ourselves what the main theatrical movements have had in common.

Above all, they have in common a revolt against some established style. With so many *avant-garde* fashions dotting the landscape of dramatic art, we might wonder whether there could be any such style. But there is, and there has been, one ever since the last quarter of the nineteenth century, if not, in fact, earlier. We call it "realism," a deceptive and difficult term perhaps for the critic and scholar but an extremely simple thing for average playgoers of the past hundred years. For that public, realism is simply the presentation in dialogue, action, and stage settings of ordinary life. The details, behavioral and environmental, are rendered with the fidelity of verisimilitude. The order of events is direct, simple, and uncomplicated—so that cause is followed by effect and there is a transparent connection between incidents.

No leap of the imagination is required to account for the vogue of this style of production. It is part of the superficial realism that characterizes popular art and literature. It reflects a world given over to the idolatry of things and the cult of practicality. It was "practical scenery," consisting, among other things, of real doors with real doorknobs, that first commended realism to the Englishmen. Realism of this order of recognizability is the bedrock of commercial theatre throughout the Western world. Let us make no mistake about it because we read other kinds of plays at college and hear discussions of advanced styles. Theatregoers of the Western world are mainly middle class. Realism was born of the middle class almost two hundred years ago, and belongs to it in heart and mind. We may escape from it now and then into an off-Broadway little theatre of 299 seats or under, but that is exactly where we are likely to remain, with very few exceptions—usually sensational ones like the New York productions of Genet's *The Balcony* and *The Blacks*.

Nor is this merely a matter of economics and social stratification. Middle-aged attitudes combine with middle class interests in establishing the context of commercial theatre. And it is amazing how quickly the young and turbulent become middle-aged and placid; or, for that matter, how quickly members of the proletariat glorified as the vanguard of civilization by Marxist ideology become middle class home-and-car owners when they have some extra dollars in the pocket or the bank.

It does not follow either that all middle class drama, or all plays that appeal to the middle-aged, are bad. No dramatic style has a monopoly on defects any more than it has a monopoly on merits. Normative realistic drama could not have survived so long without qualities that can engage human interest. It cannot even be said that this style of drama cropping up year after year with relentless repetiveness and chronic inanity must kill off its public with boredom. This is not the case, partly because there have always been unconventional plays and productions in the professional theatre to add a little spice to playgoing; and partly, no doubt, because the Philistine majority has been able to regale itself regularly with that most flamboyant of all departures from realistic theatre—the synthetic art of the musical revue and musical comedy that comprises a large part of the commercial theatre. If Mr. Babbitt is tired of a parlor comedy like *Beekman Place* he can always transfer his patronage to *Hello, Dolly!* There have always been music-hall and variety-show alternatives to sober dramaturgy. And in any event we must reckon with the possibility that even a commonplace commodity, such as drawing-room comedy or the problem play, may become irradiated with talent. If only for its own brief time and place, realistic comedy such as Maugham's *The Circle* and Sidney Howard's *They Knew What They Wanted* or a realistic problem drama such as Galsworthy's *Loyalties* or Lorraine Hansberry's *Raisin in the Sun* rose above the general mediocrity of middle class realism.

Now that we have defined the norm of theatre against which the twentieth-century *avant-gardes* have revolted, we can glance at the nature of the revolt itself.

In the theatre, the most substantial revolt occurred during the last quarter of the nineteenth century within the middle-class habitations of realism itself. And this palace revolution, so to speak, manifested itself in two virtually simultaneous phases. One of these, which developed under Ibsen and Shaw, I like to designate as "critical realism," because it emphasized intellectual inquiry and judgment as the criteria of significant art. The other phase, associated with Émile Zola and the early Strindberg, fought for a place in the theatre with the slogan of "naturalism" because it aspired to an approximation of the natural sciences in focusing on instinctual, natural forces as a way of viewing men's conduct and fate.

It is not too much to claim that the modern drama started with these two allied *avant-garde* movements. *Avant-garde* is precisely what they were, although we have tended to look upon both critical realism and naturalism as the Establishment against which it has been necessary to stage the series of insurrections we have called modernism. It is precisely as *avant-garde* upheavals that critical realism and naturalism attracted their friends and appalled their foes. That is how leading turn-of-the-century American critics such as William Winter and James Huneker received Ibsen, the latter applauding him as heroic and beneficial iconoclast (as did Bernard Shaw) while Winter denounced Ibsen as a dangerous influence and called Ibsenism "a disease injurious alike to the stage and the public." And Winter had distinguished allies in puritanical American criticism when he protested against what he called Ibsen's "variously flaccid, insipid, tainted, and nauseous plays," his "rank, deadly pessimism," and his "disordered mentality."

You will, of course, have no difficulty in observing the similarity between these charges and the charges leveled half a century later against *avant-garde* writing today, whether of the beatnik or the Theatre of the Absurd variety—in short, the same outcry against decadence, which has been more comprehensively denounced in Soviet Russia for some thirty years as bourgeois formalism. Nor will you fail to hear echoes of a similar denunciation of moral depravity in the political speeches of the election year of 1964.

The reaction against the antirealistic reactions of dadaism, expressionism, and surrealism led briefly to a retrograde realism in Central Europe known as *die neue Sachlichkeit,* or new objectivity, but also to the new *avant-garde* art of epic theatre under Piscator and Brecht in Germany; also to constructivist mechanization of settings and performances in the Russian theatre under the leadership of Meyerhold; also to the controlled theatricality of Giraudoux, Anouilh, and Jouvet in France, as well as fugitively to the poetic theatre movement of Eliot and Fry in England. And cutting across these efforts came a new *avant-garde—*notably, social realism in America during the Depression period of the 1930's, in reaction to the sophisticated theatre of the twenties; and a belated Wesker and Osborne-led social realism in England some twenty years later. (And to this I should add a brief period of existentialist realism and fantasy led by Sartre and Camus in postwar France.) Finally, to date, we have had the Theatre of the Absurd cutting across liberal realism and social optimism—a reaction against any complacent assessment of man and his future on a planet threatened with nuclear suicide.

And today we may already have to add a reaction against this reaction! So it would seem if we take into account a recent turn to social drama by the absurdists themselves, as witnessed by Adamov's play about the French Commune, *Spring 1871,* and Ionesco's *Rhinoceros*—and the rise of a grotesque form of social satire and social melodrama favored by the Swiss writers Duerrenmatt and Frisch in such works as *The Visit* and *The Firebugs.*

In the face of so bewildering a succession of reversals how can the concept of *avant-garde* revolt carry much meaning? It can, and it does, of course, provide us with evidence of a high degree of instability in twentieth-century art, which is hardly surprising in view of the instability of twentieth-century society. It can tell us, too, that we have manifested an undercurrent of romanticism, if by that term we mean a restless pursuit of vistas and values not readily available. From this point of view, critical realism, too, has been fundamentally romantic in sustaining the principles that critical inquiry is superior to social and intellectual conformity. (Even when an individual like T. S. Eliot becomes a self-announced conservative in politics and religion, he becomes a rebel in art. He deviates, he cannot but deviate, from the norm in the period's playwriting when he writes *Murder in the Cathedral, The Family Reunion,* and *The Cocktail Party,* just as he deviates from majority opinion and social practice. The conformity he advocates is not conformity to the norms of his time and place.)

A special kind of romanticism sparked the enthusiasm of proponents of social drama. They idealized the common man, attributed heroic qualities to the class-conscious proletariat, and assigned to it the historical mission of creating a new world order of millennial justice and virtue. And nothing perhaps can be considered more romantic than the very ideas of irresistible progress and the perfectibility of man intrinsic to militant social drama. Both the revolt and romanticism need to be closely defined and plainly limited before they can be usefully applied.

Revolt, in the first place, against what? I have already answered that question in calling it, on the whole, revolt against middle-class private or family life and middle-class society—whether that revolt assume the lineaments of antirealistic art or of intensified realism. By the same token, I have also suggested that *avant-garde* art has been a revolt against superficial realism.

But we can go further and describe all the vanguards qualitatively as representing intensifications of a practice or principle. Intensify realism, which is a virtually inevitable ingredient of art since its basis is the observation of our outer and inner worlds, and you get an exciting realist-naturalist *avant-garde* in the 1880's. Intensify imaginativeness in art, which is an equally important ingredient, and you get an attractive symbolist theatre in the next decades; or you get, a decade or so later, a violent, eruptive expressionist theatre. Intensify regional, local and occupational speech and you get *avant-garde* naturalistic dialogue. Intensify the language of feeling and you get poetic or impressionist or expressionist dialogue. Finally, intensify either men's affirmative or their negative attitude toward their possibilities and you attain two radically different types of *avant-garde* theatre—that of protest and hope or that of despair and negation.

If we bear in mind that intensified art, as seen from this point of view, is necessarily *avant-garde* art, we can appreciate its duplicity in the modern theatre, we can say that it has been an *avant-garde* theatre in different periods whether it was strongly realistic or antirealistic, distinctly positive or negative, definitely hopeful or despairing. We can observe this process, in fact, right now in the most advanced quarters of our theatre on both professional and nonprofessional levels. For a decade or longer the theatre has been regarded as advanced whether it favored Brecht or Beckett— that is, intensely engaged or intensely disengaged drama. Young people feel about equally advanced in dramatic art whether they put on the former's *Mother Courage* or the latter's *Waiting for Godot*. Their prime commitment has been in either case to the enticements of art rather than to the clamor of social reality. I discern no inclination to overthrow the capitalistic system when they produce Brecht, or any loss of appetite when they produce Beckett in their little theatre. It is evident that they can assimilate both Brecht and Beckett or Ionesco without any marked awareness of divided loyalties.

Both schools are real *avant-gardes* to them, although their origination and leaders may insist on sharply distinguishing between one school and another, denouncing one or the other as merely a fancied or illusory vanguard that should actually be exposed as a rear guard. This was notably the case in the controversy aroused when Kenneth Tynan attacked Ionesco in 1958 (in the *London Observer*) for moving into a blind alley or self-imposed vacuum in offering an escape from realism; for providing at best a "funfare ride on a ghost train, all skulls and hooting waxworks." Ionesco, in turn, assailed Tynan's Brechtian premises of a socially didactic theatre, contending that "a work of art has nothing to do with doctrine" and "has its own unique system of expression, its own means of directly apprehending the real." For Ionesco, Brecht (as well as the political Sartre, Arthur Miller, and John Osborne) were false messiahs of art. For Ionesco, the really advanced dramatist would be the one who attends to the ultimate reality of man's failure. "No society," he declared, "has been able to abolish human sadness, no political system can deliver us from the pain of living, from our fear of death, our thirst for the absolute; it is [he asserted] the human condition that directs the social condition, and not vice versa." To this Tynan effectively retorted: "M. Ionesco correctly says that no ideology has yet abolished fear, pain, or madness. Nor has any work of art. But both are in the business of trying. What other business is there?"

One thing is abundantly clear to any historically knowledgeable person or, for that matter, to anybody who became a playgoer some forty or more years ago: the *avant-garde* is not *avant* in the sense of newness or inviolable originality. Epic theatre, as its leaders Piscator and Brecht made clear, was not new when they created it in the 1920's by combining Ibsenite social realism with presentational techniques. For epic breadth and variety they referred to Shakespeare, and they could have referred to Aeschylus. Epic theatre is certainly not new today even if a new generation has but recently discovered it and young critics began to call attention to it after World War II when it already was a quarter of a century old. Theatre of the Absurd is not new either. It prevailed during and immediately after World War I. It was already over thirty years old when Ionesco's *The Bald Soprano* opened in a tiny left-bank Paris theatre in 1950.

To youthful zealots who have come to the absurdist theatre recently, it must be disconcerting to be told that what they have just discovered was discovered long ago. To those of their elders such as the famed theatrical scholar Allardyce Nicoll, who has taken a dim view of modernist experimentation, it is doubtless comforting to know that what they deplore is actually a dramatic style that was buried, if indeed it ever really lived, three quarters of a century ago. But there is no reason for the young to be dispirited and for the old to be complacent. Each discovery in art tends to be a rediscovery and an adaptation to new conditions or to experiences and ideas that are new to a new generation. Each generation must discover for itself what has already been discovered if it is to be meaningful and effective. This is true of both style and idea, of form and content. A valid charge against proponents of absurdism is not that their theatre fails to be spanking new (how long can newness remain new in any case!) but that it fails to be arresting or absorbing, that it usually seems overextended when it exceeds the average length of a one-act play, and that it tends to be repetitive.

The fun goes rapidly out of the game when the characters are lifeless, when the body that is being derided and kicked around is a corpse. That is where, of course, passion, imagination and invention rush to the rescue of the indubitably talented—the rare Beckett, Albee, or Ionesco—

who adopts a style of art or a form of drama that historians have considered stale. The problem is ever one of making it new rather than of finding it new.

The designation—*avant-garde* art—of course, is a matter of interpretation. Thus, the man who considers *Waiting for Godot* a rueful paean to man's heroic spirit rather than a metaphor for bleak futility, is not likely to reach eagerly for the term *"avant-garde"* as a label for the work. He will prefer to locate this play in the mainstream of humanistic tradition consisting of faith in man and sympathy with his strivings. He will observe such approvable signs of humanity in the work as the touching friendship and interdependence of Beckett's two tramps, Gogo and Didi, no matter how they may symbolize "body" and "flesh" abstrusely.

One could wonder at the inordinate success of *The Threepenny Opera* with the New York public during years of political reaction until one realized that but for isolated statements on exploitation and economic motivation this parodistic masterpiece by Brecht and Weill was dadaist mockery far more than it was Marxist propaganda. There were playgoers in New York who went to see *The Threepenny Opera* several times during its long run. Why not? They could eat their cake and have it, too— that is, they could enjoy the thrill of cynical aspersions on humanity and society without having their comfortable way of life seriously challenged or impeded; they could feel boldly safe and safely daring. This has probably been the case with many a latter-day Brecht enthusiast in America.

He could take the *avant-garde* skepticism, which is a prominent facet in a Brecht play, and ignore the Marxist message, often indeed muted or trumpeted from both sides of the mouth with a skeptical or ambiguous wink in between. It is to a large extent his ambivalences that made Brecht an arresting playwright and a great scenewright. It is his negativism, his sardonic view of both middle-class values and liberal assumptions or presumptions that has chiefly qualified him for *avant-garde* support in academic and bohemian circles.

And this brings us, finally, to the element that most closely defines *avant-garde* theatre, past and present—namely, its latent or overt nihilism, its flambuoyant irreverence, or its profound skepticism. This is what links the *avant-garde* most distinctly to the pattern of revolt I traced earlier. And so it has continued, this reflex theatricalization of civilization's bankruptcy up to the present day with the current Theatre of the Absurd. And so we come face to face with *avant-garde* dramatic art as an evocation, and perhaps an exorcism, of *Angst* in our perilous times.

The Theatre of the Absurd has not indeed taken over the commercial or popular theatre while making some inroads in it (such as the Joan

Littlewood pacifist revue *Oh What a Lovely War* and Duerrenmatt's science-fiction fantasia *The Physicists,* currently on Broadway after succeeding in England and Central Europe respectively). Especially in the relatively placid United States, the *avant-garde* still stands at the periphery of popular theatre. Nevertheless, it has been virtually the only alternative to the complacencies and ineptitudes of Philistine art. That this *avant-garde* is real enough rather than fancied can be readily granted even after noting that it offers for the most part only a warmed-over pessimism.

That the advance guard really advances, however, is very much open to question. It seems rather to lead dramatic art as well as its audiences into quagmires of desolation from which an escape must be found if theatre and society are to possess vital continuity.

A negative vitality is almost impossible to attain in art; and as a proposed advance in theatre, other than as an escape from soap opera, absurdist drama in general is, in fact, illusory. Actually and potentially, it tends more to ensure the immobilization or paralysis of dramatic art than its revitalization. Even if it has produced a few minor masterpieces such as Beckett's *Waiting for Godot* and Ionesco's *The Chairs,* even if it has been briefly invigorated by the satanic genius of a Genet in *The Maids, The Balcony,* and *The Blacks,* in principle it leads the theatre, as well as human behavior, into the numbness of nullity. Not surprisingly, therefore, there already appears to be a flight from the absurdist impasse even now when an Ionesco turns to the genre of social protest with a *Rhinoceros* and Edward Albee dramatizes personal rather than abstract tensions in *Who's Afraid of Virginia Woolf?*

Even in matters of stylistic and technical innovation, a condition of stalemate has been more apparent than a state of progression. Style was fragmented and otherwise disordered in the earlier absurdist experiments of dadaism and surrealism; and also in expressionism, which often reduced dialogue prose to stenographic stammering and poetic speech to rhythmic ejaculations some forty years before. In drama of the absurd, language has once more been undercut by moody repetitions that make progression of feeling and thought impossible; this is apparent even in such well-written plays by Samuel Beckett as *Krapp's Last Tape, Endgame,* and *Happy Days.* In some of these, words, which have been the carriers of ideas in the theatre ever since Aeschylus, have even been subordinated to mechanical sounds and movements as a preferable means of communication.

A total reduction of words to movement appears in Beckett's *Act Without Words,* in which the hopelessness of man's situation in the universe is conveyed entirely by the miming of a single hapless individual who never articulates his desires and defeats. (I might say in passing that one could take this to be the ultimate canard of the absurdists against humanity. Humanity may have been as trapped, teased, and frustrated as Beckett's miming antihero in *Act Without Words,* but has certainly been gloriously articulate, as three thousand years of world literature and world drama would prove. It is surely with his sentience and language that man has continuously triumphed, more than with anything else, over the absurdity of his condition, if indeed it is absurd.)

And Ionesco, I should add, goes even further than Beckett in the war against the great human prerogative of language, both in reducing speech to the inconsequent banality of *The Bald Soprano,* and in substituting not only gesture or mime but objects (such as multiplying furniture and a growing corpse) as a proper means of expression. Some of the effects achieved by this vanguard may be entertaining and meaningful (at least as meaningful comment on meaninglessness). But in making this concession, one cannot of course maintain that there has been any renovation of language from the latest *avant-garde.*

As for the possibility of getting technical innovations from this *avant-garde,* the only one I have come across is the anti-Aristotelian scuttling of linear progression in favor of a pattern of action that has no real beginning or ending since the movement of the play is distinctly circular. Circular action is most successfully employed in *Waiting for Godot,* and, with modifications, it does some service elsewhere, as in *Krapp's Last Tape* and *Endgame.* But circular dramaturgy is at most such an exotic innovation that it would soon lose its novelty if repeated, and prove self-defeating insofar as the objective of dramatic technique is to promote, rather than retard, the progress of action and idea in a play.

The problems of language and structure remain secondary to the total effect of what this latest *avant-garde* has been saying to us; and its limits as dramatic art derive principally from its limitation of content and philosophy.

The only difference of treatment I would expect from our Western absurdists is that as the man bent over the barrel he would see in the clear mirror of the water not himself, but somebody else—a skeleton perhaps, or simply nothing, nothing at all! And I would also expect that if the story were rendered as a play, it would lack the movement, the scenery, and the visual imagery of the motion picture—and leave the playwright and the playgoer in the bottom of the barrel.

For all that, I am paradoxically not inclined to leave this overview of *avant-gard*ism in the bottom of the barrel with an unmitigatedly dispirited conclusion. An obvious reason is that theory and practice or effect are not necessarily identical. No matter how dismal an artist's view of life may be, the creative act may prove exhilarating. The art, if really well executed, will be a positive achievement even if the philosophy is unalterably negative. Also, through the gap between the philosophy and the play, however tiny that gap may be, as in the case of Beckett's *Waiting for Godot,* may flow the chemical substance that performs art's alchemy. Some miracle of insight or empathy may transform a No into a Yes, greatly to the advantage of a play, a film, a mime, a ballet, or a book.

I know that *I* was not cast down but lifted up by *Waiting for Godot* when I saw the New York performance featuring that wonderful clown Bert Lahr, whether or not everyone would approve his being cast in the part. His humanity in the role of the tramp Gogo, who is given the mind and heart of a child, redeemed man's fallen condition for me then and there. The readiness of Beckett's tramps to wait for the ever postponed arrival of Godot reminded me of man's unostentatious endurance in an alien and puzzling, often seemingly hostile, world. Nor was this an abstruse concept for me. It was as close as the face of one I had loved and tended for many years; I was reminded of the fortitude and wan dignity of a dying old woman who dressed herself for company and sat erect until the gathering poisons of gangrene made her fall down on her bed; I am reminded as I draft these words of all the heartening things we can all recall about the fragile humanity Pascal called a "thinking reed" and could have called, just as appropriately, "a feeling reed."

In the work of Beckett that I have seen, despite the plainly intended irony of the author, I felt the same reprieve from total desolation when I observed the sweet-faced old lady Nell, the ancestral woman, peeping out of her ashcan in *Endgame,* and the talkative matron of *Happy Days* who kept on solacing herself with rosy recollections as she lay buried on the stage first up to her hips and then finally up to her neck. In *Endgame,* the sweet Nell of the Greenwich Village production prevailed with me long enough to abate for a while the bleak apocalypse that one of Beckett's approving critics has called, with apparent relish, "the death of the stock props of Western civilization—family, cohesion, filial, parental, and connubial love, faith in God, artistic appreciation and creation." Somehow the *avant-garde* does not seem so formidably negative after all when humanity takes possession of us.

We may conclude, then, that if the *avant-garde* does not move forward half as much as it thinks it does, neither does it devastate its public as much as it apparently intends. More conflicts between a presumptive *avant-garde* and rear guard are frequently stimulating and perhaps even essential to the health of art. Perhaps Emily Dickinson was right when she wrote in a letter that "It is essential to the sanity of mankind that each one should think the other crazy."

ART AND INSTABILITY IN THE
MODERN THEATRE[1]

Anyone expected to cast anchor in the turbulent and turbid sea of contemporary professional theatre is bound to be disappointing to himself and his audience. We may well ask whether the theatre has ever had much stability and whether there has ever been much point in concerning oneself with it from any long-range point of view, not to say from any fixed philosophical position.

As for the first question, the answer is quite simple: the only stable periods of any appreciable duration in the history of the theatre have been the intervals during which the theatre was dead. Each of the great ages of the theatre—and you can count them on one hand—had a relatively short and merry, or not so merry, life. If there was one institution that could not be counted on to behave with consistency and seasoned circumspection it was the theatre. It is not surprising that it was often censored and saddled with rules. Plato would have banished the theatre from his ideal republic; and this was long before the early Christian fathers lost patience with the ribaldness of the decadent Roman stage. The Greeks, who gave official status to their dramatic performances, wondered why they were so much concerned with this unruly institution associated with the cult of the god Dionysus, the god of wine, rivalry, and fertility. *Ti tauta pros Dionyson?*—"Why all this fuss about Dionysus?"—the Greeks asked.

I suspect that the question was largely rhetorical, for the classic Greeks knew they were celebrating the life-principle at their annual theatre festivals; and although they loved to order things with reason, logic, and law they knew that life is naturally unruly. They believed in giving the life-drive release while at the same time controlling it, and in the case of the drama the controls ranged from principles of taste to taboos against scenes of violence. The plays, moreover, had a specific structure in the tragic pattern of alternating "episodes" or scenes and choruses; and the stage productions had ritualistic features such as masks that formalized and distanced turbulent feeling, and costumes and boots, in the case of tragedy, that impeded spontaneous action.

[1] One of three Vincent J. Flynn Lectures delivered by the author at the College of St. Thomas, March, 1962.

Drama is the art of presenting meaningful crises to an audience, and theatre is, as it were, an organized chaos. That being the case ever since classic times, so that the drama has always disturbed the public's equilibrium before restoring it, and the theatre losing reputation almost as often as it gained reputation, so that actors were considered little better than vagabonds in Shakespeare's day unless they acquired a powerful patron, we may well ask why we should be particularly exercised over the theatre's instability today? I think there are many reasons for our concern and not all of these are necessarily uncomplimentary to the theatre.

For one thing, we really care about the theatre, even in the United States, where we have no government support for the stage while many European governments subsidize it. The theatre, although caught in a tight squeeze between its economic unsoundness and the competition of the mass media of radio, television, and movies, generally commands respect. It is the least commercialized institution after opera, ballet, and symphony orchestras, and it is the only one among these arts that deals explicitly with ideas. For another, the theatre is considered an effective educational instrument and regarded as a pleasurable means for offering instruction or correction. Those vigorous post-Renaissance educators the Jesuits discerned ample educational possibilities in the theatre, and today these possibilities are being cultivated as an important part of a liberal-arts program in thousands of American schools and colleges. I submit, however, that we are especially concerned today because of three more or less related circumstances that may be described as economic, moral, and esthetic instability.

The first factor is too familiar to require detailed discussion here. The doldrums of the professional theatre in the United States have been abundantly publicized. These may be fundamentally economic, for the theatre is a wasteful and speculative business, but it is not the bookkeeping *per se* but the cultural aspect that is truly dismaying. I refer to the reduced opportunities available to the talented, the chaotic conditions of play production that cannot but weaken morale and artistry, and the loss and deterioration of audiences. By "loss" I mean the regrettable fact that, owing to high prices, an institution that should have a large mass audience—and that had such an audience for Sophocles or Shakespeare—becomes the special preserve of a small, economically comfortable, usually middle-aged public, leaving a large and youthfully impressionable public at the mercies of television programming. By "deterioration" of the audience I mean the deplorable fact that the public dooms all but a small percentage of professionally produced plays to a quick death regardless of merit, and catapults the remaining few plays into the dubious category of the "smash hit" success that everybody feels he must see. As a result, the public does not really attend plays but "hits," while the producer, as a rule, has no alternative to producing hits than that of producing failures. This situation deteriorates the audience and demoralizes producers, playwrights, and actors.

Since the same unfortunate condition now prevails in the off-Broadway theatres on the periphery of Broadway, there is no balm in the Gilead known as mid-Manhattan. In one respect, the situation is even more regrettable since the very public, the youthful and the economically straitened one, for which the off-Broadway theatre is designed, sees few of its productions, and also becomes demoralized, patronizing only those shows that have gained a reputation for oddity or sensationalism.

Whereas the large Broadway theatre manages to lure customers to the box office with resplendent and tuneful, if intellectually hollow, musical comedies, which at least provide miscellaneous entertainment and generally innocent, if vapid, pleasure, the off-Broadway cubicles attract a following chiefly with plays steeped in cynicism or garnished with bizarre details and perfumed with the odor of decay. Only in the theatres associated with our smaller communities, our schools, and our colleges is there less pressure to bait the hook for the young. But one hesitates to say that the hook remains unbaited, because the young are likely to bait it themselves. They don't like to be left out of any enterprise that seems daring or iconoclastic. They don't want to lag behind the prevailing *avant-garde* even when it leads into a cesspool—or a madhouse. They are under great pressure to conform to the new fashion, whether of moral or philosophical vacuity. That is, they tend to become conforming nonconformists. The recent vogue of the Theatre of the Absurd type of drama, imported chiefly from the Paris of Samuel Beckett and Jean Genet, confirms one's conviction that the blame cannot be meted out merely to the Broadway or the off-Broadway theatres. It ultimately rests with the spirit of the age, the *Zeitgeist,* and involves the instability of modern society, which the theatre reflects rather than creates.

Why we should be especially exercised over the moral instability of the theatre when this has been so often the case in past periods can easily be explained. Its special manifestation in our times is not actually looseness of morals, which is surely less widespread than some plays might lead us to believe, but something deeper and, I rather think, more deadly. I would call it moral sloth or acedia. It is, briefly, *nihilism* which, contrary to the life-affirming sensuality of medieval farces and Rabelais's or Boccaccio's narratives, robs dramatic art of its vitality while making life meaningless. Humanity has long been familiar with frivolity and prurience. The conventional figure with the forked tail and the lascivious leer is a devil who can be rather easily recognized. It is against a radically different demon that our defenses are weakest. He is a less recognizable devil and he is capable of commanding some respect for apparent intellectual integrity, honest disillusion, and stoic despair. The great Goethe described him well when he made Mephistopheles say to Faust, "I am the spirit that is forever denying"—*"Ich bin der Geist der stets verneint."* In our anxious times, it is the spirit that is, in effect, forever denying that life has worth and men's aspirations value. The titillations of sensualism are about as evanescent as they are familiar. It is against the lure and challenge of the new puritanism of negation that our defenses are weakest. The evil that creates the greatest concern is essentially *new* in the Western theatre. It is the corrosion of the will, the destruction of hope, the idolatry of passiveness. It is "death-wish" theatre, and not salacious theatre, that is most profoundly disturbing.

In order to avoid doing it injustice by definition and description, I shall resort to the words of its proponents. According to the ablest American playwright associated with this school, Edward Albee, the Theatre of the Absurd expresses, as he put it in a *New York Times* article, "concepts having to do, in the main, with man's attempt to make sense for himself out of his senseless position in a world which makes no sense— which makes no sense because the moral, religious, political, and social structures man has erected to 'illusion' [that is, to deceive] himself have collapsed." This, I would say, is a fairly accurate description but for one detail: I don't find in this theatre much effort to "make sense" out of man's position in the world. To make "nonsense," yes; to make "sense," no!

I even suspect these writers of indulging in more than a modicum of pleasure and self-gratulation in failing to make sense and, in the work of some of the playwrights (certainly in the case of Jean Genet, a writer traumatized since childhood by an unwholesome family situation) I suspect a sadistic pleasure in the verdict of worthlessness and hopelessness that they render against the world. Nor is the present period (the period since 1945) the only one which has reflected this attitude in the twentieth-century theatre. It was briefly represented about forty years ago in American plays of the 1920's such as the poet E. E. Cummings' farrago of satire and fantasy *him,* and these plays were actually mild by comparison with those produced about the same time and somewhat earlier in Central Europe. In one German play, *The Seduction,* by Paul Kornblum, a young man was induced to shoot his father in the name of freedom with the slogan "Destroy the tyranny of the family," and in one mercifully unnamed play, according to an embarrassed critic, "a gentleman's liver was cut up and eaten." The German critic in question, the eminent Alfred Kerr, exclaimed "They actually produced that in the theatre. Oh, you know too little about this era in the German drama." And I couldn't help reflecting later that when a character in a pro-Nazi play of the 1930's declared that he was tempted to whip out a revolver whenever he heard the word "culture" pronounced, he could just as well have walked out of an expressionist play of the year 1915.

I should add, however, that Mr. Edward Albee was not exactly representing his own plays when he gave us his Theatre of the Absurd definition;[2] I don't believe that his poignant and exciting play *The Zoo Story* fits the definition, and I am not sure that his most recent play, *The American Dream,* does to any appreciable degree. It is also only fair to quote an apologist for the present Theatre of the Absurd from England, Mr. Martin Esslin, the author of an excellent book on the subject, who claims that this school (and here I quote him) "does not reflect despair of a return to dark irrational forces but expresses modern man's endeavor to come to terms with the world in which he lives. It attempts to make him face up to the human condition as it really is, to free him from illusions. . . ." Then Mr. Esslin expands upon this point, claiming that "the dignity of man lies in his ability to face reality in all its senselessness, to accept it freely, without fear, without illusions and to laugh at it."

It will be observed, however, that the fundamental premise here is that reality and the human condition are both devoid of sense—a tall hypothesis which men have contradicted from the beginning of civilization; otherwise, indeed, there would have been no civilization at all, no thinking, no humaneness, no love, no friendship, no family life, no decency—only mindless flux and soul-less nature red in tooth and claw. Moreover, if reality and human nature are so senseless, how is it possible to write plays about senselessness that make sense? How is it possible to write well-organized books and essays about the Theatre of the Absurd like Mr. Esslin's book and Mr. Albee's *New York Times* Sunday article?

Nevertheless, the fact that the recent negativistic plays these writers defend dramatize the absurdity cult and the "endgame" or end-of-the-world philosophy of the *avant-garde* playwrights is incontrovertible. Mr. Albee describes some of their qualities aptly when he recalls that in one of the representative plays, Beckett's *Endgame,* "a legless couple live out their lives in twin ashcans, surfacing occasionally for food or conversation"; that in another specimen, Ionesco's *Jack, or The Submission,* "a

---

2 "Which Theatre Is Absurd?" *The New York Times Magazine* (February 25, 1962).

man is seduced, and rather easily, by a girl with three well-formed and functioning noses"; and that in a third masterwork of the absurd, Genet's *The Blacks,* which has been flourishing in a small Manhattan theatre since last summer, "one group of Negro actors is playing at pretending to be Negro." And Mr. Albee's samples are by no means the most bizarre available. In one of Samuel Beckett's plays, *Krapp's Last Tape,* the hero (or should I say, the *antihero*) devours bananas like a monkey; and in the same cheerful author's *Endgame,* in which life has been virtually wiped out, a character is alarmed to find a live flea in his trousers and promptly crushes it lest it start the chain of evolution all over again, which could culminate in the human species again. Beckett's *Waiting for Godot* has been aptly described as "a despairing study of hope," and his *Endgame* as a "despairing study of despair."[3]

As for the humor attributed to many of the negativistic plays as a virtue, it is a bizarre blessing even when the plays have zest and effervescence. Humor will be found abundantly in a number of the short plays of Ionesco, but it is mixed with gall and neurosis; and it turns completely sour in his two full-length plays, *The Killer,* in which individuality becomes extinct, and *Rhinoceros,* in which the human race, except for the rare individual Berenger, becomes bestial. Humor is ample, too, in the Freudian potpourri which its author, the recent Harvard graduate Arthur Kopit, facetiously but not inaptly titled *Oh, Dad, Poor Dad, Mamma's Hung You in the Closet and I'm Feelin' So Sad.* It does, however, require at times some odd taste to be amused by the savage humor of young Kopit's masters, Ionesco, Genet, and Beckett. Characteristically, a minor character in *Endgame* declares that "Nothing is funnier than unhappiness," and a key line in *Endgame* is one character's aside, "I say to myself that the earth is extinguished, though I never saw it lit," which is matched by the other main character's words, "Moments for nothing, now as always, time was never and time is over, reckoning closed and story ended."

I fear it will take some doing to convince many of us that the Theatre of the Absurd at its apogee is especially funny except when it is successfully satirical, as it is in Ionesco's *The Bald Soprano,* in which the absurdity of the dramatic action, not to mention the intentionally idiotic dialogue, suits the subject. In this piece, indeed, the absence of meaningful forward movement is the right form for a travesty on directionless lives, and the absence of dimensional characterization is conducive to satirical laughter. The characters are not only cartoons, but *identical* cartoons. Thus a character discussed by other characters, Bobby Watson, has a wife

[3] Vivian Mercier, "How to Read *Endgame," The Griffin* (June, 1959), pp. 10–14.

named Bobby Watson, as if husband and wife were equally devoid of individuality; and the Bobby Watsons have a son and daughter named Bobby, an uncle called Bobby Watson, and also an aunt called Bobby Watson. That the play concludes, moreover, very much as it began (there is *static* or, rather, *cyclical* dramaturgy in other absurdist plays, most notably in Beckett's *Waiting for Godot* and *Krapp's Last Tape*) enforces the satire and sustains the humor. But *The Bald Soprano* is an exception in its lively and audacious theatricality.

True gaiety emanates rarely from the mid-century *avant-garde* and is the last thing to be expected from those who walk in darkness half in love with easeful death and scornful of consolations whether human or divine. Let us at least grant them the integrity of their despair or their spite (it is sometimes difficult to distinguish the one from the other) even while taking note of the self-consciousness of their desperation. Certainly their sense of futility is "time-conditioned"—that is, it is an authentic twentieth-century "endgame" (*fin de partie*) motive—by contrast with the conviction of predecadent nineteenth-century intellectuals that progress was possible and indeed imminent. It is a belief that was dear to even so rueful a naturalist as Georg Büchner, whose plays *Wozzeck* and *Danton's Death* attained the nadir of disillusionment for their times. The absurdists of our age, one hundred and twenty-five years later, could not conceivably arrive at his affirmative conclusions, with which not even Büchner's contemporaries, who persecuted him as a radical, would have been inclined to quarrel. About the year 1830, Büchner, who also held a chair in comparative anatomy at the University of Zurich, could write that "The feeling that there's life in the thing that's created is much more important than considerations of beauty and ugliness." Büchner, the "naturalist," could even declare that "one must love human nature in order to penetrate into the character of any individual," whereas the contemporary school of the absurd does not as a rule regard the character in a play as an individual, let alone "love" him; it feels compassion for him at most—and that only as the *genus homo,* "Man," who hovers in the absurdist plays midway between an abstraction and a type. Büchner was not easily discouraged by his acquaintance with reality, not even by the bleak events of the French Revolution he recorded in *Danton's Death*. "God," he wrote his family, "didn't create history to provide reading matter for young females." This *avant-garde* opinion of the year 1835 that life is a challenge to adult spirits and minds would hardly be consolatory, not to say exalting, to the *avant-garde* of 1955 or 1960.

At the same time, it would be a mistake to attribute the taste for damnation solely to the recent and avowed apostles of the absurd. O'Neill evinced a strong awareness of damnation throughout the greater part of his life, and his instability as a dramatic artist was closely related to his inability to locate a resting point other than blanket negation. O'Neill's dramatic power was indeed largely a capacity of pain and a sense of alienation from man, nature, and God. He differed chiefly from the absurdists in having an appreciable regard for humanity and a tragic sense of the grandeur of the isolated suffering individual. O'Neill took a tragic, rather than a worm's eye, view of humanity even in *The Hairy Ape,* in which his main character Yank persists in seeking an honorable place in the universe. O'Neill aimed at stark tragic art in such plays vibrant with passion as *Desire Under the Elms* and *Mourning Becomes Electra,* whereas our mid-century absurdist playwrights have tended to be passionless ones too; for if nothing is worth anything, then passion is as superfluous as is purpose.

Tennessee Williams is another nonabsurdist nay-sayer. His nihilism is personal rather than abstruse and formal, as is Beckett's or Ionesco's. Williams has not flaunted an unbreakable negativistic commitment, being ready to break any compact he seems to have made with morbid negation whenever he feels an urge to oppose despair with strongly romantic affirmations. His Don Quixote character in *Camino Real* surmounts the wall that imprisons the rest of faltering humanity. Williams is much taken with his vivid Sicilian heroine Serafina, in *The Rose Tattoo,* in whom the vital need to love overcomes her humiliation on discovering that her deceased husband had been unfaithful. Williams also fancies Maggie, the plucky heroine of his *Cat on a Hot Tin Roof,* who drives so hard toward life while her hopeless husband Brick plunges headlong into the destructive element. Nevertheless, Williams has an obvious affinity for the school that finds no solace or resting point in the universe.

Other contemporary writers also have an inclination toward negation without any commitment to a philosophy of absurdism. William Inge has a strong sense of failure and isolation, but covers it up with a folksy Midwestern quality of sympathy and a somewhat strained optimism in *Picnic, Bus Stop, The Dark at the Top of the Stairs.* Lillian Hellman has generally taken a dim view of humanity in the plays she has written from *The Children's Hour* in 1934 to *Toys in the Attic* in 1960, but has often strengthened her playwriting with her ingrained capacity for moral indignation. She has usually indicted *individuals* rather than the universe, and she has put the blame for failure on weakness of character rather than on the so-called human condition, which is a hazy concept at best. A favorite term among absurdists and their apologists, "the human condition" is a muddled concept deriving about equally from twentieth-century existentialist atheism and nineteenth-century naturalism, which has tended to exempt the individual from responsibility on the grounds that his conduct is determined by heredity, physiology, and environment.

Arthur Miller, perhaps the most "constructive" of recent American playwrights, has struggled manfully to create a theatre of positive values and personal responsibility. He has done this with a criticism of false values, such as the materialistic success-worship that appears in *Death of a Salesman;* and with heroic example in the case of his Salem witchcraft drama, *The Crucible.* He has tried to uphold rigid standards of conduct in these plays, as well as in *A View from the Bridge,* the tragedy of a longshoreman who betrayed his kinsmen out of desperate lust for his young sister-in-law. Miller has endeavored to write tragedies about common people that will give them uncommon moral stature. There has been no love of decadence in Miller's work; if anything, he has been rather overstrenuous and obvious in his moralizations. Miller is to be credited with excellent intentions and honest endeavors. Yet the very fact that he has been so self-conscious in his positiveness, which he has also defined at considerable length in his Prefaces, is symptomatic of the disorientation of our theatre and society. He has not dropped anchor naturally and inconspicuously in a norm of values and then gone ahead with his business as an artist. He has felt impelled to proclaim his values as if Judaeo-Christianity and even Hellenism had not made them known long ago, and he has placed them at the top of his dramatic register.

Nor has the situation been radically different abroad. Advanced European playwrights such as Friedrich Duerrenmatt and Max Frisch have enlivened their bleak view of humanity with irony and extravaganza. The premise of *The Visit,* the outstanding and perhaps most *somber* product of this little Swiss school of the disillusioned, is that evil can easily have its way even in civilized, humane societies, and that there is no integrity whatsoever in the grotesquely corruptible human race. As for France—that is, Paris, the headquarters of the school of the absurd—the theatre has long been preempted by nay-sayers. The ablest of these elder negativists have differed from the present-day absurdists only in their aplomb or suavity, their easy air of sophistication, and their theatrical tricksiness.

In England, to bring this brief survey closer to home, dramatic art since World War I—with brief exceptions supplied by Shaw and the transplanted O'Casey—has stumbled into one impasse after another. The first and most long-lasting impasse has been British drawing-room comedy which has trifled endlessly with domestic crises, flirtations, and adulteries. Drawing-room comedy became especially tiresome after the strenuous *Private Lives* handsprings of Noel Coward of the 1920's.

The next impasse came when the poets invaded the theatre, one school led by Auden moving to the left, and the other school led by Eliot veering to the right. The left-wing invasion was a quick and almost total failure. The right-wing scored a notable success in 1935 with Eliot's *Murder in the Cathedral* and another, if somewhat dubious, one with *The Cocktail Party* fifteen years later. But both the poetry and the drama of other more or less religious plays by Eliot and his followers left much to be desired. Midway between the Auden and Eliot contingents came Christopher Fry, but the production of his one unexceptionable poetic work, *The Lady's Not for Burning,* was followed by works of variable merit that marked a decline in the entire career of British poetic drama.

As of today, more than a quarter of a century since the first efforts to revive poetic drama as a genre, the struggle for poetry in the British theatre is virtually over. It has been followed in recent years by the contrary trend of exploiting raucous prose and sordid situations. These have appeared in naturalistic plays ranging from sociological drama, such as Wesker's *Roots,* familiar to us in America from our Depression theatre of the 1930's, to imaginative and more or less symbolical plays even more depressing, such as Harold Pinter's *The Caretaker* and *The Dumbwaiter.* The latest theatrical movement has also brought forth farces ridiculing human aspiration, such as N. F. Simpson's *One-Way Pendulum,* which was considered uncommonly hilarious in London and uncommonly tedious in New York. This venture into vaudeville cannot continue long without exhausting itself as significant art, if indeed it ever could have attained such status. And still another quickly reached impasse has been the *Look Back in Anger* type revolt. It was started in 1956 and virtually also ended a few years later by the gifted but erratic young playwright John Osborne. He has been the typical "rebel without a cause" who must either alter the line of his attack constantly or give up the policy of revolt altogether if he is not to revolt his public.

In the American theatre concurrently we have experienced four decades of frustration despite works of individual merit and a good deal of creditable striving. The sophistication of the 1920's ended in a blind alley or was thrust into it by the stock-market crash of 1929 and the ensuing Depression. Only a few of the many lively plays of the period by Kaufman, Hecht, MacArthur, Barry, and others retain any life. The drama of social protest that galvanized the theatre of the 1930's with the explosive new talent of Odets, Hellman, Kingsley, and others disappeared with our recovery from the economic depression after 1939. The war-made liberal fervor of the decade of the 1940's, insufficiently productive during the war itself, flared up later in the work of Arthur Miller and the plays of a few secondary writers. But Miller has been stalemated for some time now, while Tennessee Williams, who also emerged in the 1940's, has made little progress toward a vision of life worthy of his extraordinary talent.

Like many other American artists, Mr. Williams, despite his devotion to art, has tended to put too much reliance on instinct and to capitalize on its implosions. As a result, there have been lapses from good taste and dramatic balance even in his most carefully constructed pieces after his early retrospective play, *The Glass Menagerie*. In America we have tended to trust too much to instinct and spontaneity. A contrary estimate of instinct was made recently by Mark Van Doren at Columbia University. "Men," he declared, "have so few instincts. Nearly all we do is art. It's learned by pain and effort. We are three years into life—the entire life-span for some animals—before we learn to button a coat, four years before we can tie a shoelace."

Williams, who has wandered far and wide with his dramatic work since he made a tentative entry into the theatre in 1940, twenty-two years ago, is by no means alone in having failed to find a resting point of thought and conviction in his work. It is, in fact, an extremely symptomatic characteristic of our century's theatre that most of its important playwrights have manifested chronic instability. Instead of bringing to fruition a single style of theatre or drama, they have shifted their ground continually. Their labor has been more experiment than art. Fully achieved work needs *organic growth* rather than the straining for expression and effect to be found everywhere in the century's theatre; as a result, we have had few masterworks, but innumerable experiments.

Much unsteadiness has characterized the careers of even such major writers as O'Neill and O'Casey, both of whom attained distinction in dramatic realism only to overleap its secure boundaries and venture into the broken world of expressionism and the murky one of symbolism. Anxious experimentation has been evident even in the case of writers who have maintained a more or less fixed attitude, such as Thornton Wilder's cultivated cheerfulness, Arthur Miller's sociological rectitude, or Bertolt Brecht's avowed Marxism. Brecht came closest to dogma among distinguished contemporary playwrights, though he exemplified this instability of forms from the early 1920's to his death several years ago. Brecht, who has recently become curiously fashionable in our academic world as the leader of "epic theatre" while still impinging only very slightly on our professional stage, was a mass of contradictions. He was a provocative playwright and gifted stage director, but it is absurd to assume that he had a pass-key to modern dramatic art. He experimented in rapid succession with surrealist drama of the irrational, as in *The Jungle of the Cities,* recently produced in New York; with "teaching plays" (the so-called *Lehrstucke* we have mistranslated as "learning plays") composed in more or less oriental style; with more or less dadaist burlesque opera such as *The Threepenny Opera* and *Mahagonny;* with historical or quasi-historical drama such as *Galileo* and *Mother Courage;* and with folksy parables such as *The Caucasian Chalk Circle* and *The Good Woman of Setzuan.* In brief, it was only Brecht's intellect that came to rest in the Marxist teachings that colored but did not consistently and strictly determine the character of his work.

Brecht the theoretician of dramatic art, moreover, was often contradicted in his plays by Brecht the playwright, who thought he was "detached" when he was attached and "cool" when he was actually warm —who fancied himself a social scientist when he was, at best, actually a quizzical and complex artist. It is no wonder that even Germany has not found anyone to take his place; he himself had no "place" or center but a succession of positions to assume and discard. And it is no wonder that there has been so little Brechtian drama elsewhere despite the clamor of his Johnny-come-lately admirers. It is, indeed, ironical on the one hand that Communist Russia should have virtually ignored his work despite his Marxist trumpetings. And it is no less ironical that the most distinguished and successful Brechtian work in English thus far should be Robert Bolt's Sir Thomas More drama, *A Man for All Seasons*—a play that celebrates a martyr of the Church and elects for a spiritual rather than Marxist philosophy.

My time is running out, I fear, and so I must hasten to my conclusion. It can be expressed in the form of an answer to the question I raised at the beginning of this address: *Ti tauta pros Dionyson?* To the question, "Why all this fuss, all this continued fuss, about a Dionysus whose behavior has been so unstable and so erratic," it is possible to propose several answers.

One of these is that the century's theatre owes its very interest to its instability. It has been varied, rich, and arresting in proportion to its instability. Without producing imperishable or even completely satisfying plays, it has given us many provocative ones. Without greatly enriching the standard types or genres of drama, the twentieth century has modified and blended them, forming, for example, mordant and ironic plays that border on the tragic such as Chekhov's *The Cherry Orchard,* Molnar's

Liliom, Pirandello's *Six Characters in Search of an Author,* O'Casey's *Juno and the Paycock,* Giraudoux's *Tiger at the Gates,* Brecht's *Mother Courage,* Beckett's *Waiting for Godot,* and Bolt's *A Man for All Seasons.*

Another, by no means irrelevant, answer is that if twentieth-century dramatic art had been more stable it would not have dealt honestly with contemporary materials and reflected the century. Conformity would have been impossible for the modern theatre on an intellectually acceptable adult level. Any marked stabilization of attitudes has been possible and apparently could occur mainly on the subadult level of school plays, in denominational uplift drama, and in distinctly elementary works such as Russian collectivist plays celebrating five-year-plan projects—plays which do not contain a drop of negativism, indeed, but also possess very little art.

Moreover, it may be appropriate to conclude that if the twentieth century is to have better theatre it will first have to deserve it. That is, it will have to create or at least make possible the values and certainties that are missing in its dramatic art. Theatre, being a public art, is a barometer of society, and an unstable society gets an unstable theatre. Fortunately, however, it also gets something more. By the grace of God, in the theatre as in other walks of life not completely crushed by commercialism or intractable ideology, talent emerges in unlikely places, beauty unfolds amid ugliness, and faith blossoms in the stoniest soil. We have seen this happen indeed in the occasional masterpieces and near-masterpieces, from *The Cherry Orchard* in the first years of the century to *A Man for All Seasons* in the century's dismal seventh decade. Every play written to express a thought or emotion, as well as every honorable stage production, is an act of faith. It represents an expectation that as feeling becomes form and thought becomes art a miracle will transpire and will communicate itself to the audience. Dionysus for the Greeks was a god of miracles, and the great fuss about the theatre has continued to be a concern with the miracles it performs despite deplorable circumstances and in the very teeth of despair.

INDEX